The Letters of the First Duchess of Ormonde

Renaissance English Text Society, 40

Joseph L. Black, SERIES EDITOR

EDITORIAL COMMITTEE
Jaime Goodrich (co-chair)
Margaret Hannay (co-chair)
Anne Lake Prescott

The Letters of the First Duchess of Ormonde

Edited by
Naomi McAreavey

Iter Press
NEW YORK | TORONTO

2022

© Iter Inc. 2022
New York and Toronto
IterPress.org
All rights reserved
Printed in the United States of America

Library of Congress Cataloging-in-Publication Data
Names: Ormonde, Elizabeth Butler, Duchess of, -1684, author. | McAreavey, Naomi, editor.
Title: The letters of the first Duchess of Ormonde / edited by Naomi McAreavey.
Description: New York : Iter Press, 2022. | Series: Renaissance English text society (RETS) ; volume 40 | Includes bibliographical references and index. | Summary: "This volume is the first to bring together the entire extant correspondence of one of the most significant women in early modern Ireland, Elizabeth Butler, first Duchess of Ormonde. She was the wife of James Butler, twelfth Earl and first Duke of Ormonde, who, as Ireland's only duke and three times its lord lieutenant, was a figure of considerable importance in seventeenth-century Ireland. But far from being overshadowed by her powerful husband, Butler was a person of significant power and influence in her own right. Descended from the tenth Earl of Ormonde, she brought a hefty portion of the Ormonde estate to the marriage. As Countess, Marchioness, then Duchess of Ormonde, as well as three times vicereine and a high-status courtier, she sat at the pinnacle of Irish and English society, unmatched by any other Irish woman of the period in terms of her wealth, social standing, and power. Her surviving correspondence reveals her importance within the Ormonde-Butler family and in the social, cultural, and political life of seventeenth-century Ireland. The volume comprises more than three hundred letters written by Ormonde to her husband and family, agents and servants, and friends and clients. Spanning six decades, these letters are meticulously transcribed, edited, and annotated, and the volume includes a substantial scholarly introduction, family trees, a glossary, and other resources"-- Provided by publisher.
Identifiers: LCCN 2021027568 (print) | LCCN 2021027569 (ebook) | ISBN 9781649590183 (hardcover) | ISBN 9781649590190 (pdf) | ISBN 9781649590404 (epub)
Subjects: LCSH: Ormonde, Elizabeth Butler, Duchess of, -1684--Correspondence. | Ormonde, James Butler, Duke of, 1610-1688--Family. | Nobility--Ireland--Correspondence. | Ireland--History--17th century--Biography.
Classification: LCC DA940.5.O69 O76 2022 (print) | LCC DA940.5.O69 (ebook) | DDC 941.706092--dc23
LC record available at https://lccn.loc.gov/2021027568
LC ebook record available at https://lccn.loc.gov/2021027569

Cover Illustration
Attributed to David des Granges, painted c. 1637. Courtesy of the Office of Public Works, Kilkenny Castle. Letter from the Marchioness of Ormonde to Lord Protector Oliver Cromwell, May 2, 1652. Credited to the Society of Antiquaries of London.

Cover Design
Iter Press.

For my family,

and especially Martin, Luke, and Nicholas

Table of Contents

Acknowledgments	ix
Abbreviations	xi
List of Illustrations	xiii
Ormonde Butler Family Table and Family Trees	xv
Chronology	xxiii
A Note on Names	xxxi
Introduction: "The noblest person, The wisest female, and the best of wives that Ever lived": The Duchess of Ormonde and her Letters	1
Birth, Lineage, and Marriage	3
The 1641 Rebellion and Confederate Wars	7
Exile and Dispossession	9
Negotiating the Cromwellian Settlement of Ireland, 1652–1657	16
Retirement in Dunmore, 1657–1660: Letters to the Marquess of Ormonde	20
Restoration	23
The Lord Lieutenancy: The Culture of Dublin Castle, 1662–1668	28
The Duke of Ormonde's Dismissal: Letters to Captain George Mathew	32
Death and Legacy	42
A Note on the Text	49
General Description of the Letters	49
Editorial Principles	53
The Correspondence of Elizabeth Butler, Duchess of Ormonde	63
Early Marriage, 1629–1641	63
The Confederate Wars, 1641–1649	66
Royalist Exile in Caen, 1648–1652	70
The Cromwellian Settlement of Ireland, 1652–1657	96
Retirement in Dunmore, 1657–1660	148
Restoration, 1660–1662	193
The Lord Lieutenancy, 1662–1668	219
The Duke of Ormonde's Dismissal, 1668–1677	239
Final Decade, 1674–1684	382

List of Correspondents	405
Persons and Places	407
Glossary	421
Selected Bibliography	431

Acknowledgments

I would not have been able to complete this edition without the help of so many people who generously shared their expertise, resources, and facilities with me. To the Renaissance English Text Society I owe the most thanks, especially to Jaime Goodrich, the late Margaret Hannay, and Anne Lake Prescott, who were members of the committee that oversaw the completion of the project. Jaime Goodrich read the whole manuscript and offered salient advice, support, and encouragement through the entire process: to her I am particularly obliged. I am also extremely grateful to the RETS copy editor, William Gentrup, for his painstaking work on my edition. It is a much stronger publication thanks to his judicious interventions.

My appreciation is due to the archivists and staff in the many libraries and archives that I used over the course of my research. Special thanks go to the Manuscripts Department in the National Library of Ireland where I spent many, many weeks working on the Ormond Papers. I am particularly beholden to the friendly faces at the issue desk and to the staff who lugged heavy volumes to my table. I am also grateful to the staff of the Bodleian Library, Oxford, and the British Library, London, where I had the pleasure of working on several occasions. Lord and Lady Rosse were gracious hosts during a short visit to Birr Castle, Co. Offaly. My thanks also go to the archivists and staff at the British Museum (especially Chris Sutherns), the Huntington Library (especially Vanessa Wilkie), the National Archives, the Society of Antiquaries of London (especially Adrian James and Helen Porter), and the Staffordshire Record Office (especially Joanna Terry), who answered my queries and supplied the materials I requested. I would like to thank the staff of Kilkenny Castle, who allowed me to work in what were once the Duchess's rooms, especially Dolores Gaffney, who took me on a mission to find the site of Dunmore House and to Peter Kenny, who shared his vast local knowledge with me. Christine Reynolds of Westminster Abbey and David White of the College of Arms also provided useful information about the Duchess of Ormonde's funeral and burial.

During the course of this project I was lucky to work closely with Julie Eckerle and Ann-Maria Walsh on other projects. As scholars who share my interest in Irish women's letters, we had many stimulating conversations on the topic. They were kind and supportive colleagues and friends, and I am extremely indebted to both for joining me on this journey. Ann-Maria shared material she found in the course of her own research on the daughters of the first Earl of Cork, and Julie read my Introduction and gave valuable feedback. Marie-Louise Coolahan, Jane Ohlmeyer, and Mary O'Dowd supported the project from the outset and offered helpful advice and much-need encouragement through key stages of the process.

This edition has been enriched through the expertise of so many other researchers working on different aspects of the history and culture of early modern Ireland. Foremost of these is Jane Fenlon, who has shared with me her extensive knowledge of the material culture of the Ormonde Butlers as well as her enthusiasm for the first Duke and Duchess. Many scholars have shared their expertise in a wide range of topics, and I would particularly like to thank Evan Bourke, Ruth Connolly, Coleman Dennehy, John Cronin, Mark Empey, Joel Halcomb, Stuart Kinsella, Patrick Little, Felicity Maxwell, Bríd McGrath, Bronagh McShane, Elaine Murphy, Marion Lyons, Frances Nolan, Paul Gerard Smith, Ann Tierney, Philip West, and Timothy Wilks. The edition was shaped by conversations at conferences and seminars over many years, not least the annual Tudor and Stuart Ireland conference, and I am grateful to the organizers and delegates.

I am so very fortunate in my colleagues and friends in University College Dublin. I am particularly grateful to Jane Grogan, who has ever been an inspirational scholar and generous mentor, and to Niamh Pattwell, whose daily support helped get me through the final stages of this project. Thanks are also due to Marc Caball, Danielle Clarke, Fionnuala Dillane, Anne Fogarty, John McCafferty, and Maria Stuart among many others.

My work on the Duchess of Ormonde began long ago with my doctoral research at Queen's University Belfast. I would like to thank Clare McManus and Ramona Wray for being such scrupulous supervisors; Kate Chedgzoy and the late Siobhán Kilfeather were thorough examiners and encouraged me to pursue further work on the Duchess of Ormonde; and what was then the Arts and Humanities Research Board generously funded my research. I completed my Ph.D. alongside Edel Lamb, who remains a brilliant friend and colleague.

Finally, I wish to acknowledge the continuous support of my own family – my mum and dad, Geraldine and Kieran McAreavey, my sister Rachel Hunter, and my brothers Michael and Kevin McAreavey. But most of all I would like to thank my husband Martin Canavan for believing that I could do this (even when at times it felt that I could not) and to my sons Luke and Nicholas for bringing such joy to my life.

Abbreviations

BL	British Library, London
Bodl.	Bodleian Library, Oxford
Burghclere	Winifred Gardner, Lady Burghclere, *A Life of James, First Duke of Ormonde, 1610–1688*, 2 vols. (London: John Murray, 1912).
Carte	Thomas Carte, *An History of the Life of James Duke of Ormonde*, 3 vols. (London: J. Bettenham, for J.J. and P. Knapton, in Ludgate-Street; G. Strahan, in Cornhill; W. Innys and R. Manby, at the West End of St. Paul's; F. Giles, in Holbourn; and T. Wotton, in Fleetstreet, 1735–1736).
DIB	*Dictionary of Irish Biography Online* (Cambridge: Cambridge University Press, 2012). http://dib.cambridge.org
EO	Elizabeth Butler, née Preston, first Duchess of Ormonde (1615–1684)
Field Day	*The Field Day Anthology of Irish Writing*, IV and V: *Irish Women's Writing and Traditions*, ed. Angela Bourke and others (Cork: Cork University Press, 2002).
HL	Huntington Library, San Marino, California
HMC Ormonde	Historical Manuscripts Commission, *Calendar of the Manuscripts of the Marquess of Ormonde*, 3 vols. (London, 1895–1899); *Calendar of the Manuscripts of the Marquess of Ormonde*, new series, 8 vols (London, 1902–1920).
JO	James Butler, twelfth Earl and first Duke of Ormonde (1610–1688)
MS/S	Manuscript/s
NLI	National Library of Ireland, Dublin
ODNB	*Oxford Dictionary of National Biography* (Oxford: Oxford University Press, 2004; online edn, Jan 2017). http://www.oxforddnb.com
OED	*OED Online* (Oxford: Oxford University Press, 2012). http://www.oed.com
O'Keeffe	Eleanor O'Keeffe, "The Family and Marriage Strategies of James Butler, 1st Duke of Ormonde, 1658–1688" (Ph.D. diss., Cambridge University, 2000).
SAL	Society of Antiquaries of London

SP   State Papers
SRO   Staffordshire Record Office, Stafford
TNA   The National Archives, Kew (formerly Public Record Office)

List of Illustrations

Figure 1   Portrait of Elizabeth Preston, when Countess of Ormonde, and her son, Thomas, Earl of Ossory, attributed to David des Granges, painted c. 1637. Courtesy of the Office of Public Works, Kilkenny Castle.

Figure 2   Letter 13. Letter from the Marchioness of Ormonde to Sir Edward Nicholas, June 20, 1649. Reproduced by permission of the British Library.

Figure 3   Letter 29. Letter from the Marchioness of Ormonde to Lord Protector Oliver Cromwell, May 2, 1652. Credited to the Society of Antiquaries of London.

Figure 4   Letter 87. Letter from the Marchioness of Ormonde ("JH") to the Marquess of Ormonde, May 19, 1659. Reproduced by permission of the Bodleian Library.

Figure 5   Letter 97. Letter from the Marchioness of Ormonde to the Marquess of Ormonde, May 11, 1660. Reproduced by permission of the Bodleian Library.

Figure 6   Letter 99. Memorandum of the Marchioness of Ormonde to [Anne] Hume, [May 1660]. Reproduced by permission of the Bodleian Library.

Figure 7   Print depicting Charles II and his court, by Peter Stent. Courtesy of the Trustees of the British Museum.

Figure 8   Letter 55. Letter from the Marchioness of Ormonde to John Burdon, [April 1657], with wax seal depicting the Preston Unicorn. Courtesy of the National Library of Ireland.

Figure 9   Letter 126. Letter from the Duchess of Ormonde to Queen Catherine of Braganza, November 16, [1663]. Reproduced by permission of the Bodleian Library.

Ormonde Butler Family Table

JAMES BUTLER (1496–1546), **ninth Earl of Ormonde**[1]
m. (1530) Joan (d. 1565), daughter of James Fitzgerald, Earl of Desmond
- **Thomas Butler (1531–1614), tenth Earl of Ormonde**
- Edmund Butler, later of Cloghgrenan, Co. Carlow
- John Butler (d. 1570), of Kilcash, Co. Tipperary
  m. Catherine, daughter of Sir Cormac MacCarthy Reagh
  - James Butler (d. c. 1570–1576)
  - **Walter Butler (1569–1633), eleventh Earl of Ormonde**
- Walter, of Nodstown, Co. Tipperary
  - Elizabeth Esmond
- James, of Duiske, Co. Kilkenny
- Edward, of Ballinahinch, Co. Tipperary
- Piers, of Grantstown, Co. Tipperary and Leix Abbey in Offaly

THOMAS BUTLER (1531–1614), **tenth Earl of Ormonde**
m. (c. 1559) (1) Elizabeth (1534–1582), daughter of Thomas Berkeley, sixth Baron Berkeley
  m. (1582) (2) Elizabeth (d. 1600), daughter of John Sheffield, Baron Sheffield
  - James Butler (1583–1590), Viscount Thurles
  - Elizabeth Butler (c. 1585–1628)
    m. (1) Theobald Butler
    m. (2) Richard Preston, Baron Dingwall, Earl of Desmond (d. 1628)
    - **Elizabeth Preston (1615–1684), Baroness Dingwall**

WALTER BUTLER (1569–1633), **eleventh Earl of Ormonde**
m. (c. 1584) Ellen (d. 1631), daughter of Edmund Butler, second Viscount Mountgarret
- **Thomas Butler** (d. 1619), **Viscount Thurles**
  m. Elizabeth Poyntz (1587–1673)
- Margaret Butler
  m. Barnaby Fitzpatrick, fifth Baron of Upper Ossory

---

[1] The heirs of the Ormonde and Dingwall estates are highlighted in bold.

- Catherine Butler
  m. Pierce Power, son of Richard, Lord Power of Couraghmore
- Ellen Butler
  m. Sir Pierce Butler
- Ellen Butler
  m. James Butler Esquire, son of Lord Baron of Dunboyne
- Joan Butler
  m. George Bagnell Esquire, Lord Catherlough
- Mary Butler
  m. Richard Burke, Earl of Clanrickard
- Eleanor Butler
- Ellice Butler

THOMAS BUTLER (d. 1619), **Viscount Thurles**
m. (?) Elizabeth Poyntz (d. 1673), daughter of Sir John Poyntz
- **James Butler** (1610–1688), **twelfth Earl of Ormonde**
- Elizabeth Butler (d. 1675)
  m. (1) James Purcell, Baron Loughmore (d. 1652)
  m. (2) Colonel John Fitzpatrick (d. 1693)
- Mary Butler (d. 1680)
  m. Sir George Hamilton (d. 1679)
- Richard Butler of Kilcash (c. 1616–1701)
  m. Frances Touchet
- Eleanor Butler (1612–1682)
  m. Donough MacCarthy, 1st Earl of Clancarty (1594–1665)

JAMES BUTLER (1610–1688), Viscount Thurles (1619), **twelfth Earl of Ormonde** (1632), Marquess (1642), first Duke (Irish peerage 1661, English peerage 1682)
- *Illegitimate son by Isabella Thynne*
  m. (1629) **Elizabeth Preston** (1615–1684), **Baroness Dingwall**
- **Thomas Butler** (1634–1680), Viscount Thurles, sixth Earl of Ossory (1642)
  m. (1659) Aemilia van Nassau (d. 1688)
- Richard Butler (1639–1686), first Earl of Arran (1662)
  m. (1664) (1) Mary Stuart (1651–1668)
  m. (1673) (2) Dorothy Ferrars (d. 1716)
    - Charlotte Butler (1678–1725)
    - Three sons, Lords Tullogh, died in infancy or childhood (c. 1676, 1681)
- Elizabeth Butler (1640–1665)
  m. (1660) Philip Stanhope, second Earl of Chesterfield (1633–1714)
    - Elizabeth (Betty) Stanhope (1633–1723)
- John Butler (1643–1676), first Earl of Gowran
  m. (1675) Ann Chichester (d. 1697)

- Mary Butler (1646–1710)
  m. (1662) Lord William Cavendish, later first Duke of Devonshire (1641–1707)
  - Charles Cavendish (1669–1670)
  - William Cavendish (1671–1729), second Duke of Devonshire

THOMAS BUTLER (1634–1680)
m. (1659) Aemilia van Nassau (d. 1688)
- Elizabeth Butler (1660–1717)
  m. (1673) William George Richard Stanley (1655–1702), ninth Earl of Derby
- Henrietta Butler (d. 1724)
  m. (1697) Henry de Nassau d'Auverquerque, first Earl of Grantham (1673–1754)
- **James Butler** (1666–1745), **second Duke of Ormonde**
  m. (1) (1682) Anne Hyde (1667–1685)
  m. (2) (1685) Mary Somerset (1665–1733)
- **Charles Butler** (1671–1758), first Earl of Arran (of the second creation), and **third titular Duke of Ormonde**

Ormonde Butler Family Trees

The Kinship of the Ormonde Cousins

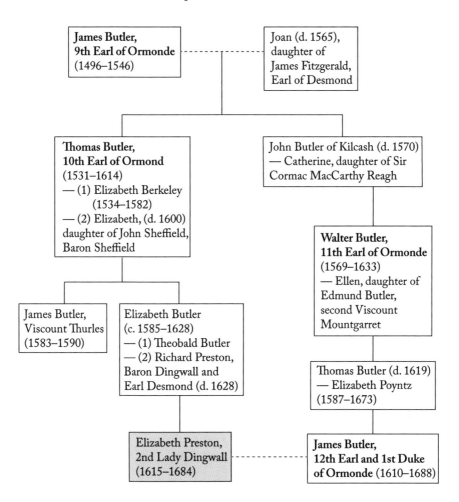

Ormond Butler Family Trees

Children and Grandchildren

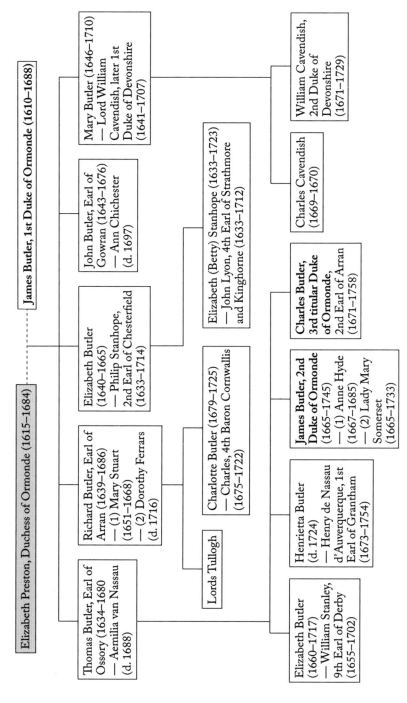

Ormond Butler Family Trees

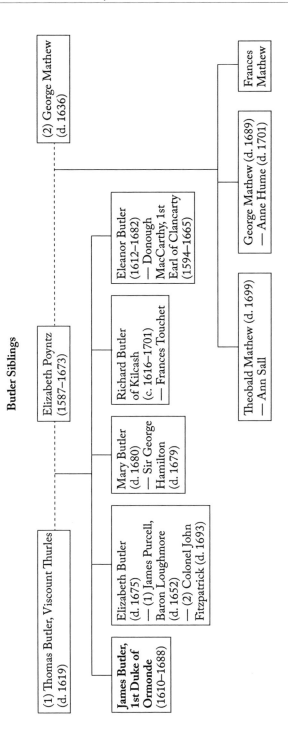

Ormond Butler Family Trees

Preston Family[1]

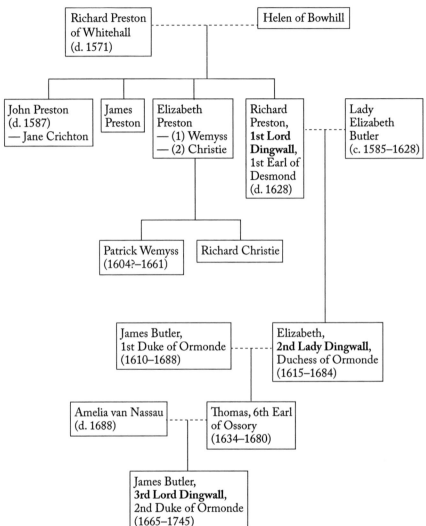

---

[1] The Preston family tree is based on information found in Timothy Wilks, *Of Neighing Coursers and Trumpets Shrill: A Life of Richard, 1st Lord Dingwall and Earl of Desmond* (c. 1570–1628) (London: Lucas, 2012), 6–7, 137–138.

Chronology

Date	Political and Cultural Events	Family Events
1610 Oct		Birth of JO
1614 Fall		Marriage of EO's parents, Lady Elizabeth Butler and Sir Richard Preston
Nov		Death of Thomas, tenth Earl of Ormonde; succession of Sir Walter Butler of Kilcash as eleventh Earl of Ormonde
1615 July		Birth of EO
1618 Oct		Bulk of Ormonde estate awarded to EO's mother
1619 June		Imprisonment of the eleventh Earl of Ormonde
Dec		Death of JO's father, Thomas Butler, Viscount Thurles; JO's succession as Viscount Thurles
1621 Dec		JO taken as a ward of the court
1625 Mar	Death of James I; succession of Charles I	
1628 Oct		Death of EO's mother and father, the Earl and Countess of Desmond; EO's succession as Baroness Dingwall, and inheritance of her mother's estate
1629 Dec		Marriage of EO and JO
1633 Feb		Death of Walter, eleventh Earl of Ormonde; JO's succession of as twelfth Earl of Ormonde
1634 July	Lord Lieutenant Wentworth arrives in Ireland	Birth of EO's son, Thomas Butler, later Earl of Ossory
1635 Jan		JO becomes a privy councillor

Date		Political and Cultural Events	Family Events
1636	May/June	Opening of Werburgh Street theatre	
1639	June		Birth of EO's son, Richard Butler, later Earl of Arran
		Performance of James Shirley's *St Patrick for Ireland* at Werburgh Street	
1640	June		Birth of EO's daughter, Elizabeth, later Lady Chesterfield
		Performance of Henry Burnell's *Landgartha* at Werburgh Street	
1641	May	Execution of Wentworth	
	Oct	Beginning of the Irish rebellion	EO in Carrick
	Dec		EO moves to Kilkenny Castle via Clonmel
1642	Jan		EO returns to Carrick
	Mar	Adventurers' Act passed by the Long Parliament	EO moves to Dublin via Waterford
	Aug	Beginning of the English Civil War	
	Oct	First Confederate General Assembly in Kilkenny	
1643			Birth of EO's son, John Butler, later Earl of Gowran
	Sept	Ormonde cessation with Confederate Catholics	
	Nov		JO appointed to the lord lieutenancy EO moves with JO to Dublin Castle
	Mar	Ordinance passed sequestering the estates of all those giving assistance to the King	

Chronology

Date		Political and Cultural Events	Family Events
	Aug	Ordinance passed setting aside a sum, not more than one fifth of the sequestered income of the "delinquent," for the benefit of his wife and children	
1646		First Ormonde Peace; publication of Henry Burkhead's *Cola's Furie* and James Shirley's *Poems &c.*	Birth of EO's daughter, Mary Butler, later Lady Cavendish and Duchess of Devonshire
1647	June	Dublin surrendered to Parliament	
	July		EO departs Ireland for England
1648	Sept		EO departs England for exile in Caen
1649	Jan	Execution of Charles I; Second Ormonde Peace	
	Sept	Cromwell storms Drogheda	
1650	May	Treaty of Breda signed between Charles II and the Scottish Covenanters	
	May	Cromwell departs Ireland	
	July	Henry Ireton appointed Lord Deputy	
	Dec		JO departs Ireland
1651	Jan		JO joins his family in Caen
	Nov		JO joins Charles II in Paris
1652	Feb		EO petitions Cromwell
	July	Charles Fleetwood appointed Lord Deputy	
	Aug	Act of Settlement Establishment of an Irish Council of State	EO leaves Caen for London
1653	Feb		Order of Parliament issued on EO's estate
	Dec	Cromwell appointed Lord Protector of the Commonwealth	

Date		Political and Cultural Events	Family Events
1654	Dec	Henry Cromwell nominated to the Irish Council of State	
		Down Survey of Ireland begins	
1655	July	Henry Cromwell arrives in Ireland	
	Sept	Charles Fleetwood recalled to England	
1656	Sept		Imprisonment of EO's eldest son, Thomas, Earl of Ossory, in the Tower of London
1657	June	Act of Settlement	EO settles in Dunmore
	Nov	Henry Cromwell appointed Lord Deputy of Ireland	
1658	Sept	Death of Cromwell; succession of his son, Richard Cromwell, as Lord Protector	
	Oct	Henry Cromwell appointed Lord Lieutenant of Ireland	
1659	May	Richard Cromwell forced to recall the Rump Parliament	
		Richard Cromwell resigns the protectorate	
	June	Henry Cromwell departs Ireland	
	Nov		Marriage of EO's son, Ossory, to Aemilia van Nassau
1660	May	Restoration of Charles II; Charles II proclaimed king in Dublin	EO reunited with JO in London
	Sept		Marriage of EO's daughter, Elizabeth, to Philip Stanhope, second Earl of Chesterfield
1661	Mar		JO elevated to Irish dukedom

Chronology

Date	Political and Cultural Events	Family Events
		JO purchases Moor Park in Hertfordshire
1662	Act of Settlement	
Feb		JO appointed as to the lord lieutenancy
July		JO and EO return to Dublin Castle
Oct	Opening of Smock Alley theatre	Chesterfield scandal
		Marriage of EO's daughter, Mary, to William, Lord Cavendish, afterwards first Duke of Devonshire
1663 Jan	Court of Claims opens in Dublin	
Feb	Performance of Katharine Philips's *Pompey* in Smock Alley	
Mar	Foiled plot to seize Dublin Castle	
1664 Sept		Marriage of EO's son, Richard, Earl of Arran, to Lady Mary Stuart
1665	Act of Explanation	
Mar	Second Anglo-Dutch War begins	Birth of James Butler, future second Duke of Ormonde
Apr	Great Plague of London	
July		Death of EO's daughter, Elizabeth, Lady Chesterfield
1666 Sept	Great Fire of London	Establishment of Kilkenny College
1667 Aug	Dismissal of Clarendon	
1668 Feb		Attempt by English Parliament to impeach JO
		Ossory appointed Lord Deputy
Aug		Death of Mary, Lady Arran, EO's daughter-in-law

Date		Political and Cultural Events	Family Events
	Dec		Marriage of JO's half-brother, George Mathew, to EO's friend, Anne Hume
1669	Feb		JO's dismissal from the lord lieutenancy
	May	Appointment of Lord Robartes to the lord lieutenancy	
	Aug		JO elected as chancellor of the University of Oxford
1670	Feb	Appointment of Lord Berkeley of Stratton to the lord lieutenancy	
	June	Treaty of Dover signed by Charles II and Louis XIV of France	
	Summer		Sale of Moor Park
	Dec		Attempted kidnapping of JO
1672	Apr	Third Anglo-Dutch War begins	
	May	Appointment of the Earl of Essex to the lord lieutenancy	
	Sept		EO's son, Ossory, appointed Knight of the Garter
1673	May		Death of JO's mother, Elizabeth, Lady Thurles
	June		Marriage of EO's son, Arran, to Dorothy Ferrars
			EO and JO return to Kilkenny Castle
	July		Marriage of Ossory's eldest daughter, Elizabeth, to William George Richard Stanley, ninth Earl of Derby
1675	Jan		Marriage of EO's son, Lord John Butler, to Lady Ann Chichester Lord John elevated to Earl of Gowran
	Apr		JO and EO return to London
1676	July?		Death of EO's son, Gowran

Chronology

Date	Political and Cultural Events	Family Events
1677 May 24		JO re-appointed to the lord lieutenancy
1678	Popish Plot	
1679	Exclusion Crisis	
1680 July		Death of EO's son, Ossory; succession of Ossory's eldest son, James, later second Duke of Ormonde, to his father's title
1682 Nov		JO's elevation to an English dukedom
1684 July		Death of EO
Oct		JO's dismissal from the lord lieutenancy
1685 Feb	Death of Charles II; succession of James II	
1686 Jan		Death of EO's son, Arran
1688 July		Death of JO

A Note on Names

When in 1629 the fourteen-year-old heiress, Elizabeth Preston, Baroness Dingwall, married her cousin, James Butler, Viscount Thurles, she was raised to the rank of viscountess. Fifty-five years later, in 1684, she died as Duchess of Ormonde, her husband having been elevated to a dukedom in the Irish peerage in 1661 and in the English peerage in 1682. Through her long life, therefore, Elizabeth Butler, née Preston, rose through all five ranks of the peerage. These were, in ascending order, baroness (usually the wife of a baron, although Elizabeth inherited the title from her father); viscountess (the wife of a viscount); countess (earl); marchioness (marquess); and duchess (duke).

Since the lives of the Ormonde Butler family were characterized by social elevation through royal favor and/or marriage, here is a list of the principal members with the dates of their titles:

Elizabeth Butler, née Preston (1615–1684)—Baroness Dingwall (1628), Viscountess Thurles (1629), Countess of Ormonde (1632), Marchioness of Ormonde (1642), Duchess of Ormonde (Irish peerage, 1661; English peerage, 1682)

James Butler (1610–1688)—Viscount Thurles (1619), twelfth Earl of Ormonde (1632), Marquess of Ormonde (1642), first Duke of Ormonde (Irish peerage, 1661; English peerage, 1682)

Thomas Butler (1634–1680)—Viscount Thurles, sixth Earl of Ossory (1642)

Richard Butler (1639–1686)—first Earl of Arran (1662)

John Butler (1643–1676)—first Earl of Gowran (1676)

Elizabeth Butler (1640–1665)—Countess of Chesterfield (1660)

Mary Butler (1646–1710)—Lady Cavendish (1662), Countess of Devonshire (1684), Duchess of Devonshire (1694)

When I refer to Elizabeth Butler, née Preston, by rank, I typically identify her as the Duchess, as this represents the peak of her social standing as well as the rank in which she spent the longest portion of her life (twenty-three years) and in which she died. When I specifically discuss her life and letters before 1661, I refer to her as Marchioness or Countess as appropriate. The same principles apply to the other members of her immediate family.

Introduction

"The noblest person, The wisest female, and the best of wives that Ever lived": The Duchess of Ormonde and her Letters

The letters of Elizabeth Butler, née Preston, first Duchess of Ormonde (1615–1684), provide extraordinary insight on the life and writing of an important aristocratic Irish woman at a time of remarkable social and political upheaval in the three kingdoms. She was the wife of James Butler, twelfth Earl and first Duke of Ormonde (1610–1688), who, as Ireland's only duke and three times its lord lieutenant, was a figure of considerable importance in seventeenth-century Ireland. But far from the retiring consort of her powerful husband, his wife was a person of significant power and influence in her own right. Descended from the tenth Earl of Ormonde, she brought a hefty portion of the Ormonde estate to the marriage to her second cousin.[1] As Countess, Marchioness, then Duchess of Ormonde, as well as three times vicereine and high-status courtier, she sat at the pinnacle of Irish and English society, unmatched by any other Irish woman of the period in terms of her wealth, social standing, and power. Her surviving correspondence reveals her importance within the Ormonde Butler family and in the social, cultural, and political life of seventeenth-century Ireland.[2]

The Duchess of Ormonde was a prolific letter-writer, and this volume brings together for the first time her entire extant correspondence, which comprises

---

[1] Technically, the couple were second cousins once removed. They shared direct lineage from the ninth Earl of Ormonde: EO was his great-granddaughter through her mother; JO was his great-great grandson through his father.

[2] In "The Place of Ireland in the Letters of the First Duchess of Ormonde," in *Women's Life Writing and Early Modern Ireland*, ed. Julie A. Eckerle and Naomi McAreavey (Lincoln: University of Nebraska Press, 2019), 159–81, I make the case for my identification of the Duchess of Ormonde as "Irish" on the basis that "Ireland, if not Irishness, is at the heart of her self-representation" (165). I argue that "whether she writes *in* Ireland or *to* Ireland, all of her surviving letters are *about* Ireland, its land, its people, its politics, and above all her family's interests in the country" (165).

more than three hundred items covering six decades. Spanning the years between c. 1630 and 1684, the correspondence traverses the 1641 rebellion and the Wars of the Three Kingdoms, royalist exile and the Commonwealth and Protectorate governments, the Restoration, and beyond, through successive waves of land settlement, and offers an important Irish female perspective on a key period of three kingdoms' history. The letters illuminate the Duchess's crucial involvement in the protection and advancement of Ormonde family interests during this turbulent period, and the volume's chronological organization helps to illuminate how the letters were shaped by changing historical circumstances and the fluctuating position of the Ormonde Butlers. Letters are written to her husband and family, agents and servants, and friends and clients, and together they showcase her fine-tuned epistolary dexterity. As she responds to the ebb and flow of the family's fortunes, the Duchess's letters are variously defensive, persuasive, diplomatic, antagonistic, assertive, passive, outraged, cynical, nonchalant, incensed, measured, passionate—this was a woman who could deploy a pen to great effect. The overwhelming impression from the letters is of a literate, intelligent, pragmatic, and resourceful woman.

The importance of the Duchess of Ormonde has long been recognized, yet she has not been subject to sustained research in her own right. *The Dukes of Ormonde, 1610–1745*, edited by Toby Barnard and Jane Fenlon, remains the definitive work on the seventeenth-century Ormonde Butlers, but its attention to the Duchess is limited. Barnard called for further research on Elizabeth Ormonde, which he rightly argued was "likely to raise higher the stature of the first duchess."[3] Eleanor O'Keeffe responded to the call in her thesis on the family and marriage strategies of the Duke of Ormonde, but it remains unpublished.[4] My edition represents the first book-length study of the Duchess of Ormonde and also the first that privileges her role as a letter-writer.[5] With the history and culture of early modern Ireland receiving greater scholarly attention, there remains a need for women's contributions to be duly acknowledged. By focusing attention on the Duchess rather than her renowned husband, I hope my edition of her letters will facilitate and encourage the development of a more refined and complex

---

[3] Toby Barnard, Introduction, in *The Dukes of Ormonde, 1610–1745*, ed. Toby Barnard and Jane Fenlon (Woodbridge: Boydell & Brewer, 2000), 1–53 (33). JO's biographers, Carte and Burghclere, also attended to EO, but only in the context of her husband.

[4] O'Keeffe's excellent thesis devotes a chapter to EO; the other three chapters address adult children and heirs; in-laws; and brothers, sisters and the Butler apanage. Damien Duffy also addresses EO as part of "The Ormond Women: Family, Power, and Politics, c.1450s–1660" (Ph.D. diss., Maynooth University, 2018).

[5] Marie-Louise Coolahan, *Women, Writing, and Language in Early Modern Ireland* (Cambridge: Cambridge University Press, 2010), also pointed out that EO required substantial research.

view of this most important Irish couple, as well as of the "public" and "private" lives of a seventeenth-century Irish noblewoman.

Her letters shape and reflect Elizabeth Ormonde's transformation from viscountess and young wife and mother to duchess and co-head of a powerful dynasty. My introduction contextualizes this transformation by outlining her lineage and marriage, her conduct during the 1641 rebellion, her experience of exile in Caen where she began the process of petitioning Cromwell for restitution of her estate, the years she spent in England after her award but before she was able to settle in Ireland, her eventual retirement to Dunmore, the improvement in fortune that came with the Restoration, the golden period of the couple's second viceregency, the Duke's dismissal followed by the couple's prolonged and difficult stay in London, and, finally, her death and legacy. In doing so, this introduction emphasizes the Duchess's role in preserving the honor and interests of the Ormonde Butler family and illuminates the vitality and material and rhetorical power of her letter-writing.

Birth, Lineage, and Marriage

Elizabeth Butler, née Preston, was descended from the Old English earls of Ormonde through her mother, Elizabeth Butler (d. 1628), sole surviving legitimate child of Thomas Butler, tenth Earl of Ormonde (d. 1614). Her father was Richard Preston, Baron Dingwall, later Earl of Desmond (d. 1628), a Scottish court noble and favorite of James VI and I.[6] Born in her father's house, St. Olave's, in Hart Street, London, on July 25, 1615, she was the only child of the marriage, and was brought up in her father's Protestant faith.[7] After the death of her maternal grandfather, the tenth Earl, her father had laid claim to the Ormonde title and estate in his wife's name. Although he failed to obtain the earldom, which was entailed in the male line, on October 3, 1618 he and his wife were controversially awarded more than half of the Ormonde estate at the expense of the elev-

---

[6] For a pioneering study of EO's father, see Timothy Wilks, *Of Neighing Coursers and Trumpets Shrill: A Life of Richard, 1ˢᵗ Lord Dingwall and Earl of Desmond (c.1570–1628)* (London: Lucas, 2012).

[7] Lady Ann Fanshawe provides the address of Lord Dingwall's house where, she writes, she and EO "were both born in one chamber." See *Memoirs of Lady Anne Fanshawe*, ed. Charles Robert Fanshawe (London: Colburne and Bentley, 1830), 50, 81–82. Lucy Moore's wonderful biography of Ann Fanshawe, *Lady Fanshawe's Receipt Book: An Englishwoman's Life during the Civil War* (London: Atlantic Books, 2018), mentions her connections with the Duchess of Ormonde and the wider Butler kinship.

enth Earl, a prominent Catholic.[8] Ten years later, in October 1628, the estate was inherited by the couple's thirteen-year-old daughter, Lady Elizabeth Preston, when her parents died within weeks of each other (her mother of illness and her father in a shipwreck in the Irish Sea). Now Baroness Dingwall, having inherited her father's Scottish title, the orphaned girl was taken as a ward of the court and placed into the care of Henry Rich, first Earl of Holland. Letters addressed to Baroness Dingwall in the months following her parents' deaths indicate the weight of responsibility that fell on her young shoulders as clients and tenants solicited for her favor.[9] They also reveal how quickly plans were revived for her to marry her cousin, James Butler, grandson and heir to the eleventh Earl of Ormonde. Her future husband had also been brought up in the Protestant faith after being claimed as a ward of the crown upon the death of his father and put into the care of the Archbishop of Canterbury. The prospective marriage promised the reunification of the Ormonde title and estate, while also ensuring that they would be in Protestant hands.[10] The couple married in Christmas 1629 when the bride was fourteen and her new husband five years her senior.[11] The earliest extant letter written by the young Viscountess Thurles (Letter 1) dates from around 1630 from Iron Acton in Gloucestershire where she and her husband spent the early years of their marriage with relatives of his mother. Addressing her letter to the eleventh Earl of Ormonde (whom she names "grandfathar"), she complains of the eviction of some of her late parents' tenants and intervenes on behalf of her paternal cousins, the Wemyss ("my kinsmen"), in a dispute that she dismisses as "soe poure a thing" (Letter 1). As she urges the eleventh Earl "to grant this my

---

[8] This account is indebted to David Edwards, "The Poisoned Chalice: The Ormond Inheritance, Sectarian Division and the Emergence of James Butler, 1614–1642," in *Dukes of Ormonde*, ed. Barnard and Fenlon, 58–64.

[9] Correspondence about the marriage negotiations from EO's advisors and agents, including Lord and Lady Esmonde, can be found in HMC Ormonde, N.S., I, 18–24, and II, 365–67.

[10] Despite the clear religio-political reasons for the marriage, a contemporary account of the couple's courtship presents the relationship as a love match, telling a story of the young suitor visiting Lady Dingwall in the Earl of Holland's house disguised as a pedlar with a love letter concealed in a glove, "which she in his drawing on the glove perceiving, pretended to have no money in her pocket to pay for the gloves, and notwithstanding the young Ladys [the daughters of the Earl of Holland] offered to lend her money, yet she retired to her chamber to fetch money, and being there, perused the letter, and soon after returned with the gloves again (into which she as cunningly conveyed an answer), which she returned to the amorous Pedlar, pretending they had an ill smell." See "Anonymous Account of the Early Life and Marriage of James, First Duke of Ormonde," ed. James Graves, in *The Journal of the Kilkenny and South-East of Ireland Archaeological* Society, N.S. 4.2 (1863), 276–92 (287).

[11] The Articles of Agreement for the marriage can be found in HMC Ormonde, N.S., II, 355–59.

request as your Lordship would have me obay your commands in anye outhar things," she demonstrates her confidence and self-assurance as heiress and landlord in her own right, as well as her acute sense of the duties and responsibilities of the position.

When the eleventh Earl died in February 1633, his grandson became twelfth Earl of Ormonde. Between 1632 and 1646 the Countess of Ormonde bore eight sons, three of whom survived to adulthood, and two daughters: Thomas, later Earl of Ossory, born in Kilkenny Castle on July 8, 1634; Richard, later Earl of Arran, born June 15, 1639; Elizabeth, later Lady Chesterfield, born June 29, 1640; John, later Earl of Gowran, born in 1643; and Mary, later Lady Cavendish and ultimately Duchess of Devonshire, born in 1646.[12] The playwright, James Shirley, dedicated a poem to the young mother during his residence at Dublin's short-lived Werburgh Street Theatre. The poem celebrates her fruitful marriage, which had at the time produced two sons, with a third, the future Earl of Arran, on the way:

> Be rich in your two darlings of the Spring,
> Which as it waits, perfumes their blossoming,
> The growing pledges of your love, and blood;
> And may that unborn blessing timely bud,
> The chast, and noble Treasure of your womb,
> Your owne, and th'Ages expectation come!
> And when your daies and vertues have made even,
> Die late, belov'd of earth, and change for heaven.[13]

The Countess's maternity is also foregrounded in a painting from the same period attributed to David des Granges, which depicts her with her eldest surviving son and heir, Thomas, Earl of Ossory, when he was a young boy (fig. 1).[14] Her expanded waistline may suggest that she was pregnant again, as indeed she probably was when she sat for the portrait. The Countess was preoccupied with multiple pregnancies, childbirth, and the rearing of her young children throughout the 1630s, and no letters appear to survive from these years.

---

[12] The first son Thomas (b. 1632) died before he was a year old. James (b. 1635), did not live above a year; another James, born on March 24, 1636, died on April 17, 1645, and was buried at Christ Church in Dublin; Walter, born September 6, 1641, died in Dublin in March 1643, and was also buried at Christ Church; and James, born in 1645, was killed in a coaching accident at six months old. See Burghclere, I, 299.

[13] James Shirley, "To the Excellent Pattern of Beauty and Vertue L[ady] El[izabeth] Co[untess] of Or[monde]," in *Poems &c.* (London: Humphrey Moseley, 1646), 36–37. The poem must have been written in early 1639 when EO was pregnant with Arran.

[14] EO was also painted by Sir Peter Lely and Henri Gascars, but the portraits have not been found. See Jane Fenlon, *The Ormonde Picture Collection* (Dublin: Dúchas / Heritage Service, 2001), 70.

Figure 1. Portrait of Elizabeth Preston, when Countess of Ormonde, and her son, Thomas, Earl of Ossory, attributed to David des Granges, painted c. 1637. Courtesy of the Office of Public Works, Kilkenny Castle.

The 1641 Rebellion and Confederate Wars

Few of the Countess of Ormonde's letters survive from the 1640s either, even though references to her letter-writing abound in the historical record, and sources recognize her as a key player during the 1641 rebellion. Eyewitnesses attest that she provided food, shelter, clothing, and money for English Protestant refugees; that she arranged for their transportation from Carrick, Kilkenny, and Waterford to Dublin or England; and that she utilized her connections with the Confederate leaders to ensure the continued safety of those under her protection.[15] The Countess and her children were in Carrick when rebellion broke out in October 1641, where she reportedly relieved five families before transporting them to Waterford for shipping to England.[16] She soon made plans to remove to Kilkenny Castle but was forced to divert to Clonmel, where she is said to have relieved a further forty English, whom she then brought with her to Kilkenny.[17] Some of those who received her charity testify that she housed, fed, and clothed more than one hundred Protestants in the Castle.[18] Her servant confirmed that "there was not two rooms in the Castle there but had been full of English families and Englishmen's goods which had been protected and saved by the said lady."[19] Lady Ormonde remained in Kilkenny Castle over Christmas and until the middle of January 1642, at which time, "the rebels growing more numerous, her ladyship being fearful of them with her family," she retreated to Carrick "for the convenience of the river and nearness to Waterford to transport herself to England or Dublin if she could."[20] Kilkenny Castle was presumably abandoned to the insurgents, where it would later become the headquarters of the Confederate Catholics. She remained in Carrick for about six weeks until just before Easter, continuing her relief efforts.[21]

The Countess of Ormonde undoubtedly owed her own protection to her kinship with Lord Mountgarret and other Catholic leaders, yet she was still vulnerable and potentially very valuable as a hostage.[22] One eyewitness testifies that "Notice being taken of the favours showed by the said lady unto the English, the Irish began to murmur and stomach at it, and restrained her from having such

---

[15] HMC Ormonde, N.S., II, 367–73. See also the depositions of John Moore, February 22, 1643, Dublin, Trinity College Dublin, MS 812, fols. 197r–199v (197v), and Thomasin Osbaldeston, March 23, 1644, Dublin, Trinity College Dublin, MS 820, fols. 008r–008v (8r), available online at http://www.1641.tcd.ie.
[16] Richard Comerford, in HMC Ormonde, N.S., II, 368.
[17] Richard Comerford, in HMC Ormonde, N.S., II, 368.
[18] Jonas Wheeler and Thomas Davis, in HMC Ormonde, N.S., II, 370, 371.
[19] Richard Comerford, in HMC Ormonde, N.S., II, 369.
[20] Thomas Davis, in HMC Ormonde, N.S., II, 371.
[21] Thomas Davis, in HMC Ormonde, N.S., II, 371–72.
[22] See Burghclere, I, 162–63.

liberty; whereupon she was driven at last to desire a pass to go by sea to Dublin, being not sure of her own safety."²³ A draft of a letter from Richard Butler, son of Lord Mountgarret, leader of the rebels in Kilkenny and Waterford, suggests something of the Countess's vulnerability in Carrick. He writes, with meaning, that he is "to wel acquanted with the richnes of your mind to err with others in the opinion that the great ^respects^ my father an I have borne you wil procure our ruin," claiming instead that he is "of soe contrary a beleefe that I protest I have a strong confidence it will be to you we shal owe for the hapines and peace of this cuntry by that favarable and trew relation I presume you will be pleasd to make of our Just resentments and moderate and equitable desiers."²⁴ Recognizing that the Countess could be a useful advocate for the Confederate cause, perhaps by using her influence with her husband, Butler implies that his lack of opposition to her plans comes with strings attached, and with a threatening undercurrent he hints at the consequences if he were to prevent her from leaving.²⁵ A testimony the Countess later prepared on behalf of the correspondent's mother, Margaret, Lady Mountgarret (Letter 32), acknowledges the older woman's role in securing the safe convoy to Dublin through her wifely influence and epistolary endeavours: Lady Mountgarret's son provided the convoy that brought the Countess from Carrick to Waterford.²⁶

Lady Ormonde stayed in Waterford for just two days, once again relieving Protestants "as far as possibly she could at that time and in that place, she herself being a stranger there and in like danger with them."²⁷ Her route to Dublin from Waterford was via Passage and Duncannon, and she made the five-day sea voyage in the company of many refugees who were traveling in her charge.²⁸ In Dublin the Countess of Ormonde continued her charitable deeds, first at her residence at Skinner's Row, then at St Mary's Abbey, and finally at Dublin Castle where she moved after her husband had been made lord lieutenant in November 1643.²⁹ There she "maintained many widows and fatherless children at her own cost and charges," according to one witness.³⁰

---

²³ Richard Comerford, in HMC Ormonde, N.S., II, 369.
²⁴ [February 1642], Edmund Butler to EO (Bodl., Carte Papers, 2, fol. 254).
²⁵ For JO's sense of his family's vulnerability, see the Earl of Ormonde to Lord Gormanstone (one of the leaders of the insurrection), Feb. 10, 1642, in Carte, III [*A Collection of Letters*], 60.
²⁶ Sir Richard Butler, in HMC Ormonde, N.S., II, 373.
²⁷ Thomas Davis, in HMC Ormonde, N.S., II, 372. For a woman's perspective on proceedings in Waterford, see Naomi McAreavey, "An Epistolary Account of the Irish Rising of 1641 by the Wife of the Mayor of Waterford" *English Literary Renaissance* 42.1 (2012): 90–118.
²⁸ Thomas Davis and Richard Comerford, in HMC Ormonde, N.S., II, 372, 369.
²⁹ Thomas Davis and Richard Comerford, in HMC Ormonde, N.S., II, 372, 369.
³⁰ William Roth, in HMC Ormonde, N.S., II, 370.

The Countess's war efforts were not limited to charity, however. She also tried to influence high-level political negotiations, allegedly trying to dissuade her husband (who at that time was commander of the royalist army in Ireland) from agreeing to a Cessation of Arms with the Confederate Catholics. According to Oliver Wheeler, "she hath been exceedingly averse, and as much as in her lay sought to divert her husband from concluding a Cessation with the Irish, apprehending the sure destruction by [sic] the English interest in this dominion."[31] Since the Cessation was agreed to in September 1643 with the hope of recruiting Irish Catholics for the royalist army in England, Wheeler's careful distancing of the Countess from her husband's royalism, especially its dangerous association with the Confederate Catholics, makes her appear more sympathetic to the Cromwellian regime by suggesting that she was suspicious of the royalist strategy from the beginning, even attempting to intervene against it. Her own letters tell a different story, as they show the Countess taking responsibility for the practical arrangements pertaining to her husband's negotiations with the Confederate Catholics in 1643 (Letter 5). The Countess is also reputed to have helped defend Dublin Castle from the Confederate Catholics in 1646. In her biography of the first Duke of Ormonde, Winifred Burghclere writes that "the idle were put to shame by Lady Ormonde, who, at the head of a band of noble ladies, herself carried baskets of earth to rebuild the fortifications."[32] She remained in Dublin Castle until it was surrendered to Parliament in June 1647.[33]

Exile and Dispossession

The Marchioness eventually settled with her children in Caen, Normandy, where her letters suggest she played an important, if overlooked, role in the Irish exile community. Caen was a Huguenot stronghold, which "[i]n addition to its proximity to the English coast and long-standing trading connections to Irish ports [. . .] offered a relatively friendly location for Protestant Royalists whose reputations preceded them in Catholic Europe."[34] Throughout her time in Caen, Lady Ormonde maintained a regular, if precarious, correspondence with Sir Edward Nicholas, Secretary of State to Charles I and later Charles II, in which she acted as an intermediary between her husband and the exiled court, relaying information in both directions. The letters to Nicholas represent only one node in the wide-ranging royalist intelligence network in which she operated, which included Sir Richard Browne, ambassador to Charles II in Paris, Sir George Carteret,

---

[31] Oliver Wheeler, in HMC Ormonde, N.S., II, 368.
[32] Burghclere, I, 315.
[33] Oliver Wheeler, in HMC Ormonde, N.S., II, 367.
[34] Mark R. F. Williams, *The King's Irishmen: The Irish in the Exiled Court of Charles II, 1649–1660* (Woodbridge: Boydell, 2014), 34.

Governor of Jersey, and others. In Caen she was also in regular contact with other Irish exiles, such as John Bramhall, Bishop of Derry, and Richard Boyle, Earl of Cork.[35] Her letters demonstrate the challenges of participating in a covert communications network and showcase the risks of sharing bad intelligence (see, for example, Letter 26). Her letters suggest something of the boredom that the exiles experienced (Letter 18). They also reveal the poverty and insecurity in which the royalists lived during their continental exile and her personal indebtedness to Nicholas for helping to secure funds for her (Letters 18, 28, and 30). Some of the letters to Nicholas are coded, using numerical cypher or aliases, which indicates her involvement in the exchange of sensitive information (Letters 13, 27; see fig. 2). Performing as an intermediary between her husband in Ireland and the court in exile, she deployed what she occasionally called her "bade [bad] lines" (Letters 7 and 15) for the service of the King.

The Marchioness's letter to Nicholas dated January 19, 1651, immediately after her husband's departure from Caen, explains her decision to petition the Commonwealth government for her estate (Letter 27). Secretary Nicholas had already been forewarned of the likelihood of this course of action, and he was no doubt sympathetic to her plight given that his own wife was already in England seeking the portion to which she was entitled.[36] In the letter to Nicholas, Lady Ormonde emphasizes her family's destitution, drawing attention to her husband's considerable financial losses and claiming that he had acted "with soe Litell Consideratione to what might Consarne his Future ^Subsistanse^ as hee hass made noe kind of provitione for it" (Letter 27). Although grounds for criticism, her husband's lack of concern for his family's welfare is more positively construed as an instance of his commendable—and self-sacrificing—devotion to the King. "I begine to See that my Nesesities will Ere Longe Forse mee to what of all the things in the world is the most Contrarye to My inclinatione," Lady Ormonde continues, her insistent use of the first person singular suggesting that it is fully her own choice to petition. This is unlikely to have been true, of course, yet it is consistent with her claim that her husband's loyalty to the King prevented him from negotiating with Cromwell, saying that he "did absolutlye refuse to Treate or acsept anye Condistions from Cromwells Partye; though very good ons

---

[35] Further letters to Bramhall are likely to be uncovered among Bramhall's correspondence in the Hastings-Irish Papers in HL, for which the current guide is incomplete.

[36] Parliament had passed an ordinance in March 1643 sequestering the estates of all those "delinquents" giving assistance to the King. However, to give the wives and children of "delinquents" some protection, the following August another ordinance was passed, which set aside a sum of not more than one fifth of the sequestered income of the delinquent for the benefit of his wife and children. See Antonia Fraser, *The Weaker Vessel: Woman's Lot in Seventeenth-Century England* (London: Weidenfeld and Nicolson, 1984), 249–50.

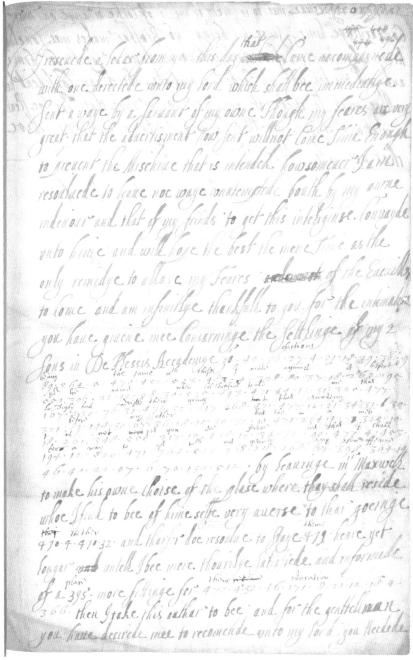

Figure 2. Letter 13. Letter from the Marchioness of Ormonde to Sir Edward Nicholas, June 20, 1649. Reproduced by permission of the British Library.

have bine offerede hime Consarninge his Estate." By presenting her husband as an exemplary royalist, she is free to look after her family's interests.

With the consent of the King and leading royalists, the Marchioness of Ormonde thus embarked on the long petitionary process. An anonymous female-authored letter written to her in Caen in late 1651 suggests that she had agents working on her behalf in London.[37] The letter (addressed "Deare Sister") may have been written by one of the sisters of Lady Isabella Thynne, née Rich, daughter of the Earl of Holland, to whom Lady Ormonde had been ward.[38] The two women had remained friends, Lady Isabella living for a time with Lady Ormonde in Caen.[39] The writer reports that during her recent stay in the capital she "saw nothing dun in your busnes, but faire words, sence it hath bin moved, and admited of a long debait."[40] She assures the Marchioness that her case remains on the agenda, however, claiming that Cromwell himself "semed much troble a bout it, and I am persuaded will not thus give it over."[41] She also professes her hope that the government "will be siveler [*more civil*] to Ladys" than it has been hitherto.[42] Armed with the assurance that she enjoyed the Lord General's sympathy and support, the Marchioness of Ormonde wrote directly to Cromwell on May 2, 1652 (Letter 29; see fig. 3). In this letter she explains that a portion of the Ormonde estate was hers by inheritance, and she requests that it not be confiscated along with the rest of her husband's property but instead used to provide a portion for the maintenance of herself and her children. As an heiress, her settlement should not have been sequestered along with their husband's own property.[43] She does not draw attention to this, however, and her decision to sue "only for relief" and "not for right" was strategic and ultimately contributed to her suc-

---

[37] "JH" to EO, [November 1651], NLI, Ormond Papers, 2482, no. 329. The letter writer informs Lady Ormonde of Lord Cleveland's "pardon," and "poore" Lady Derby's "surenther" of Castle Rushen. These contextual details date the letter no earlier than late October 1651 and probably soon after.

[38] "JH" to EO, [November 1651], NLI, Ormond Papers, 2482, no. 329. My reasons for attributing the letter to one of the Rich sisters are circumstantial. The letter is addressed "Deare Sister"; EO had been the ward of Henry Rich, Earl of Holland. The Earl of Holland had been executed in March 1649 for his part in the second Civil War; the letter-writer refers to "that unfortinate busnes" "for which my deare father died." The handwriting of this letter does not match that of an undated autograph signed letter by Lady Isabella Thynne preserved among her husband's papers at Longleat House (Thynne Papers, IX, fols. 39r–40v).

[39] Burghclere, I, 420.

[40] "JH" to EO, [November 1651], NLI, Ormond Papers, 2482, no. 329.

[41] "JH" to EO, [November 1651], NLI, Ormond Papers, 2482, no. 329.

[42] "JH" to EO, [November 1651], NLI, Ormond Papers, 2482, no. 329.

[43] Fraser, *Weaker Vessel*, 251.

cess.⁴⁴ Despite this, Lady Ormonde presents herself to Cromwell as politically naïve, asking for direction in making her application because she is "ignorant how to goe about it." She appeals to Cromwell's chivalric impulses by highlighting her vulnerability as one now "in Niede of protectione and assistanse." No mention is made of her husband; instead she foregrounds her responsibilities as lone parent and insists that if her request is granted, the estate would be used only "to raise a Subsistanse for my Selfe and Chilldren." Throughout the letter, Lady Ormonde suppresses her own royalist sympathies, yet at the same time her loyalty to Charles I may be obliquely suggested by the black wax with which her letter is sealed, signifying her mourning for the murdered King.

The letters to Secretary Nicholas and Cromwell showcase the ways the Marchioness of Ormonde refashioned her identity in the Ormonde Butler family in carefully gendered ways following her husband's defeat and designation as traitor, the sequestration of his estate, and his exile. But earlier correspondence indicates the extent to which this gendered transformation was a result of marital epistolary collaboration. Two letters from March 1649 addressed to the Parliamentarian general Lord Fairfax and his cousin, the Earl of Mulgrave (to whom the Marchioness was related), provide important context for Lady Ormonde's later petitions (Letters 9 and 10).⁴⁵ These letters are drafted in her husband's hand, with a note inscribed on the first by a secretary stipulating that "My lord would have my lady to write this letter to Sir Thomas fairfax to which purpose you are directed to Send it to her decyphered by a Safe express speedyly" (Letter 9). Evidence of judicious revisions indicates that the Marquess composed the letters with great care and with the intention that his wife should copy and send them in her own name.⁴⁶ The letters show how the Marquess thinks his wife should present herself in her correspondence with Parliament. In the letter to Sir Thomas Fairfax, he ventriloquizes his wife's voice, requesting the General's intervention so that "my lords servant may receive the mony ^remaineing^ due to him to his according to the termes set downe by the Commitee at Derby house

---

⁴⁴ Sir Robert King to William Basil, Attorney General of the Commonwealth in Ireland, October 6, 1652, in HMC Ormonde, N.S., I, 266.

⁴⁵ The second Earl of Mulgrave inherited the title from his grandfather, who was EO's great-uncle through the maternal line (his sister was EO's maternal grandmother). A letter from Edmund Sheffield, first Earl of Mulgrave, to his niece (c. 1628), arranging to meet her in the garden of Whitehall "to discuss what agreement is made in your business" (NLI, Ormond Papers, 2483, no. 469), shows that he had been a close advisor to EO when she was a young heiress.

⁴⁶ Although this is hardly unusual for the period, these letters represent the only evidence of such a practice in EO's correspondence. For discussion of this practice, see James Daybell, *The Material Letter in Early Modern England: Manuscript Letters and the Culture and Practices of Letter-Writing, 1512–1635* (London: Palgrave Macmillan, 2012), 74.

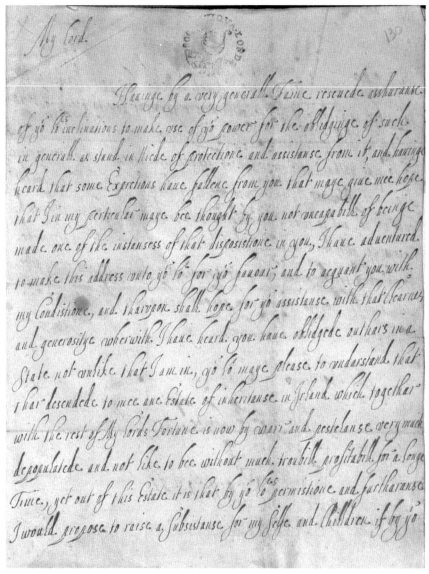

Figure 3. Letter 29. Letter from the Marchioness of Ormonde to Lord Protector Oliver Cromwell, May 2, 1652. Credited to the Society of Antiquaries of London.

~~without which~~ without which I shall bee wholy disapoynted of the meanes of subsistence designed for mee and the family left with mee" (Letter 9). By deleting "to him" and "to his," the Marquess eliminates any suggestion that the money is due to him, instead emphasizing that it is solely for the use of his wife and children. But in canceling these words the Marquess represents himself as the person who provides for his wife and children, while his wife is forced to adopt a passive voice and position as she speaks of what is "designed for mee and the family left with mee." In stark contrast, she claims in her own letter to Secretary Nicholas that her husband left Ireland having acted "with soe litell Consideratione to what might Consarne his Future ^Subsistanse^ as hee hass made noe kind of provitione for it" (Letter 27). While her husband is keen to highlight the provisions he made for his family, Lady Ormonde's letter to Nicholas betrays resentment at his lack of attention to the needs of his young family. Comparison of the letters written by Lady Ormonde and her husband points to her deliberate re-working of the model her husband provides: while he is keen to emphasize his fulfilment of duties as husband and father, she implies his neglect.

The Marchioness of Ormonde was fortunate to have the support and assistance of many high-ranking figures in Cromwell's government in England and Ireland in making her claim.[47] A Commissioner of Revenue, Sir Robert King, for example, wrote: "I did never observe more eminent virtues in any lady than are in her most perspicuous, and this I am sure (and much more of her worth) you may have from all those who know her."[48] He concludes: "It is hard that she that was born to a great inheritance shall want bread for her children because of her Lord's delinquency, and I believe was not practiced by her."[49] But Lady Ormonde would not have enjoyed such wide-ranging support if her conduct in the preceding years had been anything other than entirely unblemished.[50] Later describing her as "a person of soe much honor and meritt as I hope I need not presse any other Arguments for the shewing her any lawfull and just favour in this particular," Cromwell eventually acceded to her claim.[51] On February 1, 1653, the Commissioners of Parliament in Ireland were instructed to set aside Dunmore House, near Kilkenny, with £2,000 per annum out of the lands of her own inheritance for the use of her and her children on the condition that no part of the revenue should be diverted to her husband.[52]

---

[47] Mary O'Dowd, "Women and War in Ireland," in *Women in Early Modern Ireland*, ed. Margaret MacCurtain and Mary O'Dowd (Dublin: Wolfhound, 1991), 91–111 (103). O'Dowd contrasts EO's position with that of Lady Inchiquin, who lacked this powerful network.

[48] See Sir Robert King to William Basil, Attorney General of the Commonwealth in Ireland, October 6, 1652, in HMC Ormonde, N.S., I, 266.

[49] Sir Robert King to William Basil, October 6, 1652, in HMC Ormonde, N.S., I, 266.

[50] Sir Robert King to William Basil, October 6, 1652, in HMC Ormonde, N.S., I, 266.

[51] A copy of Cromwell's letter to Fleetwood in response to EO's letter can be found in NLI, Ormond Papers, 2499, no. 20, p. 85.

[52] See HMC Ormonde, N.S., II, 373–75.

Negotiating the Cromwellian Settlement of Ireland, 1652–1657

"I hear shee has now gott some of her owne Lande in Ir: granted her, but whither she will gett it when she com's there is I think a question," Dorothy Osborne astutely observed to her future husband, Sir William Temple, in September 1653.[53] The Order of Parliament had been obtained in February, but it was August 22, 1653, before Lady Ormonde received the documentation that enabled her to return to Ireland.[54] Then it was December 2, 1653, before the Commissioners examined the schedule of lands and rents assigned for her maintenance, at which point it became clear that the income produced fell far short of the promised £2,000 annuity: in some cases, taxes absorbed half of rents, in other cases it was nearly 80%.[55] The Marchioness of Ormonde was forced to make further petitions to both the Lord Protector and his Council and to the Irish Commissioners, including the letter to General Fleetwood published here (Letter 31): it was not until early 1655 that she was finally able to return to England to fetch her children and bring them to Dunmore.

Letters sent during what turned out to be, unhappily, a protracted stay in England from 1655 to 1657 showcase the challenges the Marchioness of Ormonde continued to face in her dealings with Cromwell and his government in England and Ireland. Letters to her valued agent, John Burdon, in Dublin, reveal the precariousness of her settlement, as well as the uncertainty caused by circumstances that she describes as having "Cast greater diffeculties upon mee, then canbee well imaginede, but by thous, whoe has bine a wittnes what a Laborious and Sad time I have had, to suport my selfe, and Familie" (Letter 66). The letters betray her desperation to retire to the relative safety, comfort, and welcome remoteness of Dunmore House; when finally able to do so, she expresses her hope and belief that at last "the worst of my ^ill^ Fortune is Past" (Letter 66). This letter, written as she was about to depart from Bristol, gives rare access to the Lady Ormonde's emotional turmoil during what was probably the most difficult period of her life.

At one point, the Marchioness of Ormonde alludes to the "one Persone that is by all soe much fearede" (Letter 40), which may refer to Cromwell: he certainly seems to be a looming presence throughout the letters. The Marchioness appears to be cautious and hyper-vigilant in her dealings with him, and other contemporary sources suggest that she had good reason to be. Thomas Morrice,

---

[53] Letter 37, *The Letters of Dorothy Osborne to William Temple*, ed. G. C. Moore Smith (Oxford: Clarendon, 1947), 83.

[54] See Carte, II [Book V], 160–61.

[55] This account is drawn from Carte, II [Book V], 160–61, and Burghclere, I, 438, where more details can be found. Official documents relating to EO's settlement can be found in NLI, Ormond Papers, 2499–2501.

chaplain and biographer of Lord Broghill (later Earl of Orrery) suggests that Cromwell had suspected that Lady Ormonde was conspiring with her husband against him. According to Morrice, Cromwell in a "fury" renounced the favors that he had given her, saying, "but I find she is a wicked woman, and she shall not have a farthing of it; and I will have her carted besides."[56] Apparently, the Lord Protector's rage only dissipated when Broghill was able to convince him that the incriminating letter that he had intercepted, and which he had believed was written by Lady Ormonde, was in fact in Lady Isabella Thynne's handwriting.[57] With the evidence in hand, Cromwell's "anger was turned into a merry drollery, and the lady Ormonde had her estate and liberty continued to her."[58]

Lady Ormonde's eldest son, Lord Ossory, was also suspected of being involved in royalist intrigue and imprisoned in the Tower of London. "[A] Nothar troubell has happenede in my Familie," wrote the Marchioness in September 1656, "as undesarvede as it was unexpectede, which was the imprisonment of my Eldest Sone, that was Carriede to the Tower one this day ^Last^ was Sennight ~~last~~ where hee has bine ever Sense and is still, but nothinge alledged against hime Nor I am most Sartane cannot bee, soe as I dout not to obtayne his release in a while" (Letter 43). According to her husband's first biographer, Thomas Carte:

> She addressed her self to *Cromwell*, answering with great confidence for her Son's innocence, upon forfeiture of her life, if he were found to be guilty, and desiring to know his crime and accusers. The Protector hoped she would excuse him in that respect, and told her that he had more reason to be afraid of her than any body. She was a person of an undaunted spirit, and replied, in a full drawing room, hundreds being present, with great assurance, "that she desired no favour, and thought it strange that she, who was never concerned in any plot, nor ever opened her mouth against his person or government, should be represented to him as so terrible a person. No, Madam, (said he) that is not the case; but your worth has gained you so great an influence upon all the Commanders of our party, and we know so well your power over the other party, that it is in your Ladyship's breast to act what you please." She answered, that she must construe it as a civil compliment; but that and a shrug was all that she could get from him for a good while. He treated her indeed with always with the greatest civility, never

---

[56] Thomas Morrice, *The Life of the Earl of Orrery*, in A *Collection of the State Letters of the Right Honourable Roger Boyle, the First Earl of Orrery, Lord President of Munster in Ireland* (London: James Bettenham for Charles Hitch, 1742), 1–50 (24).

[57] O'Keeffe persuasively suggests that the letter is evidence that JO had resumed his affair with Lady Isabella Thynne by whom he had an illegitimate son (26). An undated letter from Lady Isabella Thynne to her husband (Longleat House, Thynne Papers, IX, fols. 39r–40v) shows a resemblance between her handwriting and EO's, as well as similar orthography, which may provide another explanation for Cromwell's error.

[58] Morrice, *The Life of the Earl of Orrery*, 24.

refused her an audience; and when she went away, he always waited on her coach or chair; a respect he never paid to any body else.[59]

Carte's account of the Marchioness of Ormonde's interactions with Cromwell is by no means impartial, yet it does accord with the impression gained from her letters at this time, which suggest something of her eloquence, assurance, and quiet resolution under pressure. She did prevail in the end: Ossory was finally released in March 1657 after languishing in the Tower for six months. Ossory then obtained a passport to travel to the continent, and his younger brother, Richard, accompanied him.[60] Forbidden, of course, from joining their father in the court in exile in Brussels in case they jeopardized their mother's settlement, Ossory established himself in The Hague while Richard went to study in Paris. By autumn 1657 the Marchioness of Ormonde was finally able to take her three younger children to Dunmore.

Lady Ormonde's hopes for her new life in Dunmore were modest: "that God has designede mee, though I Covete Not great wealth, yet such a Competensie with a private Life, as may inabell mee to pay my depts and reward my such of My Sarvants as has Sarvede mee industerouslie and fathfullye" (Letter 66). Her letters to Burdon reveal her particular indebtedness to him as "one of the prinsepall" of her dutiful servants. They also give some insight into her relationship with those in her service. She has no patience with those who fall short of her high expectations: Edward Butler, for example, is described as "ussless" (Letter 66) because of his failure to collect rents from her tenants at a time of pressing need. Butler and Burdon would remain in the Marchioness's service after the Restoration, but Burdon is particularly valued by her. In May 1660 she recommends him to her husband's service, asking him "to louke with favour upon your ould Sarvant John Burdon whoe is Now as Sober and abbell a Secretarye as anye that I doe beleve you Cane light upon and willbee very ussfull to you upon Sondrie ocations" (Letter 101): she also brings Burdon to London with her. There are few references to him after that, however. A terse letter from the newly promoted Duchess to Burdon in August 1661 suggests that Burdon had perhaps overreached his mistress's favors by desiring an increased salary on top of rent-free accommodation (Letter 117). Two years later, he remained in the Duchess's service, as the last surviving letter to Burdon reveals (Letter 125). A letter to her brother-in-law and estate manager, Captain George Mathew, in February 1669 states: "If John Burdon bee soe unfitt for bussenes a Nother must Nesesarilie bee imployede" (Letter 160). Assuming this is the same Burdon, it is unclear whether he was thought unfit for service because of ill health or other deficiencies. Either way, it seems he remained in her service until at least April 1671 (he is mentioned in Letters 185 and 213).

---

[59] Carte, II [Book V], 162.
[60] Burghclere, I, 443.

Burdon was tasked with looking after his mistress's interests in the context of the Cromwellian land settlement.[61] In the background of the letters is the Down Survey of Ireland, which was taken in 1656–1658. The first ever detailed land survey on a national scale anywhere in the world, the Down Survey sought to measure all the land to be forfeited by the Catholic Irish in order to facilitate its redistribution to Merchant Adventurers and English soldiers.[62] Lady Ormonde was keen to ensure that her lands were not wrongly included with forfeited land, and her letters from this period shed light on the challenges of reclaiming confiscated land, as well as the struggles between landowners and the Adventurers that would persist for decades. That she did protect her settlement was attributable to her political connections as much as Burdon's hard work (although her satisfaction with his efforts is amply demonstrated in Letter 34). She enjoyed the favor of Henry Cromwell: just before his arrival in Ireland in 1655 she describes him as someone "whom I have a good oppinione of as to his wishing well to mee in this bussenes" (Letter 33), and in 1658 she entertains him in Dunmore, taking pleasure in telling Burdon: "hee was pleasede to make a visset hethar, and was bouth Sivell, in h and very frindlie in his expretions bouth To ^my selfe^ and of mee, as I understand when I was not presant" (Letter 79). At the same time, her surviving letters to him (Letters 39, 42, 70) suggest that she was far from secure in Lord Deputy Cromwell's favor. The Marchioness's letters reveal her particular indebtedness to her friend, Katherine, Lady Ranelagh, and her brother Roger, Lord Broghill, who had earlier defended Lady Ormonde against Cromwell's accusations, and was now named one of the trustees of her estate.[63] Thomas Page, an advisor to her husband and son, later wrote of "the great obligations [the Boyle] ^family^ has layd upon my lady in her straightned condition, particularly the Lord Broughill, and the Lady Rannlagh, which later to my knowlege may be sayd to have saved her estate from destruction."[64] At the Restoration the Marchioness of Ormonde was determined to acknowledge and reward Katherine Ranelagh's support (Letters 96 and 99).[65]

---

[61] For details of EO's settlement, see Conleth Manning, "The 1653 Survey of the Lands Granted to the Countess of Ormond in Co. Kilkenny," *Journal of the Royal Society of Antiquaries of Ireland*, 129 (1999): 40–66.

[62] Dublin, Trinity College Dublin, *The Down Survey of Ireland* http://downsurvey.tcd.ie/. Accessed February 17, 2020.

[63] Other Trustees included Sir John Reynolds and Sir John Temple.

[64] Thomas Page to JO, the Hague, October 13, 1659, Bodl., Carte Papers, 213, fols. 367–70 (fol. 368).

[65] In 1653 Lady Ranelagh was in possession of a "watch-dial without a clock" that had been gifted to her by EO. See Samuel Hartlib, *Ephemerides*, 1653 (Sheffield University Library, Hartlib Papers, 28/2/72B), available online via https://www.dhi.ac.uk/hartlib/. Accessed February 17, 2020.

Retirement in Dunmore, 1657–1660: Letters to the Marquess of Ormonde

Surviving letters to the exiled Marquess of Ormonde between 1658 and 1660 are evidence that the couple maintained a clandestine correspondence during the Marchioness's retirement in Dunmore. Only once does she allude to her "Cover," and this is when she tells Burdon that he should "not Convay or reseve anye Leters under my Cover [To or] from England of anye bodys that [are no]t this time in my Familie" (Letter 78). In her covert correspondence, the Marchioness attempts to conceal her identity and that of her family circle by disguising her handwriting, signing herself as "JH," and addressing her letters to "Sir" (once specifically naming her husband as "Mr Benss" and once as "Mr James Johnson").[66] She refers to herself in the third person, either as the anonymous "frind" of the addressee, or variously named as Mrs. Beckett, Mrs. Rashlye, or Mr. Dallison, and she constructs "JH" as a disinterested intermediary between the "Sir" addressed in the letters and his anonymous "frind." She also identifies her family and close friends through a range of aliases that are correspondingly adopted by her husband in his letters to her.

The letters indicate that marital relations were strained during the couple's long separation, with the earliest surviving letter to her husband (Letter 82) barely concealing the anger that she feels towards him. What is at issue is his interference in the lives of their elder sons; the Marchioness feels this is done without due consideration of the risk to her and the settlement that is dependent on the separation of the Marquess from his wife and children. A bigger crisis follows on its heels in the form of her eldest son's pursuit of a Dutch woman, Aemilia van Nassau, against the wishes of his mother. Although her husband gave his cautious approval to Ossory's choice of wife, the Marchioness opposed it because she believed the family could not afford the marriage. The van Beverweerds insisted that £1,200 a year must be settled on the couple, which the Marchioness argued her estate could not bear. As she made her case against the marriage, letters written from Dunmore illustrate Elizabeth Ormonde's complex negotiation of her conflicting identities as wife, mother, and nominal holder of the surviving Ormonde estate. The changing power dynamic between husband and wife is signified materially in the letters as the Marchioness places her "JH" signature at the center of the "significant space" below the text of her letters (see fig. 4), eschewing the customary deference to her husband.[67]

---

[66] The choice of the initials "JH" may have been inspired by those used by the author of the pseudonymous letter that she received in Caen that I have tentatively attributed to one of the Rich sisters.

[67] Jonathan Gibson, "Significant Space in Manuscript Letters," *The Seventeenth Century* 12 (1997): 1–10.

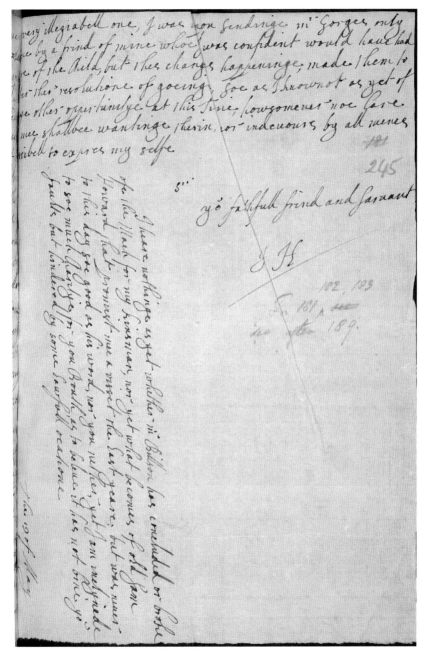

Figure 4. Letter 87. Letter from the Marchioness of Ormonde ("JH") to the Marquess of Ormonde, May 19, 1659. Reproduced by permission of the Bodleian Library.

The licence for free and open communication as the pseudonymous "JH" is borne out in the letters themselves. In the first letter to her husband on their son's marriage, the Marchioness acknowledges the young woman's virtues, before carefully delineating the reasons for her opposition to the match (Letter 85). Although she lists several objections, she focuses primarily on the issue of money, mentioning the mortgage on her estate, the expense of recovering it, and the dowries needed for her two daughters. She speaks rationally and practically, letting the evidence speak for itself, and so concludes: "for which considered, as shee hopes it will bee seriouslie by hir sone, and shuch of his frinds as are ther, will shee hopes give a stope unto his rueninge of his familie, to please his fancye" (Letter 85). She is forthright in her rejection of the proposed marriage, and allows no room for debate. It seems that the "JH" persona enables her to be more frank with her husband than she might be otherwise. By writing her own words in the third person, and as a disinterested intermediary, she simply lists her objections without qualification or apology. Although occasionally she betrays some anxiety about her forthrightness, particularly when it involves "displeasinge" her husband, she rarely wavers in her sense of her own authority, which emerges most strongly in her response to her son (Letter 83), which he rightly "interprets as an absolute denyall."[68] In the letter she reminds her son of his and his father's absence from the estate and the day-to-day business of generating an income, emphasizing her sole management of the family's Irish estates, which she claims places her in a position where only she can make an informed decision about whether or not the proposed marriage can take place.

Eventually Thomas Page, Ossory's secretary and confidante, was dispatched to Ireland to persuade the Marchioness to change her mind. Yet even when she finally conceded to the match, she continued to drag her feet. With her formal approval and signature necessary for the negotiations to proceed, she simply refused to provide either, using the difficulties of getting letters to and from the court in exile, as well as other practical constraints in letter writing, as a way of avoiding accusations of obstinacy or neglect. Her husband was evidently attuned to these manipulations as several months into the discussions and during the for-

---

[68] Ossory made the mistake of underestimating the force of his mother's opposition. Having first broached the subject with her in September 1658, Ossory reported to his father: "my mother seemed to dislike the thing but she had not received your letter . . . but when she has your sense of the thing I am sure hers will goe along with it" (November 4, 1658, The Hague, the Earl of Ossory to JO, Bodl., Carte Papers, 213, fol. 158). His confidence that his happiness depended more on his father's support than his mother's compliance was seriously misjudged, and he was ill prepared for her response, which was reported to JO: "I never saw him in so disconsolute a moode as hee has continued ever since the receite of his letter . . . if my Lady be not pleased to shew her selfe yeilding and condescendent in this conjuncture, I tremble to thinke what will be the issue of it" (November 8, 1658, The Hague, Thomas Page to JO, Bodl., Carte Papers, 213, fols. 156–57).

mal negotiations in The Hague in May 1659 she was forced to "vindecate" herself (Letter 87).[69] The letter she received from her husband admonishing her is not extant, but her response from May 19, 1659—four months to the day since her last letter—protests against any "misconstroctione" of her motives, explaining that she was "not at this time soe well in hir health as to write hir selfe by reson of a Cough that has troubled hir of Late" (Letter 87). Elizabeth Ormonde's resentment of her husband's and son's persistence is thinly veiled, the defence unconvincing, and an apology unforthcoming. Moreover, when she insists that she "never as yet did declyne the owninge and payinge of a respect where and obligation where it was soe much dew," the revision of her text reveals the reluctance with which she complies with her husband's wishes: this is not simply a "respect"; it is also an "obligation," and the speed with which she adds the word "obligation" (it is an immediate revision rather than a later insertion) betrays the displeasure that she barely attempts to conceal.

Restoration

A subtle shift in the power dynamic with her husband is signified materially in the first letter she writes at the Restoration. Elizabeth Ormonde now offers due deference to her newly "avowede" husband in the space created by his "most affectionat wife" (Letter 97; see fig. 5). The period of their estrangement she now describes as an "8 yeares absense," and deletions in her letter suggest that the absence was not just from her husband but from the King and his court as well, with her experience of exile compounded by her isolation from the royalist community. As she celebrates "our longe wisht for blessinge of the kings restoratione at length establishede to uss," she reintegrates with the royalist community and reasserts the royalism that she was for so long forced to suppress. She also now allows her two daughters to write to the father from whom they had been separated for most of their childhood.[70] A letter dated just four days before the first "avowede" letter to her husband shows that the Marchioness of Ormonde remained cautious to the last. Her letter of May 7, 1660, she expects, "will find you at a Nierer distanse then my former has done," but she doubts "how farr I may Credit it for truth your beinge soe; Sense I perswade my selfe if it were, you

---

[69] There is evidence that her husband was aware of this as a method to voice her opposition from the beginning when her son confessed to his father: "I have alreadie sayd something to her of my inclination but have not received this 2 monteths on [one] letter from her" (October 24, 1658, the Earl of Ossory to JO, Bodl., Carte Papers, 213, fols. 130–31).

[70] [May 1660], Elizabeth Butler to JO, NLI, Ormond Papers, 2481, no. 275; [May 1660], Mary Butler to JO, NLI, Ormond Papers, 2481, no. 351.

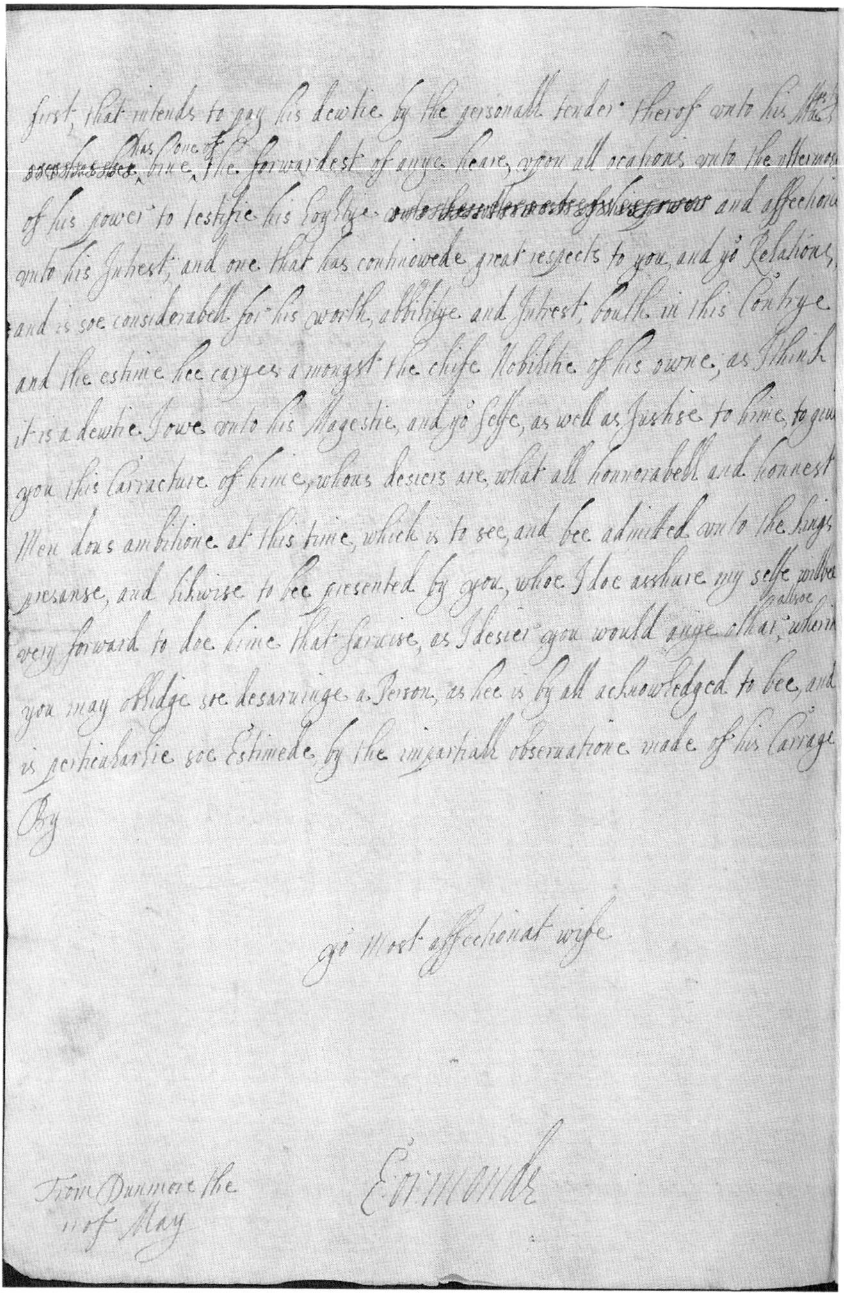

first, that intends to pay his dewtie by the personall tender therof unto his Ma:tie
has Come, hee the forwardest of anye heare, vpon all ocations, vnto the vttermest
of his power to testifie his loyltye ~~overtuereworkesyshisgraces~~ and affectione
vnto his Juhest, and one that has continuewede great respects to you, and yo Relations,
and is soe considerabell for his worth, abbilitye and Juhest, bouth in this Contrye
and the estime hee caryes amongst the chife Nobilitie of his owne, as I think
it is a dewtie I owe vnto his Magestie, and yo selfe, as well as Justice to hime, to giue
you this Carracture of hime, whose desiers are, what all honnorabell and honnest
Men deas ambitione at this time, which is to see, and bee admited vnto the kings
presanse, and likwise to bee presented by you, whoe I doe asshure my selfe willbee
very forward to doe hime that faruise, as I desier you would giue vs that, wherin
you may oblidge soe desarvinge a Person, as hee is by all acknowledged to bee, and
is perticularlie soe Estimede by the impartiall obseruatione made of his Carriage
by

yo most affectionat wife

From Dunmore the
11 of May

Ormonde

Figure 5. Letter 97. Letter from the Marchioness of Ormonde to the Marquess of Ormonde, May 11, 1660. Reproduced by permission of the Bodleian Library.

wouldbee soe kind as to Let mee know it from your owne hand" (Letter 95): the only source she trusts at this critical time is her husband.

The flurry of letters sent to her husband, as the Marchioness of Ormonde made preparations to join the court on its triumphal return to London, expresses a combination of exhilaration, anxiety, and disorientation as she anticipates the seismic changes that the Restoration will bring to her, her family, and the three kingdoms. The last letter sent to her husband just before she leaves Dublin brings these different emotions together. What particularly emerges is her trepidation about facing the hubbub of London after the relative peace and quiet of Dunmore, and she shares her preference for lodgings in Chelsea or Richmond where she would be away from "the Hurye of pepell, and the Noysomnes [noisomeness] of that great Towne" (Letter 103). She insists that her eldest son and his new wife find their own home because "the troubell of haveinge a Nothar Familie in My House is; from Comminge from a retyrede life a troubill I cannot undertake" (Letter 99). Her protestation, however, may betray her apprehension about meeting the daughter-in-law whom she had tried to prevent marry her son. Morbid fears sit alongside social unease as the Marchioness shares her concerns over the possibility of attempts on the life of the King or the Marquess himself, and she urges her husband to be wary of "wickede Spirets . . . Sectories and Phanatickes as thay are Now Called" (Letter 103). Although she expected that her husband would dismiss her "womanish feare," the Marchioness's suspicions would prove prophetic, with an assasination attempt in 1670 (see Letter 208).

The letters sent to her husband before they were finally reunited are mainly concerned with patronage as Elizabeth Ormonde took upon herself the responsibility of recommending clients in Ireland to her husband in the restored court. This comes as early as her final "JH" letter when she recommends the bearer, assuring her husband that the gentleman's "Meritt in all respects has bine such, as added unto his abilitye, and beinge Sone unto soe Reverend and worthye a Person, dous desarve your regard and furtharanse of his preferment, which I desier hee may find, and his Father allsoe, your frindshipe, in his particuler consernment" (Letter 95). One of the many letters of recommendation sent by the Marchioness in May 1660 stands out for the way it manifests materially the excited chaos of this period (Letter 101). The main body of the letter recommends one Captain Power; then a postscript acknowledges correspondence received but overlooked in the main body of the letter, "The good Neuse haueinge made mee allmost as wilde, as it has done many wisser persons;" then she writes "I pray turne the leafe," and inserts a new leaf upon which a recommendation is made for a second man, Walter Plunkett; yet another postscript is then added after the letter has been folded and sealed. The letter showcases the Marchioness's status within a lively and wide-ranging epistolary network, indicating that she can barely keep up with the demands of her new role mediating between clients in Ireland and her husband in the revived court.

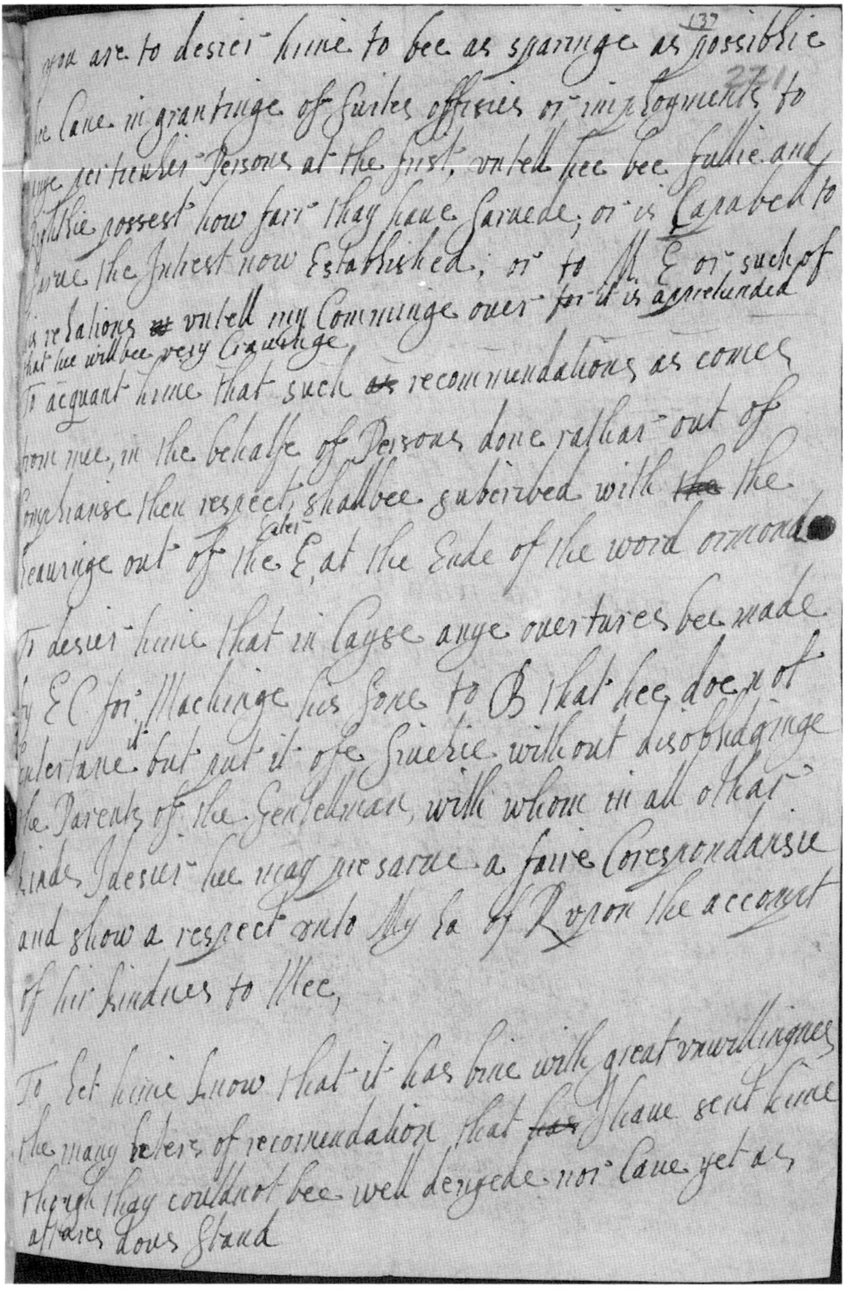
137
271
you are to desier hime to bee as sparinge as possibble
in Cane in grantinge of Suites offices or imployments to
anye perticuler Persons at the first, vntell hee bee fullie and
rightlie possest how farr thay haue Sarvede, or is Capabell to
sarue the Subiect now Established, or to M. E or such of
his relations vntell my Comminge over for it is apprehended
that hee will bee very Craueinge,
To acquant hime that such recommendations as comes
from mee, in the behalfe of Persons done rathar out of
Comphianse then respect, shallbee subcribed with the
Later
leauinge out of the E, at the Ende of the word ormond
To desier hime that in Cayse anye overtures bee made
by E C for Machinge his Sone to B that hee doe not
entertane it but put it ofe Sivelie without disobligginge
the Parents of the Gentellman, with whome in all othar
kinds I desier hee may presarue a faire Correspondanse
and show a respect vnto My La of Roxon the account
of his kindnes to Mee,
To let hime know that it has bine with great vnwillingnes
the many letters of recomendation that I haue sent hime
though thay couldnot bee well denyede nor Cane yet as
affaires doues stand

Figure 6. Letter 99. Memorandum of the Marchioness of Ormonde to [Anne] Hume, [May 1660]. Reproduced by permission of the Bodleian Library.

In the letters of recommendation she sent to her husband, the Marchioness of Ormonde invariably cites the men's loyalty to her husband and the King and highlights their role in maintaining the King's interests in Ireland. Participating in patronage networks in her own right, her letters from Dunmore and then Dublin suggest that she is best equipped to identify those Irishmen who should be rewarded for loyal service. In one letter, Lady Ormonde advocates for a client, not only because he has proven himself loyal to the King and to Ormonde, but also because he "has in your absense, and my nesesities, bine frindlie to mee" (Letter 101). Thus, it seems that she plans to use her husband's position to reward those who supported her throughout the 1650s. In a list of remembrances that she intends to be delivered orally to her husband by her close friend Anne Hume, the Marchioness writes that her husband should "show a respect unto my Lady of R[anelagh] upon the account of her kindness to me" (Letter 99). Indeed, her first priority upon hearing news of the restoration was to acknowledge the network of female friends who had supported and sustained her during the previous decade. On May 7, 1660, in a letter that pre-dates the letter to her husband by four days, Elizabeth Ormonde wrote to her servant, Stephen Smith, asking him to remind her "Cousen the Lady Turner" (most likely a pseudonym for her husband) to visit the Dowager Lady Devonshire, the Lady Marchioness of Dorchester, Lady Strafford, the Dowager Lady of Peterborough, the Dowager Lady Derby, Lady Ranelagh, Lady Anne Savile, and the Countess of Dysart, all women whom she identifies as being "soe perticularlie kind and Frindlie to Mee" (Letter 96). Thus, the Marquess of Ormonde is encouraged to make visiting this wife's female friends and supporters a priority when he returns to London.

Although the Marchioness exploits her husband's new-found power in the revived court, she apologizes for making use of it and also proposes a novel way of dealing with the number of requests for patronage that she receives. She asks Anne Hume to acquaint her husband that "such as recommendations as comes from mee, in the behalfe of Persons done rathar out of Complianse then respect, shallbee subscribed with the ~~the~~ leaving out of the ^leter^ E, at the Ende of the word ormond" (Letter 99; see fig. 6). The spelling of the Ormonde title was fluid: her husband used both spellings, while she routinely adopted the (feminine) terminal *e*. The Marchioness deploys this flexibility as a secret code with her husband in order to maintain strict control over the family's distribution of patronage while at the same time placating hopeful clients. Thus she cues her husband that her later—and half-hearted—recommendation for one Mr Burneston (Letter 100) was "done rathar out of Complianse then respect" (Letter 99). Although Elizabeth Ormonde ultimately defers to her husband's judgement when the people arrive at court, she does the initial filtering of their Irish client base.

The Lord Lieutenancy:
The Culture of Dublin Castle, 1662–1668

As Elizabeth Ormonde had rightly anticipated, her husband and family experienced a significant improvement in fortune after the restoration of Charles II, and in 1661 Ormonde was rewarded for his loyalty to the crown by being made the only Irish duke and also Lord Lieutenant of Ireland. An engraving from the 1660s by the print-seller Peter Stent, featuring the Duke and Duchess of Ormonde alongside the King and Queen, the Duke and Duchess of York, the Duke and Duchess of Monmouth, the Duke and Duchess of Albemarle, and the archbishops of Canterbury and York (fig. 7), vividly illustrates the couple's central position in Charles's court.[71]

Still, the couple were "bit players" in the King's court, whereas in Dublin, as Barnard puts it, they were "the stars."[72] They made their triumphal return to Dublin on Sunday July 27, 1662, accompanied by what John Evelyn describes as an "extraordinary retinue."[73] The Duke oversaw a significant development of Irish court life as well as the flourishing of Dublin's literary culture. The celebrated poet, Katherine Philips, came to Ireland at this time, attaching herself to the viceregal court at Dublin Castle, where she became part of a coterie developing around the Duke and Duchess of Ormonde.[74] Philips seems to have begun work on her translation of Corneille's tragedy, *La Mort de Pompée*, in Dublin, and less than a month after her arrival, she wrote that the Earl of Orrery (formerly Lord Broghill and a playwright himself) had read a portion of the manuscript and

---

[71] See Alexander Globe, *Peter Stent, London Printseller, circa 1642–1665: Being a Catalogue Raisonné of his Engraved Prints and Books with an Historical and Bibliographical Introduction* (Vancouver: University of British Columbia Press, 1985). There was also a market for prints of the Duke of Ormonde in his own right: Pepys bought a "head" of the Duke from the engraver and printseller, William Faithorne, which, in a diary entry for January 9, 1667, he describes as "the best I ever saw." See *The Diary of Samuel Pepys* http://www.pepysdiary.com. Accessed February 17, 2020.

[72] Barnard, Introduction, *Dukes of Ormonde*, 5–6. See also Toby Barnard, "The Viceregal Court in Later Seventeenth-Century Ireland," in *The Stuart Courts*, ed. Eveline Cruickshanks (Stroud: Sutton, 2000), 256–65.

[73] See *The Diary of John Evelyn*, ed. E. S. de Beer (London: Everyman, 2006), 400.

[74] Philips's letters from this time reveal much about the culture of the viceregal court. See *The Collected Works of Katherine Philips*, II: *The Letters*, ed. Patrick Thomas (London: Stump Cross, 1992). The poetry of the coterie surrounding the Duke and Duchess of Ormonde is held in the Osborn Collection, Beinecke Library, Yale University. See Andrew Carpenter, "A Collection of Verse presented to James Butler, First Duke of Ormonde," *The Yale University Library Gazette*, 75 (2000): 64–70. For an examination of the literary patronage of the Duke of Ormonde, see Jane Ohlmeyer and Steven Zwicker, "John Dryden, the House of Ormond, and the Politics of Anglo-Irish Patronage," *The Historical Journal* 49.3 (2006): 677–706.

Figure 7. Print depicting Charles II and his court, by Peter Stent. Courtesy of the Trustees of the British Museum.

urged her to complete it.[75] *Pompey* would be the first original play performed in the new theatre royal at Smock Alley when it was staged on February 10, 1663. Smock Alley theatre had opened under the Duke of Ormonde's patronage less than four months earlier as a replacement for the defunct Werburgh Street theatre, where James Shirley had been resident in the late 1630s. Like many of his peers, the Duke of Ormonde was a regular theatergoer; he also had numerous printed plays in his library.[76] Philips's letters suggest that the Duchess of Ormonde might have shared her husband's enthusiasm for the theater, since she "would not be refus'd" a copy of Philips's play and also allowed "several persons to take Copies" from the manuscript.[77] The Duchess also seems to have helped bring the play to the stage: Philips notes that "by her [the Duchess's] Order," one Monsieur Le Grande, an artist who was in the Duchess's employ, set the fourth

---

[75] Orinda [Philips] to Poliarchus [Sir Charles Cotterell], 20 Aug. 1662, Letter XIV in *Collected Works*, II, 46–49. For an edition of *Pompey*, see *Collected Works*, III: *The Translations*, ed. Germaine Greer and Roger Little (London: Stump Cross, 1993), 1–91.

[76] HMC Ormonde, VII, 513–27. In the inventory of the Duke's library in Kilkenny there are multiple copies of Corneille (possibly including Philips' translation), as well as a copy of Philips's poetry; there is also a manuscript of Orrery's play, *Altemira*.

[77] Orinda to Poliarchus, no date, Letter XIX in *Collected Works*, II, 59–61.

song of *Pompey* to music.[78] The Duchess even supported her husband's literary endeavors, it seems. In a letter written to Colonel William Legge in October 1666 before his daughter's nuptials, the Duchess writes: "My Lord is resolved sense hee Cannot Danse at hir wedinge hee will prepare a Balladt; and send it hir and hee hopes as good a one as that hee Made for hir at Moore Parke" (Letter 134). This is the only evidence that the Duke dabbled in poetry-writing, and although the Duchess indulges her husband's scribblings, her choice of the term "Balladt" and the teasing reference to his previous efforts suggest that perhaps the Duke's talents lay elsewhere.[79]

Weddings in the Ormonde Butler family also inspired the production of more distinguised poetry, such as Philips's "To the Lady Mary Butler at her marriage with the Lord Cavendish, October 1662."[80] With the poem celebrating the vice-regency of Mary's parents, a passage of the poem dedicated to the mother of the bride imagines that one of the muses or "bride maides,"

> shall your mother's glories raise,
> And much her beautie, more her vertue praise;
> Whose suffering in that noble way and cause,
> More veneration than her greatnesse drawes,
> And yet how justly is that greatnesse due,
> Which she with so much ease can govern too![81]

The Duchess is conventionally represented as beautiful, virtuous, even saint-like, but these qualities are specifically tied to her royalism and especially to the hardship she endured during the Interregnum. The poem recognizes Ormonde's dukedom and the lord lieutenacy as just rewards for his loyal service to the king, while also representing the Duchess as equally deserving of the favors she enjoys through her husband, perhaps acknowledging her contribution to her husband's success. The poem suggests that the Duchess is as well equipped to "govern"

---

[78] Orinda to Poliarchus, 31 Jan. 1663, Letter XXV in *Collected Works*, II, 74–75. Jane Fenlon, "Episodes of Magnificence: The Material Worlds of the Dukes of Ormonde," in *Dukes of Ormonde*, ed. Barnard and Fenlon, 137–59 (156, note 121), suggests that Monsieur Le Grande is possibly the painter, David des Granges (1611–c. 1671/2). For the fourth song, see *Collected Works*, III, 72–73.

[79] Philips, for example, refers to the poems published against her will as "Ballads (for they deserve no better name)." See Orinda to Poliarchus, January 29, 1663, Letter XLV, in *Collected Works*, II, 235.

[80] *Collected Works*, I, 250–51. Along with other Irish-born women including Frances, Countess of Roscommon ("Amestris"), Anne ("Valeria") and Elizabeth ("Celimena"), all daughters of Richard Boyle, second Earl of Cork, and his wife Elizabeth, née Clifford, Mary had been initiated into Philips's Society of Friends. See "To my Lady M. Cavendish, choosing the name of Policrite," in *Collected Works*, I, 213–14.

[81] *Collected Works*, I, 250–51.

as her husband, a quality amply demonstrated by her extraordinary individual achievements during her husband's exile.

The Duchess herself seems to have used the occasion of her youngest daughter's wedding to reflect on Mary's upbringing in Dunmore House, where the wedding took place at her mother's insistence (and not in Kilkenny Castle as has been assumed).[82] The Duke admitted to the groom's father that the location had been stipulated "by my wife's superstition who will needs have it in something she may call a house of her own how little soever . . . it deserves that name."[83] Although embarrassed by the relatively modest location for the wedding, the Duke was clearly willing to indulge his wife's wishes, which indicates Dunmore's importance to the Duchess.[84] It had provided her and her younger children refuge during the difficult years of the Interregnum, and it was where both her daughters came of age. It also seems to have been planned as her dowager home. Dunmore had been inherited from her mother, and was passed along the female line, which may mean that her elder daughter, Elizabeth, expected to inherit the property.[85] But Elizabeth, who had married Lord Chesterfield in July 1660, was absent from her sister's wedding because her own marriage had become embroiled in a scandal at court when her husband became suspicious of her relationship with James, Duke of York, and dragged her from court to their country estate.[86] The Duchess's only reference to what her husband describes as a "scurvy garboil" (or contemptible disturbance) is in a letter to Sir Edward Nicholas in

---

[82] See O'Keeffe, 69–70, for a discussion of Mary's wedding ceremony. Colonel Edward Cooke, sole representative of the Cavendish family at the wedding, suggests that Dunmore was chosen "in compliance to the pleasure of privacy," and admits: "but that design I confess hath not taken effect for our retiring from the crowd of Dublin hath but moved that crowd hither, and added the whole country's multitudes on to it." For his detailed description of the wedding, see Cooke to Lord Bruce, October 15, 1662, HMC, *Report 15 on the Marquis of Ailesbury, Appendix 7*, Part I, 166.

[83] October 20, 1662, Dublin, JO to the Earl of Devonshire (Bodl., Carte Papers, 199, fol. 117).

[84] For a detailed account of Dunmore, see Jane Fenlon, "The Duchess of Ormonde's House at Dunmore, County Kilkenny," in *Kilkenny: Studies in Honour of Margaret M. Phelan*, ed. John Kirwan (Kilkenny: Kilkenny Archaeological Society, 1998), 79–87. Fenlon's research suggests that Dunmore "was a large house with spacious rooms, set in a well ordered park" (80). Improvements were ongoing through the 1660s, however, so Mary's wedding would have taken place at a relatively early stage of the process.

[85] Fenlon, "The Duchess of Ormonde's House," 79.

[86] The scandal is mentioned in Pepys's diary, and a salacious account is provided by Lady Elizabeth's cousin in *Memoirs of the Comte de Grammont* (London: S. and E. Harding, 1794). For a more nuanced discussion, see O'Keeffe, 71–75. Five letters from Elizabeth Chesterfield to her friend Martha, Lady Giffard, in 1664 and 1665, speak of her experiences in the country and are published in *Martha, Lady Giffard, Her Life and Correspondence (1664–1722)*, ed. Julia G. Longe (London: George Allen, 1911), 1–17.

which she apologizes for a long silence based on ill health and "unease of Mind; for My daughter Chesterfilds unhappenes; of which I cannot but have a sense, Ecquall to the consernment that I have for hir" (Letter 121).[87] With her elder daughter's marriage in crisis as her younger daughter was due to wed, Dunmore perhaps signified for the Duchess and her daughter a promise of matrilineal protection and a guarantee of the safety and security of the maternal bond.

The Duke of Ormonde's Dismissal: Letters to Captain George Mathew

The single largest collection of letters in the Duchess's scattered correspondence are the letters written from England to her brother-in-law and Irish estate manager, Captain George Mathew, between 1668 and 1673, before and after her husband's dismissal from his second term as Lord Lieutenant. The letters address a variety of public and private issues, including her husband and sons' fluctuating political positions and conspiracies against her husband; a variety of Irish and English political matters, as well as gossip from the royal court; family news including births, illnesses (and their treatment), deaths, and marriages; issues around household management, including that of her daughters-in-law; estate management, including the payment of debts, the hiring and firing of servants, the organization of repairs and improvements, tenancy agreements; and many, many other topics. They provide ample evidence that the Duchess took a leading role in the management of the family's Irish estate and show off her aptitude for business, intricate knowledge of the family's Irish interests, and careful management of the family's sprawling estate. They indicate the wide range of duties and responsibilities attached to her varied roles as landowner, heiress, wife, vicereine, duchess, mother, and grandmother. And by giving us sustained access to Lady Ormonde's routine activities over a five-year period, they offer remarkable insight on her day-to-day life. Overall, the correspondence reveals the Duchess's abiding concern with her family's honor and reputation and illuminates her part in preserving its good name at a time when it was most under threat.

During the first few months of her correspondence from London, the Duchess of Ormonde is preoccupied with her husband's political career. For some months the Duke had been at court defending himself against charges that he was irresponsible or even corrupt in his administration of Ireland as Lord Lieutenant.[88] These charges were brought by the Duke of Buckingham, who was later supported by the Earl of Orrery. Throughout her correspondence, the Duchess

---

[87] JO quoted in O'Keeffe, 73.
[88] See J. I. McGuire, "Why was Ormond Dismissed in 1669?," *Irish Historical Studies*, 18 (1973): 295–312.

represents her husband as the innocent victim of attempts made by his political rivals to oust him from the lord lieutenancy (see, for example, Letter 152). Orrery, his rival for the post, is singled out for particularly harsh criticism, with the Duchess arguing that his attempts to discredit her husband expose him as "the most false and ingratfull ~~Person~~ ^Man^ livinge; and under that Estime I cane asshure you hee passes heare with all the considerable Persons of this kingdom" (Letter 162). Since she had been an advocate for Orrery at the Restoration, his betrayal is keenly felt.

The Duchess of Ormonde responds to such threats by keeping a tighter rein on her family in Ireland and especially her eldest son, Ossory, who was deputizing for his father in Dublin Castle. In a letter of November 1668, she complains about her son's conduct as Lord Deputy, but—in a sleight of hand that is repeated in other complaints against Ossory—focuses more on the behavior of his wife.[89] She admonishes Lady Ossory for neglecting her household responsibilities, particularly criticizing her careless governance, lax bookkeeping, and behavior unbefitting her rank and status (Letter 151). She writes that her daughter-in-law's conduct is "not the way to Live with that desensie that both is ^Now^ and willbee hearafter Expected from hir." Asking Mathew to transmit her advice to the couple "without Naminge mee to avoyde My daughters taking anye Exseptions," the Duchess recognizes the delicacy of intervening in another woman's household. Nevertheless, as her mother-in-law and, more importantly, social superior, the Duchess asserts her overarching authority as matriarch.

Although the Duchess repeatedly assures Mathew of her belief that her husband will return as Lord Lieutenant, in February 1669 she is forced to inform him of "My Lords dismiss from the goverment of Ireland, declarede by his Magestye" (Letter 159). She conveys the news without comment, instead preoccupying herself with the practical arrangements for the change of government. She gives orders for the preparation of Dublin Castle for the new viceroy, Lord Robartes, and indicates her intention to return to Ireland to oversee these activities. She begins to build a relationship with the new viceregal couple, immediately making contact with Lady Robartes to offer her the use of their goods, "which I Find was Extremlie well takene" (Letter 160). She also encourages the women in her kinship network, including her old friend Anne Hume, now Mathew's wife, to extend the hand of friendship to the new vicereine (Letter 162). The Duchess utilizes her family's position in Ireland to help her successor integrate into Irish society, perhaps with the hope of securing the couple as allies.

---

[89] Lady Ossory (1635–1688) served as lady-in-waiting to Queen Catherine of Braganza for twenty years. A chapter is devoted to her in Anna Jameson, *Court Beauties of the Reign of Charles II* (London: J. C. Hotton, 1872), 123–46. The *ODNB* entry for her husband mentions her poor financial sense, but the evidence is drawn only from her mother-in-law's letters. See J. D. Davies, "Butler, Thomas, sixth earl of Ossory (1634–1680)," *ODNB*.

Focusing on the practical arrangements, she wastes no time speculating on what might have been, nor does she betray any dissatisfaction with the King. As the months in England turn into years, however, her disillusionment with Charles's government becomes increasingly apparent. When in July 1671 she discusses the King's endorsement of Lord Ranelagh's unwelcome interventions as Chancellor of the Exchequer for Ireland, she comments: "but the kinge is pleasede with the Progect and that is all that canbee sayede for it" (Letter 217). The last straw comes with the King's response to the attempted assassination of her husband in December 1670, which was reputed to have been ordered by the Duke of Buckingham. When Thomas Blood, who confessed to the crime, was sensationally pardoned by the King, the Duchess suggested to Mathew that "the kinge had some Exterordenarye grownd for it which I wish may tend unto his Sarvise, how vilde and wicked sowever this Person has bine" (Letter 221). No doubt she expected Mathew to detect her abhorrence of the King's decision and her suspicion of his motives between the lines of her letter.

Her feelings about the treacherous Orrery are less circumspect. She gleefully relates that Orrery is "as Litell Satisfiede with this Change that ~~is~~ is made . . . as if my Lord had continowede" because, despite his schemes, he did not manage to secure the Lord Lieutenancy for himself (Letter 160). She anticipates, moreover, that the new Lord Lieutenant "willbee very Just and Frindlie unto My Lord and all his relations; and not soe indulgent ^I supose^ to My Lord of Ororye as my lord was" (Letter 162). Overall, the Duchess expresses confidence that, despite her husband's dismissal from office, the family will maintain their privileged position in Ireland. Indeed, when she briefly returns to Ireland in the middle of 1669, her description of being escorted from Dublin to Kilkenny "with all the ~~companye~~ ^Persons of qualitie^ in Towne whoe to Exprese ther respect to you [Ormonde] did bringe mee part of the way with the greatest conserne for your Leavinge the Goverment that ~~Ever~~ couldbee exprest" (Letter 166) lays bare her relief that her husband continues to be held in high regard by the country's elite.

The Duchess takes primary responsibility for the couple's Irish estates, tenancy agreements in particular. She even once complains of her husband's careless interference, assuring Mathew: "I shall hensforward bee more wachfull which I thought I nieded the Less bee when I had my Lords promiss after the Last mentioned Cheate that was put upon hime that Hee would not ingadge himselfe anye more in things of that kind without acquantinge Mee" (Letter 238). The Duchess deals with the local consequences of the Restoration land settlement, so when the disgruntled landowner, Edward Purcell, came to court threatening to "Ether kill or Pistole" her husband, it is she who asks Mathew to find out whether Purcell had rebeled in 1641, and thus whether his confiscation was justified (Letter 223). She is anxious to keep the couple's Irish affairs away from the court, and urges Mathew to deal with petitioners in Ireland rather than letting them show up in Whitehall (Letter 222). She is bombarded with petitionary letters from Ireland, telling Mathew in September 1673 that "theris a poure Madwoman kate

Foxe that torments mee with ^beginge^ Leters in verse and the Strangest superscriptions in the same Style that Ever was Siene [*seen*]" (Letter 271). Directing Mathew to give her "4 Stone of the Cast wooll and 2 or 3 Barells of Corne if ther bee anye, upon condistione that Shee writs verses to mee noe More," the Duchess stops the verse of this amateur poet but still indulges her request. The Duchess was often a charitable aristocrat and landlord, and her letters suggest that she was keen to ensure that loyalty and service were rewarded with extended leases or reduced rents (see, for example, Letter 239).

Throughout her letters, the Duchess recognizes the importance of maintaining the family's high profile in Ireland through magnificent display and hospitality, and she takes responsibility for much of this.[90] She continues to oversee repairs and improvements on the family estates, especially Kilkenny Castle and her own house at Dunmore. Her letters also reveal the petty squabbles among her servants that threaten the work, and she deals with the disagreement with William Millan, bailiff of Dunmore, and Robert Trotter, who was overseeing the building work, with characteristic efficiency (Letters 195, 202, 243).[91] Her "delight" in the development of the gardens at Dunmore (Letters 182 and 271) indicates that the renovations were as much for her personal gratification as maintaining the family's public profile; she also reveals her hopes for an imminent return to Kilkenny. The Duchess keeps track of the couple's broader interests in the city, particularly the school they established (Letters 168, 169, 174, 178 and 215) and the mooted inn (Letters 260 and 277). Building work was clearly important to the couple's maintenance of their power and prestige in Ireland, and the Duchess's letters showcase her role in such developments.

The Duchess also ensures that the family residences are always ready to welcome guests. Before her visit to Ireland in the summer of 1669, she had anticipated entertaining guests by instructing Mathew to prepare Kilkenny Castle for her arrival, "For I will make My Frinds wellcome to that Plase whilst I staye" (Letter 160). The Castle is also prepared for the entertainment of guests in the couple's absence. In August 1670, she sent instructions to Mathew that the new viceroy "shouldbee Lodged and Entertanede in the Castell" (Letter 198), and the next letter expresses approval that her son Arran entertained the Lord Lieutenant in his parents' place (Letter 199). The Duchess insists that "ther may bee allways a convenient quantitie of wine and Beare allo still kept in the Castell, that upon anye sudane ocatione, or persons of qualities Cominge thether to See the House, thay may bee offerede to drinke" (Letter 199). If Kilkenny Castle was not prepared for guests it would discredit the family, and the Duchess is anxious to

---

[90] For more on this, see Fenlon, "Episodes of Magnificence," 137–59.

[91] She keeps a tight rein on all her servants, complaining to Mathew in December 1668 about it being "soe strange a Time this is for Sarvants at as pepell of all degres complayns that thay were Never Soe Bad as Now" (Letter 155).

avoid this risk at a time when her husband was already vulnerable after his dismissal from the lord lieutenancy.

For the same reason, Kilkenny Castle was lavishly furnished in the couple's absence. In January 1669, the Duchess requests that some pieces of plate should be sent to her from Kilkenny Castle "to bee Changed For what is Now more in uss, and beter for Show" (Letter 157). She emulates fashionable tastes in London, keen for her family's houses to set the standard in Ireland. She also arranged for property to be moved from Kilkenny Castle to their houses in England. In 1672, she sends for "3 of the Diepe ~~Sutes of~~ ^Sutes of^ Hangings at killkenye, to uss heare, whilst I staye, and to bringe them Backe when I come; rather then ~~beeinge~~ bee at the Charge of buyinge soe Large ons heare, which will cost a great deale of Mony" (Letter 231). She further requests two boxes of silver sconces and white damask curtains for use in their house in London (Letter 231). Later in the month, she sends for two suits of hangings of Forest work and one Persian carpet (Letter 197). It seems that expensive pieces are more usefully displayed in London than in the empty castle at Kilkenny. Yet at the same time, she is careful that the items can be removed from the Castle "without disfurnishinge the best Romes" (Letter 235). The importance of keeping up appearances in both Kilkenny and London is crucial, as the couple attempt to maintain their position through magnificent display, in Ireland as well as England.

It was clearly a challenge for the couple to maintain the lavishness of their properties in both England and Ireland during a period consistently characterized by financial insecurity. Most of the Duchess's letters to Mathew are concerned with obtaining enough money to sustain the couple in England. Contributing to the high cost of living in London were the demands of hospitality, and she writes that her husband is "forst unto an Expense of his kiepinge a great Table not possible to bee avoyded havinge daylie the resort of all Strangers, and Embasodors and all the Nobilitie besides" (Letter 205). The Duchess also played her part in entertaining, explaining to Mathew after she arrived in Whitehall in September 1668 that she was so busy with "payinge my dewtie to My Beters, and resevinge the serimonye of vissets" that she had barely time to write (Letter 144). The obligations of being at court put the couple under enormous financial pressure, and during her trip to Ireland in 1669 the Duchess writes anxiously to her husband "of prodigious Soms that has bine transmi[tted] Sense your beinge in England, which terifies mee; with the Feares of beinge Ruenede if wee must Live Ther" (Letter 169). By the end of 1672 she writes to Mathew: "My Lord must resolve ether to betake himselfe to Live in the Contrye heare or goe into Irland for imposible it willbee for hime to Subsist at London" (Letter 258).

"If the Duchess of *Ormonde* had any fault," wrote Carte, "it was the height of her spirit, which put her upon doing every thing in a noble and magnificent manner, without any regard to the expence."[92] Subsequently, the family's indebtedness (which was figured between £100,000 and £150,000 when her husband died) was partly attributed to the Duchess's extravagant spending, a myth that the HMC editors failed to dispel by selecting her letters in such a way as to exaggerate her spending and lampoon her attempts at cost cutting.[93] To be fair, the Duchess's correspondence does seem to exhibit some striking inconsistencies in her financial management. Consider, for example, her tight-fisted haggling with a potential cook for her son Ossory, which "with much adoe" reduces his annual salary from £15 to £10 (Letter 164), against the £200 she lavished upon a diamond "George" (a typically jeweled or enameled representation of St. George, which forms part of the insignia of the Order of the Garter) when Ossory was made Knight of the Garter (Letter 259). But of course these are two very different types of spending: pay negotiations with a servant is a mundane and private affair compared to the high-profile celebration of her son's glorious installment in the Order of the Garter, with the jeweled "George" a necessary symbol of his new role. Moreover, unlike a servant's wage that would be paid out of profits from the estate, Ossory's gift was bought on credit and is only mentioned by the Duchess because she needs Mathew to find the money to pay off her creditor. Time and again, the correspondence reveals the challenges she and her husband faced in balancing the family's costly aristocratic and courtly obligations with their income, which problematizes, in turn, the narrative that the excessive spending was entirely her fault.

The letters also point to the significant emotional cost of managing the family's spending, of which it seems she bore the brunt. Throughout her letters the Duchess repeatedly expresses anxiety about the family's "depts"—a word that appears seventy times across forty-seven letters, amounting to more than a third of the letters to Mathew—and their ability to manage them. The failure to discharge debts on time could compromise the couple's reputation, so the Duchess takes it upon herself to manage the "clamor" and "noyse" of creditors. On one occasion, she confides to Mathew that in order to discharge a debt upon which her husband was six months in arrears, and "which was Like to have drawne some Clamor upon hime," she was "driwene [*driven*] to Pawne a [pair of] [dim]and Pendants" (Letter 149). Here, she takes responsibility for her husband's debts; elsewhere, she shows herself a conscientious bookkeeper, correcting the figure put on a particular debt by the evidence recorded in her own tablebook (Letter 197; see also Letters 235 and 253 for evidence of her scrupulous bookkeeping). Fears about the potentially catastrophic consequences of debt linger throughout her life. As she relates the news that the Duchess of Richmond's house was seized for debt in early 1683, her judgement of the woman's profligacy seems to be mingled with a recognition of the risks of keeping up appearances no matter

---

[92] Carte, II [Book VIII], 538.
[93] Toby Barnard, "Butler, James, first duke of Ormond (1610–1688)," *ODNB*.

what the cost. She judges that Lady Richmond has been "soe very imprudent . . . in hir Expenses" (Letter 300), and she is always anxious to protect herself against similar charges. Overall, the letters certainly illuminate the couple's spending, but they more fully represent the Duchess's efforts in bringing that spending under control.

The Duchess worries as much about the monetary affairs of her sons as their father. None of the three sons was ever entirely free from his father's financial support, and their dependence not only drained the family's income but added to their mother's anxiety. Her eldest son, Ossory, she is denounced as a "bad paymaster" because "Nether hee nor his Lady dous know what ther depts are or to whom thay owe" (Letter 151). She frequently admonishes his excessive spending and his indifference to debt management. When, against her wishes, he makes plans to move his family from Dublin to London at the end of his term as Lord Deputy, his mother predicts that "in six Months hee willbee forst to Rune in dept" (Letter 170). Once again blame is laid heavily on Lady Ossory's shoulders and, dismissing her as "a healples wife," her mother-in-law barely distinguishes her from the "Nomber of Small Children" for whom Ossory is also responsible (Letter 170).

But Ossory's financial irresponsibility is nothing compared to that of his youngest brother, John, whose money troubles—which are so serious that the Duchess fears he will end up in prison (Letter 180)—are part of a spectrum of reckless behavior, which also includes drinking, unsavoury company, duelling, and (although these are only hinted at) sexual indiscretions. There are at least forty mentions of John across thirty letters to Mathew, together amounting to nearly a quarter of the correspondence, almost all of which discuss his poor conduct. The first detailed description of his misdemeanors comes as early as December 1668 (Letter 153), although in the Duchess's very first letter from England she asks Mathew, in a postscript, "how my Son John dous Carye himselfe" (Letter 142). In her absence from Ireland she depends on Mathew for updates on John's deportment, angrily admonishing him when she hears of John's poor conduct from "Strangers" rather than his uncle (Letter 154). She also employs Mathew as an intermediary to correct her son's behavior—or failing that, to limit the damage (Letters 153, 154, 224, 234, 240, 245, 250, 252). "I have soe Mene an oppinione of his Parts as I think hime wantinge in a Capasitie of Liveinge beter," she writes in early 1671 (Letter 207). But she does not "cast ofe anye hopes of hime," as she declares in this moment of despair, later promising her son that if he mended his ways she would become his "sutor" to his father (Letter 246). Her letters certainly indicate that she and her husband took steps to help settle John's debts and finally secure him an advantageous marriage. The Duchess had been here before: her letters to Colonel Legge in 1666 focus on the ultimately doomed marriage negotiations between Lord John (for whom Legge was acting as marriage broker) and the wealthy heiress, Elizabeth Malet (Letters 132–139). Nearly a decade later, Lord John was to have more success with the new match: he married Anne Chichester, daughter of Lord Donegall, in 1675, although he would survive the marriage by only a year.

When the match for John was first discussed in May 1673, the Duchess was cautiously hopeful: "This is a greate yeare of wedings Generalie soe as I doe not dispare but that My Sonn John may gett a wife"(Letter 261). Earlier in the letter, she had shared her delight that marriages had been agreed between Ossory's daughter, Elizabeth, and the Earl of Derby, and her middle son, Arran, and Dorothy Ferrars, who was descended from "one of the best and Antiantist [most ancient] Families of England formerlie Earles of Essex, the Portion is 12 Thow^sand^ [/] Pound and but one Sicklie yonge Man hir Brother betwixt hir and 3 Thowsand a yeare after hir Fathers desease" (Letter 261). The economic advantages of the match are prioritized by the Duchess, but an alliance with an ancient English house is also valued. "My Lord and I were for Strengthninge of our Familie by the best allianse to [forti]fie it aganst the Mallis [*malice*] of Mene and Litell Pepell that has Labored [all tha]y could to Ruene [ruin] uss," she admits (Letter 261), showing the extent to which marriage alliances were used to weather the storm of political isolation. The letter also indicates the Duchess's active involvement in negotiations for the marriages of her children and grandchildren and the pleasure she took in their successful completion.

The marriage to Dorothy Ferrars was to be Arran's second advantageous marriage. In 1664 he had taken as his first wife, Mary Stuart, daughter of the Duke of Richmond and niece of the Duke of Buckingham. She was only thirteen when she married and lived with her husband's family after the wedding. As the Duchess's letters to Colonel Legge attest, their daughter-in-law was beloved by the couple. In November 1666 the Duchess is happy to report that, after a period of ill health, "My daghter Arran is thanks bee to God very well, Grows Tale, and Fatter then shee was, which makes a Change in hir Louks much to hir advantage" (Letter 136). Lady Arran's premature death in the summer of 1668 was marked by a spectacular funeral, but it left her bereaved husband reeling.[94] When the Duchess first sees her son in London she finds him "in great Sadnes" (Letter 143). For a time he goes off the rails, and his mother is forced to write in response to "reports heare, that are greatlie to his dishonner that I feare are but to Trew" (Letter 207). This she sees as an aberration, a "strange Course of Life" (Letter 207), and unlike his younger brother, Arran does get himself back on track, proving his honor through military and political service in Ireland and England. Extant letters suggest that the Duchess was closest to her middle son. She had nothing good to say about John and had little patience with the whims of her eldest son, even as she took pleasure in his successes and painfully grieved

---

[94] *An Account of the Solemn Funeral and Interrment of the Right Honourable the Countess of Arran* ([London]: Thomas Newcombe, 1668). For discussion, see Jane Ohlmeyer, *Making Ireland English: The Irish Aristocracy in the Seventeenth Century* (New Haven: Yale University Press, 2012), 459–61.

his untimely death. Arran she frequently praised for his dutiful conduct, telling Mathew in September 1668: "I perseve hime much consernede for his Familie and I have resone to beleve that hee will give a Materiall prouf of it" (Letter 143). The matter concerned a settlement on his elder brother that disadvantaged him, and the Duchess was relieved that he did not act on any jealousy, which she implies might have been warranted. There are no letters from the Duchess to Arran until the 1680s, but they reveal a tenderness that is not apparent in her letters to her other sons. Perhaps this is because she writes to Arran from a mellower old age and a period of relative contentment following her husband's promotion to an English dukedom.

The Duchess's letters to Arran are mainly concerned with updating him on the wellbeing of his wife and children. The affectionate indulgence for her grandchildren is clear from her playful description of Arran's young daughter as "Lady Blouse" (Letter 299); it is also evident in her account of another granddaughter's refusal of a suitor on the basis of his physical appearance. While she regrets the choice, she points out it was "the Part of hir Frinds to propound; but Not to Compell against hir owne inclination" (Letter 299). The Duchess also expresses her approval of the steps Arran and his wife have taken to deal with their marital troubles, no doubt drawing upon the ups and downs of her own marriage to share her hopes that the changes "will make you Both hapie, which I pray God may Continow to the Ende of both your days, and that Evrye yeare of your Liufs" (Letter 299).

The Duchess of Ormonde reports the birth of grandchildren throughout her correspondence, often at a proximity to the event that suggests she attended the births. The arrival of healthy grandchildren is a cause for celebration in the family. With the arrival of her daughter Mary's son, the Duchess specifically comments on the indulgent response of her daughter's errant husband (Lord Cavendish was notoriously unfaithful) "whoe is become the kindest husband and the Fondest Father of his yonge Sonn that Ever I saw" (Letter 175). She later delights in the sign of royal favor that comes when the King offers himself as godfather to Ossory's newborn son, who is named after his godfather, "soe as this Childe is Like to bee the first Charles that has bine of his Familie" (Letter 225). In both cases, the births offer hope for the family in challenging times. Along with good household management, it is through the production of healthy children that women can best contribute to the honor of the family. Whereas all of her sons are frequently discussed in the Duchess's letters, after marriage her daughter Mary is rarely named and then only in connection with pregnancy and childbirth. No letters to either Mary or Elizabeth have so far come to light among their mother's writing, although a couple of letters from Mary to her mother survive.[95] This reflects the lower survival rate of letters between women from the period, although

---

[95] See NLI, Ormond Papers, 2401.

letters may yet be found in the archives of her daughters' marital families. We get fuller insight into the Duchess's mother-daughter relationships through comments on her daughters-in-law, particularly Lady Ossory and the first Lady Arran, which reveal much about her expectations of the women in her family. The greater visibility of the daughters-in-law in her correspondence perhaps indicates that the Duchess saw her primary responsibility to the wives of her sons rather than to her married daughters. Still, the evidence of the letters (both her own and her husband's) suggests that the Duchess maintained good personal relationships with her natural daughters.

As well as attending the births of her grandchildren, the letters of the Duchess of Ormonde also showcase her responsibility for caring for the sick and dying. A standout example is her detailed account of the death of her nephew, James Hamilton, who lost a leg fighting in the Third Anglo-Dutch War and later died of his injuries (Letter 264). Another example is her care for her paternal cousin Sir George Preston's daughter, who nearly drowned in a shipwreck off the west coast of England before she was rescued and "broght on Shore upon a Mans Backe" (Letter 295). The Duchess frequently discusses her own bouts of ill health, as well as the illnesses of family and friends. She visits Bath to drink the spa waters, which before her first trip she claims were said to have "done Cures Ecquall unto the Burbone waters in Franse to thous whoe have had Coughs Like Mine" (Letter 270). She often speaks of the healing benefits of country air. On one occasion she removes to Hampstead on the outskirts of London, claiming that the "Plase and ^the^ quietnes of it has givene mee greater advantages in My health then all the remidies the Doctors could have precribede Mee" (Letter 275). She regularly consults with medical practitioners in London, sometimes on behalf of her friends in Ireland. She has a particularly low opinion of the doctors in Kilkenny, and when a senior member of staff at Kilkenny Castle falls ill she encourages him to come to England "to Trye what the Change of Climats may doe with the healpe of beter Phisistions then the Contrye doctors are Ther, hee beinge removede from the best of Them, beinge ^Now^ Soe farr from Dublin" (Letter 218). Later, when her friend Anne Hume, now married to Mathew, is ill, she assures her brother-in-law that she "will discourse with the best Doctors heare, and Send hir over some remidie if it be possible at this distanse" (Letter 205). Medical recipes were shared among friends, and in a letter to the Countess of Cork and Burlington the Duchess writes of benefiting more from the remedy she received from her friend's husband to ease the pain of a broken leg than he did from the remedy she shared with him (Letter 283). This letter to the Countess also reveals the Duchess's belief in purging as a remedy for illness, professing that she "hope[s] to find some benefitt by the beinge Sicke at Sea" (Letter 283). Travel was often essential to finding a location better suited to rest and recuperation, but the journey could be physically gruelling: in her letter to the Countess from Chatsworth she blames her ill-health on "the Rockinge by Land in the worst Coche way that Ever I past in cominge hether" (Letter 283). Sea voyages were particularly fraught with difficulty, yet she and her family (like the other Irish elite) were frequently required to make the arduous journey across the Irish Sea. Her letters provide insight on the necessary preparations for sea travel, including the best times to travel. Having lost her father and father-in-law to the Irish Sea, she was highly sensitive to the dangers of sea travel.[96]

Death and Legacy

The Duchess's last extant letter was written from Hampton Court on July 5, 1684, to her only surviving son, Arran, informing him of the couple's plans to return to Ireland imminently (Letter 303): however, her husband would return alone. As soon as they came to their residence in St. James's Square to settle their affairs before continuing their journey to Ireland, the Duchess started feeling unwell and took to her bed.[97] That was a Tuesday evening. She died at 7 the following Monday morning, on July 21, 1684, a few days before her 69th birthday. She was being treated for high fever, and her husband hoped that the timely application of "Jesuits' Powder" would be enough to save her life.[98] A poignant postscript on the Duke's letter updates Arran on his mother's condition: "It is now 6 in the evning and tho your Mothers temper is not perfectly good yet the Doctors beleeve the worst of this fit is past."[99] His wife died thirty-six hours later.

The Duchess of Ormonde was buried in Westminster Abbey on the evening of July 24, three days after her death. The body of her eldest son, Ossory, who had died in 1680, already reposed there; her second son, Arran, would join them in 1686, and her husband in 1688.[100] She was laid to rest in the plot from

---

[96] Her father-in-law, Thomas Butler, Viscount Thurles, drowned on December 15, 1619; and her father, Richard Preston, Earl of Desmond, drowned on October 28, 1628. See David Edwards, "Butler, Elizabeth," *DIB*, and Michael Perceval-Maxwell, "Butler, James," *DIB*.

[97] July 22, 1684, London, Samuel Douglas to the Earl of Arran (Bodl., Carte Papers, 40, fol. 281).

[98] July 19, 1684, St James's Square, JO to the Earl of Arran (Bodl., Carte Papers, 220, fols. 76–77). "Jesuits' Powder," a newfangled treatment made from the powdered bark of the South American cinchona tree, was named after the Jesuit missionaries who first used it for the treatment of malaria. The treatment had been introduced to England in the 1660s by Robert Talbor who, as court physician, successfully cured the king of malaria. It is probable that the Duchess was treated by Talbor during her final illness. See Royal Society of Chemistry, "Jesuits Powder," http://www.rsc.org/education/eic/issues/2009Jan/Jesuit-quinine-cinchona-bark-perkin.asp. Accessed February 17, 2020.

[99] July 19, 1684, St James's Square, JO to the Earl of Arran (Bodl., Carte Papers, 220, fols. 76–77).

[100] According to Ossory's *ODNB* entry, his burial in Westminster Abbey had been intended only as a temporary arrangement, but plans to move him to a permanent rest-

which her old enemy, Cromwell, had been exhumed in January 1661.[101] Given the significance of the Duchess's long battle with Cromwell over ownership of her Irish estate, it is ironic that in the end she and her family would come to occupy Cromwell's grave (although if she and her family appreciated this irony, there is no indication of it in the family archives). There are few records of the Duchess's burial. No funeral certificate exists among the records of the College of Arms; there is just a painter's workbook with a sketch of impaled arms on a shield with supporters and coronet above and the inscription "A Hatchment and Escutcheons for the private Buriall of her Grace the Duchess of Ormond who dyed upon Munday being the 21th of July 1684."[102] The service would have followed the burial service as set out in the 1662 Book of Common Prayer, but there is no record in Westminster Abbey of any music sung or the processions, and no sermon has survived.

At least two elegies were produced after the Duchess of Ormonde's death.[103] While one of the elegies was published anonymously, the author of the other was Edmund Arwacker, chaplain to the Duke of Ormonde. Arwacker was a graduate of Trinity College Dublin, where the Duke was chancellor, and prior to that had been educated at the couple's endowed school at Kilkenny.[104] Given his own Irish connections, Arwacker situates the Duchess squarely in Ireland, explicitly identifying his "Muse" as speaking in a "Hibernian Dialect" (3). For the anonymous author of the pastoral elegy, on the other hand, the Duchess's Irishness fails to resonate. Both elegies celebrate her status as consort to the Duke of Ormonde; commemorate her roles as wife, mother, and grandmother; and praise

---

ing place at Kilkenny Cathedral were not carried out. See J. D. Davies, "Butler, Thomas, sixth earl of Ossory (1634–1680)," *ODNB*.

[101] The Ormond vault (formerly called Cromwell's or Oliver's vault) is located at the east end of Henry VII's chapel in the Abbey. Names were inscribed for family members buried therein on a stone over the vault in the nineteenth century, but prior to that there were no markers and there remains no monument. My thanks to Christine Reynolds, Assistant Keeper of Muniments, The Library, Westminster Abbey, London, for this information.

[102] Coll. Arms Painter's Workbook 1634/1689.95. I am grateful to David White of the College of Arms for this information.

[103] Anon., *A Pastoral Upon the Death of her Grace the Duchess of Ormond* (London: N. Thompson, 1684), and E[dward] A[rwacker], *An Elegy on her Grace Elizabeth, Duchess of Ormond, who died July the 21st, 1684* ([London]: Thomas Newcomb, 1684). The untimely death of her eldest son, Ossory, in 1680, saw the publication of at least ten separate elegies (Ohlmeyer, *Making Ireland English*, 469).

[104] Andrew Carpenter, editor of *Verse in English in Tudor and Stuart Ireland* (Cork: Cork University Press, 2003), offers a scathing assessment of Arwacker's poetic abilities: "Arwacker was not only the most prolific poet of his age but incomparably the worst. His endless effusions in praise of the notables of the day plumb depths of almost unimaginable banality" (497).

her exemplary (female) virtues. However, for Arwacker the Duchess is of secondary importance to the Duke and his male heir, while the anonymously authored pastoral elegy fulsomely celebrates the Duchess of Ormonde's matrilineal power.

Arwacker commemorates his subject primarily as the wife of the Duke of Ormonde, identifying her as "*Ormond's* Duchess" (4). His praise for her quickly gives way to a eulogy on her son, Ossory, and then drifts further from the Duchess as it proceeds to commend her young grandson, James, who had inherited the Ossory earldom from his father and become heir to the Ormonde dukedom. "*ORMOND* and *OSSORY* in Epitome" (4), the young heir is imagined as the glorious realization of an exclusively male Ormonde patrilineage, with the generative role of the Duchess—and of the Ormonde Butler women in general—entirely overlooked by the emphasis on the male line. The anonymous pastoral elegy, in contrast, places the Duchess at the head of an Ormonde Butler matrilineage. She is given the pastoral name, "Pyrrha," who in Greek mythology is explicitly associated with female generative power.[105] Accordingly, the poem privileges the Duchess's maternal relationships with her daughters and granddaughters. It attends to the three sons in order of seniority, before turning to their younger sisters, Elizabeth ("*Phyllida*") and Mary ("*Lysca*").[106] The poem pays particular tribute to the Duchess's surviving daughter, Mary—who is given three times the space allotted to the Earl of Arran, the Duchess's only living son —and in doing so it celebrates the daughter's virtuous matrilineal inheritance from her mother, claiming that "*Lysca* was of pious PYRRHA born, / And PYRRHA's Virtues *Lysca*'s Heart adorn."[107] It is likely that a client of Mary, who was elevated to Countess of Devonshire in the year of her mother's death, is the author of the poem.[108] The elegy goes as far as to commemorate the Duchess of Ormonde as a patroness of all mothers.[109] Later, when her grandson, the young Earl of Ossory, is introduced, the Duchess is represented as an important shaping influence, with her role in finding a worthy wife for her grandson highlighted. The young woman

---

[105] In Greek myth, Deucalion and his wife Pyrrha re-peopled a world depopulated by the deluge by throwing stones over their shoulders. The stones thrown by Pyrrha became women; those thrown by Deucalion became men.

[106] "Fair *Phyllida*, who was with Ægon wed, / And blest Him with a Faithful Fruitful Bed; / Generous *Lysca* too, by Nature taught / To recommend the poor mans cause unsought" ("A Pastoral," 3).

[107] Anon., "A Pastoral," 4.

[108] Upon Mary's own death in 1710, her chaplain, Joseph Williamson, published *A Modest Essay upon the Character of her late Grace, the Dutchess-Dowager of Devonshire* (London: A. Roper, 1710).

[109] "Come then, ye Mothers, mourn around Her Tomb: / In PYRRHA's Name your Mystick Rites perform, / When to your Aid ye would *Lucina* charm / Either the lab'ring Matrons pangs to ease, / Or bless the Barren Mourner with increase" ("A Pastoral," 4).

herself, Lady Anne Hyde (*"Aminta"*), who would become the second Duchess of Ormonde, receives more praise from the poem than the male heir. The poem thus celebrates three generations of Ormonde Butler women and places the first Duchess of Ormonde as the matriarchal head of a thoroughly feminized Ormonde dynasty.

In striking contrast to the hackneyed praise Arwacker lavishes on the Duke of Ormonde over the body of his dead wife, the anonymous pastoral elegy celebrates the Duchess of Ormonde's powerful womanhood. This poem is thoroughly feminized, with the Duchess's matrilineage commemorated; women's generative powers celebrated; marriage, childbirth and childrearing positioned at the heart of the family's success; and the importance of the women of the Ormonde Butler family properly acknowledged. "Full Fifty happy years this matchless Pair / Liv'd in unshaken Love," trumpets the poem. This is an extraordinary achievement, the poem suggests, but one that might be explained by the fact that this "matchless Pair" are well matched. In the poem's unusual emphasis, the Duke has to be found deserving of his wife before she is proved worthy of him, and accordingly she takes a husband who merits her: "The Nymph found Him a Tryumph worth Her Charms, / And she alone was fit to fill His Arms."[110] Husband and wife are represented as equal partners, and their genuinely companionate marriage is presented as fundamental to the family's success. Moreover, the poem suggests that their marriage gives the couple the resilience to survive the many challenges they faced through the troubled times that formed the backdrop to their marriage.[111]

The theme of the Duke and Duchess's enduring, loving, and companionate marriage is taken up in a letter of condolence that the Duke of Ormonde received from his close friend, Michael Boyle, Lord Chancellor of Ireland and Archbishop of Armagh, after his wife's death:

> yow have now shut the gullfe; and have past the greatest difficulty of yowr life; you have lost, The noblest person, The wisest female, and the best of wives that Ever lived; one of such an unnusal goodness that her death doth worthily chalenge, not onely yowr Grace's, but the kingdoms lamentation; but all the gloryes of this world must have an end, And God in his divine wisedome hath fit to put a determination unto this; The newes thereof was a surprize and indeed of greate astonishment; but I hoped it may not be [unseasonable] for yowr Grace on this occasion to consider How long God hath bine pleased to afford yow yowr enjoyment of this greate blessing; If my [computation] fayles me not It is about 55 yeares that yow have bin happy in each other; what an age of mercyes have yow possesd togeather? How

---

[110] "A Pastoral," 3.

[111] "In all which time, PYRRHA, His charming Bride, / Oft came, and watch'd as He did, by His side; / Of his worst dangers still her part would bear, / And for all Joys She gave Him, ask'd but care" ("A Pastoral," 3).

have yee supported each other through with the changes and varietys ^of fortune?^ and have made even yowr Sufferinge easy to yow both by yowr mutuall assistances? God hath bine infinitaly kind & indulgent to yow both all those past yeares of yowr life; and I know yowr Grace to be so much a Christiane as not to repine, that now, at the latter end of yowr dayes he should make that seperation which mortallity cannot avoyd.[112]

Primate Boyle notes the unusual longevity of the couple's marriage and celebrates its buoyancy in the face of many challenges: this is the story also told through Elizabeth Ormonde's letters as they describe the fortification of the family through periods of difficulty. Although Boyle uses hyperbole in claiming her as "The noblest person, The wisest female, and the best of wives that Ever lived," the qualities of nobility, wisdom, and wifeliness are also key to the ideals of aristocratic female identity that she upholds for herself and the women of her family. Overall, the Duchess of Ormonde's correspondence testifies to her contribution to the success of her long marriage, the central importance of her husband and family and their dependence on her, and her own strength and resilience during a time of extraordinary personal, social, and political upheaval.

Conclusion

The letters of the Duchess of Ormonde form the largest body of extant writing by any woman who lived in seventeenth-century Ireland. Gathering and arranging her correspondence in one volume creates something of an epistolary life narrative for this important Irish noblewoman, but it is one fundamentally shaped by accidents of survival and recovery. Individual letters illuminate how Elizabeth Ormonde wanted to represent herself in a particular moment and to a specific correspondent and bringing her varied correspondence together reveals just how carefully she scripted herself through her letters. Casting the net widely has enabled me to gather letters from a range of different sources and repositories, and the volume encompasses letters written from her teenage years to her old age

---

[112] July 29, 1684, Dublin, Michael Boyle, Lord Chancellor of Ireland, to JO (NLI, Ormond Papers, 2439, no. 8506, p. 221). The Duke had faced the prospect of losing his wife a year before her death, confessing to his son:
> I know it is more reasonable I should own Gods great mercy in keepeing us alive so long then to bee troubled in the approaches of a seperation which can not bee farr of, I know shee thinks her self neerer her end then shee will own to mee or then I hope shee is, and that shee first resolved upon her jurny to the Bath for feare of giveing mee the greef to see her dye, tho I am prepard for it almost as well as I am for the parting that must bee betwixt my body & soule, This is too much on this subject, Gods blessed will bee don (August 2, 1683, St James's Square, JO to the Earl of Arran (Bodl., Carte Papers, 219, fol. 502).

and to a wide range of respondents including her family, friends, agents, patrons, and clients. The volume thus illuminates the many different faces of the Duchess of Ormonde. Overall, the picture that emerges is of a woman who was shrewd, even-tempered, cautious, diplomatic, exacting, loyal, proud, discreet, reserved, retiring, clever.

This edition of her letters is further intended to facilitate and encourage new research on this remarkable woman. Aspects of her life that require additional scrutiny include her relationships with her wide network of female friends and relations: many of the women writers who have received critical attention from scholars in the last twenty or thirty years—Katherine Ranelagh, Katherine Philips, Mrs. Briver, Dorothy Osborne, and Ann Fanshawe—write of their interactions with the Duchess of Ormonde, and deeper examination of these relationships would be very valuable. There could also be more research on her relationships with the women in her family—two daughters, four daughters-in-law, several granddaughters, her mother, mother-in-law, and sisters-in-law. In general, there could be more attention to all of the women in the Ormonde Butler kinship network, including Anne Hume, later Mathew, who was her ward, companion gentlewoman, and finally sister-in-law.[113] Following the biography of Elizabeth Ormonde's father Richard, first Earl of Desmond and letters she wrote to her father's nephew, Sir George Preston (brought to light in this edition), attention to the Duchess of Ormonde's Scottish connections also has the potential to be richly rewarded.

The period between her parents' death and her marriage needs to be further scrutinized, with particular attention to her agency as a young heiress. The Ormond Papers contain numerous letters to her from figures including Lord and Lady Esmond and indicate the network of connections that were competing for her service. Unfortunately, no letters written by her appear to be extant for this formative period, although something of the confidence with which she handled her new role as owner of a massive Irish estate is suggested in the responses of her

---

[113] Anne Hume, née French (d. 1701), had been EO's ward and had married Thomas Hume (d. 1668), a favorite of EO's father. She later married Captain George Mathew. See John Burke, *A Genealogical and Heraldic History of the Commoners of Great Britain and Ireland*, 4 vols. (London: Henry Colburn, 1836), III, 389. There are glimpses of EO's relationship with Anne Hume from her letter to Edward Comerford, c. 1630s (NLI, Ormond Papers, 2485, no. 47). There are also a series of letters from Walter Plunkett in Dublin to John Burden in Kilkenny in 1644 that indicate that Mrs. Hume was EO's gentlewoman companion at this time. In a postscript to one letter Plunkett writes: "I pray present my most humble service to my noble Lady to My Lady Elizabeth, and Mrs Hume" (NLI, Ormond Papers, 2485, no. 219). Lady Anne Hume lived through the Williamite War in Ireland: her petitions are discussed by Frances Nolan in "'Jacobite' Women and the Williamite Confiscation: The Role of Women and Female Minors in Reclaiming Compromised or Forfeited Property in Ireland, 1690–1703" (Ph.D. diss., University College Dublin, 2015), esp. 32–33.

correspondents. Her life in the 1640s and 1650s could also be analyzed in much more depth. Her relief efforts in the 1641 rebellion are well known, but her interaction with the Catholic Confederates, including some of her own kin, such as her brother-in-law, could be further interrogated. Her activities during her exile in Caen, especially her involvement in royalist intelligence networks, is in need of attention. Also requiring further examination is her engagement with Cromwell's government in the 1650s. More research is needed on the period between Lady Ormonde's first address to Cromwell in February 1652 and Parliament's Order of a year later. There is no record of any appearances before the Committee for Compounding at Goldsmiths, although in October 1652 Sir Robert King alludes to Lady Ormonde being "about to make her address to the General and Commissioners" in Dublin.[114] It is unclear whether she would have appeared in person or through an agent, and there is scant information about what a personal appearance might have involved. But since such appearances provide examples of public speaking or performance, more research is needed if we are to get a fuller sense of Lady Ormonde's political voice and activities at the time.[115] The Duchess of Ormonde's surviving correspondence is patchy for the viceregal period of the early 1660s; further examination of her involvement in the cultural activities at this time, and her role as patron of literature and the arts, would be very valuable. As scholarly inquiry into women and the cultures of early modern Ireland continues, our understanding of the importance of the Duchess of Ormonde and appreciation of the value of Irish women's epistolary writing can only deepen.

---

[114] HMC Ormonde, N.S., I, 266. Evidence of EO's activities in other contemporary sources await further scrutiny, including in *The Diary of Richard Boyle, 2nd Earl of Cork and 1ˢᵗ Earl of Burlington, 1650–73*, ed. Coleman Dennehy and Patrick Little (Dublin: Irish Manuscripts Commission, forthcoming), where, for example, an entry for October 17, 1654, says: "the Earle of Meath and I attended her la[dyshi]p to the Court of Claynmes, where Sʳ Jeames Barry did very well plead her cause." I am grateful to Patrick Little for the reference and also for alerting me to the extensive references to EO throughout the diary.

[115] It might be interesting to compare EO's experiences with those of Margaret Cavendish, Marchioness of Newcastle. Bruised by her failed appearance before the Committee, she represents other female petitioners as "Pleaders, Atturneys Petitioners, and the like, running about with their severall grievances, exclaming against their severall enemies, bragging of their severall favours they receive from the powerfull, thus Trafficking with idle words bring in false reports, and vain discourse." She attributes her own lack of success to being "unpractised in publick Imployments, unlearned in their uncouth Ways, ignorant of the Humors, and Dispositions of those persons to whom I was to address my suit, and not knowing where the Power lay, and being not a good flatterer." See Margaret Cavendish, *A True Relation of My Birth, Breeding, and Life*, in *Natures Pictures Drawn by Fancies Pencil to the Life* (London: J. Martin and J. Allestrye, 1656), 380–81.

A Note on the Text

General Description of the Letters

More than three hundred letters authored by the Duchess of Ormonde survive from six decades of her adult life, from around 1630 to her death in 1684. The vast majority have never before appeared in print.[1] Most of the letters are preserved among the two main archives for the Ormonde Butler family: the Ormond Papers in the National Library of Ireland, Dublin, and the Carte Papers in the Bodleian Library, Oxford. Further letters are held in the Bodleian Library's Clarendon Papers; in the British Library, London, among the Additional Manuscripts (Althorpe, Egmont, and Evelyn Papers), the Egerton Manuscripts, and the Lansdowne Manuscripts; in the State Papers, Ireland, in the National Archives, London; in the Society of Antiquaries, London; in the Dartmouth Papers in the Staffordshire Record Office, Stafford; in the Rosse Papers at Birr Castle, County Offaly; and in the Hastings-Irish (Rawdon) Papers in the Huntington Library, California.

The Ormond Papers at the National Library of Ireland contain the majority of letters by the Duchess of Ormonde, thanks mainly to MS 2503, which encompasses nearly 130 letters to her husband's half-brother, Captain George Mathew,

---

[1] Excerpts from the correspondence of the Duchess of Ormonde were first printed in HMC Ormonde, III, 437–54. With extracts of varying lengths taken from just 47 of the nearly 130 letters in MS 2503 of the Ormond Papers, this represents only a small proportion of her extant writing. Moreover, since passages are selected primarily for the light they shed on the political careers of the Duke and his sons, they skew the Duchess's epistolary output. More recently, a small sample of the Duchess's letters selected from the full range of her correspondence was published in the *Field Day Anthology of Irish Writing*, IV and V: *Irish Women's Writing and Traditions*, ed. Angela Bourke and others (Cork: Cork University Press, 2002), V, 30–34, 501–03. Privileging those letters that illuminate the duties and responsibilities of the Duchess herself as heiress and landowner, as well as wife, mother and grandmother, these best represent the Duchess's correspondence as a whole, although only eight letters are selected.

the couple's estate manager.² But there are a further 94 letters among this massive —and uncatalogued—collection addressed to various recipients, including her sons and agents, from around 1630 to the 1680s. Treasures among this collection include letters written to her agent, John Burdon, during the 1650s, which give unique insight into her experiences in Ireland under the Commonwealth and Protectorate governments. The second most important repository of the Duchess's letters is the Carte Papers in the Bodleian Library, which holds twenty-five letters, mainly addressed to her husband between the 1640s and the 1660s. Probably the most valuable of these are the coded letters sent to her husband in exile in the late 1650s, as well as letters written to him during a short trip to Ireland in 1669 after he had been removed from the lord lieutenancy. In addition to these, there are two letters from the 1660s to the Duke of Clarendon among the Clarendon Papers in the Bodleian Library. In the British Library there are letters across three collections: among the Additional Manuscripts there are two letters to the Countess of Cork and Burlington from 1677 (Althorp Papers); seven letters to Sir Richard Browne from 1650 (Evelyn Papers); one letter to Sir Philip Perceval from 1647, and one to his son and heir, Sir John Perceval from February 1660 (Egmont Papers); in the Egerton Manuscripts there are fifteen letters to Sir Edward Nicholas from the 1640s, 1650s, and 1660s; and in the Lansdowne Manuscripts there are three letters to Henry Cromwell from 1656 and 1658. There are eight letters dated late 1666 among the Dartmouth Papers to Colonel William Legge, who was representing the family in negotiations for the (ultimately doomed) match for the couple's youngest son, John. There are ten letters in the Rosse Papers to the Duchess of Ormonde's paternal cousin, Sir George Preston, and his wife, as well as to other recipients regarding Sir George's concerns; most are undated but written in the final years of the Duchess's life. Lady Ormonde's address to Cromwell can be found in the Society of Antiquaries, London. There are also three letters to John Bramhall, Bishop of Derry, dated 1650, among the Hastings-Irish (Rawdon) Papers in the Huntington Library, as well as an undated letter to Sir James Graham. Three letters addressed to the Earl of Arlington in spring 1666 can be found among the State Papers, Ireland, housed in the National Archives at Kew. The Duchess of Ormonde's formal petitions to the Commonwealth government can be found between the National Archives and the Carte and Ormond Papers, although they are not included in this edition.

The range and diversity of the letters that survive indicate the size of the epistolary networks maintained by the Duchess, and evidence therein of many other letters written by her points to the likelihood that more letters are yet to be uncovered, perhaps among the papers of the many families with whom she was

---

² Letters 176, 178, 179, 183, 184, 189, 192, 194, 195, 196, 200, 204, 208, 211, 213, 215, 216, 218, 221, 224, 226, 228, 235, 236, 238, 241, 249, 252, 253, 254, 255, 260, 263, 265, and 267 include drafts of Mathew's responses to EO's letters.

connected. As it stands, there are significant gaps in the correspondence represented in this edition, the most notable of which is the Duchess's letters to other women: her daughters, her mother-in-law, her husband's sisters and sisters-in-law, her female friends. We know from reciprocal correspondence from some of these women, as well as references to such correspondence in the surviving letters, that the Duchess wrote to them, yet no letters survive. In fact, the only letters from the Duchess to another woman are one letter to her gentlewoman companion, Anne Hume (Letter 99); one letter to Queen Catherine of Braganza (Letter 126); two letters to her friend the Countess of Cork and Burlington (Letters 282 and 283); and one letter to Lady Jean Preston, the wife of her paternal cousin (Letter 291). Significantly, all but one of these letters are found *outside* the papers of the Ormonde Butler family. The loss of letters between women in the Ormonde circle reflects traditional patterns of manuscript survival: since women's letters tend to be preserved in the archives of men, women's letters are more likely to survive if they were written *to* men, and this is particularly the case for the Duchess of Ormonde, whose letters are primarily found among her husband's papers. Such patterns of survival have the potential to skew our understanding of the Duchess's letter-writing, yet, without ignoring questions of "representativeness," it is clear that the Duchess of Ormonde left a substantial body of correspondence behind her, a diverse collection of over three hundred letters written to a variety of respondents, including her husband, sons, estate manager, servants, friends, patrons, and clients.

The Duchess of Ormonde normally writes with medium to dark brown ink in a distinctive long, slanted, and elegant italic hand. It has been suggested that she taught herself to write "by copying after print; for which reason she never joined her letters together," but her handwriting is not at all unusual for an early modern woman of her status.[3] Almost all of her letters are autograph, although the few letters that survive from the 1640s and a handful of routine business letters from the 1660s are scribal. Compared with her later correspondence, her signature on the earliest letters seems more labored. During the 1650s, she adopts a different hand to write to her exiled husband. While the hand is undoubtedly hers, the script is smaller and flatter than her usual practice: presumably, it was an attempt to disguise her handwriting since one of the conditions of the Cromwellian settlement was that she would sever contact with her husband.

Throughout the correspondence as a whole, the paper is generally of good quality. Most of the letters are written on a folded half-sheet quarto, where a full sheet of paper was cut in half and folded to form four writing sides, although the Duchess sometimes writes on a folded folio sheet.[4] Letters are folded through

---

[3] Carte, II [Book VIII], 537.

[4] For a thorough discussion of paper used in letter writing, see James Daybell, *The Material Letter in Early Modern England: Manuscript Letters and the Culture and Practices of Letter-Writing, 1512–1635* (Basingstoke: Palgrave Macmillan, 2012), 97–101 (esp. 99).

Figure 8. Letter 55. Letter from the Marchioness of Ormonde to John Burdon, [April 1657], with wax seal depicting the Preston Unicorn. Courtesy of the National Library of Ireland.

the standard "tuck and seal" method, which, as James Daybell explains, involved folding the bifolium letter twice horizontally, then twice vertically, before tucking the left portion inside the right.[5] The Duchess's letters are sealed with a range of different stamps (including the Preston unicorn, see fig. 8) using red or occasionally black wax. Black wax was a declaration of mourning, and she uses black wax in all her letters written from her exile in Caen after the regicide, including the one to Cromwell, as well as letters written after the death of her daughter-

---

Drawing on the work of H. R. Woodhuysen, who has suggested that the folded folio sheet was gradually replaced by the folded half-sheet quarto in the seventeenth century, Daybell argues that the folio format remained dominant for official correspondence throughout the entire period and proposes that women were more likely to use smaller-sized paper for their letters. Letters that were written on a folded folio sheet include Letters 4, 5, 9, 10, 13, 29, 31, 73, 88, 97, 114, 142, 146, 223, 253, 256, and 280. Letter 152 was written on a folded quarter-sheet octavo. There is no obvious reason why EO occasionally varied from her custom of writing on folded half-sheet quarto.

[5] Daybell, *The Material Letter*, 49.

in-law, the first Lady Arran, and her mother-in-law, Lady Thurles.[6] Only once, in a letter to Queen Catherine of Braganza (Letter 126), is there evidence of the use of silk or floss. Daybell proposes that their use "added a personal or emotive touch to the sealing of correspondence," and this might explain her use of silk in her letter to the Queen.[7]

The text is occasionally lost or obscured by worn or torn paper, as well as by modern binding, mounting paper, and mending tape; this is more likely to affect letters preserved among the Ormond Papers. Most leaves are numbered, often more than once: letters in the Ormond Papers have item numbers in addition to foliation, except in the case of MS 2503, where item numbers only are provided.

Editorial Principles

In preparing my edition of the letters, I aim to present a text that is accessible to the modern reader while remaining as faithful to the original manuscripts as possible. For this reason I preserve the original spelling. The Duchess of Ormonde's orthography is often phonetic ("vnkell" for "uncle," "Corronell" for "Colonel"), which was not uncommon for seventeenth-century women. Her idiosyncrasies may indicate her pronunciation of words (for example, "nide" for "need," "sense" for "since," "consarninge" for "concerning," "hir" for "her," "offier" for "offer"). Her spelling might even reveal something of her accent as a member of the Irish elite: when she writes "taught" rather than "thought" (Letter 180), her text exhibits a typical feature of Hiberno-English pronunciation. Evidence of an Irish dialect is occasionally found in her grammar: in the sentence "I have not as yet disposede of the thirtye Pound for to Satisfie" (Letter 224), "for to" is a characteristic Hiberno-English construction. There are a few instances where the Duchess of Ormonde's idiosyncratic spelling is replicated in her husband's letters ("shuch" for "such," for instance): this may indicate the extent to which her spelling shaped and was shaped by the practices of her regular correspondents.

In cases where the Duchess's orthography risks obscuring the meaning, I provide the modernized spellings of the words. For unique examples, the modernized word is provided in italics in the right-hand margin. For repeated examples, the word is marked with a small superscript circle to indicate that the word and its modernized spelling can be found in the glossary. In a few instances the Duchess of Ormonde routinely makes a compound of a verb ("willnot," "willbee," "canbee," "theris," "knownot," "doutnot"): as with modern compounds that she also employs ("cannot"), I preserve this practice. With less consistency, she also

---

[6] Letters 11, 12, 14, 17, 27, 29, 57, 68, 69, 107, 129, 130, 131, 143, 145, 146, 147, 148, 149, 152, 155, 175, 180, 181, 182, 185, 189, 190, 193, 196, 204, 249, 267, 271, 272, 274, 275, 277, and 278 were sealed with black wax.

[7] Daybell, *The Material Letter*, 106.

occasionally runs the first person pronoun into the verb ("Iam," "Iwas," "Imay"): I do not preserve the compound in these cases. She also at times splits words in two, especially when they begin with the syllable *a* ("a distione" rather than "adistion," "a ganst" rather than "aganst," "a frade" rather than "afrade," "a doe" rather than "adoe," "a greede" instead of "agreede," "a brode" instead of "abrode," "a gayne" instead of "agayne," "a Levene" for "alevene [*eleven*]"; "in stied" for "instied," "dis opoynment" for "disopoynment," "with out" for "without"): to avoid unnecessary confusion I merge these words. However, an exception is made for "a Nother" ("another"), which she routinely capitalizes: this idiosyncrasy I retain.

I retain the original punctuation. The Duchess of Ormonde rarely uses periods; instead she tends to use commas in place of periods and semi-colons in place of commas. When the ink is faded, smudged, or splattered, it can sometimes be difficult to distinguish between comma and semi-colon: when there is any doubt, I have done my best to differentiate between them according to the Duchess's usual practice. Occasionally, she utilizes line-ends in place of punctuation marks: in these cases, I add a virgule [/] in square brackets to indicate the possibility of punctuation. Otherwise, original lineation has not been preserved. In the unusual instance that a word in the original is split across two lines, it is brought together silently (so "Like [/] =lihoude" becomes "Likelihoude"). While the Duchess mainly writes the text continuously, she occasionally indicates new "paragraphs" with line breaks (either within or between lines): I attempt to duplicate this aspect of her presentation continuing the text on the next line, after a paragraph indentation.

I also retain the original capitalization, which may at times be meaningful. For example, the Duchess routinely capitalizes when she mentions her relationship with a third person ("My Lord" or "My Sone Arran," to select two examples). She also occasionally uses capitals for emphasis: when she comments upon the "admiratione and Joy" with which the population have greeted news of Charles's restoration, for instance, "Joy" is shown to be the dominant emotion (Letter 97), and when she remarks on her youngest son's refusal to change his ways—"I hear hee Lives as hee did Still"—her exasperation is clear from the capitalized "Still" (Letter 154). Sometimes capitals distinguish one word from another: for example, "To" beginning with the upper-case *T* often represents "too." There are minor issues concerning the Duchess of Ormonde's typography, however. She almost always uses an upper-case *L* when it appears at the beginning of a word ("Last Letter"): in these cases I employ the upper-case *L* to distinguish from the lower-case *l* that appears in the middle or at the end of words ("Litell"). It is a little unclear whether the Duchess means to use the long *s* (ſ) or the upper-case *S* when it appears at the beginning of the word ("Surprise"): I adopt the upper-case form in these instances. Very occasionally the Duchess uses the upper-case *L* and *S* in the middle of a word: these I silently change to the lower-case *l* and *s*. I modernize the Duchess's use of *u* and *v* ("beleve" for "beleue," "unto" for "vnto"), and *I* and *J* ("Journye" for "Iournye," "John" for

"Iohn"). Where there is some ambiguity ("maior," for example, might be "major" or "mayor"), I add a footnote to explain the choice. A bigger question concerns the Duchess's use of the initials "IH" in her interregnum letters: without any solid basis on which to choose between "IH" and "JH," I have adopted "JH" because "J" can stand for greater range of common forenames ("John" or "James"), as well as to preserve the possibility that the "J" in "JH" alludes to her husband, James. The numerals *1* and *7* occasionally cause confusion: however, since they typically refer to the date, they can often be corroborated by the endorsement. The Duchess occasionally uses numerical ciphers in her letters from the 1650s: the solutions are included when supplied by the recipient.

Words that are often used and commonly abbreviated by the Duchess of Ormonde I silently expand according to her preferred spelling: "Lo," for example, becomes "Lord," "La" becomes "Lady," "Cap" becomes "Captane," "Cor" becomes "Corronell," "Lif" becomes "Liftenant," "Thow" becomes "Thowsand." When appropriate, I also lower superscriptions, so "yor" becomes "your," "S^r" becomes "Sir," "Mis" becomes "Mistris," "Lor^s" becomes "Lordshipps," "La^p" becomes "Ladyshipp," "Com^{ie}" becomes "Commitie," "Com^s" becomes "Comistioners," and "Shill^{ige}" (or "Shill") becomes "Shillinge." Occasionally, the Duchess uses abbreviations for words that she spells inconsistently. "Par," for example, is abbreviated from "Parliament," which she variously spells "Parlement" and "Parliment," and "Bro" is spelled "Brother" and "Brothar": I expand "Par" to "Parliment," and "Bro" to "Brother." Abbreviations for words that are less commonly used I also expand, so "Mar" becomes "Marchioness" (even though she only uses the abbreviation in her letters), and "Eng" becomes "England." The Duchess of Ormonde uses different kinds of abbreviations for the months of the year: "September," for instance, is abbreviated to both "Sep" or "Sep^{ber}" (and, rarely, "Sep^{br}"). In the latter case, I expand the abbreviation and lower the superscription, so "Sep^{ber}" becomes "September;" the former, however, I leave in its original state. Similarly, "Jan," "Feb," "Oct," "No" and "Des" are untouched (although "Ia" is regularized to "Jan"), while "No^{ber}" is expanded to "November" (or occasionally "No^{bar}" to "Novembar"), and "Des^{ber}" is expanded to "Desember." The Duchess rarely uses Roman numerals: these are brought in line with her usual habits (so "xx" is replaced by "20"). In general, abbreviations that conform to modern usage (such as "m^r" or "S^t") are not expanded, although the superscription is lowered; "mi^r" is regularized to "mr." I modernize her abbreviations of numerical dates so that, for example, "Caen the 2th of May" becomes "Caen the 2nd of May." Abbreviations for first names I expand in line with her usual spelling practices, so "Ed" becomes "Edward," "Fra" becomes "Franses," "Go" becomes "Gorge," "Har" becomes "Hary," "Io" becomes "John," "Ja" (or, on one occasion, "J") becomes "James," "La" becomes "Lawrence," "Red" becomes "Redmond," "Ri" becomes "Richard," "Ro" becomes "Robert," "W^m" becomes "William," and "Pa" becomes "Patricke." Shortened names by which the person is commonly known, such as "Ned" (Butler) or "Hary" (Cromwell), are left in their abbreviated form. Surnames or the names of titles are expanded for clarity (so "Ran" is adjusted to "Ranalagh"). The occasional words in which the Duchess employs tildes (~) are expanded.

An interesting feature of the Duchess of Ormonde's letters is her revision practice, which reveals a concern for clarity, precision, and style. She corrects spelling mistakes: for example, "~~gyede~~ guide" (Letter 142). She often removes repeated words: "resoulvede . . . resoulvede" becomes "resoulvede . . . intend" (Letter 64). She is also careful how she represents herself and her relationships in her letters. Writing to her agent John Burdon, for example, whose loyal service through the difficult years of the 1650s had threatened to blur the social distinctions between them, her authority is reasserted when a polite request becomes a command: "~~I praye~~ it willbee Likwise Nesesarye" (Letter 35); this revision may also be a sign of her less precarious position as she takes control of her Dunmore estate. Also writing to Burdon, but describing the deficiencies of another servant, she decides "negligent" is not a strong enough word to describe him; instead he is "ussless" (Letter 66). And when she feels oblidged to write a letter of recommendation for a person of whose loyalty and merits she is unconvinced, she cues her husband accordingly: "~~as to asshure you~~ ^in Justis to hime^" (Letter 100). Her corrections also reveal faultlines in her representation of the power dynamics of the marital relationship. For example, when she tells her brother-in-law and Irish estate manager Captain George Mathew of the couple's efforts to sell their country house, she belatedly remembers that it is first and foremost her husband's property: "~~wee are~~ ^My Lord^ is in Treatie for the Sayle of Moore Park" (Letter 152). Similarly, in regard to finding someone to work on the couple's Irish estate, the Duchess writes to Mathew: "what you doe propose as unto his imployment ~~I doe a~~ for the presant is very well approvede of by My Lord" (Letter 217). Once again her error shows that even though she makes the decision, she ascribes ultimate authority to her husband. Corrections also reveal the difficulty the Duchess often experienced in deferring to her husband in this way, especially when his decisions differed from the ones she would have made. For instance, she tones down her criticism of an overly hasty decision that led to the loss of money when she confesses to Mathew that "had ~~his Haste~~ ^Not My Lord^ [/] bine ~~soe~~ ^a litell to^ hastie In, I am very confident hee might have had a hundreth pound a yeare More" (Letter 196): her confidence in her own superior judgement remains unshaken.

Revisions are often barely legible under the Duchess's heavy strikethroughs (often a series of diagonal slashes written over by tightly connected loops that resemble a row of joined-up *ses*). When they can be reconstructed, the canceled words are supplied and then struck through. When there is doubt about the words supplied, they are enclosed in square brackets and struck through. When deleted words cannot be reconstituted, this is acknowledged by "~~[illegible]~~," with a footnote indicating when more than one word is affected. Interpolations are signaled by the use of caret symbols (^ ^) at either end of the inserted text; the added text is also silently lowered. To avoid any unnecessary confusion (when, for instance, revisions extend over two or more lines), all interpolations are inserted immediately after the deleted word/s. I have not amended any uncorrected mistakes because they may indicate haste, fatigue, or distractedness: the mistake has simply been noted with [*sic*] and any necessary clarification is provided as a marginal gloss. There are further material signs of emotional distress that are more difficult to flag in a scholarly edition, including ink blots or unusually poor handwriting. For example, when the Duchess shares with Mathew her frustration at the conduct of her eldest son Ossory and his wife (Letter 213), she makes more mistakes as the letter progresses, and her handwriting also becomes larger and more scrawled: this may indicate the greater speed of her writing and also her reluctance to pause to trim her quill, which may reflect in her penmanship her anger and distress at this time. On the whole, the manuscripts are well preserved, although several letters are damaged by tears, burns, or general wear of the paper. Words that are lost or obscured through damage to the original are supplied, where possible, in square brackets. These words are my own, but are based on what I understand about the Duchess's writing habits and epistolary style, by the text before and after the missing words, by the length of the missing text, and by her usual orthography. When it is not possible to extrapolate the missing words, the omission is marked by "[*missing*]," and if more than one word is missing the estimated number of missing words is included, for example "[*three words missing*]" or "[*one line missing*]." Details of damage to the manuscript are supplied in a footnote at the start of the letter.

The Duchess of Ormonde's letters usually begin in the top left-hand corner of the letter with a simple salutation ("Cousen," "Brother," "John Burdon"): this is sometimes followed by a large slant (which I ignore). Occasionally—particularly when she addresses close family members, such as her brother-in-law Mathew or her son Arran—she omits the salutation altogether. Letters are often dated in the top right corner of the letter: when an addressee is named, the date typically appears at the end of the same line. Occasionally, the Duchess identifies the place of composition along with the date ("kilkeny the 3 of oct"). Sometimes this information is provided at the end of the letter instead of the beginning: in these cases, place and/or date usually sits to the left of the signature. In my edition I have not regularized the presentation of these details, nor have I highlighted their absence (except, when possible, proposing a likely date or place in the headnotes). Many letters are endorsed with dates of receipt and, when available, dispatch: this information is supplied in the headnotes, with abbreviations expanded. Dates are given in the Old Style calendar (eleven days later than the New Style). But since in the Old Style calendar the year began on Lady Day, March 25, the New Style year is also supplied to avoid any potential confusion in letters dated January through March (presented as, for example, January 27, 1659/60).

A noteworthy feature of the Duchess of Ormonde's letters is the style of her valedictions, which she incorporates in the final sentence of her letter: for example, "which I doutnot by your care willbee Efectede to the Sattisfactione of EO" (Letter 45). The importance of this rhetorical manoeuvre to her epistolary style can be glimpsed in the times she re-writes the final sentence of her letter to conform to the practice: for example, in a letter to Stephen Smith (Letter 96) she deletes "I have inserted" and replaces it with "is heare inserted by," so that it can lead into her signature. The Duchess of Ormonde typically signs herself "E:ormonde" or "EO." Reflecting her superior status, her signature is larger than the rest of the text and tends to be surrounded by white space. Throughout my edition I have adopted the "Ormonde" spelling because the Duchess preferred it: the family title is variously spelled "Ormond" and "Ormonde," and the ducal couple is now better known to historians as "Ormond," even though the first Duke also seemed to have a preference for the terminal *e*. However, the Duchess's rare—and meaningful—deviations from this rule are not regularized in the text. Pointing to the irregularity of the "Ormond/e" spelling as well as to the Duchess's personal preference for "Ormonde," in a memorandum written after the restoration in 1660, she requests that he husband be acquainted "that such recommendations as comes from mee, in the behalfe of Persons done rathar out of Complianse then respect, shallbee subcribed with the leauinge out of the leter E, at the Ende of the word ormond" (Letter 99; see fig. 6). A rather half-hearted recommendation that follows for one Mr. Burneston is duly signed "E:ormond" (Letter 100). I have not expanded the Duchess's frequent use of the initials "EO," which may indicate intimacy or haste. A striking exception to her identification as "E:ormonde," "E:O," or "E:ormond" comes in the letters sent to her exiled husband during their long separation in the 1650s: in these letters, written in her own hand, she signs herself "JH" (see fig. 4). Nothing is known for certain about the particular choice of pseudonym, and the existence of an earlier pseudonymous letter by "JH" *to* the Marchioness of Ormonde in Caen further complicates the issue.[8]

As I discuss in detail in my introduction, in the letters written by "JH," the Duchess of Ormonde manipulates the spatial conventions of the early modern letter—the rank-conscious "significant space" discussed by Jonathan Gibson and others—to assert her authority over her exiled husband.[9] These spatial conventions otherwise govern her letter-writing so that, for example, her letter to Queen Catherine of Braganza (Letter 126) has large areas of blank space to signify the Duchess's deference to her queen. This striking example of the Duchess's use of "significant space" is provided in figure 9, and the distinctive use of space is outlined in the notes to that particular letter. However, for practical reasons it

---

[8] "JH" to EO, [November 1651], NLI, Ormond Papers, 2482, no. 329.

[9] Jonathan Gibson, "Significant Space in Manuscript Letters," *The Seventeenth Century* 12 (1997): 1–10.

A Note on the Text 59

Figure 9. Letter 126. Letter from the Duchess of Ormonde to Queen Catherine of Braganza, November 16, [1663]. Reproduced by permission of the Bodleian Library.

is otherwise necessary to standardize the layout of her letters and their salutations, valedictions, and signatures. My presentation aims to replicate as far as possible the Duchess's usual habits, which means that the addressee appears on the top left corner of the page, with a blank line between the addressee and the main text. The Duchess's choice of whether or not to indent the first line of the main text does not seem to be meaningful: I standardize the correspondence by not indenting. The date, when it is provided, often comes at the bottom left hand side of the letter, either beside or below the signature: I consistently present the date to the left of the signature. This, as Daybell argues, was common practice by the seventeenth century.[10] But just as often the Duchess provides the date at the beginning of the letter at the far right hand side. This is a practice that Daybell associates with business letters, pointing out that such organization faciliated the archiving and subsequent retrieval of letters, and may suggest the Duchess's awareness that her letters would be archived.[11] The positioning of the dates at the beginning or end of the text might indicate whether the Duchess expected particular letters to be preserved or discarded, and my edition reflects that intention. Very often, salutations and/or signatures are missing from the manuscripts of the letters. It is possible that this reflects the Duchess's standard practice when writing to regular correspondents. Or is also possible that they have been lost at some stage during the archiving process.

The part of the valediction that indicates the author's relationship with the recipient (such as "your Cousen and Sarvant"), when it appears, comes below the main text and is indented. The signature is added a line below that and further indented. In most cases, the horizontal positioning of the Duchess's signature is not particularly meaningful: her usual habit is to indent her signature underneath and about an inch to the right of the end of last word of the text, and thus it appears variously on the left, centre, and right of the page depending on where the main text ends. In contrast, the vertical positioning of the signature is meaningful: when she addresses her social inferiors, the signature is positioned close to the main text, while to her social equals or betters there is a wide space between the main text and the signature, materially communicating politeness or deference. There are numerous postscripts throughout the correspondence, which either continue the text as normal under the signature, are crammed at an angle in the bottom corner of the leaf to the left of the signature, or fill the left margin. Since these decisions are related to the availability of space on the page, I have regularized the layout of the postscripts.

The overwhelming majority of the Duchess's extant letters are written in her own hand, with and without her signature (I identify these as "autograph" whether or not the signature appears). The few scribal letters mostly come from the busy period of 1661, when the Duke and Duchess were conducting their business from Whitehall, or during the crisis of the 1640s. From the 1640s there are also unsigned drafts of letters written in Lady Ormonde's name (for which the final version is not extant): two of these are penned by her husband (Letters 9 and 10) and another shows evidence of his presence during their composition (Letter 3). Pertinent details about the scribal hands are provided in the footnotes

---

[10] Daybell, *The Material Letter*, 104.
[11] Daybell, *The Material Letter*, 104–105.

for individual letters. For all of the scribal letters, I apply the same editorial principles as for the autograph letters, with original spelling, capitalization and punctuation preserved, and abbreviations expanded. Some abbreviations that appear in these letters but are not routinely adopted by the Duchess in her own writing include "wth" for "with," "w^{ch}" for "which," "y^e" for "the," "y^t" for "that," "&" for "and," "&c" for "et cetera," and "li:" for "pound;" the "-ment" at the end of words such as "agreement" and "Settlement" is also abbreviated to "m^t". These contractions are expanded accordingly.

Any addresses or directions for delivery that accompany the letters are provided in the headnotes, alongside the endorsements (usually including dates of receipt) that have been inscribed on the Duchess of Ormonde's letters, usually in the hand of the recipient. These I standardize in the following ways: I present them in a linear fashion and expand abbreviations.

The Correspondence of Elizabeth Butler, Duchess of Ormonde

Early Marriage, 1629–1641

Letter 1. May 18, [1630], Acton, Viscountess Thurles to the Earl of Ormonde (NLI, Ormond Papers, 2486, no. 195). Autograph.
To the Right honrabll my very lovinge grandfathar the Earle of ormond and osre at Carick give this.

Right Honrablle[1]

your lordshipe was pleased to at my request to engadgedg your prommis to mee that you would ^not^ put anye of my fathar and mothars frinds or sarvants out of thar° farmes but sence° your Lord beinge [in] ireland through the instigation of some mallitious° persons that hath incensed your Lordship against them hath Caused you to turne them oute: and upon your Lordships nobll promis I did asshure° them all by letars that, they should keepe theire farmes [they] being Content to pay your Lordship as much as anye others and thay° haveing deserved soe well from mee, I cannot in honner° see them suffer: tharfore I beesech your Lordship to grant this my request as your Lordship would have me obay your commands in anye outhar° things: I am advertised by a letar from my Cousen weames[2] that your Lordship keepes backe some of the land of bennis

---

[1] JO's grandfather, Walter, eleventh Earl of Ormonde and fourth Earl of Ossory (1559–1633), had lost much of his estate to EO's parents. The dispute was only resolved when in September 1629, after the deaths of both of EO's parents, Walter was granted her wardship as part of the negotiations for her marriage to his grandson and heir JO. He returned to Ormond Castle in Carrick-on-Suir where he remained for his final years. See Robert Armstrong, "Butler, Walter 11th earl of Ormond," *DIB*.

[2] Patrick Wemyss (1604?–1661) was EO's cousin, the nephew of her father Richard, first Earl of Desmond, by his sister, Elizabeth: see Timothy Wilks, *Of Neighing*

bridg from them which belongs to them by thayr° lease which I
^am^ perswaded they would not seeck if it weare not there due I
am very sorye to see your Lordship should fall in contriversie with   *controversy*
my kinsmen about soe poure° a thing for I did think your Lordship
had beene reconsiled to them soe leving all to your Lordships noble
Consideration who I know will grant ^my^ Just and resonablle
request soe with my dute and sarvis° to your lordship I rest   *duty*

        your lordships loving grandchild to Command

From Acton* the 18 of May   Eliz Thurles

Letter 2. [No date], [Carrick], the Countess of Ormonde and Ossory to Edward Comerford (NLI, Ormond Papers, 2485, no. 284, p. 47). Autograph.
To my loving frind Edward Cummorford this. [Endorsed]: Eliz Countess of Ormonde and Ossory.

Edward Commorford[3]

I spoke to you at your Last beinge heare Consarninge° a wardshipe,[4] which I undurstoud by you, dous° of Right belonge unto the kinge

---

Coursers and of Trumpets Shrill: A Life of Richard, 1st Lord Dingwall and Earl of Desmond (c. 1570–1628) (London: Lucas, 2012), 137–38. There was a clause in EO's marriage agreement that specified that "the Castle towne and lands of Danefort, and the lands of Bennetts Bridge with all the Mills and appurtenances thereunto belonging in the County of Kilkenny" were to be granted to Patricke Wemyss and Richard Christy, both nephews of EO's father, for a twenty-one-year term. They were required to pay the eleventh Earl £100 for each of the first two years of their tenure and thereafter present a pair of twenty-shilling gloves to EO every Michaelmas. See James Graves, "Some Additional Facts as to the Marriage of James, Viscount Thurles, Afterwards Duke of Ormonde, and the Lady Elizabeth Preston," *The Journal of the Kilkenny and South-East of Ireland Archaeological Society*, New Series, 6.1 (1867): 232–38 (237); and Wilks, *Of Neighing Coursers*, 137.

  [3] Edward Comerford (d. 1649) of Callan, Co. Kilkenny, had been party to the lease of Danefort and Bennetsbridge to EO's Scottish cousins (scc Note 2). He remained an agent of the Ormonde Butler family, and the Ormond Papers include a large series of correspondence between him and JO between 1630 and 1652. A detailed biography of Comerford can be found at http://comerfordfamily.blogspot.ie/2007/11/6-comerford-of-ballymack-and-callan.html.

  [4] The ward in question seems to be Anne French, a woman who would become a close friend of EO. Her potential guardian—and later husband—is Thomas Hume of Scotland. The couple's eventual marriage is outlined in John Burke, *A Genealogical and Heraldic History of the Commoners of Great Britain and Ireland*, 4 vols. (London: Henry Colburn, 1836), 3. 389–90, where it is explained that Thomas Hume was the "confidential

soe as I Conseve° Sir Phillipe Persevalle ^might^ doe mee a Curtisie° ~~in it,~~ by preferinge my Sarvant humes* to it, whome I would willinglie recummend unto hime, if I thought my request might take Efcet, not outharwise;° soe that I shall desier° you to afford ~~my~~ ^mee^ your audvise, and to Let mee know whethar you think it Likelie that I might prevaule, for I intende onlie to doe my Sarvant a benifite, soe that it may bee without prejudiss, to Sir Phillipe, whoe I think Cannot Suffer anye way in it; and this beinge all for the presant I remayne

effect

advice

prevail; only

your loving Mistres

Eliz:ormond:ossory

I intend not to write to Sir Phillipe Persevall tell° I heare from you soe as I Expect your answar

---

favourite" of EO's father, and "through the influence of that nobleman's daughter, Elizabeth, Duchess of Ormonde, [he] obtained the hand of Miss French, a great heiress, her grace's ward, in marriage":

> In consequence of which he settled in Ireland, and after the Restoration acquired large tracts of land in the county of Tipperary, under grant from the Crown, dated in February, 1665. In the same year he was presented with the freedom of the city of Dublin in a silver box, and subsequently had the honour of knighthood from the Duke of Ormond, then lord lieutenant of Ireland. Sir Thomas died at an advanced age, 4th July, 1668, as appears from a registry of his death in the office of Arms, Dublin. He had no issue, and some time before his demise, he induced his nephew, Thomas, the eldest son of his elder brother Robert to come from Scotland, under the promise of making him his sole heir. Dying, however, intestate, a considerable portion of his property devolved upon his widow, Lady Anne Hume, who obtained administration, as appears from an entry in the Prerogative Office in Dublin, dated in August, 1668. Her ladyship afterwards compromised with Thomas, the nephew, for a sum of money, and married for her second husband Captain George Mathews, half brother to the old Duke of Ormond, whereby the lands in Tipperary merged in the Landaff estate. Lady Anne survived Captain Mathews and died in the beginning of March, 1701. By her last will, which was duly registered and proved the 13th of that month, she bequeathed, after some legacies, all the estate, arrears of rent, and of dower, goods and chattels, to Sir Henry Wemys and Thomas Hume, by the description of Thomas Hume, nephew of her first husband, and appointed them her executors.

An undated letter from an Anne French to JO can be found in NLI, Ormond Papers, 2486, no. 249. Sir Philip Perceval was Master of the Irish Court of Wards, so petitions for the guardianship of wards would be sent to him. See Victor Treadwell, "The Irish Court of Wards under James I," *Irish Historical Studies* 12 (1960): 1–27.

The Confederate Wars, 1641–1649

Letter 3. [January/February] 1642/3, [Dublin], the Countess of Ormonde to William Wale (Bodl., Carte Papers, 4, fol. 173). Scribal draft: unsigned.
[Endorsed]: The Co[untess of Ormonde] to Alderman Wally 1642.

Mr Wally[5]

my servant Edmund Kennedy* hath some things of consequence in London which belong unto mee and not dareing to trust them with any messenger to convey them heather° in regard of the many Letts[6] and dangers that are in the way, is forced to detaine them uppon his hands to my no Smale prejudice I Shall therefore desire you ~~knowing~~ ^understanding^ that yow have dayly ~~recourse~~ ^Supply^ fro ~~thence~~ *from* London ~~with~~ ^of^ Such things as are usefull for yow there ~~at Chester If with any Safety yow conceave it may be done~~; to be pleased to take ~~some~~ course for the safe conveying of the said things to yow, if yow shall conceave it may be don° with^out^ ~~Safetie~~ indangering the Loss of them, that Soe they may be the Sooner transported heather unto mee ~~by yow~~ Soe in useing your best endeavours to effect this my desire yow ^Shall^ Lay an obligation uppon mee to ~~requite~~ make requitall when the least occasion Shall be offered

Letter 4. February 20, 1642/3, Dublin, the Countess of Ormonde to Edmund Kennedy (Bodl., Carte Papers, 4, fol. 398). Scribal: signed.
[Endorsed]: my Ladys to Edmund Kenedy.

~~Mr~~ ^Edmund^ Kenedy*

I receaved your letter dated the seventh of this month uppon Sunday the ninteenth of the same whereby I understand that my things are in a redynes° ~~with you~~ and are only stayed for want of conveniencie, which for the present is hard to be mett with; I shall therefore desire

---

[5] William Wale was a wine merchant who became an alderman of London in 1659. He was conferred a knighthood by Charles II in May 1660. See Alfred P. Beaven, "Chronological List of Aldermen: 1651–1700," *The Aldermen of the City of London: Temp. Henry III–1912* (1908), 75–119. British History Online. http://www.british-history.ac.uk/report.aspx?compid=67242&strquery=Wale.

[6] "Hindrance, stoppage, obstruction; also, something that hinders, an impediment" ("let, *n.*," 1, *OED*).

you to apply your selfe to the bearer Captaine Tucker⁷ who will be
redy to afford you his best furtherance and assistance in findeing out
some safe way for the transportation of them heather which I desire
may be done with as much speed as possibly you can and without
hazarding the loss of them, thus expecting your care herein I remaine

                your loveing mistris

Dublin the 20th of february 1642   Eliz

Letter 5. August 12, 1646, Dublin Castle, the Marchioness of Ormonde to Patrick Archer (Bodl., Carte Papers, 18, fol. 252). Scribal: signed.
My Ladys letter to Patrick Archer Dated 12 August 1646 Lining et cetera.

Sir⁸

My Lord intending to take a journey shortly into the Country⁹ I find
that it will be necessary to Send Some Linnin along with him, which   *linen*
I heare may be had in those parts. By the inclosed note you will finde
as well the quantyty as the rates of Such Linnin as I desire you with
all possible hast° to buy and convey unto mee, for which you Shall
receive Satisfaction uppon demand, And if this you cannot doe I
desire Suddainely¹⁰ to understand Soe much, and rest

            Your very affectionate frend

Dublin Castle 12th August 1646   Eliz:ormonde

---

   ⁷ Captain William Tucker. A letter dated 25 April 1643, from Captain William Tucker to JO (Carte Papers, 5, fols. 85–86) mentions a trunk being sent over for EO. Thanks to John Cronin for this reference.
   ⁸ Patrick Archer was a merchant of Waterford and kinsman of James Archer; James was later employed by EO to oversee improvements on Kilkenny Castle.
   ⁹ JO was heading to the Confederate headquarters in Kilkenny to renegotiate the terms of the controversial peace treaty that had been agreed between the royalists and the Confederate Catholics in July 1646. The peace treaty granted many of the political and economic concessions sought by the Confederate Catholics but prevaricated on the issue of religion, causing a rift among the Confederate Catholics between the conservative landowning leadership who endorsed the deal and the clergy who opposed it. JO arrived in Kilkenny on August 31, 1646. See Micheál Ó Siochrú, *God's Executioner: Oliver Cromwell and the Conquest of Ireland* (London: Faber & Faber, 2008), 46–48, and Burghclere, I, 309.
   ¹⁰ "Without delay, forthwith, promptly, immediately, directly, at once" ("suddenly, *adv.*," 2, *OED*).

80 yardes for napkins ~~of h~~ at 2 shillings 6 pence the yard
24 yards of broad[11] Sutable[12]
30 yards more for napkins at 3 shillings the yard
26 yards of broad Sutable

Letter 6. June 3, 1647, [Dublin], the Marchioness of Ormonde to Sir Philip Perceval (BL, Additional MSS, Egmont Papers 46931 B, fol. 8). Autograph.
For Sir Phillipe Persivall [/] thes. [Endorsed]: Lady of Ormond 3 June 1647 received 8 July.

Sir[13]

upon the ressept° of your Letar; I made my Lord acquanted with the Contents tharof; whoe hass soe great ~~grea~~ a Care and regarde of your preservatione; as hee asshurede° mee tharwass nothinge hee would make more Seariouslie° his Studie, then some waye whereby to Secure you from anye Sudayne° or future inconveniense that maye happene by your Ingadgments° for hime; which Sir wiliame usshar[14] will I know give you a more perticular accompt° of; as well of the waye propounded for Effecttinge the same; as allsoe of the willinge and rediee parformanse of anye thinge that maye give a furtharanse tharunto; wherin if the indevours° of soe unprofitabill a persone as my Selfe maye in anye ways Contribute; I asshure° you my industrye

---

[11] "Fine, plain-wove, dressed, double width, black cloth, used chiefly for men's garments" ("broad cloth, *n.*," *OED*).

[12] "Conforming or agreeing in shape, colour, pattern, or style" ("suitable, *adj.*," 1, *OED*).

[13] Sir Philip Perceval was an associate of JO, and although he had defected to the parliamentarian side in August 1644, they had remained on good terms. Until his death in December 1647, he was, according to his *ODNB* entry, "a crucial figure in Anglo-Irish politics" and "an important part of the network which kept open lines of communication between Dublin and London." He was aligned with the Presbyterian party, and his election to Parliament in May 1647 was met with significant opposition by the Independent party, who were suspicious of him on the basis of his connections with JO. See Patrick Little, "Perceval, Sir Philip (1605–1647)," *ODNB*.

[14] Sir William Ussher (c. 1610–1671) held office in Dublin in the 1650s; he was a kinsman of Perceval's wife.

shallnot bee wantinge to doe you all the Sarviss° in this that I maye
bee Caypbill to parforme; as beinge   *capable*

        Sir

        your affectionat frind and Sarvant

June the 3   Eliz:ormonde

Sir

I praye present my Sarviss to your Lady[15] to whom I would oftene
have writene but that I forboare as fearinge to prejudiss hir tharby

---

[15] Katherine, daughter of the well-connected Dublin official Arthur Ussher. See Patrick Little, "Perceval, Sir Philip (1605–1647)," *ODNB*.

Royalist Exile in Caen, 1648–1652

Letter 7. November 1648, [Caen], the Marchioness of Ormonde to Sir Edward Nicholas (BL, Egerton MSS, 2533, fol. 466). Autograph. For Sir Edward Nickcollas. [Endorsed]: Received 3 december sent November 1648 The Lady Marchioness of Ormond to me.

Sir[16]

I Considar you to° Seariouslye° imployede this morninge in makinge your severalle dispaches; to interrupt you by Comminge hethar;°[17] and tharfor I have to Easse you of that troubill; venterede° I feare upon givinge you a greatar; by thes bade Lines; which this inclosede papar is the ocatione° of; beinge ane° abstract of a Letar to mee in Shiphier° from a very good hand;[18] which with some formar surcomstanses° I shall desier° that you willbee pleasede to Considar of, and at your betar° Leasure afford mee your oppinione and advise whethar it wouldbee nesesarye to send this to my Lord and if befor the dispach of your Letars for England you shall think fitt to Injoyne° some one thar;° whom you houlde° inteligense with; to send you some advertisment of what hee hears of this perticular; it maye Contribute to the advantage of his affayrs for whome wee all Suffier;°[19] as well as the Saftye of my Lord; whoe is I am Shure° very fathfullye a frind and Sarvant of yours; as is alsoe

bad

safety

Eliz:ormonde

---

[16] Sir Edward Nicholas (1593–1669) was Secretary of State to Charles I and later Charles II.

[17] EO is clearly in the same location as Nicholas, but it is not certain that she had settled in Caen by this stage. Caen was a Huguenot stronghold, and, as Williams notes in his groundbreaking study of the Irish in the exiled court of Charles II, "In addition to its proximity to the English coast and long-standing trading connections to Irish ports, Caen offered a relatively friendly location for [Irish] Protestant Royalists whose reputations preceded them in Catholic Europe." As well as EO and her family, Caen provided refuge for Richard Boyle, second Earl of Cork, and Lord Inchiquin, as well as Catholics including JO's brother-in-law, Donough MacCarthy, then Viscount Muskerry. See Mark R. F. Williams, *The King's Irishmen: The Exiled Court of Charles II, 1649–1660* (Woodbridge: Boydell, 2014), 34–35.

[18] In other words, a reliable or trustworthy source.

[19] I.e. the king's cause.

Letter 8. March 24, 1648/9, [Caen], the Marchioness of Ormonde to Sir Edward Nicholas (BL, Egerton MSS, 2533, fol. 479).
Autograph.
For the Right Honnorabill Edward Nichcolas his Magestyes Prinsepall Secritarie of Estate thes. [Endorsed]: 14/24 March 1648/49 My Lady Marchioness of Ormond to me.

Sir

havinge resevede° many more realle Curtisiess° and favours from you then it hass bine° in my power to desarve; I hope you willbee soe Just unto your Selfe as to Exsept of this inclosede paypar;[20] and Continow° soe favorabill unto mee; as to pardon all thous° ocations° of troubill that I have givene you; and beleve; that though I maye fayle° in power; I shall never want a will to Se gratitude Nor a will to Sarve you Ecqualle unto that Respect that is professt; and shallbee still Carryede you by

accept

    Sir

        your asshurede° frind and
        humbill Sarvant

The 24 of March   Eliz:ormonde

Letter 9. March 24, 1648/9, [Caen], the Marchioness of Ormonde to Sir Thomas Fairfax (Bodl., Carte Papers, 24, fol. 202).[21] Scribal draft [in the Marquess of Ormonde's hand]: unsigned.
[Endorsed]: Sent the 24th of March 1648 in a letter to mr Smith.

Sir[22]

---

[20] Probably in the sense: "Negotiable documents, bills of exchange, promissory notes, etc., collectively; banknotes as opposed to coins" ("paper, *n.* and *adj.*," 13a, *OED*).

[21] Letters 9 and 10 were drafted by JO from Henrietta Maria's exiled court in Paris in March 1648. It is impossible to know whether EO kept to her husband's script when she copied the letters and therefore whether these drafts accurately reflect the letters she sent.

[22] Sir Thomas Fairfax, third Lord Fairfax of Cameron (1612–1671), was a parliamentarian army officer. See Ian J. Gentles, "Fairfax, Thomas, third Lord Fairfax of Cameron (1612–1671)," *ODNB*. Fairfax, whom JO described as "extremely civil and oblidging," had already been his friend and advocate in Parliament (for example, he secured JO access to the imprisoned Charles I, in Hampton Court), so he had some reason to hope for his intercession. For a summary of this period, see Burghclere, I, 325–37.

When my lord went for ffrance hee made noe question but that as on his parte he had performed to the utermost extent of what hee was by Article obleeged unto ^the contrary^ haveing bin° never soe much aleged by any^ soe the Parliment had put what on their parte remained unperformed into such a way as would require noe more solisitation from him, ~~But in case~~ ^And if^ there should hapen any delay or interuption in ^the^ payments designed him hee directed mee to aply my self to you for your assistance in removeing any such impediment being as hee sayd confident your owne justice ~~and~~ ^together with your^ care of the engaged honour of the Parliment would incline you readily to afforde it, in his ~~case as~~ particular ^case^ as in others ^of like nature^ you had done, But ~~hee it was~~ as soone as it was knowen hee was gone a stop was made of any further payments ~~notwithstanding the course setled by the Comitee at Derby house and though by leter~~ and though a servant of my lords hath atended ever since for performance of the Parliments engagement yet hee hath not ~~received any any answer~~ prevailed ~~to have the answer~~ ^for ought I heare^ soe much as bin° tould the reason why he can not, <u>My desire to you is that you will bee pleas'd soe farr to interpose that by your mediation my lords servant may receive the mony° ^remaineing^ due</u> ~~to him to his~~ <u>according to the termes set downe by the Comitee at Derby house</u>[23] ~~without which~~ <u>without which I shall bee wholy disapoynted of the meanes of subsistence designed for mee and the family left with mee, and by your favour ^and justice^ herin you will exeedingly Obleege your</u>[24]

My lord would have my lady to write this letter to Sir Thomas fairfax to which purpose you are directed to Send it to her decyphered by a Safe express speedyly[25]

Letter 10. [March 24, 1648/9], [Caen], the Marchioness of Ormonde to the Earl of Mulgrave (Bodl., Carte Papers, 24, fol. 225). Scribal draft [in the Marquess of Ormonde's hand]: unsigned.

<u>By the enclosed copy of my leter to Sir Thomas ffairfax you will</u> see how much I am like to sufer for want of what was designed by my

---

[23] Named after its Westminster meeting place, the Derby House Committee was from January 1647 the parliamentarian Executive and the predecessor of the Council of State, which was established in February 1649.

[24] The underscores are in the same ink as the main text and appear to be original: the emphasis therefore seems to be JO's.

[25] "My lord . . . speedyly": written by another hand.

Lord for ~~my~~ ^mine and my famillys^ subsistence, and you will bee
able to judge how reasonable and just it is that the Parliments should
^now at length^ performe what they ~~are~~ ^were^ oblidged ~~unto~~ by
Articles long since to have done, yet there apeared soe much dificulty
to obtaine what hath already bin° payd when my lord soliscited
performance in his owne person and by the help of the friends hee
was able to make that I ~~uterly despaire of~~ whoe am lesse knoweing ~~or
fit for~~ in the likelyest ways of prevaileing despaire of it without the
assistance of some such as ~~to the justice of~~ as [*sic*] besides the justice
of the request may have some consideration of mee that am soe
nearely concerned in it, therefore it is that I have taken the boldnes
to desire your lordships advice and assistance in this particular, ~~to
receve satisfaction if it may bee had,~~ ^That if it bee possible ~~payment~~
payment may bee made of what remaines due^ but if that can not bee
I shall desire as the next greatest favour speedily to know that it is
not to bee expected with ~~the reason why of it,~~ ^the reason^ why it is
not, that some other course may bee thought of by
          et cetera

This letter is to be after Sent To my lord of Mulgrave[26]

Letter 11. May 6, 1649, [Caen], the Marchioness of Ormonde to Sir Edward Nicholas (BL, Egerton MSS, 2533, fol. 484). Autograph. For Sir Edward Nicholass his Magestys prinsepall Secretarye of State thes. [Endorsed]: 6 May 1649 My Lady Marchioness of Ormond to me. This 100 was repaid to me by order of this lady dated the 16th of March 1660 at Bruxills by Mr Thomas Page.[27]

Sir

I doe not send you this inclosede Note; as thinkinge it a vallewabill°
Securitye for what you have bine° pleasede to trust in my hand;
but to wittness to you; that Could my power Extend in makinge
a more amppell acknowledgment I should afford it with the Same   *ample*
willingnes; and Ernest desier° I doe; that this; maye bee acsepted by

---

[26] Edmund Sheffield, second Earl of Mulgrave (1611–1658), was a parliamentarian nobleman and Fairfax's cousin. See C. H. Firth, "Sheffield, Edmund, second earl of Mulgrave (1611–1658)," rev. Timothy Venning, *ODNB*. His grandfather (from whom he inherited the earldom) was an uncle of EO, and had been an advisor during the negotiations for her marriage of JO.

[27] All EO's letters written after the regicide, and for which the remnants of wax remain, are sealed with black wax, a sign of mourning.

you; Sense° I hope ~~and beleve~~ that what Ever acsident maye befall mee; it willbee Suffisent to Ingaydge° thous° of Nearest relatione to mee; to make good; what is fathfullie intended you by hir; that most Sensearlye is *sincerely*

    your very ashurede frind
    and humbill Sarvant

the 6 of Maye   Eliz:ormonde

Letter 12. May 18, 1649, [Caen], the Marchioness of Ormonde to Sir Edward Nicholas (BL, Egerton MSS, 2533, fol. 486). Autograph. For Mr Secretarye Nicholass thes. [Endorsed]: 8/18 May 1649 Lady Marchioness Ormonde.

Sir   The 18 of Maye

I am very glade to heare that you are gotene Sayfe° to Roane;° and in that; you ought to beeleve it a Signe of my Charitye; that Can bee Soe well pleasede to heare of the wellfare of one that hass woune my ~~my~~ mony° at Boulls; Though withall I must tell you; that I shall not only indevour° to quitt[28] that depte° I owe you but to wine much more of you when wee Meete in Ireland; from whense I am very impatient to heare; and shall not fayle° the mene° time if I Cane meete with anye oppertunitye; to Send the papar to my Lord; that I resevede° from you this daye; Nor bee wantinge notwithstandinge all my quarells; when anye ocatione° shallbee offerede to make apiere° with how great Senseritye I am

   Rouen

   won

   win

   sincerity

  Sir

    your very ashurede frind
    and Sarvant

    Eliz:ormonde[29]

---

[28] "To pay (a debt, penalty, due, etc.)," ("quit, *v.*," I, 1a, *OED*).
[29] A response to her from Nicholas is drafted on the second leaf of her letter.

Letter 13. June 20, 1649, [Caen], the Marchioness of Ormonde to Sir Edward Nicholas (BL, Egerton MSS, 2533, fol. 496). Autograph. See Figure 2.
[Endorsed]: 20 June 1649 Lady Marchioness Ormond.

Sir   The 20 of June

I resevede° a Letar from you this day; ~~which~~ ^that^ Came accompaynede with one derectede° unto my Lord; which shallbee immediatlye Sent awaye by a Sarvant of my owne; Though my feares are very great; that the advertisment Now Sent, willnot Come Time Enough to prevent the Mischive that is intended; howsomever I am resoulvede to Leave noe waye unatemptede bouth° by my owne indevour° and that of my frinds; to get this inteliginse Convayde unto hime; and will hope the best the mene° Time as the only remidye° to allaye my Feares; ~~and must~~ of the Euvills to Come;[30] and am infinitlye thankfull to you for the intemation° you have givene mee Consarninge° the Settlinge of my 2 Sons in De Plessis Academye[31] your 42. 36. 27. 4. 21. 18. 29. 366. 9. 89. 264. 5. 470. 452. 523. 483. 4. 328. 80. 37. 18. 262. 95. 551, 306. 22. 12. 28. 30. 525. 493. 471. 44. 13. 31. 320. 477. 167. 230. 76. 31. 476. 32. 217. 268. 471. 477. 12. 21. 34. 31. 30. 321. 89. 194. 30. 67. 36. 18. 10. 30. 32. 90. 470. 264. 12. 320. 15. 18. 261. 348. 550. 217. 15. 438. 14. 34. 32. 90. 477. 4. 453. 194. 12. 520. 471. 364. 523. 368. 218. 268. 67. 398. 364. 14. 46. 40. 22. 57. 6. 75. 130. 512.[32] *objections being the same with those I made against it before your letter came which Colonel Traford tould me that Lord Digby*[33] *had advised their going to that Academy before any other But the arrangement is not yet gon soe farre but that I shall find a way to oppose*

---

[30] On June 5, 1649, the parliamentary army had been ordered to leave for Ireland.

[31] Lord Ossory had been educated by a French tutor in Caen for the first year of his stay, but in October 1649 he proceeded to Monsieur de Camp's Academy in Paris where he remained until December 1650. See J. D. Davies, "Butler, Thomas, sixth earl of Ossory (1634–1680)," *ODNB*. His younger brother Richard attended there also. Evelyn writes of December 13, 1649: "I went to see a Triumph in *Monsieur del Camps* Academie, where divers of the French & English Noblesse, especially my *Lord of Ossorie*, & Richard, sonns to the Marquis of Ormon'd (afterwards Duke) did their Exercises on horsback in noble Equipage, before a World of Spectators, & greate Persons, men & Ladies: it ended in a Collation." See *The Diary of John Evelyn*, ed. E. S. de Beer (London: Everyman, 2006), 252.

[32] The code is decyphered in the original and provided here in italics.

[33] George Digby, Lord Digby, was Nicholas's fellow Secretary of State, but he was favored by Henrietta Maria. This letter seems to be about whether or not EO's sons should join Henrietta Maria's court in exile in Paris.

with out giving any offense by Leavinge mr Maxwell³⁴ to make his owne Choise of the plase where thay° shall reside whoe I find to bee of hime selfe very averse to thar° goeinge 470. 4. 410. 32. *thither* and tharfor doe resoulve to Stay 479. *them* heare yet Longar ~~und~~ untell° I bee more thourilye Satisfiede and informede of a 395. *plan* more fittinge for 470. 432. 46. 171. 8. 21. 12. 18. 4. 366 *their duration* then I take this outhar° to bee; and for the genttellman you have desirede mee to recomende unto my Lord; you Needede Not have requestede mee to inquier° of my Lord of Corke³⁵ or anye outhar Consarninge hime; Sense° his beinge your Brothar³⁶ makes mee Conclude hime ~~whor~~ worthye of as much as Cane bee dune° or Sayede° for hime and will besides give my Lord ane° ocatione° wherof I am Confident hee willbee much Satisfiede of Searvinge you or anye that hass Soe Neare a relatione to you; my Selfe havinge the Same ambitione allsoe that am unfaynedlye

thoroughly

serving

    Sir

      your most ashurede frind and
        humbill Sarvant

       Eliz:ormonde

Letter 14. March 22, 1649/50, Caen, the Marchioness of Ormonde to Sir Edward Nicholas (BL, Egerton MSS, 2534, fol. 17). Autograph.
For Mr Secretarye thes. [Endorsed]: 22 March 1649/50 Lady Marchioness Ormond.

Sir

Just as I arrivede heare this day, it wass my good fortune to meete Mr Boswell³⁷ whoe brought thes inclosede Letars from my Lord; wherof tharis one unto his Magestye³⁸ ^and^ a Nothar° to Prinse Robert³⁹ the Coppye of which I thought fitt to Send you That to his Magestye beinge allsoe as I suppose ~~Som thinge~~ to the Same Effect; wherin

---

³⁴ JO?
³⁵ Richard Boyle (1612–1698), second Earl of Cork.
³⁶ Perhaps his younger brother, Mathew Nicholas. See S. A. Baron, "Nicholas, Sir Edward (1593–1669)," *ODNB*.
³⁷ An alias?
³⁸ Charles II.
³⁹ Prince Rupert (1619–1682), royalist army and naval officer.

The Correspondence of Elizabeth Butler

you will perseve° mee soe much Consarnede;° as I Cannot doupt° your Frindshipe soe farr as to make anye questione of your Care to deliver That unto the kinge and gett the outhar° Sent; which I shall accompt° a very speatialle° favour dune° hir that is

Sir

your ashurede Frind and
humbill Sarvant
EO

Sir I have sent you a Nothar Letar derectede° to my Lords Agent fearinge Least° the outhar° should miscarye; and doe desier° you to show the Coppye of my Lords Letar to the Prinse unto Mr Seymor[40] and present my Sarviss° to my Lord Berone[41] and Excuse mee to hime that I did Not write by this berare° the Time I now ~~take~~ ^have^ beinge what I take from my Sliepe it wass Soe Layte when I Came to towne   *sleep*

Caene the 22 of March

Letter 15. March 24, [1650], Caen, the Marchioness of Ormonde to [Sir Richard Browne] (BL, Additional MSS, Evelyn Papers, 78199 (827A), 4).[42] Autograph.

Sir[43]

Thes frequent importunities of mine maye with resone° Ennough make you repent of your Sevilities° to mee that should thus oftene troubill you; but that you are pleasede to allowe mee this fridome and tharfor will I hope the Easilier forgive when I punnishe you with my bad Lines as I am now forst to doe by this address; wherby to acquant you that I undarstand of a Shipe that is Laytlye Come into Dunkirke

---

[40] Henry Seymour (1612–1687), who in October 1649 had been sent to JO by Charles II in order to assess the military situation in Ireland. See W. A. Shaw and Ronald Clayton, "Seymour, Henry (bap. 1612, d. 1687), courtier," *ODNB*.

[41] John Byron, first Baron Byron (1598/9–1652), who had supported JO in his negotiations with the Confederate Catholics and brought the Second Ormonde Peace, which has been signed on January 17, 1649, to Charles II in the Hague. See Ronald Hutton, "Byron, John, first Baron Byron (1598/9–1652), royalist army officer," *ODNB*.

[42] The recipient and date of this letter have been identified by Williams, *King's Irishmen*, 93, note 56.

[43] Sir Richard Browne was Charles II's ambassador in Paris during his exile. See J. T. Peacey, "Browne, Sir Richard, baronet (1605–1683)," *ODNB*.

that hass brought in a Considarabill Pryse,[44] Callede the Sant Petar of Gallowaye° Commanded by one Captayne Nicholas Martine[45] wherin my Lord hass a Share as hee himselfe Confessess; Soe as if anye Persone ^I desier° that Some Persone^ that you imploye in his Magesties affares Thar;° might reseve° derections° from you to inquier requier° Some accompt° and if not givene to make Staye of the Shipe untell° Satisfactione bee made; but whethar this I propound maye apiere° soe resonabill as to obtayne your aprobatione and furtharanse is what it befitts Not mee to Judge beinge alltogethar Ignorant in busseness° of this kind beinge besides ane° intrestede Persone yet one that in this or a very much greatar Consarnment° should willinglye bee Concluded or advisede by you such is the Estime that is healde of you by

       Sir

          your very ashurede Frind and Sarvant
Caene the 24 of March   Elis: Ormonde

I have Sent you hearinclosede a Letar to the Captane of the Shipe which maye bee sent if you think fitt [/] if not returnede;

Letter 16. April 7, [1650], [Caen], the Marchioness of Ormonde to [Sir Richard Browne] (BL, Additional MSS, Evelyn Papers, 78199 (827A), 5). Autograph.

Sir   The 7 of aprell

I perseve° by your Letar that Captane Martine* is gone from Dunkirke; and that hee my ^maye^ possiblye Come to Jersye [/] Soe as I shall accordinge as you have bine° pleasede to advisse mee write a Letar unto Sir Gorge Cartwright* Consarninge° this bussesness: and shall desier° you to Seconde the favour you have allredye dune° mee in this perticular by informinge your Selfe and Letinge mee know what the vallew° of the prisiess are that Captane Martine hass   *prizes* takene; wherby hee maye the betar° bee brought to ane° accompt° heare or if Not in Irland if it bee his designe to returne; but Chiflye

---

[44] "A ship or ship's cargo captured legally in war" ("prize, *n.*2," 1b, *OED*).
[45] The *St. Peter* was JO's ship, which would bring him to Caen in January 1651. See Williams, *King's Irishmen*, 35, 92–93.

that you will pardone the frequent importunities I have givene you one° this Subgect; is the Serious request of

        Sir

        your very ashurede Frind and Sarvant

        E:ormonde

Letter 17. May 23, 1650, [Caen], the Marchioness of Ormonde to Sir Edward Nicholas (BL, Egerton MSS, 2534, fol. 26). Autograph. For Sir Edward Nicholass thes. [Endorsed]: 23 May 1650 Lady Marchioness Ormond.

Sir   The 23 of Maye New Style

I have resevede° the severalle Letars you intended mee beinge 4 in all datede from Breda:[46] this of mine to you makinge upe the same Nombar;° though I find but the halfe of them are Come to your hands, at which I much wondar; havinge takene the same waye to gett them Convayde as you derectede° mee; and in that of my Last, have givene you ane° accompt° of what I shall agayne° mentione fearinge Least° that should miscarye; and Let you know; that I have ~~givene~~ ^Sent^ the first Packet derectede unto my Lord by Mr Rawlings whoe went to haverdegrase[47] one Tuesday Last wass sevenight[48] and toucke° Shipinge the Next day the winde beinge then and many days Sense° good for Irland; Soe as if noe ill acsident have happenede hime in the waye; I am very Confident hee is with my Lord by this Time; and shall use the same Care to gett the duplicate Sent which I resevede upon Thursday Last; though at the presant I heare of noe oppertunitye by which I maye venter° it; I find by all your Letars soe much of your Care and Frindshipe to mee; as when I Considar how Litell° it hass bine° in my power to desarve it from you I Conclude it your Goodness, only; that makes you take mee and my Condistione Soe much into your Considaratione which I hope that hee whoe recompensess the Charitabill[49] will rewarde you For; I have Siene° some Letars to Severalle persons heare Confirminge the

---

[46] At this time home to Charles II's court in exile.
[47] Le Havre.
[48] I.e. a week before last Tuesday.
[49] God.

Treatys beinge Concluded betwixt our kinge and the Scots;[50] though your Last Letar speaks it not possitivlye, upon which it is furthar Sayede,° that his Magestye intends to remove Sudanlye° from where hee is; if soe; I shouldbee glade to bee informede how I might Send my Letars to you hearaftar; whoe the mene° Time desiers° to bee Contenowede° in your good oppinione and belevede ^to bee^ what I profess to bee that is

> your very ashurede Frind
> and Sarvant
>
> Eliz: ormonde

I will not troubill mr Seymor with a Letar at this Time it beinge but a Fewe days Sense I have writene to hime, but shall request you to remembar my Sarviss° to hime

Letter 18. June 6, 1650, [Caen], the Marchioness of Ormonde to Sir Edward Nicholas (BL, Egerton MSS, 2534, fol. 30). Autograph. [Endorsed]: Lady Marchioness Ormond.

Sir

I perseve° by your Last Letar of the 18 of Maye that you intend shortlie to remove; which I am hartilye sorrye you should have any Cause for;[51] and tharfor doe desier° to know how I maye gett my Letars Convayde to you hearafter; not that I think thay° canbee soe materiall as to bee worth the troubill that I feare thay put you ^the readinge them dous°^ put you unto, but that you maye See I am not willinge to ommitt anye thinge that maye testifie the Memorye and respect I have for you and tharfor out in the foremost Considaratione that you have allredye or maye Suffier° some inconveniense by the want of that mony° you Lent mee; my desier is; that if his Magesty intends mee anye part of that which is dewe° from hime unto my Lord and that thar° bee anye possibillitye of procuringe it wherof

---

[50] The Treaty of Breda between Charles II and the Scottish Covenanters had been signed on May 1, 1650. Charles II undertook to establish Presbyterianism as the national religion there and to recognize the authority of the Kirk's General Assembly in civil law in England as it already was in Scotland.

[51] Upon the succession of Charles II, Nicholas had not been formally sworn in as Secretary of State, although he was admitted to his Privy Council. Opposing the king's alliance with the Scots, he began to make plans either to retire to Wesel, where the cost of living was lower, or to return to England to compound for his estates. See S. A. Baron, "Nicholas, Sir Edward (1593–1669)," *ODNB*.

it should sime° you are Not out of hopes: that you Stope° soe much
of it in your hand as maye fullye discharge bouth° the first and
Seconde depte° that I owe you and that you paye your Selfe the
hundreth pound in the Same Gould° that I resevede° it from you;
which at what Rayte° sowever it maye b[e] ha[d] I will allowe for;
the same havinge yellded no[w] thi[r]tye Pistolls[52] which I had for
the Changinge; and Least° this [wa]ye I now propose should Fayle°
I am resoulvede to make it good with the very first Monys° that I
shall reseve° from Irland by returning all or at the Least some part
of it; though as yet I have Not resevede anye from thense sense° I
saw you; The Letar that Came to mee inclosede in yours wass from
the Busshope of Derye[53] wherin hee gave mee a brife° accompt°
that hee Left my Lord in good health but brought mee noe Letars
from hime nor have I had anye of Laytar° dayte then about the same
Time that Mr Boswell[54] Left Irland; but I heare for Sartane° that
thar are diveres passengars Landed at SenMalows[55] that Came from
Gallowaye° amongst whome is a ^the^ Seconde Sone of the Earle
of Arglass[56] formarlie Callede [the] Lord Cromwell whoe thay tell
mee dous intend to Come this waye by whom if [*missing*][57] I bee
informede anye thinge worthye your knowledge[58] you shall by the
Next reseve ane° accompt; Mr Raylings[59] wass by the knavrye of
the Seamen put into Rochell where hee wass the 21 of Maye from
whense hee hopede to ^bee^ goeinge within 2 days Soe as Not

---

[52] "A Spanish gold double-escudo dating from the 1530s and surviving into the 19th cent.; (also) any of various coins derived from or resembling this from the 17th and 18th centuries" ("pistole, *n.*," *OED*).

[53] John Bramhall (1594–1663), Bishop of Derry and later Archbishop of Armagh, who in January 1651 claimed: "My Lord Marquis of Ormond did commit a trust to me for the support of his noble Lady. Your Majesty was graciously pleased to approve it, and to ratify that power which he had given me. I have executed it honestly with as much discretion as God hath lent me." See Williams, *King's Irishmen*, 92; EO's correspondence with him is mentioned in 92–93.

[54] Possibly, Major Humphrey Boswell, a royalist agent and spy. See Geoffrey Smith, *Royalist Agents, Conspirators and Spies: Their Role in the British Civil Wars, 1640–1660* (Farnham: Ashgate, 2011).

[55] Saint-Malo, port town in Brittany, France.

[56] Vere Essex Cromwell (1625–1687) was the second son of Thomas Cromwell, first Earl of Ardglass (1594–1653), who had been awarded the Irish earldom in April 1645. See David Grummitt, "Cromwell, Edward, third Baron Cromwell (c. 1559–1607)," *ODNB*.

[57] This seems deliberately obliterated through a tear or burn.

[58] Two lines from "Lord Cromwell" to "your knowledge" are marked with a vertical line in the left margin.

[59] Unidentified.

havinge heard from hime Sense that Time I Conclude hime gone
at Length though I could wish it had bine° much Souner° The Last
Packet you ^Sent^ to my Lord is still in my hands for want of a
shure° ~~hands~~ ^Mesengar^ to Send it by; which Soe Soune as I Cane
Light upon shallbee immediatlye dispacht to hime; I am very much
troubled at the report of the defeate of my Lord Montros his Armye
and himeselfe Slayne but I hope it is Not true;[60] Sense that were to
Large ane° adistione° of Misfortune to the kinge and his partye if soe
Loyall and Gallant a persone shouldbee thus unseasonablye Lost;
My Lord of Corke is gone from hense to the waters; and I think that
most of the Companye heare besides will remove shortlye Non° of
them beinge designede I beleve soe Longe a Confinment to this plase
as is

       your very ashurede Frind
         and Sarvant

The 6 of June   E:ormonde

Just as I wass Sealinge this Letar I resevede° yours of the 25 of Maye
which I will answar by the Next Post and wass at the same instant
tould of the arrivall of my Lord of Mongarats Eldest Sone[61] at
Rochell whoe is Come out of Irland and willbee heare within a fewe
days I shouldbee glade to heare of your Ladys good health to whom I
praye presant my Sarviss° if it maye not bee Tresone in hir to reseve°
a remembranse from mee[62] I sent a Letar inclosede in one of mine ~~to~~
^to you For^ my Lord Hoptone[63] which I wass tould wass of Some
Consarnment° to hime which I would very willinglye know whetar
you have resevede it beinge Sent by Sir Richard Browns Convayanse

---

[60] The forces of James Graham, first Marquess of Montrose (1612–1650), had been defeated by the Scottish Covenanters at the Battle of Caribsdale on April 27. He escaped but was taken prisoner and then executed on May 21, 1650. See David Stevenson, "Graham, James, first marquess of Montrose (1612–1650)," *ODNB*.

[61] Edmund Butler was the eldest son and heir of Richard Butler, third Viscount Mountgarret (1578–1652/3).

[62] Nicholas's wife Jane (d. 1688) had gone to England to try to get an income out of her husband's estates in 1649; presumably, part of the process involved formal disassociation from the royalist cause. She would return to her husband in exile, unsuccessful in her claim, in August 1655. See S. A. Baron, "Nicholas, Sir Edward (1593–1669)," *ODNB*.

[63] Sir Ralph, Lord Hopton, a royalist army officer, was in exile with the king and a member of his Privy Council, but he left Charles after the signing of the treaty of Breda. See Ronald Hutton, "Hopton, Ralph, Baron Hopton (*bap.* 1596, *d.*1652)," *ODNB*.

and a Nothar° from mee at the Same Time to Sir Fredrick Conwalliss⁶⁴ wich° I feare hee hass Not resevede

Letter 19. June 20, [1650], [Caen], the Marchioness of Ormonde to [Sir Richard Browne] (BL, Additional MSS, Evelyn Papers, 78199 (827A), 18). Autograph.

Sir   The 20 of June

your Letar wass the first that informede mee of the kings beinge Gone for Scotland;⁶⁵ for whous Sayftye I shall praye and Longe to heare of his Sayfe° arrivall; which if you please to make mee pertaker of when it shall Come to your knowledge; I shall very thankfullye reseve° that favour from you: as I doe the Care you are pleasede to Express in what Consarnes° my Lords ocations;° about which I have writene unto Sir Gorge Cartwright;* whom I find very Siville and willinge to afforde Justiss tharin, but the Party whoe is Captayne of this Shipe in which my Lord is Instrastede; dous° absolutlye *interested* denye hime to have anye Share Tharin; and how to make it apiere° willbee the difficultye; unless my Lord Bushope of Derye Cane give anye furthar informatione of the bussenes° to whom I have allredye writene, but whethar my Letar have Come to his hands is I feare as douptfull° as this truth is Sartane° that I am Sir

your very ashurede frind and Sarvant

E:ormonde

Letter 20. June 23, 1650, Caen, the Marchioness of Ormonde to John Bramhall, Bishop of Derry.⁶⁶

My Lord

Upon the receipt of a letter your Lordship was pleased to send me soon after your arrival in Holland, wherein you gave some account of my Lord, and that you were then upon a journey into Flanders,

---

⁶⁴ Frederick Cornwallis, First Baron Cornwallis (1610–c. 1662).
⁶⁵ Charles arrived in Garmouth, in Moray, on June 23, 1650, signing the Scottish Covenant as he came ashore.
⁶⁶ The letter is edited from *The Rawdon Papers: Consisting of Letters on Various Subjects Literary Political and Ecclesiastical to and From Dr John Bramhall, Primate of Ireland*, ed. Edward Berwick (London: John Nichols and Son, 1819), 96–98.

where you hoped to advantage him; I immediately returned an answer unto that letter, and sent it unto Sir Edward Nicholas to be conveyed unto you, which I fear has neither as yet come to his nor your hands. And hearing within these few days from Sir Richard Browne that your Lordship has exprest yourself so careful of my Lord's concernments, as you had written to him, and desired that Captain Nicholas Martin's* ship might be made stay of, and secured untill he should make satisfaction of what is due unto my Lord, he being now at Jersey, and denies my Lord to have any share in that vessel, alleging it belongs unto the city of Gallowaye,° I thought it necessary to inform your Lordship thereof, and to desire that what particulars you know concerning this business, and how far my Lord is interested to a right sharing, that you will be pleased to signify so much unto Sir George Cartwright* the Governor of Jersey, who has some time since desired to receive some information from me; which I being not able to give him, having heard nothing from my Lord concerning it, gives me cause to fear that Captain Martin* is already, or will be, very suddenly dismist° from thence, so as the sooner your Lordship pleases to send to him, and such advice to me, as you think necessary, will the more advantage and oblige her that is very assuredly, my Lord, your Lordship's very assured friend and servant,

Caen, June 23   E:ormonde

My Lord,—I shall desire the favour of being informed how I may direct my letters unto you, as also to know whether your Lordship hears any thing of one Captain Thomas Plunket, with whom my Lord has ventured £900, and has sent me divers letters to be conveyed unto him, which are still in my hands by reason I know not as yet where he is, nor how to send to him.

Letter 21. August 1, [1650], [Caen], the Marchioness of Ormonde to [Sir Richard Browne] (BL, Additional MSS, Evelyn Papers, 78199 (827A), 25). Autograph.

Sir   The first of August

you are pleasede to Express a greatar regard bouth° to Mee and My Sons; then it is Ethar° in mine, or Thar° power to desarve; outhar° then as I hope thay° will retayne Soe much of Gratitude as to indevour° to Sarve you hearaftar wherin I asshure° you I shall very willinglye Joyne with Them in havinge that Creditt; I have presumede upon the fridome and incoridgment° you have by your Sevilitiess° bine° pleasede to give mee to hearin to inclose 2 Letars which by the favour of your Convayanse I desier° maye bee Sent accordinge as thay are derectede,° That to Sir Edward Nicholass Espetialye;° it beinge of Some Consarnment° to mee; whoe am desirious of Nothinge More then the good fortune of Some ocatione° wherby to Manefest My beinge

Sir

your very ashurede Frind and Sarvant

E:ormonde

Sir I forgot to tell you that I am Now fullye Satisfiede that My Lord had Noe Share at all in that Shipe of Captane Martins*

Letter 22. October 31, [1650], [Caen], the Marchioness of Ormonde to [Sir Richard Browne] (BL, Additional MSS, Evelyn Papers, 78199 (827A), 30). Autograph.

Sir   The Last of octobar

I perseve° by the Coppye of that Letar you did mee the favour to send mee that some Exseptianse is takene by the kings offisiers° at Dunkirke unto My Lord Bushope of Derys prosidings;°[67] which trulye I am troublede for; that any thinge of dispute should soe unfortunatlye happene in a bussenes° wherin My Lord is sayede° to be Consarnede;° whoe haveinge the honnor to Sarve his Magestye willnot I hope bee belevede to have intentions to infringe his Rights to presarve whous Intrests hee hass Losst his owne; in that which wass more of Sartantye° to hime then the Share of the Prisess is like to bee; Some profitts by which (it is true) I have bine° promist by my Lord of Derye and tharfor doe beleve I shall have; though as yet I never had anye benefitt by; Nor outhar° healpe then what the small remayns of my Ruenede° Fortune hass givene for Subsistanse to Mee and Mine Sense° my Comminge into Franse; soe as I Cane sattisfye you in what Consarns° my Selfe in that perticular; and I think I maye answar for My Lord in That which I am most Confident hee is abbill to make Good that he Never yet gave othoritye° to anye Persone that wass repugnant to that of his Magesties; but with a Subbordinatione to That Sufranitye which Loyaltye religione and

exception

sovereignty

---

[67] According to his *ODNB* entry, in the 1650s "much of [Bramhall's] energy was devoted to managing part of Ormond's domestic finances and mainly in acting as a prize commissioner." See John McCafferty, "Bramhall, John (bap. 1594, d. 1663), Church of Ireland archbishop of Armagh," *ODNB*.

honnor oblidges hime to Reveranse and regard beyond all private intrest whatsomever;[68] soe as what hass happenede in My Lord of Derys managment of the bussenes that hass givene offense I shall not fayle° accordinge as is desirede to Let hime know; whoe I hope will vindecate himselfe; and in declaringe the Truth Justifye allsoe the Clearness of my Lords intentions; whom absense maye make Subgect perhaps to bee misundarstoud unles by persons whoe not knowinge hime; are soe Just as your Selfe; whous Sevilities° to hime and favours to my Sons; I am shure° hee will acknowlege; as I doe with much gratitude that am

      Sir

         your very ashurede Frind and Sarvant

         E:ormonde

Letter 23. November 24, [1650], [Caen], the Marchioness of Ormonde to [Sir Richard Browne] (BL, Additional MSS, Evelyn Papers, 78199 (827A), 35). Autograph.

Sir   The 24 of No

you oblidge mee soe much by the favour of your Letars as you Nide° make noe appoligies nor bee Confynede° to the Rules that you give your selfe of deferinge to write but when you have Neuse° or bussenes;° sense° without Ethar° your Letars wouldbee very acseptabill to Mee; The Neuse that Sir Edward Wallker[69] hass brought Consarning° the kings beinge now ~~belevede~~ in a betar° Condistione then formarlye; and that of the Prinse of Oringe[70] his Death; ocations° Joye for the one; though it gives Troubell for the outhar;° as for the most part attends all that wee Figure to our Selfs of Good; The Neuse ^from Irland^ I am aptar[71] to doupt° of havinge bine° soe oftene desevede° then beleve True; though if my wishess could make it Sartane° or yours Ethar; I beleve your affectione to his Magesties Sarviss° and intrests; and favorabill inclinatione to My Lord; would make you afford Some; sense your Sevilitye° and favour

---

  [68] "Whatever" ("whatsomever, *pron.* and *adj.*," 1, *OED*).
  [69] Sir Edward Walker had accompanied Charles II to Scotland but had returned to the Hague. See Hubert Chesshyre, "Walker, Sir Edward (1612–1677)," *ODNB*.
  [70] William II, Prince of Orange (1626–1650), married to Mary, elder sister of Charles II. See Tony Claydon, "William III and II (1650–1702)," *ODNB*.
  [71] "To incline, dispose *to*" ("apt, *v.*," 3, *OED*).

to Mee and my Sons is soe great ane° argument of it; as it likwiss lays ane ingaydgment° upon Mee to bee

        Sir

                your very ashurede Frind and Sarvant

                E:ormonde

Sir I returne you many thanks for your kind invitatione of soe troubellsome a Gest as Dick[72] would have bine to you; whoe Could not bee Left anye where soe well nor soe much to his owne Contentment I am shure° as with you; but tharis ane° acquantanse of Mine heare that goes shortlie to Paris and offires to Mee to bringe hime downe in his Coche° soe as by that Menes° you willbee Easede of that Troubell   *guest*

Letter 24. December 12, [1650], [Caen], the Marchioness of Ormonde to [Sir Richard Browne] (BL, Additional MSS, Evelyn Papers, 78199 (827A), 38). Autograph.

Sir

Mr Maxwell hass informede mee how willinge you Exprest your selfe upon the First Motione to Send to make Staye of that Pryse, Laytlie Come into Rochell; untell° My Lords Share shouldbee Securede out of it; whom I find you have bine° noe Less forward to oblige in this perticular, then Sivell° to hime in all outhars,° wherof I shallnot only make hime acquantede wherby hee maye rendar you his owne acknowlegments; but as I have bine pertakar of your favours allsoe; shall indevour° ~~to acquit my Selfe~~ by takinge all ocations° to Sarve you ^to^ give testimonye of My beinge

        Sir

                your very ashurede Frind and Sarvant

The 12 of Des   E:ormonde

---

[72] Presumably, her second son Richard.

Letter 25. December 12, [1650], [Caen], the Marchioness of Ormonde to John Bramhall, Bishop of Derry (HL, Hastings-Irish Papers (Rawdon Papers), HA 14109). Autograph.
[Endorsed]: dutches of ormond.

My Lord

Fearinge my formar ^Letar^ should miscarye; I thought fitt [to] Second it; and Let your Lordshipp know; that I resevede° advertisment within thes fewe days; of a Pryse, brought into Rochell worth fivetine thowsand Pistols by one Diego Line; that hass ane° Irishe Commistione; and tharfor I suppose My Lord is to have out of it his Magestys Share; but in regard that nethar My Selfe Nor anye heare hass power to demand the Same; I thought it requisite to desier° Sir Richard Browne to send and make Staye of it the Shipe (which hee hass allredye dune°) for soe Longe Time; as tell° I shall have made your Lordshipp acquanted; that if you have not allredye heard Nor givene anye derections° Tharin or that your beinge out of the Contrye maye make it of to great inconveniense for you to Louke° aftar; that your Lordshipp willbee pleasede to Send hethar° such ane° othoritye° in writinge; Leavinge a Blank for the Partys Name as maye Collect what is dew° unto My Lord and give a discharge for it; and the Like for Jersye that maye bee kept by (and only made use of) in Cayse° anye Pryses should bee brought into that Illand; and I will aftar the ressept° of such a papar; Nominate some such Persone; as maye bee abbill and Fitt for that Trust; but one° the Contrarye; if your Lordshipp have allredye Settlede a Correspondant in Eache of these plasses° that willbee accomptabill° to you; it willnot then bee at all Nesesarye that you Send anye such warrant; but proside° accordinge to what in your owne Judgment Fitt to bee dune; and That shall perfectlye Satisfye

fifteen

    My Lord

      your Lordshipps very ashurede Frind
      and Sarvant

The 12 of Des   E:ormonde

Letter 26. December 12, [1650], [Caen], the Marchioness of Ormonde to John Bramhall, Bishop of Derry (HL, Hastings-Irish Papers (Rawdon Papers), HA 14110). Autograph.

My Lord

I am more troubled that I should have givene your Lordshipp a wronge informatione then for my owne disappoyntment; Sense° I find upon a Second advertisment that tharis noe ~~shipe~~ such Pryse Come into Rochell as I mentionede to your Lordshipp by tow° formar Letars; but one° the Contrarye; the Same Shipe sayde to bee Cast away upon the North Seas; which grose mistake that hass bine;° I Cannot Comprehend the resone° of; Nor have I hardlye patianse° Enoughe to forgive the oughtors tell° you have pardonede *authors* mee the Errour that Thar° Fault hass made mee gilltye of; that am

        My Lord

                your Lordshipps very ashured Frind
                      and Sarvant

The 15 of Des   E:ormonde

Letter 27. January 19, 1650/1, [Caen], the Marchioness of Ormonde to Sir Edward Nicholas (BL, Egerton MSS, 2534, fol. 44). Autograph.
For the Right Honnorabill Sir Edward Nicholas thes at the hague.
[Endorsed]: 19 January 1650/51 Lady Marchioness Ormond.

Sir   (28)[73]   The 19 of Jan

By my Last Letar to you writene one° Monday wass Sevenight I gave you ane° accompt° of My Lords beinge Sayflye° arrivede heare, and sent you inclosede tharin a Letar from hime; which I hope is by this Time Come Sayfe° unto your hands; from whom you will heare agayne° soe soune° as hee Comes to Paris[74] by the Lord of Inchsquine[75] whoe intends aftar a Fewe days to goe from thense into

---

[73] The numbers on EO's letters to Nicholas were added by the recipient to facilitate filing.

[74] Henrietta Maria's court in exile.

[75] Murrough O'Brien, first Earl of Inchiquin (c. 1614–1674), had refused the offer of safe conduct by Cromwell after the royalist defeat, and followed JO into exile in France in December 1650. See Patrick Little, "O'Brien, Murrough, first earl of Inchiquin (c. 1614–1674)," *ODNB*.

Holland; whoe I ashure my ^selfe^ will give you a full accompt of
all things that Consarnes° Irland; and the Nesesitiye of My Lords;
and his Leavinge that kingdom; Soe as I shallnot troubill you with
anye discourse upon that Subgect; by resone° ~~that~~ the best accompt
that I Cane give willbee to° insignifficant if tenderede by a persone
soe Litell° knowinge as I am; and tharfor shall Confyne° my selfe
to what only Consarnes my perticular; and Let you know; that My
Lord did absolutlye refuse to Treate or acsept anye Condistions
from Cromwells Partye; though very good ons° have bine° offerede
hime Consarninge° his Estate hee not thinkinge it fitt for hime to
artickell for the Securinge of his owne Intrest; when hee Saw that of
his Mastars upon the Matar Lost; and himselfe soe unfortunate as *matter*
~~outh~~ by outhors defaults[76] had made Frutles° all his indevours;° and *others*
thous° Sunderye difficultys and great wants that hee had Contended
aganst Ever sense° his Last goeinge over; in hope to presarve for the
kinge Some Intrest in that kingdom which hee at Lenght beinge noe
longar abbill to doe; nor Seeinge anye possibilitye of beinge relevede;
Chouse rathar to Expose himselfe to all haszards in Comminge a *chose*
waye ~~which hee did [illegible]~~[77] then staye; to bee a furthar wittness
of that Pepells° disobedianse and Contempt of the kings othoritye;°
which hee did with soe Litell Consideratione to what might
Consarne his Future ^Subsistanse^ as hee hass made noe kind of
provitione for it; Nor brought with hime save 5 hundreth pound *provision*
Sterlinge; which with the Nombar° of Persons to bee mentaynede°
out of it; willbee Soune at ane° Ende; Soe as I begine to See that my
Nesesities will Ere Longe Forse° mee to what of all ~~the~~ things in the
world is the most Contrarye to My inclinatione; the indevoringe°
to recover some part of my Lords Fortune; that I am perticularlye
intrestede in from such as are now the injust posessors of it; though I
am not yet perfectlye resoulvede nor am willinge to bee; whilst tharis
anye Life ~~Left in~~ or hope Left in the kings affayrs or possibilitye
that my Lord Cane procure a Livlihoude for himselfe by anye
imployment abrode;° which as yet I find to bee alltogethar unsartane°
and in this douptfull° Condistione wee are bouth° in at the presant;
I perseve° by your Last Letar that it maye prove ^hasardous^ to
.318.9.30.2.28.36.32.9.[78] Brothar to reseve° anye Letar from you or
anye Else in Shiphier;° tharfor I praye doe not venture it for what

---

[76] "A failure in duty; a wrong act or deed; a fault, misdeed, offence" ("default, *n.*," III, 5a, *OED*).

[77] Nine or ten canceled words are illegible.

[78] The code is not decyphered but it may refer to "Mr Seymors Brothar" who is mentioned in Letter 28.

Consarnes Mee; for I have soe much of regard unto the Sayftye
of anye Persone that is fathfull to the kinge; as I would not bringe
inconveniense upon anye one of them for anye advantage it Couldbee
to my Selfe; but am very well Contentede to have patianse° and relye
upon the Gentellmans owne Care; whoe I beleve will not disappoynt
Mee; Nor will you I hope; bee Less Just; then to beleve I am with
much Sinseritye

    Sir

      your very ashurede Frind
      and Sarvant

       E: ormonde

Sir aftar the writinge of This; I resevede° your 35 Letar dayted the
1/11 of Jan with one from My Lady of Inchequine[79] that Came
inclosede in it; and ane° Extract of a Letar from Mr Philip Carpentar
which I have sent unto My Lord that is by this Time at Paris from
whom I ashure my Selfe you will Shorlye heare

**Letter 28. March 29, 1651, [Caen], the Marchioness of Ormonde to
Sir Edward Nicholas** (BL, Egerton MSS, 2534, fol. 57). Autograph.
[Endorsed]: 32. 29 March 1650/51 Lady Marchioness Ormond.

Sir   (32)   The 29 of March

Though your letars shallbee allways; and are, very wellcome to mee,
yet I willnot bee soe unresonabill to Expect Them, but when at your
best Leasure (and not outharwiss°) you maye afforde Them; and
if anye oftener I shall have ocatione° to troubill you with Mine; I
shall make use of the fridome you have allowede mee of writinge
to you; I perseve° that the 2000 Peases of Eight,[80] are not yet put
ofe° nor Like to bee, without great Loss; which I Considar not soe
much the prejudiss of to my Selfe as I am Sorye for the Troubill and
disappoyntment it hass givene you; which if it shallbee Ever in my
power to repare by anye waye of Sarvinge you the inconveniensies
you have givene your Selfe to pleasure Mee; I shall indevour° the

---

[79] Elizabeth, Lady Inchiquin (d. 1685), was daughter of Sir William St. Leger, Lord President of Munster, to whom her husband had been ward; the couple had married in October 1635.

[80] Spanish dollar, widely used in many countries as international currency ("pieces of eight," *The Oxford Companion to Ships and the Sea*, ed. I. C. B. Dear and Peter Kemp (Oxford University Press, 2006) http://www.oxfordreference.com.

performanse with a very reall willingnes; and doe give you many
thanks for the Cautione and good advise you have bine° pleasede to
give mee Consarninge° my Journye into England; which I am not as
yet perfectlye resoulvede upon though I have writene to his Magesty
for his Leave as I tould you by a formar Letar, nor Cannot bee;
untell° I shall reseve° his answar and heare from some Frinds of Mine
in England; wherby to bee Sattisfiede befor I remove from hense
whethar my J~~ournye~~ goeinge maye bee of advantage to mee and not
bee forst to take the ingaydgment° Nor hinderede to returne when I
please; without which Libertye I intend not to Leave my Frinds to
~~Cast my selfe at the~~ put my selfe into the power ^of My Enimies^
Sense° that wouldbee but a very unsecure and uncomfortabill
Exchange; but soe soune° as I Cane possitivlye determine how to
Settell and dispose of My Selfe I shall not fayle° to Let you know
it; I have not heard anye thinge as yet from Mr Seymors Brothar[81]
but doe beleve I shall whenever hee is providede and Cane ~~Conveni~~
[/] Convenientlye Send; your Care and favour in writinge to hime
in that behalfe; beinge noe Less ane° obligatione then thous° Many
outhars° wherby you have ingaydgede°

    Sir

        your very ashurede Frind
        and Sarvant

        E

Sense° the writinge of this I resevede° a Letar from you of the 5/15
of this Month togethar with the accompt° of the 2000 Pesess of   *pieces*
Eight which sense your Last Letar to Mee I perseve are with some
difficultye at Lenght put ofe; and what remayns dew° to you of the
first and Last Some you Lent Mee I hope I shallbee abbill to Send
you Shortlye; the Neuse° of My Lord of Corks Death I ~~ha~~ ^beleve^
is Not True[82] for I saw a Letar that Mentionde hime but Nothing of
his beinge Sicke which wass writene but a fortnight Sense

---

[81] Presumably, this refers to a brother of Henry Seymour who was first mentioned in Letter 14. Henry had four brothers.

[82] The rumour was false: the Earl of Cork lived until 1698.

Letter 29. May 2, 1652, Caen, the Countess of Ormonde to Oliver Cromwell (SAL MS 138). Autograph. See Figure 3.
For the Lord Gennerall Cromwell. [Endorsed]: Lady Ormonde 2 May 1652.

My Lord

Havinge by a very generall Fame resevede° asshuranse of your Lordshipps inclinations to make use of your power for the oblidginge of such in generall as stand in Niede° of protectione and assistanse from it, and havinge heard that some Expretions° have fallene from you that maye give mee hope that I in my perticular maye bee thought by you not uncapabill of beinge made one of the instansess of that disposistione in you,[83] I have adventured to make this address unto your Lordshipp for your favour, and to acquant you with my Condistione, and tharupon shall hope for your assistanse with that Clearnes and generositye wherwith I have heard you have oblidgede outhars° in a State not unlike that I am in, your Lordshipp maye please to undarstand that thar° desendede to mee ane° Estate of inheritanse in Irland which togethar with the rest of My Lords Fortune is now by warr and pestelanse very much depopulatede and not Like to bee without much troubill profitabill for a Longe Time, yet out of this Estate it is that by your Lordshipps permistione and furtharanse I would propose to raise a Subsistanse for my Selfe and Chilldren if by your Lordshipp I shallbee incoridgede° to indevour° it and derectede° how most advantagiouslye to applye my selfe to it, beinge outharwiss° as ignorant how to goe about it as I am unabell° to Compass[84] it by tedious applications, soe as from bouth° thes your Lordshipp may gathar how great ane obligatione you have in your power to plase upon mee, I desier My desier° is to owe my acknowlegments in this perticular unto your Lordshipp, and to reseve° your pleasure with such Passess[85] for my selfe and Nesesarye attendants as you shall Judge Fitt, and that with what speede your Lordshipp shall think Convenient that accordinglie I maye prepare

instances

clearness

pestilence

---

[83] In a letter written to JO on May 6, 1650, Michael Boyle, a kinsman of EO's friend Richard, Earl of Cork, claims that Cromwell "pretends to be a great servant of your lady, and much to pitty her condition; the estate which she brought Your Lordship they openly profess shall not be given from her." See Burghclere, I, 391.

[84] "To attain to or achieve (an end or object aimed at); to accomplish" ("compass, *v*.1," IV, 11a, *OED*).

[85] "Permission to leave, enter, or travel somewhere; a document giving or declaring such permission" ("pass, *n*. 4," II, 7a, *OED*).

my selfe with thankfullnes to reseve the favour hearin Sought from you by

    My Lord

      your Lordshipps humbel Sarvant

Caen the 2nd of May   E:ormonde

Letter 30. September 23, 1652, Caen, the Marchioness of Ormonde to Sir Edward Nicholas (BL, Egerton MSS, 2534, fol. 129). Autograph.
For Mr Jones [/] At Antwerp. [Endorsed]: 23 September 1652 Lady Marchioness Ormond to me by my frind [about] some mony she [gave] him for me.

Sir

I have forborne writinge to you sense° my beinge heare, relyinge upon the Justiss and favour of your Sone,[86] whoe promist mee in his Letars to asshure° you of my respects, which should have bine° witnesede from my owne hand, could it have bine profitabell to you, or safe for Mee, to have sent anye Letars to you, as I find it is not, unless by a Persone I may soe saflie trust as hee whoe is pleasede to undartake the delivrye of thes Lines unto you, whom I have Likwise intreatede to give you some accompt° of my prosidings° in my bussenes,° though the Sucksess° tharof has not as yet answrede nor I feare willnot, the troubell of soe unpleasinge an adresse as I have bine driwene° to make unto your kinsman, though the worst Event Can bee noe Surprise; Sense my solissitatione has bine rathar to discharge what I owe to outhars° by imployinge my indevours° to presarve thar° Right, then anye Confidens I Ever had of prevayling soe farr as to make it of anye presant advantage unto My Selfe, that am alltogethar unprofitabell unto thous° persons that I have the greatest desier° to Sarve; ~~wherof~~ yet am most undoutedlye

    Sir

      your ashurede Frind and
       humbell Sarvant
The 23 of Sep   E

---

[86] Probably his heir, Sir John Nicholas, who at this time was employed as secretary to Sir Edward Hyde.

Sir

it has bine some part of my indevour° sense° my beinge heare, to procure wherwithall to redime° my goods that I Left ingadgede° upon very hard Termes in Franse, part wherof is within this few days though with some hazard Come sayfe° to Mee; but not as yet soe disposede of, as Leaves mee riche Ennough to paye you all the dept° ^I owe you^ but what I could procure upon soe short warninge beinge fiftye Pound; I did make offier° of unto your Sone for your usse; which out of some apprehenstione of my Condistione, hee wouldnot reseve;° but shallbee nevertheles payede upon the first derections° from you unto your Lady[87] or to anye outhar° that you shall oppoynt;° and the rest you shallbee Likwise shure° of, soe soune° as Ever it shall please God to inabell° Mee wherwithall to make you Sattisfactione

---

[87] Since Jane Nicholas was in England at this time, it is clear that EO's journey was imminent.

The Cromwellian Settlement of Ireland, 1652–1657

Letter 31. June, 1653, [London], the Countess of Ormonde to General Charles Fleetwood (NLI, Ormond Papers, 2499, no. 17, p. 173). Scribal copy.
[Endorsed]: Coppie of my Ladies Lettre to Generall Fleetewood June 1653. Touching the Lands for 2000 pounds and.

My Lord[88]

It is soe lately since I made knowne unto your Lordship my apprehensions of the prejudise I am like to suffer by the strict interpretation that is made upon the words of the Parliaments order and the giveing me lands wast° and in severall places farr distant from the howse assigned mee as it were not reasonable for me to presse or importune you further for redresse in these particulers, since I do assure my selfe that your Lordship is out of your owne inclination enough disposed to doe me all the lawfull favour yow may but lest that others to whom I am altogether a Stranger may not have the like favourable intentions, I have desired from the Lord Generall his Lordships[89] [letter] in my behalfe, which is now Sent and addrest unto your Lordship and the Commissioners there in hope to incline them to be the more favourable in their proceedings in what concearns mee when they shall understand it will not be unacceptable their being soe to thise in authority heere, as well as I suppose it will be agreeing with your Lordships likeing who is cheife there, but not intended by me that it should be delivered unles your Lordship shall approve and thinke it necessary, to whose opinion it is wholly

---

[88] General Charles Fleetwood had been commissioned as Commander-in-Chief of Ireland in July 1652, and the next month he became one of the commissioners responsible for the civil government of Ireland. See Toby Barnard, "Fleetwood, Charles, appointed Lord Fleetwood under the protectorate (c. 1618–1692)," *ODNB*.

[89] A copy of Cromwell's letter to Fleetwood in response to EO's letter can be found in NLI, Ormond Papers, 2499, no. 20, p. 85. In it, he writes: "This lady is a person of soe much honor and meritt as I hope I need not presse any other Arguments for the shewing her any lawfull and just favour in this particular."

referred by her that beggs your Lordships pardon for this freedome taken and the favour to be accompted°

>My Lord
>
>>your Lordships humble servant
>
>>>E: Ormonde

My Lord I have yet one request more to make unto your Lordship that since it is supposed that all lands in Ireland that are in the Possession of the State will be shortly disposed of that my inheritance may not be included or given from me untill I may have the Common justice and tyme° aforded me to make my Claime

Letter 32. January 2, 1654/5, Dublin, the Marchioness of Ormonde's certificate on behalf of Margaret Butler, Viscountess Mountgarret (NLI, Ormond Papers, 2500, no. 68, p. 129). Scribal copy.
[Endorsed]: Copie of the Certificate on the behalfe of my Lady Mountgarrett.[90]

At the request of the Lady Mountgarrett I doe hereby certifie, that in the beginning of the Rebellion in the yeare 1641 I being then at Kilkeny,* her Ladyship (in discourse with me) did expresse a very deepe Sence and detestation of the Crueltyes then used towards those of her Nation, the said Lady her Selfe being an English Woman; And she then declared to me, that it wrought in her soe greate a dislike of remayning in the Country, that (if She could have had any Security) she would have gone unto her freinds into England. And I have heard it credibly reported at that tyme,° and after my getting from thence hither to Dublin, that her Ladyship favoured diverse poore distressed English in her owne howse, And that (for that cause) She was disliked by many of the Country. And I doe further certifie, that after my comeing to Dublin, my Lord my husband

---

[90] EO's kinswoman, Margaret Butler, née Spencer (d. 1655), was the widow of JO's uncle, Lord Mountgarret (d. 1651). Mountgarret had been President of the Supreme Council of the Confederate Catholics, and it was he who gave EO and her family protection and who ensured her safe convoy to Dublin in 1642. Viscountess Mountgarret's case appeared before the Committee for Compounding on October 6, 1652, and again on January 17, 1654/5: see *Calendar of the Proceedings of the Committee for Compounding, 1646–1660*, ed. Mary Anne Everett Green (London: Her Majesty's Stationery Office, 1890). For biographical information on his widow, see Sean Kelsey, "Butler, Richard, third Viscount Mountgarret (1578–1651)," *ODNB*.

Shewed me a letter of her Ladyships, which it Seemes She had written, whiles I was deteyned in those partes, and appeared to be in answeare to one of her husbands, and intercepted by Some of the English Party under my Lords Commaund, which letter (to the best of my remembrance) was to this effect, That She earnestly desired her husband to use his best endeavours to get me of° from thence, and the English with me intimating unto him, that the performance of Soe charitable an Act would be more to his honour, then it could reflect prejudice upon him, admitting that the Irish for soe doeing, should plunder him, as in Such case they threatned to doe, Which desire of her Ladyship he accordingly Answeared, and by the blessing of God and his Assistance, both my Selfe and the English with me were delivered, and Safely conducted to the Waterside. And this I certifie this 2 day of January 1654.

                Signed E ormonde

Letter 33. August 11, [1655], [London], the Marchioness of Ormonde to John Burdon (NLI, Ormond Papers, 2484, no. 226, p. 153).[91] Autograph.
[M]y Sarvant John Burdon.

[*four lines missing*] beinge out of Towne I did apprehend might have [caused a] delaye in the delivrye of them, I doe very much wondar a[t] what you tell mee Consarninge° hime, that was onse° my Tenant, but doe not feare anye prejudges that his Juglinge cane doe if My Lord Hary[92] doe Continow° as I hope and doe beleve hee will to bee my frind, and w[93] whom I have a good oppinione of as to his wishinge well to mee in this bussenes,° and doe not find that anye thinge dous° yet apiere° to give mee Cause to olltor° it, Nor by what relatione I have hetherto° resevede° from you, to make mee doute,° but rathar to Expect good Suckses° towards the obtayninge wherof, I am suffisentlie satisfiede that thar° nethar is, nor willbee anye indevours° of yours wantinge, and that shallbee Ecqualie acseptabell with Mee; as if you did prevayle, in my Letar sent you by the Last

juggling

---

[91] There is a large tear at the top of the leaf that has obliterated four full lines in each of two pages as well as part of three further lines in each page.

[92] Cromwell's son Henry Cromwell had arrived in Ireland in the summer of 1655, and, after the departure of Fleetwood that September, was "in effect, though not always in name, chief administrator of Ireland." See Peter Gaunt, "Cromwell, Henry (1628–1674)," *ODNB*.

[93] Presumably, someone whose name begins with *W* (unidentified).

Post I acquantede you of the answar that Sir Thomas resevede from his unkell,° which did nethar satisfie hime nor mee, wherupon hee and a Nothar° has joynede bouth° thar Intrests agayne,° and writene Soe [*four lines missing*] that bussenes of the [*three words missing*] thinge that stays mee in Towne; for [*three words missing*] have allredie Sent to Acton,* but I am still layboringe and [t]ryinge all ways ~~in this~~ ^and doe hope to Efect some good in this^ perticular; I pray take care to deliver this inclosede unto My Mothar[94] or get it sent sayflie° to hir, if shee bee not ~~still~~ at Dublin, and Let the ould Doctor[95] know that I resevede his of the 25 of July, and will shortlie return hime an answar of it

The 11 of August   EO

Letter 34. September 21, 1655, [London], the Marchioness of Ormonde to John Burdon (NLI, Ormond Papers, 2321, no. 1147, p. 225). Autograph.
For your Selfe. [Endorsed]: Her Ladyships of the 21 September 1655.

John Burdon

I have sent the List of my Lands within the Countye of Tippararye, by mr Carr,[96] unto mr Averye;[97] whoe Promises, that hee will indevour,° that Noe Injurye shallbee dune° mee by the Adventerors,°[98]

---

[94] EO's mother-in-law, Elizabeth, Lady Thurles. See "Elizabeth, Lady Thurles — Her Ancestry and Her Role in the Rebellion of 1641," in *Thurles: The Cathedral Town; Essays in Honour of Archbishop Thomas Morris*, ed. William Corbett and William Nolan (Dublin: Geography Publications, 1989), 40–45.

[95] The unnamed "ould doctor" is mentioned on a number of different occasions. It is likely that he is Gerald Fennell, the family's physician, who is first named in Letter 47. He had served as a member of the Supreme Council of the Confederate Catholics in the 1640s but by the 1650s he was living in Dublin where he was held in high esteem by the Cromwellian administration. See Mary Ann Lyons, "The Role of Graduate Physicians in Professionalising Medical Practice in Ireland, c. 1619–1654," in *Ireland and Medicine in the Seventeenth and Eighteenth Century*, ed. James Kelly and Fiona Clark (Farnham: Ashgate, 2010).

[96] Mr. Carr is mentioned in eight letters but his identity remains obscure. From internal evidence, it appears he was EO's agent in the mid-1650s, perhaps her legal representative.

[97] Possibly Timothy Avery who was part of the Cromwellian government of Ireland and was based in Dublin. See Crawford Gribben, *God's Irishmen: Theological Debates in Cromwellian Ireland* (Oxford: Oxford University Press, 2007), 233, note 77.

[98] Speculators who loaned money to the English Parliament in return for a promise of land in Ireland. Following the Cromwellian conquest of Ireland starting in 1649,

and now, that you have have [*sic*] made upe the Lists soe Exzact° for
mr worslye* and Doctor Petete,⁹⁹ as thay° may with Ease distinguish,
what Lands in Each Baronye are Mine, from thous° of the Stats,° I
hope it will prevent anye furthar prejudise that I might otharwise
have bine° Liabell unto by Thar° Mistakes; and Leave mee in the
greatar possibelitye of beinge put into the Possestione of ~~my~~ what
belongs unto mee, upon such Termes at the presant, as the State and
I Cane agree; wherof your Letar gives Mee some hopes; upon the
incoridgment° that mr worslye has givene you, and his advise that
you should applye your Selfe unto Corronell Herbert¹⁰⁰ and desier°
hime to move the bussenes° unto the Counsell, as I doe beleve hee
has allredie, or will Sudanlie°¹⁰¹ doe; Soe as I doe very well aprove
of the way you have takene in followinge mr worslys advise; which
I Seconded by your Care and dilegense, wherof I have a great
Confidense, will with Gods assistanse bringe this bussenes I hope
unto a good Effect, and I beleve with Less oppositione then if it
had bine agitatede heare; and tharfor I would by noe menes° have
you to returne, untell° you have broght it unto some Conclustione,
or that you find your Stayinge thar in Ordar tharunto, willbee Noe
Longar Nesesarye, I have Considerede the propositione made for
Drilands Britas, and doe think the offier° is Faire, soe the Persone   *Brittasdryland*
bee not undar anye incapasitye of stayinge in the Contrye by the Late   *(Co.*
^Proclimation^ which you must inquier,° and See if hee couldbee   *Kilkenny)*
Tyede to Builde a Stone House, otharwise the Cabans that are Now,   *cabins*
though a Conveniensie to hime at the presant, willbee noe advantage
hearaftar unto the Plase, as you may Let hime know, is Consevede°
by

E.O

---

in 1653 Ireland was declared as subdued, and the lands were allocated in what became known as the Cromwellian Settlement. See Trinity College Dublin, *The Down Survey of Ireland* http://downsurvey.tcd.ie. Accessed February 17, 2020.

⁹⁹ Sir William Petty, medical doctor and surveyor of Ireland, whose "Down Survey" replaced Worsley's. See Toby Barnard, "Petty, Sir William (1623–1687)," *ODNB*.

¹⁰⁰ Colonel Thomas Herbert had been serving in Ireland since the summer of 1649 and was clerk of the governing council of Ireland. See Ronald H. Fritze, "Herbert, Sir Thomas, first baronet (1606–1682)," *ODNB*.

¹⁰¹ "Without delay, forthwith, promptly, immediately, directly, at once" ("suddenly, *adv.*," 2, *OED*).

This inclosede Letar is from mrs Herbert,[102] which I praye bee Carfull to deliver; and Let Corronell Harbert know, that if hee will returne an answar you will get it Sent in my Packete by the Same Mesengar

The 21 of Sep

Letter 35. September 21, 1655, [London], the Marchioness of Ormonde to John Burdon (NLI, Ormond Papers, 2321, no. 1148, p. 233). Autograph.
For your Selfe. [Endorsed]: Her Ladyships 21 September 1655.

John Bardon

[you will hearinc]losede reseve° my Letar to mr Archar,[103] which aftar you have perusede, you may seale upe and deliver if you doe aprove tharof, and when you returne mee from mr Archar the Coppie desirede I praye it willbee Likwise Nesesarye that you Sertifie° mee, what by your best discovrye and inquirye you Cane gathar of mr Archars Condistione, whethar hee hath provede his good affectione,[104] or is otharways previledgede by Articles from beinge transplantede or upon what sartane° grownds° hee is inablede° to dispose of his Intrest, wherof hee offiers° mee the refussall in the Mills, as likwise of what yearlie vallew° Thay° now are, and what ells Else you shall conseve° fitt for mee Clearlie to bee advertisede of, Consarninge° the Same

The 21 of Sep   EO

---

[102] Presumably, Colonel Herbert's wife, Lucy, née Alexander (d. 1671). See Ronald H. Fritze, "Herbert, Sir Thomas, first baronet (1606–1682)," *ODNB*.
[103] Walter Archer?
[104] In other words, proved that he did not rebel in 1641.

Letter 36. March 10, [1656?], [London], the Marchioness of Ormonde to John Burdon (NLI, Ormond Papers, 2484, no. 223, p. 131).[105] Autograph.
[For my] Servant John Burdon [/] thes.

[*six lines missing*] soe will most of the [rest] allsoe if you heare anye thinge from mr Gilliarde[106] and [will] reseve° an accompt° of this berar° whom I sent one° purpose with thes papers becaus I wouldnot have you Come out this ill wethar,° but staye at once and atende [your] owne health [*illegible*][107] ^and^ make your whole bussenes° untell° it shall please God to restore it to you, according as is the wisshes of

The 10 of March   E:ormonde

Letter 37. March 30, [1656?], [London], the Marchioness of Ormonde to John Burdon (NLI, Ormond Papers, 2484, no. 233, p. 209).[108] Autograph.
For John Burdon thes. [Endorsed]: Her Ladyshipps of the 30th of March Received 17 April.

John Burdon

your Letar of the 18 of March expectede upon Monday Last came not to my hands untell° the Thursday followinge, soe as I couldnot souner° then by this returne, informe you of the resept tharof and the countarpayne[109] of the Lease and Letar of Aturnye,° which I did that Eveninge carye unto Sir Orlando Bridgman,[110] whoe made some olltoratione° in the Layter° of thes; but is now writene over faire to bee offiered° unto Sir John Reynalds,[111] and the rest of the

---

[105] Severe damage to the MS has resulted in the loss of significant portions of text, particularly to the top and left corner of the page.

[106] Unidentified.

[107] Four deleted words are illegible under EO's heavy strikethroughs and the discoloring of the MS.

[108] There is large hole in the leaf that has resulted in the loss of up to eleven words per line in more than twelve lines of text, mainly in the first page. It is unclear how many words are lost from the postscript.

[109] "A duplicate, or exact copy" ("counterpane, *n*. 1," 2, *OED*).

[110] Sir Orlando Bridgeman, a renowned conveyancer, helped his royalist friends protect their estates from alienation or forfeiture. See Howard Nenner, "Bridgeman, Sir Orlando, first baronet (1609–1674)," *ODNB*.

[111] Sir John Reynolds (1625–1657), a parliamentary army officer, had been rewarded for military service with confiscated Irish lands, including in Carrick. He was a valued

Trusties° whoe I am indevoringe° to gett togethar that Bouth° may bee Signede by Them, though whethar it canbee dispacht befor the Post dous° goe, I am rathar doutfull then sartane° of, it fallinge out at soe bussie a time, with thous° persons whoe has relatione unto the Parlement and Court; as untell this great bussenes° now in hand bee broght unto a fynall conclustione as it is belevede it will within a very few days all things beinge as thay° say agreede upon; it willbee hard the mene° Time to gett anye Speache with them

    I am very sensibell of thous tow° disadvantages, that you forsee, is Liklie to [bee] a Prejudise unto mee, as Namelie such Lands as are possest by the Souldiors,° wherof tharis resone° to beleve thay willnot forgoe the possestione, untell thay have gaynede° reprysalls, the othar is that of such of the Lands as are wast° in the Countye of Carlogh and Tipperarye, it willbee hard to gett Tenants to take them for a yeare, unles thay may have 3 or 5 years Lease, which I am convinst out of that respect and to the raysinge° of some rent at the presant wouldbee nesesarye to give, yet it would allsoe bee ~~fitt to~~ bee consideredede; whethar the doeinge of that may not hindar the mene Time ^some^ Suffisent Persons whoe perhapes would take them in Lease ^(and give a valluabell consideratione)^ if thay might have presant possestione which oppertunityes are not at all times to bee Lightede upon, but of this you cane betar° Judge then I cane doe at [this distanse soe as] what you shall advise in this perticular I shall give my Consent unto; as [six words missing] to bee Cutt at Arcloe° and may bee spared without harme to the [six words missing] towards the payinge of the Stats° Rent provided that such a Course may bee takene [five words missing] of it, as I may bee advantaged, and not Coussenede° and that some honnest Man, may [three words missing] mene time, that may bee trustede to oversee that worke and to give an accompt°

    I had very Latlie° a Large discourse with A[112] and the othar gentellman ^Severalie^ [eight words missing] did desier° to take to whome I representede my Nesesitye [nine words missing] unto the State to Sett[113] it immediatlie with the rest [eleven words missing] with some Frinds of mine aboute it; whoe [eleven words missing] the most advantage I alledginge besides an [eleven words missing] thay did advise mee rathar to devide, and Lett [eleven words missing] anye

---

supporter of successive commanders in Ireland, including Henry Cromwell, to whom his wife's sister was married. See G. E. Aylmer, "Reynolds, Sir John (1625–1657), parliamentarian army officer," *ODNB*.

  [112] Unidentified.
  [113] "Letting, lease" ("set, n.1," 3a, *OED*).

one persone; by menes° wherof, it wouldbee Souner [*eleven words missing*] ^owne^ power To resarve what demenes I pleasede; and that [*ten words missing*] conveniensie and profitt from my selfe, which by Subdevidinge [*eight words missing*] the only way by which anye one person whoe would take it in Grose would [*four words missing*] advantages by it, wherof aftar some time spent [*two words missing*] of the bussenes bee [*three words missing*] that tharwas resone in that advise that had [*three words missing*] but withall desirede, that [*two words missing*] some frinds of his had intrusted hime to deale [*six words missing*] thay had resevede° some incoridgments° from hime to depend upon that [*six words missing*] where thay had the greatest desier to Settell, hee did desier Leave to propose unto mee [that hee m]ight be permitted to have the Towne and some 6 Thowsand Ackers° about it, unto which I answered; that I couldnot consent unto that Motione; for that wouldnot only hindar the Lettinge of the Rest, but overthrow my designe which was to draw Traydsmen thethar,° and to oblidge Evrye severall Tenant of them accordinge unto his houldinge° to build a Stone House, and soe within a Short Time to make a Towne thar;° then hee requestede to know of mee, what quantitye of Land wouldbee allowede to anye one Tenant or undartaker that would settell thar, I tould hime that at the presant I couldnot resoulve hime by resone the bussenes was not as yet nor couldnot soe sudaynlie° bee put into a Forme as aftar a Litell° time, I did Expect it wouldbee; soe as haveinge thus fullie discourst the bussenes with hime, I desirede to know at Last, what it accordinge unto this resolutione that I had takene; hee would have mee doe for thous frinds of his, that hee appirede Consarnede° for; which in brife° was this, that I would write unto you to Sett unto such Persons as should Come unto you in his Name, soe much of that Land for this yeare only as you should think fitt, and upon such termes as you and thay should agree; which I promist I would doe hee tellinge mee that hee did beleve that thous persons would hearaftar deale for such proportions as othars did; and would paye thar Rents honnestlie; ~~all~~ which ^Last^ I consevede° to bee a motione soe resonabell, as all things considered; I was much sattisfiede to bringe my selfe ofe° upon soe Easie termes; and tharfor I would have you to give them all the Content you cane, when thay doe aplye themselfs to you, soe farr as may bee noe prejudise unto my affares, and Let them know, that you had derections° from mee soe to doe upon A accompt but what Ever you reseve° from mee in the behalfe of the [whoe came]

demesnes

^recommended^ you are to understand it, but as a thinge of Forme, which to [acquant you of] may possiblie bee Sent you from

The 30 of March   E:ormonde

Corronell Aboots* has writene to mee to picke [missing] to be acknowledged by mee and My Sone for [missing] which I will take advise whethar I shall [missing] Letar advisede mee to it, I loukede° [missing] in the Counterpayne of the Lease, and I doe [missing] Killkeny [illegible] Namede tharin [missing] with the Bargine, and Soe are all my [missing]

Letter 38. April 2, [1656?], [London], the Marchioness of Ormonde to John Burdon (NLI, Ormond Papers, 2484, no. 237, p. 241).[114] Autograph.
For John Burdon. [Endorsed]: Her Ladyshipps of the 2nd April.

John Burdon

I am [six words missing] winkworth* the 28 of March, whous [missing] is in a way soe unusstiall° and upon [six words missing] Condesend as perhapes he dous° [five words missing] or Nothinge, soe as I doe [seven words missing] unto hime, as by command [eight words missing] Come himselfe and Build your [six words missing] to take it For hime, to [eight words missing] preferensie of it, may not Loose mee the oppertunitye [four words missing] this May [five words illegible] [three words missing] from Dublin yesterday [eight words missing] anye thinge that [eight words missing] howsomever I have sent them to you as I [four words missing] for Ballinehinshe, which mr Butler[115] did [five words missing] Limmericke acordinge to the instroctione y[ou] [four words missing] but that the mesenger whoe broght it did ac[quant] [four words missing] intended to bee heare within 2 days made [four words missing] to kiepe° it by mee to make uss° of when [four words missing] inclosede unto Corronell Flower,* and Show him [four words missing] which is all that my presant indisposistione [four words missing] to Say, beinge in much payne with the Jour[nye] [three words missing] in my Fase°

        The 2 of Aprel   EO

---

[114] The MS is very badly damaged with more than a third of the leaf missing from top to bottom on the right-hand side, which amounts to approximately four to eight words missing from the end of each line.

[115] Dispossessed Catholic.

Letter 39. July 9, 1656, London, the Marchioness of Ormonde to Henry Cromwell (BL, Lansdowne MSS, 823, fols. 322–323).[116]
Autograph.
For the Lord Henrye Cromwell. [Endorsed]: Countess of Ormond to my Lord.

My Lord

His Highnes and the Counsell haveinge grantede an Ordar upon my Petistione referinge ^it to^ and impowringe the Deputye and Counsell of Ireland to proside° tharupon as thay° shall see Cause, I should have bine° the presentar of it my selfe unto your Lordshipps, but that for the ^more^ spiede° have sent this Berar° to attend and know your Lordshipps and the Counsells pleasure what you, and Thay shall think fitt to doe upon what is now transmitede unto you; Not beinge in a redenes° as yet to Solisset it in persone, though I have the intentions of it, as beinge hopefull that your Lordshipps will find nothinge in my desiers° when you shall have considerede them, but what will appiere° soe resonabell as may inclyne you to countenanse and befrind mee hearin that with much thankfullnes doe acknowledge to have found; soe oblidginge to mee in my formar consarns° as I Cannot dout° you willbee Less to mee in This; when tharby you cannot hindar but on the contrarye but furthar and increase the Stats° [dutye] ^Revenue^ by permitinge mee to become Tenant unto my owne Estate duringe My Lords Life, I beinge willinge to give as much Rent or more ^for it^ then anye othar will; not out of anye Expectatione I have to bee a presant gayner° tharby, but to presarve it from a Totall wast° and Ruene,° which is otharwise ^a^ Like to happene when noe sartantye° of time canbee grantede, wherby to incorage° Tenants to Settell upon it and make improvments, soe as if I may by your Lordshipps menes° obtayne thisat favour, it shall with much gratitude bee ownede, to you by

My Lord

    your Lordshipps humbell Sarvant,

London the 9 of July   E Ormonde

My Lord I have one favour more to desier of your Lordshipps that my Sarvis° may bee Presented unto My Lady Cromwell[117]

---

[116] In this letter, EO utilizes blank space to signify deference and respect.
[117] Elizabeth Cromwell, née Russell (1637–1687).

Letter 40. August 5, 1656, [London], the Marchioness of Ormonde to John Burdon (NLI, Ormond Papers, 2321, no. 1166, p. 387).
Autograph.
[Endorsed]: Her Ladyships Dated 5th Received 12th August 1656.

John Burdon   The 5 of Agust

yours of the 23 of July gave mee Nottis° of your arrivall, which I perseve° by a Letar I resevede° from mr w[118] fortunede to bee at a very seasonabell Time, to prevent anye Error that might happene through the mistake of the Clearks of the Commitye for Setteing out of Lands for the Souldirye,° now that you are not only permittede, but desirede by hime, to bee as Constantlie thar° as your othar bussenes° will admitt, to informe them, of such as are speasifiede° in my Decree, when thay° falle upon anye of the Contryes where my Lands dous° Lie, soe as if anye Error bee, thay willbee apte to cast the blame upon you to ~~free~~ Excuse themselfs, which to avoyde;° I praye bee very wachfull and Carefull of this affare, sense° tharis few things relatinge to my fortune, that is of more Consarnment° to mee; I perseve you have delivrede the most of my Letars, but that the uttarmost that they could gayne° upon that one Persone that is by all soe much fearede;[119] was but his promise that hee wouldbee passive in the bussenes, which hee has profest hee would heartofore, but never kept his word, nor I beleve Never will, and for the way that hee advises I know nothinge of it, not haveinge heard anye thinge as yet from his Nephue, and when I doe supose what comes from the othar, willnot bee much to my Satisfactione, Soe as I wouldnot have you to Slakene your prosidings° Thar, out of anye Expectatione of good that the answar of his Letar wil bringe, unles for othar resons you shall think fitt to doe it, for a while, wherof you beinge upon the Plase Cane best judge to whous discretione I referr it, though Sir orlando Bridgman is of the oppinione, that the followinge of it willnot more indayngar the bringinge in questione the Decre ^then^   *endanger* the ~~the~~ Mentioninge of it at the Counsell which oftene happens in othar pepells° Cayses° will doe, which I perseve has ocationed°

---

[118] The initial first appeared in Letter 33 and remains unidentified.

[119] Oliver Cromwell? The phrase is reminiscent of lines written to EO some years earlier when the anonymous female letter-writer wrote: "I know no thing Can make me visit the Gennarall, unless it may be to sarve you, he being a person I yet never say [saw] but onse by chance, pasing by, nor ame I so mambistious [sic] to desire such high things, if I can avoyd them and yet for all this, if I can find I may serve you by a sight of him, I will be armed to doe it" ("JH" to EO, [November 1651], NLI, Ormond Papers, 2482, no. 329).

allredie some dispute that might have ^bine° a grownd° For^ ~~causede~~
it, had not my Lord Hary[120] discoridgede it, and for desiringe anye
confirmatione of it, when the Parliment Sitts Sir orlando dous think,
would make them Judge it of Less forse° then it is, and accordinge
the ussiall way of thar prosidings would bee referede to a Comitie,
which if ill Chosene, may prove as distroctive° to my Intrests, as
the greatest ills that I could Feare, besides that it is Supposede that
thay willbee soe imployede in the affares of the Publicke, as it is
thought thay willnot admitt of private bussenes, but of this; thar
willbee Time to Considar, when you see a Litell° farthar what the
Counsells intents are, and whethar thay bee inclinabell to proside°
upon the Ordar or Not, I had writene unto Major Morgine[121] by this
Post, had I not bine tould, as I was yestarday, of his beinge Come to
Towne, whom I shall indevour° to speake with befor his returne for
Irland, I would gladlie know what was the most that was offerede
for Arckloe,° for I perseve that it has bine Exposede to the veye,[122]
with what accompt° you are abbell° to give of my small affares in the
Contrye and how my buildinge at Dunmore* goes forward, wouldbee
an advertisment very acseptabell unto

EO

Sense the writinge of this the Gentellmans Nephue was with mee
and showede mee the Letar hee resevede from his unkell,° which was
to this Effect [/] that hee did mee all good offises in gettinge Settlede
what the Parliment did grant Mee but as to the rest, hee had in
Publick declarede his oppinione and from that hee couldnot resede,   *recede*
but sayede° thar was to bee a Parliment Shortlie, to which I might
have recourse, and if anye thinge were dune° by them, it was not then
his part to opose, nor would hee presume to advise in this, but Left
it to the Consideratione of othars, which was all that the Leter did
Mentione Consarninge° Mee; I praye deliver the inclosede as it is
derectede° and get an ansar° returnede

---

[120] Henry Cromwell.

[121] Sir Anthony Morgan, a trusted supporter of Fleetwood and Henry Cromwell, had been involved in the early stages of the land settlement in Ireland. See Patrick Little, "Morgan, Sir Anthony (1621–1668)," *ODNB*.

[122] "A formal inspection or survey of lands, tenements, or ground, for some special purpose" ("view, *n.*," I, 1a, *OED*).

Letter 41. August 2, [1656?], [London], the Marchioness of Ormonde to John Burdon (NLI, Ormond Papers, 2484, no. 215, p. 65).¹²³ Autograph.

For John Burdon.

[*four lines missings*] my Lady of Rannelagh* goes, whi[ch she]e beleves willbee one [*day missing*] com senight;° whoe will Let your tronke on goe bee Sent with hir owne Goods which ^and^ willbee the Securest way, for shee is to goe in a Shipe of warr; I have defered writinge as Longe as I could this day, in hope to have recevede some accompt° from you; but the wind beinge Contrarye, has it should sime° hinderede the Comminge of the Post, and by that Menes° gives mee at the presant nothing more to Say, untell° I heare from you agayne,° and then you shallnot fayle° of resevinge° a Spidie° answar from

The 2 of Agust   EO

Letter 42. August 19, [1656], Dublin, the Marchioness of Ormonde to Henry Cromwell (BL, Lansdowne MSS, 823, fols. 324–325). Autograph.

My Lord

At my beinge the othar day, at the Phenixe,* I had an intentione but wantede the oppertunitye of speakinge with your Lordshipps, which in consideratione of the small time you have to spare from publicke bussenes,° I did suppose might bee with Less troubell [*illegible*] to you, this verball addrese, then wouldbee my personall waytinge upon you, made mee of tow° Errors, to willinge to Chuse° what I consevede° might bee the Least; and by thes Lines, brifelie° make knowne unto your Lordshipps, what my desiers° are, that when anye fitt ocatione° shall bringe into Consideration how this Estate of Mine, the inheritanse wherof beinge ajudgede and Decrede for mee and my Childrene, shallbee disposede of, for the Time that the States Intrest dous° Continow° which Cane bee noe Longar, then dueringe° My Lords Life, that I may bee permittede at the presant, to become Tenant Tharof, for such Time, as the State shall think Fitt, or had power to Grant; which wouldbee more for thar° advantage, to bee Securede and assartanede° a Rent out of it; Then to Loose the whole profitt as now upon the Mattar Thay° doe; the Lands beinge allmost all wast,° unless some perticular plasess,° that are possest by offisiers,°

---

¹²³ Most of four lines of text are lost due to a large tear at the top of the leaf.

and Souldiers,° that payes noe Rent, but Evrye one that pleases without Ordar, Cutts downe, and distroys the woods, and upon the devistions° that are made, dous Cause to bee Survayede Lands that belongs to mee; and ads it, to thar owne proportions, soe as the disputs hearaftar is Like to prove Endless, and the distroctione° Ireparabell, that will falle upon this ruenede° Fortune [t]hat I, and my Chilldrene, are intrestede in, wherof when I acquantede My Lord Deputye,[124] as I did the othar day, I found hime very Sensibell; in relatione unto the States disadvantage [at t]he presant, as well as Mine in the Future; Soe as if my becominge Tenant unto it, might bee an Expedient to prevent Bouth;° as to anye soe rationall as your Lordshipps is; I suppose it will apiere° to bee; I shall then hope, and have the greatar asshuranse, that my desiers not beeinge repugnant, but advantagios to the publicke Intrest; your Lordshipps will in this perticular befrind, hir, that requests this favour of you, and is
My Lord
Your Lordships humbell Sarvant

Dubline the 19 of Agust   E:ormonde

Letter 43. September 23, 1656, [London], the Marchioness of Ormonde to John Burdon (NLI, Ormond Papers, 2321, no. 1170, p. 417).[125] Autograph.
For John Burdon. [Endorsed]: Her Ladyships 23 of September 1656.

John Burdon   The 23 of Sep

befor I was out of my feares for my Daughtar Betye[126] whoe has bine° dayngeroslie Sicke, but is now I thank God recovrede, a Nothar° troubell has happenede in my Familie, as undesarvede as it was un expectede, which was the imprisonment of my Eldest Sone, that was Carriede to the Tower one° this day ^Last^ was Sennight last where hee has bine ever Sense° and is still, but nothinge alledged aganst hime Nor I am most Sartane° cannot bee, soe as I dout° not to obtayne his release in a while, sensc his restrant is suposed to bee only upon distast of his Fathars presant actings,[127] to which hee nor   *distaste*

---

[124] Charles Fleetwood.
[125] There is a tear at the top middle of each leaf (affecting all three pages of the letter) which has been partially repaired with mending tape.
[126] Elizabeth, her eldest daughter, who was around fifteen or sixteen at this time.
[127] Ossory was accused, with little grounds, of being involved in a royalist conspiracy.

his relations heare,° beinge anye ways acsesarye I hope willnot make
his imprisonment of Longe Continowanse,° the Charge wherof
~~beyo~~ beinge beyond what my Nesesities cane Mentane,° which I
doutnot willbee considerede, soe as the mene° Time, Least° the
Rumor of this, might Make hime suspectede Gilltye by such as are   *guilty*
at a distanse and strangers to hime as hee is Not, but securede as
generalie all persons are of his years and qualitye, that have the Like
relations, and has not actede for the commonwealth [/] I thought it
Nesesarye to give you this informatione of the Cause, to the Ende
that you may Sattisfie such as are his Frinds, and disprove thous°
that are his Enimies if anye hee have, that [*two words missing*] [C]
ould report ~~the Contrarye~~ ^otharwise^ as it is not unliklie but some
[pur]poslie doe to hindar my bussenes° though I hope that noe such
inderect° arts shall prevayle to obstroct what is by ordar allredie
grantede, the Coppie of which I resevede° from you by the Last
weeks Post, and am very well Sattisfiede tharwith; but not ~~soe m~~
^at all^ Soe, with the accompt° of my affares in the Contrye nor of
mr whelers* dealinge, but when you Come upon the Plase, and shall
have resonede° it with hime, and furthar informede your Selfe how
I may have redrese aganst hime and othars I hope you will then put
things into such a way as I may have right dune° mee, I have sent you
such an othoritye° under my hand, for to Treate with the Commitie
as you desirede, which should have gone by the Last Post but that
your Letars comminge soe Late it Couldnot bee gottene redie Time
Ennough, I would gladlie know what is dune upon my Letars to
mr Plunket[128] and mr Bellingham[129] datede this day was fortnight
~~consarnge~~ consarninge° the procuring for mee a hundreth Pound
to bee payede unto the Tresuror at Dublin which if hee Couldbee
perswaded to forbeare tell° such Time as my Rents dous° Come in,
I would allow anye Consideratione for it rathar then troubell my
Frinds, but if noe offier° of this kind will Sattisfie hime I would then
have you to follow the instroctions of my formar Letar and by ^the^
menes° of the above namede persons to gett the Monys° payede

---

[128] Probably Walter Plunkett, EO's agent. Letters between Plunkett and Burdon from c. 1644 indicate that Plunkett was involved in finding EO a residence in Dublin (NLI, Ormond Papers, 2485, nos. 85, 213, 219, 229, 245). He remained in her service until at least November 24, 1657, when he wrote again to Burdon, this time anticipating EO's arrival in Dunmore (NLI, Ormond Papers, 2485, no. 249). He was appointed to the office of Prothonotary of the Common Pleas in 1660 at the recommendation of EO (see Letter 99).

[129] Possibly, Daniel Bellingham who is mentioned in Letter 115 in terms of the repayment of a debt.

unto hime and when you have soe dune, to See the Ordar strock
out of the Booke and Sir Hary wallers* bond to bee Canselede and
delivrede unto hime whoe was bound for the Mony,° and Let mee
know what depts° a[re to be paid ou]t of the Next Ensuinge Rents,
and what I may Expec[t] [*missing*] above, I have not time by resone°
of my Solisitations in my [Sons] behalfe to write unto My Mothar,[130]
tharfor I would have you to give hir an accompt of what I have now
writene consarninge ^My Sone^ ~~hime~~ and ~~to~~ Let hir know that you
doe it by Command from mee whoe in respect of my relatione may
Expect it from mee

**Letter 44. October 29, 1656, [London], the Marchioness of
Ormonde to John Burdon** (NLI, Ormond Papers, 2321, no. 1174,
p. 443). Autograph.
For John Bardon. [Endorsed]: Her Ladyships 29 October Received
15th November 1656.

John Burdon

Sense I had a sight of your Letar to Stivene Smith* of the 11 of
oct I made the Survayer Generall[131] acquanted with that part of
it that mentions the giveinge my Lands in upper ossory unto the
Souldiorye,° at which hee simede° much to wondar, and beleves, if
anye such thinge bee, that it has bine° ocationede° by some neglect
of thous° Rules hee gave bouth° unto you, and his Clerke, wherby
if obsarvede, that prejudise had bine preventede though I am apt
to beleve it Nether, but rathar a willfull mistake in some of the
Comistioners in the Contrye for settinge forth the allottments for the
Souldiorye, that has ~~not~~ done it, without makinge anye distinctione
of mine, from thous of my Lords Lands, out of a desier° to get what
thay° fansiede to bee convenient for them selfs, without consideringe
how [*illegible*] the Tytell° stands, and if Soe; I Conseve° thar° willbee
noe way to Rescew them out of thar hands, but by gettinge the   *rescue*
Survayer generall to put a Stope° to the passinge of anye such, as I
have by Letar this day intreatede hime to doe and for movinge to
have the referees[132] to bee Changed, and othars Chosene wherby the
bussenes° may goe on, I would by noe menes° have you doe it, for
severall resons that I could tell you, but shall forbeare all but one;

---

[130] Her mother-in-law, Elizabeth, Lady Thurles.
[131] Benjamin Worsley, Surveyor General of Ireland.
[132] "*Law.* A person to whom (either alone or with others) a dispute between parties is referred by mutual consent; an arbitrator" ("referee, *n.*," 1b, *OED*).

that it is aganst the judgment of the wissest and best Frinds that I
have heare, whoe advises that instede tharof, you doe as throwlie *thoroughly*
informe your selfe and prepare all things as redie as possiblie you
Cane aganst the Referees goeinge over, which I now beleve willbee
shortlie, I have bine movede by one you know, to treate Consarninge°
the Farme ~~that~~ where I have noe othar Land but it, within that
Countye, which I did in as faire a way as I could declyne, alledginge
it not convenient for mee soe to doe, untell° the agrement were first
made betwixt ~~mee~~ the State and Mee, howsomever this Party tould
mee that hee would send to thous frinds of his the mene° time, to
trye the uttarmost that thay would give for it, to which I made noe
replye, but fell upon othar discourse persevinge as I did, that hee
himselfe is intrestede, soe as I desier to bee perticularlie informede
by you of the Extent and Situatione of the plase, of the Buildings
that are tharupon, the qualitye and quantitye of the woods and the
priveleges and profitts that belongs unto it, what the Chife° Tenant
made of it, and what it may now yeald, and what the improvments
ought to bee, and to what vallew,° that all beinge represented and
put into writinge, I may show it unto some Frinds heare, that may
instroct mee what to demand and insist upon, whous oppinions I
will aftarwards transmitt unto you befor I conclude anye thinge
consarninge it, for I considar the well managinge of This, not only as
a Rule for mee to goe ~~for~~ by, as to the Settinge of the rest, but that
which is the Likeliest to yeald mee a Considerabell profitt of anye
that will falle ~~into m~~ in the dispose of

The 29 of oct   EO

**Letter 45. November 25, 1656, [London], the Marchioness of
Ormonde to John Burdon** (NLI, Ormond Papers, 2322, no. 1188,
p. 77). Autograph.
[Endorsed]: Her Ladyships 25th November Received 8th December
1656.

John Burdon

yours of the 12 and the 19 of Novembar Came this day togethar to
my hands, and in them a full answar unto some formar and Late
Letars that I sent you consarninge° my affares in the Contry and
of that bussenes° dependinge at Dublin which last, I perseve° you
have upon soe good Grownd° resoulvede to Sett on Foote agayne;°
upon the arivall of ^one^ ~~a Nother~~ of the Referees; as I am very
well sattisfiede that you should proside° tharin, as allsoe of your

Care and dilegense in the Manadgment tharof; and am very well
pleasede with the agreement that is made with mr wheler;* it beinge
all things Considered betar° then I Expected; I hope the Gentellman
you Mentione will declyne his importunitye of gettinge Letars
of recommendatione, for should anye such Come; I would by noe
Menes° ingadge° my selfe that way; for I have very good Grownds
to make mee resoulve the Contrarye; as allsoe not to Entar into a
Treatie much Less conclude with anye Tenant, untell° I have first
made my agreement with the State, for that wouldbee to informe
Them, unto my owne disadvantage; besides that the resarvinge to my
selfe a Power will still kiepe° an Expectatione in many, whoe upon
that accompt,° may prove Sarvisabell,° wheras if onse° disposed of
cane oblidge but ~~wone~~ one, though dueringe° this Suspense, I would
have you continow° to informe your selfe as Exzactlie° as you Cane
of all perticulars Consarninge it, for Mr A has made mee some
proposalls, but not such as is at all to be likede of, which howsomever
I touke to Considar of ~~and will send you by a Frind the Coppies
of within thes few days~~; but made it apiere° how inconvenient it
might bee for bouth;° to treate upon perticulars much Less conclude
whilst othars remayne intrestede and are still Possest, though by
what I have bine° informede, I perseve this Persone has kept ofe°
Many that ~~would~~ had a Mind to have takene it, and I doe very much
feare will ~~governe his Frindshipe~~ furthar or retard the bussenes, as
may Conduse most to his owne benifitt and advantage, but of this,
noe Notise° is to bee takene, but to Shift ofe from passinge anye
ingadgment,° wherof I have bine hethar° to warye, and shallbee
soe Still, I Like not Jonas whelers* offier° for kells, first that he
requiers° an abbaytment of tene pound for the first 10 years for his
improvments, when hee has made Non° towards the reperation of
the buildings then what hee made mee to paye for, and Next it is
inferiour to what himselfe did offier mee when I was at Donmore,*
where hee offerede to give a hundreth Pound for the first yeare
sixcore for the Second and a hundreth and thurtye for the Resedeue *six score*
of years, my demand beinge then a hundreth and fortye from hime,
Not intendinge to have Let it for Less then a hundreth and fiftye to
a Nothar,° which it was then vallewede° to bee worth, but that hee
soe ordered it, as hee kept ofe othars from biddinge for it, and is of
soe wranglinge a humor as I Confess I Like him not for a Tenant,
and his Brothar in Law that is his Partener[133] ^much^ worse; and
tharfor hee maye provide himselfe when hee pleasess Else where, the

---

[133] Jonas Wheeler's brother-in-law is unidentified.

Mene° Time I praye Let Edward Butler* know my Mind ~~or~~ tuching°
this perticular and doe you bouth joyne your indevours° in harkninge
out and providinge mee a Nothar Tenant, ^in his Rome°^ [134] Tharis
a very ~~Suffisent~~ honnest Gentellman on° mr Payne[135] that willbee
over in Aprell Next, and the mene Time has writene unto a Frind
of his Thar,° that is an offisier,° to See what Lands of mine are to
bee Sett,[136] that wouldbee Convenient for hime, ^to^ whom I gave
~~a~~ ^tow^ Letars one derected° unto you and a Nothar unto Edward
Butler, that hee should bee afforded a veue° of them, but have not
heard whethar anye such did Come unto your hands the Gentell
man haveinge bine with mee yestarday to inquire, whoe wouldbee a
very fitt Tenant for Callan if thous° whoe has it would part with thar
Intrest upon resonabell Termes, which I wish I could bee informede
of, yet Soe as it may not bee knowne unto ~~thous~~ the presant Tenants,
whoe it is that Louks° aftar it, as Consarninge the dispute that is
Like to oppene betwixt mee and Sir Gorge Askew[137] I Cane give noe
derections° tharin, but Leave it to bee composede in such a faire waye
~~as~~ as you propound, which I doutnot by your care willbee Efectede to
the Sattisfactione of

The 25 of No   EO

present My Sarvise° unto My Lady of Ranalagh* to whom I intend to
write and Send my Letar by a ~~Nothay~~ Nothar way

**Letter 46. December 2, [1656], London, the Marchioness of
Ormonde to John Burdon** (NLI, Ormond Papers, 2322, no. 1192,
p. 103). Autograph.
For John Bardon. [Endorsed]: 2nd December 1656 received 15th
From her Ladyship.

John Burdon   London the 2 of Des

I doe very well aprove of your resolutione grownded° upon thous°
resons that you have givene mee in your Letar of the 25 of Novembar
for the prosecutione of My busenes° at this Time; the Counsell it
should sime° beinge favorablie disposede, and at Leasure to Considar

---

[134] "A piece of rented land; a farm holding" ("room, *n.1* and *int.*," 6c, OED).

[135] Unidentified. This is the only letter in which this Mr. Payne is mentioned.

[136] "To let on lease, lease, let" ("set, *v.1*," 57a, OED).

[137] The naval officer Sir George Ayscue had recently received a pension of £800 from Parliament, £300 in Irish lands. See J. D. Davies, "Ayscue, Sir George (c. 1615–1672)," ODNB.

and give Ruels in it; I heare Nothinge of anye mony° returnede as yet *rules*
to Dublin for payinge the Lady[138] and mr Standishe* to whom it is
dew,° which makes mee feare that I shall suffier° in my Creditt for my
Tenants backwardnes to paye thar° Rents, thay° perhapes presuminge
upon Edward Butlers* unwillingnes to Prese them in that perticular,
though I hope you will Considar how much I am Consarnede,° and
make hime sensibell tharof, as allsoe that an indulgense to them
whoe pretends, but are not in soe reall wants; willbee noe Less then
Crueltye to mee and Mine; whous only subsistanse Now, is what wee
have to Expect from thense, I shallnot say more to you at this Time;
by resone° tharis ~~a frind of~~ an acquantanse of Mine to goe for Ireland
the Latar° Ende of this weeke by whom you shall heare agayne° more
at Large [from]

EO

**Letter 47. December 12, [1656?], [London], the Marchioness of
Ormonde to John Burdon** (NLI, Ormond Papers, 2484, no. 225,
p. 145).[139] Autograph.
For John Burdon [/] thes.

Steward

Just [*one line missing*] in your health with the payne of your Shoulder,
as makes you unabell° to goe the Journye you intended, into the
Countye of Tipperarye, and that you are putinge your Selfe at this
time under a remidie,° which I wish ~~my~~ ^may^ Suckside,° to your
good; though you chuse° a very ~~bade~~ ^Could°^ Time for it, which
I doe beleve your Phistione will disaprove whous advise it will *physician*
Consarne° you to have ~~otharwise~~ and the best I am tould is one
Doctor ~~Madinge~~ Madding[140] whoe Lives at watterford a Learnede
and Experinst Person, and best aprovede of by Doctor Fenell,* of
anye in thes Parts, hime you should doe well to have in Time, for
thous° of Less Skill, may possiblie give you Ease for the presant, but

---

[138] Lady Ranelagh.

[139] There is some wear and tear to the top and bottom of the leaf, which has resulted in the loss of most of the first line of text and perhaps another line of text at the end of the letter (at the bottom of the first page and top of the second page).

[140] Unidentified. A database of medical practitioners in England, Wales, and Ireland, c. 1500–1750, is being developed by the University of Exeter at http://practitioners.exeter.ac.uk/.

not Cure you quite; I unders[t]and mr Feake[141] is made resever° of the Stats° Rent, and that hee has an assignment upon mee, by which I am to pay 6 hundreth and ode° pound, towards the makinge upe wherof, I did hope the advanse of ~~thous~~ the years Rent of thous Lands that are to be Sett in the Countye of Tiperarye [*one line missing*][142]

The 12 of Des   E:Ormonde

I pray get the inclosede Sent

Letter 48. December, 1656, [London], the Marchioness of Ormonde to John Burdon (NLI, Ormond Papers, 2322, no. 1197, p. 141). Autograph.
For your Selfe. [Endorsed]: Her Ladyships Received 22nd December 1656.

John Burdon

I writ unto you the Last weke by mr Burneston[143] sense° which time I had some discourse with the Survayer generall,[144] from whom I desirede to know, what accompt° was returnede hime, consarninge° such of my Lands in upper ossory as I heare are sett forth unto the Souldiors° for thar° arrears, whoe informes mee that it happenede ~~upon~~ by the mistake of the Survayers in the Contrye, whoe returnede them as belonginge unto Mr Floranse Fitspatricke,[145] soe as it is Consevede° that the only way to have redrese, willbee to informe your Selfe perticularlie what the Lands are, and to whous Lott thay° are fallene and then to address your selfe from mee unto the severall Partys, to, give them Nottise° tharof, whoe if thay doe Petistione in Time the Counsell doutles° will give them a Consideratione Else where, but if thay willnot desier° it, but trust to what thay have thus takene, thay must stand to the hazarde of it, whoe beinge timelie warnede cannot pleade ignoranse of the Tytell° nor Expect anye favour from mee or Mine; The Act consarninge the Securinge of the Souldyors° and Adventerors°[146] is not as yet agreede upon, but willbee

---

[141] Mr. Feake was evidently involved in the government of Ireland but is otherwise unidentified.

[142] The words "[giv]ene Some healpe, if" are discernible.

[143] Mr. Burneston is mentioned again in Letter 100—where he is again the bearer of a letter—but he is otherwise unidentified.

[144] Benjamin Worsley, Surveyor General of Ireland.

[145] Presumably, a transplanted Catholic.

[146] The Act of Settlement, 1657.

I supposse very Shortlie; tell° when I shall defferr my goeinge into
the Contrye where Else I intended to have bine,° I have bine within
thes few days agayne° importunede by A[147] Consarninge the Farme,
which I tould the Person I couldnot make anye Bargine for, untell° I
knew upon what Termes I was to have it, nor untell I were informede
of the vallew° and perticulars of it, but that I would inquier° the
betar° to inabell° mee to treate with hime hearaftar consarninge it,
though by his offier° to mee which I sent you but a few days sense
I see noe great Likelihoude that we shall agree, howsomever I it
wouldbee to my Sattisfactione and advantage to know what Rent to
demand for it what Terme of years to give and what Condistions to
insist upon as to buildinge and improvement for thar are undartakers
heare that would give Securitye for the payment of the Rent and
makinge good the Condistions and I am confident would Sticke at
Nothinge that resonablie couldbee demanded for it, thar beinge some
of them that has sent unto mee a bout it, and that are indevoringe°
as I heare to informe them selfs of the quantitye of Ackars° which
if you could gett out of the Survayers Booke[148] may prove of great
advantage to mee, I have not resevede° the Last weeks Letars if anye
were intended mee, nor is anye by this Post as yet come to the hands
of

EO

sense the Endinge of this Letar I resevede one from the Lord Hary
Cromwell not in his owne but his Secretarys hand, which came
without Seale, but signede by his Lordshipe[149] a Copie of which I
have hearinclosede sent you, which soe soune° as you reseve° I would
have you to advise upon such an answar, as you conseve° may bee
fitt for mee to returne, without ingadginge° of my selfe which at
noe hand I shouldbee willinge to doe, to the Person recommended;
nor to anye othar, and send mee the draught tharof by the first
Conveniensie

---

[147] Unidentified. The initial is used again in Letters 50 and 59.
[148] "A legal document, *esp.* a charter or deed by which land is conveyed" ("book, *n.*,"
1d, *OED*).
[149] EO seems suspicious of the lack of seal, which were used (along with a signature)
to authenticate letters. As Daybell points out: "Letters not bearing the correct seal were
suspect, with no assurance that their contents had been read and sanctioned before sending." See Daybell, *The Material Letter*, 107.

Letter 49. December 24, 1656, [London], the Marchioness of Ormonde to John Burdon (NLI, Ormond Papers, 2322, no. 1198, p. 149). Autograph.
For your Selfe. [Endorsed]: Her Ladyships 24th received 29th December 1656.

John Burdoṅ

The wind has bine° soe Crosse for this Last weeke past, as I have misst hearinge from you soe as I have the Less to Say at this time, ~~but~~ yet Conseved° it nesesarye to acquant you, that yours of the 10 of Des is come unto My hands; as I hope is mine to you sent from hense this day fortnight, an answar wherof it somthinge Cons[arninge] mee to have within some resonabell Time the which I doe [asshure°] my selfe you will returne as soune° as is possibell

    I perseve° the bussenes° that you now attend is Like to prove more tedious then you did at the first beleve, and I am the more convinst tharof by the ^private^ practisies that I disserne in perticular Persons to contrue it soe; the betar° to worke thar° owne advantages which may possiblie foresloe,[150] but willnot I hope have power hindar it quite; I gess° the resons whye you have Left out thous° Lands in the queenes Countye,[151] and I aprove very well of your Soe doeinge, and the Like I should advise might bee allsoe of a Plase callede Tulloe Lease which was Soulde° by My Lord and mee some years Sense;° I find by as much as I cane gess ~~by So~~ ^[illegible]^ ~~delay of~~[152] the Commities intended way of prosidinge° ~~that it~~ is to ~~Sett~~ ^Lease^ the Lands for ~~4~~ ^7^ years accordinge the [us]iall Purchase of a Life, though I should have Likede it betar ~~without~~ to have Farmede it dueringe° the Stats° Intrest then to have had it Limetede unto a sartane° Time, though in such Caysess° the persons intrestede must not bee thar owne Chuseres,° and I doutnot but you doe very well considar all the advantages and disadvantage that may hapene in this agrement and will prevent ~~as~~ the Last of thes as much as [illegible][153]; you doe well to ommitt the Lands Morgedged it being agreeinge with my frinds advise heare as well as Thar, a[nd for] thous in the Possestione of the Souldiors° I think, if thay° were [ashured] would not bee grantede, unles thar were an intentione in the State to take some Course to Sattisfie them Else where, which thay apiere°

construe

limited

---

[150] "To make slow, delay, hinder, impede, obstruct; to slacken" ("for'slow / fore'slow, v.," 2, *OED*).
[151] Queen's County, now Co. Laois.
[152] A deleted word cannot be discerned against the browned MS.
[153] Two words are obscured by smudges in the letter.

not forward to doe, whethar it bee that thay are not movede in it as
my thinks° thay shouldbee by the Partys themselfs or ~~that~~ if thay
were that thay mene° not to give anye redress ~~which Last I am not
willinge to beleve~~ I know not; only this ~~that~~ I doe, that unles some
Justiss bee done as unto this perticular it willbee a wronge ~~unto all
Partys Consarnede~~ ^bouth° unto Mee and them^ which I hope
willbee considerede; I heare Nothinge as yet whethar My Lady
Ranalagh* and mr Standish* bee Payede what is owinge them, which
gives mee Just Cause of beinge dissattisfiede that my rents are soe
Slolie payede when soe Longe aftar thay are dew° nothinge Can bee   *slowly*
resevede° Ethar° to presarve my Creditt or give mee Subsistanse,
this forberanse beinge of worse consequense then ~~Pep~~ perhapes is
undarstoud by Edward Butler,* when done towards a pepell° that will
pleade Costome for it, and by ~~the~~ Exampell, will all of them take
a Libertye to ~~h~~ Paye but what and when thay please, which willnot
only prove a disapoyntment but Ruene° unto

EO

I praye gett the inclosede Letar sent as it is derectede° [/] The Bill for
Settlinge the Souldiors° and adventerors° is Not as yet broght into
the ~~Hose~~ Parliment House but when it is I hope I shall obtayne to
know the Contents, which stays mee still in Towne, My Sone is well
I thank God but still where hee was,[154] remembar mee to the Doctor

The 24 of Des

**Letter 50. January 6, [1656/7], [London], the Marchioness of
Ormonde to John Burdon** (NLI, Ormond Papers, 2484, no. 228, p.
169). Autograph.
For John Burdon. [Endorsed]: Her Lordshipps of the 6th January
received 12th.

John Burdon

your first and Second Letar datede the 17 of Des Came to my hands;
as did Likwise that of the 10 of the Same; which gave mee a full
informatione of the state of my affares, as allsoe of the returnes
that has bine° made of Arckloe° what it is sayede° to have bine Sett
for in the yeare 1640 beinge soe farr beyond what Carryes anye

---

[154] Ossory had fallen ill of an ague in October, and, according to Carte, EO had obtained a promise from Cromwell for his release, although he was not actually set at liberty until the following spring. See Carte, II [Book V], 162.

provabilitye° of Truth as I hope willbee undarstoud by thous° Persons with whom you have to deale, in hope wherof, I shall uss° all the indevours° I Cane to gett them perswaded to moderatione by some heare, whoe I beleve has Intrest in Them, which had bine Souner° attemptede by mee, but that the Frind I most relyede upon[155] has bine out of Towne for some weeks Past, but is Now returnede [/] I have not had Time sense° the ressept° of your Letar, to know Sir Orlando Bridgmans oppinion consarninge° the acknowleginge of a Fine; but this you may be Confident of, that noe such thinge shallbee Condesended to by mee if tharbee a possibilitye for mee to avoyde° the doeinge of it as I doe beleve tharis, I cannot but wondar that in all this Time Edward Butler* has not returnede the Mony° that is to bee payede unto Mr Standish* and the Lady,[156] which makes me hopeles of resevinge° anye thinge Seasonablie from thense for my releufe° when thous assignements that are to bee payede Thar° are soe Longe delayede, which if not remediede, will dishartene mr Bellingham* or anye othar Frind from doeinge mee a Curtisie,° should I bee prest° to desier° ~~the~~ it upon the like ocatione°

    I perseve by the accompt° that you have givene mee of the worke at Dunmore,* that the Carpentar raysinge° the ould Bourds in the Dieninge Rome° finds the Cross Beames, walle Plates and othar Timbar much decayede, though the Supporters or Pillars undarneath you Say bee indifferant goo[d] yet where thous decayes are, it is absolutlie fin in my oppinione to have it repayrede with New, which I conseve° cannot bee much Charge by resone° the woode is my owne, and tharfor I would have it to bee made firme and Substantiall otharwise what Charge is allredie bisstowede upon the House willbee but to Litell° Purpose, and tharfor have now writene unto Edward Butler Consarninge it and to Pay Corronell Flower* the 12 pound dew° to hime for his Plow of Oxene, but for the othar 14 Pound that hee demands it Consarnes° not mee; but is a ~~Recknowinge~~ Reekninge° betwixt hime and Bucke* whoe tells mee hee will write by this Post and Sattisfie hime as to that Perticular, Let the inclosede ^to Edward Butler^ which I have left unsealede that you may See it, goe accompaynede to hime with a Letar from your Selfe, and a List of what depts° is dew to Mr Carr* and othars wherin I would have the Intrest that is dew unto mistris Bullone[157] to bee included; and bee shure° you you Press the payment

dining

fine

---

[155] Unidentified.
[156] Lady Ranelagh.
[157] Mrs. Bullone is only named in this letter. Her identity remains obscure but she was evidently a creditor to EO.

of what is owinge unto the Lady, that shee may reseve° it soe soune°
as mr Bellingham is Sattisfiede, which to heare were accordinglie
performede, would much please

The 6 of Jan   EO

**Letter 51. January 13, [1656/7?], [London], the Marchioness of
Ormonde to John Burdon** (NLI, Ormond Papers, 2484, no. 221,
p. 115). Autograph.
For John Burdon. [Endorsed]: Her Lordshipps.

John Burdon

I forgott to tell you that I resevede° a Letar a good while sense,° from
sir Robert Sterlinge[158] and Sir Bryse Cougharane[159] unto which I
have not as yet returnede an answar, nor was willinge to doe, least°
anye advantage might bee takene by them to have ingadgede° mee
unto the grantinge of thar° desiers;° but now, that I have ansarede°
the Lord Hary Cromwells letar, I thought it nesesarye to send you
thars, Letars ^to mee^ to the Ende you may returne mee the draught
of such Cautious answars unto Bouth,° as you think willbee requisit
for mee to make or Else to write such a one from your Selfe by
derectione° from mee, as you think fitt and willbee best sort with
my ocations° at the presant, and Soe as A[160] may not thinke himselfe
dissoblidgede tharby, whom it wouldnot bee Sayfe° to make my
Ennimie ^at this Time^ noe more would it on the othar Side prove
convenient to presarve his Frindshipe to much to my owne Loose,
soe as if you Cane ordar the bussenes° that it may remayne still in
my owne power, is that, which wouldbee most for my advantage, I
resevede a Letar by Captane Southwells[161] Sone from a Lady that
you know has a great power with mee[162] whoe desiers in his Fathars
behalfe, what in Justise Cannot bee denyede hime, which is the
Continowanse° of his Intrest in that Farme; hee giveinge for it as
much or More then anye othar will doe; soe as by That, I am apt to
beleve that the knight whoe desiers it for himselfe has not obtaynede

---

[158] Colonel Robert Sterling had fought with JO and been knighted in 1649. See
Thomas Carlisle, *The Life of John Sterling* (London: Chapman and Hall, 1851), 9–10.

[159] Sir Bryce Cochrane (or Cockram), described as "New Scots" in David Stevenson,
Scottish Covenanters and Irish Confederates (Belfast: Ulster Historical Foundation, 1981,
repr. 2004), 280.

[160] Unidentified.

[161] Unidentified Cromwellian officer.

[162] Lady Ranelagh?

Captane Southwells Consent to have it, though it should sime° by your Letar that hee alledges hee has but of this thar willbee Time Ennough to discourse the bussenes betwixt them, and find out the truth when the greater is onse° dispacht

The 13 of Jan

Letter 52. January 27, 1656/7, [London], the Marchioness of Ormonde to John Burdon (NLI, Ormond Papers, 2322, no. 1210, p. 231). Autograph.
For John Burdon. [Endorsed]: Her Ladyships 27th January 1656.

John Burdon

Sir Bryse Cougharane has bine° with mee Consarninge° the takinge of Arcklow,° which in generall Termes hee Says hee will give as much for, as anye will doe, but I returnede hime an answar much unto the same Effect of my Letar sent unto the Lord Hary Cromwell and soe that bussenes° remayns in Suspense betwixt uss though I am tould that the Protector[163] will send unto mee in this Gentellmans behalfe, but I heare nothing from hime as yet;

  Thar° are Some heare whom if I were Ennough instroctede how to Treate and what to demand for that Plase would give Securitye to paye what Rent shouldbee agreede for ^Ethar°^ heare, or in Ireland, and advanse halfe a years Rent befor hand; which are Condistions not to bee Slightede,

  The Act of Atayndar[164] is has bine onse° Read in the House as it is to bee agayne° by opoyntment° tomorough, which is much

---

[163] Lord Protector Oliver Cromwell.

[164] The Bill of Attainder of the Rebels in Ireland was read before the House of Commons on January 21, 1656, and again a week later. See *Journal of the House of Commons* (London, 1813), VII, 481. The Bill had been prepared by the Committee for Irish Affairs, which was represented at the House of Commons by Lord Fleetwood and Major Morgan. The reading of the Bill had been postponed from the week earlier, when Fleetwood had stressed its "absolute necessity," for "without which no purchaser or adventurer could be secured, and this was a bill of great concernment to that nation." Morgan had added: "It is of great importance; no greater can be in the whole nation, than to unite your interests and people together. It costs you now 1700*l. per mensem* to protect your interest there. The Irish interest grows, the English is at a stand." See *Diary of Thomas Burton Esq*, I, July 1653–April 1657, ed. John Towill Rutt (London: H. Colbum, 1828), 337–38. "An Act for the assuring, confirming, and setling of Lands and Estates in Ireland," which was written into law on June 9, 1657, can be found in *Acts and Ordinances of the Interregnum, 1642–1660* (London: His Majesty's Stationery Office, 1911), II, 1100–1110.

Cryede out upon by very Many, yet not thought Ridged Ennough
by Some, soe differant are the humors of Peepell as I am very — *people*
unwillinge to appier in makinge anye request unto the Parliment
if my Intrest Can bee Sayfe° without it, as it is hopede it will by a
sartane° Clause that is in it, the which I am advisede rathar to rest
sattisfiede with, then proside° furthar at the presant; when My Name
Consideringe my relations, wouldbee more Like to Exasperate then
obtayne Justice from them; yet if I find that my Right willbee Lost
or indayngerede without some perticular Proviso bee Enterede ~~to Secure it~~ in the Act wherby to Secure it I am then resoulvede to put
it to a ventar, for soe in such a Cayse° I am advisede to doe, I find — *vendor*
the ~~Layd~~ Ladys Brothar¹⁶⁵ very Frindlie to Mee in all my Consarnes°
by whous Menes° I have asshuranse of ~~the~~ tow° very considerabill
persons, whoe willbee over Shortlie, that I am Confident will doe
all thay° Cane to furthar my bussenes Thar, ~~and~~ ^in^ obtayninge
mee a favorabell dispache tharof, for thay are faire and Just in thar
dealings, tharis noe Letars that I heare of from Ireland this weke,
but soe Soune° as I reseve° anye from you, thar shall with the first
Conveniensie, bee an answar returnede you fro

The 27 of Jan   EO

**Letter 53. February 10, [1657], [London], the Marchioness of
Ormonde to [John Burdon]** (NLI, Ormond Papers, 2484, no. 231,
p. 193).¹⁶⁶ Autograph.
For your Selfe. Her Ladyshipps.

[John Bur]don

In my Letar to you ^of^ this day sennight, I [*three words missing*]
of the Copie you sent me of the Referees Report unto [*missing*]
con[sarninge] my bussenes,° whoe I am of the oppinione dous°
indevour° [*two words missing*] at the [*missing*] on° of them thar°
prosidings° tharupon, out of the hopes [*two words missing*] that
this Act will have influanse to the distroyinge of My Chilldrens
Right which by the Savinge that is in it, a Coppie of which I have
hearinclosede sent you, I am tould by my Counsell Leaving out the
word such, which I am promist shallbee, when the Bill is committede

---

¹⁶⁵ Presumably, Lady Ranelagh's brother, Roger Boyle, Lord Broghill, later Earl of
Orrery (1621–1679).
¹⁶⁶ The top corners of each leaf are torn, which has resulted in the loss of a couple of
words at the beginning and end of four lines of text on each of three pages.

dous Secure Mine and my Chilldrens Right from Sufferinge by the Penalltys of it, Soe as I have bine° advisede not to Petistione at all for thous° resons that I have formarlie givene you, if without it I may bee Secure; but if otharwise then I must put it to the hazard, and Cast my selfe upon the Justise of the Parlement, but as to That, thar willbee Time Ennough befor the Act bee Read the thirde Time in the House,[167]

    Tharis allsoe tow° more redie to bee broght in allsoe; the one for Securinge the Souldiors° the Extract of which is Left with my Counsell to give thar Judgments of, whethar my Intrest bee indayngerede tharby or Not, whouse sense° tharupon I have not as yet had, Sir Orlando Bridgman beinge Sicke, soe as I cannot satisfie you at the presant, nor my selfe, as unto that perticular; though I observede in the readinge of it, a Saveinge of all Decrees givene by the Court for ajudicatione of Clames° in Ireland, which my thinks,° shouldbee Suffisent to presarve my Right, but what That of the Adventerors is, I Cannot as yet informe my selfe, but shall~~bee~~ doe, soe Soune° as it has bine onse° Read, which I feare is somthinge Strict more than ordenarye, because it is kept soe private, and has not past the same Commitie that the othar tow° has done; Soe as to wache ~~and presarve hope~~ ^in hope^ to prevent the the [sic] increasinge dayngers that thretens Ruene° to my Fortune by [missing] gives mee as Layborios a Taske as anye that [three words missing] I doe not dout° but to presarve my owne [three words missing] the indevours of my Advarsarys aganst mee [missing] doe [you goe] on; with the same asshuranse, and I dout not but [God] will send mee, by your indevours a good Suckses;° I perseve° tharis one of my Tenants, whous Carrage has not bine alltogethar what I could have wisht it, for his owne Sacke, as well as Mine, howsomever I doe not disaprove, but shall make good the abaytment you offerede hime of fortye pound a yeare of his formar Rent, provided I find that hee dous make good his word in forwardinge, and not obstoctinge the dispach of my bussenes, which beinge thus delayede, I hope the Counsell will Considar, and allow ^to mee^ some abaytment for the first yeare; Espetialie° if I bee to paye the Contributione and my Share of the Taxe besides, that is now to be Layede upon Ireland over and above what is allredie, which is Sayede° willbee Twentye Thowsand Pound to bee Raysede° within ^3^6 months; beinge

laborious

sake

---

[167] The Act of Settlement, 1657 was an "Act of the Cromwellian Parliament for the Assuring, Confirming and Settling of lands and estates in Ireland." The Act received its Third Reading on June 8, 1657, and received the assent of the Lord Protector the following day.

the Proportione that is Charged upon that Contrye towards the 4
hundreth Thowsand Pound that is to bee raysede within the three
Nations for the Caryinge on of the Spanish warr,[168] but not to bee
impossede° for anye Longer Time upon Ireland as dous not Nide;°
the Miserye and povertye of that Contrye considered [/] I had a
very uncomfortabell accompt° from Edward Butler* of my Tenants
refussinge, and delayinge to paye thar Rents, and such; as makes
mee forsee an impossibilitye for mee, for want of Menes° to goe over
or Subsist heare; My Misfortuns, and the Nesesitye of my affares
^constrayninge^ mee to bee from my Familie which ocations° a
greatar Charge, and My Sones imprissonment beinge an adistione°
to bouth,° is like to bring a Sudane° Ruene upon uss unles the good
providense God [missing] some way for our releufe;° you will find
[two words missing] unto Edward Butlers Letar, the Effect of his to
Mee; wh[ich when] you have reade, I would have you to Seale and
S[end] hime, [He]e writs mee word that Jonas wheler,* offiers° for
the [two words missing] sixcore pound a yeare for the first tene years,
and sixcore [missing] [af]tarwards; and advisses mee to let hime have
it Soe; which hee Says is as much as it is worth, or that anye will
give, but I have returnede hime noe positive answar, untell° I know
whethar My Sister Butler[169] will like it or Not, tharfor I pray Let mee
know hir resolutione hear[ein] as soune as you Cane, and with it your
owne oppinione Consarn[in]g° the disposinge of it, in cayse° shee doe
declyne the takinge of it from

The 10 of Feb   EO

**Letter 54. April 6, 1657, [London], the Marchioness of Ormonde
to John Burdon** (NLI, Ormond Papers, 2322, no. 1222, p. 295).
Autograph.
For John Burdon thes. [Endorsed]: Her Ladyships 6th April 1657.

John Burdon

---

[168] Anglo-Spanish War (1654–1660).

[169] Lady Frances Butler, née Touchet, the English Catholic wife of JO's younger brother, Richard Butler of Kilcash. Her husband's estates were confiscated after his exile, and she was transplanted to Connacht. For a detailed account of her experiences, see John Cunningham, *Conquest and Land in Ireland: The Transplantation to Connacht, 1649–1680* (Woodbridge: Boydell and Brewer, 2011), 105–6. Letters from Lady Frances to EO and Burdon in 1655 can be found in NLI, Ormond Papers, 2481, nos. 283, 389, and 293.

the Last Letar that I resevede° from you, came accompaynede with
the Counterpayne of the Lease made by the State unto Sir John
Reynalds* Captane Halsye* and Corronell Bridges[170] in trust for
mee; which togethar with the Letar of Aturnye,° wherin ^I have
Causede^ your Selfe and Humes* was ^to bee^ Naymede, is Signede
by the tow° formar, but for Corronell Bridges hee was unwillinge,
and did refuse, alledginge some resons for his soe doeinge, not worth
the repeatinge; soe as I was advisede to prese hime noe furthar, My
Counsell heare, beinge of oppinione that if anye one of the five did
Signe; it wouldbee Suffisent, made mee returne it, as it is, unto mr
Carr,* to gett it, if hee Cane; furthar perfected by the othar tow that
are Thar,° and then to have it Enterede in the offise, according as
you Left derections° with hime that it shouldbee,

The Act of Atayndar has bine° twise read in the Parlement
and Committed, which in Generall words did Carrye such a
Latitude as was consevede° might involve my Estate within the
forfiture,° Soe as I was advisede to indevour° the gettinge of a
Perticular Proviso to bee Enterede in the Act to Secure Mine and my
Chilldrens Intrest aganst the Penallties of it, which is accordinglie
insertede by Consent of the Commitie, a Coppie wherof I have sent
unto mr Carr, with derections that it shouldbee first Showne unto
Sir Maw^ris^ Eustas[171] and aftarwards bee Sent you; I resevede
a Letar Latlie° from Corronell Aboots,* wherin hee desiers° that
bouth° My Sone and my Selfe would acknowlege a Fine[172] for the
betar° Confirmatione of his Lease, the which I have not denyede the
doeinge of, but have takene time to Considar of, untell° I see the
Counterpart of it, which I have desirede mr Carr might bee fortwith
Sent mee; it haveinge bine Left in the Litell° blacke ^Trunk^ that
ussede to stand in Nan Jones[173] Chamber ^at mr Plunkits hous^
which if hee doe speake with Sir Mawris Eustas aboute, I doe beleve
that hee Cane healpe hime to; I doe obsarve in the Lease that it is

---

[170] Colonel John Bridges was in service in Ireland in 1655 and represented Sligo and Roscommon in the Second Protectorate Parliament in 1656.

[171] Sir Maurice Eustace had been a close associate of JO during the Confederate wars. He had been imprisoned by parliamentarian authorities, but thanks to the favor of Henry Cromwell he was able to resume his legal practice in Dublin in 1655. He would be appointed Lord Chancellor of Ireland in October 1660. See R. M. Armstrong, "Eustace, Sir Maurice (1590x95–1665)," ODNB.

[172] "a fee (as distinguished from the rent) paid by a tenant or vassal to a landlord on some alteration of the tenancy, e.g. the transfer or alienation of the tenant right" ("fine, n.1," II, 7a, OED).

[173] Unidentified.

dated from the 25 of March and the Rent to bee payede by Ecquall
Portions on the 29 of ~~Sep~~ Sept followinge though I am to Entar but
at May, which willnot only prove an inconveniensie, but ~~a~~ ^some^
Loss; which I doe hope the State will ^hearaftar^ Considar; Mr
Moore of Banke Halle,[174] has writene a Letar unto my Lord of
Meath* to speake to mee in his behalfe Consarninge° the Farme of
Collaghmore, which I wish you would send mee word what Rent
and Fine to demand for it, for a Lease of one and twentye or one
and thirtye years hee beinge very well abbell to paye for it, I have
not ommittde by Evrye Post writinge to you for this 6 or 8 wekes
Last Past, soe as such ^Letars^ as you have faylede° of resevinge° ~~I doe Conc~~ you may Conclude are Lost by the way or Else fallene into
othar hands; the Contrarye of which if I couldbee Sattisfiede of from
you, would much Please

The 6 of Aprell   E:ormonde

Letter 55. [April, 1657], [London], the Marchioness of Ormonde
to John Burdon (NLI, Ormond Papers, 2484, no. 242, p. 273).[175]
Autograph.
For My Sarvant John Burdon thes.[176]

Immediatlie after you went from [hense] I resevede° The inclosede
from Captane Hallsie* whoe des[iers] an answar by the returne of
the berar;° whome hee has Sent, the which I would after you have
advisede with Corronell Flower* and Ned Butler* to ~~returne~~ send
hime such an answar of, as you and Thay° shall think fitt, ^and
doe it^ by command from mee, whoe am not well this day, which
may Excuse my not writinge unto hime my Selfe, as for the tow°
parsells° besides thous° holldene[177] by hime at presant hee desiers° the
tenansye of tow more, namlie Ballitarsny and the 3 Ackers° in   *Ballytasney*
Rathkeran, which if I bee not mistakene some othar of the English   (Co. Kilkenny)
                                                                                Rathkieran
in thous parts did desier Soe as if it may bee thought inconvenient   (Co. Kilkenny)
for one persone to hould° soe many ~~plasses~~, this gentellman may
bee ~~tould~~ informede by you, as unto thes last, that I am not free to
dispose of them beinge preingadgede   *pre-engaged*

---

[174] Unidentified.
[175] There is minor wear and tear to the top of the leaf.
[176] Sealed using the Preston unicorn emblem. See Figure 8.
[177] The past participle of "hold" ("hold, *v.*," OED).

Letter 56. April 15, 1657, [London], the Marchioness of Ormonde to John Burdon (NLI, Ormond Papers, 2322, no. 1227, p. 329).[178] Autograph.
For John Burdon. [Endorsed]: Her Ladyships of the 15th Received 26th Aprill 1657.

John Burdon

I was Carfull to dispach away so soune° as it was Signede, the Counterpart of the Lease, and Letar of Aturnye;° which was sent the Last weeke unto Mr Carr,* accordinge unto your derections;° sense° which Time, nor the weke befor, I have ~~have~~ not heard from you; which makes mee Conclude you are now in the Contrye; Tharis of Late some Liklihoud of a [M]ache° for your yonge Master[179] ^That^ ~~whoe~~ is in all respects fitt for hime [Bou]th for ~~hir~~ ^the Gentellwomans^ Extractione persone, and presant fortune beside [hir] Estate that [is] very antiant° and Considerabell, that will desend to hir aftar hir Parents Death, whoe dous° appiere° to have great [inclynation] to make an allianse with uss; haveinge besides an [Estime] for the Persone of my Sone; but are [*illegible*][180] [how] thay° doe proside° <u>Not knowinge what my Estate is at presant or what it willbee worth hearaftar, what depts° it dous stand [Char]ged with, or what allowanse might bee givene out of it at [presant] towards the yonge coupells Mantenanse</u> all which it you [co]uld ~~yo~~ informe and give mee some accompt° of as possiblie you may betar° doe now then formarlie; and send mee brifelie° [st]atede the Condistions that my Estate is in, what it now yealde [*three words missing*] [w]hat [*missing*] undertake it worth aftar 3 or 7 years would [*four words missing*] to have [in Cayse°] of othar [*three words missing*] like [future]; whe[tha]r This doe [*one line missing*] Effect or Not, which if it doe, will with more Ease, and Less inconveniensie healpe on the othar, wherof I formarlie acquanted you; tharfor I pray take some paynes to Sattisfie mee in thes Perticulars, without Letinge anye persone undarstand

---

[178] There is significant wear to the MS, especially around the bottom edges of the leaf, which affects the first page of the letter.

[179] Her eldest son, Ossory. The match to which EO alludes is probably the daughter of Thomas Wriothesley, fourth Earl of Southampton, most likely Elizabeth (1646–1690), only surviving daughter of Southampton's second marriage. For details of Southampton's daughters, see Lois G. Schwoerer, "Russell, Rachel, Lady Russell (*bap.* 1637, *d.* 1723)," *ODNB*.

[180] Wear and damage to the manuscript means that two words are not clearly discernible, but it may contain the word "Tender."

the Reasone of it, unles the ould Doctor,[181] to whom if you find it
Nesesarye, I doe give you Leave to Communicate but unto Noe
othar, the Contents of this Letar that comes from

EO

**Letter 57. April 22, [1657], Kensington, the Marchioness of
Ormonde to John Burdon** (NLI, Ormond Papers, 2484, no. 232,
p. 201). Autograph.
For John Burdon. [Endorsed]: Her Ladyshipp of the 22th of Aprill.

John Burdon

It has pleased God to make my Sones fallinge very violentlie ill of
a Fever about a weeke sense° that ^which^ is now turnede into a
Tertione Ague, to have bine° the Cause of obtayninge hime ^his^
Libertye for the Recovrye of his health, but upon Bond, to returne
when somonede° tharunto by the Liftenant of the Tower, Soe as
I was advisede to remove hime immediatlie from thense, as I did,
and broght hime hethar° to kinsington, unto My Aunt the Lady
of Mongravs[182] House, from whense if hee bee not to weake to
Travell, hee is desirious and soe am I; that hee should goe downe
to Acton,* for much Companye, is not only prejudistiall unto his
health, which is hard to bee kept from hime soe neare the Towne,
but may perhapes ocatione° a Spidier° Recall then wouldbee unto his
or his frinds Sattisfactione, hee is at this Time in his Fitt; which is
bouth° violent and Lastinge, yet to one of his youth and Strength
I hope it is not dayngerous, I was in some troubell to find by your
Letar dattede from Acton Arckloe° the 30 of March, and a Seconde
of the 4 of Aprell that you had not then heard of a good while from
mee untell° a thirde of f the 11 of this month came by the Last Post,
that Sattisfiede mee that tow° of Mine had bine Sense° resevede;°
and soe I hope are more that were intended you by this time; in
one wherof, I did answar that perticular consarninge° the wast°
Lands, as allsoe informede you how I had takene ofe,° bouth thous°

---

[181] Gerald Fennell?

[182] Presumably, the house of Mariana Sheffield, née Irwin, second wife and widow of Edmund Sheffield, first Earl of Mulgrave (d. 1646). The Earl of Mulgrave was EO's great uncle. His sister, Elizabeth Sheffield (d. 1601) was EO's maternal grandmother, the second wife of the tenth Earl of Ormonde. There is a letter from Mulgrave to his (great) niece c. 1628 arranging to meet her in the gardens of Whitehall to discuss the agreement for her marriage to JO (NLI, Ormond Papers, 2483, no. 469).

tow Gentellmen from Expectinge that Farme, that you have Sent
mee Latlie° the perticulars of; by alledginge that I wouldnot Let
it in Bulke unto anye one, but in p severall proportions, and trulye
I doe remayne still of that oppinione, that it willbee the only best
Course soe to doe for the improvment of the Plase, and raysinge°
of the Rent, which whenever it is assartanede,° willbee fittar to bee
ingadgede° ^for raysinge of Mony°^ if thar° bee ocatione for ^for it^
then anye othar; soe as the greatest skill in the well manadginge of
and Settinge of it, willbee in the Choise of such Tenants as willbee
[Propor] orderinge the Subdevistions and makinge Choise of Abbell   *subdivisions*
and fitt Tenants for Eache Proportione soe as ^and tharfor^ the
more ^Pepell°^ that you doe incoridge° to Bid for a Share ^tharof^
the betar° you will come to undarstand the uttarmost that may bee
made of it; the Situatione beinge by your relatione very advantagious
good; as are othar Convenienses that are thar allsoe, tharis Letell in
the ^your^ 3 Last Letars, but what I have allredie tould ^you^ my
Sense of as you will find if my tow Last dous° as I hope thay° will
Come to your hands; Exseptinge that busseness° of Durow which if   *Durrow*
it may bee Carryede on in [tha]t way which you propose I shall like   *(Co. Laois)*
very well, ofe provided you doe not tharby ^revive^ a Nothar° Intrest
that may prove more unto my disadvantage then that which is now
pretended by Corronell Axtell;[183] for by mr walls[184] Lease the rent
resarvede was as I take it but fortye 90 Pound a yeare, soe as if that
should hould° good, it would barr anye presant inhandsment of it,   *enhancement*
unles mr Bucklye[185] and the othar would resigne thar Intrest and
give way to the othar gentellman to uss° thar Names in it ^only^ and
then, I Confess I shouldbee betar Sattisfiede that hee whoe has it at
the Presant shouldbee outede[186] upon that Score then anye othar; as
for My Tenant the knight,[187] I Cannot at this distanse precribe° you
anye Rule how to accord with hime, but doe Leave it to your owne
discretion by resone° I doe not know what it is that hee Expects or
^that^ would Content him; unles it bee to paye Nothinge, and that
is an Easier bargine then I feare canbee afforded hime at the Presant,
I am Sorye Captane Southwell* knowinge that you had instroctions

---

[183] Colonel Daniel Axtell had opposed Henry Cromwell's policies of accommodation and resigned in November 1656; he would return to Ireland in 1658. See Alan Thomson, "Axtell, Daniel (bap. 1622, d. 1660), parliamentarian army officer and regicide," *ODNB*.
[184] Unidentified.
[185] Unidentified.
[186] "Driven out, ejected; extracted" ("outed, *adj.*," 1, *OED*).
[187] Unidentified.

to Lett but for a yeare wouldnot take it that Farme which hee had
formarlie rathar then Suffier° himselfe to bee disposest soe as if hee
doe Suffier an inconveniensie tharby hee Maye thanke himselfe, this
inclosede Came from mr Patricke Briane,[188] whous Brothar if hee
bee as willinge as hee is abbill may give well for the Farme that hee
desiers,° soe as I thought it not amiss to Send his Letar to you, that if
you thinke anye informatione nessesarye to bee givene mee of it, you
may Send it unto

kinsington the 22 of Aprell   E:ormonde

**Letter 58. May 11, [1657], Acton, the Marchioness of Ormonde
to John Burdon** (NLI, Ormond Papers, 2322, no. 1230, p. 347).
Autograph.
For John Burdone. [Endorsed]: Her Ladyships Dated 11th May
Received 4th June 1657.

John Burdon

as I was upon my way hethar° to Acton* a Letar from Corronell
Flower* overtoucke° mee, that Mentionede his haveinge had Latlie°
some discourse with Mathew Harisone* whoe tould hime, that hee
had resevede° Latlie from a Brothar of his fore hundreth Pound that
the Lord Chichestar[189] had a desier° to take into his hands and to
give hime Intrest for, at the Rayte° of tene in the hundreth, but that
if I had ocatione,° hee would Let mee have it upon thous° Termes
Souner° then anye othar, wherfor I praye send to hime tuchinge° this
particular whom I would willinglie give all such Securitye unto of
Land as I am Capabell of, and as othar Persons dous° acsept, if that
will Sattisfie hime, That Mony° beinge what if it might bee had, that
I would oppoynt° for payinge of Doctor ^yarner^[190] and rediminge°
of the Morgadge° hee has of Callan accordinge the Covenants
which oblidges mee soe to doe at all hollantyd[191] Next, wherin if I
should Fayle,° hee might perhapes make as much discourse unto my

---

[188] Unidentified.

[189] Arthur Chichester, Earl of Donegal, or perhaps his son. Chichester had been granted the earldom in March 1647, but this title would not have been recognized by the Cromwellian government. See J. M. Rigg, "Chichester, Arthur, first earl of Donegal (1606–1675)," rev. R. M. Armstrong, *ODNB*.

[190] Abraham Yarner, a physician who arrived to Ireland in the 1650s. He was later president of the College of Physicians in Dublin. See Lyons, "Role of Graduate Physicians."

[191] All Saints Day, November 1.

prejudise, as hee did onse° befor, without Cause, consarninge° the hundreth Pound that hee was with Sir Franses willobye[192] Bound for, at my request, beinge an inconveniensie that I doe desier to avoyde° if it bee possibell for I like not anye [illegible] of Pepell[193] I hope you have by this Time put Corronell Flower* into that way, wherof you acquanted mee, whoe I find has a great desier to bee my Tenant at Durogh; as I have that hee shouldbee Soe, hee not Expectinge as hee Says to have it but Soe, as to give what it is worth, and tharfor what you cane doe to gayne° hime his desier in That willnot only bee Sattisfactorye unto hime, but a Sarvise° unto mee allsoe, My Sone has his Ague[194] still and his Fitts bouth° violent and Lastinge, I wishe the ould Doctor[195] were with hime, of whous Skill and Care theris a great oppinione heald by

Acton* the 11 of May   E:ormonde

Letter 59. June 20, 1657, [Acton], the Marchioness of Ormonde to John Burdon (NLI, Ormond Papers, 2322, no. 1234, p. 371). Autograph.
[Endorsed]: Her Ladyships of the 20th June Received 1st July 1657.

John Burdon

I have resevede° your Letar of the 30 of May, togethar with Edward Butlers* accompt,° wherby I perseve° that My Tenants are in Areare from the Last Allhollantyde,° unto This Last May, and Soe willbee Still I am Confident; unles some such Course bee takene of distrayninge[196] as you now have resoulvede upon, the which if Edward Butler would have begane Souner,° mi it might have Savede mee the Loss of 6 hundreth Pounde Areare that I doe beleve I am not now Like to gett, though Less abbell to want bee

---

[192] Sir Francis Willoughby had been governor of Dublin Castle and major general of the king's army in Ireland.

[193] Four or five cancelled words are illegible through EO's heavy strikethroughs.

[194] "An acute or high fever; disease, or a disease, characterized by such fever, esp. when recurring periodically" ("ague, *n*.," 1, *OED*).

[195] Gerald Fennell?

[196] "To constrain or force (a person) by the seizure and detention of a chattel or thing, to perform some obligation (as to pay money owed by him, to make satisfaction for some wrong done by him or by his beasts, or to perform some other act, e.g. to appear in court); to punish by such seizure and detention for the non-performance of such obligation" ("distrain, *v*.," II, 7a, *OED*).

without; considringe the great Charge I have to Mentayne,° then
anye that ~~refusses~~ ^kieps from^ mee my dew,° upon pretense of
thar° owne povertye; and tharfor I pray Let not Sir Patricke wemes*
bee forborne[197] ~~with~~, but proside° with hime, as with the rest, for it
is not the first Time that hee has made promises to paye his Rent
if hee might bee allowede some Longer time, ~~but~~ and when that
was grantede hime, hee was as farr from makinge Sattisfactione
as befor; Tharis a Gentellman on° Mr Gookin;[198] to whom I ~~am~~
have bine° very much behouldige for his Frindshipe to mee, in all
my Late Consarnes° heare whoe has recommended a kinsman of
his that is of his owne Name, and a very Suffisent Man as hee tells
mee, to bee my Tenant, to thes 3 small Farmes, the Names wherof
I send you hearinclosede, that if thay° bee Not allredie Sett for this
yeare, or part of thous° Lands that ^are promist unto^ My Lord
Hary Cromwell, ~~[has a desier to take]~~ to take that then ~~you will~~ this
gentellman may have the Profer[199] of them, hee giveinge as much
as a Nothar° will, of which particular, I praye send mee an accompt
by the Next, that I may the betar° Sattisfie Mr Gookin whoe has
writene unto mee Latlie° Consarninge° this bussenes;° as My Lord
of the Ards,* ~~is~~ ^has^ done, Recommendige mr Cawfild* to bee
my Tenant for the whole or some Part of Arckloe,° and soe has My
Lord Moore[200] in the Same persons behalfe, unto My Sone; whous
answar, togethar with Mine, are now Sent you to See; ~~be~~ that if
you doe aprove tharof, thay may bee delivrede or Suspendede ~~as you~~
which of the tow° you doe think best, Sir Bryse Cougharane ~~is~~ has
a Companye, and is gone into Franse Soe as I thinke hee will louke°
noe more aftar a Farme and whethar anye of A[201] his Frinds has
bine yet with you I wouldbee very glad to know; I undarstand that

---

[197] "To bear with, have patience with, put up with, tolerate" ("forbear, *v.*," 2, *OED*).

[198] Probably Vincent Gookin, a close ally of the Boyle family, especially the Earl of Cork and Lord Broghill. He was author of *The Great Case of Transplantation in Ireland Discussed* (London: I. C., 1655), in which he argued that Ireland would be a more stable and prosperous place if Irish Protestants had a say in its government. In 1658 Gookin was appointed surveyor-general of Ireland and worked alongside William Petty in setting out forfeited land for plantation; before that, he was part of the commission for settling the army's land claims. See Patrick Little, "Gookin, Vincent (c. 1616–1659)," *ODNB*.

[199] "An act of offering or presenting something for acceptance, or of making a proposal; an offer, a proposition" ("proffer, *n.*," 1, *OED*).

[200] Henry Moore, third Viscount Drogheda (d. 1675), had succeeded his father, who died in battle in August 1643. See David Murphy, "Moore, Sir Charles, 2nd Viscount Moore of Drogheda," *DIB*.

[201] Unidentified.

Captane Moore²⁰² is in great Rage that his Farme is Set this yeare unto a Nothar though it was by his owne Negligense, whoe had ~~Notis ^timl^~~ Timelie Notise° givene hime from mee if hee would have Loukede° aftar it, to have oppoyntede° Some one Thar, to have agreede for it, whoe I heare dous° Expect allowanse from mee, for: his Buildings and improvments, which I conseve° it is not Sayfe° for mee to promise, not knowinge how farr, such a president° may bee of inconveniensie to Mee, in the Like Cayses;° ~~though~~ ^yet^ on the Contrarye I shallnot refuse to doe in this, what Ever my Frinds Thar shall advise mee ^To^ though the Rent beinge to goe unto the State, whoe has much ogmentede° it upon mee; my thinks° it is Thay, and *augmented* not I; that ought to make hime Sattisfactione, upon whous othoritye° and noe invitatione or incoridgment° of Mine, hee did Settell Thar; I hope you are by this Time, abbell to Let mee know, what Supplye of Monye° may bee returnede mee, and when, I may Expect it, as allsoe some accompt of what Mathew Harisone* did offier° to ~~put [out] [illegible]~~²⁰³ ^Lend Mee^ of which, as allsoe upon what Termes, I did by tow° Severall Letars acquant you, but have not sense° heard anye thinge From you Consarninge that perticular, though it is wisht and Expectede from you To

The 20 of June   E:ormonde

Letter 60. June 29 [1657], Acton, the Marchioness of Ormonde to John Burdon (NLI, Ormond Papers, 2484, no. 229, p. 177).²⁰⁴ Autograph.
[Endorsed]: Her Ladyshipps of 29th June Received July.

John Burdon

yours of the 5 and 17 of this month came togethar this Last Post unto my hands, which gives mee an accompt° of your havinge resevede° Mine that mentionede the offier° made mee by Mathew Harisone,* which now, that you are come to Dublin, will I hope bee broght unto a good and spidie° conclustione; which at this time wouldbee very Nesesarye for my ocations,° in Many Respects

---

²⁰² A Cromwellian soldier with a competing claim to land on EO's estate. The issue appears to have been resolved by Letter 65 when he is named again.

²⁰³ Three canceled words are illegible under EO's heavy strikethrough.

²⁰⁴ There are identical tears (caused by the seal) at the bottom of both leaves, which has resulted in the loss of up to four or five words per line in six lines in each of three pages.

I perseve° you have had a Taske noe Less difficult, then I did beleve ^it^ wouldbee; to kiepe° Faire with a companye of such unresonabell Pepell° as you have had to deale with; though when Reprisalls²⁰⁵ are grantede, which you Say willbee of Course, I shall not then much considar the displeasinge of some of them, whoe tell° then; it willbee perhapes more convenient to humor then it wouldbee Sayfe° to disoblidge ~~sense the Lands~~ which may the betar° bee done sense° the Lands, beinge sett but for one yeare, will kiepe them still in expectatione and make them Less apt, to doe mee ill offisies,° then otharwise thay° wouldbee, tharfor you are to make the best uss° you cane at the presante of such; as may prove ussfull, and give them good words, but as few promises as you Cane; for I see thay are for thar° owne Ends, and noe otharwise, are to bee considered;

I find by the accompt that you have givene mee, that all that will falle dew° of the Last Estars Rent, the Payments deducted, will amount but to 223 besides the 338 [pounds] 13 [shillings] arears for the yeare endinge the Last of octobar Last, unles that Major Redmond²⁰⁶ willbee contented to acsept the halfe of what is owinge hime, and forbeare the rest, untell° Allholantyde° Next, and Mistris Bolline²⁰⁷ the Intrest only of what is dew unto hir, as I doe beleve shee would, if spokene unto by you, and soe would possiblie my Sister Pursell,²⁰⁸ bee contented with ^a^ part of ^what^ is dew unto hir if Ned Butler* would write unto hir; but for what is owinge unto the Lady²⁰⁹ I would by all menes,° have the whole some° payede unto hir, and with as much spiede° as possiblie it can bee gatharede in, and that [done] ~~to~~ Then to send mee what remaynes, were it but by fifftye pound a [missing] by Bill [of Exchan]ge, to bee payede at ^London^ unto Stiven Smith,* which y[ou] [three words missing] [Stan]dish for a small allowanse if you will speake unto [four words missing] will not Crupell to uss° hir power with hime; [three words missing] furnishe mee for my want of Mony° in expect [three words missing] some befor now from thense; and my beinge [three words missing] I cannot supplye my selfe has redust° me unto very great Strats,° and tharfor I pray Let all my Tenants that has not payede thar Rents, bee

Easter's

scruple

---

²⁰⁵ "The action, practice, or right of seizing by force foreign nationals or their goods, in retaliation for loss or injury caused by them or by their compatriots" ("reprisal, *n.*," I, 1a, *OED*).
²⁰⁶ Presumably, a Cromwellian officer.
²⁰⁷ Unidentified.
²⁰⁸ EO's sister-in-law Elizabeth, widow of James Purcell, Baron Loughmore, who had died in 1652, was among those transplanted to Connacht.
²⁰⁹ Lady Ranelagh.

distrayned[210] upon, and some Course taken to Recover thous° Arears
that are dew upon them, otharwise you will find that thous to whom
you have Sett the Stats° Lands, will prove bad paymasters; by othars
Exampell, and then you may immagine of how ill a consequense, if
not Ruene,° such a disapoyntment would bringe upon mee,
  you are not to Creditt what Sir Patrick wemes* dous°
alledge, of my owinge of hime a hundreth ~~Pound~~ and tene pound,
for that is only to put you ofe,° and to gayne° Time, I haveinge found
a perticular discharge for that dept,° writene all with his owne hand
beringe date the 17 of Agust in the yeare 1640 besides a nothar°
generall discharge allsoe; but Let hime not know soe much; but urge
hime to to [sic] tell you, when this mony was Lent ~~and whethar it
was his owne or anye~~ and to make that dept apiere° by produssinge
somthinge undar my hand, otharwise you may tell hime, you
cane give noe allowanse for it, but must distrayne, in regard I sent
you word, that I ought° hime Nothinge, but that hee dous mee;
a hundreth and tene pound of his Rent dew befor the Rebelione,
all which with the rest, I would forgive, soe hee would give upe
his Farme, but if that willnot bee harkenede unto by hime, then
indevour° to gett some one at Dublin whoe has redie Mony to buye
hime oute;
  I shouldbee glad if thar were anye way for mee to avoyde°
ansaringe° the Sute° that Corronell wogan[211] has commenst aganst
mee, sense I cannot but ~~think~~ beleve, besides that Shuninge of much
troubell, that it it [sic] wouldbee sayfier,° then by allowinge such
a president,° ~~to make my selfe Like~~ in ~~all~~ the Like Cayses,° which
may by the contrivanse, of my ould Frind ^May^ bee made of worse
consequense to mee, tharfor bee well advisede as in that perticular;
The Captane you tell me of, whoe was Latlie° heare is generalie
obsarvede in his discourse to varye much from Truth, and soe it
should sime° hee dous [in his] writinge allsoe [and] as much from
honnestye I am shure,° that should [one word] upon [out] of respect
~~to~~ with design to have intrapt mee [four words missing] to make his
best advantage of all I saye [four words missing] with wittneses by; as
indede tharwas Non,° [three words missing] with hime, though hee
sayede° that tow° of his [three words] not haveinge anye but a youth in
the [three words missing] whoe dynede heare   *dined*

---

 [210] "Constrain" ("distrain, *v.*," II, 8b, *OED*).
 [211] Colonel Thomas Wogan had received satisfaction for arrears in army pay in the form of lands in Ireland. See J. Peacey, "Wogan, Thomas (b. c. 1620, d. in or after 1669), army officer and regicide," *ODNB*.

My Lady of Rannalagh has Earnestlie recommended mr Sands hir Brothar in law²¹² [to] bee my Tenant at Arckloe,° soe as you may make uss° of hime with the rest and see what hee will give, and speake with Doctor yarner* mr Backster²¹³ and mr Bellingham* as allsoe with mr worslys* Frinds that amongst all thes you may [obt]ayne some considerabell offiers;° for that Farme of Arckloe°

consarninge° your owne desiers,° to have Leave to make uss° of the [ce]darwood of Cloane grownded° as you say upon a promise I made you of it, I must injeniouslie tell you, that I doe not at all remembar anye such thinge, though it might very well bee that you had an intentione [to] have spokene unto mee for it but did forgett it, or Else possiblie did [im]ploye some body whoe did ommitt to move it for you, though the [bu]ssenes is not considerablie Ecquall in vallew,° unto the Noyse,° that it would make, and the Sensure that it would bringe upon you, for desiringe; and blame upon mee for giveinge a way what is Estimede soe convenient for my owne [uss], it beinge the only wood that Lies neare Dunmore,* you undarstandinge [as] well as I the humor of the pepell; soe as I know your owne discretione [ad]mitt I had givene you a Reall promise of it, as in that thar has bine° [a] mistake, would I am shure,° make you declyne what you could not [pr]osecute with Neare soe much as benifitt unto your selfe one way; as it would [be] disadvantagious unto you a Nothar, and tharfor if it bee the Lacke of [an]ye presant supplye, that you may have put you upon the desier of this, Let mee but know what it is; and I will find out a betar way to Furnishe you; untell I cane performe what I intend of gratifinge, and providinge betar for you

Clone (Co. Kilkenny)

ingenuously

Tharis a Gentellman on° mr Page²¹⁴ that is allredie or willbee shortlie at Dublin, whoe I praye bee Sivelle° To, and desier all my Frinds to bee the Like, for hee was designede to have accompaynede My Sones in thar Travells, and is a very honnest abbell and worthye person,

I s[uspect] thar may be [som]thinge dew unto mr Plunket* and mr Carr* for letars [*four words missing*] all Care to see payede unto them; I doe hope [*four words missing*] who is now at London [*missing*] and imployede a [*four words missing*] thar, I may bee abell° [to suck]side° as I have [*four words missing*] you Cane furnishe mee [with so]me Mony, to [*three words missing*] my Comminge over

---

²¹² Robert Sandys was the husband of Elizabeth Jones, half sister to Lady Ranelagh's husband.
²¹³ Unidentified but possibly Baxter who is mentioned in later letters.
²¹⁴ Thomas Page, a friend and confidante of EO's eldest son, Thomas, Earl of Ossory.

into Ireland where besids that my ocations makes it Nesesarye I shouldbee, my inclinations dous ~~allsoe;~~ make mee desier it allsoe;

I reseved a Letar from the Lord Angers* recommendinge mr Bridgman²¹⁵ to bee my Tenant for the Farmes of Lisneva williamstowne Tobinstowne hearldstowne and Portruskene in the Countye of Carlagh,²¹⁶ with a Nothar from himselfe unto the same Efect, which ^if^ you have not allredie soe disposede of for this yeare, as thay are past Recalle, I desier that mr Bridgman may bee preferede unto, upon such termes as hee and you cane agree, and if My Lord Angers bee not at Dublin, deliver this inclosede unto mr Bridgman for it Consarnes° hime, to whom I had not Leasure in perticular to write, as you may suppose by the Lenght of this Letar to you from

Acton* the 29 of June   E:ormonde

I pray remember mee to the ould Doctor²¹⁷ and bringe mr Page* acquanted with hime; and mr Carr [/] aftar the Endinge of my Letar, I thought it Nesesarye to Send you my Lady of Ranelaghs* Letar to mee, ~~which I wa~~ and my answar unto that of hirs, that you may ^the betar^ governe your Selfe, amongst the Number of thous, whoe dous all desier to Settell in that Plase ^of Arckloe°^ and to ordar things, Soe as may bee most for my advantage

Letter 61. July 4, [1657?], [Acton], the Marchioness of Ormonde to John Burdon (NLI, Ormond Papers, 2484, no. 216, p. 71). Autograph.
For John Burdon [/] Thes. [Endorsed]: her Ladyshipps of 4 received the 18th of July.

John Burdon

I am much sattisfiede to find as I did by yours of the 24 of June that reprisalls are granted unto the Souldiors° which will remove one of the greatest inconveniensies that I apprehended my selfe Subgect unto of haveinge dispute with Them which by this Menes;° will I hope be avoyded,° It wouldbee Nesesarye that I knew whethar anye of the Adventerors° have part of My Lands in the Countye of Tipararye, for though tharbee noe perticular Act yet past, to Secure unto them what they are possest of, yet it was much Prest° this Last

---

²¹⁵ Unidentified, but evidently a client and associate of Lord Aungier.
²¹⁶ Lisnavagh, Williamstown, Tobinstown, Heraldstown, Portrushen, all in Co. Carlow.
²¹⁷ Gerald Fennell?

Parlement, and willbee agayne° at the Sittinge of the Next, which willbee within this 6 Months, I perseve° that Mistris Commorford²¹⁸ has indevorede,° if not allredie done mee some prejudise with the Persone that most desiers° it, which as unto the the Mayne° of my Intrests, I know shee Cannot though ^in^ some things I beleve shee may, as unto what dous° Consarne° the Morgedges, however I could wishe that you would informe your Selfe the best you Cane, and if it bee not to Late to prevent hir Mischife, gett Mr John Mandevile* whoe has some Creditt with hir, or some othar if anye you know that is more fitt, to represent the Scandall that by it, shee will draw upon hir Selfe, in Injuringe of a Familie that was the Rayser° of hirs, and hir Husbands, and upon which I ^hee^ had a perticular dependansie, and if the Consideratione of that, willnot make hir Sease° hir Mischife, I have noe more to Say, but to indevour° my owne Securitye the best I Cane, and Leave hir unto the reward, that at one time or othar willbee the recompense of Trecherye, and ingratitude, and that will ^bee^ begerye and Contempt, in the Ende, as might bee wittnesede in Many, that shee has knowne, and I could Name for Exampells,

  I hope Mr Harisone* willnot goe ofe° from his offier,° if hee should, and that my Rents is Like to falle soe Short, and bee soe ill payede as you tell mee, and I find, suffisentlie to my inconveniensie would implunge mee in such Strats,° as I cannot but with Horror think upon, tharfor as you are Carfull of all my other Consarnes, I praye bee Noe Less industrious as unto That of My Suplye; by tryinge it upon anye resonabell Termes I might bee healpt with Mony,° which my thinks° might bee had from Mr Mandevile or some othars Thar;° in which the ould Doctor²¹⁹ and Ned Butler* might possiblie prove assistinge whoe has Intrest with Them, I doe not wondar at mr whelers* wranglinge about his Lease, but rathar then have anye furthar dispute, provided hee doe paye what is dew,° you may remitt part, or all the Acats,²²⁰ and if that willnot ~~willnot~~ Sattisfie, then some othar Menes must bee ussede to Compell hime, if in soe doeinge I may not indaynger the pullinge of greatar inconveniensies upon my Selfe one way, then I Cane ^reape^ benifitt the othar which I know you are warye Ennough to Considar to whom this bussenes° is referede by

---

 ²¹⁸ Perhaps Austacie Comerford, the widow of Edward Comerford of Callan (d. 1649).
 ²¹⁹ Gerald Fennell?
 ²²⁰ "Bought provisions; provisions that are not made in the house, but have to be purchased fresh when wanted, as meat, fish, etc. Hence: all provisions except the home produce of the baker and brewer; foreign foodstuffs, delicacies" ("acate, *n.*," 2, *OED*).

EO

I would gladlie See the perticulars of Edward Butlers* accompts,°
which you may Send when anye of your acquantanse dous Come over
The 4 of July

**Letter 62. July 13, [1657], [Acton], the Marchioness of Ormonde
to John Burdon** (NLI, Ormond Papers, 2484, no. 230, p. 189).
Autograph.
For John Burdon [/] this. [Endorsed]: Her Ladyshipp 13 July.

John Burdon

I did reseve° from Stivene Smith,* tow° days Sense,° a Coppie of a
Late ordar of the Counsells, made upon a Petistione preferede by
you on my behalfe, which I hope will produse a good Effect, if the
persons to whom it is referede to Sertifie;° bee as Just tharin, as I
hope thay° willbee, I resevede° a proposall from mr Cawfilde,* and
one mr Boullton,²²¹ for the Tenantinge of the whoule Lord^shipe^
of Arckloe,° a Coppie of which, I have hearinclosede sent unto you,
with my answar back unto them, for you to See, and to deliver, or
Not accordinge as you think best, to whous discretione I doe referr
it, I am much Consarnede° to have a spidie° accompt° from mr
Harisone* whethar the Mony° hee made mee offier° of may bee had
or Not, and that some supplye out of my Rents may bee spidilie°
Sent mee, for otharwise it ^this unsartantye°^ will to Longe retarde
my takinge some resolutione in ordar to the Settlinge of my Selfe
and familie, which it is now highe Time to doe, befor the Sommer
doe Pass, tharfor some accompt ^answar^ as to thes perticulars, is
desirede and Expectede from you To

The 13 of July   EO

I Pray tell the Doctor that the Letar ~~Hee Sent~~ to humes* was
immedeatlie Sent by mee, unto Doctor Fogurtye,²²² by John

---

²²¹ Unidentified.
²²² Catholic physician William Fogarty (d. 1678). See Peter Elmer, "Promoting Medical Change in Restoration Ireland: The Chemical Revolution and the Patronage of James Butler, Duke of Ormond (1610–1688)," in *Early Modern Ireland and the World of Medicine: Practitioners, Collectors and Contexts*, ed. John Cunningham (Manchester: Manchester University Press, 2019).

Butler,²²³ whoe delivrede it into his owne hands and broght mee word that hee would take Care to Send it Sayfe° unto My Sister²²⁴

Letter 63. [July] 22, 1657, [Acton], the Marchioness of Ormonde to John Burdon (NLI, Ormond Papers, 2322, no. 1235, p. 379).²²⁵
Autograph.
[For John] Burdon. [Endorsed]: [Her Ladyships] 22nd July 1657 [*missing*] August.

John Burdon

[*one line missing*]²²⁶ Corronell Flower* [*one line missing*] you have ad[vised] [*missing*] of [*eight words missing*] [of it] which hee [*eight words missing*] mee that [*one line missing*] [la]tlie Consarninge° the Mony,° has [refusede] hime [*three words missing*] [it] shallbee [*missing*] at Mickellmas° Next soe [*three words missing*] the mene° time that [ashur]anse Ethar° of Land or othar that my [*missing*] or My [*missing*]   *assurance*
Capabell to give may bee agreede upon betwixt hime and you on my behalfe and the writings²²⁷ sent over to bee Signede by uss heare and then returned to Lie in Corronell Flowers hands to bee [del]ivrede unto hime when the Monys° is payede to prevent [de]laye or disopoynment which in many respects should it happen would prove highlie prejudistiall to Mee, [It] [*three words missing*] writene unto you more at Large, as [unt]ell I heare [*three words missing*] [ag]ayne tharis nothing more at the presant [*three words missing*] by

EO

I did by [advise] of m[rs] [*three words missing*] Sir John Tempell;²²⁸ which bore [*five words missing*] in one to hime, but has not as yet [*five*

---

²²³ A kinsman of the Ormonde Butlers.
²²⁴ Perhaps Lady Francis Butler.
²²⁵ The MS is severely damaged by wear and tear, with significant portions of text lost at the top middle and bottom right of the page.
²²⁶ As many as eight or nine words are illegible in each of the blank spaces.
²²⁷ "A written paper or instrument, having force in law; a deed, bond agreement, or the like" ("writing, *n.*," II, 8b, *OED*).
²²⁸ Sir John Temple (1600–1677) was one of the trustees of EO's estate. He had been appointed as a commissioner for the settlement of the estates belonging to delinquents in Ireland on November 1653. In 1655, he regained the office of Master of the Rolls, thanks in part to a highly commendatory letter from Cromwell. In June 1656, Temple was appointed a commissioner for determining disputes over the land settlement arising among the adventurers. See Robert Dunlop, "Temple, Sir John (1600–1677)," rev. Sean Kelsey, *ODNB*.

words missing] [wher]for I pray inquier,° and send mee an accompt°
[*two words missing*]

The 22 of J[uly]

Letter 64. August 8, 1657, [Acton], the Marchioness of Ormonde to John Burdon (NLI, Ormond Papers, 2322, no. 1236, p. 385). Autograph.
[Endorsed]: Her Ladyships of the 8th Received 18th August 1657.

John Burdon

By your Letar of the 29 of July I perseve° that tharis an Ordar of Counsell made upon the Comistioners report, whoe are tharby forthwith, to Sett out othar Lands; to the Souldiorye,° in Leue of Mine; in the same Baronys or Neare, where thous° Lands dous° Lie, though the Comistioners report, which you tell mee you Sent mee a coppie of, is not come unto My hands but the Counsells ordar only, upon which, that was grownded° ~~did~~ ^(is)^ wherof I gave you an accompt° is a formar Letar that I hope is with you by this Time; as allsoe of the ressept° of the Bill of Exchange²²⁹ which was acsepted; and the Mony° Sense° payede, It is a great incoridgment° to mee to Come over, that I see by your indevours,° my affares Liklie to Suckside° soe well, as that thous Lands of Mine that were possest by the Souldiors° tharis hopes willbee Recovrede from them; and tharfor I am Now soe fullie resoulvede upon my Journye over as this weke I begine to Packe upe my Goods which I ~~am resoulvede~~ ^intend^ to Send by the way of Bristoll* but whethar I shall Imbarke Thar° or at Chestar My Selfe I am not as yet sartane,° but must bee Gyded accordinge as ~~will~~ ^shall^ bee Judgede most Sayfe,° but Cannot Move untell° I gett Mony, tharfor I pray hastene with all the Spiede° you Cane some Supplye over to mee, that I may bee ~~thar~~ ^in Irland^ befor the winter Stormes; and Least° the wethar° or othar acsident might Staye mee Longer, then wouldbee Nesesarye for mee to bee Thar, to desir an abaytment of My Rent, consideringe how great a proportione of what is mentionede in my Lease is kept from mee, I will Send such Letars, unto the Lord Hary Cromwell, and othars as you have advisede mee the Mene° time, which may bee kept by you, and deliverede when you see most Convenient, or kept

lieu

guided

---

²²⁹ "A written order by the writer or 'drawer' to the 'drawee' (the person to whom it is addressed) to pay a certain sum on a given date to the 'drawer' or to a third person named in the bill, known as the 'payee'" ("bill, *n*.3," 9a, *OED*).

backe, accordinge as you shall See Cause; I have resevede° Edward Butlers* accompts° by the Last Post, but have not as yet had time to Examine them, ~~I have~~ ^I send^ hearinclosede ~~sent~~ Some derections° ~~unto Edward Butler,~~ ^unto hime^ to provide Fieringe[230] of all Sorts at Dunmore,* and to Laye [it] Beare,[231] and for othar provistions I suppose thay° may bee Soune° had when I am Thar, I am buyinge to ^2^ Chockhorsses More unto the tow° I have allredie, and doe hope   *coach–horses*
I may Compase to Make them sixe when I come into Ireland Soe as it wouldbee Nesesarye that the ouglie Stabell that is at Donmore*   *ugly*
shouldbee made to Sarve untell I bee abbell to make a betar,° which if I live, shallbee with othar amendments in that Plase ~~bee~~ indevorede° by

The 8 of Agust   EO

I have great obligations unto the Ladys Brothar[232] whoe is now goeinge over, and will I am Confidint befrind mee as farr as hee Cane in all my Consarnes° soe as by hir Menes,° I would have you to addrese your Selfe to hime as you find ocatione,° for hee has a great intrest thar, as well as heare with thous in greatest power

Letter 65. August 19, [1657], [Acton], the Marchioness of Ormonde to [John Burdon] (NLI, Ormond Papers, 2484, no. 240, p. 261).[233]
Autograph.
For John Burdone.

J[ohn Burdon]

[*one line missing*] you carryede [*four words missing*] reade at Counsell which denyall I take for a bad signe [*missing*] grownd° for mee to suspect the persone that you doe not to bee what hee pretends, but a Litell° time will make a furthar discovrye, tell° when, I shall with patianse° Expect what the Event of this bussenes° of mine willbee, that possiblie is obstroctede by Humes* his Naybor, that went hense Latlie,° whous perswations may, and I beleve has wroght some couldnes° in the Person you tell mee, you did obsarve to bee soe, when you made your Last addres to hime, howsomever I am very

---

[230] "Material for a fire, fuel" ("firing, *n.*," 7a, *OED*).
[231] "*to lay bare*: (a) to denude, remove the covering from; (b) to expose to view, reveal" ("lay, *v.*1," 25a, *OED*).
[232] Probably Lady Ranelagh's brother, Roger, Lord Broghill.
[233] Text is missing from three lines at the top of each page due to damage apparently caused by the seal.

well satisfiede of your diligense, and the punctuall accompt° you
give of your prosidinge° thar° and Care allsoe of what consarnes°
my affares in the Contrye [which] I hope when [Mister] Farrar
and Edward Butler* returnes you answar of the Late Letars you
Sent them, I should reseve° [some] furthar informatione [from
you] tuchinge° that perticular [and] shouldbee glade to heare that
such ^of the Soulderye°^ as have settled into [my lands] would by
Captane Moors* exampell desier,° as hee has dune,° to have a reprisall
else where, which wouldbee much for thar securitye as well as my
advantage; Corronell Sankye[234] is in Towne but has not as yet sent,
nor delivrede mee any Letar [from] the gentellman that you tould
[mee] had by him, sent mee [one] but when ^hee^ dous,° I shall let
you know it and will indevour° to gett from you think it Neses[arye]
[eight words missing] My Lord of Broghall* [three words missing] when
hee come will I hope bee assistinge [unto]

EO

I heare mr Gorge Carr* is comminge over but doe not beleve it, by
resone° that I have had noe mentione of it, Nethar from you Nor
himeselfe; I am well pleasede to heare that you are Liklie to gett
Deale Bourds[235] at Dublin for flowringe which the Souner° thay° bee
sent downe to Dunmore* [the] betar,° befor the wethar° grow worse

**Letter 66. September 16, 1657, [Bristol], the Marchioness of
Ormonde to John Burdon** (NLI, Ormond Papers, 2322, no. 1240,
p. 413).[236] Autograph.
[Endorsed]: Her Ladyships 16th September Received 1st October
1657.

John Burdon

[I recevede your] Letar of the 1 of Sep this Month, as Stivene
Smith* Sends mee word hee has done the 2 hundreth Pound, that
my Lord of Meath* has Lent mee, which was payede accordinge
his Lordshipps Letar in that behalfe, unto mr Bathurst,[237] wherof I

---

[234] Cromwellian soldier.
[235] "a thin board of fir or pine" ("'deal-' board, *n*.," *OED*).
[236] There is a small tear to the top of each leaf that has resulted in the loss of approximately three words from the middle of the first line of text on all three pages of the letter.
[237] Presumably, Samuel Bathurst, who is later recommended by EO for the position of postmaster of Dublin. See *The Post Office in Ireland: An Illustrated History* (Newbridge: Irish Academic Press, 2016).

dout° Not but Smith has acquanted you from London, Souner° then
this Letar of mine cane doe, by resone° of my beinge at soe much
a greater distanse; Nor shall I nide° to tell you how acseptabell a
Curtisie° My Lord of Meath has done mee in This; Nor how sensibell
I am of your indevo[r]s° allsoe; sense° without this supplye, had
Come, it had not bine° possibell for mee ^to^ have removede, nor
will it yet to Come soe well a way with soe much Creditt as I desier°
of in Settinge my selfe free Cleare out ^of^ Marchands° Books and
such Like ^as^ which 2 hundreth more, wouldnot only doe what
inabells mee ^inabell° mee to doe, but allsoe^ to bringe over much
of Nessesarye provistione for my house, as Groseries and the Like,
which are very Cheape at Bristoll,* but Diere° at in Ireland, as I
understand, and for othar things, I have made that Competent[238]
provistione as I shall not Nide to Laye out anye Mony° for one yeare
[three words missing] in redenes,° to transport mee from Bristoll to
waterford, but the wethar,° in Cayse° all othar things were redie, is
not soe Settlede as it Canebee Sayfe° for mee to venter,° it beinge
heare at the presant very Boysterous, soe as fearinge I might bee
hir not bee in Ireland befor Mickellmas,° I hope you will not relye
upon Edward Butler,* to reseve° and Collect the Stats° Rent, but goe
downe your Selfe into the Contrye at the Time, or befor thay° fall
dew° to warne the Tenants Least° I should at the first, fall under an
areare and which may bringe mee into Troubell; sense ^I see^ I am
not [illegible][239] [pepell] ^to depend upon his^ performanse whom I
have intrusted in my affares that should have appierede soe negligent
^bine Soe ussless^ in healpinge mee; at a Time; wherin the Nesesitye
of my ocations° ^made it^ Soe absolatlie requisett, as in sense I   *absolutely requisite*
Left Ireland Nevr to have resevede° on° peeny of my owne, from   *never*
thense, but what by your indevours was takene Lent Mee, which yo
Cannot Consideringe my Charge, and the unexpectede acsidents
of Expense in, or that fell upon mee, by my Sones imprisonmett
and afterwards his fallinge Sike, [two words missing] My Familie   *sick*
hethar,° and the preparations for my Journye at presant, but have
Cast greater diffeculties upon mee, then canbee well imaginede, but
by thous,° whoe has bine a wittnes what a Laborious and Sad time I
have had, to suport my selfe, and Familie, Free from fallinge undar
anye Contempt, or Clamor of Mene° persons, soe as if it shall please

---

[238] "Sufficient but not going beyond this: fair, moderate, reasonable, enough" ("competent, *adj.*," 3b, *OED*).

[239] Seven or eight words are illegible under EO's heavy strikethroughs.

God to Send mee Sayfe into Ireland, where I hope My Steward²⁴⁰ with my Goods, are by this Time; I doe verylie beleve that the worst of my ^ill^ Fortune is Past and that God has designede mee, though I Covete Not great wealth, yet such a Competensie²⁴¹ with a private Life, as may inabell mee to pay my depts° and reward my such of My Sarvants as has Sarvede mee industerouslie° and fathfullye as God willinge I intend of which Nomber as I accompt° you one of the prinsepall, soe you shallbee pertaker of my good intendments towards you; I have sent the inclosede oppene for you to See, which soe soune° as you have read, I would have you to Seale, and delever, unto as it is derected;°

    I shouldbee glad [*two words missing*] [the] order ^of Reprisall^ were gotten out, befor my Comminge, though I am satisfiede that the delaye is noe fault of yours; I hope you have resevede my Letars of the 12 and 29 of Agust with my Last Exseptinge this of the 5 of Sep, though you have not mentionde them in such of the Laytest° Letars of yours as has come unto the hands of

The 16 of Sep   E:ormonde

Letter 67. [1657?], [no place], the Marchioness of Ormonde to John Burdon (NLI, Ormond Papers, 2484, no. 214, p. 61). Autograph. For your Selfe. [Endorsed]: Her Ladyshipp.

John Burdon

I would have you to Present my Sarvise° unto My Lord of Meath* and Let hime know that I sent to know ho you to inquier° after his Lordshipps health after his and deliver the inclosede unto his Lady,²⁴² but not when hee is presant, because it Consarnes° My Lady Jeane Moore²⁴³

---

   ²⁴⁰ "An official who controls the domestic affairs of a household, supervising the service of his master's table, directing the domestics, and regulating household expenditure; a major-domo" ("steward, *n.*," 1a, *OED*).

   ²⁴¹ "A sufficiency, without superfluity, of the means of life, a competent estate or income" ("competency, *n.*," II, 3a, *OED*).

   ²⁴² Mary Brabazon, née Chambre, Countess of Meath, daughter of a wealthy settler, Calcott Chambre of Carnew Castle, Co. Wicklow. She married Edward Brabazon in 1632, bringing with her a very large dowry.

   ²⁴³ Lady Jane Moore (b. c. 1641) was the daughter of the Earl and Countess of Meath. She married Randall Moore, son of the Second Viscount Moore of Drogheda and his wife Alice.

Retirement in Dunmore, 1657–1660

Letter 68. March [1658?], [Dunmore], the Marchioness of Ormonde to John Burdon (NLI, Ormond Papers, 2484, no. 239, p. 255).²⁴⁴ Autograph.
For My Sarvant John Burdon thes. [Endorsed]: Concerning Mr Recorder Byttle.

John Burdon [*missing*] of March

This berar° mr Recordar²⁴⁵ whoe has bine° very frindlie to mee in all my Consarnes° heare is desirious to bee my Tenant for some Lands, Ethar° in the Countye of ~~kill~~ Carterlough, or killkenye, wherfor, if hee doe fortune to Come time Ennough beefor all Mine bee Sett, I would have you to indevour° to accomodate hime, and in Cayse,° that Cannot bee at the presant, I doe beleve if you doe advise hime to deale with Sir Patricke wemes* for the Remayndar of the years that are unexpirede of his Lease, it willbee as fitt a Plase for hime, as anye hee Cane Picke upon, in regard hee desiers° a House; besides ^that^ the Changinge of a bad Tenant for a good wouldbee Likwise a Sattisfactione and advantage unto

Cheatharlach (Co. Carlow)

E:ormonde

Letter 69. [June 12, 1658], [Dunmore], the Marchioness of Ormonde to John Burdon (NLI, Ormond Papers, 2484, no. 220, p. 107). Autograph.
For My Sarvant John Burdon [/] thes. [Endorsed]: Her Ladyshipp Dutchess of ormond.

John Burdon

~~yesternight~~ on Teusday Last Mr Leslye²⁴⁶ came hethar,° but could only obtayne a fortnights time to Stay, soe as if I had knowne of

---

²⁴⁴ There is minor damage to the MS caused by the seal.
²⁴⁵ Recorder Byttle is not oterwise identified.
²⁴⁶ Henry Leslie (1580–1661), Church of Ireland Bishop of Down and Connor, was a staunch opponent of non-conformity and a firm royalist. He had returned to Ireland from exile in the early 1650s and was given a pension by the Cromwellian government, but he continued to defend episcopacy and the Church of Ireland. In 1659 he preached against the Presbyterian habit of extempore prayer, and published a sermon the following year as *A Discourse of Praying with the Spirit and with the Understanding* (London: John

it, I shouldnot have advisede his Comminge downe at all, though his sudayne° returne from hense agayne,° will I hope Justifie mee that I intend not to imploye hime, Nor shallnot, in anye kind; but Entertayne hime as I would doe anye othar Stranger whilst hee Stays, ~~and~~ I hope you did immediatlie ^upon your Cominge to Towne^ deliver my Leter unto Mr Gookine,* as what wouldbee very seasonabell if it have fallene out to bee ~~by the~~ befor, as Thay° might Supposs; his beinge heare; as you ~~are~~ know it was dispacht from hense befor I had anye ~~thou~~ knowlege of his beinge at Libertye; Captane Parker[247] has payede the fortye Pound, and desirede that his Lease might bee drawne and gottene redie by Friday Next, at which time hee would Call ^heare^ in his way to Dublin for it, which I returnede hime word couldnot bee untell° your returne; butt I gess° by his Earnestnes that hee may possiblie press to have it drawne Thar;° and if Soe, it cannot bee refusede if hee brings his Artickells upon which the same is to bee grownded° whoe desiers° Likwise, to have the kiepinge° of the Courts[248] accordinge as Corronell Abotts has, whose bargine I am not willinge [to make a] presedent yet if I thought it might bee Noe cause of any prejudis unto mee but a Conveniensie unto the Gentellman, I shouldbee willinge to allow hime that, but not for years, but duringe pleasure, and that to bee by a perticular warant[249] and Not a Clause in his Lease; I suppose that Corronell Flower* willbee at Dublin by the Time that this Leter will, whous artickells for Durow I doe desier may bee drawne, and Sent mee down to bee Signede, the Rent to bee threscore and tene Pound [/] the years one and Thirtye, hee to Laye out in buildinge and repayringe 2 hundreth Pound with such othar usstiall° Clauses as inclosinge and the Like, as is Speasifiede° in all othar Leasses, and the rent resarvede to bee above all maner of Taxe or Contributione; Just now I saw a Leter from you to Buck,* wherin I perseve° that you intend not to deliver my Leter unto my Lord Deputye,[250] untell you heare from mee agayne, which is the Cause of my dispachinge ~~of this berar~~ away this ~~Leter that it may be ansared Soune as you Cane~~

Crooke, 1660). See Alan Ford, "Henry Leslie," *DIB*. Thanks to Mark Empey for help with the reference.

[247] Cromwellian soldier and EO's tenant, mentioned again in Letter 71.

[248] "A clear space enclosed by walls or surrounded by buildings; a yard, a court-yard" ("court, *n*.1," I 1a, *OED*).

[249] "Command or permission of a superior which frees the doer of an act from blame or legal responsibility; authorization, sanction; an act of authorization" ("warrant, *n*.1," 7a, *OED*).

[250] Lord Deputy Henry Cromwell.

~~that it may bee~~ ^to let you know that I would have that othar to bee delivrede^ befor mr Leslys* returne to Dublin whoe willbee Thar on Saterday, and Soe will Corronell Flower allsoe to whom deliver the inclosede from

wedensday Night   E:Ormonde

Letter 70. June 16, 1658, Dunmore, the Marchioness of Ormonde to Henry Cromwell (BL, Lansdowne MSS, 823, fols. 64–65). Autograph.
For his Excellency the Lord Henry Cromwell Lord Deputye of Ireland [/] this present. [Endorsed]: 16 June 58 Countess Ormond.

My Lord   Dunmore the 16 of June

Hearinge Latlie° of the confinment of Mr Lesslye* a Devine, and one whoe upon the recomendatione of severall of his owne profestione, and othars of qualitye, Livinge in thous° parts where hee did, to bee a persone Learned, of peasebell and Seville° conversatione, and a Singell Man; I did promise to Entertayne at my beinge Last at Dublin; to bee my housald Chaplen aganst whom; I understand that theris some offense takene; but what the perticulars are, or may bee, I am as Ignorant, as innocent of beinge anye ways an acsesarye unto what may bee made his Crime, if anye hee shallbee found Gilltye of; soe as my humbell desier° unto your Lordshipps is; that noe part of your displeasure aganst hime whoe is to mee a Stranger, more then that I doe remember to have ~~heard onse and~~ Siene° hime at Dublin aboute twelfe years sense° and then heard hime preach; hee beinge at that time under the Notione of[251] one of my Lords Chaplenes; yet never had unto the best of my remembranse, but at my comminge Last from Dublin in all my Life, anye discourse with hime; may not involve Mee and consequentlie prejudis mee in your Lordshipps estime; whoe Singlie without the othoritye° of the plase you hould;° I carrye to great a respect For, to Intrest my selfe for anye aganst whom your Lordshipps may Ethar° in your private, or publicke capasitye have anye exseptianse aganst, soe as unles your Lordshipps shall become sattisfiede of his beinge as innofensive, as hee was Carracterede,° and I belevede hime to bee; I shall declyne the entertayninge of him; as I hope your Lordshipps will the admittinge

---

[251] "A general concept, category, or designation, *esp.* one under which something is comprehended or classed; a classificatory term. Frequently with *of*" ("notion, *n.*," 1b, *OED*).

anye beleufe to my prejudis in This, or anye othar perticular, to which othars offense; and not my owne; may by my ill willers bee agrevatede to my disadvantage; whoe notwithstandinge, all that the unhappenes of my condistione cane Throw upon mee; your Lordshipps shall never find; but allways redye to testifie my selfe

My Lord,

your Lordshipps most humbell Sarvant

E:ormonde

Letter 71. June 19, [1658], Dunmore, the Marchioness of Ormonde to John Burdon (NLI, Ormond Papers, 2484, no. 217, p. 79). Autograph.
For My Sarvant John Burdon [/] thes. [Endorsed]: Dutchesse of Ormonde [/] her Ladyship touching Captain Parker [/] 19 June.

John Burdon

The Last weeke I writ unto you consarninge° this Gentellmans[252] desier° to have his Lease, and Libertye to kiepe° Courts; which if givene hime in the way of warant othorisinge hime soe to doe; and to bee duringe pleasure[253] only, I doe Conseve° it Cannot prejudis mee, but will Sattisfie hime, whoe beinge my Tenant and a Sivell° Man, I shouldbee willinge to doe in That, or anye other resonabell thinge; whoe I perseve° has an Intent, by resone° that hee wants wood ^upon his Farme^ to Move My Lord Deputye for Some, out of thous° Lands that are Now his Lordshipps and from whense hee did formarlie furnishe himselfe, whoe desiers your assistanse which I would have you ^are^ to afford hime as farr as you may in This, and in soe doeinge you will Please

authorizing

Dunmore the 19 of June   E:ormonde

---

[252] Captain Parker.
[253] "at will, at discretion" ("pleasure, *n*.," P6, *OED*).

Letter 72. June 19, [1658?], Dunmore, the Marchioness of Ormonde to John Burdon (NLI, Ormond Papers, 2484, no. 218, p. 91).[254] Autograph.
For My Sarvant John Burdon [/] Thes at Dublin. [Endorsed]: Her Ladyshipps 300 pounds etc payable unto the Treasury.
[*One line missing*] wherin tharis 3 hundreth Pound, a good part wherof, beinge in English Mony° I doe beleve you may Change with advantage for ^such^ Pesesses of Eight as willbee resevede° Thar,° if you doe it befor you make ^Tender^[255] of the Mony into the Excheker, otharwise I doe beleve that thay° will allow you nothinge for it ^Ther^ and soe soune° as more ~~May~~ Canbee gottene ~~is~~ wherof tharis yet ~~more~~ dew;° it shallbee Sent you; This with what Sir Patricke wemes* has promest to Pay; Sir Hardres wallers* Rent, and what mr Gookine* and the Tenants of Arckloe° dous° owe, I doe beleve will goe Neare to make upe the first payment, which to dispach the Souner° if Mr Bellingam* will Lend mee what is wantinge; as I doe beleve hee will if it Exside° not a hundreth Pound I will returne it to hime agayne° within fortine days or three weeks at the farthest, I thought it Nesesarye to Send you Captane Issaks[256] Artickells for Crokswood that Corronell Flower* and your Selfe advisinge together you may the beter° know what Rayts° to put upon it in Cayse° that Major Redmonds* beinge now at Dublin might Speake unto Ethar° of you Consarninge° it, Mr Lesslye* went hense yesterday, soe as I hope my Leter unto My Lord Deputye willbee delivrede; as I wishe it may, befor his comminge thethar;° I shallnot Nide° to tell you how much a worse bargine I am like to have of the Tyths°[257] then you did know of, sense° [*two lines missing*] Soe as it willbee fitt for you to Sieke some redress tharin whilst mr wilson[258] is Thar, I have advisede with mr John Briane[259] that was Latlie° at Crokswood; what rayts to Sett upon that Plase, the which I now send you, though not to Limmett Corronell Flower nor your Selfe to what is tharin Mentionede, but that by it and the Artickells you may the beter Judge, what willbee fitt for you to demand for it, on the behalf of

seek

---

[254] Two lines are missing at the top of each page due to damage to the MS.
[255] "An offer of money, or the like, in discharge of a debt or liability, *esp.* an offer which thus fulfils the terms of the law and of the liability" ("tender, *n.*2," 1b, *OED*).
[256] Unidentified.
[257] "Any levy, tax, or tribute of one tenth" ("tithe, *adj.*1 and *n.*1," B2, *OED*).
[258] Unidentified.
[259] EO's agent at Kilkenny.

E:ormonde

I Send you hearinclosed the key of the Tronk

Dunmore the 19 of June

Letter 73. June 24, 1658, Dunmore, the Marchioness of Ormonde to John Burdon (NLI, Ormond Papers, 2323, no. 1288, p. 305). Autograph.
For John Burdon thes. [Endorsed]: Her Ladyships Dated 24th Received 25th June 1658.

John Burdon

In your Leter of the 29 of this month you tell mee that you had bine° with Mr Gookine,* whoe promisede the delivrye of my Leter unto My Lord Deputye the Monday followinge; but in a Layter° of yours datted the 22 of the same; I undarstand that you went into Chappellizard[260] your selfe, and presented it, soe as the contradictione I find in the accompt° you have givene mee of That bussenes;° makes mee doute° the gentellman unto whom you were adrest, was not soe ~~frind~~ frindlie; as I did beleve hime; in declyninge to doe mee the Curtisie° that I did desier° of hime, or ellse, that thar° was some mistake, soe as I desier to bee furthar sattisfiede as unto this perticular; as I hope My Lord Deputye Shall have noe othar, then resone° to bee; with my actions, which willbee Clearer testimonys of my innosensie; then it canbee the Contrarye what is spokene, by such as are my Enimies, upon the Score[261] of thar desier to posses themselfs of my Fortune, ~~and tharfor shall [forse] my selfe to [illegible]~~[262] I perseve° you are Like to have some difficultye to settell that bussenes of Arckloe,° which if it couldbee dispossede unto Captane Hassells[263] Singlie; you might then have a very faire pretense to breake ofe° with the othar tow; unless thay° will stand unto thar first agreement, and that, my thinks° ^if^ thay willnot, might Justifie my disposinge of it to a Nothar,° rathar then Loose a whole years Rent for thar wranglinge, but ~~in~~ This, I Leave ~~it~~ to bee Managede as Corronell Flower* and your Selfe shall think fitt; ~~whous~~ whous healpe willbee Nessesary in this bussenes; by resone hee has soe offtene treatede with them; and that it should bee broght unto Some

disposed

---

[260] One of the official lodgings of the lord deputy in Dublin.
[261] "by reason of, for the sake of, with regard to" ("score, *n.*," II, 12, *OED*).
[262] Five or six cancelled words are illegible under EO's heavy strikethroughs.
[263] Cromwellian officer. See Clarke, *Prelude to Restoration*, 206.

Conclustione as spidilie° as may bee; I hope you have by this Time resevede° from the Carger²⁶⁴ the 3 hundreth Pound I sent towards [the] makinge upe of the Stats° Rent, beinge all that I could gett or am Like to reseve° yet this fortnight, soe as if Major Redmonds* would pay the Sevincore pound° ~~who~~ for soe much it is as I remember that is Charged upon hime ^which^ ~~That~~ with Sir Hary wallers* Rent, and what I supose mr Bellingaine* would Lend for a fortnight or 3 wekes if spokene unto; would discharge the first payment, which if made would bee a great Ease and sattisfactione to mee, that would by noe Menes° Motion for a respitt for what is behind, unles thar were a very great Nesesitye for it, in regard this is not a proper Time for mee to Expect Curtisies;° I have of Late made some inquirye into the Tytell° of Grangtolokany the which I find to bee Curche° land; belonginge unto the Abye° of Duske Neare Grage ~~which My Grandfather had by t~~ and that the Tyths° allways went with the Land, and soe mr Davide Routh²⁶⁵ still heald them; as did the presedent Tenant ~~besides~~ whoe is yet alive, and many wittneses besides, that cane testifie the same; soe as ~~as~~ Captane Mathews²⁶⁶ beinge now convinst of his Error, that should have begede That for a discovrye that all the Contrye knows to bee my Right; has writene unto mr willson²⁶⁷ to desier backe his Bonds; which Leter togethar with one from mr Hackett;²⁶⁸ soe soune° as you have read; I pray Seale and gett them Bouth° delivrede as spidilie as you Cane; befor that Mr willson dous° Leave Dublin; which perhapes may bee beter° givene hime by some othar hand then your owne, that hee might the Less suspect them gottene by my procurment; and then, soune after to adrese your Selfe to hime to stope° the returne, which if done cannot then bee recovred out of the Stats hands but by Sute;° and I hope that as to thous° othars that Captane Evans²⁶⁹ has Sett without order as I am tould and had Joynede unto a Nothar Parishe; you will take some Course in; otharwise shall not only Loose my Right, but much of the Rent that I must pay out of them; as will apiere° by the Gentellmans Leter unto Edward Butler* which I sent you formarlie; and unto which I doe referr you for your beter ~~inforati~~ informatione as unto that perticular ~~I have sent you~~ ^you will I hope reseve^ some

sevenscore

precedent

---

²⁶⁴ "One who has a charge on an estate or revenue" ("charger, *n.*2," 4, *OED*).
²⁶⁵ Probably David Rothe (1573–1650), Catholic Bishop of Ossory. See Thomas O'Connor, "Rothe, David," *DIB*.
²⁶⁶ Presumably, not her brother-in-law.
²⁶⁷ Unidentified.
²⁶⁸ Unidentified.
²⁶⁹ Cromwellian officer.

papers consarninge° Collishill bege which if thay bee not of uss° thar; I desier may bee kept sayfe° or Else returnede agayne° by this berar,° I am Crediblie informede that tharis much of my wood at Lackath at this time Cuttinge downe by tow° Irishe Men whous Names you will find by the inclosede,[270] for whom I am advisede to gett a writt, which willnot only give a Stope to the Mischife that thay are now doeinge, but will frightene othars from the Like; and doe send you a Leter allsoe of Liftenant Corronell Stivens[271] ~~wherin you may perseve that his~~ ^whous^ holldinge of Garanbegha is rathar to gett as much as hee cane by what is Non° of his owne, then anye pretense that hee has to it for his ~~Ar~~ Arears; soe as if upon the Seeinge My Decree and Lease from the State, hee dous refusse to give possession [/] I think hee may and ought to bee compelled unto it, or Else to Show Cause unto the Contrarye, Mr waters[272] was heare upon monday Last with intent to have gone to Dublin; but some ocatione° hindringe hime when hee went backe unto killkenye, made it his request that some spidie° Course might bee takene whilst you were at Dublin ^with Captane Follia^[273] whoe will pay mee noe Rent, and yet kipes° possessione of Dunnohill; alledginge that hee has it by Lease from you for [a] yeare to Come, and yet refusses to paye the Contributione that is Layede upon it, tellinge the Comistioners, as hee did mee, that hee only [to]uke it beinge wast° to See if hee could gett Tenants wherby to doe mee a Sarvise° by it, but ~~do~~ not otharwise; soe as allthough hee dous thus contradict himselfe; yet hee makes a Shift to Injure mr waters and I bouth; and Says that by agrement with you hee is Likwise to Carye his Crope free ofe Grantstowne, and Soe intends; wherfor tharis an Nesesitye that some spidie Course may bee takene for redress in this or Else mr watters will quitt his bargine whoe desiers ~~that~~ to reseve some accompt from you how the bussenes is derectlie;° and what ~~[illegible] Sattisfactione~~[274] hee may Expect the which I pray consider of, and returne an answar with what spiede° you may; whoe says furthar, that Captane Folia* without Leave unles hee has it from you; dous Grayse all his Stocke upon the Land of killfekill, which will ocatione a

Cooleeshal Beg (Co. Kilkenny)

graze

---

[270] See Vandra Costello, *Irish Demesne Landscapes, 1660–1740* (Dublin: Four Courts, 2015), 93–116, which indicates that EO's concern about the loss of woodland was fairly typical of Irish landowners of the seventeenth century.
[271] The lands awarded to Lieutenant Colonel Stephens and his company are listed in John P. Prendergast, *The Cromwellian Settlement of Ireland* (London: Constable, 1996).
[272] Unidentified.
[273] Cromwellian officer and EO's tenant.
[274] Two words are illegible under EO's heavy strikethroughs.

greater Contributione to bee Layede upon it then hee is a war of, for hee is Extremlie dislikede of by all the Gentellmen of that Contrye; and I feare will Cast it upon the few Tenants that are ^Ther^ and alledge himselfe unconsarnede° [wit] as not beinge Tennant, but graysinge his Cattell ~~upon~~ tharon as beinge wast Grownd° and hee distrest beinge outede of his othar Farmes; which hee Says were promist him, Mr waters I find has a Mind to take this Farme, whoe at the forst did offier° 2 hundreth for it the f Next yeare, and if that might Not bee had, hee would deale for the Farme of Capragh, but I gave hime Noe answar as to Ethar,° not thinkinge it convenient that hee should know that you were intrestede in the prinsepall of them; in regard, hee tould mee that Captane Southwell* kieps° divers persons ofe that would take it, intendinge as hee gives out that hee will insist upon his ould Lease; but that will Signifie Littell, when his one° Leters refussinge it shallbee produsede the which I hope you have and ~~the [illegible] Rent shallbee [illegible]~~[275] ^will kiepe° to Show^ one thinge I thought fitt to give you cautione of that if Mr watters and you doe Come to anye agreement, that the tow° Small Parsells° belonginge unto Castelleur may bee Strock out of your Lease to avoyde° anye dispute hearafter I desier to know what discourse My Lord Deputye had with you at the 2 time that you were oppoyntede° to wayte° upon hime, which you may give mee an accompt of at Large by the returne of this berare,° with more convenuiensie then by the Post, by resone hee Shall Stay yor Leasure for it; by whom Likwise I shouldbee glad to heare whethar his Lordshipp dous intend to come downe into thes parts this Sommer or Not; Tharis soe many ocations° that will mulltiplye bussenes upon you that it will Consarne you as new derections° are Sent you to take Memorandoms of Eache; wherby Nothinge that is Nesesarye may bee ommittede Nor forgotten, as willinglie I know thar shallnot in what Consarnes

first

Dunmore the 24 of June   E:ormonde

---

[275] Approximately two then four canceled words are illegible under EO's heavy strikethroughs.

Letter 74. June 26, [1658?], [Dunmore], the Marchioness of Ormonde to John Burdon (NLI, Ormond Papers, 2484, no. 217a, p. 85).[276] Autograph.
For John Burdon [/] thes. [Endorsed]: Dutchesse of Ormonde [/] Her Ladyshipps 26 June.

John Burdon

on Thursday Last I sent you [*missing*] othar papers, [*missing*] from Captane [*two words missing*] a nothar° from mr Hackett unto mr [*missing*] whoe cominge yesternight to killkenye, couldnot reseve Them, soe as I desier° thay° may bee returnede mee with the first oppertunitye, and that I may know whether you have gotten that Surtificate from mr willson consarninge° the Tyths° which you Say hee promist you, which if ommittede when he was ther, willbee as unto that bussenes° of some prejudis unto

Certificate

The 26 of June   E:ormonde

Letter 75. [1658?], [Dunmore], the Marchioness of Ormonde to John Burdon (NLI, Ormond Papers, 2484, no. 234, p. 217). Autograph.
For My Sarvant John Burdon [/] thes. [Endorsed]: Her Ladyshipps.

The Lissense° which as I remember Leaves mee and My Lord; Power to make Leasses for terme of years I might not make a Lease of soe much of it, as I now Rent from the State for one and twentye, or one and thirtye years, to some persons in trust for payment of depts° and raysinge° Portions for my yonger Chilldren; without all the Trusties° Joyninge with mee; Save only such as thay° have impowrede to act for them in things of the Like Nature, as your Selfe and Humes;* which if that bee admitted; to bee bindinge in Law aganst the Stats° overthrowinge of it, ~~shall~~ willbee then suffisent for my Purpose, you tell mee of a Bill preferede aganst mee in the Excheker by Corronell Stubers[277] ~~which~~ ^That^ you doe beleve is about the Commons of Callan ^the^ which you doe advise might rathar come into a devistione,° then a Sute° betwixt uss, and trulye I am of your oppinione, if it couldbee broght unto That; but whethar thar° might not bee some advantge takene by hime; if such a motione should

---

[276] Some words in the first three lines of the letter are illegible or missing due to water damage to the MS.

[277] Colonel Peter Stubber. For further information, see Clarke, *Prelude to Restoration*, 208.

come from mee doe not know, but think it Nesesarye that you should informe your selfe; and then to proside;° in the best and Securest menes° to have it rathar ~~soe~~ composede in a fare way; then desided by Law, I understand not what that dispute is consaringe° killbride; but did conseve° that after the Lease of Egectment[278] was Signede upon the Plase; that the Partye pretendinge, was made Plantive, and if Soe, I beinge in possestione I doe ^beleve^ that the othar when hee hears, that it is ~~Settled and~~ in Captane Hassells* hands, will have the mind to spend anye mony° in goeinge to Sute for it, I perseve° my Lady willoby* is Not as yet come to Towne, but willbee I hope befor you doe Leave it, and then some accompt° of what I did write unto hir ~~as best~~ willbee expected by

E:ormonde

one argument ^more^ aganst my grantinge of Sir Henrye Tichborne[279] Power, to make advantage of the woods in that Large Mesure that hee desiers;° is that when hee or his Assigns, shall have Made Mony of the wood; hee may ^then^ Cast upe his Lease and Leave the plase ~~so mu~~ Some hundreths worse then hee found it, and Soe make his gayne° Sartane° by my Loose of what would yeald mee Mony as well as hee, I have ~~a~~ Sent hime an answar unto his Leter but would not have it to bee delivrede unles Corronell Flower* dous° aprove tharof whoe beter° knows his humor then Ethar° you or I dous

---

[278] "The act or process of ejecting a person from his holding" ("ejectment, *n.*," 1a, *OED*).

[279] Sir Henry Tichborne (1581?–1667) had fought in Ireland alongside JO and been involved in negotations with the Confederate Catholics, but after the defeat of royalists in Ireland, he managed to convince Cromwell of his loyalty. In 1650 he composed an account of his activities during the Irish wars—later published as *A Letter of Sir Henry Tichborne to his Lady, at the Siege of Drogheda* (Drogheda: John Fleming, 1772)—to support his petition for a reward for military service in the Protestant cause in Ireland. His petition was successful, but thanks to the opposition of the Dublin commissioners, it took the direct interventions of Cromwell for him to finally receive Beaulieu, Co. Louth, in February 1658. See Terry Clavin, "Tichbourne (Tichborne), Sir Henry," *DIB*.

Letter 76. July 10, [1658?], [Dunmore], the Marchioness of Ormonde to John Burdon (NLI, Ormond Papers, 2484, no. 222, p. 123).[280] Autograph.
For John Burdon [/] thes.

[*Two lines missing*] and payede into the Excheker [*two words*] which you are to have from Captane Hasells,* and that othar from Major Redmon[d]* which done, and the Lord Chife° Barons[281] warant takene forth, which you tell mee was promist you; thar° willnot then remayne much more for you to doe ^Thar^ but the Settlinge of that bussenes° of Arckloe,° which I hope is by this time at an Ende, and the tryinge what My Lady willobye* will doe towards the furnishinge mee with Mony,° which at this time, is one of my greatest Consern[s]° and tharfor must with all dilligense and industrye bee indevoured° by you; an to that Ende I desier° that Corronell Flower* may bee advisede with, how to move Sir Hary Tichborne* to pay the hundreth Pound of remayninge of the first years Rent which is dew° of hime by the Artickells, the which my thinks° hee should not Scrupell to doe sense° I have condesended in giveinge more to hime then I was oblidgede unto, I doe not as yet heare of Major Redmonds beinge Come home [*two lines missing*] inquired of Edward Butler* whether you gave [hime the] Counterparts of Captane Folies* lease and hee says derectlie° that you did Not, Nor has mr Butler of Thurles anye papers at all that Consarnes° that bussenes that hee knows of, unles you Sent hime anye, you will find by the inclosede what arrears of Rent is dew out of the Countye of Tiperarye and how Litell° Liklie I am to reseve° anye Mony from Portomny, tharfor as unto this Last, I wish you would Send mee word what Course is best to bee takene for the gettinge of it, as allsoe what redrese I am to Expect for that Tyth° of knocktofer which beinge devided as it is, tharis noe persone will Medell with, soe as it remayns unsett and soe is like to bee for this yeare, to my loss of six and twentye pound; mr watts of waterford upon whom I gave an assignment[282] refusses to pay anye thinge; alledginge that you doe know that he has sattisfiede all demands; and would have it to be understoud that hee has payede it to you, and severall othars in your absense dous° alledge [*three lines missing*] I have sent you a Leter [*three words missing*] I not well understandinge what hee menes° by desiringe you to kiepe° his Bond,

---

[280] Two full lines and parts of two other lines are missing on each of three pages due to a tear on the MS.

[281] Miles Corbett had been appointed Chief Baron of the Irish Exchequer in 1655. See Robert Armstrong, "Corbet, Miles," *DIB*.

[282] "Legal transference of a right or property" ("assignment, *n.*," 2, *OED*).

I conseved° best to bee left unto you to answar [/] I am glad to find that Doctor yarner* and Mr Mandeville* are soe Moderate as not to prese mee to pay them thar mony at the presant, and shouldbee likwise much sattisfiede to resone° the oppinione of Counsell Consarninge° that perticular of my haveinge Power to make ~~Leases~~ a Lease of Part of my Estate ~~in~~ for Sartane° yeares in Trust for such usses as was formarlie mentionede by

E:ormonde

Send mee word whethar Sir Hardres waller* has payede his Rent and the Tenants of Arckloe° what did rest dew upon them
The x of July

Letter 77. July 17, [1658?], [Dunmore], the Marchioness of Ormonde to John Burdon (NLI, Ormond Papers, 2484, no. 236, p. 233). Autograph.
For My Sarvant John Burdon [/] thes. [Endorsed]: Her Ladyshipps.

John Burdon

If I could wonder at anye ill fortune that has bine° under the Exsiersie° of soe many, I should at the unsartantye° that I apprehend my selfe in, consarning° the bussenes° of Arckloe,° and consequentlie bee ~~trouble~~ Sensibell of the Prejudis that the Suspentione of what I was to have resevede° from thous° whoe touke it, is Like to bring upon mee, by retardinge the payment I am to make into the Excheker, and the Stayinge you ther unto the hinderanse of my affares heare, but that it is is vane for anye to Expect Justis from thous that has it Not, unles thay° bee Complede unto it by Law, and   *compelled*
tharfor I wish that Corronell Flower* and your Selfe would bringe it unto Some Conclustione on° way or othar, that you might returne; for heare are divers that dous° Expect, and has Sent to have thar° Leases

     The Survayer is gone with Edward Butler* into the County of Tiperary to Survay the lands Ther, from whom I Expect a weklie accompt,°
     Captaine Folia* willnot allow the mony° hee Lent unto Richard Butler to goe in Part of payment of his Rent but thretens daylie to arest hime wherfor ~~and for his delayinge~~ I conseve° it fitt to take out a writ aganst hime, whereby to make hime apiere° at Dublin the Next Terme, if hee bee not an offiser in Pay; if so; you are to gett the Lord Deputies Leave to Sew hime, for I find hee [thinks]   *sue*

to Carrye away his Rent by Rantinge which some of his Naybors I heare has reprovede hime for, somthinge Severlie,

 I perseve° that my Lady willoby* will furnish mee with fiftye Pound ~~which is~~ ^and tharfor^ fitt, Shee have my bond for, untell° furthar Securitye bee givene hir, the which ~~if when~~ if the Payment into the Excheker Canbee ~~otharwise~~ Made without it; I desier° may bee upon the resept tharof transmittede over unto Stivene Smith,* and that an accompt may bee givene mee if it may bee, or Not [/] I would not have you to move for reprisall for Caringroe for it is generalie knowne the one halfe of it to belonge ^formarlie^ unto the Lord of Mongarat ~~and~~ from whous Lady[283] I have Latlie° resevede a request that I would oppoynt° someone, Ethar° to ~~Compound or~~ Treat for the Sayle of hir Joynture or to Sett it for the best advantage, wherfor I could wish that mr Browne* would informe mee ^of the^ Names of the Lands that ~~is grantede~~ Shee has now Possestione of, and I will trye if I Cane gett one to Sett them for hir, if Not I will give hir a timlie accompt that shee may imploye some othar which is all, that in ordar unto hir Sarvis° Canbee performed by

      E:ormonde

I am somthinge doutfull that Non° has takene possestion for My Lady of Mongarate wherfor that wouldbee knowne and whoe the Person is

the 17 of July

Letter 78. July 24, [1658?], [Dunmore], the Marchioness of Ormonde to John Burdon (NLI, Ormond Papers, 2484, no. 235, p. 225).[284] Autograph.

John Burdon

I perseve° that you have pay[ede] five hundreth pound into the Tresurye; and that you and Corronell Flower* has at Length agrede with mr Hughs but upon giveinge tow° hundreth pound Bond that such furthar asshuranse shallbee made unto hime of the Farme that hee has takene of mee within 7 yeares; as his counsell shall advise,

---

[283] Elizabeth Butler, née Simeon (c. 1606–1674), third wife of Edmund Butler, fourth Viscount Mountgarret (c. 1595–1679) whose land was confiscated when he went into royalist exile.

[284] There is some wear to the right margin of each leaf, which occasionally obscures a word at the beginning or end of a line throughout all four pages of the letter.

whoe perhapes beinge Ignorant of the Condistione of my Estate, may requier° beyond what I am capabell to give them, and from this presed[ent] Sir Hary Tichborne* will insist to have the Like; which Consideringe that I have from Nethar of Thes person[s] anye Bonds for performanse of Covenants on [missing] Parts, I Confes I think it very Litell° resone° that I should give anye othar then the demise[285] it Selfe ~~as as unles I give soe to othars~~ ^unto them^ ^yet^ however, sense° you and Corronell Flower has ingadged° your Selfs I will Signe a Deede of indemptnitye wherby to Save you harmles, allthough I doe not think that Hughes[286] ^his^ Maner of deallinge ought to have had [thes] great condesendanses yealded unto, and if [I] belevede Captane Hassells* to have bine° Chiflie [in] the Least Ecqualie intrestede, I should have bine very unwillinge to ^have^ made anye bargine with that othar Persone whoe Caryede himselfe soe unworthilye, and truly I doe very much resent Sir Hary Tichborns Not ansawringe of my Leter, ~~nor~~ which noe ways Sorts with that Sivlitye that my respect unto hime might have givene mee Cause to Expect, but I see the humors of pepell° are apt to Change with the Times, and thay° [whoe] are under misfortuns are heald fittest to bee injurede and Neglectede, which it should sime° [is] Like to ^bee^ my ~~fortune~~ ^Fate^ on all hands; I heare that [the] Tenant of Balynihinely is upon partinge with his Bargine for tow hundreth pound, without makinge mee the Profier of it, as hee conseves° hee may doe and Soe dous° othars understand thar° are waranted ~~to give~~ ^(to by thar agrement) provided^ thay resarve unto them selfes but on° yeare of the one and twentye; Soe as my thinks° thar shouldbee Some Clause of greater Limetatione as to that perticular [missing] the Decree that you tell mee mrs Hindshaw[287] [has gottene] of the Tyths,° I think it ought Not to hinder your takinge out a Lease of that of knocktofer Sense I doe beleve that it was only Mentionede in hir Deede by mistake, and however cannot [do] good to hir in Law aganst mee; sense ~~it was~~ the Securitye made unto hir did presede ^my^ Mariage and consequentlie ~~it~~ was not in my Lords power to give at that Time; however it may not bee a Miss for you to Speake with the gentellwoman about it, whoe unles shee bee Less sivell° ^and Just^ then shee ought to bee; willnot I supose give mee anye disturbanse in what I doe posses; I send you hearinclosede [missing] I resevede° from Edward Butler,* wherin you will find [missing] hee Expects to reseve° the twentye Pound dew° for the rent of Dery

---

[285] "Conveyance or transfer of an estate by will or lease" ("demise, *n.*," 1a, *OED*).
[286] Unidentified.
[287] Unidentified.

Illand; soe as you Nide° not [*missing*] Doctor Gorge²⁸⁸ anye furthar about it ~~but know~~ I am much Injurede by the Last Survays that has bine takene in the Countye of Tipperarye and the Cuttinge down of my woods by some of the offisiers° whom it is in vane to questione untell° I have My Lord Deputys Leave, which I shall suspend the desier° of; untell such time as you returne the which [as] Soune° as you have Ended your bussens in [that and] that with Sir Henry Tichborne ~~and m~~ I wish [it] bee as spidie° as you Cane make it for Severall resons, I am well pleasede that you have transmitted the fiftye Pound over unto Stivene Smith* that you resevede from My Lady willoby,* to whom you are to Confer, and see what Securitye will Sattisfie hir for it, My Eldest Sone²⁸⁹ is in great want of Mony,° and I in noe small troubell that I Cannot releve hime, which I have no possibilitye of doeinge unles Sir Hary Tichborne [shall] bee perswaded by Corronell Flower to pay it upon this ocatione° without which I shouldnot have [dem]anded it, tharfor I pray trye bouth° your Intrests ^[with h]ime^ [and] See what may bee done, and Send the Boxes hethar° that came out of England as soune as you Cane wherin tharis tow small Gillt Picture Frames 2 Plane handcharers,²⁹⁰ and Coufs, and a Bundell of Crewells²⁹¹ which you will find derectede° unto

cuffs

The 24 of July   E: ormonde

I hope you doe not Convay or reseve anye Leters under my Cover [To or] from England of anye bodys that [are no]t this time in my Familie; if [you] [d]oe; thar may fall greter inconvenies by it then [you] are awar of for some resons that I shall hearafter tell you

inconveniences

---

²⁸⁸ Unidentified.
²⁸⁹ Thomas, Lord Ossory, who was living in the Hague.
²⁹⁰ Handkerchiefs ("handkercher, *n.*," *OED*).
²⁹¹ "A thin worsted yarn, (according to Bailey) of two threads, used for tapestry and embroidery; also formerly for making fringes, laces, vestments, hosiery, etc." ("crewel, *n.*1," 1, *OED*).

Letter 79. July 31, [1658?], [Dunmore], the Marchioness of Ormonde to John Burdon (NLI, Ormond Papers, 2484, no. 238, p. 247).[292] Autograph.

For John Burdon thes.

John Burdon

upon [*missing*] [L]ast, the Lord Deputye Came unto killkenye, and upon Thursday in the afternoun hee was pleasede to make a visset° hethar,° and was bouth° Sivell,° ~~in h~~ and very frindlie in his expretions° bouth To ^my selfe^ and of mee, as I understand when I was not presant, I am by noe menes° sattisfiede with the Strictnes of mr Hughs his dealinge that should urge mee to acknowlege a Fine to make good his Lease, which is never done without the Lessie doe give a Fine in hand which hee did not, but the advanse of a hundreth pound ^of the Rent^ for a few months, but however his mony° beinge resevede,° upon soe urgent an ocatione° as to paye into the Tresurye it must, if hee will insist upon it bee done accordinglie, only this I desier,° that the Covenants of his Lease may bee strict as to that of payinge his Rent, Buildinge within a Sartane° Time ^and^ not [*illegible*][293] it without makinge the first tender of it to mee, and Next, that what I have condesended unto consarninge° the giveige Sir Hary Tichborne* power to make uss° of such of the wood as is allredie Fallene and Lies on the grow[nd] [*one line missing*] formarlie Exsepted [*four words missing*] a warant by it Selfe for mee to [*three words missing*] hime Soe to doe [*two words missing*] Captane Evans [*two words missing*] and kiepe° from mee the Tyths° of Baytas [*two words missing*] ever belonginge unto that of knocktofer soe as if that couldbee insertede by Name in the Lease ^from the State^ It would prevent a Sute° that otharwise must fall betwixt uss, I pray doe all you Cane to gett that hundreth Pound, or to Leave order that it may bee resevede from Mr Foxteth,[294] for my Sons presant wants, is very afflictinge unto

lessee

giving

E:ormonde

The Last of July

If my busses at Dublin were dispacht your Comminge a way wouldbee very Nesesarye bouth for my ocations° and your owne, I

business

---

[292] Parts of one line of text is missing on the recto side and five on the verso side due to a tear at the top of the MS.
[293] It looks like "alli . . . ge" with the missing letters overwritten or deleted.
[294] Unidentified.

pray send mee such a bond redie drawne as may bee fitt for mee to Signe for the fiftye pound that I resevede from My Lady willoby,* and bringe downe with you the bundell of [olde] writings that [*five words missing*] and left in the Tronke of papers that stoud° in my Chamber at Dublin I beinge like to have some uss° of them heare

Letter 80. August 9, [1658?], Dunmore, the Marchioness of Ormonde to John Burdon (NLI, Ormond Papers, 2484, no. 219, p. 99).[295] Autograph.
For My Sarvant John Burdon [/] Thes.

John Burdon

[I res]evede intematio[ne]° from a frind at Dublin, that a [propositi] one were then in hand to bringe in questione my whole Tytell° unto Arckloe;° upon the accompt° of its beinge My Lords, and Not Mine; intendinge to grownd° the Sute° ~~up~~ aganst mee upon some Antiant° Entayle which cannot bee done, but by overthrowinge the adward° which ~~be~~ haveinge bine° admittede as the Mayne° Poynt upon which my Clame° was grownded,° and My Decree grantede in the Court of Clames, I cannot but beleve, that Ethar° tharwas a mistake in the persone whoe informede mee, or some intentione to find out this, for a way to take away the rest of my inheritanse ~~allsoe~~ from mee; and that which at this distanse dous° give mee the greater apprehentions that Some prejudise is intended mee; and as I am tould; Chiflie Contrivede by the Litell° wrech my Tenant that is Corronell Flowers* Contreman; is; your not comminge ^hethar^ as you did intend upon Satterday Last, has made mee to dispache this berar° purposlie to bee Sattisfiede in this perticular, as allsoe, whethar Arckloe bee one of the Five Maners that by a spetiall° Deede was Settlede by my Grandfathar[296] upon his Hiers, which beinge in ~~the~~ Generall; did Intytell° my Mothar, as unto Soe much; admittinge that Noe adward had bine; ~~Next~~ but if upon the Right of such as are pretended freeholders, backt by such injust Persons as themselfs; I am like to bee troubled [/] [*one line missing*] informatione of what Past aganst [the Earle of or]monds[297] Time wherof I am perswaded that mr Browns* unkell° that Lives Neare Dublin Cane give Some accompt; If you have resevede° the hundreth Pound from Sir Henry Tichborne* the gettinge of which I doutnot but you doe make your

wretch
countryman

---

[295] Part of one line of text is missing due to damage to the MS.
[296] Thomas Butler, tenth Earl of Ormonde.
[297] JO's grandfather, Walter Butler, eleventh Earl of Ormonde.

bussenes° I desier° that threscore pound of it may bee immediatlie
Sent over for unto Stivene Smith;* and the othar fortye sent hethar°
unto mee; by the first returne of the Carryer, for I stand ingadged°
unto some workmen whoe are Now to bee discharged thay° haveinge
done thar° Tasks; and I not provided of Mony° Nor Cannot bee soe
Sudaynlie° anye othar way ^to pay Them^ tharfor if you Come not
your Selfe I pray send mee word what I may or may not depend upon
tuchinge° this perticuler, as allsoe what Course you have takene with
the Tenants of Arckloe and whethar the Rent of killsallagh bee as yet
payede or Not that it may bee made knowne unto

Dunmore the 9 of Agust   E:ormonde

**Letter 81. [1658?], [Dunmore], the Marchioness of Ormonde
to John Burdon** (NLI, Ormond Papers, 2484, no. 246, p. 301).
Autograph.
For My Sarvant John Burdon [/] thes. [Endorsed]: her Ladyshipps
concerning Powerstowne.

John Burdon

as I remember I gave you some derectione° consarninge° the Farme of
Powerstowne, the which, I did promise unto the ould Lady Gallmoy
and hir Sone the berar° hearof,²⁹⁸ as to whom you with whom you
had best to Treate and when you find upon what termes hee desiers°
it, and ^in^ what hee way I may doe hime a Curtisie,° without
drawinge daynger upon hime, or inconveniensie upon my Selfe,
that you come preparede to give mee an accompt,° and some advise
in that perticuler, and the mene° time, that you desier his patianse,°
from concludinge anye thinge with hime this day, in regard of the
Mulltiplistye of bussenes° that at the presant falls upon Corronell
Flower* and your Selfe, untell° tomorogh, and then you will proside°
accordinge to such instroctions as you Shall reseve° from

EO

---

²⁹⁸ Presumably, Anne Butler, widow of Sir Edward Butler, first Viscount Galmoye,
who had died in 1653, and her son. EO shared a grandfather with Viscount Galmoye,
although his was an illegitimate line.

Letter 82. August 21, 1658, [Dunmore], the Marchioness of Ormonde ("JH") to the Marquess of Ormonde ("Mr Benss") (Bodl., Carte Papers, 213, fols. 103–104).²⁹⁹ Autograph.
for Mr Benss [/] thes. [Endorsed]: My Wife 31/21 August Received 24/14 November 1658.

sir

It has bine° want of an ~~am~~ oppertunity and not of care, to sattisfie you, that yours of the 10 and 11 of May beinge the last that I reseved° from you are come unto my hands as allsoe the coppie of the olde Bonde, that I sent unto you for a good while sense;° the which beinge as it is attestede willbee suffisent as I am tolde to justifie the dept,° soe as you Nide° not anye new obligatione—
   I heare that mr Ashforde³⁰⁰ is now plasede much unto his owne sattisfactione and his unkell° Astins³⁰¹ content, soe as in that respect I shallnot argue aganst what hee has done, though as to the prejudis that a third pr person³⁰² is Like to reseve° tharby, somthing might bee sayede,° as allsoe, against that yonge Mans vissitinge mistris Allepe,³⁰³ which if well considered had in prudense bine beter° forborne, knowinge how bad a constroctione hir Grandmother Baytes³⁰⁴ will make of it, This gentellwoman mistris Allepe havinge writ latlie° unto hir Aunt Damport,³⁰⁵ that shee might have Leave to goe to sarvis,° in hopes to beter hir fortunes that way, without beinge chargebell unto hir frinds,³⁰⁶ which Thay,° not knowing but

---

 ²⁹⁹ In the letters to her husband from this period, EO refers to her family and close friends through a range of aliases that are also adopted by her husband in his letters to her. With the same people identified by different names within and between letters, and the deliberate obscuring of their gender (her eldest son is occasionally referred to as "her," for example), identities are often difficult to pin down securely, and are sometimes impossible to identify altogether.
 ³⁰⁰ Their middle son, Richard? JO had decided to remove Richard from his studies in Paris so that he could be closer to him in the exiled court. EO was deeply unhappy with a move that she feared might put her settlement at risk, and in this letter she criticizes her husband's decision to remove Richard ("mr Ashforde") from Paris, and for facilitating a meeting between him and his elder brother, Thomas, Lord Ossory ("mistris Allepe"). She also rebukes her husband for apparently encouraging her eldest son's desires to go into military service.
 ³⁰¹ JO?
 ³⁰² EO?
 ³⁰³ Ossory?
 ³⁰⁴ Perhaps Cromwell or the Commonwealth authorities?
 ³⁰⁵ EO?
 ³⁰⁶ EO.

that hir kinsman mr Turner³⁰⁷ might have incoridgede° and givene
his approbatione To; did desier° mee to indevour° [to] know the truth
tharof; which I not beinge abbell° to comp[as] unles by your Menes,°
I shall intreate you to give mee the best ~~accompt~~ ^informatione^
you cane tuchinge° this perticuler, that the Girls Frinds, may not
troubell themselfs in vane, to presarve fo[r] hir, what perhapes is not
regarded by hir ^selfe^ nor other[s]³⁰⁸ but in such a cayse,° that Thay
may bee frelie and clearlie dealt withall, and mistris Dallison,³⁰⁹ Left
at Liberty to dispose of that small Livinge that shee now posseses,
by takinge for it a some° of mony° to pay hir depts, and if anye thing
remayns to let it bee put out into good hands for hir tow° yonger
childrens portions Eliz and Mary,³¹⁰ which if done; I find shee
would retyre hir selfe, and sojorne with some frind, without beinge
burdensome to such of hir relations, as allthough perhapes wouldbee
willinge, yet are not abbell to releve hir; I am sorye I cannot sarve
the gentellwoman you writ to mee about,³¹¹ in what shee desiers soe
sudanlie° as I have a will to doe, by resone° of the distanse that I am
at from where [h]ir Litell° Boy³¹² is Nurst, besids the bad season that
it is Now with us for soe yong a Child to Travell, but when I goe
next into thous° parts where hee is; as it is not improvabell° but my
troubells will forse° mee ~~Eare~~ Err Long, I will then use my indevors°
tharin, and send you [a] beter accompt° of that perticuler, then
canbee givene at presant by

    your fathful frind
     and Sarvant

the 21 of Agust   JH

your old acquantanse mr Brackley³¹³ willbee shortlie at London whoe
for his owne conveniensie and with the consent of his Frinds heare,
~~hee~~ intends with his wife to reside, whoe willbee Carfull in anye of
your consarns° if you have [but] anye time ocatione° to imploye hime,

---

³⁰⁷ JO?
³⁰⁸ Ossory's inheritance, which was dependent on his mother's settlement.
³⁰⁹ EO herself.
³¹⁰ EO's two daughters, Elizabeth and Mary, were eighteen and twelve, respectively.
³¹¹ This may refer to the young son of Susanna and George Lane, who married in 1655. Susanna was the daughter of Edward Nicholas, with whom EO had become friends during her exile in Caen.
³¹² Perhaps a reference to EO's youngest son, John?
³¹³ Unidentified.

whom mr Duton[314] will know where to Find I should bee glad to know how your best Frind[315] dous°

Letter 83. [October 1658], [Dunmore], the Marchioness of Ormonde to the Earl of Ossory (Bodl., Carte Papers, 213, fol. 449).[316] Autograph.
For the lord of ossorye [/] thes. [Endorsed]: My Wife to my Son without date.

Sone

I am sorrye that I should find Cause to differ in oppinione from othar of your Frinds, as to the Mach° proposede for you, and wherto I perseve° you have your selfe an inclinatione; but knowinge somthinge more of the Condistione of the Fortune that must give you Subsistanse, and the incombranses° that are upon it, then perhapes thous° at a distance or your selfe ~~can do [illegible]~~[317] ^Cane doe^; shall first represent the Same to you, and then make Them, and your selfe the Judges, whethar the Portione mentionede, admittinge it were to bee at your Parants dispose as by the Laws of that Contrye it should sime° it is not, could[b]ee Suffisent to disingadge° the Morgadges° that are upon it, beinge noe Less then twentye Thowsand Pound befor, and sense° the warr, besides the yearlie Rent of Thirtine hundreth and fifftye pound to be payede out of it unto the State, ^as allsoe^ ~~and~~ depts° ~~besides~~ contractede for some years Mantenanse and expense of Recovringe it; and your tow° Sisters as yet unprovided for; all which considerede, will I hope prevent impossibilities from beinge expectede, or impossede° upon mee, of allowinge a Considerabell mantenanse, and Settlinge a Joynture upon the Lady, when the Portione cannot inabell° mee to doe it, unless it were ~~more considerabell~~ ^greater^ then it is, which togethar with a Nothar° exseptione; which I shall forbeare to Mentione, knowinge it willbee Gesst° at by you;[318] I conseve° in Justise you cannot expect my Consent, when the giveinge it to your disadvantage wouldbee to make mee not soe to you; and the rest of your Brothers

differ

---

[314] Unidentified.
[315] Charles II, perhaps?
[316] The letter is undated but must have been written no later than October or early November because Page's letter written to JO upon its receipt is dated November 8 and mentions having received EO's letter the day before.
[317] One or two canceled words are illegible.
[318] Presumably this refers to the illegitimacy of Aemilia van Nassau's father.

and Sisters, over whous Fortunes your well, or ill dispossinge of your selfe will have influanse, and tharfor I shall uss° noe othar [Cons] then ^thes^ Resones° to perswade you not to ingadge your Selfe this way, that you propose, and if that willnot prevayle, you must then stand or falle by that Fortune that you Ellect for your Selfe, sense it is that I find noe Resone to give my approbatione To, but shall my indevours° to Supplye you, soe Longe as you remayne a Singell Man, and rathar, if you were in anye othar Plase, then where you are,[319] I haveing had I allow it ^I^ think, as a presage of some misfortune, allways an unwillingnes of your goeing thethar,° as by severall of my Leters unto mr P unto [sic] your Selfe and Mr Page* may apiere,° allthough I doe not accompt° it Soe, out of anye disvallew[320] or exseptione I have unto the persone of the Lady; but that you should have ingadgede your selfe soe farr in your affectione, as I perseve that you have done; befor you had knowne whethar this Mache couldbee Suttinge with your Fortune or Not, which in prudense unto your *suiting* Selfe, and Jusstis unto your Familie, ought to have Governede you, *justice* beyond that of your Pastione,° and that it may yet, is the prayer, and hope of

                your affectionat Mothar

                    E:ormonde

Letter 84. November 21, [1658?], [Dunmore], the Marchioness of Ormonde to John Burdon (NLI, Ormond Papers, 2484, no. 224, p. 137).[321] Autograph.

John Burdon

I Expectede your [*missing*][322] the Next day aftar you went from hense [which] relyinge upon; made mee kiepe° your letars intend[ede] for to Dublin, and for England soe as I am Now drivene to Send them by a [hirede] Mesenger whoe I much feare willbee Stopt ^goeinge on Sonday^ and besides, have kept some Gentellmen in delay of resevinge° answars from mee untell° Monday, suposinge you would [have] bine° hear befor that time that ^whom^ it may prove of all Consequense unto mee, to disapoynt anye longer, as mr Corbett*

---

    [319] The Hague.
    [320] "Depreciation, disparagement" ("disvalue, *n.*," 1, *OED*).
    [321] There is wear and tear to the MS, particularly in the top right-hand corner of the leaf, which has resulted in the loss of some text.
    [322] Someone's "arrival"?

whoe broght a longe with hime mr Butler³²³ of Balynihinely; and
othars, as allsoe a Sarvant of Doctor Fenells;* whous Cattell is
Seasede° upon by Sir Renalds* his Steward and hee Sends to mee
to know what he shall doe, which I suspended the giveinge anye
derections° in, as makinge accompt° you would have bine heare this
day, tell° his importunitye made mee bid [*two lines missing*]³²⁴ of
derections I couldnot but give Messenger ^hee^ urginge that the
Cattell wouldbee Starvede unles some spidie° Course were takene
soe as only your Staye that bee of great Nesesitye, I desier° that your
repaire hethar° may bee Spidie unto

the 21 of No   E:ormonde

**Letter 85. November 26, 1658, [Dunmore], the Marchioness
of Ormonde ("JH") to the Marquess of Ormonde ("Mr James
Johnson")** (Bodl., Carte Papers, 213, fols. 168–169). Autograph.
For mr James Johnson [/] thes. [Endorsed]: My Wife 26 November
1658 Received 10 January 1659.

Sir

your tow° leters of the 11 of oct are both come unto my hands with
a copie of the Diede, the former you sent beinge defective, was   *deed*
tharfor not thoght fitt to bee prodused in Court, and whether this
second may bee of forse;° not beinge an origenall, your lawyers must
determine, with whom I shall the next terme advise consarninge°
it; and for also beinge in some wonder that you have not heard
from mee in many weekes, is an omistione, that I hope you will   *omission*
excuse, when you shall have considerede what a frind I have lost of
my unkell° Badlie,³²⁵ that ocationed° my sielense° for some Time,
which I shall now indevour° to repare, by writinge oftener, sense° it
is a troubell, I find you willinge to admitt of; and as to your othar
comands, I shall give you the [s]ame clear accompt° tharof, as in all
things ellse [t]hat you please to injoyne° mee, by acquantinge you
that accordinge your desiers,° I showede your frind the proposals of a
mach° for hir elldest sone; and first, [r]epresented the extractione of
the person, hir fortune [a]nd the condistione how it stoud,° as I did
Likwise [t]he vertew° and Beuty of the yonge gentellwoman [a]nd the
pastion that hir sone had for hir, all which, beinge then Left unto hir

---

³²³ EO's tenant.
³²⁴ Some words that are discernible are "I doe not know."
³²⁵ Unidentified.

to Consider [of], I then prest° as farr as was fitt for mee to know hir
sense tharupon, which in brife° was this; that [a]s to the first, shee
consevde Just cause of exseptione as to the desent of the Ladys father,
which however not perhapes the less estimede in a Nother° contrye,
would make it of reproch heare;[326] and secondl[ie] as to the fortune,
which hee ^shee^ hears at the most is bu[t] tene Thowsand pound
of which nethar the husban[d] nor his parents canbee the beter°
more then wha[t] the intrest of soe much cane bringe, shee conseves°
very inconsiderable, to the freeinge of an estate Morg morgedged
for noe Les befor and sense the warr th[en] twentye Thowsand
Pound, besids depts° contracted for some years mantenanse, and the
expense of recovring[e] it by Sute,° and the yearlie rent with which
it stand[s] Charged, besides tow° daughters, yet unprovided for [/]
which considered, as shee hopes it willbee seriouslie by hir sone, and
shuch[327] of his frinds as are ther, wil[l] shee hopes give a Stope° unto
his Rueninge° of his [fortune] familie, to please his fancye, sense
himselfe kno[wes] that beter Maches°[328] were offerede hime befor hee
went to travell, and shee belevefs not without Some resone° may still   *believes*

---

[326] Aemilia's father was the illegitimate son of Maurice of Nassau, Prince of Orange.

[327] This is a spelling ("shuch" for "such") also employed by JO (see, for example, Bodl., Carte Papers, 213, fol. 246), which illustrates the way EO's orthography was shaped by the letters she received from her husband and other regular correspondents.

[328] One prospective match was a daughter of Thomas Wriothesley, fourth Earl of Southampton, of whom Ossory writes "whoes alliance I should more covet then any persons in England if I could like the young woman who I have seen often, or if I were not so absolutely given over to this person as it is impossible for me ever to love any other, but this being, I thinke it were an unworthines in me to marry any deserving person upon score of a fortune which will not prevent boath of us being miserable if there be not a mutuale kindenes" (March 3, 1658/9, The Hague, the Earl of Ossory to the Marquess of Ormonde, Bodl., Carte Papers, 213, fols. 216–217). Ossory conveniently forgot the Southampton match in an earlier letter to his father in which he swore:

> as to the matches offered me I assure you my mother told me of all them, the most considerable was Mr Fretswels [John Frescheville, later first Baron Frescheville (1607–1682)] daughter who has eighteen hundred pounds a yeare, but that he would not settell upon her but would engage some of it for eight thousand pounds ready mony and if he died without children would leave her the . . . but besids this there was ^is^ out of it on if not tow daughters to be provided for another was sir walter Pys [Sir Walter Pye (1610–1659)] daughter who he sayd he would by disinheriting of his son make her worth more then twenty thousand pounds but in that he over shot himself, however besids if that were I should never dispose of my self that way for a reason I would give you if I could speake to you, which I am sure would make you be of my opinion as my mother also is, other things have bin endeavoured by her but none came neare any thing, people boath fearing our alliance, and beleeving irish fortunes littell considerable" (January 17, 1658/9, The

bee had, more Sutabell° in respect of the advantages of thar° allianse, then what th[is] stranger cane bringe, soe as upon the whole Matt[er] I find shee dous° not for thes resons aprove of t[he] propsistione, which ~~and~~ I thought it befitted mee to tell you, and if I have relatede in this, what may bee ethar° displeasinge unto your selfe, or the yong gentellman; I bege your pardon for it, the which I am incoridged° to hope you will grant, when to a person that has actede noe furthar then what your owne comands has warented mee to; in fathfullye returninge an accompt of what I was desired, as to the best of my understandinge I have now don,° and shall with the same in integritye acquitt my selfe, on all ocations° else, of your consernes° as may answer, the profestione of my beinge

        sir

                your fathfull humbell sarvant

the 26 of No   JH

Letter 86. January 19, 1658/9, [Dunmore], the Marchioness of Ormonde ("JH") to the Marquess of Ormonde (Bodl., Carte Papers, 213, fols. 202–203).[329] Autograph.
[Endorsed]: My Wife 19 January Old Style 1658 Received 10 March New Style 1659.

sir

I perseve° that a Leter of mine sent you in agust last, came not unto your handes untell° November Following [s]ense when I had a recompense for that ill fortune, by [r]esevinge tow° from you, one of the 7 of No, the other of the 27 of the same, wherin you have givene your selfe [g]reater troubell to satisfie mee as to the Course that my

---

Hague, the Earl of Ossory to the Marquess of Ormonde, Bodl., Carte Papers, 213, fols. 200–201).
Ossory's rejection of each of the potential matches suggests that JO took seriously his wife's objections and weighed up other options.

[329] This is EO's response to JO's letter of November 2, which was itself a rejoinder to hers of August 21, which had been delayed for some months. JO's letter had provided a lengthy justification of his actions with regards to their elder sons in which he defended himself against the accusation that "in the disposition of both their Neeces [their sons] hee had not enough considered his [EO's] satisfaction or security" (November 2, 1658, the Marquess of Ormonde to the Marchioness of Ormonde, Bodl., Carte Papers, 213, fols. 166–167).

[y]ongest Nephue[330] has taken then I expectede, sense° what [p]leases you, and himselfe, shall find from mee Noe [c]ontradictione; haveinge onse° representede as I did, what I thought did become mee to doe; and soe I have Latlie° [c]onsarninge a Nother° person allsoe,[331] that was onse comitted [to] my charge by his Parants, whoe I perseve is as farr ingadged° in his affectione, as the fortune that hee [i]s Heir To, is with dept,° and how [illegible][332] this [l]ast, will sort with the portion that is spokene of, [t]he accompt° that I, and othars the Trusties° has now ~~sen~~ sent of the perticulers of what it yealds at presant [a]nd may bee expected for the future will best show; [w]hich for your satisfaction, is heare transmitede to [y]ou, and had bine° souner,° but that wee wanted the conveniensie of a mesenger to send it by; and one to reduse the same into forme, whoe upon othar ocations° was for some time absent, untell very Latlie; unto which accompt, is Likwise added, a seduell° of the Partys parents depts; contracted sense the times of thar° Nesesitye, with desier° from uss, whoe are Left oversiers by his Mother of the estate; that such regard may bee had, unto the payment tharof, that in cayse° it shallbee thoght fitt that this mach° proposed should goe on, that care may bee had in the first plase to see them discharged; where[by] the Frinds ingadged, may not suffier,° is what wee cons[eve] and doe hope, willnot bee louked° upon unresonable but Just in uss to inssist upon; sense by what was borrowede, is this estate recovrede and the Chilldren bine mantayned and suported, all which, beinge considerede and the tow° daughters as yet unprovided for; it is hoped that ^by ~~by~~^ your care of the yonge Gentellman, and well wishes unto his Familie, that nothinge shallbee concluded unto the disadvantage tharof, ~~upon~~ ^upon^ provabilities° only of good, which are but unsartane° things, and cannot when thay° fall out contrarye as to oftene thay doe; [best] abbell to recompense a Lastinge ill, espetialie° in a bussenes° wherin it is not the fortune of a singell person, distroyed tharby, but of a whole posteritye, which I think is a Mater° to° Serious to bee arguede with the yonge Man himself at this distanse, espetialie when his pastion ^perhapes^ for the Lady Caryes hime beyond thous° considerations, and Resons that ought prinsipalie to governe, when in a bussenes upon which depends the hapenes° or   *happiness* Missery of his life which First; allthough not to bee ^alltogether^ plasede in wealth or a fortune; yet not usstialie° Lastinge, where a Competensie is wanted unto the quality of the persons and tharfor

---

[330] Richard, and the decision to remove him from his studies in Paris.
[331] Ossory and his proposed marriage with Aemilia van Nassau.
[332] Approximately four canceled words are illegible.

I conseved° it more nesesarye to make this adrese to you, whoe might advise and acquant hime, with what is now sent, then to himselfe, as belevinge allsoe, that you willbee noe les carfull to presarve the papers, that consarnes° hime, then I have bine fathfull in statinge things rightlie that are contayned tharin, that in Cayse thar shouldbee noe ocatione° to make uss° of them, then ~~Ether~~ to burne; or secure Them soe as thay may not by acsident fall into other hands, ~~ether now or hearafter,~~ which may prove very prejudistiall unto the persons consarned,° The berar° is chosen rather for his integritie then knowlege of the estate, the other tow, that are more soe, not beinge to bee sparede without great inconveniens at this Time, will I hope satisfie you of my indevour° to make you Soe, wherin my small Sarvises,° may contribute towards it, as beinge very fathfulllye [*sic*]

      sir

      your fathfull frind and Sarvant

the 19 of Jan   JH

I must not forget to tell you ~~that yo~~ of the kindnes of mr Drakes old Mistris,[333] that offered hir Daughter to this yong Man, and to setell upon hir tow and twentye hundreth a yeare ^~~at hir parents desease~~^ upon which estate; tharis woods, and a fine house, wich° is to come to hir after the parents desease, that offered besides 5 hundreth a year, for thar presant Mantenense ~~which~~ ^but^ was not acsepted by resone° thar was not wherwith at presant to pay depts and provide for his Sisters portions, The Bond you Latlie sent mee is Come unto my handes

Letter 87. May 19, 1659, [Dunmore], the Marchioness of Ormonde ("JH") to the Marquess of Ormonde (Bodl., Carte Papers, 213, fols. 244–245). Autograph. See Figure 4.
[Endorsed]: My Wife 19 May Received June 1659.

sir

your Leter of the 11 of march in answer unto one of mine of the 19 of January I did immediatlie returne you an accompt° that I had reseved,° and recommended it unto mr Dutton[334] to bee sent unto you, which I hope is by this time come unto your hands, and will sattisfie you that I am soe, with your prosidinge° in the conserne° of

---

[333] Perhaps Sir Walter Pye (1610–1659)?
[334] Unidentified.

my kinsman had you not afforded mee anye further accompt as you have Latlie° done by a nother° of yours of the 30 of March, wherby I perseve° that you have imployed mr Gorge Billson[335] to treat one my cousen[336] his behalfe, with the parents of the Gentellwoman that I perseve hee has still great pastione° for, with instroctions to conclude the bussenes° for his and his families advantage or Else to breake it ofe° the Mach,° which beinge put into the hands of soe fathfull a person to manage as hee is, cannot but bee abundantlie sattisfactory unto mee and the rest of his Frinds, whoe will arrogate[337] nothinge unto themselfs, in the disposinge of the Portion, then what shall reseve° your approbatione and consent, that has bine° made acquanted with the condistione of the Estate how it stands, in all the Parts thereof, and the perticuler ingadgments° contracted for the recovry of it, soe as I have nothinge more to adde, but to expect to heare from you, what willbee the event of what is now proposed for hime, and wherto I find hee has soe great inclinations as if Crost,° will ocatione° hime noe smale disturbanse, as the concludinge it unles upon good termes will his Ruene° ^wherfor^ ~~soe as~~ all I cane doe at the presant is to pray for hime, and to vindecate my sister Dampart,[338] whom you doe blame, for not beinge soe kind as to answer your Leters which gives you, as you say ocatione to beleve, that shee ether aprehendes daynger from the corespondanse, or is indiferant whether it continow° or Not, to which, shee beinge not at this time soe well in hir health as to write hir selfe by reson of a Cough that has troubled hir of Late, and dous° Still has desired mee to returne you this answar, that as shee never as yet did declyne the owninge and payinge of a respect ~~where~~ and obligation where it was soe much dew,° soe is it as Litell° possibell that the discharginge of such, canbee to hir a thinge indiferant, and therfor dous hope, that noe acsident that may have Caused the Loos° or interseptione of hir leters, may meete with anye such misconstroctione from you; I doe beleve as you doe, that if Mistris Beckets eldest Daughter[339] had

---

[335] JO's brother-in-law, George Hamilton. Hamilton had been chosen to negotiate the terms of Ossory's marriage along with JO's secretary, George Lane; they were sent to The Hague in May 1659. For a detailed discussion of the marriage negotiations, see O'Keeffe, 58–63.

[336] Ossory.

[337] "To claim and assume as a right that to which one is not entitled; to lay claim to and appropriate (a privilege, advantage, etc.) without just reason or through self-conceit, insolence, or haughtiness" ("arrogate, v.," 2, *OED*).

[338] EO herself.

[339] Her daughter, Elizabeth.

but a competent portione that mr Anetts Frinds Sone³⁴⁰ would bee
inclyned to make adresses Ther and espetialie° if hee saw hir; but
Liveinge where shee dous cannot but Loose hir manye oppertunities
of preferment, which hir parents povertye and depts,° kiepinge°
them in the Contrye is the ocatione of,³⁴¹ the rest beinge under some
^dis^advantage allsoe by the want of such healpe as is Nesesarye
for ther educatione though ther Mother ^(takes care of them and)^
mantanes° them desentlie,° whoe are all very well Naturede Children,
I did propose in my former Leter that if the Portion requirede with
the gentellwoman that my kinsman dous make adresses unto cannot
bee had upon beter° termes then the ingadgment of soe much of the
Estate as may secure to hir the prinsepall; then to take it; allowinge
the Intrest therof to goe for the mantenanse of the yonge Coupell
which will yeald greater advantage to bee soe disposede of where
8 or tene in the hundreth is givene then where it is as I am tould a
third part Less, but this is only offerede unto your consideratione
in Cayse° of the worst and not to bee ~~made uss of~~ ^proposede^
otherwise; ~~or proposed~~ It wouldbee Nesesarye that mr Archer³⁴²
would change his hand, it beinge as you know a very illegiabell one, I
was upon Sendinge mr Gorges³⁴³ only Sone by a frind of mine whoe
I was confident would have had care of the Child, but thes changes
happeninge, made them to alter ther resolutione of goeinge, Soe as I
knownot as yet of anye other oppertunitye at this Time, howsomever
noe Care in mee shallbee wantinge therin, nor indevours° by all
menes° possibell to expres my selfe

   sir

     your fathfull frind and Sarvant

       JH

I heare nothinge as yet whether mr Billson³⁴⁴ has concluded or broke
ofe the Mach for my kinsman, nor yet what becomes of old Sam

---

³⁴⁰ Philip Stanhope, second Earl of Chesterfield.
³⁴¹ Although Chesterfield had not yet met Elizabeth, according to Daniel O'Neill he was more "satisfied" with her "than any match he or his friends had thought of" (May 16, 1659, Daniel O'Neill to the Marquess of Ormonde, Bodl., Carte Papers, 213, fol. 242). Negotiations could not proceed, however, until the couple met.
³⁴² Unidentified.
³⁴³ Lord John?
³⁴⁴ George Hamilton.

Howard³⁴⁵ that promist mee a visset° the Last yeare, but was never to this day soe good as his word, nor you nether, yet I am inclynede to soe much Charitye for you Bouth,° as to beleve it has not bine your faults but hindered by some Lawfull ocatione

The 19 May

Letter 88. August 1, 1659, Dunmore, the Marchioness of Ormonde to George Hamilton ('James Offaly') (Bodl., Carte Papers, 30, fol. 470).³⁴⁶ Autograph.
For my respectede Cousen Mr James offlye [/] thes at the Hage.
[Endorsed]: My Wifes 1 August Received 26 December 1659.

Cousen

Sense you were pleasede to take the troubell upon you'of treatinge with Mounsiuer Beverward on the behalfe of my Sone, wherby to know what portione hee would give with his Daughter, and upon what Termes the same shallbee advanst, I could doe noe Less haveinge resevede° a proposall from hime, by mr Page;* then give you an accompt° therof, which as unto evrye perticuler is consented unto by mee; as you will find by the paper that is returnede in answar tharunto; which this berar° is desirede by mee to Show unto you, soe as it will appiere° that I have not offerede less but rather more, I feare then ~~willbee~~ ^Can bee made^ good; the Causualtye of the Times considerede, and the incombranses° of depts° that lies upon the Estate at presant, out of which, I pay ~~yearlie~~ five hundreth and fifftye Pound ^Intrest^ yearlie, besides the Stats° Rent of Thirtine hundreth and fiftye more; unto which twelfe hundreth being added for my ~~Sons~~ ^Sons^ Mantenanse when Mariede; tharwill remayne but a very inconsiderabell proportione for mee to Live upon, and mantane° the rest of my Familie, besides the unsartantye° of what willbee raysede° out of the whole; by resone° of the povertye of the pepell° and the Taxes, which are soe highe; as noe person canbee sartane° of what thay° are to reseve,° soe farr I find it short of what

---

³⁴⁵ JO? He had recently made a secret visit to England and perhaps had hoped to visit Ireland on the same trip.

³⁴⁶ According to Edward Edwards's handwritten calendar in Bodl., JO is the intended recipient of this letter, and this has not been challenged by O'Keeffe and others. But since George Hamilton, not JO, was in The Hague negotiating the marriage, it is most likely that Hamilton was the primary recipient, even if it was evidently forwarded to JO in Brussels. It seems to have been hand-delivered by Thomas Page on his return to the Netherlands after his visit with EO in Dunmore.

is payabell by ther leases ~~Soe as in~~ ^Nor in^ this Cayse;° ~~it~~ dous° ~~not~~
^it^ troubell mee my owne redusment;³⁴⁷ sense° to that I cane I thank
^God^ Chierfullie° Submitt; if by it, my Chilldrene and Familie may
bee advantaged; but the misfortune of not beinge abbell to performe
my ingadgements° unto the State, and next unto the Ladys Frinds,
whom my Sone is consarnede° For, is what, I Confess I doe much
feare and apprehend, sense to faylle° in performinge with the first
of thes, would take from mee a power of acquitinge my selfe as to
my undertakings to the Layter;° and by that menes° not only injure
them; but Ruene° my Selfe, and yet if the pepell were abbell, and
wouldbee Just in payinge ^accordinge^ to Covenants, I shouldnot
~~then~~ ^Nide°^ bee under the perplexities of thes Feares; soe as in this
Strate,° it is referede to you to Consider; and order as you think fitt,
the Manadgment of this affare; of my Sones; wherby this Mach° of
his, may bee renderede of most advantage; sense I know you want not
affectione unto his persone and familie, to make ~~you indevour~~ you
uss° your best indevours° hearin; The Portione offered I Confess is in
it Selfe Considerabell; though not what will free the Estate of anye
of the former ingadgments; nor of my perticular depts, contracted ~~in~~
^Sense^ the Times of my Nesesity espetialie° when allowinge out of
it the one halfe, or more, of it for my Eldest Daughters preferment,
and defrainge besides the Charge of my Sons wedinge, and the   *defraying*
payinge of his depts, all which accordinge unto the competatione that *computation*
mr Page and my selfe has made tharof ~~comes not to~~ ^will not Come
to^ less then 18 hundreth Pound; 13 hundreth wherof is the depts
that hee has contracted Ther; soe as ther will remayne but Litell°
~~for him to rescue~~ ^of it behind^; out of which; tharis a Creditor to
whom I owe a Considerabell Some one mr Austin, now in Holland a
Marchand;° to whom I desier° to make some Sattisfactione, by resone
that hee has bine° longe out of his Mony,° and that it might bee soe
orderede by the Mother of the yonge Gentellman,³⁴⁸ that I heare
dous oftene speake and inquier° after my Daughter, as hee might bee
perswaded to make a ^Private^ Journye over hethar,° upon pretense
to See the Contrye; rathar then Expect my goeinge into England,
which I Cannot doe without Ruene to my Intrest, should I Leave
my Estate at this time; besides the charge of such a Journye; which
would much increase my depts, and that if hee intend Soe to dispose
of himselfe; that it bee indevorede° ~~that~~ that 2 years time may bee
gaynede° for payment of the Last 2 Thowsand ^of hir Portion^ and 5

---

[347] "Decline, reduction in fortune" ("reducement, *n.*," 5, *OED*).
[348] The "yonge Gentellman" is Lord Chesterfield; the "Mother" is Katherine, Lady Stanhope.

or 6 ^Thow^³⁴⁹ More to bee takene upe at the usstiall° Intrest that is
Payede in Holland, which Last; my thinks° if mounsiuer Beverward
willnot give as an adistione° unto his Daughters Portione, hee should
Lend upon Land Securitye heare; or bee assistinge to procure it
from some other; which ~~would pay~~ ^to discharge^ such of my depts
~~heare~~ as I pay unresonabell intrest For, which beinge computede with
Sarvants wages besides, I cane hardlie without some such healpe
bee abbell to kiepe° House, much less mantane° my Sone John*
in Franse³⁵⁰ which I have a great desier Fo;° that Ther hee might   *for*
Learne his Exsersies° and bee committed unto the Goverment of
this Gentellman mr Page;³⁵¹ soe as your advise and furtharanse in all
thes severall perticulars, as allsoe in a Nother° that I have intreated
hime to acquant you ^~~of~~ with^ I cane the Less dout° you will afford,
when the Nesesitye of thes desiers of Mine, shallbee considerede by a
Person soe well abbill to judge of them, and soe frindlie as you have
exprest your Selfe in the consarnes° of my Chilldrene and Familie,
whoe willnot I hope bee wantinge in thar° gratitude to you for the
Same though thay want at presant the power of Sarvinge you; ~~of~~ as I
doe ^allsoe^ much unto my regrett that am

        Sir

              your kinswoman and Sarvant

Dunmore the 1 of Agust   E:ormonde

Sir I have bine desirede by my Sone to make addres by leter unto
Madam Beverward as I have done, but how Significant I know not,
beinge noe competent Judge ~~of~~ ^in^ that ~~Language~~ wherin I am soe
Litell° practisiede; and therfor doe desier it may reseve the advantage
of your healpe in Correctinge and amendinge the Errors of it,
which May bee writene over in some womans hand, and afterwards
delivrede when it shallbee judgede the most Seasonabell and bee
pleasede I pray to remember mee unto mr Gorge langton and his

---

   ³⁴⁹ Thousand.

   ³⁵⁰ EO hoped to send her youngest son to study at the academy in Paris where his elder brothers had studied.

   ³⁵¹ After his visit to EO, Page wrote to JO of his youngest son:
his only infelicity is that hee is backward in his studyes which has bene occasioned by some mens ill dealing with my Lady and I am afrayd the losse will be irrecoverable as to the learned languages, because the exercises of a Cavalier will take up most part of his time. Yet what is necessary either to use or ornament for a person of his quality, may be gained out of the moderne tongues, to which hee expresses great inclinations (Bodl., Carte Papers, 213, fol. 369).

wife, whous Litell Sone³⁵² I have desirede mr Page to take, to his Care, whoe will I hope bouth° of them arrive Sayfe°

Letter 89. August, 1659, [Dunmore], the Marchioness of Ormonde to John Burdon (NLI, Ormond Papers, 2324, no. 1317, p. 83).³⁵³ Autograph.
For John Burdone thes. [Endorsed]: Her Ladyships 11th August 1659.

John Burdon

Captane [warine]³⁵⁴ and is still in arreare of his Rent, though hee promist to paye it a Month Sense° at Dublin, and Sense that time Edward Butler* went to hime to demand it, but hee put hime ofe° allsoe, promisinge to Satisfie what was dew° of hime soe Soune° as hee went Next to Dublin as hee intended as hee sayede° to doe very Sudanlie,° it beinge Sense that a fortnight, and as I understand hee is not as yet gone ^thethar°^ Nor intends to goe as is supposede by some of his Naybors wherfor you Liveinge neare unto hime and Ned Butler* beinge Sent by mee a Nother° way, I desier° that you would goe to Captane warine* from mee, and Let hime know that my ocations° are Soe great for Mony° to at this Time as I desier hee would pay mee my Rent heare, rathar then at Dublin, it Sense hee faylede° to doe it at the Time when hee first promist, by resone° that ^the^ Harvest is Now Comminge in, workmen to bee payede, and the Nesesarye Provistione for my House to bee made, Soe as I Cannot Suspend anye Longer the Rent that was to have bine° payede in May Last, which I would have you to Press as Earnestlie [*seven words missing*] mee his answar, the Some dew is [*two words missing*] pound, and if hee should make abaytment for the Land that Corronell Redmonds* has pecourede you are to tell hime you have *procured* noe instructions for it nor doe but ^to allow for [*illegible*]³⁵⁵^^it^^^ and tharfor if hee Expects anye such thinge, it willbee fitt for himselfe to ^Come and^ speake with mee aboute it; which is all at presant from

      E:ormonde

---

³⁵² EO's youngest son, John?
³⁵³ There is minor wear and tear to the leaf, which obscures most of the first line of text and part of the second line of text on the second page of the letter.
³⁵⁴ Captain Edward Warren? EO's tenant.
³⁵⁵ One or two words are rendered illegible by EO's heavy strikethroughs.

Thursday Morninge

I pray send a Leter for mee to Signe unto mr Adkins[356] for the twentye Pound that remayns dew of hime for the Rent of Lackagh whoe promist above 3 weekes Sense to have Come hethar° and have payede it but has faylede ~~mee~~ Contrarye unto his promise and my Expectatione wherfor Let hime know that I desier that the second Messenger that [was] ^is now^ sent on purpose to hime may Not returne with an Excuse as the former did Sense that willnot bee well resevede° by Mee whoe Expects ~~bebeter~~ beter° performanse from hime

Letter 90. October 11, 1659, [Dunmore], the Marchioness of Ormonde to John Burdon (NLI, Ormond Papers, 2324, no. 1318, p. 91). Autograph.
For John Burdon thes. [Endorsed]: [*illegible*] 1659.

[John Burdon]

I have hearinclosede sent you [a draught] of a Petistione, unto which it is thought requiset that the Names of the Persons shouldbee insertede upon whom the de[falt actions] are to bee, which I not beinge abbell to doe, without Edward Butlers* and your healpe, have therfor sent it to you, as allsoe to have added unto this draught what Else if anye ^thinge^ more you find Nesesarye for the presant ocatione,° and furtharanse of it, that it may bee spidilie° returnede unto

The 11 of oct   E:ormonde

Letter 91. January 4, 1659/60, [Dunmore], the Marchioness of Ormonde ("JH") to the Marquess of Ormonde (Bodl., Carte Papers, 213, fols. 508–509). Autograph.
[Endorsed]: My Wife 4 January 1659 Received 16 March 1660.

sir

your havinge bine° soe Longe absent from the plase of your abode,[357] made mee desist from writinge to you of Late and the rather, because

---

[356] Unidentified tenant.

[357] In August 1659 JO had left Brussels for Calais with Charles II as one of only three advisers (Daniel O'Neill and Silius Titus were the other two). Since the overthrow of the protectorate and the restoration of the Long Parliament in May 1659, there had

I did beleve that your other frinds ~~at a~~ ^that are^ nearer ~~distanse~~
^you^; would give you a more timelie, and perticuler accompt° of
your Nephues³⁵⁸ consarnes,° then I could, that am soe farr removede
from you Bouth,° though my care and willingnes has not bine
wantinge to contribute what I could unto the settlinge hime, as hee
is Now, in that way,³⁵⁹ that I found was ~~abr~~ agreable to his owne,
and your Likinge; soe as theris noe more to bee informede by mee,
but to perfect what shalbee further required on the behalfe of the
gentelwoman,³⁶⁰ which I am redie to doe, soe soune° as anye one
shallbee imployede hether by [you]r frinds upon that accompt, I
heare of noe adres as yet made unto ~~mis~~ Miss Becket,³⁶¹ by Mr
Annets Frinds Sone,³⁶² though perhapes ther would be, if with
conveniensie the yonge [cou]pell might see Eche other, which in
the Loe condistion that hir frinds is in, and thes unsetled Times,
cane hardlie [bee]; by hir remove, nor would it bee resonabell at
all, unles upon som greater sertantye, and then; I doe beleve thay°   *certainty*
would indevour° a complianse by goeinge [as] farr as hir unkell°
Robertes³⁶³ his House at the Springe, where my cousen John
Rashly³⁶⁴ is at presant, to take the the first oppertunitye to goe for
franse, ther to Meete the person that is to have the charge of hime,
whoe is a fine youth as this berar°³⁶⁵ cane tell you, that accompanys
hime thither, and from thense is imployed to som other of the Boys
relations,³⁶⁶ to bringe an ~~accompt~~ accompt of ther wellfare unto ther
frinds, by whom I shouldbee glad to heare from you, and reseve°
your Command[s] if anye I may sarve you in, it was my fortune to
See your wife³⁶⁷ not Longe sense;° whoe was then very well, but
troubled that shee had not heard from you of some months, though
I satisfiede hir that it was rather to bee belevede the Changes of late

---

been reports from England of planned royalist risings, and the king wanted to be within easy reach of England when those risings took place. During his time in France, JO was sent to Paris on the king's behalf to re-establish relations with his mother, Henrietta Maria.

[358] Ossory.
[359] Ossory was married on November 7, 1659.
[360] The marriage settlement.
[361] Elizabeth, her daughter.
[362] Chesterfield. "Mr Annet" is Daniel O'Neill: he was a good friend and later husband of Katherine, Lady Stanhope, Chesterfield's mother.
[363] JO's maternal uncle, Sir Robert Poyntz, of Acton.
[364] EO's son John?
[365] Thomas Page?
[366] Ossory?
[367] EO herself.

that hinderde [the Posts] Leters from comminge, then anye want of
Care in you to sende, as I doe beleve, as allsoe that mr Buncklye³⁶⁸
dous° by this ~~time~~ ^time^ repent that hee did not holde his Farme
still, and compond for his arrears, as hee might you know have done
upon resonabell termes, with my Cousen Samuell;³⁶⁹ sense thay whoe
has it now, I doe beleve will not quit soe advantagious a bargine
soe easilie as hee did; but whethar that will prove good paymasters
I cannot as yet [say] but doe hope the best, and that my cousen
Austin will have a good indusment to settell himselfe, and come to
louke° after his estate, which beinge Left unto the manadgment of
Sarvants cannot doe soe well, as when the masters Eie° is over them
for of the tow° best Tenements hee had, a considerable part of the
chife° of them is fallene,³⁷⁰ and the second totalye out of repare,³⁷¹
soe as theris but only the Litell° farme House³⁷² left that has bine
Latlie° reparede by old mistris Rashlye³⁷³ that is in anye tolorabell
condistione, and that is now a pretye plase, but wants ^a^ Stabell and
gardine, which shee intended to have made this next sommer the
materialls beinge redie, but cannot proside° for want of Mony,° which
accompt I thought fitt to give you, by resone° I know you wish the
Person well whom it conserns,° and Lives so neare hime, as you may
acquant hime tharof, as I desier° you would doe, and mee that right,
as to beleve I am very sinserlie

        Sir

                your fathfull frind and Sarvant

the 4 of Jan   JH

sir

I have sent unto the Frind that I imploye to bee accomptabell° unto
you of what has past thorough his handes and to suplye you with
what you desier for your owne ocations°

---

[368] Unidentified.
[369] Unidentified.
[370] Kilkenny Castle?
[371] Carrick-on-Suir?
[372] Dunmore House.
[373] EO herself.

Letter 92. February 10, 1659/60, Dunmore, the Marchioness of Ormonde to Sir J[ohn] Perceval (BL, Additional MSS, Egmont Papers, 46938, fol. 3). Scribal: signed.

Sir[374]

I have received many complaints, as well of the wast° committed on the Woods of Killiny (parcell of the Lordshipp of Lackagh) as of the encroachments made upon the Land; And amongst the rest of twenty Oakes cutt downe by order (as t'is said), from Mr Parsons of Birr,[375] and of twenty more, that are markt for the like end: Whereof I thought fitt to give yow notice desireing that yow (being in possession of the Land) will take a Speedy course to prevent as well the wast, as the encroachment lest heereafter the prejudice may be greater (when these things shall come to be inquired into) then now it seemes to bee which that it might be avoided is the desire of

 Sir

   your very Assured Freind
   and Servant

Dunmore 10th february 1659 E:ormonde

Letter 93. April 13, 1660, [Dunmore], the Marchioness of Ormonde ("JH") to the Marquess of Ormonde (Bodl., Carte Papers, 214, fol. 42). Autograph.
[Endorsed]: My Wife 13 April Old Style Received 12 May New Style 1660.

Sir

It is not Longe sense° I gave you an accompt° of the ressept° of the first Leter that I had from you sense your returne from your travells, as I shall doe now of a second that came newlie unto my hands, beinge offered soe good an ocation as the sendinge it by this berar,° in which I perseve° it is your desier° to have Ned Dampart[376] to put

---

[374] Sir John Perceval (1629–1665) was the eldest son and heir of Sir Philip Perceval, with whom EO corresponded in 1647.
[375] Lawrence Parsons (d. 1698), later first baronet.
[376] EO.

himselfe into a redenes° to meete you at Esterlie,³⁷⁷ which hee bid mee to tell you hee would indevour° but thought it not fitt as yet to Stir, untell° hee should heare from you agayne,° though many of his other frinds has importunede hime to come upon the same accompt

    I thank you for the Care that I perseve you have had of My Neesses³⁷⁸ preferment, soe as nether to have slighted the mach° that I thoght would have bine° proposed by the yonge Mans³⁷⁹ Frinds nor apieringe° more forward then was convenient; in which I doe very much commend and aprove your Cautione, and doe hope that though this have not sucksided,° a beter° may, this Late misfortune hee has had, renderinge a mach with hime Les desirabell then befor, though somthinge may perhapes bee pleaded in his excuse,³⁸⁰ however I shallnot hinder other adresses if anye bee made, that I think hir frinds and selfe, will Like of in anye expectatione of hime, but will give you an accompt therof, whoe will err Longe bee I hope where you may personalie reseve° it,

    I am sorye that my frind John³⁸¹ did not visset° you as sertanlie if my Leter that I sent after hime had come unto his or his [illegible] fellow travelers hands ~~hands~~ hee would have done, and I am confident will yet, whoe I heare is at presant with his Eldest Brother³⁸² that I am tould is very hapie in his Mach, and soe I doe hope will the rest of that familie bee allsoe,

    Mr Dallison³⁸³ your partener, has some Marchand° Goods but is ~~Loth~~ unwillinge to remove them with himselfe, as suposinge it wouldbee both troubelsom and chargibell, but intends to leave them heare, where the rates of such comodities are higher, unles upon the sartantie° of beter markets in England, you shall advise the contrarye, wherof hee desiers to bee informede by you, as I doe to

---

³⁷⁷ Presumably this means to head eastward, i.e. towards London. EO had been urged by her husband to settle her affairs in Ireland and go to England. See Bodl., Carte Papers, 214, fol. 7.
³⁷⁸ EO's daughter Elizabeth.
³⁷⁹ Chesterfield.
³⁸⁰ Chesterfield had recently caused a scandal by killing Francis Wolley, the son of a Hammersmith doctor, in a duel over the price of a mare. See Anon., *The Occasion and Manner of Mr. Francis Wolleys Death, Slaine by the Earle of Chesterfield at Kensington, January 17 1659* (London: IC, 1660). He had been forced to flee England and subsequently sought a pardon from Charles II at Breda.
³⁸¹ EO's youngest son, John.
³⁸² Ossory.
³⁸³ EO?

know, how my vallantine Samuell[384] and his sarvant Richard[385] dous°
like of on° a Nother° and when I may expect to see you and them,
whoe shouldbee very wellcome to my poure° House,[386] the mene°
time, I pray bee kind to thous° that has bine Frinds to mee in cayse°
it bee your fortune to see them befor I doe, the prinsepall wherof, mr
Allepe[387] or Brakly[388] cane informe you, I had befor your Last Leter
came givene mr Bluett[389] my consent to take the imployment that
was offerede hime, and am upon termes of agreeinge with another
whoe is aprovede of by himeselfe and others to bee fitt to sucksíde°
hime in the plase for which hee was intended, I am goeinge the Next
weeke to see my frind Astins Mother[390] whoe is very well, and soe
are the rest of hir relations, whous Daughter inlaw[391] I heare has
finnisht the repares of hir House and made it very handsome,
I am very well pleased that what I offered to my cousen Drakes[392]
servis, was made uss° of by hime, and shallbee noe les Forward to
contribute further therto in that, or anye thinge Else that may fall
within my power, which I beseche you tell hime, and beleve I am

     Sir

       your fathfull Frind and Servent

the 13 of Aprell   JH

Sir I asshure° my Selfe you have an accompt from beter hands of
the Mach that is Like to bee betwixt mr Abdy and my Naybors
Daughter mistris Efton[393] to which I heare that hir Grandfather
Squire ~~Epham~~ Epsham is agreeinge allsoe and will adde to the
Portion yet notwithstanding some of the Eftons covetious frinds
doe grumbell and has a good mind to hinder it, if thay° could, but
the yong cupell beinge resolved it is thought it Cane hardlie bee   *couple*
prevented

---

[384] "A person of the opposite sex chosen, drawn by lot, or otherwise determined, on St Valentine's day, as a sweetheart, lover, or special friend for the ensuing year" ("Valentine, *n.*," 2a, *OED*). Presumably, EO is referring to her newlywed son, Ossory.
[385] EO's second son Richard.
[386] Dunmore.
[387] Unidentified.
[388] Unidentified.
[389] Unidentified.
[390] EO's mother-in-law, Elizabeth, Lady Thurles.
[391] EO herself.
[392] Unidentified.
[393] Unidentified.

Letter 94. March 28, [1660], [Dunmore], the Marchioness of Ormonde ("JH") to the Marquess of Ormonde (NLI, Ormond Papers, 2482, no. 115, p. 321). Autograph.
[Endorsed]: anonymous. J H. 28 March.

Sir

It was not this Gentellmans fault, nor Mine, that you heard not from mee when hee went first, but some acsident at that time, which did not permitt therof; but now, that I am offered this oppertunitie, I must not ommitt to give you an accompt° of your frinds and relations beinge in health, and Next, to recomend this berar,° as a person qualifiede in all respects worthye of your and your Parteners Trust and Estime and to Let you know, that your prudent answer sent by him unto your Creditor mr Childe,[394] has givene hime abundant Satisfacti[on] insoemuch, that I doe confidentlie beleve, that hee, and the rest, will compound[395] the 3 thowsand Pound dept,° and allow time for payment ^therof^ and therby aprove themselfs honnest in ther dealling with you and hime; soe as you will find noe cause I hope, to blame, what indevours° has bine° ussede by your Frinds to sarve you in This, wherof my Cousene Adrean Scot[396] has I asshure° you ~~in this~~ bine very instrumentall, ~~and~~ ^Soe as it^ wouldbee of advantage unto your affares to gett hime recommended by mr Aplby,[397] unto mr Chedell[398] and the rest if soe you shall think fitt, to some imployment, Hee beinge a Man as desarvinge as capabell of it,

I hope James Brakly[399] has bine with you befor this Time, whoe will give you an accompt of othar your small conserners,° and will bringe mee your derections° as to what may relate therunto, and that you will Let mee know when I may expect mr Abdy[400] whom you tould mee Longe sense° had a Mind to take a Farme; after whom I doe inquier,° but heare noe sartantye° of his cominge [/] I was tould but knownot how true; that mr Driver[401] has writene unto you about a Litell° bussenes° that consernes a diferanse betwixt himselfe and one Samuell Howard,[402] whom it wouldbee a very good worke to

---

[394] Unidentified.
[395] "To come to terms as to the amount of a payment; to make a pecuniary arrangement" ("compound, v.," 12, *OED*).
[396] Possibly one of EO's paternal cousins.
[397] Unidentified.
[398] Unidentified.
[399] Unidentified.
[400] Unidentified.
[401] Unidentified.
[402] Unidentified.

reconsile and in that respect, and for othar resons; I wish you may
bee an instrument of attonment betwixt them, to the satisfactione
of Both; otharwise a Sute° in Law may posiblie arrise; that willbee
both Chargebell and troubelsom which wouldbee beter° a voyded I
should think as the Cayse° stands, but this I only offier,° ~~and Leave to~~
^(but Sobmitt unto)^ your beter Judgment, my Chalenor⁴⁰³ is well,
and professes much to you and your Frind,⁴⁰⁴ and truly I think is very
Sinsere in it, and soe are Many more that I shall forbere to Name
at this time, haveinge I feare tyrede° you with readinge my ill hand
and tedious leter which I hope you will the rather Excuse, sense my
giveinge you this troubell prosides° not out of anye offistiousnes, but a
reall conserne that is had for your wellfare, and shallbee Ever by

    Sir

      your fathfull frind and Sarvant

the 28 of March   JH

Letter 95. May 7, [1660], [Dunmore], the Marchioness of Ormonde ("JH") to the Marquess of Ormonde (NLI, Ormond Papers, 2482, no. 117, p. 337). Autograph.
[Endorsed]: Anonymous J H May 7th.

Sir

I hope this Leter will find you at a Nierer distanse then my former
has done, and that theris by this time a possibility that I may Err
Long bee agayne° restored unto the comfort of seeinge you, in ~~this~~
^The^ Plase where I heare you now are,⁴⁰⁵ but knownot how farr
I may Creditt it for truth your beinge soe; Sense° I perswade my
selfe if it were, you wouldbee soe kind as to Let mee know it from
your owne hand; howsomever I shall venture this Leter, as I have
done tow° former ons° very Latlie;° which I hope will obtayne mee a
Comfortabell returne in bringinge mee a confirmatione of your and
your Parteners⁴⁰⁶ wellfare, for whom I am not a Littell Conserned,°
as allsoe to reseve° your derections° and commands when and where

---

⁴⁰³ "A maker of chalons"; a chalon was a "blanket or coverlet for a bed" ("chaloner, n." and "chalon, n.", *OED*). Perhaps a reference to herself, i.e., the maker of the "cover," "JH"?
⁴⁰⁴ King Charles II.
⁴⁰⁵ London.
⁴⁰⁶ King Charles II.

you will oppoynt° mee with your tow Neeses[407] to attend you, whoe wants not affection to make ther visset° more spidie,° but thinks it beter° to stay untell° they may performe it with Less troubell to you, then perhapes ther more spidie repayre ~~where you are would bring~~ ^wouldbee to^ untell such time as you ~~bee~~ ^are^ beter settled, that are in ther persons and humors such; as I hope you will like well of, I mene° the yonge ons,° but but [sic] for the condistion of ther Aunts[408] fortune, it is much impayred of Late by the Changes ^heare^ and Poverty of the pepell,° but that is not considered ecquall to the advantage and Content that a Settellment would bringe, which wee all doe hope willbee Efected, by the wisdom of the Parlement, which I pray ^God^ to grant [/] Sir I must in Justis unto this Gentellman Let you know, that his Meritt in all respects has bine° such, as added unto his abilitye, and beinge Sone unto soe Reverend and worthye a Person, dous° desarve your regard and furtharanse of his preferment, which I desier° hee may find, and his Father allsoe, your frindshipe, in his perticuler consernment;° wherin you willnot only oblidge Them, but likwise much Sattisfie Mee; that am

     your fathfull Frind and Sarvant

The 7 of May   JH

Theris an acquantanse of yours mr Milo that will wayte° upon you Shortlie

Letter 96. May 7, 1660, [Dunmore], the Marchioness of Ormonde to Stephen Smith (NLI, Ormond Papers, 2324, no. 1334, p. 199). Autograph.
For Mr Stiphene Smith thes. [Endorsed]: My Ladys letter to Mr Smith Dated the 7 of May 1660.

Sir

It beinge liklie that you will See My Cousen the Lady Turner[409] befor I shall, I doe desier° that when Shee Comes to Towne you willbee hir remembransier to visset° thous° persons of qualitye that

---

[407] EO's daughters, Elizabeth and Mary. Letters sent to their father at this time can be found in NLI, Ormond Papers, 2481, nos. 275 and 351.
[408] EO.
[409] JO?

was soe perticularlie kind and Frindlie to Mee as a List of whous
Names ~~I have~~ is heare inserted by

E:ormonde

The dowager Lady of Devonshire[410]	Lady Marchioness of Dorchester[411]
and Lady Straford[412]	
The Dowager Lady of Peterbrogh[413]	Lady Darby the Dowager[414]

---

[410] The dowager Countess of Devonshire, Christian (Christiana) Cavendish, née Bruce (1595–1675), was a firm royalist: her house in Roehampton, Surrey, became a center of royalist intrigue, and it is possible that she facilitated the correspondence between EO and her husband at the king's court in exile. A sign of the continued friendship between the dowager Countess and EO after the restoration, EO's youngest daughter, Mary, would marry the dowager's grandson. For more biographical information on the dowager Countess, see Victor Stater, "Cavendish, Christian, countess of Devonshire (1595–1675)," *ODNB*, and for a contemporary biography, see Thomas Pomfret, *The Life of the Right Honourable and Religious Lady Christian, Late Countess Dowager of Devonshire* (London: William Rawlins, 1685).

[411] The Marchioness of Dorchester, Katherine Pierrepont, née Stanley (b. 1631), was the second daughter of the dowager Countess of Derby, and the sister of the Countess of Strafford, who are also listed as friends by EO. Katherine had been present with her mother and sister during the siege of Lathom House in 1644. In May 1650 she and her sisters were imprisoned by parliamentarian order; their father, the seventh Earl of Derby, was executed for high treason in October 1651. In September 1652 her mother arranged for Katherine's marriage to the royalist nobleman, the Marquess of Dorchester.

[412] The Countess of Strafford, Henrietta Maria Wentworth, née Stanley (1630–1685), was the eldest daughter of the dowager Countess of Derby. She was with her mother and sister during the civil war years and was married in the mid-1650s to the second Earl of Strafford.

[413] The dowager Countess of Peterborough, Elizabeth Mordaunt, née Howard (1603–1671), was the widow of John Mordaunt, first Earl of Peterborough (d. 1643). While her husband fought for parliament, her son defected to the royalist cause only months before succeeding to the earldom. In 1644 he married Lady Penelope O'Brien (c. 1622–1702), daughter of the fifth Earl of Thomond (d. 1657), who had remained loyal to JO during the wars in Ireland. See Victor Stater, "Mordaunt, Henry, second Earl of Peterborough (*bap*. 1623, *d*. 1697)," *ODNB*.

[414] The dowager Countess of Derby, Charlotte Stanley, née de La Trémoille (1599–1664), was the widow of James Stanley, seventh Earl of Derby, who had been executed in 1651 for his royalism. Throughout the Civil Wars she had been active in the royalist cause and is renowned for her defence of Lathom House in Lancashire, which was besieged in March 1644. While a chronicler, writing in 1660, praised her "more than Feminine Magnanimity," at the time she was accused by an enemy propagandist of having "stolen the Earl's breeches when he had fled . . . into the Isle of Man, and hath in his absence play'd the man at Lathom." Lady Derby left Lancashire for the Isle of Man in July 1644, during which time nearly all of the Stanley estates in England fell to the parliamentarian army: Lathom House finally capitulated in December 1645. After her

My Lady of Rannelagh
My Lady Savell[415]
My Lady Dysert[416]

The 7 of May

---

husband's execution, she returned to England to compound for her family's estates, but heavy debts forced her in 1655 to retire to her estates at Knowsley, where she lived quietly for the rest of the Interregnum. See John Callow, "Stanley, Charlotte, countess of Derby (1599–1664)," *ODNB*. The nature of her relationship with EO is unclear, but the two women clearly shared similar experiences during the 1650s as they tried to protect their estates and ensure the safety of their children. An anonymous correspondent had thought to inform EO of "poore" Lady Derby's "surenther" of Castle Rushen ("JH" to EO, [November 1651], NLI, Ormond Papers, 2482, no. 329).

[415] Presumably, the elder Lady Anne Savile, née Coventry (*d.* 1662), who was the widow of Sir William Savile (1612–1644), third baronet of Thornhill, who died in arms for the king. She became celebrated as a heroine of the Civil War when she was besieged by the parliamentarians in Sheffield Castle. According to Peter Barwick:

> This gallant Lady, famous even for her warlike Actions beyond her Sex, had a little before been besieg'd by the Rebels in *Sheffield* Castle, which they battered on all Sides by great Guns, though she was big with Child, and had so little Regard for her Sex, that in that Condition they refused a Midwife she had sent for, the Liberty of going to her. Yet this unheard of Barbarity was so far from moving her, that she resolved to perish rather than surrender the Castle: But the Walls being every where full of Cracks with Age, and ready to fall, the Soldiers of the Garison began to mutiny; not so much concerned for their own Danger, as for the lamentable Condition of this noble Lady, so near the Time of her falling in Labour; for she was Brought to Bed the Night after the Castle was surrendered.

See Peter Barwick, *The Life of the Reverend Dr. John Barwick, D.D. sometime Fellow of St. John's College in Cambridge* (London: J. Bettenham, 1724); and also Joan Kirby, "Savile family (*per. c.* 1480–1644)," *ODNB*. It is less likely but possible that EO might mean the younger Lady Dorothy Savile (1640–1670), who had married George Savile on December 29, 1656: she was the daughter of Henry Spencer, first Earl of Sunderland. See Mark N. Brown, "Savile, George, first marquess of Halifax (1633–1695), politician and political writer," *ODNB*.

[416] The Countess of Dysart, Elizabeth Tollemache, née Murray, was the eldest of the five daughters of William Murray, first Earl of Dysart, and she inherited her father's titles on his death in 1655, becoming Countess of Dysart in her own right. Throughout the wars Lady Dysart maintained a friendship with Oliver Cromwell, which provided a cover for her royalist activities. In 1653 she became an active member of the secret organization known as the Sealed Knot, carrying on a coded correspondence with exiled supporters of Charles II. By 1659, her marital home at Helmingham seems to have become a hub of royalist activity. See Rosalind K. Marshall, "Murray, Elizabeth, duchess of Lauderdale and suo jure countess of Dysart (*bap.* 1626, *d.* 1698)," *ODNB*.

Restoration, 1660–1662

Letter 97. May 11, 1660, Dunmore, the Marchioness of Ormonde to the Marquess of Ormonde (Bodl., Carte Papers, 30, fol. 645). Autograph. See Figure 5.
For the Marquise of Ormonde [/] thes. Endorsed: My Ladys Dated 11 May 1660. By the Lord of Ardes.

My Deare Lord

I beleve it will sime° strange to you to reseve° an avowede address from mee, whous misfortune ~~and Sufferings~~ has bine° such, as besides my 8 yeares absense ~~from you~~; it was made penalle° for mee to write, or reseve Leters from you, That by the great and good providense of God that Bondage[417] under which the three kingdoms as well as my selfe has Sufferede, shouldbee now by his Mercye removede, and our Longe wisht for Blessinge of the kings restoratione at the Length Establishede to uss, is such a motive of admiratione and Joy to all; and perticularlie to mee, as is unexpresabell, and indeede hardlie to bee contaynede within moderate [bo]unds, soe as I suspect my selfe not to write sense, though however, I supposs you [a]re sattisfiede that I ~~mene well and~~ have soe much affectione for you, and dewtye° for your Master,[418] that I mene° well to you Bouth;° though my reveranse unto the one, forbides the presomtione of anye Congratulorye addresse, but That, which with all humilitye and hartye zeale, I shall and doe offier° upe to heavene for Longe life, and Prosperitie ~~to~~ unto his Sacrede Magesty, which I hope you willbee Soe Just to mee, as to Let hime know, untell° I may have the honner° to kiss his hands, which I shall indevour,° with all the Spiede° I cane, as what I Covete beyond all the things ~~of~~ ^in^ this world, next That of Seeinge you, which expretione,° I know to bee Less a compliment, but more of Truth; ~~then if it were Mixt with Flaterye~~, and in that respect beter,° then if mixt with flateries

penal (punishable)

presumption

My Lord

This Nobell Person My Lord of the Ards,* whoe beinge the first, that intends to pay his dewtie° by the personall tender therof unto his Magesty, ~~soe has hee~~ ^has^ bine ^one of^ the forwardest of anye

---

[417] "Subjection to some bond, binding power, influence, or obligation" ("bondage, *n.*," 3a, *OED*).
[418] The newly restored King Charles II.

heare, upon all ocations° unto the uttermost of his power to testifie his Loyltye ~~unto the uttermost of his power~~ and affectione unto his Intrest; and one that has continowede° great respects to you, and your Relations, and is soe considerabell for his worth, abbilitye and Intrest, bouth in this Contrye and the estime hee caryes amongst the chife° Nobilitie of his owne; as I think it is a dewtie° I owe unto his Magestie, and your Selfe, as well as Justise to hime, to give you this Carracture° of hime, whous desiers° are, what all honnorabell and honnest Men dous° ambitione at this time, which is to see, and bee admitted unto the kings presanse,° and Likwise to bee presented by you, whoe I doe asshure° my selfe willbee very forward to doe hime that Sarvise,° as I desier you would anye othar ^allsoe^ wherin you may oblidge soe desarvinge a Person, as hee is by all acknowledged to bee, and is perticularlie soe Estimede, by the impartiall observatione made of his Carrage By

                your Most affectionat wife

From Dunmore the 11 of May   E:ormonde

Letter 98. May 14, 1660, Dunmore, the Marchioness of Ormonde to the Marquess of Ormonde (Bodl. Carte Papers, 214, fols. 188–189). Autograph.
For the Marquis of ormonde [/] thes. [Endorsed]: My Lady Marquiss Dated 14 Received 26 May 1660.

My Lord   Dunmore the 14 of May

Though Sir Charles Cootes[419] Late Actings in the publicke affares, has givene soe great a testimonye of his good affections unto his Magesties sarvise° ~~has~~ ^as^ I dout° not has sattisfiede the kinge, as allsoe your selfe therof, yet is a Justise, I owe him upon that accompt,° and his profestione of respects to you in perticuler, Manefested likwise, by his Sevilities° to Mee in all my Consernments,° to let you know, the good oppinione I hould° of hime, and his Brother

---

[419] Sir Charles Coote had supported the parliamentarian cause and had been a close friend of Henry Cromwell (over whom he may have used his influence to assist EO). He declared his support for the restoration in February 1660, for which he was well rewarded by Charles II. In July 1660 he was reappointed President of Connaught; in August his estates were confirmed; and in September he was created Earl of Mountrath. As Lord Justice of Ireland from October 1660, he governed Ireland with Lord Broghill (now Earl of Orrery) and Sir Maurice Eustace. See Patrick Little, "Coote, Charles, first earl of Mountrath (c. 1610–1661)," *ODNB*.

Corronell Richard Coote as desarvedlie dew° unto Bouth° Ther Meritts, and therfor recommended unto your Regard by

your affectionat wife

E:ormonde

Letter 99. [May 1660], [Dunmore], memorandum from the Marchioness of Ormonde to [Anne] Hume (Bodl. Carte Papers, 214, fols. 221–222). Autograph. See Figure 6.
[Endorsed]: My Ladys remembrances to Mistress Humes et cetera.[420]

you are to desier° hime to bee as sparinge as possiblie hee Cane in grantinge of Suites offises or imployments to anye perticuler Persons at the first, untell° hee bee fullie and Rightlie possest how farr thay° have Sarvede, or is Capabell to Sarve the Intrest now Established; or to M E[421] or such of his relations w untell my Comminge over for it is apprehended that hee willbee very Cravinge

To acquant hime that such as recommendations as comes from mee, in the behalfe of Persons done rathar out of Complianse then respect, shallbee subcribed with the the Leavinge out of the ^Leter^ E, at the Ende of the word ormonde

To desier hime that in Cayse° anye overtures bee made by EC for Machinge° his Sone to B[422] that hee doe not Entertane ^it^ but put it ofe° Sivelie° without disoblidginge the Parents of the Gentellman, with whom in all othar kinds I desier hee may presarve a faire Corespondansie and show a respect unto My Lady of R[423] upon the accompt° of hir kindnes to Mee,

To Let hime know that it has bine° with great unwillingnes the many leters of recomendation that that [sic] has I have sent hime though thay couldnot bee well denyede nor Cane yet as affares dous° Stand Soe as you are to make my Excuse for it

---

[420] The editors of *Field Day* (V, 33) suggest that the memorandum was for Lord Ranelagh, but "Mistress Humes" is clearly named as recipient. Mistress Humes is probably the heiress, Anne Hume, née French (d. 1701), who had been EO's ward, and had married Thomas Hume (d. 1668), a favorite of EO's father. See John Burke, *A Genealogical and Heraldic History of the Commoners of Great Britain and Ireland*, 4 vols. (London: Henry Colburn, 1836), 3. 389. There is no salutation or signature on the memorandum. EO leaves blank space between most points on her list.
[421] Sir Maurice Eustace?
[422] Their daughter Elizabeth (Betty).
[423] Lady Ranelagh.

you are to acquant hime that I doe Conseve° and Soe dous othar his
frinds more Judginge then my Selfe that hee shouldbee generalie
plausibell ^to all^ and admitt of the applicati[ons] of such as ^has^
relatione unto this Contrye yet Soe, as to kiepe° himeselfe as free
from promisses and ingadgments° unto Perticular Persons, as
may bee, untell hee doe reseve° an impartiall accompt of Evrye
ons° Carrage and Intrest wherby the kinge and himselfe may the
beter° know how to Plase favours and rewards where thay are most
^desarvedlie^ dew° which I shall make it my bussenes° to procure; by
the healpe of some ~~Frin whous~~ that knows beter then I doe, and by
my owne perticuler observatione

To tell hime that Sir Paule Davise[424] is honnest, and willbee
tractabell to what hee will have hime doe, that I thinke Sir James
Bary[425] willbee Soe Likwise; and that great uss° may bee made of
Corronell Hill[426] ^Sir John Clatworthye^[427] and the rest ^of that
Gange°^ whoe must bee all of them kindlie resevede° by hime   *gang*

To desier hime to resarve some imployment ^for^ Corronell Flower*
and Major Harmon[428] and some othar of the Honnestest of his
Frinds heare

~~To desier him to Lay his Command upon John Sayres to gett mee a good Cooke~~

To desier hime to write unto his Mothar and to such othar of his
relations as hee thinks Fitt, and in perticular unto the olde Doctor as
a Most affectionat and fathfull Person to hime and all his

If you Cannot be Sudanlie° at London I pray send a way My leter
unto My Lady of Ranalagh* by the Post

To desier My Lord to order the way of his ^Eldest^ Sones Liveinge
by himselfe, by reson I am alltogethar unprovided Ethar° of house

---

[424] Sir Paul Davies, appointed Secretary of State for Ireland in 1661 (*Field Day*, V, 33).

[425] Sir James Barry (1603–1673), lawyer and recorder of Dublin; chairman of the Dublin Convention, which voted unconditionally for the restoration of Charles II in 1659; appointed Irish Privy Councillor and Chief Justice of the King's Bench and created Baron Santry in 1660 (*Field Day*, V, 33).

[426] Colonel Arthur Hill (c. 1601–1663), a colonel in the parliamentary army; MP for counties Down, Antrim and Armagh (1654); created constable and Irish Privy Councillor in 1660 (*Field Day*, V, 33).

[427] Sean Kelsey, "Clotworthy, John, first Viscount Massereene (*d.* 1665)," *ODNB*.

[428] Thomas Harmon, Cromwellian officer (*Field Day*, V, 33).

or furniture, fitt for ther resseptione,° Nethar will I adventure upon it on anye Termes that thay should Live with mee fearinge thay might not Like of it, which my Experianse in the world has ~~made me made~~ ^givene^ mee more resone° to feare then Expect the Contrarye though I am a bundantlie Satisfiede of the Ladys worth and discretione soe am I noe Les of his good Nature and obedianse, yet the troubell of haveinge a Nothar° Familie in My House is; ~~from~~ Comminge from a retyrede life a troubill I cannot undertake but willbee willinge to healpe and assist them by my advise wherin it shallbee Sought and bee as kind to hir as to hime, shee beinge a Person Not like to desarve othar from mee

To desier my Lord to make a returne of kindnes unto My Lord of Broghall* in what applicatione hee shall make to him

To desier hime to Stope° the disposall of the Prothonotars[429] offiss° in the Court of Common Plees in Ireland and to Preferr mr wallter Plonket[430] to it whoe had the Promise of it formarlie from hime, and has bine very desarvinge his regard by the Frindshipe hee has exprest for his Sake unto mee and all his relations heare

To desier hime to Countenanse and favour Sir Franses Hambellton[431] as a Fathfull sarvant to the kinge and soe has bine his Sone allsoe

To desier hime to lay his commands upon John Sayres the kings Cooke to provide a good one for mee

---

[429] A prothonotary was a principal notary or chief clerk or recorder of a court of law ("prothonotary, *n.*", 1, *OED*).

[430] Walter Plunkett was appointed to the office of Prothonotary of the Common Pleas in 1660 (*Field Day*, V, 33).

[431] A royalist, Sir Francis Hamilton was granted charge of a troop of soldiers in 1660 (*Field Day*, V, 34).

Letter 100. May 20, 1660, Dublin, the Marchioness of Ormonde to the Marquess of Ormonde (NLI, Ormond Papers, 2324, no. 1339, p. 235). Autograph.
For the Lord Marquis of ormond thes. [Endorsed]: My Ladys Dated 20 May 1660. By Mr Barneston.

My Lord   Dublin the 20 of May

This Berar° Mr Burneston apprehendinge that his dependansie on the Late Governer heare, might now Cast a prejudis upon hime, has desirede mee to Say somthinge on his behalfe, which I shall soe farr doe, ~~as to asshure you~~ ^in Justis to hime^ to prevent such an inconveniensie, as to Sertifie,° that to the best of my observatione, hee was a disliker of the prosidings° of thous° Times, and a Person affectionat unto that Intrest that is now Established, which Carracture° togethar with ~~the~~ Many Sivell° offisies° Performede by hime to mee, and othar of your relations I desier° may recommend hime unto your Regard, and bee a Motive to induse you to Excuse the troubell that upon this ocatione,° is givene you by

                 your Sinsearlie° affectionat wife

                        E:ormond[432]

Letter 101. May 21, 1660, Dublin, the Marchioness of Ormonde to the Marquess of Ormonde (Bodl., Carte Papers, 214, fols. 87–88). Autograph.
For the Lord Marquis of ormonde [/] thes. [Endorsed]: My Ladys concerning John Bourden and Mr Plunckett et cetera.

My Deare

I have made many addresses to you of late by severall persons, but by non° I am shure,° that is more fathfull one unto the kings Intrest, and your Selfe, then this berar° Captane Power,* whoe is soe transported with the hopes of Seeinge you, as knowinge I couldnot oblidge hime more then by giveinge hime the oppertunitie of it, have Chossene hime to bee the Mesenger of This, and the deliverer of some other perticulars, which I have intrustede hime with, more fitt to bee tould you, then put in writinge, soe as I will make the troubell of this leter the ~~brifer~~ briuefer,° and only desier,° that I may reseve° your derections° consarninge° my comminge over, whoe am the mene°

---

[432] EO had alerted her husband to the significance of the "Ormond" spelling in Letter 99.

time indevoringe° to put My Selfe into a redenes° to obbay the first
sommons that shall Come from you, and to intreat, that you will
reseve with kindnes such, as has in your absense, and my ~~Extremities~~
^Nesesities^, bine° frindlie to mee, wherof Bouth° Bucke* and
Stivene Smith* are abbell to informe you, as one mr Chidslye that
Maryede My lady Savelle[433] and mr Edward Heath[434] ~~are such as~~
^bouth which^ I have bine very much oblidged unto, the layter° ^of^
thes, I find has somthinge to propound, that hee beleves willbee for
your advantage as well as his owne, but what it is I know not, but
desier that if it appiere° resonabell and rationall in your Judgment,
that you will give hime such furtharanse therin, as may bee to his
Sattisfactione, and the desier ^Now^ made in his behalf by

          your trulye affectionat wife

          E:ormonde

I must not forgett to give you an accompt,° and thanks for your leter,
sent by Bucke, though I Confess I had allmost forgott to doe it, The
good Neuse° haveinge made mee allmost as wilde, as it has done
many wisser persons I pray turne the leafe

Theris a gentellman that had onse° ^a^ relatione to you, mr wallter
Plunket* ^and^ ~~that~~ had your Promis for the Prothonotars offiss°
in the Court of Common Plees in Ireland which his Father had,
and hee as worthye to hould° upon the accompt of his honnestye
and loyaltye as anye Man I know heare and one whoe has retaynede
the greatest affectione for your Person, and kindnes to mee and
all your relations and Frinds that it was possibill ~~for~~ to Exprese,
wherfor I beseche you to make good your Former promise to hime,
by interposinge soe far, as noe othar may gett it from hime, or bee
Joynede with hime, which I doe thus timelie intersede in; by resone°
that I heare that Patricke Tallon[435] a Clarke[436] brede under his Father   *bred (reared)*
dous° hope by mr Anslows[437] menes° and Sir Mauris Eustis* whous
Neese hee maryed, to gett himselfe Joynede in the Patent, and soe

---

[433] Presumably, Lady Dorothy Savile (d. 1670), who had in 1656 married George Savile, later first Marquess of Halifax. See Mark N. Brown, "Savile, George, first marquess of Halifax (1633–1695), politician and political writer," *ODNB*. Mr. Chidsley was presumably the minister who officiated the wedding.

[434] Unidentified.

[435] Unidentified.

[436] "Since the Reformation, in England generally = 'clerk in holy orders', i.e. a deacon, priest, or bishop" ("clerk, *n*.," 1b, *OED*).

[437] Unidentified.

by the Exsecutione of it would make it of litell° or noe profitt at all unto mr Plunket,* wherof I pray have an Eie° ~~of~~ ^after^ it, that the grant may not bee givine from hime, and that you willbee pleasede to louke° with favour upon your ould Sarvant John Burdon* whoe is Now as Sober and abbell a Secretarye as anye that I doe beleve you Cane light upon and willbee very ussfull to you upon Sondrie ocations° whoe I doe therfor intend to bringe a longe with mee

Just now I resevede° 2 leters from you by mr Carpenter[438] the Contents wherof I shall obaye in Makinge all the hast° over that I Cane

Dublin the 21 of May

Letter 102. May 23, 1660, Dublin, the Marchioness of Ormonde to the Marquess of Ormonde (Bodl. Carte Papers, 214, fols. 208–209). Autograph.
For the Marquise of ormonde [/] thes. [Endorsed]: My Ladys Dated 23 May 1660 Concerning Sir Theophelous Jones.

My Lord

Amongst thous° many that have bine° zealous in the restitution of his Magestyes Intrest, and the promotinge of his Sarvise° heare, I doe not find that anye appierede° more active; and was more considerablye instrumentall in Carringe° it on, then this Gentellman Sir Theophelous Jones[439] in the Capasitiye wherin hee was; and therfor, though I doutnot but his Magestye willbee forward to Manefest his good acseptanse therof, and you noe less willinge to doe hime all Frindlie offisies° yet the handsomnes of his Carrage in this late actione oblidges mee to doe hime the right of recommendinge hime to your Regard, in which I hope you will Excuse this Troubell, with others of this kind, that has bine put upon you by

        your Sinsearlie° affectionat wife

Dublin the 23 of May   E:ormonde

---

[438] Phillip Carpenter, a bearer of JO's letters to EO.
[439] Aidan Clarke, "Jones, Sir Theophilus (*d.* 1685)," *ODNB*.

Letter 103. June 4, 1660, Dunmore, the Marchioness of Ormonde to the Marquess of Ormonde (Bodl., Carte Papers, 214, fols. 227–229). Autograph.
[Endorsed]: My Ladys Dated 4 Received 12 June 1660 Concerning the postmaster of Dublins place for Mr Bathurst.

My Lord

In obedianse unto your commands sent mee by mr Phillipe Carpenter,* and by such as I resevede° Sense° by a Leter from you datted at Bruslls; I am now redie to imbarke for England, nothinge stayinge mee, but the Comminge from Dublin to waterford, of a Frigatt to Carrye mee, that is daylie expected, soe as I hope it willnot bee Longe, befor I reseve° your furthar derections° at my Landinge at Bristoll,* whethar you will have mee to make my first repayre to Acton* or to London, sense I cannot soe much Crose my owne Sattisfactione as to dout° of his Magestys and your beinge allredie ther, though I have not as yet the positive asshuranse therof, but doe with great impatianse° Expect it; I heare that London is soe Crowded and all the best Lodgings allredie takene upe, as in Care of My Chilldrens health and my owne; I could wishe ^for^ a House or Lodginge Ethar° at Chellsie or Richmond⁴⁴⁰ or anye where to bee out of the Hurye⁴⁴¹ of pepell,° and the Noysomnes of that great Towne, though I shallnot bee Soe tyede to My owne desiers° ^in That^ in that as to the plase of my abode but with Submistione unto what may Sort best with your liekinge and Conveniensie; My Lady your Mothar is Now heare, and as well in health, and Chierfull° in Humor, as Ever I saw hir, and for the rest of your frinds I shall give you an accompt° of them Ere longe, the mene° Time, I pray excuse mee for troublinge you with soe many Leters of recommendation on the behalfe of perticuler Persons, most some wherof I could not avoyde° as things stands heare at the presant, and som othars, were extortede from mee by importunitye, soe as you must Show your Charitie in forgiveinge My Error, as I hope you will your owne prudense ^and diligense^ in a Care of the Person of your Gratious Master, in the first Plase; and Next of your Selfe to prevent towards Ethar, anye Mischife that Might bee attempted by anye villans, wherof you Cannot but beleve, notwithstandinge the generall Joy that is for the kings restoratione, but, that ther are ^some^ wickede Spirets ^still^ therfor I praye have a Care; to have fathfull Pepell about you (and where,) and with whom you Eate or Drink, and

noisomeness

---

⁴⁴⁰ Both Chelsea and Richmond were outside the city of London.
⁴⁴¹ "A confused crowd, a mob" ("hurry, *n.*," I, 1b, *OED*).

though perhapes you will Louke° upon this advise of Mine as
^Prosidinge° from^ a womanish feare and growndless° Suspition, yet
I bege of you Not to Slight it, in what Consernes° the kinge and your
Selfe, for I have had ocatione° to observe much of the dayngerous
humores of the Sectories and Phanatickes as thay° are Now Called;
God if it bee his will, Protect all good Pepell from ther Mischifes,
your two Daughters are bouth° in good health, and longs very
much to See you and ther Brothers, of whom you have Mentionede
Nothinge in your ~~leter~~ tow° last leters to mee; whoe have givene you
a longer troubell by this; then I intended, or Cane bee in discretione
Justifiede by

    your Sinsearlie° affectionat wife

Dunmore the 4 of June   E:ormonde

My Lord

Just as I was sendinge a way this Leter I resevede° one from you
dattede the 27 of May from Canterburye to my infinite sattisfactione
^to finde therin^ that the kinge ~~an~~ with his Brothars and your
Selfe are Sayflie° Landed, for which great Mercy, God Make uss all
thankfull to hime, to whom This Blessinge of the kings peasebell   *peaceable*
restoratione must bee ascribed; you Nide° urge Noe arguments
to hastene mee over ^then your beinge in England^ sense° I am
redie upon the first Notise° of the Ships beinge come to waterford
to Meet it Ther, I am desirede by the Post Master of Dublin mr
Samuell Bathurst* to request your favour to hime, that his Plase may
bee Continowede° and not givene from hime, whom you will find
soe ~~Stronglie~~ generalie approvede of bouth for his honnestye and
abbilitye as I doutnot will obtane your Regard of hime, to whom I
have in my perticuler bine° behouldinge for his Care of what leters
~~was derected to Mee~~ have bine derected° unto

    your

    EO

Letter 104. October 9, 1660, [London], the Marchioness of Ormonde to John Burdon (NLI, Ormond Papers, 2324, no. 1351, p. 343). Autograph.
For My Sarvant John Burdon thes. [Endorsed]: Her Ladyships Dated 9th Received 22nd October 1660.

John Burdon

I resevede° but one Leter from you sense° you Left this plase, soe as I have but Litell° to Say in ~~ansuer~~ answar of the Contents, but that theris a Leter Signede by his Magestye conserninge° the rents payabell into the Exchek[er] and the arreares, accordinge as you did desier° might bee procurede, which shallbee very shortlie Sent, as is now a Coppie of the Leter for the revertione[442] of one of the offisies° that you desirede, the orrigenall wherof, I thought fitt to send by a Shure° hand, for feare of Miscarage which I doe asshure° you did cost mee some paynes to procure, which had it not bine° gottene when it was I have good resone° to beleve, wouldnot have bine obtaynede in regard the kinge has resolvede to grant noe revertions therfor the Less is sayede° of this the beter°
    as for answaringe of Sir Henry Tickborns* demand I shallnot adventure to doe it, ~~but by~~ unles by advise from you and the rest, in regard I find non° heare that are willinge to Laye out mony° in that Contrye, therfor Let mee know in Cayse° that hee doe importune my Lord or mee, what answar willbee fitt to give hime, and to uss° the best indevour° you Cane the mene° time to prevent the Plase from beinge Left wast,° or the woods from distroctione,° bouth° ther and Else where; I perseve° that mr Butler of Balynehinchye[443] has bine threteninge of Captane Gilliard[444] whom I desier may bee incoridgede° in the Tenansie, untell° mr Butler can ^prove^ ~~make~~ his Tytell° to bee beter then ours, which his Carrage Considerede, and what is to bee Sayede agenst hime hee willbee very hardlie abbell to doe; The accompt° of the depte° dew° to my Lord from the kinge is now statede, and redie to bee givene unto My Lord Chanselor of England upon Thursday next, whoe wee hope willbee assistinge to procure uss sattisfactione, in the mene° time wee have securede all

---

[442] "An estate granted to one party and subsequently granted in turn or transferable to another, esp. upon the death of the original grantee; the right of succeeding to, or next occupying, such an estate" ("reversion, *n.*1," I, 1a, *OED*).
[443] Dispossessed Catholic.
[444] Cromwellian officer.

the Morgadgs° and obtaynede a grant of all thous° prisewins⁴⁴⁵ that were exemptede out of the antiant° Patent which it is intended shall Pass under the great Seale heare, to bee in rolled in Ireland, by which you may perseve that I have not bine negligent in ~~my~~ the conserne° of our Estate in ~~getti~~ putinge my Lord in Mind to move for what is soe Nesesarye to the presarvatione of his Fortune, of which I pray make my olde Frind the Doctor⁴⁴⁶ acquanted ~~with~~ and Let mee heare from ^you^ of all such affares as Conserns°   *enrolled*

The 9 of Oct   E:ormonde

Letter 105. November 3, 1660, [London], the Marchioness of Ormonde to John Burdon (NLI, Ormond Papers, 2324, no. 1357, p. 387). Autograph.
For My Sarvant John Burdon thes. [Endorsed]: Her Ladyships 3rd November 1660.

John Burdon

I refer you to my othar Leter, as to the ansawringe of thous° poynts wherof I perseve° that Sir william Flower* and your Selfe are in dout,° and by This, shall only Let you know, that the bussenes° of revertione that you desirede of mr Mauls⁴⁴⁷ offisse° is obtaynede, and the Coppie of the kings Leter sent you inclosede in one of Mine about ^3^ weeks Sense,° the origenall beinge in my Costodie, and shallbee sent when mr Plonket* goes; theris a Nothar,° that I have obtayned for mr Browne* the Aturnye° that he may bee permitted to Plead, ~~which~~ ^that^ I intend to Send by the same hand, ^the^ which I pray Let hime know, as allsoe mr Taffe⁴⁴⁸ the Minister of killkenye, that the Parsonage of Callan that hee desirede; was givene unto one mr Asshe⁴⁴⁹ as antiant° chaplene of My Lords above 2 Months befor his Leter desiringe that hee might bee preferede unto it, did come unto my hands [/] I wish that Mojor Abbell warine⁴⁵⁰ had not fallene into that misfortune of beinge suspectede and Committed for actinge   *Major*

---

⁴⁴⁵ Prisage was "an ancient duty levied upon imported wine, in later times correlated to and often identified with butlerage" ("prisage, *n*.1," 1a, *OED*). The Ormonde Butler family's right to prisage dated back to the family's arrival in Ireland as part of the Anglo-Norman conquest.
⁴⁴⁶ Gerald Fennell?
⁴⁴⁷ Unidentified.
⁴⁴⁸ Unidentified.
⁴⁴⁹ Unidentified.
⁴⁵⁰ Cromwellian officer.

what has givene offense, sense it has dasht what I and some othars
heare were indevoringe° with ^good^ provabilitye° of Sucksses ^for
hime^ had not this ill bussenes hindered, which you may as from
your selfe intemate° unto hime; if you think it fitt Not otharwise;
and remember mee unto Sir william Flower and his Lady, which is
all I have time to Say at this presant beinge Now callede a way to
wate° upon the [quine]⁴⁵¹ that is Now come to this Plase, where I am
intended to Settell this winter, and affter, as it shall please God to
dispose of

   E:ormonde

I pray send mee word whethar° John Meagh⁴⁵² bee imployede and
how hee is Satisfiede, for I take hime to bee bouth° abbell and
honnest

The 3 of No

**Letter 106. [1660?], [London?], the Marchioness of Ormonde
to John Burdon** (NLI, Ormond Papers, 2484, no. 227, p. 161).
Autograph.
For John Burdon [/] thes. [Endorsed]: Her Ladyshipp.

John Burdon

Sense the Closinge of my othar Leter, mr Corbett* Came hethar°
whoe understandinge of your beinge in thous° Parts did not prese
mee to anye perticulars consarninge° his Farme, nor was I willinge
to discourse anye thinge that might incoridge° hime to a treatye
only made a Shift to Let hime know what I had bine° offerede fo
for Balinekineye and Showede hime the Leter I now send you whoe
upon the readinge of it, did Say that hee would give as much as anye
othar Should that ment to be a Saver and not a Looser by it; and
that he would Sarve mee upon the Score of his respect as farr as
anye that should make mee offers in the way of Bargininge which I
undarstoud to bee the suplyinge mee with Mony° Soe as ~~accord to
that I pray~~ accordinge to that I praye Let hime bee Spokene with that
I may know what suplye may bee had from hime and how Soune,°
whoe I find to bee Extremlie desirious to gett mr Butler out of that
Plase, ~~whoe~~ that is allredie as hee Says very troubellsom, ~~and if~~ this

---

⁴⁵¹ Henrietta Maria, the Queen Mother.
⁴⁵² Unidentified.

leter of mr Jacksons* you may make uss° of but doe not Show it to mr Corbett by resone° that hee has allredie Siene° it

EO

Letter 107. November 21, 1660, Whitehall, the Marchioness of Ormonde to John Burdon (NLI, Ormond Papers, 2324, no. 1364, p. 427). Autograph.
For My Sarvant John Burdon thes. [Endorsed]: Her Ladyships 21st November 1660.

John Burdon

I have showede your Severall Leters unto My Lord, whoe has takene advise in the instructions that are now sent you, which as unto one perticular, is the Sueinge of Corronell Aboots,* to overthrow the Fyne ^of Nenagh^ which I could wishe might rathar bee avoyded,° as I conseve° it may bee, if Sir william Flower* and your selfe upon discourse, could draw hime to acsept of what is resonabell for his improvments, or to still bee ^Continow°^ Tenant to it, ^still^ giveinge as much as ^the Farme^ it is worth, which Last, I Conseve would of the tow° bee the best for uss, in regard that by that menes,° wee may have pretense to avoyde° the giveinge of that plase unto hime whoe formarlie had it, and whous Lease is not as yet expirede, nor wouldbee insistede upon, if hee Saw an aparant advantage to uss by Aboots offier,° beyond that which hee ^himselfe^ would give besides the avoydinge° of a Sute,° which I confess I would gladlie Shune if it bee possibell, therfor I pray uss° your best indevour° hearin, and send mee an accompt,° as allsoe how My Lords Rents dous° come in, I am glad to heare that the Copie of the [*missing*]⁴⁵³ Leter consarninge° your owne bussenes° Came sayfe° unto your hands as will I hope the origenall allsoe, which shallbee sent by mr Plunket* whoe goes hense upon Monday Next, I am still in a confustione soe great, with Companye and the vexsation of attendanse upon such as beinge heare I must obsarve, as I cannot write soe oftene; nor soe much as I did formarlie, howsomever I pray doe not you Slakene to Let mee heare, how my Lords affares goes Ther, and whether Ned Butler* keep doe punctuallye pay the Intrest Mony° that I gave him derectiones° to discharge in the dew° Times when that the Same is dew, sense° his performanse in that dous much import

whithall the 21 of No   E:ormonde

---

⁴⁵³ This is the result of a small tear, perhaps caused by the wax seal.

Letter 108. January 29, 1660/1, Whitehall, the Marchioness of Ormonde to Sir William Flower, Sergeant Major Thomas Harman, Edward Butler, Matthew Harrison, and John Burdon (NLI, Ormond Papers, 2325, no. 1371, p. 31).[454] Scribal: signed.
For Sir William Flower Knight Sarjant Major Thomas Harman Edward Buttler and Matthew Harrison Esquires and to Mr John Burden or to any of them to be opened and imparted to the rest. Dublin. [Endorsed]: 29 January Received 15th February 1660.

Sirs

[I] have received your joynt letter of the 16th of January, [which] I have considered of with my Lord, and upon examinat[ion] of the severall particulars contained therein; and in [the] adjoyned schedule of mortgages made to English, wee find [the] severall Summes by you ascertained amount to fowertene thowsand one hundred pounds, besides what remaines due of the severall debts for which Sir Phillip Percivall* became bound which are not stated; and besides all debts and mortgages due to Irish and what is claimed by the Earle of Midlesex[455] the executors of mr Miller[456] and mr Henshaw[457] and the Executors of Sir Robert Parkhurst;[458] Soe that upon the whole matter wee doe not See that by paying of any of those debts, more rent then the interest at ten in the hundred is to be gained, except in what may Concerne F[oulkes] Court, Burrishoule, Gauran ^the lands^ and Prizewines engaged [for] Sir Phillip Percivalls Security (which engagement may [hin]der the letting of the land at improoved values) and except the tythes° mortgaged to Mrs Henshaw[459] of which [noe] particular is Sent. It is therefore necessary before [any] order can be Sent hence for disposeing of any of the [M]ony returned by Bill of Exchange or of any rents [rec]eived or to be received, first that the account with [Sir] Percivall be Stated to which if he will not readyly come, he must by Such course as shall be advised be brought to it, that upon produceing his counter Security the engagement to him and debts to others may appeare. Secondly that [the] Sonne of

---

[454] A copy of this letter in the same scribal hand is NLI, Ormond Papers, 2325, no. 1370, p. 23. This has been used to supply words that in the original (signed) version are lost as a result of wear and tear to the left-hand side of the leaf or obscured by the mending tape.
[455] Lionel Cranfield, third Earl of Middlesex (1625–1674).
[456] Unidentified.
[457] Unidentified.
[458] Unidentified.
[459] Unidentified.

the late Bishop of Meath be speedyly brought to [ascertaine] his debt, whilest Doctor Fennell* and Patrick Darcy[460] are to wittnesse that the 3500 pounds for which Gauran et cetera stand ingaged is part of the 5000 pound for which Burishoule is ingaged and the nature of this Security is particularly to be [Examined] and transmitted with the exactest computation that [can] be made of the present and improoveable ^value^ of Burishoule Gauran et cetera. Thirdly that a rentall be speedyly Sent over, distinguishing the free from the engaged revenue and Setting downe as neere as may be the certaine the doubtfull, and the desperate rents. Haveing thus answered all the partes of your dispatch, I desire you as Soone as you can to lett me know upon what conditions Sir Henery Tichburne* had his two shares of Arclo° and [what] you think is reasonable to be insisted upon for the Setting of them. I desire you likewise to consider of the inclosed which I received this day from Mr Wheeler[461] and to doe [for him] what you think is just and fitt to be done therein [and] alsoe to Send me your answere to the inclosed quer[ie] concerning Crechanagh et cetera. And Soe I remaine

            Your loveing frend

Whitehall January the 29th 1660.   E:ormonde

Letter 109. February 26, 1660/1, Whitehall, the Marchioness of Ormonde to Thomas Meredith (NLI, Ormond Papers, 2325, no. 1374, p. 55). Scribal: signed.
For Sir Thomas Meredith Knight. These at Dublin. [Endorsed]: My Lady to Sir Thomas Merredith 26 February 1660.

Sir

I received your letter of the 9th of January but very lately, As soone as It came to my hands I communicated your desires to my Lord who is Soe Sensible of your condition that he hath Sent the inclosed direction to Such as he hath entrusted with the mannagement of his estate to permitt you to injoy your farme without any disturbance,

---

[460] Unidentified.
[461] Jonas Wheeler.

and to allow you what ^competent^ [ter]me you shall think fitt for the payment of the eighty pounds you mention. And Soe I remaine

        Sir

        Your frend and Servant

Whitehall the 26 of febr 1660   E:ormonde

Sir Thomas Meredith

Letter 110. February 27, 1660/1, Whitehall, the Marchioness of Ormonde to Sir William Flower, Sergeant Major Thomas Harman, Edward Butler, Matthew Harrison, and John Burdon (NLI, Ormond Papers, 2325, no. 1375, p. 61). Scribal: signed.
For Sir William Flower Knight Mr Edward Butler Mr Mathew Harrisson and Mr John Bourden and to any of them to be imparted to the rest. Att Dublin. [Endorsed]: [My Ladys] Dated 27 February Received 12 March 1660.

Sirs

Your letter of the 6th of february with the Schedule of Lands fitt to be charged with my daughters[462] joynture came not to my hands till the 23th of then communicated the same to my Lord, and wee are both of your opinion that it is better to charge the lands therein mentioned with a rent charge of 1500 pounds a yeere for her joynture then to assigne the lands themselves for that purpose. And therefore you are upon advice with Councell to gett such an instrument as is requisit prepared and transmitted hither with all convenient expedition to be perfected, inserting Carrick* for her joynture Howse with the Parke.[463] I desire that a lyst of the mortgages upon the Prezewynes may be speedyly Sent unto me and that mr Wailsh* may   *prisewines*
be made acquanted with my haveing received his letter of the 6th of febr Soe lately that I cannot returne him any answere thereunto untill the next oportunity, And Soe I remaine

        Your very assured frend

whitehall the 27 febr 1660   E:ormonde

---

    [462] EO's eldest daughter, Elizabeth, who married the Earl of Chesterfield around this time.
    [463] Ormond Castle, Carrick-on-Suir.

Letter 111. March 8, 1660/1, [Whitehall], the Marchioness of Ormonde to John Burdon (NLI, Ormond Papers, 2325, no. 1378, p. 79). Autograph.
For John Burdon thes. [Endorsed]: My Lady Marchioness 8th March 1660.

John Burdon

I resevede° tow° of your Leters togethar of the 27 of Feb, the one ~~con~~ men[tioned]e an accompt,° ~~and answar~~ of some perticulars requirede from you in some former Leters of my Lords, which I will take a Time to Show and advise with hime in, the othar is about a consarnment° of your owne ~~about the~~ ^consarninge a^ ^tuching°^ ^a^ Plase ~~that~~ in revertione that the kinge gave you a Leter For, after which I have sent to make inquirye, and will doe all I Cane by my Lord of Corks[464] menes° and othars to Secure it for you, beinge all that is at this time furthar Nesesarye to bee Sayede° unto you by

The 8 of March   E:ormonde

I desier° to have a List sent mee of such of my depts° as has bine° payede sense° I Left Ireland, and of what are remayninge, which may bee done by takinge a veue° of the Note of them which ~~wh~~ was Signede and Left by mee with Ned Butler* when I Came away

Letter 112. May 4, 1661, Whitehall, the Duchess of Ormonde to Sir Willam Flower, Sergeant Major Thomas Harman, Edward Butler, Matthew Harrison, and John Burdon (NLI, Ormond Papers, 2325, no. 1389, p. 155).[465] Scribal: signed.
For Sir William Flower Knight Sarjant Major Thomas Harman Edward Buttler and Matthew Harrison Esquires and Mr John Burden or any of them to be opened and communicated to the Rest. Dublyn. hast° hast.

Sirs

This is to lett you know that My Lord hath given Letters concerning Bansagh to Mr Theobald Buttler[466] and therefore you are not to

---

[464] Richard Boyle, second Earl of Cork. *The Diary of Richard Boyle, 2nd Earl of Cork and 1st Earl of Burlington, 1650–73*, ed. Coleman Dennehy and Patrick Little (Dublin: Irish Manuscripts Commission, forthcoming) has evidence of a close relationship between EO and the Earl of Cork through the 1650s and beyond.

[465] There is minor tearing to the MS, and text is also obscured by mending tape.

[466] Unidentified.

dispose thereof to any othar person un[til] he shall arrive there himselfe with those Letters which wilbe about the latter end of this [month /] I remaine

    Your assured frend

Whitehall the 4th of May 1661 E:ormonde

Sir William Flower et cetera

Letter 113. May 7, 1661, Whitehall, the Duchess of Ormonde to Sir William Flower, Sergeant Major Thomas Harman, Edward Butler, Matthew Harrison, and John Burdon (NLI, Ormond Papers, 2325, no. 1391, p. 169).[467] Scribal: signed.
For Sir William flower Knight Serjant Major Thomas Harman Edward Butler and Mathew Harrison Esquires and John Bourden Gentleman or any of them to be imparted to the rest. Att Dublin. [Endorsed]: Her ladyships Dated 7 Received 22 May 1661.

Sirs

You have formerly received some d[irectio]ns concerning the Setting of Some lands in Arclo° unto one mr Burnely.[468] And [in reg]ard it is possible that he being a Stranger [may not] be able to procure security there [to your] satisfaction, I desire you will not withstanding Conclude your agreement with him obleegeing him to give my lord such Security heere as for the performance thereof as he shall approve. And soe I rest

    Your assured frend

whitehall the 7 May 1661   E:ormonde

Letter 114. May 7, 1661, Whitehall, the Duchess of Ormonde to John Walsh (Bodl., Carte Papers, 31, fols. 170–171). Scribal Copy. [Endorsed]: Coppy of my Lady Dutchess Letter to Mr Walsh 7th May 1661.

Sir

I have Received your Letter of the 19th of Aprill, and have Communicated the Same together with the Note of severall

---

[467] There is minor tearing to the MS, and text is further obscured by mending tape.
[468] EO's tenant.

particulars you sent to mee inclosed unto my Lord, who as he is
very sensible of your great care and paines in the management of his
~~Consernments~~ Concernements,°[469] So you may be Confident, hee
wilbe ready to Reconpence it unto yow in any Occasion, wherein
~~your~~ ^his^ Friendship may bee of Advantage to yow. The Course of
Correspondence settled between ^Dr Fennell*^ yourselfe and the
Trustees, in Order to a Communication with each other, concerning
such overtures of Composition as shalbe made unto either of yow,
will certainly both facilitate and Expedite that worke. My Lord hath
considered what yow have written upon Occasion of the Note given
yow concerning the Ten[ure] of Crehanagh and the Parcells thereof,
which it Seemes you found by Severall off[ices] and ancient Rolls
to be held of the mannor of Carrick* in cheif, as well in Relation to
the pretentions of Reynolds[470] and fox[471] as Mr Buttler[472] the ancient
proprietors, whohaveing as yow Say taken Lands in Connaght in liew
of them [illegible] to be concluded by the Declaration. Yet my Lord
thinks that by his Majesties Grace his owne [tenure] is Reserved unto
him. But if in the Settlement the land should fall to Fox his [lott]
concernes it wilbe good to deale with him, if hee will take Reason for
it, in which Bargaine my Lords Tenure is to be Considered.

    As to Balimoran late the Inheritance of Pierce Buttler[473]
which you say was in Renolds possession, my Lord would have you to
See who is interested therein, and to use all Industry in compassing
the Purchase of the ancient Proprietor, if hee have any such Right,
as is comprehensiflie within the Declaration; I pray Lett my Lord
Chancelor and my lord ~~mountrath~~ Mountrath[474] [sic] know how
thanckfull my Lord is unto them, for the favour of their Interposition
for the [prevention] of the prejudice which wee were likely to Receive
by the meanes of Captain Castle.[475] And now haveing Answered the
particulars of your Letter, I shall beginn with the Note yow Sent
inclosed, and in answer to that concerning Mr Thomas Buttler, Sonn
to the Lord of Galway; his Interest by assignment of his Father, of
Severall Mortgages, amounting as he saith to 1500 pounds, my Lord
is contented if the Same shall appeare unto you to be true, ^that you^

---

[469] This correction of EO's usual spelling of "consernment" suggests that this might be a copy of an autograph original.
[470] Unidentified.
[471] Unidentified.
[472] Unidentified.
[473] Unidentified.
[474] Charles Coote, first Earl of Mountrath (c. 1610–1661).
[475] Unidentified.

conclude the agreement proposed, of paying him for his Interest 100
pounds in hand and secureing unto him 900 pounds upon Lands
in the County of Catterlogh, if the lands there benot already too
mush in tangled [first] provided that you be assured that hee tooke   *much*
noe Lands in Connaght, and that his Interest may be Secured by the
Declaration. As to the agreement with George Cummerford⁴⁷⁶ of
Holy Crosse my Lord desires approves of all the parts thereof, except
his haveing the farme for this yeare, in Regard of ^your^ present
Tennant whome he would not Remove for Soe short a time, but
rather allow Cummerford a reasonable Compensation for it; so it may
be free for his Lordship to dispose of hereafter[.] And he doubts not,
you would not made an Agreement with Commerford, if youdid not
find his Interest Secure and not intangled.

    Upon Occasion of the Proposition made by Hugh Oneale of
Ballineale,⁴⁷⁷ my Lord desires that all opportunityes might be taken
by the Trustees for the gaining of as much land about Carrick,* as
possibly they can, Soe the titles of such as they deale with there, be
Secure, and he desires you to Signify unto him, whither mr James
Tobyn of Garrangibbon⁴⁷⁸ tooke any Lands in Compensation of
the 180 pounds paid in Consideration of the 6 pounds13 shillings 4
pence yearely Rent you mention, and in the meane time, not to deale
with him, untill you Receive his further sense thereupon. My Lord
doth approve of the agreement made with Thomas Buttler⁴⁷⁹ for the
Yeares yet unExpired in his Lease of Derryclony Masterstowne and
Ballihourin, and thinks it may be of considerable Advantage that a
Compensation^osition^ may be made with Such mortgagees as do
offer to compound; But whoever tooke lands in Connaght and had
consideration for any Mortgage, he wo^u^ld have noe Compensation
given to them at all, But to Such Mortgagees as have had noe
Compensation for their Mortgages, he would have them agreed
withall, upon as easy Tearmes as may be, or any Composition rather
then None.

    Finding in the Note that you Sent concerning the mortgages
of the Prizewines, those of Limbrick mortgaged unto William
Haly;* I think fitt to let you know, that my Lord hath given him a
Compensation for it here and that he hath made alegall Resignation
of his Interest therein, which I desire you to make knowne to
Matthew Harrison, to the end he may endeavour to Compound with

---

⁴⁷⁶ Unidentified.
⁴⁷⁷ Unidentified.
⁴⁷⁸ Unidentified.
⁴⁷⁹ Unidentified.

the Rest who haue mortgages upon any Part of the Prizewines in Ireland and Soe I remaine

    Your assured friend

Whitehall 7th May 1661   EOrmond

Letter 115. June 10, 1661, Whitehall, the Duchess of Ormonde to Sir William Flower and Matthew Harrison (NLI, Ormond Papers, 2325, no. 1402, p. 247). Scribal: signed.
For Sir William Flower Knight and Matthew Harrison Esquire or either of them. these at Dublin. [Endorsed]: My ladys dated [10] of June 1661.

Sirs

I have received your Letter of the 5th of this month wherein you take Notice of a Letter of mine of the 3rd of June directing you to pay Alderman Bellingham* 2216 pound and in regard I do not remember that any other summe hath been writt for but the two thousand pounds lately charged by that Alderman upon Sir Thomas Vyner* I desire to know how the 216 pound comes to be added and that hereafter when hee shall transmitt any moneyes for Our Use hee will appoint a shorter time of payment wee beinge much prejudiced by the length of time given to Sir Thomas Vyner upon the last Bill of Exchange. The proffer made by my Lady Thurles* of accepting two parts of three of what is due unto her by ^Bond^ from my Lord is so reasonable that wee must desire you take as speedy a Course as you can for her Ladiships Satisfaction accordingly and I desire you to let us know as soone as you can how much her Ladiships whole debt amounts unto As to the cheife rent payable by Mr Boulton[480] out of Corronell duffe[481] you are to consider my Lords Act of Parlament whereby hee was restored to his possessions and if you find that a Retrospect in that case is warranted the[re]by I know no reason why hee should not be oblidged to pay the Arreares due since the death of the late Chancelor But if you find no warrant in that Act for the demand of such Arreares you shall do well to take any ^resonable^[482] Composition hee shall ~~voluntarily~~ offer unto you rather then bring

---

[480] Unidentified.

[481] Unidentified.

[482] This is inserted in EO's hand in the same ink as her signature. The subsequent deletion also appears to be in her hand: the word is crossed out using her distinctive looped ses.

the Business into dispute. Mr Jonas wheeler[s]* wife desired mee
to accept of a Surrender of her Lease and to give her Husband
Consideration for his Improvements which I was not willing to do
but do now referr him to you and the rest of the Commissioners to
treat and conclude with him upon those particulars as you shall think
just and reasonable [/] I remaine

                Your very assured Friend

Whitehall the 10th of June 1661   E:ormonde

Letter 116. August 3, 1661, Whitehall, the Duchess of Ormonde to Sir William Flower, Sergeant Major Thomas Harman, Edward Butler, Matthew Harrison, and John Burdon (NLI, Ormond Papers, 2325, no. 1413, p. 337). Scribal: signed.
For Sir William flower Knight Sarjant Major Thomas Harman Edward Buttler and Matthew Harrison Esquires and Mr John Burden or any of them to be communcated to the rest. at Dublin.
[Endorsed]: My Lady dutchesse hers Concerninge Arckloe and other things 3 August 1661.

Sirs

Your Letter of the 20th of July last I have received which being perused by my Lord is well pleased and accordingly directs that you conclude with Captain Saules[483] upon the Tearmes you propose, that is to say to pay him Eight hundred pounds for one thousand five hundred thirty and four Acres wherof three hundred pounds in hand and the rest in twelve months time without Interest and that you deale likewise with him for the two thousand Acres belonging to his Troope so you can bargaine upon so easy tearmes as you signify in your Letter

      You are likewise without delay to conclude with Collonel owen[484] for Eight hundred and fifty Pounds as you propose to be paid to him in Consideration of the third part of the five thousand pounds for which Burrishoule is mortgaged to Martin* Provided hee secures to make good the Bargaine as Councell shall Advise You are to use the more Expedition in this (so it be with Security) in regard Mr Martin is already upon his journey thither, who (as wee have just cause to suspect) will endeavour to obstruct your Bargaine and would upon no tearmes yeild to an Abatement of any part of the Totall

---

[483] Unidentified.
[484] Unidentified.

Summe and sayes that Collonel Owens can pretend to noe Interest in it.

By the Account you give concerning Arclo° it seemes that Sir Henry Tichburne* and Mr Foxleth⁴⁸⁵ will not Surrender unless the interest of the undertennants be saved to them and halfe a yeares Rent abated. By former Letters it was signified unto you that wee would be at no losse by the Surrender and in case Mr Burnaby⁴⁸⁶ his agent did not agree to discharge the Easter Rent and allow the Interest of the undertenants so it were insisted upon) then were you to leavy the whole Rent [owed] of Sir Henry Tichburne without abatement. yet do not wee understand by your Account what answer Mr Burnabys Agent gave you in this Particular However now that Mr Burnaby is here hee shalbe spoken unto concerning it In the meane time delay not the bringing in ^and demanding^ of the ^full^ Rent ~~any longer~~ of Sir Henry Tichbourne for the future

I understand by a Letter from Ned Butler* that the house of Carrick* is in a Ruinous Condistion The Season of the yeare being so farr past that there can be no considerable Reparation made at present I desire that such Course be taken as may preserve it from more distruction till next Spring and the like Care to be taken of the house of Cloghrenan.⁴⁸⁷ I rest

    Your asshured° Frind

Whitehall the 3 of August 1661 E:ormonde

Letter 117. August 6, 1661, [Whitehall], the Duchess of Ormonde to John Burdon (NLI, Ormond Papers, 2325, no. 1415, p. 351). Autograph.
For John Burdon thes. [Endorsed]: Her Ladyshipp 6 August 1661.

John Burdon

I saw a Leter from you Latlie° unto Edward Butler,* consarninge° your Rent, wherin you desier° to know my plesure whether I will continow° your first Sallerye° or Not, which ^(did determin)^ upon the giveinge you a Lease at Dublin of the Farme of killfe kell ~~which~~   *Kifeacle* (Co. Tipperary)

---

⁴⁸⁵ Unidentified.
⁴⁸⁶ Unidentified.
⁴⁸⁷ Cloughrennan Castle, Co. Carlow, had been built in the fifteenth century by the Ormonde Butlers. See *Anthologia Hibernica: Or Monthly Collections of Science, Belles-Lettres, and History* 3 (May, 1794), 319, which also includes a plate illustrating the ruins of the castle.

^that^ you were to hould° rent free duringe plesure, and the benefitt givene you besides therby, you did rest fullye satisfiede with; as Doctor Fenell* did tell mee, and as I toucke° for Granted; haveinge then Exprest my selfe in that perticuler, and was made knowne to you ^then to be^ as the intent of

The 6 of Agust   E:ormonde

Letter 118. September 16, 1661, Whitehall, the Duchess of Ormonde to Sir William Flower, Sergeant Major Thomas Harman, Edward Butler, Matthew Harrison, and John Burdon (NLI, Ormond Papers, 2325, no. 1420, p. 379). Scribal: signed.
For Sir William flower Knight Sarjant Major Thomas Harman Edward Buttler and Matthew Harrison Esquires Mr John Bourden or any of them to be communcated to the rest. Dublin. [Endorsed]: receaved this Letter the 10th of October with the [instr]uctions. My Ladys Letter aboute my Lady Thurles debt. 16 Sept 1661. Duchess of O.

Sirs

I presume your delay of sending an Accompt° of our Rents proceeds from some maine Obstacle you meet with It is of that Consequence to have it whereby wee may be able to Judge what wee are to trust to that I must againe desire you to make it your Care with as much Expedition as you can to send it. I desire that you will likewise send an Account as neere as you can of what Mortgages or debts my Lady of Thurles* and Mr James Buttler of Thurles do pretend[488] unto and by what Title or upon what Security they stand and what Overtures of Composition they or either of them do make. You are to proceed in compounding with Mortgagees and others our Creditors as speedily as you can according the inclosed instructions and from time to time to returne an Account of what you do therein unto

Your loveing Friend

Whitehall the 16th of September 1661   E:ormonde

Sir William Flower

---

[488] "To put forward as an assertion or statement; to allege, assert, contend, claim, declare; *esp.* to allege or declare falsely or with intent to deceive" ("pretend, *v.*," 1, *OED*).

Letter 119. October 12, 1661, Whitehall, the Duchess of Ormonde to Sir William Flower, Sergeant Major Thomas Harman, Edward Butler, Matthew Harrison, and John Burdon (NLI, Ormond Papers, 2326, no. 1426, p. 13). Scribal: signed.

For Sir William Flower Knight Sargeant Major Thomas Harman Edward Buttler & Matthew Harrison Esquire & Mr John Bourden or any of them to be communicated to the rest. at ~~Dublin~~ ^Kilkenny^.

Sir

Upon Complaint heretofore made by Lieutenant Colonel Stevens* that by your Directions the tyeth of Grange tillhanny was sett to another notwithstanding that by his Lease from mee he was to enjoy it I signifyed unto you that I conceived it but Justice that hee should have the Benefitt of his Lease yet I am now informed by him that your Answer upon receipt of those Directions was that the Tyethes were already sett upon the Account of Mrs Hensham[489] by Richard Cumerford[490] and that my Lord would not allow of that or of any other Lease made by mee which though I cannot give credit unto yet I have thought fitt to give you notice of it that yo^u^ may both let mee know what you said unto him and take some such speedy Course as hee may have no cause of Complaint. I have by former Letters severall times desired that you would appoint some certaine person in Dublin upon whom wee may rely for to receive such Letters and dispatches as Should be sent from hence and would dispose of them there according to directions [/] this I must againe renew unto you and desire that you will thereof returne a speedy Account unto

tithe

Your loveing friend

Whitehall the 12th of October 1661   E:ormonde

Sir William Flower

---

[489] Unidentified.
[490] Unidentified.

The Lord Lieutenancy, 1662–1668

Letter 120. November 12, 1662, [Dublin], the Duchess of Ormonde to Sir Edward Nicholas (BL, Egerton MSS, 2538, fol. 195). Autograph.
For Sir Edward Nicholas. [Endorsed]: 12 November 1662 The Dutchesse of Ormonde leter to me upon the Newes of my removal from being Secretary of State.

Sir[491]

The favour of your Last Leter of the 10 of october I had not the good Fortune to reseve° untell° the day that I went from hense into the Contrye; otharwise I had souner° exprest to you my trouble for the Contents of it, that brought mee the unwellcome Neuse° of your beinge to quitt your Plase of Secretarye;[492] I willnot answar for your Good frind at Bouas; but I will asshure° you, that all that I converse with ^heare^ was Sorrye and Sensible of it; and soe I doe beleve were manye more upon a publick accompt,° as well as ther perticuler frindshipe to you; of which I Nomber, I cane pertend to bee but the Least considerable; yet as much consernede° for you as anye canbee; Sense° my vallew° of you was not grownded° upon ~~upon~~ your Power, but that integritie and worth that your Enimies cannot but allow you allways to have had, and your Frinds Estimede you For, which added to the obligations of soe many favours as I resevede° from you when I was abrode,° and sense your returne home, are Motives that dous° ingadge° mee to bee allways

        Sir

                your much oblidged frind and
                     humble Sarvant

                    E:ormonde

Sir I desier° my Sarvis° may bee remembred unto my Lady Nicholas*

The 12 of No

---

[491] These letters to Nicholas have a wide indent under the greeting as a sign of respect.

[492] Against his wishes, Nicholas was replaced as Secretary of State by a younger man, Henry Bennet, first Earl of Arlington, a favorite of Charles II and close friend of EO's eldest son, Ossory.

Letter 121. January 21, 1662/3, [Dublin], the Duchess of Ormonde to Sir Edward Nicholas (BL, Egerton MSS, 2538, fol. 211).
Autograph.
For Sir Edward Nicholas. [Endorsed]: 21 January 1662 Dutchesse of Ormond full of Noble kindnes to me.

Sir

My indisposistion of health, added to my unease of Mind; for My daughter Chesterfilds* unhappenes; of which I cannot but have a sense, Ecquall to the consernment° that I have for hir, will I hope obtayne your Excuse, and favorable constroctione of my not owninge Souner,° the favour of your Last Leter; sent mee by James Bucke,* which otharwise I shouldnot have soe Longe deferede; allthough my makinge you a returne; dous° rathar ade° unto your troubell; then signifie anye thinge that is worthye of your acseptanse, othar then as I know you to have soe much indulgense for Mee, as to admitt, and Excuse my Errors; when thay° proside° out of my kindnes (and not ill will to you;) for what ever othars may doe if anye therbee soe Bad; as to declyne thar° vallew° and respects to you, I doe asshure° you that I nethar am; Nor Ever willbee of that Nomber, but as much a wellwisher of yours, and as desirious to Sarve you in what may Lie in my power; as you were allways forward to oblidge Mee ^the Last^ beinge what is; and shallbee Ever, with much thankfullnes remembrede; and ownede by

       Sir

               your asshured° Frind and humble Sarvant

The 21 of Jan   E:ormonde

Sir I desier° that by you My Sarvise° may bee remembred unto My Lady Nicholas*

Letter 122. January 21, 1662/3, [Dublin], the Duchess of Ormonde to the Earl of Clarendon (Bodl., Clarendon Papers, 79, fol. 29). Autograph.
For the Earle of Clarendon Lord Chanceler of England. [Endorsed]: Dutchesse of Ormonde January 21th 1662/3.

My Lord[493]

I remember a Letell befor I toucke° my Journye hether, your Lordshipp toulde mee that befor a yeare should come about, My Lord should have a habitatione of his owne in England, I did not comprehend how it would bee, but now hearinge of a Plase callede More Parke* is to be sould,° and that it is a pleasant ~~plase~~ ^seat^ at a convenient distanse from London, I take the Libertye to mind you of what you sayde; and to desier° you would speake with Sir Charles Harbert,[494] whoe was onse° Master of it ~~whoe~~ ^that^ cane give your Lordshipp the best accompt° of it; The Mony° for it shallbee provided within six Months, and might bee Souner,° but that I hope the charge of transmitinge which is five in the hundreth may in that time bee savede, your Lordshipp will pardone this freedom I use, and the trouble I give you prosiedinge partlie from your owne indulgence; and very much from my beinge

    My Lord
      your Lordshipps very reall and humble Sarvant
The 21 of Jan   E:ormonde

---

[493] There are approximately four lines of blank space between the greeting and the main text of the letter, and this use of blank space is replicated on the top of the second leaf; a similar amount of blank space is also found between the main text of the letter and the signature. The use of material space indicates EO's deference to Clarendon.

[494] Sir Charles Harbord, Surveyor General. See https://www.historyofparliamentonline.org/volume/1660-1690/member/harbord-sir-charles-1596-1679.

Letter 123. March 1, [1663], [Dublin], the Duchess of Ormonde to Sir James Graham, High Sheriff of County Louth (HL, Hastings-Irish Papers (Rawdon Papers), HA 14112).[495] Autograph. [Endorsed]: dutches of ormond to Sir James Grahame about a Salieri[e] being alow'd to the Goveraner of drogheda.

Sir[496]   The [2] ^First^ of March

you doe mee but Right, when you are pleased to beleve mee willinge to bee sarvisable° to you in anye thinge that I cane, in order whereunto I showed My Lord your Leter, that mentioned your Consernes,° whous answar unto mee was; that theris noe allowanse in the Establishment for a Governer of Droighedath [/] besides   Droichead Átha
that hee findinge noe president° for it; in the Late Lord Liftenants   *(Drogheda)*
Time, hee cannot without the kings imediate Order give anye such; whous Commands Comes soe frequentlie to hime for disposinge of Compaynes as Leavs hime not free to ingadge° himselfe befor hand, which beinge his owne words, I have noe other part therin; then to acquant you of it; and to asshure° you from My Selfe, of my asshured° beinge

                 Sir

Letter 124. August 26, 1663, [Dublin], the Duchess of Ormonde to Sir Edward Nicholas (BL, Egerton MSS, 2538, fol. 231). Autograph. For Sir Edward Nicholas. [Endorsed]: 26 August 1663 Lady Dutchesse of Ormond with much kindnes.

Sir   The 27 ^26^ of Agust

upon the ressept° of your Leter of the 8 of Agust, I toucke° the best oppertunitie I could after I had advisede with such heare as I know to bee your Frinds; Namelie Sir Paule Davis[497] and Sir Gorge Layne,* to speake unto My Lord as I did in your Consernment,° whoe bid mee to Leave that bussenes° to hime; for hee was mindfull of it, and intended to give you an accompt° therof himselfe, which I doe hope

---

     [495] The bottom of the letter appears to have been trimmed, resulting in the loss of the valediction and signature.

     [496] Sir James Graham was the son of the Earl of Menteith. He married John Bramhall's daughter, Isabella. See John McCafferty, "Bramhall, John (*bap.* 1594, *d.*1663)," *ODNB*. Sir James was High Sheriff of Louth in 1663 and Mayor of Drogheda in 1671. Since JO was not serving as lord lieutenant in 1671, it is likely that the letter dates from 1663 or thereabouts.

     [497] Sir Paul Davies, Secretary of State for Ireland.

hee has accordinglie done; and soe sattisfinge a one, as willbee to your Content; howsomever untell° I heare it Soe from your owne hand; I shall continow° the beinge his rememberansier, in what relates unto your perticuler; it beinge all that my small Talent or power cane render mee capabell to sarve you in, unto the full extent of which; you may rest confident of the frindshipe and indevours° of

   Sir

     your ashured Frind and humble Sarvan

     E:ormonde

Letter 125. October 31, 1663, [Dublin], the Duchess of Ormonde to John Burdon (NLI, Ormond Papers, 2332, no. 1803, p. 13). Autograph.
For John Burdon thes the Last of oct. [Endorsed]: Her Graces letter Dated 31st October Received 2nd November 1663.

John Burdon

Theris some ocatione° at this Time wherin your repayre hethar° willbee Nesesarye in ordar to some consernes° of My Lords and Mine wherfor I pray Let your Comminge bee as Soune° as you Cane Convenientlie if ^and^ your health Permitt, which willbee very well takene by

   E:ormonde

Letter 126. November 16, [1663], [Dublin], the Duchess of Ormonde to Catherine of Braganza (Bodl., Clarendon Papers, 92, fols. 69–70).[498] Autograph. See Figure 9.
For hir Magestye. [Endorsed]: Lady Ormond to the Queen.

As your Late danger ocationed° a generall grife;° soe has your deliverense out of it bine° as universall a Joy to all,[499] and to mee in perticuler, that have allways had for your Persone soe great an honner° and admiration of your vertews° as I cannot but beleve that the great providense of God has prolonged your Life to make thes kingdoms hapie, by the Blesinge they soe much desier,°[500] which together with all the happenes and prosperitie that this world is capabell to adde unto what you doe allredie injoye, is and shall[bee wisht] for by mee, that humblie beges your Magesties pardon for the presumtione of this address, and your Justise to beleve that non° is, or canbee more devoted to you, then is with all humilitie and fathfullnes

    Madam

        your Magesties most humble and most
         obedient Subject and Sarvant

The 16 of November   E:ormonde

---

[498] There is significant blank space in this letter. The top half of each page is blank, which is a sign of humility. It looks like the letter was trimmed by perhaps a little over an inch after the letter was sent and received. There is no direct greeting to the Queen, yet EO's customary diagonal slash (above which the greeting is usually placed) is at the top left-hand corner of the first leaf. In addition, the address on the outside of the letter is not centred as is EO's usual practice (even within the folds). Furthermore, the top edge of the letter is uneven, which indicates that it was cut when the letter was folded. It is therefore possible that the deferential space at the top of each leaf was even larger than now appears. The letter is sealed with red wax and silk ribbon.

[499] The Queen had fallen seriously ill of a fever in October, and in her delirium thought she had three children; there was already speculation by this time that she was infertile. See S. M. Wynne, "Catherine (1638–1705)," *ODNB*.

[500] The birth of a royal heir.

Letter 127. January 5, 1663/4, [Dublin], the Duchess of Ormonde to Sir Edward Nicholas (BL, Egerton MSS, 2538, fol. 239). Autograph. For Sir Edward Nicholas. [Endorsed]: 5 January 1663 My Lady Dutchesse of Ormond Noble favour [regarding] my [Concerns] in Ireland.

Sir   The 5 of Jan

I hope you willnot blame my Sielense° in not Souner° ansaringe° yours of the 21 of November when I shall tell you the true Cause, which was an unwillingnes to troubell you untell° I could see some provabilitye° of Sarvinge you, by which Rule I ought to have suspended it still, but that My Sone Arans* goeinge has tempted mee to tell you, that the presant povertie of this plase,⁵⁰¹ and the great unsetellment that all the publicke bussenes° is in upon which anye Mony° canbee raysede;° ocations° soe uneversall a disapoyntment, as untell the Act⁵⁰² bee agreede upon theris Litell° hopes to prevayle, though it is that, of your Consernment° only, that ocations my inquirye, and that I shall Continow,° untell I cane send you some beter° accompt° of your perticuler affare, as at ~~Longe run maye~~ Length I hope to doe at the Least my best indevours° shallnot bee wantinge, though to inconsiderable I feare to desarve your acseptanse; yet as farr as my small Tallent or power cane inabell° mee to Sarve you theris nothinge condussibell therunto but shall on all ocations bee put in practise by

    Sir

        your very asshureded° Frind and
            humble Sarvant

        E:ormonde

Sir I desier° my Sarvis° may bee remembred unto My Lady Nicholas*

---

⁵⁰¹ I.e. Ireland.

⁵⁰² After the Act of Settlement (1662), a Court of Claims was established to investigate who was eligible for recovery of their lands. However, the commissioners found more eligible Catholics than there was available land. The Act of Explanation (1665) stated that Cromwellian settlers (with some named exceptions) had to give up one third of the lands they had received after 1652 to compensate the eligible Catholics.

Letter 128. April 4, 1666, [Dublin], the Duchess of Ormonde to the Earl of Arlington (TNA, SP Ireland, 320,85, fols. 198–200). Autograph.
For My Lord Arlington. [Endorsed]: April 4 66 Dublin My Lady Duchess of Ormonde Sends her Recognitions to your Lordship for your kindnesses to my lord Ossory and his Lady, as to my Lord John.

My Lord   The 4 of Aprell

I find in all my Son and daghter Ossorys* Leters such acknowlegments of your Lordships kindnes and frindshipe to them Both, seconded with such testimonies of your favour unto my sone John* allsoe, as I should injure the gratitude I have for you upon ther accompt° and my owne if I should think the retributione of words were suffisent to make it appiere,° and therfor I shall avoyde° the giveinge your Lordshipp to tedious a trouble of that kind, and only asshure° you, that in all the returnes of Sarvis° and respect to you thereis noe person you shall find to ther capasitie more redie to paye it you then my selfe, I am very glad my Son ossorys* offier° was refusede of goeinge to Sea was refused⁵⁰³ [/] it beinge a statione of sarvinge the kinge wherin I think hee could prove Least ussfull where nether Intrest nor Experiense could have intytled° hime, The honner° of beinge admitted a Gentellman of the Bedchamber in his Fathers Rome⁵⁰⁴ upon the condistions mentioned in your Lordships Leter unto My Lord is an advantage hee ought to reseve° as I dout° not hee dous,° with all hum^ble^ thankfullnes and gratitude unto his Magestie which I am very sensible hee owes in a great mesure unto your Lordships good assistanse; The Mache° you were pleasede to propose for my Son John* I have consulted my Lord in; and find upon the consideratione of the Dept° yet restinge upon his Fortune [/] the unsartanties° of Monys° comminge in out of which the same should^bee^ discharged [/] his Rents besides fallinge and ill payede by resone° of the great and generall povertie of the kingdom by the presant warr and inhebitione of transportinge Cattell from   *inhibition*
hense into England as thay° did formerlie; forses° hime out of these considerations to rather to decline that advantage that by

---

⁵⁰³ For an account of Ossory's impulsiveness in offering himself for naval service, see J. D. Davies, "Butler, Thomas, sixth earl of Ossory (1634–1680)," *ODNB*.
⁵⁰⁴ "An office or post considered as belonging to a particular person, esp. by right or by inheritance" ("room, *n.* 1, and *int.*," A, IV, 11, *OED*).

your Lordships my Lord Crofts⁵⁰⁵ and Mr Cofferers⁵⁰⁶ indevours°
with some provabilitie° might have takene Effect; then adde to his
ingadgment° soe considerable a Some as wouldbee expected, and
might resonablie bee Soe by the yonge Ladys Frinds [/] soe that my
Sone must content himselfe to stay a while, and wee deferr to see
hime soe settled as your Lordships good intendments towards hime
had designed in this second overture of makinge his Fortune; when
the Mach° with my Lord Hawlys* Grandchild faylled which for some
resons I cannot bee Sorrye For;⁵⁰⁷ I hope by this time Madamosell
de Beverward⁵⁰⁸ is Landed and that I shall befor it bee Longe have
ocatione° to congratulate and wish you Joy of hir; tell° when it will
not befitt mee to detane you Longer from your grater consernes,°
though you have bine° soe oblidginge as to Consider thous° of Mine;
beyond what couldbee expected or desarvede by Soe ussless a person
as is

   My Lord

     your Lordships humble Sarvant

      E:ormonde

**Letter 129. June 6, 1666, [Dublin], the Duchess of Ormonde to
the Earl of Arlington** (TNA, SP Ireland, 321,31, fols. 83–85).
Autograph.
For My Lord Arlingtone [/] Thes. [Endorsed]: 6 June 66 Lady
Dutchesse of Ormond. Hath nothing to request beyond the
continuance of your Lordships favour.

My Lord   The 6 of June

I did injoyne° my Sone Ossorye* to make my Excuse unto your
Lordshipp that I did not by the Last weekes Post acknowlege the
favour of yours of the 15 of May ~~but~~ ^which^ my beinge but Newlie

---

⁵⁰⁵ William Crofts, Baron Crofts (d. 1677). See Stephen Porter, "Crofts, William, Baron Crofts (*d.* 1677), courtier," *ODNB*.

⁵⁰⁶ Unidentified.

⁵⁰⁷ Lady Elizabeth Malet had a reputation for sexual indiscretion. For the details of her suitors and marriage, see *The Letters of John Wilmot, Earl of Rochester*, ed. J. Treglown (Oxford: Oxford University Press, 1980), 10–17. See also O'Keeffe, 64–65.

⁵⁰⁸ Isabella van Nassau (1633–1718), sister of EO's daughter-in-law, Lady Ossory, whom Arlington would marry on April 16, 1666, in the middle of the Anglo-Dutch War of 1665–1667. See Alan Marshall, "Bennet, Henry, first earl of Arlington (*bap.* 1618, *d.* 1685)," *ODNB*.

returnede out of the Contrye and my Surprise at my Lords goeinge
soe sudanlie° unto Carickfargus⁵⁰⁹ respetede your resevinge° soe
Earlie a returne as in gratitude and good Manners I ought to have
made you for confirminge from your owne hand what I am soe
well pleasede to heare, as your belevinge your selfe as hapie in your
Mariage as I was Ever confident that the vertew° and discretione of
your Lady would make you, added unto that Sense of honner° as I
know you have to vallew° hir for beinge Soe, your Lordship is pleased
to bee soe oblidginge in your Frindshipe and kindnes to my Sone
and in your advise to mee conserninge° hime as the demonstratione
I reseve° of your favour by what you Extend to hime Leaves mee
nothinge to request beyond the continowanse° of it, Save the Justise
to mee of ~~still~~ beinge still accompted°

    My Lord

      your Lordships reall and humble Sarvant

       E:ormonde

Letter 130. June 16, 1666, Dublin, the Duchess of Ormonde to the Earl of Arlington (TNA, SP Ireland, 321,37, fols. 103–105). Autograph.
For My Lord Arlingtone. [Endorsed]: Dublin June 6 66 My Lady Dutchesse of Ormonde.

My Lord   The 16 of June

It was not my Fortune to heare of my Sone Ossorys* beinge at Sea
untell° sonday Last that in a Publick Leter I heard hime Namede,
which I confess did a Litell° surprise Mee, and ~~Left~~ ^kept^ mee
in some unease, untell relevede that same Eveninge by the arrivale
of a persone that asshurede° mee of his beinge sayfe,° and sense°
confirmede by his returne, I shall not argue aganst what is past, but
doe hope I shallnot bee thought the Less Loyall, if I wishe hee may
not attempt the Like agayne° but resarve himselfe to Act if ther
shallbee ocatione° where hee may bee instrumentall to bringe more to
ingadge° then himselfe Singlie, and I am apt to flatter my selfe with
a beleufe that it is your Lordships oppinione allsoe, and if Soe, I doe

---

⁵⁰⁹ Carrickfergus, Co. Antrim, the seat of Sir Arthur Chichester, Earl of Donegal.

not dout° but it will have Creditt with hime, and your Lordship I hope, the Charitie for mee, as to pardone all the Errors of you find in

    My Lord

        your Lordships reall and humble Sarvant

            E:ormonde

My Lord I bege your Leave in this to present My Sarvise° to My Lady of Arlington[510]

Letter 131. September 20, [1666?], [Kilkenny?], the Duchess of Ormonde to the Duke of Ormonde (NLI, Ormond Papers, 2484, no. 244, p. 287). Autograph.
For the Duke of Ormonde [/] thes. [Endorsed]: My Lady Dutchesse to my Lord concerninge debt due in England.

[Sense] your goeinge I have devided out of the paper[s] Intrest Mony° what is best to bee retainede unto Bucke* and what to James Clarke[511] that ther may bee noe confusion in accompts,° That to ~~Backe~~ Bucke, willbee 365 10 Shillings and that to James Clarke willbee 144.03.11 which makes upe in the Totall what is Mentioned in the paper, That I gave you which if you doe aprove of I shall then desier° that your derections° for the resept of the Mony Ether by Bills or otherwise may bee accordinglie, I pray when Sir Allen Brodericke[512] goes for England ingadge° hime to put My Lord Chanselor[513] in Mind to Send you his Picture

The 20 of September

---

[510] The new Lady Arlington, Isabella Bennet, née van Nassau (1633–1718).
[511] EO's household steward.
[512] Sir Allen Brodrick (1623–1680) was Surveyor General of Ireland. See http://www.historyofparliamentonline.org/volume/1660-1690/member/brodrick-allen-1623-80.
[513] The Lord Chancellor Sir Edward Hyde, Earl of Clarendon, was a patron of Sir Allen Brodrick.

Letter 132. September 24, [1666], Kilkenny, the Duchess of Ormonde to Colonel William Legge (SRO, Dartmouth Collection, D(W)1778/I/i/203).[514] Autograph.
For Corronell Lege. [Endorsed]: Duchess of Ormond. September 24th.

Cousen   The 24 of September

I am shure° you willnot bee unsatisfiede to know that all your Frinds heare are well, and espetialie° that my daghter Arran[515] is Soe; whoe has bine° this weeke past and is still in a Course of Phisicke, with soe good suckses;° as I doe beleve you Never saw hir louke° soe well as shee dous° at this presant, nor Cane you wishe hir more Chierfull° nor in a more provable° way of a perfect recovrye of hir health which is noe small Joy to Mee [/] wee are yet heare at killkenye where I doe beleve the Ayre° to bee beter° then at Dublin makes mee willinge to Stay some Time in Care of my daghters health, as well as my owne, shee beinge as much my conserne° as anye thinge in this world Canbee, for noe body canbee more oblidginge and Consequentlie more honnored and belovede in a Familie then shee is, in this of ours; I supose you are Now at oxford where you Cane give some gess° of what My Sone may Expect from My Lord Halys* profestions, that if not answarede by Effects; you will in the worst Event that may

---

[514] Colonel William Legge enjoyed a longstanding friendship with JO and his family, and was broker for the marriage of EO's youngest son, Lord John Butler, who in the summer of 1664 had been proposed as husband to a highly sought-after heiress, Elizabeth Malet. Described by Pepys as the "great beauty and fortune of the North," she had inherited estates said to be worth £2,500 per year from her father, John Malet of Enmore, Somerset. O'Keeffe, 64–65, describes the circumstances of the breakdown of negotations with Elizabeth Malet, who would later marry John Wilmot, second Earl of Rochester. By Pepys's account there were no hard feelings between Elizabeth Malet and Lord John: "But it was pleasant to see how every body rose up when my Lord John Butler, the Duke of Ormond's son, come into the pit towards the end of the play, who was a servant to Mrs. Mallet, and now smiled upon her, and she on him" (*The Diary of Samuel Pepys: Daily Entries from the 17th-Century London Diary*, February 4, 1666/7, http://www.pepysdiary.com).

[515] Mary Butler, née Stuart (1651–1668), had married EO's second son, Richard, Earl of Arran, in September 1664 at the age of thirteen. In a letter to Colonel Legge on March 15, 1666/7, JO wrote that she "growes a lovely person and continues so good, that if I had a hundred children or but one, I could not love any of them better then I doe her. I never saw so much discretion in so few yeares, nor so little of humor or trouble in any of her sex of what agesoever. I know you will be glad to heare it, I am sure I am highly delighted to find it" (cited in HMC, *The Manuscripts of the Earl of Dartmouth*, 3 vols. [London: His Majesty's Stationery Office, 1887], 1. 16).

hapene consider of some way how hee may come ofe° handsomlie, sense° I cannot but aprehend that hee will meete with difficulties, where some are ingadged° to oppose hime, that you very well know, and therfor I nide° not Name, but relye upon your Frindshipe and advise, which willbee of great advantage to hime, and of Ecquall Sattisfactione unto

    Sir

      your Cousene and Sarvant

       E:ormonde

I pray remember mee to my Cousen Lege[516] and to your daughter[517] whous Companye is oftene wisht for heare [/] I have writene twise to My Lady Duches of Richmond[518] sense my Landinge but doe feare my Leters came not to hir hands

Letter 133. October 3, [1666], Kilkenny, the Duchess of Ormonde to Colonel William Legge (SRO, Dartmouth Collection, D(W)1778/I/i/205). Autograph.
For Corronell Legge thes. [Endorsed]: Duchess of Ormond October 3rd.

Cousen   kilkeny the 3 of oct

This is my second Leter to you sense° my arivall, my former mentioninge to you the conserne° of my Sone John* of which I shall not at this time trouble you to say more untell° I heare from you tuchinge° that affare, as I doutnot I shall when it is Nesesarye; by this inclosede from mee to your daghter with what is transmitted to you by my Lord from his unkell° you will find it in your owne power to [Con]clude or decline the Mache° proposede for hir, soe as accordinge unto what shee best aproves and you resolve I desier° that my unkell Poynes[519] may heare spidilie° from you, and that you will

---

[516] Possibly his eldest son, George Legge (c. 1647–1691), later Lord Dartmouth.

[517] This is most likely "Mall," or Mary, Legge (c. 1647–1715), whom EO later names in Letters 134, 138, and 139.

[518] Lady Arran's mother, Mary Stuart, née Villiers, Duchess of Lennox and Richmond (1622–1685).

[519] The Poyntzes of Iron Acton, Gloucestershire, were the maternal family of JO, and they had strong Catholic loyalties. The uncle to whom EO alludes has not been identified but is presumably a brother of her mother-in-law, Elizabeth, Lady Thurles.

beleve mee in this as in all that Consernes you or yours to bee very Sinsearlie°

    your Cousene and Sarvant

      E:ormonde

I have sent your daghters[520] Leter to mee ~~that~~ and mine to hir which Last I desier you would seale and Send unto hir, that knowinge what has past betwixt uss you may the beter° know ^how^ to governe that affare as I desier you would with all Satisfactione to hir, and remember my Sarvis° to My Cousen Lege[521]

Letter 134. October 7, [1666], Kilkenny, the Duchess of Ormonde to Colonel William Legge (SRO, Dartmouth Collection, D(W)1778/I/i/206). Autograph.
For Corronell Legge thes. [Endorsed]: Duchess of Ormond Oct 7th.

Cousen   kilkeny the 7 of october

The same day that I sent a way my Leter of the 4 of this Month I fortuned to reseve° one from you of the 16 of the Last, that Mentions the ressept° of Mine by my Nephue Hambelton[522] and that My Sone was gone unto Sir william Portmans[523] from whense Corronell Pigott[524] whoe Came Latlie° over tells mee that hee went and was Entertanede twise at Sir John wards[525] House, where thay° spent ther time a dansinge and were very Merye but what hopes My Sone John* has of the yonge Ladys[526] favour I know not, for I never heard word from hime sense° I saw you, but doe beleve well, if hee follow your advise and derections° as I doe hope hee will, as to the Mache° proposed for your Daghter My Last Leter ~~will~~ with othars that was then sent you, will Sufisentlie satisfie you that theris nothinge my

---

[520] "Mall," or Mary, Legge (c. 1647–1715)?

[521] George Legge (c. 1647–1691)?

[522] Probably James Hamilton (c. 1642–1679), eldest son of JO's sister Mary and her husband Sir George Hamilton.

[523] Sir William Portman, sixth baronet (1643–1690), of Orchard Portman, Somerset, was one of the most influential gentry in south-west England. See Robin Clifton, "Portman, Sir William, sixth baronet (1643–1690)," *ODNB*.

[524] He has not yet been identified, but there are letters to a Colonel Piggot from JO preserved among the Carte Papers in Bodl.

[525] Sir John Warre was Elizabeth Malet's step-father and had married her mother, Untia (or Unton), née Hawley, after the death of her father in March 1656.

[526] Elizabeth Malet.

unkell°⁵²⁷, and all his relations soe much desiers° as the Mach° may goe on, as will apiere° by his owne Leter, ~~to my lord~~ in hopes wherof, hee has broke ofe° that treatie that hee was upon when wee came to Bristoll,* soe as I referr you to that accompt,° which I asshure° my selfe is with you or willbee befor this cane come unto your hands and remayne very asshuredlie°

                your Cousen and Sarvant

                    E:ormonde

My daghter Arran° is Mended beyond Expectatione by the Phisicke shee has takene and Louks° beter° then Ever I saw hir I pray turne the Leafe

I desier you will remember mee to My Cousen Lege and to My Cousen Mall⁵²⁸ and Let hir know that My Lord is resolved sense hee Cannot Danse at hir wedinge hee will prepare a Balladt; and send it hir and hee hopes as good a one as that hee Made for hir at Moore Parke*

Letter 135. October 25, [1666], Dublin, the Duchess of Ormonde to Colonel William Legge (SRO, Dartmouth Collection, D(W)1778/I/i/211). Autograph.
Fo[r] Corronell Legge thes. [Endorsed]: Duchess of Ormond October 25th.

Cousen   Dublin the 25 of o[ct]

I am very sensible of your Frindshipe and favour to my Sone John* in the Care that you have had to Manadge that affare wherin hee is conserned,° the Suckses° of which I hope I shall now heare, sense° My Lord Haly* and you have conferede together, and that hee simes° to bee Satisfiede with what you have proposed, however should it fayle,° it cane prove noe Surprise to mee knowinge the Humor of that Person with whom you have Treate⁵²⁹ nor make mee Less accompt°

---

⁵²⁷ Poyntz, first mentioned in Letter 94. His first name has not been identified.
⁵²⁸ Since Mary Legge would marry Sir Henry Goodricke in 1668, it is possible either that negotiations with the Poyntzes broke down or that the marriage was short lived. Goodricke's friend and fellow Yorkshire MP, Sir John Reresby, would later describe her as "the finest woman, one of them, in that age" (cited in J. D. Davies, "Goodricke, Sir Henry, second baronet (1642–1705)," *ODNB*).
⁵²⁹ Presumably, Sir Francis Hawley.

of your indevours° for hime⁵³⁰ whoe I heare has had a dayngerous
fall latlie° ofe° his Horse and brusede his Fase,° of which I hope and
Longe to heare of his recovrye, as I doe of the conclutione of the
Mach° with my Cousen Poyns⁵³¹ and your daghter whous happenes
and your comfort in Seeinge hir Soe ^is I ashure you^ ~~beinge~~ very
hartilie the wisshes of

      your Cousen and Sarvant

        E:ormonde

I am forst to make this leter briffer° then I did intend havinge at
this time a returne of my Cough sense my cominge to this Towne
which Ayre° I find dous° not agree with Mee[/] My Daghter Arran°
is perfectlie well thanks bee to God, and is handsomer then Ever you
Saw hir

**Letter 136. November 22, [1666], [Dublin] the Duchess of
Ormonde to Colonel William Legge** (SRO, Dartmouth Collection,
D(W)1778/I/i/219). Autograph.
For Corronell Legge thes. [Endorsed]: Duchess of Ormond.
November 22nd.

Cousen   The 22 of November

I resevede° by the Last Post yours of the 3 of November from
Oxford whether it should sime° My Son John* was not then come,
but stayede at Sallsbery⁵³² by that unhapie Fate hee gott⁵³³ of which
I hope hee is by this time soe well recovrede as hee is now with
you; and knows his doome from My Lord Haly* from whom My
Expectations are not great, but if it hapene beter° I shallbee very
well pleasede, and however owne with much thankfullnes your
Conserne° and indevours° for hime and have Litell° more to Say
then if you obsarve and bee convinst that theris greater resone° for
hime to declyne then further persue his pretentions⁵³⁴ that then the
Souner° hee returnes hether the beter [/] I have writene twise to My
Lady Duches of Richmond* sense° my cominge over and onse° in my
Journye ~~but~~ to give hir an accompt° of hir Daghters health but Never

---

⁵³⁰ Her son John.
⁵³¹ Presumably, the son of the uncle mentioned above, a maternal cousin of JO.
⁵³² Salisbury, a cathedral city in Wiltshire, England.
⁵³³ I.e. the failure of Lord John's engagement.
⁵³⁴ A veiled reference to Elizabeth Malet's reputation, perhaps.

resevede anye returne from hir which I tell you rather to Justifie my selfe that I have not omitted my respect to hir, then to charge hir with anye unkindnes to mee, My daghter Arran° is thanks bee to God very well, Grows Tale, and Fatter then shee was, which makes a Change in hir Louks° much to hir advantage, I find a returne of My Coughe which makes writinge uneasie to mee and therfor I must conclude, and ~~being~~ briflie asshure° you of my beinge very realye

your Cousen and Sarvant

EO

I pray remember mee to all yours and Let Mee know how that affare with My unkell° goes forward

Letter 137. November 25, [1666], [Dublin], the Duchess of Ormonde to Colonel William Legge (SRO, Dartmouth Collection, D(W)1778/I/i/220). Autograph.
For Corronell Legge thes. [Endorsed]: Duchess of Ormond November 25th.

Cousen   the 25 of November

you will within a few days see My Son John,* whous Pastione° for his Mistris and hopes of hir favour to hime makes hime Steale away from hense, and goe privatlie to London ther to gayne° an oppertunitie if hee Cane of Speakinge with hir, and resevinge° his doome from hir selfe; that hee May proside° in his addresses accordinge as hee Finds incoridgment° or declyne them if therbee Cause, in which affare hee is to bee governede (and will; by your advise) whoe I hope willbee soe oblidginge unto this yonge Son of Mine, as to afford ^it^ hime, that hee may owne his good Fortune if this Mache° Suckside° as all his relations dous° ther obligatione to you upon the Like accompt,° which has givene you a perfect Intrest in Ther Frindshipe and Estime, and perticularlie in That of

your Cousen and Sarvant

E:ormonde

Letter 138. November 29, [1666], Chapelizod, the Duchess of Ormonde to Colonel William Legge (S.R.O., Dartmouth Collection, D(W)1778/I/i/221). Autograph.
For Corronell Legge thes. [Endorsed]: Duchess of Ormond November 29th.

Cousen   Chapelizard* the 29 of No

The leter you Mentione from my Lord Hawlie* which in your absense my Lord Arlington* openede and transmitede to mee, ~~is~~ Came yesterday unto my hands, and has confirmed what I allways suspected; his insenseritie in this bussenes° and therfor is rather the Subgect of my Contempt then ~~Surprise~~ ^wonder^, other then that hee should have Createde a troubell to himselfe and others when he Nieded° not, My Lord has Sent for My Sone over, whoe I hope has bine° advisede by you in retyringe himselfe ~~to~~ and makinge a vissit to his Sister[535] which was sartanlie° the best course hee could take as things has fallene out; I am tould you have some thoughts of cominge hethar° Shortlie I pray if you have realye anye such intentione, Let mee know it, sense° Non° of your Frinds wouldbee glader to See you then my Selfe, I shall not remove the Juells° from where thay° are, though the Party had noe order from mee to plase them Ther untell° I know whether you Mene° to Come that I may committ them to your Costodie to bringe over or Else think on some othar way, the Leters you will reseve° from a Nother° hand will I supose Suffisentlie satisfie you that My Cousen Poyns continows° his designe of waytinge upon you soe Soune° as may bee fitt for hime to apiere° ther being Nothinge that cane Render hime more considerable to uss; then if hee shall have the good Fortune of beinge Likede of by you and My Cousen Mall without whous free Consent, Let mee Conjure you Never to Entertane his adress; soe much hir Content, is wisht and Considered by

                              your Cousen and Sarvant

                              E:ormond

I Cannot write to your Lady[536] this Post as I intended, but I shall by the Next to whom I pray remember my Sarvis° and to My Cousen Mall

---

[535] This must refer to Mary because their elder sister, Elizabeth, had died the previous year.
[536] Colonel William Legge's wife was Elizabeth (c. 1616–1688), eldest daughter of Sir William Washington of Sulgrave Manor, Northamptonshire.

Letter 139. December 18, [1666], Dublin, the Duchess of Ormonde to Colonel William Legge (SRO, Dartmouth Collection, D(W)1778/I/i/226). Autograph.
For Corronell Legge thes. [Endorsed]: Duchess of Ormond December 18.

Cousen   Dublin the 18 of Des

Sense my Sone John* went from hense, ther was a Packet of Leters derected° unto hime, which in his absense I opened wherin ther was one from Sir John warr[537] to My Lord and a Nothar° from hime to My Sone, soe contrarye unto what his actions sime° to Second, as I thought it ~~if~~ Nesesarye to Send you the Copies of Both, and in cayse° of a Refusall from the yonge Lady to command my Sone to come away imediatlie which in that cayse I hope hee will obaye My Lord haveinge as I understand done the like, but if beter° happene hee shallbee then countenanst and healpede ~~by~~ with what shallbee Nesesary for hime, whoe has a supplye sent hime, Suffisent for the Presant untell° wee heare further, what his Suckses° is Like to bee, Least° a Larger proportione might tempt hime to ^Extravagansie^ ~~Stay when it may bee Fitter for hime to come a way~~; for I dare not bee to confident of that yonge Mans discretione; and therfor doe deale thus freelie with you, on whous Frindshipe to advise hime I doe much hope and relye, as what will I am Shure° prove much to his advantage if hee Follow it as I doe hope and expect hee will, I tould hime I had Sent the Copies of Sir John wars Leters to you which if hee has the Curiositie to See you may Show them to hime, whoe has great obligations to you for the care you have of his conserne° as has all his relations in his behalfe and shallbee allways perticularlie ownede by

                    your Cousene and Sarvant

                    E:ormonde

I pray remember My Sarvis° to My Cousen Legge and tell my Cousene Mall that Shee is oftene wisht For by hir Frinds heare

---

[537] Sir John Warre, stepfather of Elizabeth Malet.

Letter 140. April 16, 1667, Kilkenny, the Duchess of Ormonde to Edward Butler (NLI, Ormond Papers, 2342, no. 2444, p. 287).
Autograph.
For Mr Edward Butler thes. [Endorsed]: her Graces order to pay mony to Captain Morton for Dunemore 16th Aprill 1667.

I send you hearinclosed an order Signede by My Lord for 2 hundreth pound and fiftye Pound to bee payede unto mr Morton[538] for the Finishinge of this House and that of Dunmore,* which I pray make as spidie° as possible you Cane; that this Plase may bee redie and Fitt to reseve° My Lord and the whole Fam[ilie] by June Next, at which Time hee intends to bee heare and Soe dous° allsoe

killkeny the 16 of Aprell   E:ormonde

Letter 141. April 22, 1667, [Kilkenny], the Duchess of Ormonde to Edward Butler (NLI, Ormond Papers, 2342, no. 2455, p. 357).
Autograph.
For Mr Edward Butler thes. [Endorsed]: her Graces letter to Edward Butler aboute money to Captain Morton 22 April 1667.

Ned Butler*   The 22 of Aprell

This is to desier° your Care to furnish Mr Morton* for the Finishinge of the worke at killkenye with that Mony° spesifiede° in My Lords Last order that was Sent you befor My Leavinge killkenye, in regard My Lord dous° Continow° his purpose of removinge his whole Familie Thethar° the begininge of June, by which Time mr Morton* hopes to have all the worke done, which will give the adistione° of 18 very handsome and Convenient Romes° much wantinge hetherto,° your y Care in this beinge not douted° by

E.O.

---

[538] Captain John Morton (d. 1669) was a contractor and possibly an architect. See his entry in Rolf Loeber, *A Biographical Dictionary of Architects in Ireland, 1600–1720* (London: Murray, 1981), p. 78. See also Jane Fenlon, "Episodes of Magnificence: The Material Worlds of the Dukes of Ormonde," in *The Dukes of Ormonde, 1610–1745*, ed. Toby Barnard and Jane Fenlon (Woodbridge: Boydell and Brewer, 2000), 137–59 (151, note 92).

The Duke of Ormonde's Dismissal, 1668–1677

Letter 142. September 3, 1668, [Minehead], the Duchess of Ormonde to Captain George Mathew (NLI, Ormond Papers, 2503, no. 1). Autograph.
For Captaine George Mathews These. [Endorsed]: [my Ladys] Letter of the 3 September 1668.

Brother   The 3 of September

I send you hearinclosede a proposall from mr Crouke* My Lords Tenant of the great Iland which if you aprove of, hee is redie to pay his Mony° heare, if Not Send your demand backe and I will desier° Sir Gorge Layne* to treate with hime; and Let mee heare from you consarninge° this perticuler as soune° as you Cane, This Gent[leman] has payede 75 pound ^heare^ and 15 pound hea in Ireland for quit rent[539] by the Comistioners o[rder] dated the 30 of September 1668[540] this I tell you to prevent anye mistake in accompts° [/] I hope the kings Leter is with you by this Time to remove the Stope° of prefer[anses][541] For the fiftye thowsand Pound and willbee such a Countenanse unto the Rays[inge]°of it as I should think might the Less Nesesitate you to take Irish Securitie [/] ther will questionles bee more redie Mony broght in, then will answar what is dew° unto My Lord; and then you might haveinge redie Mony bee abble to disingad[ge] such depts° of incombranse° as Lies most heavie upon the Estate, which I doe soe much desier might bee Left Free; as I confess out of that consideratione and som others I am for the partinge with Moore Parke,* for which 12 Thowsand I think ma[y] be had, but 13 is demanded and I beleve will with such a Part of the Goods a[s] may bee well parted with, will paye ofe° all the depts that My Lord dous° owe hear[e] and stope a growinge Charge[542] but this I willnot proside° further in, untell° I may know My Son ossorys* Mind, whoe may at anye time hearafter Fitt himselfe w[ith] a Plase

---

[539] "A (usually small) rent paid by a freeholder or copyholder in lieu of services which might otherwise be required; a nominal rent paid (esp. in former British colonial territories to the Crown) as an acknowledgement of tenure" ("quit-rent, *n.*," 1a, *OED*).

[540] Since September 30, 1668, post-dates the letter itself, it is likely that the year is wrongly ascribed.

[541] "A prior right or claim to something; *spec.* a prior right or precedence to payment, esp. of a debt" ("preference, *n.*," 2a, *OED*).

[542] "Pecuniary burden; expense, cost" ("charge, *n.*1," 10a, *OED*).

heare Less Expendsive and more convenient, for the House[543] is soe deca[yed] as to make a New Roufe and that douted° to whether if wee did the walls w[ould] beare it, and mend the Tarrases ^as^ will cost at the Least a Thowsand Pound, and if it bee not done in some resonable time the House will Fall, and this is the T[ruth] of the bussines true state of the Plase; therfor I pray discourse it with My [Lord] and Let mee know his, and your oppinion that it may the beter° gyede guide

roof
terraces

          your affectionat Sister

            E:ormonde

I pray send mee word how my Son John* dous Carye himselfe, what is become of Captane Morton* and how the Skoule house[544] goes on, as allsoe how the worke is Lelft and the Materialls that was Left of the buildinge

left

Letter 143. September 12, 1668, Moor Park, the Duchess of Ormonde to Captain George Mathew (NLI, Ormond Papers, 2503, no. 20). Autograph.
For My Brother Mr Gorge Mathews [/] thes. [Endorsed]: My Ladyes of the 12 of September 1668. Dublin.

Brother   Moorparke* the 12 of Sep

I arivede at Minhead[545] the Sonday morninge after I parted with you, where I was driwene° to Stay untell° the wedensday followinge; to give My Cochhorses° on° days rest that came not into the Harbor tell° tow° days after Mee; soe as I came not hether untell Teusday Last, where I intend to Stay untell Monday Next, and then to goe

---

    [543] Ormond Castle, Carrick-on-Suir?

    [544] Kilkenny College had been established in John Street, Kilkenny, in around 1666. Catering for the Protestant population of Ireland, it quickly established itself as the best school in the country: Jonathan Swift (1667–1745), writer and dean of St. Patrick's Cathedral, Dublin, attended the school from the age of six until fourteen, and the playwright and poet, William Congreve (1670–1729), also attended the school from about 1681. In establishing the school, the couple were following a Butler family tradition of promoting education in the city: in 1538 Piers Butler, eighth Earl of Ormonde, and his wife Margaret had founded a school to the west of St. Canice's Cathedral. Kilkenny College continues to this day, albeit at a different location. See http://www.kilkennycollege.ie/index.php?option=com_content&view=article&id=50&Itemid=69.

    [545] Minehead, a port town in Somerset, England, presumably the route through which EO traveled from Ireland.

to London ~~whether~~ My Lord is gone this day to wayte° upon the
kinge whoe has bine° abrode° at Bagshott[546] and other plasses° a
huntinge ever sense° My Lord Left the Towne soe as noe bussenes°
couldbee don;° My Lord Arlington* beinge gone to his owne house
in the Contrye To;° but preparations on Foote when the Court
returns ^to^ prosecute all the designes that are Layede aganst My
Lord and the Lord of Anglisie,* soe as a very Litell° time will make
a full discovrye of what My Lords Enimies are able to doe aganst
hime [/] which for anye thinge that I Cane yet apprehend willbee
more Liklie to prejudise themselfes, then Ruene° hime [/] though
theris nothinge that Thay° will, and dous° more indevour,° haveinge
ingadged° themselfes soe Farr ~~will beleve themselfes unsayfe if hee Stands~~ and therfor will Laye the Strength of ther whole Intrest upon
it [/] I Found My Sone Arran* in great Sadnes[547] when I came whoe
intends to goe for Ireland very Sudanlie° though I did what I could
to disswade hime from it; his Chife° resone° is to Settell his affares *dissuade*
ther and discharge his depts° and to returne hether agayne° when that
is done and attend the Parlement untell hee Sees what willbee don°
for or aganst his Father and afterwards has I find some thoughts to
Travell; I perseve° hime much consernede° for his Familie and I have
resone to beleve that hee will give a Materiall prouf of it, Espetialie°
to his Eldest Brother; Therfor I pray doe all you Cane to prevent anye
ill offiss° that may bee indevorede° by such as may intend Ruene to
Them under the pretense of kindnes by raysinge of Jelosie betwixt *jealousy*
them which ther are some perhapes ~~in~~ Ther, whoe may Cunninglie
indevour, I will Name Non° for I suppose it not hard for you to
Gees° ~~what~~ ^whoe^ I Meane [/] I did fullie discourse with my Lord
consarninge° the Settellment made at My daghter Arrans* Marage
and desirede his advise how and in what Manner I might order what
was fitt to be Sayede° unto ~~hime~~ ^My Son Arran*^ consarninge that
perticular ~~that yo~~ but hee advisede mee to say nothinge to hime of
it at this Time, and gave mee very good resons for it, and bid mee
to write to you, not to tuche° upon anye thinge of that to hime nor
to Suffier° mr wellch* to doe it Nether untell you have derections°
from hime; and bee derected° in the Manner of it in Cayse° it bee
Neseserye to doe it at all, but in way of discourse as it may Fall out
~~for you~~ To make hime know the condistione of My Lords fortune
and the great depts that are upon it may bee very Fitt for you to doe,
and to offier° hime all the healpe that you cane give hime by your

---

[546] Bagshot Park was royal hunting lodge in Somerset, England.
[547] Mary Butler, née Stuart, Countess of Arran, had died earlier in 1668.

advise as to the Settlinge of his owne privat affares at presant and payinge of his depts;

Letter 144. September 19, 1668, Whitehall, the Duchess of Ormonde to Captain George Mathew (NLI, Ormond Papers, 2503, no. 2). Autograph.
For My Brother Mr Gorge Mathews. [Endorsed]: my Ladys of the 19 of September 1668. Dutchess of Ormonde.

Brother   whithall the 19 of Sep

It was Monday Last befor I came hether where I have bine° soe imployede in payinge my dewtie° to My Beters,° and resevinge° the serimonye of vissets,° as I had not Time and Scarslie have yet to *ceremony* write unto anye of my Frinds, The Leter of Aturnye° I gave unto My Lord soe soune° as I came to Towne, whoe tells mee hee has signede and returnede it to you by the Last Post, I cannot as yet give you an accompt° of our weeklie Expenses heare Not haveinge had an howeres° time to Louke° into that affare but doe resolve to make it my bussenes° soe Soune as Ever I cane only I must tell you that I have bine soe good a Manager of my owne, as payinge the Charge of Both the Shipes which cost mee threscore and 5 pound and 10 Shillinge a head dewtie for Evrye Horse ^besids^ of My owne I broght threscore pound of my 2 hundreth with mee hether, which has purchast mee all that I shall Laye out upon my Selfe untell° Cristmas Next [/] I have Not Seene your Frind and Mine⁵⁴⁸ as yet, but resevede° a request from hir to gett the kings Leter for Passing the Fee of all thous° Lands that shee houlds° by Lease from the Crowne which I immediatlie movede My Lord in, whoe tould Mee that hee belevede it a very improper time for hime to desier° anye thinge of the kinge in his owne behalfe or in anye others, when all his actions were ransa ransaktt ransact into by his greatest Enimies and that hee belevede Nothinge that should come recomended by hime of this Nature but wouldbee opposede and Not only Soe but might more provablie° bee a menes° to questionc what wass allredie granted then obtane beyond it, and therfor advisede the Person a Suspense as much sayfier° at this time unto the Person consernede,° then anye further prosidinge° in that affare couldbee; which accordinglie I have bine free to tell your

---

⁵⁴⁸ Possibly Lady Anne Hume, who is specifically named in Letters 109, 113 and 116, and whom Mathew later married.

Frind by Leter My Sonn Arran* and My Lord of Cayhier⁵⁴⁹ went hense for Ireland yesterday of whous sayfe° arivall I much Longe to heare beinge very apprehendsive of this Season of the yeare that for the most part proves Stormye and shouldbee glad to know how you advanse in the affare consarninge° Captane Powers* Mony° that out of it the Tradsmen heare may bee Sattisfiede whoe are upon that accompt very much importuninge

>your affectionat Sister
>
>E:ormonde

Letter 145. October 26, 1668, [London], the Duchess of Ormonde to Captain George Mathew (NLI, Ormond Papers, 2503, no. 3).⁵⁵⁰ Autograph.
For My Brother Mr Gorge Mathews [/] thes. [Endorsed]: [my Ladys of the] 26 of October 1668.

[Brother]

yesterday [*five words missing*] by whom I [writ] unto My Sone who [will] give you [an acc]ompt° of as much as wee know heare con[sarn]inge what relats unto My Lords owne perticuler and what is soe Litell° [agreed] as Leaves uss [more in a] Conjecture then s[art]antie of what willbee the Event as to [his hope] as I shallnot speake my thoughts to you in that nor anye other subgect I consider unfitt for others veue° by this comm [*two words missing*] of convanse sense° I   *conveyance* have some resone° to dout° it will not be sayfe° to doe, which caution I did forget to g[ive] unto My Sonn and therfor doe intreate you from mee to doe it, I resevede° a Leter from you of the 10 of this Month from killkenye wherin I find you have bine° very bussie in Settlinge of My Lords affares Ther and to indevour° to suplye hime with Mony° which willbee Nesesarye as to his Suport heare untell° hee dous° take some further resolutione how ^and where^ to Settell himselfe and that dous depend upon the kings plesure whether hee shall continow,° or quit the Goverment; the Mene° Time I desier° to have a Checkrole⁵⁵¹ Sent mee of all the Sarvants that are now in the

---

⁵⁴⁹ Pierce Butler, fourth Baron Cahir (1649–1676). He married Elizabeth, daughter of JO's half-brother Theobald Mathew, in 1663. See *Burke's Irish Family Records*, 5th edn. (London: Burke's Peerage, 1976), 793.

⁵⁵⁰ There is significant wear and tear to the top of the leaf, which affects two to three lines of text, as well as minor damage to the outer edges of the MS.

⁵⁵¹ "A list of the servants of any large household" ("check-roll, *n.*," 2, OED).

Familie Ther, and of such of them as are provided for by offisies° in the Armye or otherwiss and of such as are in the Gards, I hope you have accompted° with the Recevers° for the Accate⁵⁵² Mony and that Soe Soune° as it is broght In that you will gett it Transmitted To

your affectionat Sister

E:ormonde

Letter 146. October 27, 1668, Whitehall, the Duchess of Ormonde to Sir George Preston (Birr Castle, Rosse Papers, A/1/39). Scribal: signed.
For Sir George Preston Baronett.⁵⁵³ Att Dublin. [Endorsed]: A letter from the Dutchess of Ormond to the Lady Preston 27th October 1668 about her patent.

Sir   Whitehall 27. October 1668

I have received your letter of the 29 of the last moneth together with the draught of a letter which yow sent inclosed which I have perused, and there being severall particulars inserted therein not contain'd in your former Pattent, I perceive the party who drew it, did not well consider [the] condition of Affaires, which are such at present that there is very great difficulty in procureing [new] Graunts; But if you will Send me a draught, [comm]itting that additionall parte, and containing only [ca]uses to strengthen your former Graunt, with referrence [to] your clause in the Act of Parliament, which I wish [m]ay be mentioned, because it may possibly render that you desire the more reasonable, and consequently facillitate the passing of it, I shall

---

⁵⁵² "Bought provisions; provisions that are not made in the house, but have to be purchased fresh when wanted, as meat, fish, etc. Hence: all provisions except the home produce of the baker and brewer; foreign foodstuffs, delicacies" ("accate, *n.*," 2, *OED*).

⁵⁵³ Sir George Preston of Craigmillar was the nephew of EO's father, Richard Preston, Lord Dingwall; his father, John Preston of Whitehill, was EO's uncle, her father's elder brother. George succeeded through his father to the lands of Preston and Craigmillar but sold the properties of Preston and Whitehill in 1662 to Robert Preston of the Valleyfield family and Craigmillar in 1660 to Sir Andrew Gilmour. He must have relocated to Ireland around this time. See *Burke's Irish Family Record* and *Scots Peerage* 3, 119–21. For further information on the Prestons of Craigmillar Castle, see Wilks, *Of Neighing Coursers*, 6–8.

upon receipt thereof endeavour to doe you all the Sarvice I can as being

    Sir

      Your affectionate Cousin

Sir George Preston   E:ormonde

Letter 147. October 31, 1668, [London], the Duchess of Ormonde to Captain George Mathew (NLI, Ormond Papers, 2503, no. 4). Autograph.
For My Brother Mr Gorge Mathews. [Endorsed]: My Lady Dutchess of the last of October 1668.

Brother   The Last of Oct

Mr Crouke* is not willinge to deale upon thous° Termes that you propose; My Lord went from hense upon Thursday Last to Hamtoncourt[554] to devert himselfe in huntinge and takinge the Ayre° as Nesesarye for his health; and returnes when the kinge dous° from Newmarkett* on Teusday Next, Hee toucke° with hime your Last Leter to mee, and sayede° hee would answar it himselfe soe as haveing it not by mee at the presant I cannot say much in returne of it; but tell you that I think it but resonable that if the Charge in Gatharinge in of Captane Powers* Mony° and the Fees that is dew° unto the kings offisiers° dous amont° to what is considerable it is but Just that hee as well as my Lord should allow his Share [/] My Lord toucke Notis° of what was payede unto the workmen over and above the Estimate but did not say more then that hee hopede and was glad hee should at Length bee Ride of Captane Morton* and all his Chargeable Reeknings,° I am very glad to heare that My Sonn Arran* is soe much consernede° for his Familie and Soe Sensible of his Fathers Condistion Soe as I think you cannot doe anye thinge more convenient and Secure to the Estate then to Sett out the three Thowsand Pound a yeare to hime in Land which My Lords Counsell heare says is Settled upon him and good in law by the deade of Settellment that was made at My Sone Arrans* Mariage a Copie of which I sent you a Fortnight Sense° but for the 2 Thowsand that was by it to have bine° added; My Lord cannot be compeled but is free to doe in That as hee pleases but this Last perhapes were beter° not to speake of, but to Settell what wee are oblidged unto First

                     rid

---

[554] Hampton Court Palace.

whilst my Sonn Arrane is soe Moderate and Soe well disposede to
a consideratione of his Familie as gives mee hopes it may be done
more resonablie Now then hearafter and therfor my opinione is
that you proside° in that affare as Soune° as you Cane for Many
resons and then Leave it to hime to Manage himselfe when it is his,
that wee may bee at noe more Trouble to make upe his allowanse,
Captane Morton is come to Towne and Expects his hundreth Pound
remayninge dew to hime For his Sallerye° which I will pay hime,
I say Nothinge to you of your Frind by resone° I know you have
an accompt° of the Resone of the Parties Staye for a while whoe is
very well and bussie in doeinge you Sarvis° in ~~La~~Providinge things
Nesesarye to Carrye over upon the best Termes [/] all things heare in
referanse to My Lord is as thay° were when I writ Last, and I am very
asshuredlie°

   your affectionat Sister

    E:ormonde

you will receve by this Post a Copie of the rest of the writings that
remayne in Corronell Legs[555] hands that conserns° the settellment
made ~~in~~ at My Son Arrans Mariage; which you may Show unto what
Counsell you think Fitt but you Nide° not owne that thay came from
Mee

Letter 148. [November/December, 1668], [London], the Duchess of Ormonde to Captain George Mathew (NLI, Ormond Papers, 2503, no. 130).[556] Autograph.
For My Brother Mr Gorge Mathews. [Endorsed]: Dutchess of ormonde.

[*one line missing*] of the 24 and 28 of the Last Month which My
Lord tells mee hee will answar himselfe ~~which~~ ^and Therfor^ Leaves
mee the Less to Say only to tell you, that I find by the Steward and
Controwlers[557] Leters very great complant of want of Mony° to pay
Tradsmen, and Sarvants wages which amonts° to 2 Thowsand five
hundreth Pound, Part of which, if it couldbee had to give some

---

[555] Colonel William Legge served as marriage broker for the family, as Letters 132–139 show.

[556] There is significant wear to the top of the MS (which has been partially repaired by mending tape), which has resulted in the loss of one to two lines of text on the top of each page.

[557] "A senior official within a household" ("comptroller, *n*.", 1a, *OED*).

satisfactione for the presant wouldbee a great Creditt and advantage at this Time, which my thinks might bee raysede out of my Lords Entertainment for 3 months to Come if Sir Gorge Cartwright⁵⁵⁸ wouldbee soe frindlie as to advanse it, as I doe hope hee wouldbee if spokene unto about it, and therfor you may doe well to Trye, sense° theris nothinge canbee more important then the desent support of the Familie Ther whilst My Sonn Continows° in the Goverment, Theris some Plate;⁵⁵⁹ the Perticulers of which is Mentioned in the inclosede Note that I beleve may bee ingadged° for 7 or 8 hundreth Pound and possiblie Sir Daniell Treswell* would Lend Mony upon Soe good Securitie to reseve° Intrest for it, I doe Likwiss propose to you the Morgadginge° of Land or Housses in anye of the Townes where My Lord has an Intrest if Mony may bee Raysede upon thous° Termes and may bee redimede° when my Lords affares are in a beter° settellment then at presant soe as the inconveniensie of That, cannot bee soe great as the apperanse of a trouble povertie and beinge Criede out upon for depts° to mene° peple wouldbee at this Time unto uss all My Lord and all his relations and this I find to bee his owne Sense as well as it is Mine whoe aproves of what I now propose unto you [*two lines missing*] Parlement is Prorogued⁵⁶⁰ which hightens much the discontents of the Pepell° whoe are not apt to bee sattisfiede with anye thinge, I beleve it willnot Now bee Longe befor I shallbee abble to informe you of the Sartane° Time of My Lords returne which you may bee Shure° for Many Resons shallbee hastened as farr as his owne indevours° Cane Contribute and Mine that am

        your affectionat Sister

        E:ormonde

I hope you have resevede° My Leter dated as I take it about the 7 of this Month and that My Lady Humes* is Sayflie° Landed which I much Longe to heare [/] I pray Let mee bee informede when Lawrence Roche* has Finisht his worke and the perticulers of what

---

⁵⁵⁸ Sir George Carteret, first baronet, had been vice-treasurer of Ireland since June 1667. See C. H. Firth, "Carteret, Sir George, first baronet (1610?–1680)," rev. C. S. Knighton, *ODNB*.

⁵⁵⁹ "Gold or silver vessels and utensils" ("plate, *n*.," I, 2a, *OED*). For further information on the family's plate, see Conor O'Brien, "In Search of the Duke of Ormond's Wine Cistern and Fountain," *The Silver Society Journal* 15 (2003): 63–67, and Thomas Sinsteden, "Household Plate of the Dukes of Ormonde," *The Silver Society Journal* 23 (2008): 123–29.

⁵⁶⁰ "To discontinue the meetings of (a legislative or other assembly) for a period of time or until the next session, without dissolving it" ("prorogue, *v*.," 3a, *OED*).

hee has done [/] I send you a Leter of mrs Farers* that Expreses what hir desiers° is but Leave it to you to doe what you think Fitt

Letter 149. November 14, 1668, [London], the Duchess of Ormonde to Captain George Mathew (NLI, Ormond Papers, 2503, no. 5).[561] Autograph.
For My Brother Mr Gorge Mathews. [Endorsed]: [My Lady Dutchess of the] 14 November 1668.

Brother   The 14 of November

yours of the 3 and 7 of November came together unto my hands upon Thursday Last soe did the accompt° of the weeklie Expense of the House sense° my Cominge a way, which I doe think (as you doe) might be Lessenede were the Clarke of the kichine[562] as Just as hee ought to bee; but I beleve is Not; and therfor I doe hope to Send one over, that shall beter° discharge that imployment then hee, and is a Single Man; but I would not advise you to Let Connowaye[563] know that theris an Intent of partinge with hime; untell° I bee Shure° of this other, and then I will Send you Notis,° I am in hope to gett Moore Parke* Solde, which would Ease uss of a good part of our dept° and stope° a growinge Charge, My Lord was in Arreare of the Last halfe years Intrest which was Like to have drawne some Clamor upon hime, which came in all to 4 hundreth and sixtie ode° Pounds which to discharge I was driwene° to Pawne a [payre of diam]and° Pendants worth [*six words missing*][564] have lived out Nomber the   *outnumber*
Table, and doe kiepe° Noe Supers, Nor Eate but privatlie, but when My Lord dines within, I have Furnisht this House from Moore Parke with ~~Goods~~ Bedinge and Goods from thense and have avoyded° as much as I could devise the Layinge out of Mony;° as to what I have the orderinge of; which I kiepe a perticuler accompt of; I am of opinione that you will See My Lord returne Lord Liftenant agayne° in Spight° of all his Enimies, this in brife° is as much as I shall venter° to Say, and what I suppose will Satisfie you, I could wish

---

[561] There is significant wear and tear to the bottom of the MS, which has resulted in the loss of one or two lines of text at the bottom of each of the two pages.

[562] The clerk of the kitchen would have had charge of the records, correspondence, and accounts of the kitchen ("clerk, *n.*," 6a, *OED*).

[563] Current clerk of the kitchen.

[564] A signed promissory note dated September 28, 1668, shows that EO pawned a pair of diamond pendants and a diamond fosset ring, valued at £700, to borrow £500 from Sir Stephen Fox. See HMC Ormonde, III, 290–91.

that in raytinge the weeklie Expense ~~ofe~~ that was Sent Mee I could
have knowne how much in redie Mony was disburst for the uss° of
the Table and other ~~Expenses~~ Nesesarye Charges [/] your Frind⁵⁶⁵
went from hense on Monday Last to Acton* ^and^ from Thense
intends For Ireland with the first oppertunitie which I wish may bee
sayfe° and Spidie° that [is]

        your affection[at Sister

            E:ormonde]

**Letter 150. [November] 1668, [London], the Duchess of Ormonde
to Captain George Mathew** (NLI, Ormond Papers, 2503, no. 6).⁵⁶⁶
Autograph.
For My Brother Mr Gorge Mathews. [Endorsed]: [M]y Ladys of the
[*missing*] [Nov]ember 1668. Dutchess of Ormond.

[Brother

My] Lord go[es] [*two lines missing*]⁵⁶⁷ the payments that a[re out] of
it, which I find unto my great trouble dous° Exsiede the ressept° soe   *exceed*
as I see noe possibiltie of Support unles by payinge ofe° the depts°
that are upon Intrest with the Mony° that is dew° unto My Lord and
Sellinge offe of Moore Parke,* which I am indevoringe° by all the
Menes° I cane to doe, though this is Loukede° upon as soe unsettled
a Time as very few Pepell° will Part with Mony; heare is greate
discourse of My Lords beinge to Leave the Goverment, but the
kinge has Never spokene unto hime as yet consarninge° it, and trulie
I think will not upon that Subgect, though theris a great Factione
that presses hime to it, but as yet I doe not ^heare^ ~~Find~~ thay° have
prevaylede, ~~I find~~ In the List of the wages ^Find^ returned fiftie five
pound a yeare to Lawrence Roche* wheras it is but fiftie, and that to
continow° Noe Longer then tell° hee has perfected the worke that
hee is Now upon and to prevent anye Longer delay therin, I have
sent hime from hense what hee gave mee a Note of and have writene
to Luke Archer* for to deliver hime some more Leafe Gould° which
Captane Morton* Left in his Coustodie; but of my Intent to Part
with hime I doe not think it convenient that it Shouldbee spokene

---

   ⁵⁶⁵ Lady Anne Hume.
   ⁵⁶⁶ There is significant damage to the MS, which has resulted in the loss of most of
three or four lines of text in two of three pages.
   ⁵⁶⁷ Some words that are discernible through the damage are "sent him of" and "alle
of his."

of untell° the worke that hee has now in hand bee at an Ende [/] The
Gardener at Dunmore* sent mee a Note of Frute Trees [*four lines
missing*]⁵⁶⁸ which willbee suffisent [for the] presant and for Lones and   *loans*
other small Nesesaries ~~I desier you~~ to give the steward derections°
to provide and send them to the Gardener and to have an accompt°
from hime how the plantinge worke dous goe forward at Dunmore
and what Course is takene to distroye the Rabets Ther which My
lord would have to bee without delaye Now that the warine° is
planted in a Nother° Plase, My thinks 10 pound a yeare wages is to
great an allowanse for the kiepinge° of soe small a Proportione of
Corne as is at killkenye, soe as the ballife° ther is to bee trusted; and
were Capable to give an accompt might I should think discharge that
Plase to, with the healpe of Mr Archers⁵⁶⁹ Care some Times to see
and derect° what were fitt to bee done, and soe may My Gardener at
Dunmore [/] the Orchard and ^kichine^ gardine at kilkenye* as I
doe designe hee shall soe soune° as Lawrence Roche is gone which
will save his and Adam Sixes* wages, I heare that Mrs Swettnance⁵⁷⁰
is left at Chapellizard,* to what Ende I know not, Now that the
Childrene are removede Thense that cane desarve hir wages, ther for
I pray let mee know what hir bussenes° is that I may Consider how to
dispose of hir, I have Never heard word of, Nor from my soun John
sense° I left Ireland though to bee satisfiede that hee spends his Time
well is a great Conserne° unto

EO

I obsarve that to discharge the dept dew unto workmen and [which]
comes to 15 8s ^Pound^ which is upon noe other accompt that I
remember [Then what] related unto the charge of the Funerall⁵⁷¹
which I could wish had bine° soe inserted that my Lord might have
knowne for what that some° became dew

---

⁵⁶⁸ Words that are barely discernable include "Gardiners" and "relyede."

⁵⁶⁹ A military engineer and architect, Captain James Archer (fl. 1632–1680) was a Roman Catholic and native of Kilkenny; he was a kinsman of the Waterford merchant, Patrick Archer, to whom EO wrote in the 1640s. See his entry in Loeber, *Biographical Dictionary*, 14–17; and also Fenlon, "Episodes of Magnificence," 151.

⁵⁷⁰ Nurse who presumably looked after Ossory's children.

⁵⁷¹ Presumably, the lavish funeral of Lady Arran. See *An Account of the Solemn Funeral and Interrment of the Right Honourable the Countess of Arran* ([London]: Thomas Newcombe, 1668), and Jane Ohlmeyer, *Making Ireland English: The Irish Aristocracy in the Seventeenth Century* (New Haven: Yale University Press, 2012), 459–61.

Letter 151. November 22, 1668, [London], the Duchess of Ormonde to Captain George Mathew (NLI, Ormond Papers, 2503, no. 7). Autograph.
[Endorsed]: my Lady Dutches of the 22th November 1668 received 4 January about Lady Ossory et cetera.

The 22 of November

Theris transmited to you by my Lords derections° an accompt° of what Mony° hee has payede for My Soon° Ossory* sense° his cominge Last over that was dew° befor that Time ~~and was~~ for the kiepinge° of his Horses and the charge of his Stabels with what hee has Layede out sense, That som accompt may bee made with hime, I find hime indepted° to Many Tradsmen heare whoe complans of hime to bee a bad paymaster and I cannot but feare and suspect hime soe because that Nether hee nor his Lady dous° know what ther depts° are or to whom thay° owe; though the greatest Part is hirs whoe gave to Large a power unto hir Sarvants to goe on the Score without Loukinge° or Correctinge the Bills hir selfe; and this prejudis willbee still, unles you Cane prevayle with one or both of them to Manadge ther Expenses with more Care and to bee Consernede° [with] the Goverment of the Familie which I doe feare My daughter willnot aplye hir selfe To, for I heare Shee Eats more in hir Chamber then at the Table, ^which^ is not the way to Live with that desensie *decency* that both is ^Now^ and willbee hearafter Expected from hir, and I beleve ther depts at Dublin are great, soe as I know not what Course of Life thay cane propose unto themselfs if thay Rune° out of all, Compas⁵⁷² after ~~all~~ the healpe that thay have had from uss both in Ireland and heare [/] This I tell you, that by understandinge how ther Condistione is, you may give them both some advise from your Selfe without Naminge mee to avoyde° My daughters taking anye Exseptions as posiblie shee might at my findinge Fault, though I doe asshure° you I may very Justlie ~~unto~~ ^of^ hir Neglect and want of Conduct in hir affares which has made a great discovrye of hir weaknes heare and is generalie takene Notis° of at the Court at which I am much troubled; I desired you in a former Leter to Call the Severall Resevers° to an accompt fo the Accats Mony which I ussede to reseve° for my perticuler uss° but upon the Last passinge of the accompts I heard Nothinge from you consarninge° Mr Crooke* of the great Illand would take Grenagh for a Frind of his if it were to bee

---

⁵⁷² "'Moderate space, moderation, due limits' (Johnson); esp. in *within* or *out of compass*: i.e. within or beyond the bounds of moderation" ("compass, *n.1, adj.*, and *adv.*," 2, *OED*.

Lett, which I promiss to acquant you of whous answar I desier° may bee sent mee consarninge it, I am still of the same opinione I was in my Last Leter that you will See My Lord returne in the Same Power that hee left you

    I perseve° My Sone Arran* is soe well disposed of himselfe to Relinquish the 2 Thowsand pound a yeare out of his regard unto the incombranse° that Lies upon the Fortune that is to desende unto his Elder Brother, as though it Cannot bee his unles wee make it Soe by addinge to what wee have alredie done, yet it may bee beter° to Let hime resigne as his owne free act accordinge as I find hee intends then that it should by you or anye Else bee questionede his Tytle to it, for then perhapes hee may Fansie that his Parents ~~were~~ ^are Less^ ~~Indevoringe~~ ^kind^ to take from hime what thay had else givene hime and that may make hime Stand more Strictlie upon the Termes hee is to reseve the 3 Thowsand pound a yeare by, which must bee made good unto hime, therfor to kiepe° all things Faire betwixt hime and his Brother Let this affare bee manadged with that prudense and Cautione as is Fitt in a busenes° of this Nature

Letter 152. November 9, 1668, [London], the Duchess of Ormonde to Captain George Mathew (NLI, Ormond Papers, 2503, no. 24).[573] Autograph.
For My Brother Mr Gorge Mathews. [Endorsed]: Dutchess of o 9 November 1669.[574]

Brother   [The 9] of November

I am very glad to Find by your Leter of the 17 of this Month that you have Securede some part of the Mony° that is dew° unto My Lord; and doe hope that by My Lord Chanselors[575] Example in payinge what was his proportion that others whoe are abble will doe soe Likwise; My Lord has given Sir Gorge Lane* derections° to goe unto Mr Philips[576] and Show hime mr Rians[577] oppinione and bringe his upon that perticuler, which shall within a few days bee transmittcd unto you, Captane Morton* diede the Last weeke of a

---

[573] There is some damage to the top of the MS, and the mending tape further obscures the text. The first line of the second page is mainly affected.

[574] The year cited in the endorsement must be incorrect because the letter is clearly written before JO's dismissal in March 1669.

[575] Presumably, this is the Lord Chancellor of Ireland, Archbishop Michael Boyle.

[576] JO's legal counsel.

[577] Unidentified.

Fever, My Lords Enimies are very industerious° to gett hime out of the Goverment and all his out of Comand in Ireland tell° when thay° Say thay Cannot goe on in ther bussenes° (what that is I Cannot tell but what is generalie belevede, is the distroction° of all, if Gods Mercye and the kings wisdome dous° not prevent them; I wish our depts° might bee payede ofe,° and then wee shouldbee the beter° abble to ~~bide~~ defend our selfes ~~wee are~~ ^My Lord^ is in Treatie for the Sayle of Moore Park* [*six words missing*] beter to be parted with then kept, by an Expres that is Shortlie to goe from hense you Shall heare further From

            your affectionat Sister

              E:ormonde

sense the writinge of this ~~and~~^I^ was sendinge a Leter to My Lady Humes* belevinge hir to bee at Acton,* ~~I understand Shee was~~ ^but am Tould shee is^ gone for Ireland, of whous sayfe° Landinge I shouldbee glad to heare, I pray when you see My Sister Frances Butler[578] Let hir know that Sir Redmond Everards[579] Petistione shallbee delivered when it is Seasonable to doe it, which at the presant My Lord Says it is Not and that is the Resone° whye it it Suspended, and ~~noe~~ ^Not anye^ Neglect of his Consernment°

Letter 153. December 4, 1668, [London], the Duchess of Ormonde to Captain George Mathew (NLI, Ormond Papers, 2503, no. 9). Autograph.
[Endorsed]: [My Ladys] Dated 4 Received 16 Dec 166[8].

Brother   the 4 of Des

I forbeare sayinge anye thinge to you of Neuse° by resone° it is writene to such of our Frinds as will impart it to you, but recomend to you at this time (My Sone John*) that I desier° you will assist by your good Counsell and rectifie (if you Cane) his Error in the Negligent way of his orderinge his affares which I doe heare has made hime to increase his depts° sense° Last thay° were ajusted[580] by you; and will Sartanlie° bringe some Shamfull disgrase upon hime; now that ~~wee~~ his Father and I are absent, and in a Condistione

---

[578] Lady Frances Touchet, wife of JO's younger brother, Richard Butler of Kilcash.
[579] Sir Redmond Everard, Second Baronet (d. 1687).
[580] "To settle, balance, or audit (an account or financial record)" ("adjust, *v.*2," 1c, *OED*).

besides not abell° to pay his depts if hee dous° not himselfe uss° some
[inde]vour towards it, I heare hee Eats constantlie at a Taverne which
is not only the most Chargeble but the most discreditinge way of
Liveing, wheras the Lodginge and bourdinge in Some [pri]vat House
which I Longe sense proposed, would sartanlie have bine° the fittest
~~course that hee could take~~ ^For Hime^ provided hee wouldnot kiepe°
Ieregular howers° or bee disorderlie; which it is high time for hime   *irregular*
to give over, sense it has both [redus]ede hime in his Fortune by
kiepinge° hime still in want ^and^ ~~[also]~~ Lessened his reputatione,
amongst all persons that are [cons]iderable; for it is heare reported
that hee is givene ^soe much^ to drinkinge ^as hee^ ~~and~~ Minds
Nothinge Ellse; this you may Judge is noe small trouble to his Frinds,
I pray Brothar bee Soe Charitable as onse° more to trye what may
bee done to make hime Sensibell of his Faults, and healpe hime in
prescribinge some beter° way how hee may Live within The Compas
of his Fortune then as hee dous; otherwiss Let hime Never Expect
that his Parents will bee Consernede° for a Person that vallews° not
his Contianse or his honner° [/] to say anye thinge to himselfe I feare   *conscience*
is Niedles° and therfor I chuse° to Exprese to you what is Extremlie
the grife° and Conserne° of

    your affectionat Sister
      EO

I wish I knew what My Sons depts are at the presant and what
hee dous propose unto himselfe for the Future as allsoe what your
opinione is of mr Osborns* Justis to hime

**Letter 154. [December 4], 1668, [London], the Duchess of
Ormonde to Captain George Mathew** (NLI, Ormond Papers, 2503,
no. 10). Autograph.
For Captane Gorge Mathews [/] thes. [Endorsed]: My Lady
Dutchess [Dated] 4 December Received 31 January 166[8] about
Earl Arran and Lord John.

[Brother]   The [4 December]

The tow° Frinds that My Sonn Arran* did relye upon in the
Consernes° of his Fortune heare one of them beinge Latlie° Dead
and the other not Like to Live tow days, makes his Cominge over
very requisit in order unto his owne Consernes, and therfor I have
with my Lords approbatione writene to hime this day about it;
Sense° I doe not See that his Stay thar° canbee of soe considerable

an advantage unto his Fathers affars as his Longer stay^absense^ willbee a prejudice unto his owne ^heare^ besides that I conseve° his remove from Some Companye that I heare (to my great trouble) that hee frequents To, wouldbee a hapenes° for hime to be removed from; and what to doe with my Sone John* I Cannot tell, for I heare hee Lives as hee did Still and kiepes° the villdest[581] companye, though I Cannot but hope that you and the rest of his Frinds doue° Conserne your Selfes for hime and his Brother a and dous° tell them what is Sayede° of Both, though you Mentione Nothinge of them to Mee or ther Father, but Leave uss to heare ill of them by Strangers which is the more grivious to uss;   *grievous*

Letter 155. December 5, 1668, [London], the Duchess of Ormonde to Captain George Mathew (NLI, Ormond Papers, 2503, no. 11).[582] Autograph.
For My Brother Mr Gorge Mathews [/] thes. [Endorsed]: 5th of December 68 Dutchess of Ormonde.

Brother

I doe conclude My Lady Humes* arrivede in Ireland by this time to whom I pray Ether to Send or deliver this inclosede to hir; I cannot tell you for Sartane° that My Lord willbee Continowed° in the Goverment though it is generalie soe sayede° and belevede both in the Court and Towne, by resone° I see soe great Changes as I cannot beleve anye thinge Shure,° but if this shall hapene to prove soe, it may bee ownede to his innosensie in Not haveinge provede Negligent or Corrupt in his Goverment rather then to anye favour hee has Found from anye Man that dous° yet appiere;° but Let this bee kept to your Selfe for it may perhaps bee beter° the world should beleve hime beter befrinded then I dout° hee is; I have discovrede sense° my cominge hethar° that the Clarke of the kichine has takene a Shillinge ^in the Pound^ Poundage[583] for all the Tallow hee Sould° at Dublin

---

[581] Most vile: "Of actions, conduct, character, etc.: Despicable on moral grounds; deserving to be regarded with abhorrence or disgust; characterized by baseness or depravity" ("vile, *adj.*," A1a, *OED*).

[582] There is minor wear to the top of the MS, which obscures a few words from the top of the second page.

[583] "A payment of so much per pound sterling, or so much per cent in other currencies, upon the amount of any transaction in which money passes; a commission, or fee, of so much a pound or so much per cent" ("poundage, *n.*1," 1b, *OED*).

and the Pantler⁵⁸⁴ soe much in the Pound Likwise which Causede
our Lights to bee soe bad that was takene from a Chandlor⁵⁸⁵ one
Cooke that Lived Neare the Castell and was Sense Changed and
the Coustome givene unto a Nother;° it were worth [*four words
missing*] but [*missing*] not privatlie done it is ods that the Clarke of
the kichine and the Pantlor will give this Man his Lessone soe that
[hee] willnot discover the Truth; I am indevoringe° to gett one in
Connoways* Plase and to Louke° the best I cane that My Lord be
not Coussened° heare, though I have soe Litell° healpe as I much
Feare wee are wronged ^for^ all the Care that I cane take to the
Contrarye; soe strange a Time this is for Sarvants at as pepell° of all
degres complayns that thay° were Never Soe Bad as Now, I pray send
mee word how thay are ther in My Sons Familie and what order is
kept by Them, with what othar accompt° you shall think Fitt to bee
transmitted consarninge° domesticke affares unto

    your affectionat Sister and Sarvant

      E:ormonde

I have intreated My Lady Humes* if Shee Finds it for hir
Conv[eniense] to Stay at My House at kilkenye⁵⁸⁶ as Longe as shee
pleases and to Make uss° of what Ever provistione is Ther

**Letter 156. January 6, 1668/9, [London], the Duchess of Ormonde
to Captain George Mathew** (NLI, Ormond Papers, 2503, no. 12).⁵⁸⁷
Autograph.
[Endorsed]: My Lady Dutches of the 6 January 1668.

after I had Ended my Leter I was bidene by My Lord to [write unto]
you of a very [sufficent] Baylife that offiers° hime selfe to Sarve ~~my Lord~~ ^Hime^ that is a husbandman, and has himselfe Farmede tow°
hundreth pound a yeare Neare unto the Lord Culpepers,⁵⁸⁸ whoe
gives hime an Exterordenarye Carracture° for his honnestie and
knowlege in Cattell, and all Manner of Contrye affares; and Soe

---

 ⁵⁸⁴ "An officer in a large household who was in charge of the bread or pantry" ("pantler, *n.*," *OED*).
 ⁵⁸⁵ "One whose trade it is to make or sell candles" ("chandler, *n.*1," 2a, *OED*).
 ⁵⁸⁶ EO's own Dunmore House.
 ⁵⁸⁷ There is some wear to the MS, which partially obscures some words at the top of each page. The mending tape used to repair the MS further obscures the text.
 ⁵⁸⁸ Thomas Colepeper, second Baron Colepeper (1635–1689), Governor of the Isle of Wight (1661–1667) and Virginia (1675–1682).

dous° a Nother° of My acquantanse that Livede in Hampshire in the Same Contrye; hee has a wife but noe Chilldrene; hee is about fiftye not givene to anye visse;° hee demands thirtye pound a yeare wages; the same hee has heare at presant, if you think such a persone soe qualifiede, may desarve that Sallerye° I pray Let mee reseve° your oppinione and advise in this Perticuler, as soune° as you Cane, For theris tow Persons that at this Time are strivinge to have hime, and hee suspends the ingadginge° of himeselfe for a Month in hope to bee resolvede [by that] Time, I doe not Conseve° the Strengthning of the Roufe of the [north] Hall of killkeny canbee anye considerable Charge and the Peesinge of the Cupp[ells⁵⁸⁹ that] are decayed and [Stript] from what supports them is all the presant defects, soe as the unslating of the Roufe soe farr as that Fault is, willbee the greatest Part of the Charge; and that I doe Conseve ther willbee a Nesesitie For, but nothinge more then what you may Find to bee Soe; would I advise to bee done; unles the Cleninge and whitinge of the inside of the Hall when the worke is Finnisht by resone° that Rome° must bee much of it pulled downe when sowever that House Comes to be inlardged

piecing

Letter 157. January 10, 1668/9, [London], the Duchess of Ormonde to Captain George Mathew (NLI, Ormond Papers, 2503, no. 30). Autograph.
For My Brother Mr Gorge Mathews [/] thes. [Endorsed]: My Lady Dutches of the 10th of January received 25th 1668.

Brother   the [10 of Jan]

My Lord and I both dous° soe much apprehend the daynger of the Roufe of the olde Hall of the Castell of killkenye as hee desiers° it might bee Securelie repayrede and Mended; with as much Spide as may bee; ther beinge Timber Ennough ther to doe it, which was Left of other workes, and I doe beleve, that Taylor the Carpenter, would contrive the doeinge of it as well or beter° then anye workman that is Ther; provided that hee bee artickeled⁵⁹⁰ with and give Securitie to performe the agreement, and mr Archer* to over See the worke and deliver out the Materialls for it; that a such an accompt° may bee kept therof; that wee may Not bee Coussened° by the workmen;

---

⁵⁸⁹ "One of a pair of inclined rafters or beams, that meet at the top and are fixed at the bottom by a tie, and form the principal support of a roof; a principal rafter, a chevron" ("couple, *n.*," II, 8, *OED*).

⁵⁹⁰ "To negotiate or arrange, esp. *with* a person" ("article, *v.*," 3b, *OED*).

nor bee betrayede into a greater Expense then theris a Nesesitie
For, I send you hear inclosede a Note of some Peeses of Plate that
I desier to have sent mee to bee Changed For what is Now more in
uss, and beter for Show, heare is litell° Neuse,° but that the Duches
was broght to Bed on wednesday Last of a daughter,[591] and that mr
Simmons whoe did very barboroslie kill My Cousen Bromiche in a *barbarously*
Taverne and the tow° acsesaries are all Fled,[592] the wether heare is
could° unto soe great a degree as I have not found the Like of it in
England, which gives My Lord hopes that the Frosts are in some
proportione Ecqualinge it in Ireland that Soe his Snow Housses[593]
ther may bee Filled; I have Noe further to trouble you at this time
havinge ~~troubled you~~ ^writene to you^ soe Latlie° but to asshure° you
of my beinge

    your affectionat Sister

      E:ormonde

I pray remember mee to My Sister[594] and if Shee bee not well
Enough to write hir Selfe; send mee ~~word to what distemper troubles hir~~ some accompt of hir

Letter 158. February 5, 1668/9, [London], the Duchess of Ormonde to Captain George Mathew (NLI, Ormond Papers, 2503, no. 32). Autograph.
For My Brother Mr Gorge Mathews. [Endorsed]: My Ladys of the 5 of february 68. Duchess of o.

I thank you for your Care, in providinge a House for the Duchman[595] whoe ^I^ intend to bringe over with Mee and doe hope that My

---

[591] The Duchess of York's daughter, Henrietta, died in infancy.

[592] Pepys writes: "Here Mrs. Smith tells us of the great murder thereabouts, on Saturday last, of one Captain Bumbridge, by one Symons, both of her acquaintance; and hectors [ruffians] that were at play, and in drink: the former is killed, and is kinsman to my Lord of Ormond, which made him speak of it with so much passion, as I overheard him this morning, but could not make anything of it till now" (*Diary of Samuel Pepys*, January 11, 1668/9).

[593] For a short discussion of ice houses see Costello, *Irish Demesne Landscapes*, 69.

[594] Presumably, Anne Hume, now Mathew's wife.

[595] Fenlon speculates that this may refer to Abraham van Uylenburgh, a Dutch painter, who styled himself "Painter to the Duchess of Ormond." She notes that the Uylenburghs were a distinguished family of painters and picture dealers in Amsterdam (connected by marriage to Rembrandt), and proposes that Uylenburgh may have been

Lord willbee over very Shortlie in what Capasitie sowever, though
my beleufe is still that it willbee the same it was Notwithstandinge
all that you heare unto the contrarye, and I think I have some resone°
to bee of that oppinione which it is Not convenient for mee to write,
My Lord bid mee to write unto the Controwler as this day I have don
to Laye⁵⁹⁶ in Beare° at killkenye the Next Month and to Fill both
the Sellers° [/] a Proportion of wine willbee Likwise Nesesarye to
bee in a redenes;° and the Securinge of the Roufe of the great Hall
Ther as requiset as or more, then anye thinge consarninge° which
I writ formerlie to you and doe agayne° seconde my request that in
your owne presanse° it may bee veuede° and soe much done as may
kiepe° it from the daynger of Fallinge; The Times are now soe bad
and apprehended will grow worse as kiepes backe anye purcharsiers
from buyinge of Land soe as I feare wee must bee forst to kiepe
Moore Parke* Still untell° wee Cane Light upon a Chapman⁵⁹⁷ which
a very good Frind of My Lords and an abble Man is indevoringe° to
Find out, the Morgadge° Mony° that is upon it, is part of it Called in,
soe is some other of the depts° for which My Lord of Devonshire⁵⁹⁸
is Bound which willbee troubellsom to My Lord; I am very well
pleasede to Find that you have payede the ^the^ Doctor Mony to and
mr Lovet,⁵⁹⁹ I hope that what is dew° upon My Lords Entertainment
will suplye the wants of the Familie at Dublin and paye ofe° in Part
the Sarvants wages and other the depts that are the most pressing

The 5 of Feb

**Letter 159. February 16, 1668/9, [London], the Duchess of
Ormonde to Captain George Mathew** (NLI, Ormond Papers, 2503,
no. 13). Autograph.
For My Brother Mr Gorge Mathews. [Endorsed]: my Ladys of the
16 February 1668.

Brother   The 16 of Feb The 16 of Feb

---

employed as an agent for the acquisition of paintings. See Fenlon, "Episodes of Magnificence," 156.

⁵⁹⁶ "To make arrangements or plans *for*" ("lay, *v.*," 38c, *OED*).

⁵⁹⁷ "A man whose business is buying and selling; a merchant, trader, dealer" ("chapman, *n.*," 1a, *OED*).

⁵⁹⁸ William Cavendish, third Earl of Devonshire (1617–1684), the father-in-law of EO's daughter Mary. O'Keeffe, 105, argues that the Ormondes expected their in laws to help them obtain credit.

⁵⁹⁹ Unidentified.

My Leter to you upon saterday ~~Last~~ did I supose prepare you for
what happened on sonday Last; which was My Lords dismiss from
the goverment of Ireland, declarede by his Magestye; and the Lord
Roberts⁶⁰⁰ Namede to suckside° hime; with the Tytell° of Lord
Liftenant, I cannot as yet informe you of the sartane° time when his
Lordshipp willbee Ther; but soe soune° as I doe know; you shall have
spidie° Nottis° sent you, The mene° time it willbee Nesesarye to gett
Ether the Phenixe* or Chapelizard* House⁶⁰¹ in a redenes° for My
Sonn ossory* and as many of his Familie as the Plase hee Chusses°
Cane contane [/] the rest may Lodge in the Towne; and hee to kiepe°
but a private Table whilst hee is Ther, and soe dismiss as manye
Sarvants of all kinds as may be sparede and give oppertunitie to have
our Goods removede out of the Castell unto Dunmore* ^at the Least
such^ ~~soune that~~ ^as^ will take upe the most Rome° by resone° That
House is Emptie; and the best of the[m to] kilkenye;* that Dublin
Castell may bee the souner° Clearede for the new Governer which will
^allsoe^ put our owne affares into a Good forwardnes, aganst I come
my selfe which shallbee God willinge about the Midell of the Next
Month, I doe beleve that what provistione of Cole Biere [hay]⁶⁰² otes   *coal; oats*
wine or the Like will possiblie bee bought by the Person employede
by the New Governor For his uss, as allsoe the [Chairs] Bedstids   *bedsteads*
for sarvants Tabells and such Loumber which it may not be amiss   *lumber*
to Consider, and sett some vallew° upon; all the Locks and keyes
I likwise payede For, and perticularlie thous° belonginge unto My
Lords Closset and my owne Chamber with the Iorne Backes in the   *iron*
Severall Chimnyes, by the Next I shall posiblie know more and then
you shall accordinglie heare Furthar From

        your affectionat Sister

          E:ormonde

I pray remember mee to My Sister to whom I was not willinge to
write what I am shure° will not please hir

---

⁶⁰⁰ John Robartes, second Baron Robartes of Truro (1606–1685), had already served briefly as Lord Deputy in 1660, although he was removed from office before he even went to Ireland. His appointment as Lord Lieutenant on May 3, 1669, therefore came as some surprise, although it was only to last a year. See Anne Duffin, "Robartes, John, first earl of Radnor (1606–1685)," *ODNB*.

⁶⁰¹ The Phoenix and Chapelizod were the offficial lodgings of the viceroy in Dublin. Barnard writes: "The Ormondes' failure to acquire an Irish townhouse of their own betrayed their assumption that the government of Ireland, together with its physical appurtenancess, belonged naturally to them" (Barnard, Introduction, *Dukes of Ormonde*, 41).

⁶⁰² Word supplied by HMC Ormond, III, 441.

Letter 160. February, 1669, [London], the Duchess of Ormonde to Captain George Mathew (NLI, Ormond Papers, 2503, no. 33). Autograph.
For My Brother Mr Gorge Mathews [/] thes. [Endorsed]: My Lady Dutchess her letter. February 1669.

Brother

[I] still hould° my resolutione of goeinge for Ireland about the Midell of the Next Month Soe as I doe hope to bee ther time Enough befor the Lord Roberts* his arrivall to healpe in the orderinge of the affares of the Familie, and the removinge of it with and Modelinge of it as may sute° our presant condistione, I doe not Sartanlie° know when the New Governer willbee Ther; som says not tell° May, but I desier° that noe time may bee Lost to put killkenye into a Redenes° to reseve° My Sonns Familie and my Selfe For I will make My Frinds wellcome to that Plase whilst I staye; My Lord of Ororye[603] is as Litell° Satisfiede with this Change that is is made and the Duke of Buckingham* as if my Lord had continowede;° and I am of opinione that thay° will Find Cause at the Least I wish it may fall out Soe, and soe I am Shure° dous° Many More; If John Burdon* bee soe unfitt for bussenes° a Nother° must Nesesarilie bee imployede Sir Gorge Layne* will give you an accompt° of mr Floyds* answar to hime, from whom hee has resevede° noe mony° as yet, and I feare willnot; when anye Person Comes from the Lord Roberts to make provistione for hime I would have the Steward and Controwler to bee Sivell° in offeringe hime anye ordenarye assistanse that hee [Should Nide°] as I have done the Lady Roberts* of anye thinge [in] the castell belonginge to uss that may untell° hir owne Goods Comes bee ussfull to hir which I Find was Extremlie well takene [/] I think the Phenixe* willbee a much Fitter Plase for My Sonn to bee at when he Leaves the Sword then Chapellizard* and I am not unapt to beleve but Corronell Jeferes[604] would Lend it Furnisht as it is for soe Short a time as wouldbee Niedfull° for My Sonn Singlie to make uss° of, (his Lady and Chilldrene), beinge Fitter to remove with mee to killkenye som Time befor the New governors arrivall, then to be ther at that Time, which may bee very well contrivede by my goeinge over soe Longe befor his cominge; whoe cannot goe Souner° then May ^as is thought^ for hee has a great Familie of Children [/] an Estate to settell and a Plase to part with heare that is Loukede° after by Many, but I cannot informe you soe Perticularlie by This, as I doe hope to

---

[603] Roger Boyle, Earl of Orrery (1621–1679), formerly Lord Broghill.
[604] Colonel John Jeffreys of Chapelizod.

doe by the Next Post and therfor shall adde noe further unto your trouble at this Time but remayne

> your affectionat Sister
>
> E:ormonde

Brother I pray Let mr John Briane* know that the Bill hee Sent was acsepted beinge what remaynede dew° for woole and that a [*missing*]⁶⁰⁵ was returnde a good while Sense° and that the uskebath⁶⁰⁶ is Come sayfe° [that mr Ar]cher did Send

Letter 161. March 6, 1668/9, [London], the Duchess of Ormonde to Captain George Mathew (NLI, Ormond Papers, 2503, no. 14). Autograph.
For My Brother Mr Gorge Mathews. [Endorsed]: My Lady Dutches her Letter of the 6 of March 1668.

Brother   The 6 of March

severall of your Leters cominge together to my hands yesterday Late gave mee not time to answar all the perticulars of them this day with my owne hand, beinge upon some bussenes° consernede° to bee at My Lady of Devonshiers⁶⁰⁷ this for noune; and therfor have *forenoon* desirede Sir Gorge Layne* to performe it for Mee; soe as I have only to ade° in this, my desier° that the Nots°⁶⁰⁸ which my Lady Layne⁶⁰⁹ has of Mine one as I take it beinge for 2 hundreth and a Nother° for one hundreth may bee atestede by you; ~~accordinge~~ the Mony° I had from hime was to paye ofe;° the wages of such of my Lords Sarvants as was Sent with My Sone ossory* into England, and the other upon a dept° that My Lord did owe unto a Poure° widow, all which hee well remembers, I supose My Lady Layne dous° not press anye spidie° payment therof, only aymes° at the beter° strengthninge of hir Securitie for the dept, I doe not think it Convenient that My daghter ossorye* Should remove from Dublin

---

⁶⁰⁵ There is a small tear caused by the seal.
⁶⁰⁶ Whiskey, from the Gaelic *uisge beatha* or "water of life" ("usquebaugh, *n.*," *OED*).
⁶⁰⁷ It is uncertain whether this is the Dowager Lady Devonshire or her daughter-in-law.
⁶⁰⁸ In relation to money or finance, a note was "a written promise to pay a certain sum at a specified time" ("note, *n.2*," V, 19b, *OED*).
⁶⁰⁹ Sir George Lane's second wife, Susanah (1627–1671), daughter of Sir Edward Nicholas. See John Cronin and Terry Clavin, "Lane, George 1st Viscount Lanesborough," *DIB*.

Nor the Goods bee carryede from thense untell° I come by reson
the Lord Roberts* desiers to buye such Furniture as wee cane spare
and provistions allsoe which willbee a Conveniensie unto uss Both, I
intend god willinge to bee at Holyhead* the ~~16~~ ^6^ of Aprell where
a Shipe willbee in a redenes° to bringe mee over, I have Sent to the
Controwler to Laye in more Beare° at kilkenye* suffisent for my Stay
3 months Ther and for My Sons Familie when I Leave them; wine
and all othar provistions allsoe; soe as it willbee Nideles° to Laye in
anye thinge at Chapellizard* but to have the Plase well kept; that
My Lord Roberts may Find it Soe whoe I have some resone° to hope
willbee a Frind; Mr Ompton Crooke* was with mee Just Now whoe
wouldbee willinge to take the Farm of Granagh but willnot give anye
more then a hundreth pound a yeare Rent and to bee Liable unto all
Taxes; all perticulars Else Sir Gorge Layne will acquant you of by
derectione° from

        your affectionat Sister

           E:ormonde

**Letter 162. March 9, 1668/9, [London], the Duchess of Ormonde
to Captain George Mathew** (NLI, Ormond Papers, 2503, no. 15).
Autograph.
[Endorsed]: The Dutches of Ormond her Letter of the 9th March
1668.

I heare theris some retrenchments made in the Familie sense° this
Change of the goverment ~~wh~~ by Lesseninge of the Nombers of them
which I doe aprove very well of, and the more; that I hope it is done
with your approbatione and advise that I am shure° will consider that
the best ~~are to~~ ^Sarvants^ in ther severall kinds are to bee retaynede
to make upe a Familie proper for My Soon° ossorye* to kiepe° at
kilkenye* when hee parts with the Goverment (for ther) I doe take for
granted hee must reside; at the least, untell° such Time as his Fathers
Mony° is Securede and the kingdom Settlede; in his hand whom
the kinge has honnored with that Trust and whoe I am perswaded
willbee very Just and Frindlie unto My Lord and all his relations; and
not soe indulgent ^I supose^ to My Lord of Ororye* as my lord was;
hee understandinge very well what that Person has bine° from the
begininge and what hee is still; the most false and ingratfull ~~Person~~
^Man^ livinge; and under that Estime I cane asshure° you hee passes
heare with all the considerable Persons of this kingdom and [I hear

he is] degected at the disapoyntment that hee has mett with,[610] and   *dejected*
soe are all his adherents; which is some satisfactione yet; and more
I Expect willbee in the downfall of some Ere Longe that has bine
My Lords Enimies whilst hee presarves I thank God a reputatione
beyond what anye of them cane Blast,[611] and has, at this Time the
kindnes and respect of all this Natione beyond what hee Ever had
[/] I desier° you will Send Sestions[612] order to Furnish the Castell of
killkenye to bee in a redenes° to reseve° mee My Sone and his Familie
by the Midell of the Next Month; and that all Nesesarye Provistions
for the House may bee Layede in according^lie^ [/] Though I doe
not beleve that My Lord Roberts* canbee ther untell the Layter°
Ende of May, tell° when My Sone is to Continow° in the same power
and to bee allowede as former Lord Depeties were; and to dispose
of all commands duringe that time; soe as I doe hope hee may ~~bee abble to~~
gett a Company for Captane Jones[613] Ether in the Gards
or in the Armye which hee shall himselfe Chuse; and some Lower
imployments for such other of My Lords Sarvants as may bee sparede
and is not as yet provided for, I pray tell my sister Mathews that my
Lady Roberts* did inquier° for hir with great kindnes and promisises
[*sic*] hir selfe much Content in haveinge hir Companye and Estime
for shee knows Non° ther but hir Selfe and My Lady of Desmond[614]
[She is a very][615] vertious and a worthye Person and goes preparede
to bee verye oblidginge to all our relations and soe I doe hope thay°
will all bee to hir; the discontents of the pepell° ^heare^ are very
great and ther haterede of the Duke of Buckingham* far beyond anye   *hatred*
thay had for the Lord Claringtone[616] or anye other; God knows what
it will Ende in, but is thought in noe good unto his Grase [/] The   *Grace*
Generall is very ill, and not Like to Recover, whoe the Sucksidinge°
person shallbee is not as yet knowne; but Conjectured [/] I pray
remember mee to My sister, whoe Corronell Fits Patricke* tells mee

---

[610] The Earl of Orrery had hoped to replace JO as Lord Lieutenant of Ireland.

[611] "To bring infamy upon (character, reputation); to discredit effectually, ruin, destroy" ("blast, *v.*," II, 8b, *OED*).

[612] William Sestions, servant at Kilkenny Castle.

[613] Unidentified.

[614] Mary Feilding, née King, first wife of William, second Earl of Desmond, later third Earl of Denbigh (1640–1685), and daughter of Sir Robert King.

[615] Words supplied by HMC Ormonde, III, 441.

[616] Edward Hyde, first Earl of Clarendon (1609–1674).

has now hir health very well, which is much unto my sattisfactione that am very consernedlie° hirs and

>your affectionat sister

The 9 of March   E:ormonde

Letter 163. March 16, 1668/9, [London], the Duchess of Ormonde to Captain George Mathew (NLI, Ormond Papers, 2503, no. 38[b]).[617] Autograph.
[Endorsed]: My Lady Dutches the 16 march received 1 April 1669.

I thought it fitt to acquant you that I have agreede with a Clarke of the kichine for 20 pound a yeare; and will bringe over with mee a Larder[618] Man allsoe; upon as resonable Termes as I cane agree if you doe find that the Layter° of thes willbee ussfull For My Sons Familie when hee Settells himselfe at kilkenye* where I doe hope hee willbee contented to spend some time untell° hee Sees the publicke and his Fathers affares beter° Settled then at the presant thay° are, The hopes of Sellinge Moore Parke* makes Mee defar my Journye untell the 20 of the Next Month and the rather, that the New Governors goeinge Cannot bee Soe sudane° as at the first I did beleve, besides the great unstedenes of affares are Such, as wee hardlie as yet know what wee may accompt° to bee Sartane;° and therfor I think it best to know the full resolutions that willbee takene heare; which wee are made beleve are Changed sense° the kings goeinge to Newmarket* in very Considerable things as to the Goverment[619] [/] [*one line missing*] as to what may [relate] unto our perticuler consernes° and soe Soune° as that is knowne which wee doe Expect willbee in some time after the kings returne you Shall heare agayne° very Soune From

defer

unsteadiness

>your affectionat Sister

>E:ormonde

remember mee to my Sister

---

[617] There is some wear to the top of the MS, which renders the top line of the second page unreadable. There may have been a salutation or date at the top of the first page that is now lost.

[618] "A room or closet in which meat (? originally bacon) and other provisions are stored" ("larder, *n.*1," 1a, *OED*).

[619] In other words, "We understand that considerable changes to the government have been agreed since the King went to Newmarket."

Letter 164. March 20, 1668/9, [London], the Duchess of Ormonde to Captain George Mathew (NLI, Ormond Papers, 2503, no. 38[a]).[620] Autograph.
[Endorsed]: my Lady Dutches of the 20 march received 1 April 1669. Dutchess of ormond to George Mathew.

Brother

In my Last I gave you an accompt° that I had bargenede with one to bee Clarke of the kichine, for 20 pound a yeare, and Now I am offerede a yonge Man that has skill to ~~powede~~ powder[621] Meate and to kiepe° the wett Larder, hee is a Cooke besides; and has sarvede as a Cayterer 7 years in a Gentellmans House that gives a very good   *caterer* Carracture° of hime the wages hee demanded was 15 pound a yeare, but with much adoe I have broght hime to 10 if you think that such an offisier° willbee Niedfull° in My Sons Familie when hee Settells at kilkenye* I pray send mee word as Soune° as possiblie you Cane That I may Ethar° bringe hime over when I come; or give hime his answar which hee desiers° may bee soe soune as may bee; that in Cayse° I doe not Entertane hime hee may bee at Libertye to dispose otherwise of himselfe

Letter 165. [March 1669], [London], the Duchess of Ormonde to [Captain George Mathew] (NLI, Ormond Papers, 2484, no. 241, p. 269). Autograph.
[Endorsed]: My Lady Dutchesse her letter.

I am prest° to give an answar unto a Person that I am offerede, to bee Clarke of the kichine and I doe not well know what to resolve consarninge° hime; for if my sone willnot Stay in Ireland; then it willbee Niedles° to Entertane hime, and if hee doe settell himselfe in anye other Sarvise° it willbee hard to gett the ~~a Nothar~~ ^like of This Person^ that is fitt for such an imployment, therfor if you Cane gess;° or Find out, what My Sonn dous° propose unto himselfe I shouldbee glad to reseve° some private intematione° of it from you that I might order my owne affares accordinglie, and Leave hime to Manadge his as he pleases; for I nether have nor Cane have anye House heare that

---

[620] This letter has been bound with one written four days earlier on March 16 but delivered to Mathew on the same day (April 1). Each letter is endorsed separately, which suggests that they were sent and delivered separately.

[621] "To sprinkle (meat, etc.) with salt or powdered spice, esp. for preserving; to salt; to corn or cure" ("powder, *v.*1," 3a, *OED*).

is Neare the Court Large Enough to contane anye more in Familie
then what I have at presant, Nether will I Ever submitt agayne° unto
the trouble of kiepinge° anye other ~~Familie~~ Espetialie° whilst I am
out of Ireland; It is possible that My Lord Roberts* may buy the
Cowes and cattell that is at Chapellizard* if not it wouldbee best
to remove all and discharge all the Sarvants that are Ther Exsept
the Gardener only, and Swetnam⁶²² whoe may when that Familie is
dissolvede stay at the Castell of Dublin untell° I Come

**Letter 166. May 31, 1669, Kilkenny, the Duchess of Ormonde
to the Duke of Ormonde** (Bodl., Carte Papers, 243, fols. 12–13).
Autograph.
For the Duke of Ormonde [/] thes. [Endorsed]: My Wife 31 May
Received 11 June 1669.

kilkeny the Last of May

upon friday Last I came from dublin accompanede with all the
~~companye~~ ^Persons of qualitie^ in Towne whoe to Exprese ther
respect to you did bringe mee part of the way with the greatest
conserne° for your Leavinge the Goverment that ~~Ever~~ couldbee
exprest, sense° my arrivall heare I have had tow° Leters from you the
one of the 22 the other of the 25 of this Month and have Seene that
of yours unto My Brother Mathews* with whom I shall discourse
befor I say anye thinge to you consarninge° the Contents therof and
tell you at presant that I found this Plase in very good condistione,
and your Jese house; ~~Full~~ out of which I had some this day, theris the   *geese*
greatest improvments of plantings at Dunmore* that Ever I saw in
Soe Short a time and has made it very bewtifull by the great Nomber
of Trees and the order that thay° are Sett in; I goe on wedensday
Next to Caricke* and from thense to Thurles,* and Next for England
Godwillinge soe Soune° as Ever the yaught°⁶²³ comes about as it will
from Dublin to waterford with the first wind, I perseve° the bargine
for the buildinge of your Lodgings is allredie made soe as what is
don° in That cannot bee recaled, I send you hearinclosed a paper
that a Frind of yours gott in Monster° amongst the Lord of Ororys*
Creaturs,⁶²⁴ that willbee thay say presented by some Nobellmen and

---

⁶²² Servant at Dublin Castle.
⁶²³ "A light fast-sailing ship, in early use esp. for the conveyance of royal or other important persons" ("yacht, *n.*," OED).
⁶²⁴ "A person who owes his or her fortune and position, and remains subservient to, a patron; a person who is ready to do another's bidding" ("creature, *n.*," 4a, OED).

gentellmen ^heare^ unto the Parlement of England [it] was givene mee but this day; soe as I cannot as yett Fastene upon ~~that~~ ^the^ person that gave the Coppie of it, but hope I shall know whoe it is befor I goe, from hense; ~~most~~ it is all but one continowede° Lie, how ever I pray Let it bee kept by you (at the Least untell° I come); and not throwne a way for it is possible I may Find the oughters and gett proufs whoe thay are ~~whoe are~~ to confirme what is a[t] presant but suspected; upon consideratione of your Leter to My Brother Mathews consarninge My Son Ossorys* allowan[se] I Find it very hard on both Sids, (on yours) to allow hime 3 thowsand ~~which~~ ^a yeare though^ as it is proposed is a beter° bargine for you then as his payments was befor, when you have not soe much your selfe out of all your Estate; on the other Side, how hee cane with anye Sattisfactione Live upon the one halfe of this; which was all that you stoud° oblidged to Pay hime; wouldbee as uneasie unto hime ~~on the other Side~~, his Charge beinge increast and his depts° somthing in England, when at the same time that you doe retrench his mantenanse you allow his Second Brother[625] what you take from hime; whoe has besids the full advantage of his Ladys Portion and nothinge abayted° hime for all the Charge that his preferment did Cost you which I doe feare my Son ossorye ~~has som~~ may have such a resentment of, as may if discontented upon the accompt° of breakinge what has past betwixt [his] Brother and hee; bee more unfixte then Ever, as to the Settlinge of himselfe and Familie; and bee an ocatione° perhapes of makinge an Envie and Breach in your Familie which should anye thinge of that kind happene ^would^ Ruene° it more then all the other disadvantages it Cane Suffier,° and therfor I think it is my part to Laye befor you all the ^ill^ consequensies that may bee fearede from what his wants; or apprehentione of your want of kindnes to hime; may ocatione; and bege of you to think seriouslie of it, and then conclude upon what you doe think to bee best; that hee may not have ~~The Shadow of anye~~ ^That for a^ pretense; to goe a Ramblinge for Lack of Menes° to kiepe° hime heare, which if afforded I hope will take him ofe° from thous° vane thoughts

authors

sides

---

[625] EO's second son, Richard, Earl of Arran.

Letter 167. June 9, 1669, Kilkenny, the Duchess of Ormonde to the Duke of Ormonde (Bodl., Carte Papers, 243, fol. 18). Autograph. For the Duke of Ormonde [/] thes.

sense I writ last unto you I went to Carrike where I had a veue° of a very Ruenous° House, in the outward apperanse of it, but presarvede from anye greater or more dayngerous decayes as to the fallinge of it, The Orchard is not Fine; but well planted with good Fruite; but the Parke⁶²⁶ is I think the finest one of the bignes that Canbee Sene anye where, and the drie wall the best of anye that Ever I saw and all Finnisht and the grownd° fullie Stokede with brave   *stocked*
Large Fatt Diere;° I had a Sight allsoe of 5 of your yonge Colts som
3 som 4 yeares old 3 Philis and 2 Horse Coults very handsom in   *fillies; colts*
others oppinione as well as Mine, otherwis perhapes you would noe more beleve them Soe, then you doe the wine ^to bee good^ that I commend ^to bee soe^ my Skill in both beinge much a Like, I Laye on° Night at kilcash⁶²⁷ and the ^Next^ Night at Thurles* where I found my Lady your Mother well unto a wonder consideringe hir Age and very inquisitive after you [/] the Next day I came backe hethar° where I have bine° tyrede° with readinge Petistions; and somthinge pourer° in stocke then I was by what I have givene away a Mongst my poure° kindred and Frinds, whoe I hope are somthinge relivede by it; I willnot trouble you with an accompt° of your greater Consarnments° sense° I hope to doe it by discourse with you very Shortlie, nothinge Stayinge Mee Now but the yaughts° comminge about, which I doe Expect with the first wind and Seeinge of My Sonn Osory* befor I goe; I have resolvede on My Stages when I come one° the other Side but I willnot Send them to you Nor Name when the Coche° shall meete mee at my Landinge untell° I have resolvede of the Sartane° time when to take Shipinge Though I have had more trouble then plesure sense my beinge heare; yet you will Find ther was some Resone° for my Cominge

The 9 of June

---

⁶²⁶ As Costello points out, the seventeenth-century understanding of a "park" was of land specifically for the preservation of game. See Costello, *Irish Demesne Landscapes*, 164.

⁶²⁷ Kilcash Castle, County Tipperary, was the residence of JO's younger brother, Richard Butler of Kilcash (c. 1616–1701), and his wife, Frances, née Touchet. See *Kilcash, 1190–1801*, ed. John Flood and Phil Flood (Dublin: Geography Publications, 1999), 42–47.

I heare from a very good hand that Sir St John Broderic[k]⁶²⁸ is to
bee made a vicount I pray inquier° after it and hinder it if you Cane,
for many Resons not fitt for mee to Mentione, by this way

**Letter 168. June 15, 1669, Kilkenny, the Duchess of Ormonde to the
Duke of Ormonde** (Bodl., Carte Papers, 243, fol. 22). Autograph.
For the Duke of Ormonde [/] thes. [Endorsed]: 15 June.

I have bine° heare on Friday next willbee 3 weekes Expectinge the
yaught° which by contrarye winds has bine hetherto° hinderede
from makinge a Passage to waterford, and has kept mee the greatest
part of this Time from hearinge from you which has bine of all; the
most uneasie to Mee; I have not as yet Namede when to bee at the
waterside but deferede it, untell° I heare onse° More from you, as I
doe with great impatianse° hope I shall very Soune,° that accordinglie
I may governe my Selfe and give you Nottis° when and where the
Coche° shall meete Mee at My Landinge, I have had my health very
well Ever sense° I saw you; and have applyede my selfe to what Litell°
Conserns° heare that I was capable to be ussfull in, and Espetialie°
in such perticulers as I had your derections° in, wherof I hope to
bringe you a good accompt,° The Skoole⁶²⁹ goes on very prosperoslie
and Scollers cominge Evrye weeke from all Parts of the kingdom all
beinge Gentellmens Sons of the best qualitie;

kilkeny The 15 of June

**Letter 169. June 18, 1669, Kilkenny, the Duchess of Ormonde
to the Duke of Ormonde** (Bodl., Carte Papers, 243, fols. 24–25).
Autograph.
[Endorsed]: 18 June.

                       kilkenye the 18 of June

The Last post broght mee yours of the 1 and 5 of this Month that
mentions the ressept° of some of mine sent you befor and at the time

---

⁶²⁸ St. John Brodrick (d. 1712) of Ballyannan, near Midleton, Co. Cork, came from Surrey where he retained estates and close connections. He received a substantial grant of property in Co. Cork in 1653, which he expanded after the Restoration, when his eldest brother, Alan, was a commissioner for settling the affairs of Ireland. His son Alan Brodrick would become first Viscount Midleton. See D. W. Hayton, "Brodrick, Alan, first Viscount Midleton (1655/6–1728)," *ODNB*.

⁶²⁹ Kilkenny College.

of my Leavinge Dublin; sense° my cominge hether I have givene
you an accompt° of Caricke,* and of your affares heare, which I hope
is come unto your hands; the rest I shall deferr the discoursing of
untell° I see you, nothinge stayinge mee but tell° the yaught° comes
which the contrarye winds has hindered hetharto;° I supose My Sonn
ossorye* willbee now convinst that it is not practicable what hee did
propose unto himselfe of haveinge a Command ~~abrode~~ in Flanders,
though at the same time I dout° hee designes what willbee allmost
as prejudistiall unto ~~you~~ hime and to his owne; and your Intrests;
which is to carrye his wife and Familie into England and Live at
London, at the Least (Leave hir ther) where Shee has a mind to
bee and goe himselfe to Itelie, [Illegible] for in this Plase I find that   Italy
Nether of them has a mind to Staye; though I doe asshure° you thay°
have not wanted such incoridgments° as might a bundantlie satisfie
anye resonable persons; I heare the House thay Picke upon to Live in
Ther, is the Lord Midelltons[630] and to take it redie Furnisht whoe has
put hime upon that Choise I cannot tell and am Louth to Suspect,
Sir Arthur Forbus,[631] This is kept a Secret from Mee but possiblie
James Clarke* may know somthinge of this from mr Page;* whoe is
the only Counselor that my Sone Chusses° because hee Finds hime
complyinge with his humor in all things [I have] I heare Nothinge
of the kings Leter as yet, though the Securinge of That; which you
are to have by it, is of Soe absolute an Nesesitie towards your Support
in England as without it theris Noe possibilitie for you to Subsist,
~~I~~ your Intrest Monye° allowanses to your Chilldrene anneweties to
others and Sarvant[s] wagess a Mountinge unto as much as your
Commings In, whi[ch] ^Last^ is Liable unto great unsartanties,°
and your Payments Not Soe your fiftye Thowsand Pound is now in
some way of beinge Collected but what with 4 yeares Intrest the
Comistioners Fee and the Excheker payments My Brothar Mathews
dous° not beleve ther will come cleare to you above the one halfe, hee
tells mee of prodigious Soms that has bine° transmi[tted] Sense your
beinge in England, which terifies mee; with the Feares of beinge
Ruenede° if wee must Live Ther, your Son[n] Johns depts° at Dublin
is 15 hundreth Pound and a Thowsand at London, towards which;
and to Support himselfe he has but 7 hundreth dew° to hime by his
Pay and what ~~is dew~~ ^remaynes^ unto hime out of his Anewetie,° soe
as I am in great Feare upon the comminge over of the New Governer
Lest his Creditor[s] should Fall upon hime and desier° Leave to

---

[630] Sir Thomas Myddelton (1586–1666).
[631] Sir Arthur Forbes (1623–c. 1696). See John Gibney, "Forbes, Sir Arthur 1st earl of Granard," *DIB*.

Arrest or Seue hime for his depts, which I see noe possible way to prevent [/] I perseve° hime troubled and Sensible of his condistione but very unknowinge how to order well his owne affares and haveinge noe applicatione to it, Nor to anye thinge but to Ease and plesure; perhapes your giveinge hime some Rules and advise upon the new Governors Comminge how to behaufe himselfe in the well discharge of his Command might not bee amiss, but very Nesesarye [/] I pray Let my Brother Mathews* know that you are Consernede° for the Skoole and that untell such time as it bee Endowede that you would have the Master and the ussher to bee punctualie payede ther Sallerye;° which as I take it, is a hundreth to the Master and fortye unto the ussher[632] which last, is Not Entered in the payments, Nor willnot bee unles you do your selfe oppoynt° it; for I planlie See the Roman Catholiks are not pleasede at the Erectinge of this Skoole and trulie I feare unles you doe apiere° your Selfe consarnede° in patronisinge of it, that it will bee greatlie Eeclipsede,° soe soune° as Ever the Shipe Comes into the River of waterford I will then give you Notis° that the Coche° may bee Sent mee, the Mene° Time I thought it Not a Miss to Send you this inclosed derectione° for my Journye givene mee by my Brother Toby Mathews[633] which I intend to gide° my Selfe by; unles you doe derect° mee the Contrarye

sue

behave

plainly

eclipsed

Letter 170. June 20, 1669, Kilkenny, the Duchess of Ormonde to the Duke of Ormonde (Bodl., Carte Papers, 243, fol. 26). Autograph. For the Duke of Ormonde [/] thes. [Endorsed]: 20 June.

on Saterday Night the yaught° arivede at Duncanon and on Teusday next com senight° I intent Godwillinge to imbarke if the wind bee Fare, as I had don° some days Souner,° but that I was advisede to Stay untell° My Son Osorys* and my Brother Mathews* returne from Dublin from whense my Sonn and mr Jones[634] Came but one° Saterday and goes backe tomorogh to prevent an inconveniensie that is designede you in the bussenes° of your payment which it is hopede willnot only bee prevented but that affare bee broght unto a good Conclutione; I desier° the Coche° may meete mee at Millford as soune° as may bee, I find My Soon° very unsettled in his resolutions as to his Stayinge heare or goeinge into England which Last hee has

---

[632] "An assistant to a schoolmaster or head-teacher; an under-master, assistant-master" ("usher, *n.*," 4a, *OED*).

[633] JO's half-brother, Theobald, elder brother of George Mathew.

[634] Unidentified.

great inclinations For incoridged° therunto by My Lord Arlingtons* desiringe and wisshinge hime ther and mr Pages* approvinge of what Ever My Son dous° Fansie whoe hee alltogether trusts and advises with (a weake Counselor you may Say) but a very ^unluckye^ one I feare hee willbee, and his Brother in Law[635] as bad (a Frind) if hee perswads hime to Leave a Plase where hee may Live Soe Noblie and presarve your Intrest and his owne; to goe where in six Months hee willbee forst to Rune° in dept° if anye body will trust hime and not bee abble to gett ofe° with the Charge of a healples wife and a Nomber of Small Children, God kiepe° you in health and Send mee well to you

The 20 of June

Letter 171. July 24, 1669, London, the Duchess of Ormonde to Captain George Mathew (NLI, Ormond Papers, 2503, no. 16). Autograph.
For My Brother Captane Gorge Mathews [/] thes. [Endorsed]: My Ladyes of 24 July 1669 received 31 July 1669.

Brother   London the 24 of July

soe soune° as I came to towne, which was on wedensday Last I delivrede thous° papers and accompts° that you Sent by mee unto My Lord; som of which; that did requier° the spidiest° answar hee has perusede and has sent you his derections° therupon; the rest hee will Louke° over, which I shall mind hime to doe as I find hime at best Leasure; mr Rians[636] Morgadge° is this day sent, and soe is My Lords derections to you consarninge° My Son Osorys* allowanse, and the not discountinge of the tow° thowsand Pound out of it that hee pretends[637] unto as hee is Deputie; Soe as I hope when hee is thus farr complyede with by his Father, hee willnot take anye course that Shallbee contrarye unto his liekinge; you will heare from himselfe consarninge the bussenes° of the quit rents out of which hee Expects payment accordinge to the kings Leter which it is to bee wisht might bee Past by Patent before the Lord Roberts* goes over to prevent

---

[635] Arlington.
[636] Unidentified.
[637] "To put forward as an assertion or statement; to allege, assert, contend, claim, declare; *esp.* to allege or declare falsely or with intent to deceive" ("pretend, *v.*," 1, *OED*). EO is not suggesting that Ossory is making a false statement, although she tends to use the word to cue her recipient of what she thinks are mistaken claims.

anye stope° ^of it^ that may be givene by hime, I hope you will find Sir Gorge Cartwright* to bee Frindlie unto My Lord; whoe may Contribute much to the advantage of his consernes° in this and other payments, to whom I doe not dout° but you will applye your Selfe as you find ocatione;° My Lord has writene unto my Brother Hambellton* after the ressept° of whous answar hee will take some course ~~accordinglie in~~ about the bussenes of the Farme, The widow Fenills[638] Pretentione[639] is ansared;° and the lease of Balikife is now ingrosinge[640] but cannot bee redie time Enough to goe by this Post but shall by the Next, what Consernes the Lords of Dunboyne[641] and uprosorye[642] My lord had not time as yet to Consider, but will shortlie and returne his answar, ~~My lord~~ whoe has thought Fitt upon Mr wellches* aplicatione to hime by Leter to ~~Continow~~ allow hime his Rent of Lafalie which is fiftye Pound a yeare, I will trouble you noe further at the presant but rest

     your affectionat Sister

      E:ormonde

Letter 172. August 2, 1669, [London], the Duchess of Ormonde to Captain George Mathew (NLI, Ormond Papers, 2503, no. 17). Autograph.
For My Brother Captane Gorge Mathews [/] thes. [Endorsed]: Lady [ormond dated 2] received 18 [August 1669].

Brother   London the 2 of Agust

Sir Gorge Layne* Carryes over with hime My Lords derections° to you in the Conserne° of My Lord of uprosorye and the Lord of Dunboyne soe as ther rests Nothinge in My hands of what was Materiall but you have resevede° My Lords derections ^In^ ~~ther upon~~ though with more Regard of others Intrest then his owne benefitt, I shouldbee glad to heare what Suckses° has bine° in My Lords affares sense° I Left that kingdome; I find hee dous° very well aprove of

---

[638] Unidentified.

[639] "The assertion of a claim as of right; a claim made; a demand" ("pretension, *n.*1," 4a, *OED*).

[640] "The action of writing out a document in a fair or legal character" ("engrossing, *n.*," 2, *OED*).

[641] Piers Butler, fifth Baron Dunboyne, had been outlawed for fighting with the Confederate Catholics in the 1640s.

[642] Barnaby Fitzpatrick, seventh Baron Upper Ossory (d. 1696).

Sellinge of his Tythes° Soe as it were to bee wisht that you would when other bussenes° of greater moment is dispacht indevour° to gett a Chapman for them, wee Cannot as yet gett anye that will purchase Moore Parke* though I have and doe still indevour to, The Lord Liftenant⁶⁴³ thay° Say will goe over Shortlie and then I hope I shall know what resolutione my Sone Ossorye* will take as to his owne Settelment [/] I will trouble you noe further at this Time but rest

        your affectionat Sister

            E:ormonde

Letter 173. August 10, 1669, [London], the Duchess of Ormonde to Captain George Mathew (NLI, Ormond Papers, 2503, no. 18). Autograph.
For My Brother Captane Gorge Mathews [/] thes. [Endorsed]: My Ladyes of the 10 August received 29 August 1669.

your Leter of the 3 of Agust came to my hands on Sonday Last, soe as I could not take Copies in Soe Short a Time of the Controwlers accompts° that you desirede, and therfor have by this berar° Liftenant Corronell Ballye⁶⁴⁴ sent you the origenall with a brife° of the Acates, I am very glad that My Lords Patent⁶⁴⁵ for the five Thowsand a yeare is allredie Past, but unles you cane deale with Sir Gorge Cartwright* to advanse the halfe of it dew° at Michellmas though not usstialie° payede into the Excheker tell° halfe a year after I doe not See how My Lord cane Subsist ther beinge nothing to bee Expected out of his Rents makes it of absolute Nesesitie to See how hee may bee otherwise Supplyede [/] the bills you Sent from Murphye⁶⁴⁶ willnot bee acseptede but are returned which comes unto on° halfe of the ~~Mony~~ ^Som° that^ you transmitted Last, I am very glad to find that My Sonn ^Osory^ is at Lenghth Contented to Live at kilkenye* and with the allowanse that is Settled upon hime how litell° sowever it pleases Mr Page;* I would gladlie know what hopes you have of ^my^ beinge repayede the Mony° I lent unto my Cousen Esmond⁶⁴⁷ and

---

⁶⁴³ Lord Robartes.
⁶⁴⁴ Unidentified.
⁶⁴⁵ "A document conferring some privilege, right, office, title, or property" ("patent, n.", I, 1a, *OED*).
⁶⁴⁶ Unidentified.
⁶⁴⁷ An heir of the Protestant Laurence Esmonde, Baron Esmonde of Limerick, who had married, before December 1628, Elizabeth, second daughter of Walter Butler, the fourth son of James Butler, ninth Earl of Ormond. See J. J. N. McGurk, "Esmonde, Lau-

whether you have discovred anye more payments that was made unto anye of My Lords Creditors in time of the warr by the Menes° of Mr Comerford of Holycrose⁶⁴⁸ or anye other sense° my Comminge a way, of which some hopes was given unto

your affectionat Sister

The 10 of Agust   E:ormonde

Letter 174. August 23, 1669, [London], the Duchess of Ormonde to Captain George Mathew (NLI, Ormond Papers, 2503, no. 19). Autograph.
For My Brother Captane Gorge Mathews [/] thes. [Endorsed]: my Ladyes 23 August 1669.

Brother   The 23 of Agust

I have hearwith sent you a Note of Such Monys° as I have payede sense° My Cominge over, as I will doe the Bonds them selfes by the Next Post; which depts° were discharged out of such a Proportione of the Plate that I broght over with mee that some parsells° of it beinge brokene and Consequentlie unussfull; and the rest what might bee very well Sparede; soe as haveing Satisfiede thes Tradsmen, and the Intrest Mony° besides dew° for the greater Somes has givene my Lord much ease (and reputatione ^allsoe^) I am ussinge all possible indevours° to Sell Moore Parke* but as yet I Cannot Light upon a Chapman though My Lord wouldbee contented to take what hee payede for it, but I hope I shall Erre Longe Suckside° in gettinge it ofe° our hands which wouldbee a great conveniensie for uss ^to My lord at this time^, I shouldbee glad to heare that the Priswines were Let and that you could deale for Sellinge all the Tythes° that my Lord dous° hould° by Lease only, and that you had Fixt upon Some Abye° Land to Settell upon the Skoole, that might Secure unto them a hundreth and fortye Pound a yeare which I desier° you will Consider of, and at your Leasure to returne an accompt° of these perticulars to My Lord or to mee that am

your affectionat Sister

E:ormonde

---

rence, Baron Esmonde of Limerick (c. 1570–1645)," *ODNB*. The Esmondes had acted as brokers in the marriage of EO to JO.

⁶⁴⁸ Unidentified.

Letter 175. [September] 14, 1669, [London], the Duchess of Ormonde to Captain George Mathew (NLI, Ormond Papers, 2503, no. 21).[649] Autograph.
For My Brother Mr Gorge Mathews. [Endorsed]: Lady Dutches 14 [September] 1669.

[*three lines missing*] Time was very Nesesary and putinge Milo Powers* Mony° into a waye of beinge colected though you have bine° drivene to allow for it was very fitt to bee done consideringe the difficulties of gettinge Mony I hope when you have gatherede it In you will secure soe much of it as may paye ofe° the Tradsmen ^heare^ that has My Lords Bond; and are very troubelsome, I think the fewest payments that are fixede upon the restored Irishe[650] the beter;° for many Resons sense° this Last Leter of the kings will countenanse my Lords pretentione ~~his payment~~ ^of^ beinge allowede the First; I shouldbee ^glad^ to know what the weeklie Expense of the Familie is at Dublin and in what Methoud thay° are governede sense the New Steward came into his imployment and how you Find hime Fittede for it, I doe not dout° but you are Mindfull of the dept° dew° unto Sir Danniell Treswell* and will order it Soe; as I may bee disingadged° of it, Now that My Son Arran* is Ther, and that upon the Lettinge of the Prisewins for a Nother° yeare that you make your bargine for the advanse of one halfe of the Rent in hand as hethar° to has bine done, I have not as yet sene Captan Morton* but doe heare hee Left Ireland befor Mr Tillson[651] came ^from thense^, My Lord is Still at Newmarket* but Expected heare the Later End of the weeke [/] My daghter Cavendish* was broght to Bed of a Son yesterday to the great Joy of all that Familie and of hir Lord whoe is become the kindest husband and the Fondest Father of his yonge Sonn that Ever I saw,[652] your Frind resolves to go over [*eight words missing*] say anye thinge to you of other Neuse° [*four words missing*] by whom you shall heare agayne° from

EO

---

[649] There is wear and tear to the top of the MS, which renders two to three lines of text on each page of the letter unreadable.

[650] Those Irish who benefited from the restoration land settlement, mainly Old English royalists.

[651] Unidentified.

[652] Charles was the first son born to Mary, EO's second daughter, and her husband, William Cavendish. He would die the following year. See David Hosford, "Cavendish, William, first duke of Devonshire (1641–1707)," *ODNB*.

I shall send you over by the Next Post the full Coppie of the Settellment made at the Mariage of My Sone Arran to bee Showne unto mr wellch* and will the Like of all the rest of the writings that relats to it, that are in mr Grimes⁶⁵³ his hand which I am promist whoe was one of the Trusties°

Letter 176. October 12, 1669, [London], the Duchess of Ormonde to Captain George Mathew (NLI, Ormond Papers, 2503, no. 22). Autograph.
For My Brother Mr Gorge Mathews. [Endorsed]: My Ladyes Dated 12 Received 20 October 1669.

The [1]2 of Oct

Sense I writ Last unto you I was forst to take upe a Thowsand Pound; and to ingadge° Plate for it, to pay 5 hundreth Pound ~~pound~~ prinsepall of the Sixe Thowsand dew° unto the Exsequtors° of the ~~Late~~ Bushop of Rochester⁶⁵⁴ whoe by a Late agreament with My Lord is contented to bee payede ofe° by a thowsand pound a yeare and 2 hundreth more wantinge five for the Intrest; the rest of the Payments of this kind out of this Some above mentionede I send you heare inclosed a Note of, which I desier° you will kiepe° by you togethar with a former accompt° I sent you of what depts° of My Lords has bine° payede out of some olde plate that was Sould° ofe upon that ocation sense° my Last comminge over; if you bee remembred a Litell° befor I Left Ireland I desirede you to Call mr Olliver wheler* unto an accompt about a Morgadge° hee pretends a Right unto (but has Non°) unto a Farme Neare kilkenye Called Bonetsrathe and Loupstowne which hee injoys upon a forfitt° Intrest, therfor I pray Let it bee Louked° after when the greater bussenes° will allow you Leasure to do it, Theris one mr Halye* of Limricke whoe had a Morgadge that was Considerable ~~whoe~~ ^Hee^ resevede° 2 hundreth Pound from My Lord the first yeare of the kings Comminge in upon Condistione that if hee did not make good his Tytell° in the Court of Clames,⁶⁵⁵ as being a Nosent⁶⁵⁶ ^~~which~~^

---

⁶⁵³ Unidentified.
⁶⁵⁴ John Warner, late Bishop of Rochester, had died in October 1666. His estates descended to his nephew John Lee, Archdeacon of Rochester. The debt relates to Moor Park (see Letters 186 and 189).
⁶⁵⁵ Court of Claims, where dispossessed Catholic landowners pleaded their case. This followed the Act of Settlement, which was passed by the Irish Parliament in 1662.
⁶⁵⁶ "A guilty person, a criminal" ("nocent, *n.* and *adj.*," 1, *OED*).

(hee did Not,) that then hee would give upe his writinges ~~and~~ but as yet Never did, it was mr John welch* that made the bargine with hime, that if you think fitt to speak unto, will beter° informe you Consarninge° this affare, that is Now Mentioned to you by

your affectionat Sister
E:ormonde

Letter 177. September 28, 1669, [London], the Duchess of Ormonde to Captain George Mathew (NLI, Ormond Papers, 2503, no. 23). Autograph.
For My Brother Captane Gorge Mathews [/] thes. [Endorsed]: My Ladyes dated 28 September Received 8 October 1669 about mr Mandevill particular bills et cetera.

Brother   The 28 [of September]

I have hearwith sent you a perticular of My Lords resepts of all such somes of Mony° as hee has had sense° hee Last Left Ireland; from your Selfe and mr Page* with ~~That~~ what hee had besides out of his Entertainment [/] It has provede an inconveniense to uss the disapoyntment of the supplye that you thought to have had from mr Mandevile* though that is the Least that I feare wee are Like to Suffier° by hime, I confess I was mistakene very much in the abbilities of the Person; which may be remided (though Late) in a   *remedied*
beter° Choise, which is wholie Left to you; whoe cane best of anye body Judge beinge upon the Plase, and haveinge had soe much Experiense; what person or Persons if tow° will bee Niedfull,° will best acquitt themselfs in that imployment of Resever;°[657] the Last Leters broght an accompt° of the Lord Liftenants being arrivede; soe as I doe conclude My Sone Ossorye* ~~Gone~~ at killkenye from whense hee is Expected heare; I wish the dept° of 2 hundreth Pound that ~~is~~ was Lent by mr Mandvile* might bee payede hime by [*illegible*] by resone° I would not bee under anye obligatione to hime of that kind when hee quits My Sarvis,° I am afrade that Sir Gorge Cartwright[658] dous° intend to Sell his Place which if hee doe I dout° it will fall into a worse hand, but this is not to bee spokene of, some says Sir william

---

[657] "An official appointed by a government, landowner, etc., to receive tolls, rents, or other monies due; a collector; (also) a treasurer" ("receiver, *n.*1," I, 1a, *OED*).
[658] Sir George Carteret would sell his vice-treasurership of Ireland for £11,000. See C. H. Firth, "Carteret, Sir George, first baronet (1610?–1680), naval officer and administrator," *ODNB*.

Pete[659] willbee the Purchasier, but I beleve it Not hee, ~~what~~ I pray send mee word how all things are at kilkenye,* and beleve I am and willbee allways

        your affectionat Sister

           E:ormonde

Letter 178. November 27, 1669, [London], the Duchess of Ormonde to Captain George Mathew (NLI, Ormond Papers, 2503, no. 25).[660] Autograph.
[Endorsed]: Received 9 December 1669.

[Brother]   The 27 of November

I send you heare [a Petition read] in the House of [Commons] consarninge° the Lord of [Ororye]* whoe is still under Coustodie yesternight Late;[661] one mr Hambelton[662] broght me a Leter from you of the 20 of this Month; and at this very Instant I reseved° by the Post a Nother° of yours of the 12 of the Same, The Copie of the kings Last Leter in My Lords Conserne° shallbee Sent you, The answar you are to give unto My Lord of Ellye* whoe desiers° satisfactione for his House that was burnede, is; that his Lordshipp is Left unto the Law to have his remidie;° the Bills you tell mee was to bee Sent for 800 pound are not as yet Come to my handes; though very requisit to bee had at this Time when thay° are; you Shall know it, I pray take Care that what depts° were Left unpayede at Dublin upon My Lords accompt,° may bee discharged; as allsoe the Sallerye° of the Skooule° and Sarvants wages, I will acquant My Lord with the Cautione you give consarninge the bussenes° of the Regument; and that othar,   *regiment* you mention of the bargine with Sir Gorge Layne* about the small parsell° of Land hee houlds° and by the Next, will Send you an

---

    [659] Sir William Petty (1623–1687), natural philosopher and administrator in Ireland; also responsible for the survey of Ireland in the 1650s. See Toby Barnard, "Petty, Sir William (1623–1687)," *ODNB*.

    [660] Parts of two or three lines of text from the top of all three pages are obscured or missing due to a torn seal, general wear, and mending tape.

    [661] On November 25, 1669, Orrery was faced in the English Parliament with a bid to impeach him, primarily for misconduct as president of Munster. See T. C. Barnard, "Boyle, Roger 1st Baron Broghill 1st earl of Orrery," *DIB*. For a transcript of the petition, see T. B. Howell, *A Complete Collection of State Trials*, 21 vols. (London: T. C. Hansard, 1816), 6. 913–14.

    [662] Unidentified.

accompt; what Canbee Charged upon My Lord for Materialls had
out of the kings Store to Sarve his own ocations° for the buildinge at
Dunmore,* and making [*four words missing*] bee made good, Ether
[*two words missing*] allowanse givene for it, as I doe beleve therwas
(as to the first of thes) by Harison* the Controwler; whoe I heard had
takene some Course about it with Captane Mongomrye[663] at Dublin
Clarke of the Stores for what Hary Hippon[664] had delivrede out of
the Store at waterford to Captane Morton* for My Lords uss, to bee
returnede agayne,° soe as you would doe well to have thes Persons
spokene unto, and mr John Briane* allsoe to informe you of as much
as hee knows Consarninge this Perticuler; that restitutione may
bee made without Noyse,° which our Enimies may otharwiss make
Some great Matter of, I am glad you have Let the priswins° and
ajusted accompts with Sir Patricke Maladie[665] and others [/] Captane
Jackas* has this day givene My Lord a Petistione and mee a Nother,
unto which is afixt an accompt of his Losses which I hearinclosed
Send you; I beleve hee is incoridged° to complayne and soe is mr
kelye of Aghrime* whoe My Lord tells mee hee had a Leter from
yesternight, but the Contents hee had not Leasure to informe mee
of, but possiblie ther Plots willbee spoyled as ^and^ Soe will I hope
bee; My Lord of Roscomon[666] To; whoe is Cominge over to accuse
My Sone Arrane* and all [his offisiers°] [*five words missing*] the Copie
of the kings leter that you [*two words missing*] Sent you yet My Lord
would request a coppie of it from the Lord Liftenante and send hime
word what answar hee gives you [/] I must heare rectifie a Mistake of
Mine by tellinge you that it was one mr Bourke,[667] not mr kelye* that
Sent My Lord a Leter of complaynt yesternight, it is hee of Burrows,
and that it willbee fitt for you to advise with Counsell what answar
to give to the Lord of Ellye,* by resone° that upon discourse Just Now
with my Lord consarninge upon what Termes hee had that House;
hee remembers Not whether it was Lent hime or assignede hime for
quarter; for rent I never heard hee Payede ^anye^ or was demanded
of hime; hee removed from Skinner Roe[668] thether in the Heate of

---

[663] Unidentified.
[664] Unidentified.
[665] Sir Patrick Mullady of Robertstown, Co. Meath.
[666] Wentworth Dillon, fourth Earl of Roscommon (1637–1685), close friend of the Earl of Orrery with whom he was related by marriage. See Stuart Gillespie, "Dillon, Wentworth, fourth earl of Roscommon (1637–1685)," *ODNB*.
[667] Unidentified.
[668] Skinners' Row, opposite Christ Church Cathedral in Dublin, where the City Council met. See Christine Casey, *Dublin: The City within the Grand and Royal Canals*

the warr and Comanded the Armye in the Justisies Time [/] this I *Justices*
thought nesesarye to tell you, as I think it were that my Lord Should
know in writinge from that Lord what his pretentione and desiers
are, that it may bee the beter° Considerede what answar is best and
Sayfest° to givene hime; for hee is a person as Liklie as anye to take
advantage of this present Time; My Lord tells mee that if you think
it fitt hee dous° that Sir Gorge Layne may have that small Parsell of
Land for the 200 hee offiers° and to bee abatted° soe much of his dept

Letter 179. December 18, 1669, [London], the Duchess of Ormonde to Captain George Mathew (NLI, Ormond Papers, 2503, no. 26). Autograph.
For Captanie George Mathewes. [Endorsed]: 18 January 1669.

Brother   The 18 of Des

beinge at this presant very much indisposede by a great Could;° I did
not think to have writene to you my selfe by this Post but that mr
Martins* importunitie has prevayled with Mee to Let you know; that
it very much consernes° hime in Some bargine hee is makinge heare;
to have thes inclosed Bills to bee acsepted in part payment of the 5
Thowsand that My Lord is owinge hime; which are drawne upon a
good allowanse of Time; in hope you may complye therwith, but in
regard of the great scarsitie and unsartantie° of the Cominge in of
My Lords Rents; and the great payments that goes out of them, I
tould hime that I couldnot give hime anye answar as to his desiers;°
untell° I had Sent first into Ireland and had an accompt° from thense
whether anye such Bills (if Sent) couldbee answered or Not, the
Copies of which are hearinclosed, consarninge° which I desier to
heare from you soe soune° as you cane convenientlie, James Clarke*
will this day give you an accompt of the resept° of the Severall Bills
of Exchang that came by the Last Post; beinge all acsepted Sayfe
(save one) for a hundreth and twentie Pound; which not onlye only
disapoynts uss of Soe much by not beinge acsepted; but to Charge
besides, and Loos° of Time to James Clarke in Loosinge the most
Part of severall days from othar ocations° of the Familie to rune° after
thes pedlinge⁶⁶⁹ Fellows that has noe Credit, I wish I knew what
Sattisfactione you Expect from mr Mandevile;* sense° Soe great an

---

and the Circular Road with the Phoenix Park (New Haven: Yale University Press, 2005), 23.

⁶⁶⁹ "Of a person: occupied with things of little consequence or value; trifling, petty, ineffectual" ("peddling, *adj.*2," 2, *OED*).

Arreare is Not to bee forborne by uss as the Cayse° Stands, your Lord Liftenant is Not Like to trouble you Longe,⁶⁷⁰ Nor doe you Nide° to Feare that Lord Ororye* will Suckside° hime, Sense the Parlement w~~ill~~ and his own Late Follie will hinder That, which is Neuse° that I do Supose will as Litell° troubell you as it dous°

       your affectionat sister
             EO

Letter 180. December 29, 1669, [London], the Duchess of Ormonde to Captain George Mathew (NLI, Ormond Papers, 2503, no. 27). Autograph.
For My Brother Captane Gorge Mathews [/] thes. [Endorsed]: My Ladyes dated 29 December Received 17 January 1669.

Brother   the 29 of Des

The order that is now sent by the kinge unto the Lord Liftenant will as is consevede° heare; bee sufficient to remove all the obgections that his Lordshipp has made unto both the Payments that are dew° unto My Lord, soe as I hope that by your indevours° to Secure his Anneuelle allowanse, and what is dew unto Sir Robert vinner,⁶⁷¹   *annual*
that wee shall Find some Ease of our depts;° I have ussede all the indevours I could to gett Moore Parke* Solde, and cannot yet, thes Times beinge not for Purchasiers; soe as wee must have patianse° untell° wee cane Light upon a Chapman⁶⁷² for it; James Clarke* will by this Post give you an accompt° how the payments has bine° upon the Severall Bills of Exchange⁶⁷³ that were ^Latlie°^ Sent over by you; I hope My Last Leters are come unto your hands befor this time; and that wee shall know in what condistione mr Mandevile* is to make Sattisfactione for that great Arreare that hee is fallene into, which is very Considerable to bee Loukede° after, I heare that My Sonn John* pretends that theris 7 hundreth pound dew to hime

---

   ⁶⁷⁰ Lord Robartes would be recalled from the post in May 1670 and replaced by John Berkeley, Lord Berkeley of Stratton.
   ⁶⁷¹ Sir Robert Vyner (1631–1688), goldsmith and banker, had by this time become the crown's largest single individual creditor and one of the country's largest-scale private bankers. See G. E. Aylmer, "Vyner, Sir Robert, baronet (1631–1688)," *ODNB*.
   ⁶⁷² "A purchaser; a customer" ("chapman, *n.*," 4, *OED*).
   ⁶⁷³ "A written order by the writer or 'drawer' to the 'drawee' (the person to whom it is addressed) to pay a certain sum on a given date to the 'drawer' or to a third person named in the bill, known as the 'payee'" ("bill, *n.3*," 9a, *OED*).

as [fees] of what the Land did yeald that was assignede hime; and if
Soe; I feare that his bad manadgment will not only redow[ble] to his   *redouble*
presant Loos° but to the Future allsoe; for it [is] not well Tenanted
and put into good hands the Plase willnot yeald Neare the vallew° of
it; and hee one° the other Side has nothinge ^save his Comand^[674]
to depend upon but his allowanse; which if hee fayle° of, will ~~give
hime a pretense of~~ [~~illegible~~][675] ^Forse° hime to Rune° in dept^ upon
which at the [least] wee must Ether pay or Suffier° hime to Lie in
Prisson; Soe as upon the whole Matter I think it were beter° that
hee should reseve° his Anewetie° from you in Mony° Evry halfe
yeare, then Medell with the Land though this I offier° only to your
consideratione and wouldnot have it to goe further Least° if hee
should know ~~the Last~~ of this it might incoridge° hime the more
unto an Expense which I have but to° much resone° to Feare hee is
inclynede [/] [That] I know not whether I writ to you formerlie upon
this subgect or Not makes mee Mentione it to you at this Time and
to desier° that your oppinione as to this perticuler may bee returnede
unto

        your affectionat Sister

           E:ormonde

The Order Mentioned couldnot bee Sent as I ~~taught~~[676] beleved it
would have bine by this days Post by resone the Counsell dous° not
Sitt untell wedensday Next, at which Time it willbee Signede and
Sent away on this day Senight;°[677]

---

[674] Lord John was captain of the troop of horse-guards in Ireland.

[675] Two or three canceled words are illegible under EO's heavy strikethroughs and mending tape.

[676] The spelling of the canceled word, "thought," offers a brief glimpse into EO's Irish pronounciation.

[677] Two Bills of Exchange are enclosed with the letter, both dated from London, December 15.

Letter 181. January 8, 1669/70, [London], the Duchess of Ormonde to Captain George Mathew (NLI, Ormond Papers, 2503, no. 28). Autograph.
For My Brother Captane Gorge Mathews [/] thes. [Endorsed]: My Ladyes dated 8 Received 30 January 1669.

Brother   The 8 of Jan

Theris soe Litell° time allowede mee this day, from resevinge° 3 of your Leters one of the 1 the 2 and 24 of Des and the answaringe of them by this Post as I feare I shall ommitt some perticulers, but must not, to give you an accompt° that the Bills for 500 which came incloused in yours of the first of the Last Month above Mentioned *enclosed* is Sent this day to bee acsepted, (as are all the former) though with some trouble and Charge to, befor the Mony° couldbee reseved° [/] The state of Captane Jackuis* his case I have, and shall deliver it unto my Lord when it is convenient; Sir Patricke Moledie[678] resevede 200 at his goeinge from hense which I sent you word of a good while sense° but doe feare that my Leter Came not unto your hands, if hee resevede anye more, Sir Gorge Lane* willbee abble to informe you of whom it willbee Nesesary that you inquier;° I have the Last accompt of the Severall Resevers° but beinge soe Newlie come unto My hands I have not yet the time to Consider of it, but doe thinke you have done very well in imployinge others, rather then Continowinge° thous° whoe has bine° soe Negligent in My Lords Conserns° as to Suffier° such an arreare to bee [/] I am very well pleasede to find that you have takene order to pay into the kings Stores what Nesesaryes was had thense for the uss° of the Buildinge, and that all the Sarvants wages are discharged allsoe; I doe not dout° but the Order which goes by this days Post will remove all obstroctions in the Payment of My Lords Mony soe as wee may Find some Ease of our depts,° the Intrest wherof as to what is dew° heare Comes to above a thowsand Pound a yeare besides a Thowsand ~~pound~~ a yeare More that My Lord is by a Late agreement with the Exsectors° of the late Bushope of Rochester to pay of° the prinsepall which in 6 years Cleares ofe° that dept and Stricks of° soe much of the Intrest which was thought a convenient Bargine, wherby to gayne° Soe Longe a Time, for the discharginge of it; soe as a Care must bee takene that my Lord may bee supplyede accordinglie to pay 500 Evry halfe yeare as hee did in October Last [/] My Sonn ossorye* speaks of Sendinge for his Lady at the springe and takinge of a House for hir but I doe beleve hee will

---

[678] Unidentified.

find cause to olltor° his mind befor that Time and therfor it is the Less disputed by

        your affectionat Sister

        E:ormonde

Letter 182. January 11, 1669/70, [London], the Duchess of Ormonde to Captain George Mathew (NLI, Ormond Papers, 2503, no. 29). Autograph.
For My Brother Captane Gorge Mathews [/] thes. [Endorsed]: My Ladys dated 11 Received 30 January 1669.

Brother

after I had Sealede upe my other Leters this Night, I resevede° one from Baxter* that acquants mee that you had payede all the Sarvants wages at Caricke* Dunmore* and kilkenye,* and that upon a veue° of the Lists of ^all^ that are in the severall plasses,° you thought it fitt Ethar° to reduse william Griffiths[679] wagges or discharge hime quite, and imploye wiliam knowles in the plantinge worke; and Adam Sixe* at kilkenye, The first of thes I think is honnest; but I am Shure° in Noe degree soe knowinge in his profestione as this other is, and what may bee Savede in his wages may Soune° bee Lost by ~~the~~ knowles his Ignoranse or Negligense, as the Bowlinge grine[680] ^onse^ was; that hee undertoucke° the kipinge° of, and for Adam Sixe, hee was Never Good for anye thinge, but to Sharke[681] what hee could for himselfe; and that made mee part with hime, and for that resone° am Not willinge to take hime agayne;° but to Continow° Griffith if hee have noe ill qualities that I knownot of, for hee is more Skillfull in his profestione and Espetialie° in That of Plantinge then anye that Canbee ordenerylie Lighted upon in that Contrye, and is ^ther for^   *ordinarily*
of the greatest uss° Ther, which I thought it might bee Nesesarye to Let you know is My Sense;° by resone that I desier° that Sort of improvment may goe forward, as what is a delight unto

        your affectionat Sister

Teusday Night Late the 11 of Jan   E:ormonde

---

    [679] Gardener on EO's estates.
    [680] For a discussion of bowling greens, see Costello, *Irish Demesne Landscapes*, 56–58.
    [681] "To steal, pilfer, or obtain by underhand or cheating means" ("shark, *n*.1," 2b, *OED*).

Letter 183. January 29, 1669/70, [London], the Duchess of Ormonde to Captain George Mathew (NLI, Ormond Papers, 2503, no. 31). Autograph.
[Endorsed]: My Ladyes of the 29 January Received 11 ffebruary 1669.

Brother   The 29 of Jan

I did a good while sense,° send you a request that mr Martine* to whom My Lord dous° owe a considerable some of Mony° did make to hime, that he might Charge upon hime tow° Bills of Exchange of 5 hundreth pound a Peese° allowinge some Months Time for the payinge of them, and to strike ofe° soe much of the prinsepall of the dept,° the coppies of which were transmitted to you, and a returne from you desirede befor My Lord would give anye answar unto hime therin; sense which time the Gentellman has bine° oftene heare to know what hee might depend upon [/] therfor if that ^his^ proposall bee come unto your hands, I pray Let mee reseve° such an accompt° from you, as may bee showne hime ^Consarninge° it^ [/] My Lord Barcklye[682] is preparinge for his Journye into Ireland whoe I doe not dout° will kiepe° a beter° correspondansie with My Lord then his predesesor[683] did, My Lord Dunkelins[684] Mariage has Extremlie troubled all his Frinds heare My owne Lord beinge as much conserned° as if hee had bine his Sonn and as Sensiblle of the afflictione it must bee unto My Lord ^of^ Clanrickerd[685] [/] the Ruene° that this unhapie yonge Man has broght upon himselfe and his Familie, My Lord and Lady Barcklye[686] has desirede the assistanse of Baxter* to advise the Person that thay° intend to imploye about the makinge of provistions for hime and bargonninge for the Goods that are Ther which it is supposed willbee Sould,° soe as

---

[682] John Berkeley, Lord Berkeley of Stratton (1607–1678), had been appointed Lord Lieutenant in January 1670 and arrived in Ireland the following April. See D. W. Hayton, "Berkeley, John, first Baron Berkeley of Stratton (*bap.* 1607, *d.* 1678)," *ODNB*.

[683] The previous Lord Lieutenant, Lord Robartes.

[684] Richard Burke, Lord Dunkellin, was the eldest son and heir of the seventh Earl of Clanricarde. In January 1669/80 he was privately married to Elizabeth Bagnall, the daughter of a servant of the court.

[685] William Burke, seventh Earl of Clanricarde (d. 1687), was connected by marriage to the Ormonde Butlers.

[686] Lord Lieutenant Berkeley had married Christian(a) (1639–1698), daughter of the wealthy East India merchant Sir Andrew Riccard, and widow of John Gayer and Henry Rich, Lord Kensington, in around 1659. Lady Berkeley was a Catholic. See Hayton, "Berkeley, John," *ODNB*.

by my Lords derectione° I have writene to hime that to repayre to Dublin soe soune° as hee heares from My Lord Barcklys Steward whoe is ordered to give hime Nottis° soe soune as hee arrives, I have at this Time some hopes of puttinge ofe[687] of Moore Parke* but not soe great a Sartantie° as I wish; My Sone had takene a House for his Lady and intends to Send for her as Soune as beter wether is, the Rent hee pays for it is a hundreth and 10 pound a yeare, which ^it^ is Competent for the bignes of it, and convenient for such a Nomber as hee intends to kiepe; though with the best Manegrie[688] thay Cane uss° I am afrade thay willnot bee abble to Live within the Compas of ther allowanse; though hee has ^gottene^ Settled upon hime Sense his comminge over a Thowsand pound a yeare for his Salerye as hee is ^a^ Gentellman of the Bedchamber which willbee well payede hime[689] heare, The wind has bine Soe Cross[690] of Late, as has kept mee from hearinge what Suckses° the Late order from the kinge and Counsell has had in my Lords Conserne° though it bee much ^much^ wisht and Expected by

   your affectionat Sister

    EO

Letter 184. February 22, 1669/70, [London], the Duchess of Ormonde to Captain George Mathew (NLI, Ormond Papers, 2503, no. 34). Autograph.
For My Brother Mr Gorge Mathews. [Endorsed]: My Lady dated 22 february received 10 march 1669.

Suposinge that some of My Lords Mony° may by this time bee reseved° by you, I thoght it Nesesarye to Let you know upon what Termes some Marchands° heare would pay Mony to reseve° it Ther, which is offered for 4 pound and fore pound ten in the hundreth

---

[687] "To dispose of (a commodity) by sale; to sell" ("to put off", 9b, in "put, *v.*," *OED*).

[688] "The judicious use of resources; thrift, economy" ("managery, *n.*," 1b, *OED*).

[689] The salary attached to the office was £1000, payable at the Exchequer. Ossory had been appointed on April 11, 1666. His duties included assisting the King at his dressing, waiting on him when he ate in private, guarding access to him in his bedchamber and closet, and providing noble companionship, generally. The offices of gentleman of the bedchamber were in the gift of the Crown. See "The Bedchamber: Gentlemen of the Bedchamber," in *Office Holders in Modern Britain*, vol. 11 (rev.), *Court Officers, 1660–1837* (London: University of London, 2006), 14–19, accessed via *British History Online* http://www.british-history.ac.uk/office-holders/vol11/pp14–19.

[690] "Of the wind: Blowing across the direct course, contrary" ("cross, *adj.*," 1c, *OED*).

and to pay ~~upon t~~ ^at^ tene days Sight soe as if you cannot gett it
returnede upon beter° Termes from Thense you may take this offier°
or refuse it accordinge as you shall find to bee the most convenient [/]
only one thinge I desier° you will observe in the Next Bills that part
of Them may bee drawne ~~upon~~ soe as to bee payede ~~also~~ within a few
days to accomodate our presant ocations°

The 22 of Feb

**Letter 185. March 1, 1669/70, [London], the Duchess of Ormonde
to Captain George Mathew** (NLI, Ormond Papers, 2503, no. 35).
Autograph.
For My Brother Captane Gorge Mathews [/] thes. [Endorsed]: My
Ladys dated 1 received 10 march 1669 about Hugh Neale.

The First of March

I reseved° your Leter of the 12 of this month but upon Friday Last,
soe as I couldnot answar all the perticulers of it for want of an
oppertunitie to speake with My Lord untell° This day whoe bid mee
to tell you ~~what~~ what his sartane° payments are yearlie of Intrest
and prinsepall ^dept°^ which you will Find to bee Somede° upe in
the inclosede Note, and by that you will Find what willbee further
requisit for My Lord to have from Thense, over and above his 5
Thowsand pound a yeare, The Bills you Sent Last unto My Lord
for 5 hundreth Pound Hee has givene into James Clarcks hands
to gett acsepted, whoe will give you an accompt° therof, as allsoe
of the resept° of that hundreth Pound you Mention of your owne
Mony,° which hee resevede and has charged himselfe withall, The
controwlers Sallerye° of a hundreth pound a yeare is to bee allowede
hime upon My Lords accompt from the Time that My Daghter
Ossorye* Comes a way, and for the rest of the Sarvants I have ~~sent~~
put some derections° in writinge which I thought fitt you Should See,
that you might ade° to it or Leave out what you think Convenient
and afterwards send a Copie of it unto the Controwler, I am glad
you have dismist° mr Mandevile* and have ajustede accompts with
John Burdon;* Mr Martine* is very desirious to have 2 Thowsand
Pound of his prinsepall within a yeare to purchase an offiss° heare
that hee is agreeinge For alledginge that hee has My Lords and My
Sons Ossoryes* Bond to bee payede the whole within a Twelfmonth
which Time is Past, pray send mee word what answar to give hime
whether his desiers° may bee complyede with or Not; I knownot

what to Say consarninge° My Sone Johns* affare⁶⁹¹ sense° it depends
Much upon what Estate wee are abble to Settell upon hime which
upon the ocatione° of gettinge hime such a Fortune cannot be Less
then a Thowsand pound a yeare at presant and as much more in
Future could our Estate beare with the giveinge a way of soe much,
as I feare it Cannot unles ther were somthinge of Portione at in hand
that might healpe to the payinge of our depts, soe as I Cane only
wish hime the good Fortune of such a Mach° as is discourst of for
hime; sense wee are unable to give him That which the Ladys Frinds
may with resone° Expect [/] Sense Hughe Neale⁶⁹² is not abble to
Exsecute the Plass° hee has, it is but resonable that a more Capable
Person should bee Chosene which is Left to you to oppoynt,° and
because Neale has bine° an olde Sarvant, I leave it to your discretione
to allow hime or abayte° hime in his Rent somthinge duringe his Life
which I beleve willnot bee Longe accordinge unto what you Shall
think Fitt

**Letter 186. March 28, 1670, [London], the Duchess of Ormonde
to Captain George Mathew** (NLI, Ormond Papers, 2503, no. 39).
Autograph.
For My Brother Captane Gorge Mathews. [Endorsed]: My Ladys 28
march received 8 April 1670.

The 28 of March

My Lord dous° proside° in his treatie for the Sayle of Moore Parke*
and the Duke of Monmoth* very Fond of haveing it, the only
obstakell° that I apprehend in concludinge of the bargine, is the
ingadgment° that is upon it unto the Exsequitor° of the Late Bushope
of Rochester whoe was contented to allow My Lord 6 years Time to
pay the depte° that is upon it at ^by^ a Thowsand pound a yeare, but
willnot change his Securitie Nor allow anye other person the Like
conveniensie, Soe as wee are Endevoringe to trye by some other way
how to Ease the purchasier by gayninge hime some time for payment
[and] transferinge over our depts to hime that thay° may bee noe
more ours and I hope wee Shall Light upon it, and Satisfie this other
person allsoe, which is at the presant our only dificultie, I send you
heare inclosede by My Lords derections° Captane Hassells* Leter to
My Sone Ossorye* whous request my Lord and I both dous referr to

---

[691] This is probably Lord John's mooted marriage to Anne Chichester, daughter of the Earl of Donegal.

[692] Long-serving servant.

you to Consider, and shall ratifie what [ab]atment you Shall think
Nesesarye for his incoridgment° as farr as you shall Judge hime to
bee desarving of it; I find My Lord dous much inclyne to make a
Journye over this Sommer but cannot as yet resolve the Sartane° time
untell° it bee declarede when the Parlement will Next Meete but at
all adventurs hee would have his Sellers° fillede with Beare° whilst
the Season of the yeare is Fitt for ~~brewinge~~ ^it^ which I pray Let the
Controwler have your derections For, I showede My Lord your Leter
of the 13 of March whoe will himselfe answar the other perticulars
mentionede therin, mr Matine* beinge in great wants of Mony°
borrowede fiftie Pound of My Lord whous acquitanse°[693] I heare
Send you, that it may bee repayede out of what hee is to reseve° of the
[rent] of Bureshoule, Coouper and My Daghter Ossorys* G[oods] are
arrived, but were 3 weeks in ther Passage to [Bristol*] [/] Sir Gorge
Layne* did the Last yeare reseve from mr Floyde* that was My Lords
Resever° 3 hundreth Pound which hee desiers° may bee allowede
hime upon accompt° and 28 pound more which hee payede ~~heare~~
to hime heare allsoe for the Fine of his House at kilkenye,* therfor
desiers that hee may have a Lease of it for 3 Lives as others has, and
not bee turnede out of possession

**Letter 187. April 16, 1670, Hampton Court, the Duchess of
Ormonde to Captain George Mathew** (NLI, Ormond Papers, 2503,
no. 40).[694] Autograph.
[Endorsed]: My Ladys dated 16 received 24 Aprill 1670.

[I] have takene [the oppertunitie] of My Lords goeing with the
kinge to Newmarket* to Come Hether to Hamptoncourt for my
health beinge indisposed of Late for want of Ayre° and Exersise
which this plase will afford mee the benifitt of with Litell° trouble
or Expense for I am in the House kiepers° Lodgings which I hyer°
by the weeke, and have only 5 Sarvants in all to attend Mee [/]
My Lord has agreede for the Sayle of Moore Parke* to the Duke of
Monmoth,* (Goods and all) for which hee is to have 13 Thowsand
2 hundreth Pound [/] it is the kinge that Buys it for the Duke Soe
as it is the Lords of the Tresurye that wee are Now a Treatinge
with; and doe hope will Secure our payments which is the mayne°

---

[693] "A document showing that a debt has been paid; a receipt in full, barring further demand for payment; a written or printed release" ("acquittance, *n.*," 1, *OED*).

[694] There is some minor wear to the top of each page of the letter, and the text in these lines is further obscured by the mending tape.

conserne° that is to bee Loukede° after, as I doutnot but it will bee
by Sir Gorge Layne;* whoe is intrusted in that affare by My Lord;
My Lord Liftenant[695] went from hense on Monday Last soe as ~~wee E~~
you may Expect his arrivall very sudanlie° and I hope [prepared
to be oblidging to] My Lords relations for soe hee confessed that
[three words missing] doe not change Men, that are strangers to it
as posiblie it May; ~~heare~~ Ther has bine° Some dissatisfiede Persons
as Prindergest[696] and one Commin* that alledges great Sarvissis°
that thay° have done for which rewards has bine promist them by
the Former Comistioners that had the Manadgment of My Lords
Estate some by Edward Butler* ~~and~~ Doctor Fennell* and John
wellch* but noe performanse and though I have very Litell oppinione
of the [illegible][697] of Ether of thes, (Nor of kelye of Arighrim*)
yet I Confess I am for Sielensinge° Them if anye thinge that is
Moderate cane doe it, and therfor doe wish that you would in all
thes mens Cayses° send My Lord your oppinione what you would
have hime give or by the othoritie° you have from hime that you
would Conclude with them upon the best Termes that you Cane, for
I Find that some of them are incoridged° by my Lords Enimies to
make a Clamor which were beter° to Suppres than Suffier,° Theris a
Nother° affare that I am tould willbee Complaynd of by the English
in Monster,° incoridged you May bee Shure° by the Lord of Ororye*
that theris Exactede for the Mart Earles[698] 3 pound where theris of
Right but a Marke or 20 shillinges a peese° dew,° This is a thinge of
some importanse and Fitt for Counsell to give ther oppinions In, and
after to bee ajusted by you as Soune° as may bee, sense° as an antiant°
Right is to be presarved; soe a Care must bee Likwiss had not to
wrest it beyond what the Law and it will beare, ~~but~~ and to bringe it
if you Cane unto Such a Sartantie° as may bee with moderatione and
Justis to Both Partys; I sent you Latlie° a List of what Sarvants were
to bee retaynede upon My Lords accompt° and of such as were to
bee dismist° at my Daughter Ossorys* cominge a way, the upholster
Coopers[699] wayges was to bee allowede by uss by resone° you know
hee was imployede in the vallewing° and orderinge of the Goods of
the Castell that wass disposede of and has bine sense his Cominge
imployede [two lines missing] for ackates still dew upon mr [missing] *acates (bought*
when the last accompts were [takene] I pray at your Lesure inquier°   *provisions)*

---

[695] The new Lord Lieutenant, Berkeley.
[696] Unidentified.
[697] The word may begin with *Q* or *O*.
[698] An abbreviation of "Earl Marshal"?
[699] Unidentified.

after it, and what all The Goods at the Castell[700] was Sould° For ~~and~~ what depts° are payede by the Controwler and what remayns that hee May as well as others bee accomptable° for what hee has resevede,° Mr Slingsbye* that I find mentionede in one of your leters did by Milo Power* present mee with the great Cabenet that is in the drawinge Rome° at kilkinye,* that a kinsman of his gave hime; which hee vallewede at Sixtie Pound; and though it was not worth soe much, yet I desier° that in what bargine you make with hime, that soe much may bee allowed for it, by resone I heare the Gentellman is poure° and that it was not in my power to doe hime anye Curtesie° that might requite it

The 16 of Aprell

Letter 188. May 7, 1670, [London], the Duchess of Ormonde to John Brian (NLI, Ormond Papers, 2352, no. 3007, p. 71). Autograph.
For Mr John Briane at killkeny thes. [Endorsed]: 7th May 1670 Her Graces 80 pound to mr Jackson uppon this and a bill.[701]

Mr Briane*

Findinge by your Leter of the 12 of Aprell ~~which gave~~ an accompt° of what Monys° of Mine remaynes in your hands ~~out of which~~ I have charged a Bill upon you for Eightie pound payable unto mr Jackson* which I desier° you willbee punctuall in Seeinge it payede accordinglie, Soe I rest

              your very asshured° Frind

The 7 of May 1670   E:ormonde

---

[700] Dublin Castle.
[701] The signed bill is enclosed with the letter.

Letter 189. May 14, 1670, [London], the Duchess of Ormonde to Captain George Mathew (NLI, Ormond Papers, 2503, no. 41).[702]
Autograph.
For My Brother Captane Gorge Mathews [/] thes. [Endorsed]: My Ladys dated 14 may received 3 June 1670.

The [14 of May]

I have for a few days deferede to returne an answar unto a Leter I resevede° from you datted the 27 of Aprell untell° I could give you the Sartantie° of My Lords agreement for the Sayle of Moore Parke* which is agreede ^resolved^ upon as betwixt the Duke of Monmoth* and hee, but now rests how to sattisfie the Exsequitor° of the Bushope of Rochester to whom the Plase is Ingadged° for 6 Thowsand pound; and hee not willinge to part with it it for anye other Securitie though a beter,° is Tendered to hime; by the knavrye of a Person that hee Trusts; but wee hope to overcome this presant difficultie; and that by the Next I shallbee abbell to give you a beter accompt° that of the Conclution of that affare and that you will think it parted with upon good Termes; you had an accompt from James Clarke* of the ressept° of the Last Bills of Exchange that you Sent for five hundreth pound that was Charged upon mr Jacksons* Corespondant, I have not as yet, but I intend to Call for the 2 Nots° I gave to Sir Gorge Layne* under my hand for 3 hundreth Pound which you tell mee you have allowed in a Purchase of some [*two words missing*] hee has Bought of My Lord [*two words missing*] Commins Cayse° is otherwiss then was at the first understood Soe as My Lord will write to you himselfe to bee more perticularlie informed in some Things that hee alledges though hee Cannot this Post beinge somwhat indisposed but not in daynger of an Ague (which wee did Feare) it beinge the generall desease throughout all the Counties in England, The kinge goes on wednesday to Dover to meete[703]

---

[702] There is minor wear and tear to the letter resulting in the loss of some words from the first line of the second page.

[703] Charles had gone to Dover to meet his sister, Henrietta, Duchess of Orléans, the sister in law of King Louis XIV of France. There, the secret treaty of Dover would be signed. See John Miller, "Henriette Anne , Princess, duchess of Orléans (1644–1670)," *ODNB*.

Letter 190. June 11, 1670, [London], the Duchess of Ormonde to Captain George Mathew (NLI, Ormond Papers, 2503, no. 42). Autograph.
For My Brother Captane Gorge Mathews [/] thes. [Endorsed]: My Ladys dated 11 Received 14 June 1670.

The 11 of June

I forgott to tell you that I spoke unto Sir Gorge ^Lane*^ for the tow° Notes that hee had under My hand, the one for a hundreth pound, and a Second for tow hundreth, which dept° I understoud from you was Latlie° payede by you whoe asshured° Mee that hee had allredie delivered them unto you which was the answar that I reseved° from hime in that perticuler, Moore parke* is now Solde for alevene° thowsand 5 hundreth Pound; and soe much of the Furniture as was Left from what I brought hether for our presant uss° came to 17 hundreth Pound more; Soe as the whole some had for the Plase and Goods is thirtine Thowsand 2 hundreth Pound which is all but 5 ^five^ hundreth; that is for the uss of the House allredie disposede of for the payment of the depts a perticuler of which Sir Gorge Lane has promist Mee to Send you this Night, I wish I could heare of the discharge of some of our depts ther, by the Cominge in of the Mony° upon the halfe years Rents and the thowsands of the quit Rents that is dew° unto My Lord which has bine° hetherto° soe Sloe in gatheringe, as it is Not only like to Eate out of it Selfe, but to disapoynt uss of a Subsistanse heare if the Last of thes should Fayle° uss, therfor I doe not as yet heare of My daghter Ossorys* Landinge but I Expect her within a Few days

slow

Letter 191. June 18, 1670, [London], the Duchess of Ormonde to Captain George Mathew (NLI, Ormond Papers, 2503, no. 43). Autograph.
[Endorsed]: My Ladys dated 18 June received 5 July 1670.

The 18 of June

In my Last I gave you an accompt° that Moore Parke* was Solde, and desirede Sir Gorge Lane* to send you a List of such of the depts° heare as was discharged, which I suppose will Satisfie you as unto soe much; I wish ther Couldbee some way Found out to pay ofe° the rest of what remayne dew° heare; and then I dout° not but wee Should Live within our the compass of what our Estate will beare; without runing in dept, Now that the Charge of Moore Parke is at an Ende and that wee are ~~Now~~ Lent a Part of Clarington House[704] whether wee remove the Next weeke, which will save uss the Rent wee pay for this wee have hetharto° Livede in; which was 2 hundreth and fiftye pound a yeare; besides other Charges insident unto it, My Lord has bine° in Treatie with Alldermane Bucknell[705] to advanse hime alevene° Thowsand Pound for the 15 Thowsand that is to bee payede hime out of the quit Rents in 3 years; but he offiers° as yet but tene Thowsand five hundreth, and Says hee will give noe More; and thus it rests at Presant, pray Send mee your oppinione of this Bargine, as I doe you ~~you~~ hearinclosede a List of the remayninge depts that you may the beter° Judge of what is proposed, This Allderman is hee whoe Farmes all the kings revenew in Ireland and ~~would Far~~ would take the Pryse wines for 6 years; but My Lord not knowinge what to demand for Them; has Suspended his answar in that perticular unto hee heares from you and bee advisede upon the Condistions that hee is to Insist upon [/] I find My Lord is of oppinione; that with what is dew to hime of the first 5 Thowsand and what willbee over and above the discharge of the ~~depts h~~ remayninge depts heare in Cayse° that mr Bucknell and hee doe agree for the advanse of what is above Mentioned that then hee will have Suffisent to kiepe° hime heare for a Nother° yeare, and then Hee resolves ^the yeare^ after, to goe for Ireland; supposinge by that Time, the other Mony° may Come in of the fiftie Thowsand towards the furtharinge of which hee willbee heare redie to imploye his Intrest, I pray dispach your answar unto a Late Leter that My Lord Sent you consarninge° mr Commin* whoe is still heare importuninge my lord and

your affectionat Sister

E:ormonde

upon veuinge° the perticulers of the remayninge depts if the bargine dous° goe on betwixt Allderman Bucknell and My Lord for a 11 Thowsand pond [sic] wich° is the Some insisted upon to bee advanst I find ther willnot remayne anye thinge over and above towards our Mantenanse as I did ~~first~~ think ther would; yet Nevertheles if what

---

[704] Clarendon House had been built for the Earl of Clarendon between 1664 and 1667; he had gone to France in 1667 when he fell out of favor with the King. The mansion, which stood in Piccadilly was the grandest private residence of its era, reputed to have cost £40,000 to build.

[705] Sir William Bucknell (1633–1676), alderman of London, was a farmer of the revenues of England and Ireland. See http://www.historyofparliamentonline.org/volume/1660-1690/member/bucknall-sir-william-1633-76.

was formerlie payede ^away^ in Intrest canbee allowede towards our Mantenanse ~~with~~ added unto what is owinge uss of the first 5 Thowsand pound that is dew out of the quit Rents I hope it will kiepe uss for a yeare to Come

Letter 192. June 25, 1670, [London], the Duchess of Ormonde to Captain George Mathew (NLI, Ormond Papers, 2503, no. 44). Autograph.
For My Brother Captane Gorge Mathews [/] thes. [Endorsed]: My Ladys dated 25 June received 5 July 1670. Charged from thence.

The 25 of June

I did accordinge as you desirede mee in your Leter of the 11 June ~~delivered~~ ^deliver^ thous° writings consarninge° Sir Gorge Lane,* whoe is gettinge them Ingrost⁷⁰⁶ in Parchment whoe tells mee that hee gave you upe the Origenall Notes that hee had under My hand, but for the Coppies that were attested by you, hee knows not what is become of them; but hee will Seearch amongst his papers and when hee Finds them hee ~~will~~ ^promises to^ bringe them to mee, but I rather beleve that hee has Left them in Ireland with his Lady,⁷⁰⁷ I pray dispach over your oppinion consarninge mr Commin* for hee Stays heare to know My Lords plesure, and is very poure,° My daghter Ossorye* willbee in Towne to Night, My Lord resevede° yesterday a Leter from you of the 18 of this Month that requiers° soe much consideratione as hee tould Mee hee thought hee shouldnot be abbell to answar it by this post but will I doe hope by the Next, the Sudane° death of Madam⁷⁰⁸ has put the kinge and Court into great Sadnes, and has ocationed° great Suspitions of hir beinge poysoned, sir Gorge Lane tould mee that hee had by my Lords derectione° ansarede° your Leter consarninge mr Mandevile* and has acquanted you of fiftie pound more that Mr Martine* has reseved from My

---

⁷⁰⁶ "Written out large, written in a legal hand; expressed or incorporated in a legal document" ("engrossed, *adj*.," a, *OED*).
⁷⁰⁷ Sussanah Lane, née Nicholas (d. 1671).
⁷⁰⁸ Henrietta, Duchess of Orléans (1644–1670), sister of Charles II, had only recently returned to the French court when on June 19 she complained of a violent pain in her side, immediately after drinking iced chicory water, and cried that she had been poisoned; she died in the early hours of the following morning. King Louis, anxious to dispel the rumors of poison, ordered a very public autopsy, after which a number of doctors, both French and English, declared that she had died of natural causes. See John Miller, "Henriette Anne, Princess, duchess of Orléans (1644–1670)," *ODNB*.

Lord Sense° My Lord A[ngers] went from hense Soe as hee has had in all as I take [it] 4 hundreth and fiftie ode° pound of the depts° wee owe [/] I pray inquier° when you goe into the Contrye after [the] Prisses° of wooll in Monster,° and ~~info~~ trye whether [anye] in thous parts would buye in the Countye of kilkenye [for] mr Briane* sends mee word the most that hee has bine° offerede is but 8 and sixe pense the Stone at which [I] much wonder, for it is very Diere° in this kingdome [and] the Trade heare for Cloth never greater then it is Now

Letter 193. June [26], 1670, [London], the Duchess of Ormonde to Captain George Mathew (NLI, Ormond Papers, 2503, no. 45). Autograph.
For My Brother Captane Gorge Mathews [/] thes. [Endorsed]: dated [26] of June received 2 of August 1670 about Captain ffoxton and Bodken. Dutchess of ormonde.

This berar° Captane Foxen* who [has on] all ocations° Exprest himselfe very Frindlie unto My Lord and to all his relations is Mariede unto the daghter of one mr Bodkine* whoe ~~it should~~ By what I understand had made some improvments upon a Small proportione of Land about 208 Ackers° that was Sense° Found to bee My Lords and is Sett at presant by you unto a Nother,° but for what Time or upon what Termes, this berer Cannot informe mee, but acquantinge My Lord therof I find hime inclynede upon Captane Foxens accompt° that his Father inlaw shouldbee preferede unto unto [*sic*] the Tenansie of it upon such resonable Termes as you and hee Shall agree if you bee not further ingadged° which by his derections° and my regard unto This Gentellman ~~is~~ ^(is made known, and)^ recomended to you by

        your affectionat Sister
                E:ormonde

Letter 194. July 6, 1670, [London], the Duchess of Ormonde to Captain George Mathew (NLI, Ormond Papers, 2503, no. 46). Autograph.
For My Brother Captane Gorge Mathews [/] thes. [Endorsed]: My Lady dated 16 received 26 July 1670 about Sir Ralph ffreeman and Gardner Caricke.

The 6 of July

Theris one Sir Ralphe Freeman[709] an antiant° acqantanse of My Lords with his Lady, whoe is now goeinge for Ireland and ther intends to Live for some years untell° thay° have Freede an Estate of Thers heare that I am tould is considerable, for whous beter° Conveniensie; My Lord has Lent them Carrick House,* with Liberty to make uss° in his absense of the Pigon House warrin and Gardins allsoe, The Man that now kieps Them, as I am informed is not to bee trusted; for a gentellman whoe is Now heare; tould mee that hee offerede hime to Sell hime Trees from Thense; and that hee had Sould° unto divers gentellmen in the Countye of Tiperarye and watterford; and soe Littell hee minds anye thing of the Gardins but what dous° yeald himselfe Profitt, as hee Lets all goe to ruene,° without takinge anye paynes himselfe; and Expects his wages and the profitts of the Plase besides; which Last I see noe resone° For; wee are now removed to Clarington House,[710] where theris very good Ayre,° which I doe hope will Cure My Lord of his Cough, which dous troubell hime at this Time, and somthinge of the Goout° with it, but the Doctor dous asshure° mee theris noe daynger, I pray hastene over the hundreth Pound to Pay My Soon° Johns* depts;° and some answar of Mr Comins* bussenes° whous povertie and Charge in Stayinge heare makes hime very importunat to bee dispacht

---

[709] A client of JO, perhaps the son and heir of Sir Ralph Freeman (d. 1667), who served in Ireland under JO during the civil wars. See C. E. Challis, "Freeman, Sir Ralph (d. 1667)," *ODNB*.

[710] Piccadilly was little more than a country lane during the time the couple resided at Clarendon House, which had been built on an eight acre site.

Letter 195. July 18, 1670, [London], the Duchess of Ormonde to Captain George Mathew (NLI, Ormond Papers, 2503, no. 47). Autograph.
For My Brother Captane Gorge Mathews [/] thes. [Endorsed]: My Ladys dated 18 received 26 July 1670 about Trotter and Millen et cetara.

The 18 of July

I have resevede° a complaynt from Trotter the Paynter[711] of the Crosnes of Millan* that kieps Dunmore House,* of Severall perticulers that hee has done to the prejudis and Spoyle of the worke as hee conseves° in Spight° unto hime, though in Effect the Loos° is Like to bee Mine, but beinge at this distanse I cannot bee my selfe a Judge whoe is Most in Fault, and beinge unwillinge to part with Trotter whoe I know to bee very abbell in his profestione and knowinge besides in things of Buildinge; I wouldnot have hime so farr discoriaged as to quitt my Sarvise° untell° hee have compleated all the Finishings that is to bee done unto that House and Mendinge what may bee Nesesarye at kilkenye* allsoe; as to what may Niede° New Colleringe without or within dours, and therfor I doe intreate you when you goe Next unto kilkenye that you will Call them Both befor you; and Examine the grownd° of ther discord, and accordinge as you Find whoe is most in Fault, that you will Ether make them to Live quietlie together hensforward; or Let mee know ~~whoe is most in fault and~~ your oppinion which of the tow° is Fittest to be parted with,[712] I heare Millan is unsatisfiede that his wife has noe wages but if hee knew how much More his owne Entertainment is, then the greatest Person heare dous° allow for the kieping° of an Emptie House hee would not repyne but bee ~~satisfiede~~ ^well pleased^ with what hee has, I have hearinclosed sent you a copie of mr Martins* resept° of fiftie Pound which hee had Sense° My Lord Angers*

crossness

coloring

---

[711] Robert Trotter (fl. 1672–1686) was a Dutch painter who acted as EO's building overseer. See his entry in Loeber, *Biographical Dictionary*, 109; and also Fenlon, "Episodes of Magificence," 156, note 121, and "'Her Grace's Closet': Paintings in the Duchess of Ormond's Closet at Kilkenny Castle," *Bulletin of the Irish Georgian Society*, 36 (1994), 30–47 (45).

[712] In Mathew's response to EO's request, dated from Kilkenny on August 19, 1670, a draft of which is appended to EO's letter, he writes: "I have beene ^~~all~~ a greate parte of^ this day Examining the difference betweene Trotter and Millen and doe finde very little grounds of either of either [sic] Side for any misunderstanding ~~Soe that I Saw~~ ^I did See^ betweene them; and I presume for the future they will live well togeather from troubling your Grace with any Complaints of that nature."

went; upon the ocatione° of his wifs death[713] to defray the Charge of hir Buriall and to Carye hime out of Towne soe as by the writinge hee Signede formerlie and what this Note dous Mentione you may become satisfiede of what hee has resevede in all

Letter 196. July 30, 1670, [London], the Duchess of Ormonde to Captain George Mathew (NLI, Ormond Papers, 2503, no. 48). Autograph.
For My Brother Captane Mathews [/] thes. [Endorsed]: My Ladyes 30 July received 10 August 1670 about my Lord Johns coming; Dunmore wall.

The 30 of July

Sense I writ Last unto you, I resevedº a Bill of Exchange for 2 hundreth pound one wherof is payed with som ode° Mony° besides accordinge as you did derect° to discharge tow° depts° of My Sonn Johns,* whous Notes givene under his hand unto the Severall Partys I doe hearwith Send you, My Lords Arrears that I formerlie mentioned to you is in a very Liklie way to bee Securede soe as I hope you will Find hee has bine° a good Manager for himselfe of Late, Hee beinge very Intent upon the payinge of his depts, and warye not to Contract More his Expense beinge as moderate as is possible Consideringe that hee is Tyede to his Plase to kipe° his Table, Hee has agreede with Allderman Bucknell* for the farminge of his Priswins° as thay° were Let the Last yeare and hee to pay the halfe years Rent in hand, which had ~~his Haste~~ ^Not My Lord^ [/] bine ~~soe~~ ^a litell° to^ hastie° In, I am very confident hee might have had a hundreth pound a yeare More, I understand from Baxter* that theris some Nesesitie of Takinge down the side wall of the Court at Dunmore* and strengtheninge what may otherwise indaynger the House by Resone° Captane Morton* made them dige in Levelinge of the Court below the Foundation, soe as what the Charge of Securinge of it may come unto, I desier° you will give order may bee allowed, it beinge My Lords Plesure allsoe, whoe I did yesterday acquant therwith [/] I am come Just now from Seeinge My Sister Cloncarthye* whoe tells mee that your wife was dayngeroslie Sicke Latlie° [/] I pray Let mee know by the Next what it was that aylled hir; and how Shee dous° Now, for I shall remayne in great unease untell° I heare of hir Recovrye

---

[713] Aungier's first wife, Jane had died in 1669. See Toby Barnard, "Aungier, Francis, first earl of Longford (c. 1632–1700), politician and administrator in Ireland," *ODNB*.

Letter 197. August 6, 1670, [London], the Duchess of Ormonde to Captain George Mathew (NLI, Ormond Papers, 2503, no. 49). Autograph.
For My Brother Captane Gorge Mathews [/] thes. [Endorsed]: My Ladys dated 6 August received 11 1670. pleased at the accompts sent.

The 6 of Agust

My Leter sent you the Last weeke will Satisfie you of the resept° of My Son Johns* Mony,° and how it has bine° disposed of, The Controwlers accompts° I acquanted you ~~a good while sense~~ ^allsoe^ [/] ~~that I~~ ^were^ reseved,° as I have ~~done~~ sense,° an Inventorye of such Goods as was Left at Dublin in Sir Mawris Eustas his House,⁷¹⁴ which I sent hime derections° to remove forthwith; that Thay° may not inconveniens the Gentellman whoe is now Ther, and to Send them by Sea whilst the wether is Good, and plase them at Dunmore* where much of that kind of Lumber⁷¹⁵ willbee ussfull the Castell of kilkenye* beinge allredie Furnisht, and out of what is broght from Dublin I beleve ther may bee some Goods that may sarve to Furnish a Few Romes° at Clonmell;* The accompt you Sent My Lord of the State of his Fortune was very perticuler and Satisfactory unto uss Both, My Lord is this day concludinge with Allderman Bucknell* ~~and~~ for a 11 Thowsand Pound to pay ofe° his depts° heare, and is in a faire way to discharge that which is owinge unto the Earle of St Allbans⁷¹⁶ allsoe out of his Arreares that I formarlie Mentioned to you, it beinge now Securede and Plast° upon such a Found⁷¹⁷ as it is belevede his Lordshipp willbee Sattisfied with; wherof My Lord himselfe will give you a further accompt by the Next Post, Soe as if anye Considerable part of the fiftie Thowsand Pound doe come In, within anye resonable Time, I hope my Lords depts in Ireland will allsoe bee discharged or at the Least a Considerable part of Them, of which I wish mrs Hindshaws⁷¹⁸ and Sir Thomas⁷¹⁹ Somes may bee the first, I have charged a Bill upon you for soe much of the Accate

---

⁷¹⁴ The Lord Chancellor of Ireland had died in June 1665. The house to which EO refers was probably the mansion Sir Maurice Eustace built on what later became Eustace Street in Dublin, where he had lived since 1660. See Terry Clavin, "Eustace, Sir Maurice," *DIB*.
⁷¹⁵ "Disused articles of furniture and the like, which take up room inconveniently, or are removed to be out of the way; useless odds and ends" ("lumber, *n*.1," 1a, *OED*).
⁷¹⁶ Henry Jermyn, Earl of St. Albans (1605–1684).
⁷¹⁷ Foundation ("found, *n*.1," *OED*).
⁷¹⁸ Unidentified.
⁷¹⁹ Unidentified.

Mony as remayns in your hands havinge takene it upe heare from mr Lindsie;* In the List of the depts I find my Lady Fouskeys[720] to bee mentioned 6 hundreth Pound wheras I think it was but 4 hundreth and Soe I find it Enterede in My owne Tabell Booke[721] soe as I wish that you would See the Bond your Selfe, Mr Jarvis[722] was heare Latlie° but Cannot Now bee heard of, soe as I dout° unles you have other Securitie then his owne it will prove a desperate dept [/] I asshure° my selfe that you have by this Time resevede a full accompt of what ^agrement^ My Lord made with mr Lindsie, and of all the Severall Bills that has bine transmitted by you, sense I made it my Care Ether to give you Notis° therof My Selfe, or to Make James Clarke* to doe it, whoe has Entered Them all in a Bouke° according the Severall Times that thay have bine deue,° with all other such Soms besides, as hee has resevede, which I kiepe° my Selfe wherby to charge hime; I pray Let mee know by the Next how My Sister dous,° and remember mee to hir [/] I was in hope your Leter of 27 of the Last Month would have givene some accompt of hir but it did Not

Letter 198. August 10, 1670, [London], the Duchess of Ormonde to Captain George Mathew (NLI, Ormond Papers, 2503, no. 50).[723] Autograph.
[Endorsed]: 10 August 1670 for mistress Lady Dutchess of Ormonde.

My Lord [*one line missing*] Liftenant did intend a Journye into Monstor, dous° beleve hee willbee Nesesitated to take kilkenye in his way ^and therfor^ dous think it Fitt that his Lordshipp shouldbee Lodged and Entertanede in the Castell* which as well, as in his owne absense; and the Shortnes of the Time cane admitt of which it is his desier° and mine Both may bee Countenanst by your beinge Ther and My Sone Arran,* and that you will Conserne° your Selfe by giveinge such derections° unto Baxter* and others as you Shall Judge Nesesarye for makinge Fitt provistion for his reseptione,° and well

---

[720] Possibly Sydney, Lady Fortescue, wife of Sir Thomas Fortescue of Dromisken, Co. Louth, daughter of Colonel Kingsmill. See John Burke, *A Genealogical and Heraldic Dictionary of the Peerage and Baronetage of the British Empire*, 6th edn (London: Burke's Peerage, 1839), 424.

[721] "A book of writing tablets; a notebook" ("tablebook, *n*.," 1, *OED*).

[722] Unidentified.

[723] The MS is subject to wear and tear (significantly worsened by clumsy repair work) that has resulted in the loss of the letter's first line (on the first page) and the last lines (on the second page).

orderinge of the Entertanment [/] I have Sent the best derections that I could at this distanse to Baxter as to what may conserne the bussenes° of his Manadgment, and to Sestions* to Furnish the House with as much Spide as hee Cane, as when My daghter Ossorye* wass Ther, Mony° I feare willbee the hardest matter to gett, but upon this ocatione° [lines missing]

Letter 199. August 13, 1670, [London], the Duchess of Ormonde to Captain George Mathew (NLI, Ormond Papers, 2503, no. 51). Autograph.
For My Brother Captane Mathews [/] thes. [Endorsed]: My Ladyes dated 13 received 22 August 1670.

when My Lord went first into Ireland after the kings cominge over, hee toucke° upon hime My Soon° Ossorys* depts,° and a Mongst them 2 hundreth pound that hee was owinge unto Gorge Stowell,* which I find inserted in the Last List of My Lords depts that you sent over, at which time an accompt° was made upe with all My Soons Creditors, and in perticuler, with Allderman Walle,[724] to whom Gorge Stowell did owe twentye pound, which hee desirede that I would make my dept by giveinge mr walle a Note under my hand for it ^(as I did)^ and Stowell would abayte° it out of the accompt of what wee ought° hime (but I think has not,) soe as I intreate you if you find that hee has not as yet allowede for it, that Soe much may bee deducted out of his Next Payment ~~and~~ ^that^ I ~~will~~ ^may^ Satisfie Allderman walle and take upe My Note by a Leter that I resevede° yesterday from Baxter* dated the 30 of the Last Month I understand that My Lord Liftenant was Entertaned at kilkenye* at My Son Arrans* Charge which My Lord Bid mee to tell you that Hee ^would^ allow For, as intendinge the same thinge himselfe as you will Find by his owne Leters, which it should sime° came Not soe Timelie as was hopede to have intemated° his plesure in that perticuler, Hee bid mee allsoe to desier° you to give derections° that ther may bee always a convenient quantitie of wine and Beare° ~~allo~~ still kept in the Castell, that upon anye sudane° ocatione,° or persons of qualities Cominge thether to See the House, thay° may bee offerede to drinke,

The 13 of Agust

---

[724] Sir William Wale, Alderman of London.

Letter 200. October 1, [1670], [London], the Duchess of Ormonde to Captain George Mathew (NLI, Ormond Papers, 2503, no. 52). Autograph.
For My Brother Captane Gorge Mathews [/] thes. [Endorsed]: My Lady Dutchess.

The First of Oct

My Lord was at Newmarket* when I reseved° your Leter of the 17 of the Last month, which I did the day followinge Transmitt unto hime, and wherof you will by this Post reseve° his answar unto the most Materiall perticulers therof; only theris one thinge I wonder you shouldbee in dout° of, Consarning° what payments you are to make unto mr Lindsie,* Sense° James Clarke* has in tow° Severall Leters informed you, and shallbee agayne° abstracted out of the Boouke ~~th~~ that I kiepe° by Mee of all such Somes as hee has resevede; sense My Lords Last Cominge into England the Time when, and from whom hee has resevede it Ether by Bill of Exchange or otherwiss soe as a perticular shallbee sent you; soe Soune° as Ever hee returnes which I doe hope willbee within a few days; I suppose ther willbee shortlie some Monys° dew° for Accates which I intreate you to transmitt over to mee, soe Soune as it Canbee gathared In; I did about a fortnight or 3 weekes [~~agone~~] sense, Louke° over the inventorye of the Goods that was Left unsolde at Dublin; and out of the whole, did oppoynt° such Parsells° as I thought would desentlie° Furnish My Lords House at Clonmell;* but have not as yet heard from the Controwler, to whom I made the derections° as playne as was posible for mee to doe at this distanse, which I hope hee has Showede you if it bee come unto his hands (for Soe I bid hime) mr Bryane* sends mee word that you have givene derections that the Plantinge of Trees from the Gardine Dore at Dunmore* unto the Dyninge River[725] should goe on this Season, which I am very much pleasede at, and doe hope to See the Next springe, I perseve° The woole is Not as yet Solde; it yealdinge a Lower Prise° then it did the Last yeare which I wonder at, for it is very diere° heare;

---

[725] Dinan River, Co. Kilkenny.

Letter 201. October 22, 1670, [London], the Duchess of Ormonde to Captain George Mathew (NLI, Ormond Papers, 2503, no. 53). Autograph.
For My Brother Captane Gorge Mathews [/] thes. [Endorsed]: My Ladyes about Leases and Subseryes dated 22 Received 29 October 1670.

The [22] of Oct

I have Litell° to Say this Post but to acquant you that My Lord and I have this day Signede and Sent away an othoritye° unto My Son Arran* and your Selfe to Signe Leases in our absense, and that wee both have perfected the writinge unto Sir Gorge Lane* that you Sent over a good while Sense,° at which Time I desirede from hime the tow° notes which hee had under my hand, which hee did affirme unto Mee that hee had allredie delivred upe unto you; which I doe suppose you did forgett to tell Mee, The accompt° that you desier,° of what mony° has bine° resevede° heare from mr Lindsie* is Sent you by James Clarke;* the Compounding[726] with the 49 Men which the Lord Roberts* did attempt to doe my Lord a prejudis, is Now Effected by the Lord Liftenant whoe has it Should Sime° drawne the Counsell to Joyne with hime in it; a Perfect Tricke of My Lord of Ororye,* and Lord Inchequins[727] though acted by other hands ar under the Spetious[728] pretense of the kings advantage when at the same time thay° forspone[729] hime as well as My Lord to gett at the Last the overplus[730] for themselfes but this affare willnot goe on as thay Expect, for the designe is very well understoud heare; though Many that pretends and some that I realie doe beleve are My Lords Frinds; has bine Coussened° into this Suberiptione[731] by beinge made beleve it was for his advantage when in Effect Nothinge Couldbee more opposit unto it; I pray remember mee to My Sister and Send

---

[726] "To settle (a matter) by mutual concession; to compromise" ("compound, *v.*," 7, *OED*).

[727] Murrough O'Brien, first Earl of Inchiquin (c. 1614–1674).

[728] "Having a fair or attractive appearance or character, calculated to make a favourable impression on the mind, but in reality devoid of the qualities apparently possessed" ("specious, *adj.*," 2a, *OED*).

[729] Possibly "To wear out with toil, etc." ("forspend | forespend, *v.*," b, *OED*).

[730] "That which remains over; an amount left over from the main amount, or from what is allotted or required; an additional or extra quantity; a surplus" ("overplus, *n.*, *adj.* and *adv.*," Aa, *OED*).

[731] "Misrepresentation or suppression of the truth or facts; an act or instance of this" ("subreption, *n*.1," 1, *OED*).

mee word how Shee dous° from whom I have not heard ~~this good~~ of
Late, makes mee dout° hir not beinge well

**Letter 202. October 28, 1670, [London], the Duchess of Ormonde
to Captain George Mathew** (NLI, Ormond Papers, 2503, no. 54).[732]
Autograph.
For My Brother Captane Gorge Mathews [/] thes. [Endorsed]: My
Ladyes of the 28 October / 12 November 1670.

The [28] of Oct

I have Loukede° over the papers wherin Trotter* and Millan* doe
charge on° a Nother,° and I find them soe frevelous; as the grownd° *frivolous*
of ther quarall arrisinge from ther owne frowardnes, rather then ther
Conserne° that I shouldnot bee Cousenede;° and therfor I have givene
James Clarke* order this day to write such a Leter unto the Paynter as
will make him Live more quietlie untell° I come over my selfe; if not
I must think of a Nother way in Cayse° of anye further complaynt:
I am contented that all Acates that you may conseve° fitt to bee
collected (in kind) may bee Soe; provided you have Land that you
cannot turne unto beter° uss° ~~May for~~ then for the kiepinge° of them,
but if otherwiss; I think it wouldbee beter husbandrye to take Mony°
in Lew° of them; as it wouldbee for the smaller dewties° as Poultrye
and the Like; I have had noe accompt° as yet from mr Briane* of the
Sayle of the woole this yeare but I doe beleve I shall; I did send the
Controwler a perticuler of such Goods as I thought wouldbee fitt
for My Lords House at Clonmell;* but have had [no] accompt from
hime [about] how farr hee has ob[served] [*three lines missing*] hee has
writene to you an answar unto that Last of your Leter that Consernes
mr John wellch,* whous way of prosidinge° I Confess to you I doe
very much apprehend; yet must bee soe warilie manadged by you;
as hee may not find wee are dissatisfiede, Ether with his dullnes;
or worse faults in thous° that acts under hime, untell My Lord
Comes over himselfe; yet to have a Care in Cayse of the acsident of
his death; that My Lords writings may bee Securede, which I doe
much feare are to bee found; or misslayede; according as it Sutes° *mislaid*
the advantage of thous relations of his that hee trusts, and beleves
are honnest, though theris but to much resone° for some to beleve
are Not ^Soe^; The bussenes° of accompt betwixt the Lord Anger*
[and] you, I doe Supose willbee ajusted; and soe I doe [*three lines*

---

[732] As many as three or four lines of text from the bottom of two pages are lost because the MS is badly torn.

missing] My Sone Osorye* is N[ot yett] arivede but daylie Expected, My daghter Cavendish* is with Childe, but is still in Darbyshire [/] all the rest of My relations I thank God are well [/] I pray remember mee to my Sister of whous good health I shouldbee glad to heare

Letter 203. November 19, 1670, [London], the Duchess of Ormonde to Captain George Mathew (NLI, Ormond Papers, 2503, no. 55). Autograph.
For My Brother Captane Gorge Mathews [/] thes. [Endorsed]: My Ladyes dated 19 November received 5 December 1670.

The 19 of No

I heare you are now at Dublin Ingadged° in a troubellsome affar of my Lords consarninge° the Securinge of his Mony,° wherin I hope you will at Length have good Sucksess;° though some Late prosidings° Ther has somthinge retarded the payments; if I Cane speake with Sir Gorge Layne* befor the Post dous° goe I will Send you a List of all the depts° that My Lord has payede sense° I ^Hee^ came Last over and what remayns the Like I wish you would returne to Mee of what you have discharged ^Ther^ and what rests still to pay [/] I wish the Estate designed for My Sonn Arran* were Settled to hime, and the tow° Maners of Bureshule and Ahrime were Soe to My Sonn John,* to avoyde° anye prejudis unto Ether, whilst My Lord and I are both willinge to Joyne in the doeinge of it which the death of Ether may weakene Ther Securitie In; as I am tould makes mee much Conserned° to have ther Estats Settled soe as Not to bee indayngered by ^anye^ acsident; I hope My Lord will goe over in the Springe it beinge much his desier,° as well as it is Mine that am

your affectionat Sister

E:ormonde

Letter 204. December 13, 1670, [London], the Duchess of Ormonde to Captain George Mathew (NLI, Ormond Papers, 2503, no. 56). Autograph.
For My Brother Captane Gorge Mathews [/] thes.

The 13 of Des

The Bill of Exchange you sent mee for 200 pound came to my hands yesterday very seasonablie, which I delivrede this day to James Clarke* to gett acsepted; Mr Harisons* assignment of 300 a yeare

untell° a thowsand pound shouldbee payede was givene hime when
My Lord came Last over into England as I remember, which is 5
yeare Sense,° soe as the prinsepall and Intrest ~~considered~~ allowede,
That dept° cannot but bee by this time discharged as I conseve;°
and therfor I intreat you to informe mee as soune° as you cane
whether wee may Charge mr Pages* dept upon the same assignment
accordinge the Manner as was by mee Latlie° proposed to you; the
60 pound that Baxter* Layede by; for My Lady Foskues⁷³³ Intrest
(but was not payede by hime) I doe hope hee has accompted° For, if
Not, I dout° not but you will calle upon hime For it; as consarninge°
the [*illegible*]⁷³⁴ which is Like to bee broght in charge aganst My
Lord I cane give you Litell° or Noe accompt,° save that I heard Sir
Thomas Humes* onse° Say that mr Mathew Bary⁷³⁵ oght° sixe or   *score*
Sevene core pound upon that accompt but that hee could gett noe
payment from hime and as I take it hee sayede° somthinge unto the
same Effect of John Connell⁷³⁶ consarninge the Like; but of this Last
I am Less Sartane,° by which I conclude hee had the manadgment
~~of~~ ^for^ some time of that affare though posiblie the Controwler
mr Harison* might have had it afterwards, soe as it is Like that
amongst Sir Thomas Humes his his [*sic*] papers somthinge may
bee gatherede to informe you beter,° I ~~think~~ think it wouldnot bee
sayfe° upon noe beter recomendation then the Porters, to Intrest his
Sonn that is a Stranger with soe greate a Charge as all the Goods,
untell hee bee beter knowne, and that ther bee some Experiense of
his Skill to distroye the Mothes which if hee dous° performe will   *moths*
deserve a recompense as Shall bee agreede upon when hee is Sett
a worke, and ~~afterward~~ afterwards as you shallbee satisfiede of his
honestie Sobrietie and knowledge in upholsterye worke hee may
bee Entertanede or Not, and Ross Browne⁷³⁷ to Continow° as Shee
was, for I doe beleve hir to bee a very fathfull Sarvant, though a
froward one; Sir Samuall Morland⁷³⁸ shallbee ~~shallbee~~ spokene unto

---

⁷³³ Unidentified creditor.
⁷³⁴ It looks like "Port corne."
⁷³⁵ Unidentified.
⁷³⁶ Unidentified.
⁷³⁷ Unidentified servant.
⁷³⁸ Sir Samuel Morland (1625–1695), natural philosopher. "One of Morland's main talents in these years was for the construction of mechanical engines for the supply or removal of water for domestic or industrial purposes. Hydrostatics and hydraulics became his forte . . . His subsequent improvements to the house included a table in the dining-room with its own fountain, and a moveable kitchen." See Alan Marshall, "Morland, Sir Samuel, first baronet (1625–1695)," *ODNB*.

Consarninge what you think willbee Nesesarye for suplyinge the tow° Houses of killkenye and Dunmore* with water

Letter 205. January 7, 1670/1, [London], the Duchess of Ormonde to Captain George Mathew (NLI, Ormond Papers, 2503, no. 57). Autograph.
For My Brother Captane Gorge Mathews [/] thes. [Endorsed]: my Lady dutchess of the 7 of January 1670.

The 7 of Jan your Leter of the Last Month was Longe on the way otherwise you should have resevede° a spidier° returne; I have perusede the List of the depts° ~~that you have discharged~~ and am very well pleasede to find that theris soe considerable a Some dischargede, which together with such payments as you have takene Securitie for, and what My Lord has payede of his depts heare; gives mee some hopes that what remaynes of our ingadgments° may bee ~~payede out ofe~~ ^discharged^ in a few yeares which renderes our condistione more Easie to uss, then I could have Expected consideringe the disadvantage of My Lords Liveinge heare; where wee are forst unto an Expense of his kiepinge° a great Table not possible to bee avoyded° havinge daylie the resort of all Strangers, and Embasodors and all the Nobilitie besides; My Lord has not as yet had Time to Consider of the List you Sent hime of the Lands to bee Sett forth unto my Soun Arran,* Nor of the remaynders which Last is a perticuler very considerable allsoe by resone° of thes Holydays; but I willnot fayle° to Mind hime of it when I see it a Convenient Time, I am very Sorrye ~~to~~ that my Sister has soe ill health as to bee soe oftene Subgect unto Fitts of vomitinge, but it beinge a desease soe generall heare this yeare gives mee great hopes of hir Recovrye, and that after Shee will find hir Selfe much beter° then shee was befor, for Soe divers of my acquantanse are heare whoe were very Loe broght, and but very few that has diede of that distemper, Nor of vapers[739] (though this Last) dous° bringe great apprehentions of daynger unto the persons themselfs though the Doctors thinks nothinge of Them; The

---

[739] "Exhalations supposed to be developed within the organs of the body (esp. the stomach) and to have an injurious effect upon the health;" "A morbid condition supposed to be caused by the presence of such exhalations; depression of spirits, hypochondria, hysteria, or other nervous disorder" ("vapour/vapor, *n.*," 3 a and b, *OED*).

Duches⁷⁴⁰ beinge Soe very ill with thous° Fitts, as She allarames the
Court with hir dieinge in Them, but the worst is hir owne Fansie of
beinge in daynger arrissinge from the Splene⁷⁴¹ which Shee has unto   *arising*
a great degree; I pray Let mee reseve° some accompt° from you how
shee is, and I will discourse with the best Doctors heare, and Send
hir over some remidie° if it be possible at this distanse and the mene°
time very hartilie wish and pray for hir Recovrye as beinge very
consernedlie° hirs, and

> your affectionat Sister
>
> E:ormonde

**Letter 206. January 20, 1670/1, London, the Duchess of Ormonde
to John Brian** (NLI, Ormond Papers, 2353, no. 3095, p. 267).
Scribal: signed.
For mr John Bryan att Jenkins towne neere Kilkenny. [Endorsed]:
Her [*illegible*] for 62 pounds 15 shillings and 10 pence.⁷⁴²

Mr Bryan*   London January the 20th 1670

I have drawne a bill of Exchange uppon you for sixty two pound
fifteene shillings and tenne pence to be paid to the order of mr John
Lyndsey* in Dublin [/] I pray doe not fayle° the payment which is all
att present from

> Your loving freind
>
> E:ormonde

**Letter 207. January 21, 1670/1, [London], the Duchess of Ormonde
to Captain George Mathew** (NLI, Ormond Papers, 2503, no. 58).
Autograph.
For My Brother Captane Gorge Mathews [/] thes. [Endorsed]: My
Lady dated 21 January received 30 1670.

Brother   The 21 of Jan

I supose this Leter of mine will find you at Dublin, where I hope this
Terme will give you a good oppertunitie to dispach the bussenes°

---

⁷⁴⁰ Anne Hyde, Duchess of York, who would die two months later, at the end of
March 1671.

⁷⁴¹ "Regarded as the seat of melancholy or morose feelings" ("spleen, *n.*," 1b, *OED*).

⁷⁴² The signed Bill of Exchange in enclosed with the letter.

that carryes you thether, ~~Though~~ ^when^ ^Though^ I beleve you
will meet with all the obstakells° that cane bee put in your way
^Ther^ ~~though~~ ^yet^ for all That^ I dout° not of anye remove of them
that cane be givene from hense (when desirede) soe as untell° that
affare of the Mony° bee onse° broght in, or Securede My Lord dous°
dout whether his Journye over may not bee beter° deferede then
undertakene; wherfor I doe the more wish that bussenes were onse
put past daynger that My Lord might have noe more to doe with
anye Governor Ther, but bee free as other Men are to goe or Stay as
thay° Please [/] The Persons whoe made that atempt upon My lord
are Some of them knowne but are not as yet takene,[743] I have Sent
you the writinge Signede for Mr Grantam,[744] and am very Glad to
heare of My Sisters Recovrye, My Lord is very well pleased and soe
am I with what you design, in buildinge of Bricke Houses at kilkenye
in the Rome° of thous° thatht° Cabens[745] that are pulled downe,
which if done for St Johns Strete allsoe; would Secure the Scoule°
from the daynger of beinge Firede which as it is may by such Naybors
bee in Some hazard and it may bee worth your consideratione
whether it might Not bee Convenient to take such Land from the
Corporatione[746] where Cabbans wouldbee built Neare unto where
Stone Housses are; to prevent the Mischife that soe frequentlie
dous hapene ~~therby,~~ ^by Them^ I have writene Latlie° to My Sonn
Arran* and acquanted hime of the reports heare, that are greatlie to
his dishonner that I feare are but to Trew, I pray take noe Notis° ~~of~~   *too true*
that you know anye thinge of my resentinge of his strange Course of
Life but Let mee know what Efects it has had, My Leter was Sent
by the Lord Montallaxander[747] whoe I doe hope is Ther Longe befor
This [/] as for My Sonn John,* I have soe Mene° an oppinione of his
Parts as I think hime wantinge in a Capasitie of Liveinge beter [~~ther~~

---

[743] On the evening of December 6, 1670, JO had been ambushed on his return to Clarendon House by five men who intended either to murder him or to hold him for ransom, but he fought back and the men fled. A committee of the House of Lords was appointed to investigate the crime and soon discovered the names of the leading perpetrators: Thomas Blood, Thomas Blood junior, and Richard Halliwell. They evaded arrest, however, and a price of £1000 was set upon their heads. See Alan Marshall, "Blood, Thomas (1617/18–1680)," *ODNB*.

[744] Unidentified.

[745] "A permanent habitation of rough or rudimentary construction; a poor dwelling. Applied esp. to the mud or turf-built dwellings of slaves or impoverished peasantry, as distinguished from the more comfortable 'cottage' of working men" ("cabin, *n.*," 2a, *OED*).

[746] The Corporation of Kilkenny.

[747] Hugh Montgomery, second Earl of Mount Alexander (1651–1717).

a Brode] soe as I have cast ofe° anye hopes of hime but the other I would wish were out of that Plase and Companye in hope That the advise of his Frinds ^heare^ may have some power to prevayle with hime, whous Reson I take to bee beyond that of his yonger Brothers; whous depts° heare are great, and I feare are Increast Ther allsoe sense° I Left Ireland the Truth of what consernes° this Last, I ought not to bee kept a Stranger To, soe as some informatione from you Consarning° hime and his deportment is desired by

>your affectionat Sister

>E:ormonde

Letter 208. [January], 1670/1, [London], the Duchess of Ormonde to Captain George Mathew (NLI, Ormond Papers, 2503, no. 59). Autograph.
[Endorsed]: My Lady about Ludlowes 500 received 2nd ffebruary 1670.

Sense the writinge of this mr Ludlow* has desired mee to pay hime heare the Intrest of the 5 hundreth Pound that hee Lent unto My Sonn Ossorye* which upon ^the^ agreement ^you made^ with My Soon° when I was Last in Ireland was to become My Lords dept,° but unto what Time I doe not well remember, which being beter° to bee payede Ther then heare by resone° of the charge of Exchange[748] I shall intreate you to Enter it in the List of the depts, and paye hime the Intrest Ther hensforward, I did forgett what I intended to tell you in My Leter that My Daughter ossorye* is with Child ^and that^ yesternight therwas tow° Roges broght to Towne one wherof My Lord dous° beleve to bee the Person that assallted hime, though hee denyes the Fact yet theris such Surcomstanses° as will wee hope to make some discovrye

rogues

---

[748] "The action of giving or receiving coin in return for coin of equivalent value either of the same or a foreign country, for bullion, or for notes or bills; a bargain respecting this; the trade of a money-changer" ("exchange, *n.*," 3a, *OED*).

Letter 209. February 6, 1670/1, [London], the Duchess of Ormonde to Captain George Mathew (NLI, Ormond Papers, 2503, no. 60). Autograph.
For My Brother Captane Mathews [/] thes. [Endorsed]: My Lady 6th february 1670.

Brother   The 6 of Feb

I am very glad to Find by your Leter of the 18 of the Last Month that you had then soe good hopes of My Sisters Recovrye which I doe hope and Longe to heare is perfected; I Never ~~heard word~~ ^knew^ of the Lease of Nenagh that Captane Coole* gott signede by My Lord untell° I resevede° your Leter, Nor dous° My Lord understand it to bee other, then the Last was; that was past unto My Brother Hambellton* upon the Late agrement that was made with hime; but with some olltoratione° only to Secure it from beinge made Liabell [unto] My Brother[s] depts,° the counterpart of which Captane Coole did not Leave, but I have desirede it might bee Sent for which is accordinglie done, and when it comes I shallbee then beter° abble to informe you and my selfe in that perticuler; My Lord tells mee that hee hass answarede all other the perticulers of your Leter soe as it willbee Niedles° for mee to adde anye thinge therunto, but in the kiepinge° of my promiss unto Mr Southcout[749] whoe complanes very much of the hardnes of his bargine that if you find it to bee Soe, I desier° that hee may for his beter incoridgment° to Continow° My Lords Tenant ~~that hee may~~ bee abayted° somthinge of his Rent This yeare or as much of it as was remitted unto hime the Last [/] It is much to bee fearede that My Lord of Castellhavene[750] is Cast away goeinge for Ireland and with hime 6 Packets Lost; as you are not to wonder that you have not resevede answar unto Some of your Former Leters; sense° My Lords goeinge over is for some resons that he has givene you Like to be rather about the Ende then the begininge of Sommer I wish that you would speake with the Controwler and mr Briane* and ~~Soe~~ bee informed by them what Sheepe and Cattell might bee made Mony° of in the proper Season which I supose willbee at Easter or Soune° after as allsoe to accompt° with the Controwler about the Accates [when] you Come

---

[749] Unidentified tenant.

[750] James Touchet, third Earl of Castlehaven (1613–1684). His sister was the wife of JO's brother, Richard Butler of Kilcash. The rumors that he was lost at sea were false.

into the Contrye, and to Let me know your Sense in what is in thes perticulers desirede by

>your affectionat Sister
>
>E:ormonde

I think in the Seduell° of the depts that you have payede ~~that~~ the incombranse° that was upon Carberye House[751] is takene ofe,° soe as My thinks you Could doe beter then Sell it, and Satisfie such of My lords Creditors you think to bee the most Nesesarye; if it couldbee Contrived as without your desiringe it that it might bee knowne what will Satisfie mr kelye of Aghrime,* and that hee would make his request unto My Lord ~~Ether forst~~ unto that Efect I doe think it wouldbee much beter to stope° his Clamor, then Leave hime upon Soe great uncartantie, though his beinge in that Condistione has bine° much his owne Stubernes

uncertainty
stubbornness

Letter 210. February 14, 1670/1, [London], the Duchess of Ormonde to Captain George Mathew (NLI, Ormond Papers, 2503, no. 61). Autograph.
For My Brother Captane Mathews [/] thes. [Endorsed]: My Ladyes the14th february 1670. My Lady Dutchess dated 14 february received 20th 1670.

>The ~~4~~ 14 of Feb

I thank you for Letinge mee know of my Sisters Recovrye whous Last Illnes gave mee much feare for hir, I find you in some hopes of gettinge in a considerable part of My Lords Mony° by Ester° Next if noe new interuptione doe hapene to hinder it, as I am willinge to beleve willnot, unles the Rumors of mr Tabotts[752] indevours° to breake the Settellment of Ireland may worke anye change, as my thinks it shouldnot consideringe how unliklie or rather imposible it is for such Extravagant designes as hee goes upon should Ever take Effect, though Countenanst by the Duke of Buckingham,* I have soe imperfect a Memorye of the bargine you made with My Sonn Ossory* upon his acseptanse of 3 Thowsand pound a yeare for his allowanse, in Lew° of 4 that was promist hime and havinge

---

[751] Carberry House, Skinners' Row, Dublin? It was later owned by the Earl of Kildare.
[752] Richard Talbot (1630–1691), later Earl and Duke of Tyrconnell. See James McGuire, "Talbot, Richard duke of Tyrconnell," *DIB*.

noe Copie of that agrement, I cannot positivelie say whether you
did or Not consent to make that dept° My Lords and to free hime
from the 5 hundreth pound which hee borrowede from mr Ludlow*
when My daghter and hee was Last heare in England and therfor
I desier° to bee beter° informed by you in this perticuler that I may
know what answar to make unto this Gentellman whoe presses mee
much unto the payinge hime Intrest for this dept of My Sons; I spake
unto hime yesterday about your bussenes° in which I find theris noe
posibilitie of doeinge anye good at presant, the Manadgment of
affares heare beinge much Changed, soe as your best Frinds heare
thinks it Sayffier° for you to rest your Selfe quiete with the Grant you
have, then have anye thinge Movede beyond it at this Time, when
it is the Ayme° of a Factione heare to have all grants recalled; which
My Lord of Anglisie* and which ^That^ possiblie you will have
difficultie to beleve with others are much For, you have done very
well in displasinge mr wellches* Nephue after the findinge hime soe
faultie as hee has bine,° and the same Rule I hope you will Follow
with others that hee imploys if you Find them a Like [*illegible*]⁷⁵³ [/]
I have resevede° the Draft of the Deade of Settellment for My Son
John* but shallbee in ~~in~~ noe great hast° to gett it perfected untell° I
heare a beter Carracture° of his behavour then what is reported of
hime heare of his drinkinge and quarilinge⁷⁵⁴ which must bee unto
a very Extravagant hight when it should make hime affront one of
his owne relations, upon what it begane betwixt hime and Corronell
Fitspatrick* I Cannot tell, but feare that his Manner of Livinge
Cane promiss noe beter Effect, then daynger and dishonner unto his
Person and Consequentlie trouble unto his Frinds and relations

**Letter 211. March 8, 1670/1, [London], the Duchess of Ormonde
to Captain George Mathew** (NLI, Ormond Papers, 2503, no. 62).
Autograph.
For My Brother Captane Mathews [/] thes. [Endorsed]: My Ladyes
dated 8 received 17 April 1671.

Brother   The 8 of March

haveinge made some inquirye after Captane Cole* I shall tell you
very freelie what I find his Carrage has bine,° which was to gett this
Last Lease of Nenagh from My Lord upon a Leter Sent by hime

---

⁷⁵³ One word is illegible under the binding tape.
⁷⁵⁴ This may specifically refer to duelling ("quarrelling / quarreling, *n.*," *OED*).

from My Sister,⁷⁵⁵ setinge forth the Sadnes of hir Condistione and
this done; as a thinge unknowne unto hir Husband, when on the
Contrarye I have some resone° that makes mee beleve that it was his
Contrivanse, and that hee put hir upon it, which was soe Manadged
by this gentellman, as it was kept from my knowlege whoe as oftene
as hee came unto My House did Never Soe much as make the Least
applicatione to mee, which I confes I thought somthinge Strange;
consideringe that hee was in some imployment in My Lords affares;
untell° I understoud the bussenes° that hee had undertakene (and
gott don) and then I desirede Leave from My Lord to Send to hime
for a Counterpart⁷⁵⁶ which it Should sime° hee had not Left, as
consevinge it requisit (as I tould my Lord) that you should not bee
kept Ignorant of what hee had thought Fitt to doe in favour of his
Sister, Least° your not knowinge of it, might upon the Fayler° of
hir Husband; give you grownd° to Settell that Farme for my Lords
advantage that might bee Contradicting to this Late act of his, and
Soe beget an intangellment in [his] affares and bringe by that Menes°
a troubell upon you Both [/] [the] which Copie I gott, and Sent you,
~~after~~ Sense° which time, this Gentellman desirede to speake with
Mee, and intended (as I suppose) to have made some appoligie for   *apology*
undertakinge a bussenes of that Nature unknowne to Mee but as
I couldnot aprove therof, soe I made very Litell° replye but upon
his great profestions of Compastione and Sarvis° unto My Sister
Hambellton* I tould hime Shee was beholdinge to hime and Soe wee
parted; I Never haveing Sine° hime Sense, but doe heare that James
Hambellton* and his wife⁷⁵⁷ dous° ~~aupla~~ aplaude this gentellman for
such a Frind as thay° acknowlige all to hime; and Nothinge to My
Lord, at the Least thay Never touke anye the Least Nottis° of this to
Mee; but as I was tould yesterday James Hambellton has gott hime
to bee knighted; which begins to make mee Suspect that the report
of this Captans⁷⁵⁸ beinge Lunaticke is true, or otherwiss my thinks
for anye Fortune that hee hass, hee had beter° have bine without that
Tytell;° ~~alltogether~~ I pray have an Eie° after this Mans actings, and

---

⁷⁵⁵ Presumably, JO's sister, Mary Hamilton: she is mentioned later in the letter.

⁷⁵⁶ "The opposite part of an indenture;" "each of the indented parts of a deed of contract, etc., in its relation to the other part; *esp.* that which is not considered the principal part or original, e.g. the executed copy of a lease or receipt retained by the grantor as a counter-security" ("counterpart, *n.*," 1, *OED*).

⁷⁵⁷ James Hamilton (c. 1642–1679), JO's nephew by his sister Mary and Sir George Hamilton. He had married Elizabeth Culpepper, daughter of Sir John Culpepper, and a maid of honour, in 1661. See Éamonn Ó Ciardha, "Hamilton, Sir George," *DIB*.

⁷⁵⁸ Presumably, Captain Cole.

if you find further Cause to bee unsatisfiede with hime put hime
ofe;° for it rests whole in your owne power for hee has noe Creditt
with My Lord but what your approbatione has givene hime and
Consequentlie Cane retayne it Noe Longer then whilst you doe allow
it him [/] I thought it fitt to give you this relatione, which I desier°
you will kiepe° unto your Selfe, and bee Soe Just to mee, as to beleve
I am, and willbee allways

    your affectionat Sister

      E:ormonde

Letter 212. March 4, [1670/1], [London], the Duchess of Ormonde to Captain George Mathew (NLI, Ormond Papers, 2503, no. 36). Autograph.
For My Brother Captane Gorge Mathews [/] thes. [Endorsed]: My Ladys dated [4 March] received 13 about Sir Ralph freeman the french one et cetera. Dutchess of ormond to George Mathew.

        the 4 of March

I heard Latlie° but Not from Sir Ralph Freeman* himselfe, that hee
and his Lady were unsatisfiede with thous° domesticke Naybors of
French[759] that are Latlie plassede in the House of Caricke,* which I
suppose had not bine° done, but upon Nesesitie to provide and Secure
Them untell° Some other plase Else where may bee had for Them,
and in such Cayse,° I wish that the Controwler might bee Sent one°
purpose thether; Soe to Settell and order them a quarter,[760] as Sir
Ralfe Freemans Familie and Theres may not bee troubellsom unto
on° a Nother° for hee is a person of qualitie and well Estimed of
heare; and ~~thay~~ that thay° may have the uss° of the Gardines, or as
much of them as thay please to order for ther owne uss or all of them
~~in o~~ whilst wee are absent if thay willbee at the Charge of kieping°
a Gardener, and the Pigone House[761] To; for I know the Lady is a

---

[759] Sir Ralph Freeman and his family were sharing the house with French Huguenot families.

[760] "A measure of land in Ireland" ("quarter, *n.*," I, 5b, *OED*).

[761] Costello, in a section on dovecoats and pigeonhouses in *Irish Demesne Landscapes*, points out that a lease of land did not automatically confer a right to take its game (70). EO is specifically conferring that right on Sir Ralph Freeman and his wife.

discrete and a very Neate[762] woman and a person that I should be very glad to oblidge that am

> your affectionat Sister
>
> E:ormonde

Captane Cole* has promist to Send a copie of the writing that hee got My Lord to Signe unknowne unto Mee or ~~anye~~ Sir Gorge Lane* for which resone° and Somthing Else that I shall tell you hear after I Like hime Less then I did

Letter 213. April 2, 1671, [London], the Duchess of Ormonde to Captain George Mathew (NLI, Ormond Papers, 2503, no. 63 [incorrectly numbered 62]). Autograph.
For My Brother Captane Mathews [/] thes. [Endorsed]: My Ladyes dated 2 received 12 April 1671.

Brother   The 2 of Aprell

I understand by a Leter that I reseved° Latlie° from mr John Briane* that theris a considerable Nomber of wethers[763] out of the Stocke of Dunmore* that must be Solde ofe,° or removed to make rome° for this years increase; and that the Souner° it bee done the beter° it will bee for the Nombers that remayne, therfor I pray give your derections° Ether unto hime or Baxter* as soune° as you think Fitt in that affare; and Let them bee accomptable° unto you for what is had for them; to bee Transmitted over to mee as soune as it is resevede, for I supose My Lord has informed you with the resons hee hass to Suspend his Journye over for some Longer time then I did beleve, such are the great unsartanties° and Changes that hapens heare, as it Cannot bee thought sayfe° for his Intrests to remove from hense untell° ~~th~~ affares bee beter Settled That relats unto that Contrye, which at the presant hangs in ~~niede~~ ^some^ kind of Suspense; I understand that the New warine° at kilkenye* dous° not thrive,[764] what the resone° is I know not, but doe think it very requisit if That Plase bee not Fitt that some other Neare the Towne shouldbee had for that uss; which I pray advise with mr Briane and Baxter In, and Let one of them reseve°

---

[762] "Of a person: inclined to refinement or elegance" ("neat, *adj.* (*n.2* and *int.*) and *adv.*," I, 2a, *OED*).

[763] "A male sheep, a ram; esp. a castrated ram" ("wether, *n.*," 1a, *OED*).

[764] Costello speculates that the reason for the warren's failure was unsuitable soil. See her discussion of rabbit warrens in *Irish Demesne Landscapes*, 171–77 (176).

derections from you in that perticuler, it beinge a Conveniensie that very Nesesarye to bee had consideringe the badnes of the Markets ^Thar^, My Sonn Osorye* is not as yet returnede out of Holland and Flanders, whoe intends to See Franse as I heare but to what purpose unles to Spend Mony° I know not and to Sattisfie a ramblinge and unsettled humor, which hee Still retayns and Runes° much in dept° I feare and is Cousenede° and soe is My daghter by ther Sarvants, and how to healp it, I Cannot tell for I find Nether of them ^beinge^ inclined to troubell themselfs with ther owne affares but bee undone by ther owne Negligense, I doe not as yet heare of My Sonn Arrans* Arrivall but doe Expect hime Evrye day, The Duches[765] diede yesterday about 3 of the Clocke in the afternoune haveinge bine° at dinner at the Lord Burlingtons* but the day befor [/] very few did beleve Shee could Recover, but did not think hir death would have bine soe Soune; I pray remember mee to my Sister; and bee ^you Both^ asshured° of the Frindshipe and kindnes of

E: Ormonde

I desier° to have a List of thous° Lands that are of My owne inheritanse Comprehended in that Estate that is to bee Settled upon My Sonn Arran, which mr John Briane mr Welch* or Burdon* Cane I suppose draw upe in an howers° Time, and what the Rents was in the yeare fortie; with and what thay° doe Now pay

Letter 214. April 15, 1671, [London], the Duchess of Ormonde to Captain George Mathew (NLI, Ormond Papers, 2503, no. 64 [incorrectly numbered 63]). Autograph.
[Endorsed]: My Ladyes dated 15 received 28 April 1671 about Sir Robert viners and Sir George Hamilton Deliver debts provisions kilkeny et cetera.

Brother   The 15 of Aprell

I showede My Lord your Leter of from killkenye of the 4 of Aprell wi and a copie of Sir Robert viners* Articles for the 25000 whoe beinge this day oppoynted° to Meete upon a publicke consernment,° could not wright unto you him selfe, but bid mee to desier° you to Send hime over the accompt° as it now Stands betwixt Sir Robert vinner and hime, Sir Robert beinge Now convinst (that hee ought ^Not^) Nor Cane demand more then Singell Intrest accordinge

---

[765] Anne Hyde, Duchess of York, died after a long battle with what was probably breast cancer. See John Miller, "Anne, duchess of York (1637–1671)," *ODNB*.

unto which you are desirede to ~~Send~~ State it betwixt Them; what
you propose is all I cane Expect from My Sonn John* towards the
Sattisfinge of the dept° that hee is owinge unto Dicke Delaes his
widow⁷⁶⁶ whoe I shall indevour° to Satisfie untell° the Mony° Canbee
transmitted over to hir, The Copie of the Lease My Lord Signede in
favour of My Sister Hambellton,* I Sent you Soe Soune° as Ever it
Came unto My hands which I am Confident was intended to have
bine° consealed had I not takene Notis° when I knew that such a
thinge was Signede by My Lord and obtaynede Leave from hime
to gett that Copie by which you [are to] Satisfie your Selfe and mee
whether it doe remitt the Arrears dew° upon Sir Gorge Hambellton*
or Not; and accordinglie to order that affare as much unto My Lords
advantage as you Cane [/] I doe heare that Sir James wemes⁷⁶⁷ has
bine Carfull and has payede severall of his other depts; and I wonder
Much that hee Shouldbee Negligent in payinge a Rent which has
bine made Soe Moderate to hime and where a Time has bine givene
~~hime~~ the beter° to inable° hime to it, I Confess I wish hime well, but
all things Considered doe not know upon what accompt to Move My
Lord to doe hime anye favour beyond what you have in your Sevilitie°
Extended towards hime; soe as anye application hether wouldbee
but to referr hime backe agayne° to you to doe as you Should find
resonable and therfor doe wish that hee might bee advised not to
make anye unnesesarye addres in that Perticuler, My Lord would
have some resonable Proportione of Beare° and wine to bee allways
in his House at kilkinye,* For the great Changes and unsartanties°
of thes presant Times are Such; as it is Not Posibell for the Most
forseeinge Person in the world to to [sic] determine what Course
willbee best to take or Plase to goe To 3 Months to Come, soe as a
Convenient retreate must aganst all acsidents bee in a redines though
this is to bee Communicated only to your Selfe and Not to others;
that you may the beter know how to Gide° affares accordinglie; if
you Cane rayse anye Mony for My particuler usse ~~I pray Send it Mee~~
out of My Stocke I pray send it Mee, and if you Pay it Ther, unto Sir
Franes Bruster⁷⁶⁸ and Charge the Bills upon mr Lindsie* hee will
Exchange it for 4 in the hundreth accordinge unto the agreement
made with hime which hee will perform untell his yeare bee out,

---

⁷⁶⁶ Unidentified.
⁷⁶⁷ Sir James Weymss was a paternal relative of EO. She had a cousin, Patrick Wemyss (1604?–1661), by her father's sister, Elizabeth (see Wilks, *Of Neighing Coursers*, 137–38): Sir James was presumably his son.
⁷⁶⁸ Sir Francis Brewster (d. c. 1704), alderman of Dublin. See C. Ivar McGrath, "Brewster, Sir Francis," *DIB*.

My Sonn Osory* arrivede heare yesterday and I Expect My Sonn
Arran* ^daylie^ [/] heare is Many things discourst of, but I dare Not
write Nuse,° ~~but desier you to bee very~~ yet doe think it Nesesarye to
give you a Cautione whom you trust when you Come to Dublin, for
I doe asshure° you that the greatest ills that are Liklie to befall that
kingdom ~~is liklie and~~ dous° reseve° its Risse from the Natives of it;   *rise*
whoe has formarlie bine ~~thems~~ the Causurs of ther owne Ruene° but   *causers*
Never more Liklie to doe it Irecovarablie then Now, if ther Fooulish   *irrecoverably*
and Extravagant desiers and indevours [bee lett] Prevayle, whilst
thay° are deluded, with the hopes of [what] is Not at all intended
Them, whoe are made uss° of to quite the Contrarye Ends, then thay
beleve; and to Sarve a Nother° Sort of Pepell° whoe wants Estats and
will have it from thous° that are allredie Settled rather then Fayle,°
but I beleve ther Progets will ~~Fayle~~ bee at an Ende when thay have   *projects*
tryede them unto the uttermost, and therfor I willnot further inlarge
my selfe upon that Subgect at the presant but remayne

      your affectionat Sister

        E:ormonde

**Letter 215. [mid-May], 1671, [London], the Duchess of Ormonde
to Captain George Mathew** (NLI, Ormond Papers, 2503, no. 66).
Autograph.
For My Brother Captane Gorge Mathews [/] thes. [Endorsed]: My
Ladyes received 27 May 1671 Cabins Kilkeny Kelly Aghrim Birne
Carloe.

Brother

I cannot but wonder to find by your Leter of the 9 of this Month[769]
what should make mr welch* to undertake a Journye hether for soe
Short a time as hee designes to Stay but when I shall have informed
my selfe when hee Comes I will Let you know it; The State of the
Liberty Court I delivred into My Lords hands soe Soune° as I
reseved° it which was on thursday morninge whoe bid mee to tell you
that hee would advise upon it with the abblest Lawyers heare; the
Seduell° of the adwarded° Lands in the Countye of Carlogh I have
allsoe resevede; I pray continow° your indevours° to prevayle with
the Corperatione of kilkenye to pull downe, or at the Least ~~wisse~~
to remove the Thatht° Housses out of St Johns Strete otherwiss the

---

[769] A draft of Mathew's letter to EO dated May 9, 1671, can be found in NLI, Ormond Papers, 2503, no. 66.

distroyinge of ours willnot the more Secure the Skooule° from the
acsident of Fyier which is soe usstiall° in that Towne Evry yeare, in *fire*
my Last Leter to you writen on Teusday I gave you an accompt° of
the Bill of Exchange you Sent for 2 hundreth Pound, one wherof
you tell mee is for Accats, but the ocatione° of the House and other
Disbursments of that kind was soe pressinge as I did not take it for
my perticuler uss° ^but^ ordered James Clarke* to reseve° it; which
I desier° you will Secure to mee Som other way as Soune as may
bee convenient, and that you will speake with mr Briane* aboute
the Sayle of the woole this beinge the proper time of the yeare for
Sellinge of it, which it is reported heare dous° yeald a good Prisse°
[/] I think it wouldbee very Nesesarye that mr kellye of Aghrim*
^and one^ Birne⁷⁷⁰ in the Countye of Carlogh that is Now heare and
produsses some promissis made to hime for Sarvis° done My Lord
from mr welch and others imployed by My Lord might bee agreede
with upon the Plase rather then come over hether to Clamor and
Starve unless healpt by uss with what may carye them Backe and by
mistake ~~may~~ perhapes gayne° more then thay° Cane Justlie pretend
unto, besides the advantages that My Lords Enimies will make of
ther complaynts unto his prejudis [/] I Send you hearinclosed a brife°
of Blouds* confestione consarninge° his attempt upon My Lord *confession*
which is all that hee dous as yet acknowlege, when I know More you
shallbee further informed by

        your affectionat Sister

        E:ormonde

Theris some worke to bee done at Dunmore* that I have writene
unto the Controwler about, which I would allow for Ether out of the
woole Mony° or the Sayle of Cattell it beinge but a Small Matter, by
resone° I wouldnot disapoynt other ocations°

---

⁷⁷⁰ Unidentified.

Letter 216. June 6, 1671, [London], the Duchess of Ormonde to Captain George Mathew (NLI, Ormond Papers, 2503, no. 67).
Autograph.
For My Brother Captane Gorge Mathews [/] thes. [Endorsed]: My Ladyes of the 6th of June 1671.

The 6 of June

My Lord has takene upon hime to answar your Leter of the 26 of the Last Month which Leaves mee the Less to Say, but to Let you know that I am very Sensibell of the trouble you undergoe, by the Controwlers beinge Sicke mr Brians* and your owne Sarvant Smiths[771] but am in hope to heare by the Next Post of ther Recovry [/] James Clarke* beinge at this time very ill allsoe, which puts our affares heare into some disorder; when you Canbee at Leasure, I wish you could order Mee some supplye of Mony° out of what is dew° upon accats, and for what ~~My~~ ^May^ bee had for the increase of the Stock at Dunmore* and for the woole of this yeare (which Last,) My thinks should yeald Mony at this time, My daghter Cavendish* was Latlie° broght to Bed of a daghter and is Both of them I thank God very well, I am goeinge this day out of Towne to See My olde Lady of Devonshire* makes mee Conclude this Leter in some hast°

Letter 217. July 1, 1671, [London], the Duchess of Ormonde to Captain George Mathew (NLI, Ormond Papers, 2503, no. 68).
Autograph.
For My Brother Captane Gorge Mathews [/] thes. [Endorsed]: My Ladyes the 1 July received 7 1671.

The 1 of July

your Leter of the 17 of June advertised mee of mr John Brians* death which I am hartilie sorrye For, as a Person that I allways had a very good oppinione and kindnes for grownded° upon his honnestie and abbilitie in all such affares wherin hee was intrusted; what you doe propose as unto his imployment ~~I doe a~~ for the presant is very well approvede of by My Lord, as it is by Mee that the Controwler should take Care of My Stocke at Dunmore;* I have acquanted Sir Gorge Lane* with what you desier,° that the [Leasse] you are in treatie for may goe on, and Not [put it] ofe° for a Small matter whoe will order it accordinglie [and give] you an accompt° I am very well pleasede

---

[771] Unidentified.

that you have satisfiede mr Slingsbye,* whoe I suppose wanted what
you payede hime from Mee; I understand that when the Last assisess   *assizes*
was at Clonmell* that the Charge of the House came to fortye Pound
more then the allowanse, the Controwler beinge Then soe ill that
hee couldnot bee Ther at that Time to attend that affare however I
desier it may bee payede, that noe Clamor may bee for anye thinge of
that kind, sense° I ~~hope~~ ^beleve^ Nothinge of the Like will hapene,
when hee is abbell to Come abrode° agayne,° as I doe hope hee
willbee Shortlie, I was this day informed of a Marchand° in London
of good Creditt that will Exchange a Thowsand Pound ~~at~~ and pay
it heare at one and thirtye days Sight after it is resevede° Ther by
his Corespondant at waterford, ~~which~~ consarninge° which I have
Sent James Clarke* to find out the person and to give you a further
accompt by this Post, if it bee possible[/] if not you Shall have it by
the Next, the Lord Ranelaghs[772] bussenes° goes on, as Litell° to the
Satisfactione of honnest Men heare as of thous° in Ireland; but the
kinge is pleasede with the Progect and that is all that canbee sayede°
for it [/] I Longe to heare that the Mony° you are to reseve° bee onse°
Securede for tell° then wee cannot Stir from heare the resons beinge I
suppose very vissible to you the [like] what Contradictions of Orders
dous° happene daylie [/] I desier ^that^ mr Archer* may reseve your
derections° to Paye the Duch Paynter[773] quarterlie as mr Briane did
[/] The Deane of Cristchurch willbee Bushope of Ossory when the
olde Man dies, whoe it is heare belevede is past Recovrye which
willbee a great advantage unto that Plase[774]

---

[772] Richard Jones, first Earl of Ranelagh (1641–1712), had made a proposal to the King, which, when accepted in September 1671, effectively privatized the Irish exchequer. Its provisions, which allowed the undertakers to receive all Irish revenue and pay all Irish charges, included payment of a fixed sum of £80,000 to the King for the right to collect all Irish arrears. In return for an annual payment of £10,000, Ranelagh was secretly indemnified against any personal liability for shortfalls in the revenue. See John Bergin, "Jones, Richard," *DIB*.

[773] The Dutch painter, Abraham van Uylenburgh, styled himself "Painter to the Duchess of Ormond," but he is supposed to have died before February 3, 1669. See Fenlon, "Episodes of Magnificence," 156.

[774] Griffith Williams would live till March 29, 1672, when he was succeeded as Bishop of Ossory by John Parry. The former was a controversial figure, who authored a number of incendiary publications. See Terry Clavin, "Williams, Griffith," *DIB*.

Letter 218. July 4, 1671, [London], the Duchess of Ormonde to Captain George Mathew (NLI, Ormond Papers, 2503, no. 69).
Autograph.
[Endorsed]: My Ladyes dated 4 July received 9 July 1671.

The 4 of July

In my Last Leter I acquanted you of a Marchand° of good Creditt heare that would pay a Thowsand Pound, one and thirtye days after that his Corespondant should have reseved° it in Ireland; ~~all~~ wee to allow at the rayte° of 6 in the hundreth if you pay it at Dublin; and but 5 if at waterford; but Consideringe how Longe a time hee will have after hee shallbee advertisede that the mony° is reseved by his Factor My Lord would not make the bargine with hime at the Least untell° you were made acquanted ther with; and your oppinione of this offier° returned hether tuchinge° this perticuler, I heare the Controwler Continows° ill Still, makes mee think that his Cominge over into this kingdom might bee Nesesarye and if Soe I wish you would perswade hime to Trye what the Change of Climats may doe with the healpe of beter° Phisistions° then the Contrye doctors are Ther, hee beinge removede from the best of Them, beinge ^Now^ Soe farr from Dublin

Letter 219. July 11, 1671, [London], the Duchess of Ormonde to Captain George Mathew (NLI, Ormond Papers, 2503, no. 70).
Autograph.
For My Brother Captane Gorge Mathews [/] thes. [Endorsed]: My Ladyes about Walter Archer 11 received 17 1671.

The 11 of July

I acquanted you in a former Leter that My Sonn Osory* alledged that upon the Last agreement made with hime; that the five hundreth pound that hee ought° unto mr Ludlow* shouldbee plasede upon My Lords accompt,° and made his dept,° and hee to bee discharged therof, wherupon I sent hime the Coppie of that agrement which I resevede° Latlie° from you which I beleved would convinse hime of the Contrarye as it should sime° it did that ther was noe such Covenant in it, but now hee says ther wass verball one made after the writings were Signede which mr John wellch* and mr Page* cane wittnes unto which purpose hee has writene unto the former of Thes, wherfor I intreate you to recolect your Selfe and to speake with mr John wellch conserninge° this perticuler, for I remember nothinge of it; heare is a gentellman come over mr wallter Archer*

recomended by his Brother in law mr Grase* of Courtstowne and
incoridged° ^as I Gess°^ by the Factions Party heare to complane
of some ill deallinge hee should have reseved from My Lord; in
beinge promist by mr wellch, that if hee would deliver upe his
writings ^as hee did^ of a Morgadge° of 9 hundreth Pound hee
had upon the Milles of killkenye and Lands Neare unto the Towne   *mills*
that hee Shouldbee restorede unto his Estate; mr Grasses Leter to
hime the Copie of which with mr Archers Petistione beinge Sent
you; dous° implye as if I should Likwiss have made hime the Like
Promiss; which I never did to hime in all my Life upon anye ^such^
Condistione; but in generall Termes that I shouldbee willinge to doe
hime anye good offiss° I could in anye thinge of his Just profestions
consernes° (as trewlie I did) though My want of power and his want
of understandinge to Follow his owne bussenes° made my indevours
to have gottene hime to bee one of the Nomenies Frutles° unto hime;   *nominees*
and this is all that I cane stand Charged with as unto this perticuler
of mr Archers, soe as I am Litell° beholdinge unto mr Grase for
makinge hime beleve as mr Archer pretends hee did, that I had
positivelie promist to have hime restorede, a Thing that was as Litell
in my thoughts to undertake, as in My Power to performe or the
otherof perhapes it may bee Nesesarye to inquier° of Edward Butler*
what past betwixt mr Archer and thous° whoe had the Manadgment
of My Lords Estate in the C Soune° after that My Lord was
Restorede unto it; for if I bee not mistakene some mony° was offerede
hime accordinge unto the Rule that was Sett downe in Cayses° Like
his, of Forfited° Intrests;

**Letter 220. July 11, 1671, [London], the Duchess of Ormonde to
Captain George Mathew** (NLI, Ormond Papers, 2503, no. 71).
Autograph.
For My Brother Captane Gorge Mathews [/] thes. [Endorsed]: My
Ladyes dated 11 received 17 July 1671. My Ladyes dated 11 received
17 July 1671 about Rates bills Lord Burlington.[775]

The 11 of July

Just now My Lady Burlington* came to tell mee from hir Lord,
that hee had indevored° and did now beleve that hee could gett
some Mony° returned hethar° for five in the hundreth, but the
Some hee did not Name, soe as if you please to take Notis° to hime

---

[775] A draft of Mathew's letter to Burlington is appended.

^his Lordshipe^ in a Leter from your selfe, that you have resevede° this advertisment from Mee, of My Lord Burlingtons* indevour° in thous° parts to accomodate uss, uss, as hee has done himselfe in gettinge Bills upon soe resonable Termes and to bee derected° by his Lordshipe where and to whom Ther you are to pay what Some hee cane gett transmitted, I doe beleve willbee the spiediest and most Secure way to Suplye My Lords ocations° ^heare^ whoe wants it much at the presant;

Letter 221. July 24, 1671, [London], the Duchess of Ormonde to Captain George Mathew (NLI, Ormond Papers, 2503, no. 72). Autograph.
For My Brother Captane Gorge Mathews [/] thes. [Endorsed]: received 5 August 1671 Stowell.

The 24 of July

The papers that came inclosede in your Leter to Mee of the 12 of this Month my Lord has takene into his owne hands and will give you an accompt° of Them himselfe and what hee thinks best to doe therupon [/] I am very glad you have Securede My Lords writings in Cayse° of mr wellches* death, whous recovrye Cane hardlie bee Expected from the weaknes that hee is in soe as it may not bee a miss to think of such a Person as for integretie and Parts may bee Fitt to bee intrusted and to offier° such a one to My Lords consideration and I will indevour° the mene° time to hinder if I Cane, anye ingadgment° tell° I heare from you consarning° this perticuler, I send you hearinclosed a Petition from Gorge Stowell;* whoe I desier° may bee complyed with as farr as My Lords ocations° cane permitt hee beinge a poure° Man and the dept° Longe dew° to hime, I pray send mee word whether anye thinge Canbee [Not] had for Sheepe or woole which I did hope I might have had some mony° for, but doe now begine to dout° but our New undertakers⁷⁷⁶ will hinder all Trade instied of makinge the kinge Rich will beger Everye Man and Ruene°   *beggar* the kings Intrests at Length, I heare Nothinge of the Controwlers Recovrye, makes mee wish hime heare where the Change of Climate [and use] of the best Phisistions° I doe beleve would restore hime to his health; I am much Satisfiede with the hopes you have givene mee that My Lords Mony is Liklie to Come without anye more obstakells° that soe wee may have the Prospect of beinge out of that

---

⁷⁷⁶ "One who undertook to hold crown lands in Ireland in the 16th and 17th centuries" ("undertaker, *n.*," 4a, *OED*).

great dept to Sir Robert viner* which if discharged the rest would
goe ofe° in degrees, and My Lord then Left at more Liberty for hee
is yet to take some resolutione where to Settell himselfe; I supose you
willbee a Litell° surprisede when you heare that Bloud* is pardoned;
for Soe are most pepell° heare that desier the resons are Not made
acquanted with the Resons that indust his Magestie to Show soe   *induced*
much Clemensie towards hime when wee are all Strangers; and
therfor must beleve the kinge had some Exterordenarye grownd° for
it which I wish may tend unto his Sarvise,° how vilde and wicked
sowever this Person has bine;°[777] The Lord Liftenant[778] goes for
Ireland the 20 of the Next Month

Letter 222. August 19, 1671, [London], the Duchess of Ormonde
to Captain George Mathew (NLI, Ormond Papers, 2503, no. 73).
Autograph.
For My Brother Captane Gorge Mathews [/] thes. [Endorsed]: My
Lady 19 August received 7 September 1671 about accats Walter
Archer and one for Mr Plunket.

The 19 of Agust
I heare returne you the acquitanse° signede for mr Plunket* and doe
consent unto what hee desiers° in Putinge all the severall Peeses
of Plate that hee has Payede mr Chiferent[779] and ^that^ has bine°
hetherto° resevede° into one; I perseve° that Baxter* has somthinge to
bee accomptable° for remayninge in his hands for the Acates, which
I intreate you to ajust with hime and to transmitt it over to mee, or
Else to acquant mee that it is, that I may assigne the payment of
it Ther as I find may bee most convenient, I am glad that you have
Found a Person that for integritie and Parts you doe Judge fitt to bee
trusted with the kiepinge° of my Lords writings in Cayse° that mr
welch* should die, but when that is, I think it willbee fitt to give My
Lord Nottis° and have his approbatione befor you put hime into that
imployment, the beter° to prevent anye exseptione that malistious°

---

[777] On August 26 Blood received a full pardon and a grant of Irish lands worth
£500 per annum. Blood's biographer locates his subject's good fortunes in the context of
the Declaration of Indulgence that was issued on March 15, 1672, which was intended
to placate non-conformists on the eve of a new war with the Dutch, and to prevent them
from allying with the Dutch, as many had done in the previous war. See Alan Marshall,
"Blood, Thomas (1617/18–1680)," *ODNB*.
[778] Lord Lieutenant Berkeley.
[779] Unidentified.

pepell° may take; of which, that unhapie Contrye dous° afford good
Store; My Lord is Now soe well thanks bee to God that hee Nides°
not goe unto the Spaw nor had hee Ever anye thoughts of it, I send *spa*
you a Copie of Pursells⁷⁸⁰ petistione delivered unto the kinge, The
Fellow was sent unto the Tower where hee is still a Prissenor though
Newgate [or] Bedlam had bine a Fitter prissone for hime, and trulie
there are but tow Many of such Foouls and knaves Sett on ^to^ *too*
Exclame aganst My Lord without Cause, God defend hime from
ther Mallis,° My Sonn ossorye* has never as yet spokene unto My
Lord about the takinge upon hime that dept° of five hundreth Pound
dew° unto mr Ludlow* what Ever his intentions were, soe as untell°
you have My Lords order for it I doe not think it can bee sayfe° for
you to paye it; I am Sorye you had not timlie Nottis from My Lord
Burlington* that Bills of Exchange might have bine had for 5 in the
hundreth befor you did deale with others, but possiblie some other
ocatione° in thous° parts may bee Lighted upon hearafter, I suppose
you are about this time Settinge of the Prisewins for a Nother° yeare
and if you could gett the advanse of one halfe of the Rent to be
payede in hand as it was formerlie; would bee ^a^ very convenient
way to rayse Mony;° wee are much vext with petistioners that Comes
over sett on as I verylie beleve from ^by^ some that are our Enimies
Ther and incoridged° by the Like heare to make a Noyse° and
Clamor, My Lord cane give noe derections° in mr wallter Archers*
Bussenes° untell mr John welch bee in a condistione to Sertifie° the
true State of it, the mene° Time I am shure° mr Grace* has givene
under his [Oath] a great untruth when hee charges mee with a
Promis I never made that I would gett mr Archer restorede unto his
Estate if hee would give upe his writings, (a thing) I never proposede
to hime Nor Nieded° I; sense° I knew his Morgadge° was soe Clearlie
forfited;° as it was not Materiall whether hee gave them upe or Not,
and whye hee had not that consideration that My Lord did allow
unto othars that were in the Like condistione I know not, but doe (I
Confess) think it resonable it shouldbee givene hime, but when he
comes over himselfe you will beter understand how to deale ^Treate^

---

⁷⁸⁰ Edward Purcell, only surviving son of Philip, was the last male of the Ballyfoyle family. Dissatisfied with the outcome of the Act of Settlement, which restored him to a portion but not his entire estate, he is reported to have visited the house or castle of Ballyfoyle with a party of men armed with swords and pistols to take possession of it, violently attacking the family of the grantee. Forced to flee Ireland in order to escape prosecution, he came to London where he pressed his suit with JO. See William Carrigan, *The History and Antiquities of the Diocese of Ossory*, 4 vols. (Dublin: Sealy, Bryers and Walker, 1905), 3. 472–73.

with hime ~~and I wish you will your Selfe~~ whoe will adrese himselfe
to you, and I wish May bee favorablie dealt with

**Letter 223. August 11, 1671, [London], the Duchess of Ormonde
to Captain George Mathew** (NLI, Ormond Papers, 2503, no. 74).[781]
Autograph.
For My Brother Captane Gorge Mathews [/] thes. [Endorsed]: My
Ladyes dated 11 received 19 August 1671.

The 11 of Agust

[I have] accordinge unto your desier° in your Leter of the 26 of the
[Last Month] dated from Clonmell* perusede My Sonn Arrans*
Leter unto you [and your answar] of it to hime with That other of
mr Hartstongs,[782] which gave mee [Niede° to] discourse with My
Sonn about it; as I did at Large, and found hime [soe] right convinst
of his Fault that upon what wass misrepresented to [hime] hee
should have givene creditt unto it soe farr as to have Charged [you
in a] soe unkind and unfrindlie Manner (as hee did) when he Now
Sees [that what] hee accusede you of is deniede by mr Hartstronge
under his [hand soe as] I am sartane° you will reseve° Satisfactione
from himselfe and therfor Leaves mee noe more to Say; but to
intreate you to Excuse what is past sense° I hope you shall Never
find from anye of Mine the [like] misunderstandinge; My Lord is
resolvede to part with noe more [Mony°] unto mr Martine* untell°
the Sute° bee determinede betwixt his Mother and hime though
this Gentellmans wants makes hime very importunate [/] [It is] a
great Comfort to mee as thes Times are; that by your Industrye the
remaynder of My Lords Mony is Like to come in, or at the Least
to bee securede which menes° hee willnot bee Nesesited to have
anye thinge to doe with [the New] governor,[783] or anye favour to
desier of hime; the Controwler [dous° advise] the Sellinge ofe° such
a Nomber of the Sheepe at Dunmore* beyond what the Land now
kept for that uss° cane well Feede and [if you] doe aprove therof I
desier that you will order hime to Sell them [as Soune°] as hee Cane;
therwas a strange paper the other day delivrede [to the kinge] by
one Pursell, Sonn to Philipe Pursell of Balyfoyle* Hee [demanded]

---

[781] There is significant wear to the MS. Text is missing all the way along the left margin of the first page and the right margin of the second page. Words have been supplied using the context.
[782] Unidentified.
[783] Lord Lieutenant Berkeley.

that this Magesty would command My Lord to give hime Backe his
Famlie a plase called killcolindoufe or Else hee vouede in this [plase]   *vowed*
that hee would Ether kill or Pistole My Lord, wherupon the [king
ordered] for the Lord Arlington* to have this Fellow committed,
but what [willbee] don° with hime I cannot tell, this hapninge the
day that My Lord and I came hether to the Lord of Allsberyes⁷⁸⁴
House [when] wee reseved° this accompt° sent My Lord from my
Sonn Ossory* [whoe] was presant with the kinge when this paper
was givene hime [Hee] Named Nothinge of the Estate that the
Souldiers° and adventurers [claimed] but this inconsiderable Farme
that is in My Lords possestion [the vallew°] of which I desier to bee
informed of, and upon what Termes [My] Lord dous holde it, Not
that it is intended that hee shall bee [rewarded] for his Rantinge but
for our perticuler Satisfactione for [*missing*] knew that it had Ever
belonged unto his Familie; a Nother° perticular may bee Nesesarye to
know, whether this yonge Mans Father [was] not a Plunderer of the
English at kilkinye the first yeare of [rebellion]⁷⁸⁵ which I doe beleve
that Olliver whieller* cane tell if hee [*missing*] [/] The tow° Bills of
Exchange charged upon one in Southaricke came to My hands Just   *Southwark*
as I was goeinge into my Coche° to come hether and was delivrede
by mee unto James Clark*s hands soe as you Shall reseve a further
accompt of them by tomoroghs post

**Letter 224. August 26, 1671, [London], the Duchess of Ormonde
to Captain George Mathew** (NLI, Ormond Papers, 2503, no. 75).
Autograph.
For My Brother Captane Gorge Mathews [/] thes. [Endorsed]: My
Ladyes dated 26 August received 7 September 1671 about Lord John
and rent mony most received of Sir William.

The 26 of Agust
you will reseve° an accompt° of the ressept of the Severall Bills of
Exchange you Sent Last from James Clarke* and of Ther beinge
acsepted, as you will from Sir Gorge Layne* of the widow that was;
of one Hackett,* that is at the presant Mariede unto a Nother,°
and intends to goe for Ireland; Soe as That bussenes° which you
mentioned to bee in some dout,° willbee soune° Clearede when Shee

---

⁷⁸⁴ Robert Bruce, first Earl of Ailesbury. See T. F. Henderson, "Bruce, Robert, second earl of Elgin and first earl of Ailesbury (*bap.* 1626, *d.* 1685)," rev. Victor Stater, *ODNB*.

⁷⁸⁵ 1641 rebellion.

comes Ther hir Selfe; your Last Leter unto My Lord gives mee some
resone° to beleve, that this ~~Leter~~ will find you at Dublin, made mee
willinge you Should See what I have writene unto My Sone John,*
what Effects it will have upon hime I know not; but doe feare but
Litell;° however when you have read it I desier° that you will Seale
and gett it sayflie° delivered by what hand you shall think Fitt; in
a Late Leter I mentioned to you the Letinge of the Priswins° and
raysinge advanse mony° of the halfe yeares Rent out of Them, not
rememberinge, that My Lord had Sett them allredie unto Sir william
Bucknell* the remaynder of whous Rent from the Time hee touck
them ~~beinge~~ ^will^ as I take it become dew° at Mickellmes° Next,
soe as if you could returne it over hether by Bills upon resonable
Termes wouldbee very convenent for My Lords ocations° untell°
the rest of his Rents Canbee gottene In or that wee cane make anye
agrement ~~to prevayle~~ with hime to pay it heare, which Last shallbee
indevored° I have not as yet disposede of the thirtye Pound for to
Satisfie My Sone Johns dept,° but intend to doe, I hope the Changes
heare by New Leters and orders Sent from the kinge willnot hinder
My Lord from resevinge° the remaynder of his Mony, which if onse°
Secure, wouldnot only free hime of Soe much dept but of haveinge
anye thinge to doe with the Chife° Governor which Last good
Fortune, as well as the former, is much wisht by

> your affectionat Sister
>
> E:ormonde

**Letter 225. September 5, 1671, [London], the Duchess of Ormonde
to Captain George Mathew** (NLI, Ormond Papers, 2503, no. 76).
Autograph.
For My Brother Captane Gorge Mathews [/] thes. [Endorsed]: My
Lady Dutchess dated 5 received 20 September 1671 about Lady
Ossory brought bed.

> The 5 of September

The Good fortune that is has pleased God to Send Mee this day by
My daghter Ossorys* beinge this Morninge broght to Bed of a Sone
(Large) and Like to Live,[786] has put all other bussenes° soe much

---

[786] Charles Butler (1671–1758) would become second earl of Arran and third titular Duke of Ormond. Éamonn Ó Ciardha, "Butler, Charles 2nd earl of Arran 3rd duke of Ormond," *DIB*, suggests that Charles was born in Dublin, but this must not be the case. EO must have attended her grandson's birth.

out of My head, as I must defer writinge upon anye other Subgect
untell° by the Next Post, The kinge has invited himselfe to bee the
Godfather, soe as this Childe is Like to bee the first Charles that
has bine° of his Familie [/] The Lord Liftenant went for Ireland
yesterday; Sir Ralphe Freeman* whoe went hense the Last weeke
made great acknowlegments of your Sevilites° to hime; whoe if I bee
not mistakene is a very honnest Gentellman and will desarve it from
you

**Letter 226. September 23, 1671, [London], the Duchess of
Ormonde to Captain George Mathew** (NLI, Ormond Papers, 2503,
no. 77). Autograph.
For My Brother Captane Gorge Mathews [/] thes.

Brother   The 23 of September

I send you hearinclosed a Leter[787] from My Lady Fouskies
daughter[788] unto My Sone Osorye* by which I find resone° to beleve
that hir Father in Law and hir selfe are agreade sense° Shee desiers°   *agreed*
that the Intrest of the Mony° Lent by hir Mother and dew° sense
May 1670 may bee payede for hir uss° unto Sir Thomas Foskye[789]
which if you ~~Find to~~ bee ~~Soe~~ ^of the same oppinon^ and This Leter a
Suffisent othoritiye° to discharge My Lord I think the payment were
best to bee accordingly [/] The widow Hackett* (that was,) cannot
by resone of hir ill health goe over time Enough to bee in Irland by
the Time that you have prefixt, but willbee by Cristmas if Shee Lives
Soe Longe; and suffisentlie prove all that you cane Expect from hir,
James Clarke* is at the presant attendinge My Lord at Newmarket,*
where hee is Like to Staye this 3 weekes; soe as I dout° you Cane
hardlie reseve° what you desier consarninge° a Note of his ressepts° of
Bills from you sense ~~the~~ 1670 untell° his returne, unles I Cane send
it you out of the Extract of The Booke of his ressepts which I kiepe°
acknowledgd under his owne hand and That I will Examine and
Send you an accompt,° all though I dout not but what you kiepe your
Selfe is ~~asExczatt~~ ^soc^ Exzact;° as you Niede° noe other, more then
to Satisfie you that Both agrees, I know not what to say to you in the

---

[787] The enclosure is not preserved.
[788] Possibly the daughter of Sydney, Lady Fortescue. See John Burke, *A Genealogical
and Heraldic Dictionary of the Peerage and Baronetage of the British Empire*, 6th edn (London: Burke's Peerage, 1839), 424.
[789] Sir Thomas Fortescue (d. 1710), Knight of Dromiskin Castle, Co. Louth, son of
Sir Faithful Fortescue (c. 1581–1666).

perticuler of the Stope° that is made in the payment of My Lords
Mony the affares of the Excheker beinge soe Changed by the Lord
of Ranelaghs* prosidings° and Progects as I Cannot tell you what a
Confutione it has made, and will doe a much greater if things dous°   *confusion*
goe on as thay° begine, but I supose my Lord will give you ~~more~~ ^a
beter°^ information then I cane how you are to proside° ~~in~~ at the
presant in that affare of his; I pray remember mee to My Sister and
asshure° your Selfe of my beinge

        your affectionat Sister

          E:ormonde

I heare nothinge as yet of the Sayle of the Sheepe nor woole which if
~~dispo~~ Sould° wouldbee Convenient in Many respects

**Letter 227. October 3, 1671, [London], the Duchess of Ormonde
to Captain George Mathew** (NLI, Ormond Papers, 2503, no. 79).
Autograph.
For My Brother Captane Gorge Mathews [/] thes. [Endorsed]: My
Ladyes 3 / 11 October 1671 about Walter Archer.

        The 3 of Oct

I writ unto you formerlie consarninge° mr wallter Archer* whoe
I doe supose has by this time made his applicatione unto you for
allowanse as others has had upon forfetide° Morgedges which is his
cayse,° and therfor I pray Let ~~asshure~~ hime bee as favorablie dealt
withall in that Perticuler as anye other has bine,° by resone° hee did
with the first deliver upe his writings, and Let mee know when, and
upon what termes you have concluded with hime; My Lord is still
at Newmarket* where the kinge intends to Stay untell° the Ende of
this Month, I know I niede° not desier° you to hastene over Bills of
Exchange Sense° you are your Selfe soe Carfull to doe it upon the
best Termes when Monys° dous° Come in, I wish you could informe
mee when the Sheepe and woole ~~wouldbee~~ ^willbee^ Sould° which if
thay° could bee put ofe,° wouldbee convenient for My ocations°

Letter 228. October 14, 1671, [London], the Duchess of Ormonde to Captain George Mathew (NLI, Ormond Papers, 2503, no. 80). Autograph.
For My Brother Captane Gorge Mathews [/] thes. [Endorsed]: My Ladyes 14 / 20 October 1671 about Parsells lands et cetera.

The 14 of Oct

Sense mr welch* is recovrede My Lord bid mee tell you whoe is himselfe still at Newmarket,* that hee thinks it shouldbee his worke to Call to Mind how the Parsells° of Lands mentioned in the Note you Sent, came into his Clame° and whye a certificate and Patent did not Follow such allowanse; sense° if hee bee not much mistakene hee beleves mr welch tould hime that Shanballyduff was Clearlie his and that therwas good Evedense to prove it, but not as his olde Estate, for as to That, hee toucke° out nether patent nor certificate as hee remembers [/] My Lord ~~bids mee tell you that hee~~ ^dous° allow and^ is Content with the Bargine you made with mr kely of Arighme* and will make it Good; The inteligense you resevede° of My Lord Ranelaghs* arivall with the Lord Liftenant in Ireland you know by this time is Not true;[790] nor dous My Lord beleve, that anye thinge cane bee done to gett acquitanses° untell° the Treatie with the Lord Angers* bee at an Ende, which Shure° must bee very Soune;° if it bee intended that his contract shall goe on, or that anye payments shallbee made in Ireland

Letter 229. December 2, 1671, [London], the Duchess of Ormonde to Captain George Mathew (NLI, Ormond Papers, 2503, no. 81). Autograph.
For My Brother Captane Gorge Mathews [/] thes. [Endorsed]: My Ladyes dated 2 received 18 December 1671 about Dunmore and lett accates and stocke et cetera.

The 2 of Des

My ill health has of Late hindered mee from ansaringe° of your Leters, which continows° still by a Coughe which kiepes° mee a prissoner to my chamber; though with Some hopes of beinge beter,° it deminishinge within this few days [/] I confes I doe a Litell° wonder *diminishing*
that what the Controwler did himselfe move; as what he consevede°

---

[790] Berkeley had been absent from Ireland from June to September 1671 while he had been attending the King at court. See John Gibney, "Berkeley, Sir John 1st Baron Berkeley of Stratton," *DIB*.

to bee Convenient that Part of the Stocke of Dunmore* shouldbee
Sould° that my derections° beinge for it; the Season shouldbee
Pass and That not don,° nor the woole Solde or anye Mony°
returned for the Accats though it was promist when hee came to
Dublin, but posiblie the Care of his owne consernes° in Maters° of
that kind has Slaknede his indevours° in that of Mine, for I   *slackened*
plenlie diserne by Effects the diferanse betwixt the Manadgment   *plainly*
of thous° affares when thay° were in mr Brians* hands and how thay
are Now; Soe as I am Not without Some thoughts if you aprove
therof and will assist mee in it to Sell ofe° all My Stocke when the
time of the yeare is fitt for it, and Let the Land; and take Mony
for the Accats yearlie, untell° wee come over our Selfs; Sir Gorge
Lane* has undertakene to gett such a Seale made as you desier° of
My Lords Armes; which Soe Soune° as it is done shallbee Sent you;
but hee is Soe Scrupelous in Sendinge your writings, as hee willnot   *scrupulous*
venture them by anye Person but such a one as you Shall Name,
and derect° hime to deliver them To; which you may Ether to the
Lord Angers* or Sir Arthur Forbus; I pray Let Mee know when you
think you Shallbee abble to returne more Mony out of My Lords
^Mickellmas°^ Rents and to what Proportione that our bussenes°
heare may bee orderede accordinglie

**Letter 230. February 3, 1671/2, [London], the Duchess of Ormonde
to Captain George Mathew** (NLI, Ormond Papers, 2503, no. 82).
Autograph.
For My Brother Captane Mathews [/] thes. [Endorsed]: My Lady 3
February 1671 Trotter.

Trotter* the Paynter haveinge bine° with mee has givene mee an
accompt° of what worke hee has done ^Finisht^ at kilkenye* and
Dunmore* and has resevede° My instroctions what is further to
bee done by hime in Both Plasses,° whoe beinge Now acquanted
in the Contyre, and haveinge some knowlege Arch in Maters° of
Buildinge and consequentlie may prove ussfull unto the Controwler
in assistinge thous towards thous° repayres in Both Housses that
theris a presant Nesesitie for, to prevent a greater Charge and
inconveniensie I have Entertanede ^hime^ for a Nother° yeare; and
givene hime derections° to Show you what order I have givene hime
as to what hee is Now to begine upon; whous Sallarye I desier° may
bee Continowede° unto hime, and payede as formerlie out of the
Profitts of My woole and Stocke; which is increast unto what poure°
Mounsiuier le Grand* had, whoe is not Like to Live many howers°

and has Left mee his Hiere, therwas a years woole dew° to hime or More of which I supose Luke Archer* can give some accompt

The 3 of Feb

Letter 231. February 10, [1671/2], London, the Duchess of Ormonde to Captain George Mathew (NLI, Ormond Papers, 2503, no. 83).⁷⁹¹ Autograph.
For My Brother Captane Mathews [/] thes. [Endorsed]: The Dutchess of Ormond London 10 February.

London the 10 of Feb

It beinge not posible [yet] for my Lord to prefixe what Month to goe into Irland though I doe conclude it must bee this next Sommer, and that wee have noe Longer ^the^ usse of My Lord St Allbans Goods, then to the Last of March, I have bine° advised to Send over for 3 of the Diepe ~~Sutes of~~ ^Sutes° of^ Hangings at killkenye, to uss° heare, whilst I staye, and to bringe them Backe when I come; rather then ~~beeinge~~ bee at the Charge of buyinge soe Large ons° heare, which will cost a great deale of Mony;° when I came from kilkenye;* I Left tow° Boxes of Sillver Conses in the Rome° where My Lords writings are Now kept, 4 payre of Large ons with Tope peeses and dubell Seockets; and 4 payre more of a Lesser Sort with duble Seockets without Topes all which; I desier° may bee put in to a Stronge deayle⁷⁹² Cayse,° and sent to Dublin unto Captane Baxter,* whoe has order to send them; and the Caysess° of Hangings over to Mee; the Plate is intended to bee Changed; for what willbee more ussfull I pray hastene your derections° for the Sendinge them with all spiede° with the white damaske Curtans that are Mentioned in Lows⁷⁹³ Note [to bee] Seourede heare and [*three words missing*] anye where else and that vallantine Smith* [enter into] the Invntory or in some Boouke besides, what is Sent over, that ther may bee noe dispute upon accompt° ^Ther^ with hime whoe has the Charge of the Goods, I am I thank God soe much beter° then I was, as I have ventered° abrode° the Last weeke in My Cheare,⁷⁹⁴ and not bine the worse for it; and shall attempt it, as oftene agayne° as a warme day will incoridge° mee

sconces
pair(s)

inventory

---

⁷⁹¹ A tear on top of the leaf has obliterated two or three words on each of the first two lines on the second page.
⁷⁹² "As a kind of timber: The wood of fir or pine" ("deal, n.3," 2, *OED*).
⁷⁹³ Unidentified.
⁷⁹⁴ "A chariot or car" ("chair, *n*.2," *OED*).

Letter 232. February 17, 1671/2, [London], the Duchess of Ormonde to Captain George Mathew (NLI, Ormond Papers, 2503, no. 84). Autograph.
[Endorsed]: My Lady February 17 1671 Walter Archer.

Brother   The 17 of Feb

I resevede° the Last weeke a Leter from mr wallter Archer* complayninge; that after mr John Wellches* report of his Cayse° you offerede hime only a Third part of his Morgadge,° wheras hee urges that 2 parts has bine° givene unto others, whoe did not soe timelie nor soe willinglie give upe his writings as hee did; and therfor Expected more favour, which at his goeinge from hense I promist hime, Ecquall unto ~~wh~~ the most that other Morgedges had; which hee alledges was to Some Persons in the same condistione the allowanse of 2 parts which I wish hime the benifitt of; and will imploye all my Intrest with my Lord to procure for hime; and to Send you an othoritie° to conclude with hime upon thes Termes; hee ~~takinge his payment a~~ allowinge such a competent Time for the payment therof, as you and hee shall agree; and if this doe not Sattisfie I shall hould° my Selfe obsalved from prosiding° further in   *absolved* his behalfe; ~~there Leavinge~~ ^but Leave^ hime to take what other Course hee pleases, wherfor I desier° that when you have spokene agayne° with this gentellman, ~~you will~~ and acquanted hime with the Contents of this, if you thinke it fitt (not otherwiss) that you will then returne ~~mee~~ his answar unto

      your affectionat Sister

       E:ormonde

Letter 233. February 20, 1671/2, [London], the Duchess of Ormonde to Captain George Mathew (NLI, Ormond Papers, 2503, no. 85). Autograph.
For your Selfe. [Endorsed]: My Lady 20 ffebruary 1671 Lord John.

            The 20 of Feb

I doutnot but you heare that My Sonn Ossorye* has takene the command of a Shipe,[795] and that My Sone Arran* goes Likwise to Sea with the Duke[796] whous hazards is the more uneasie to Mee;

---

[795] Ossory was appointed captain of the *Resolution* in January 1672. See J. D. Davies, "Butler, Thomas, sixth earl of Ossory (1634–1680)," *ODNB*.

[796] James, Duke of York (1633–1701), later King James II.

that my thirde Sone⁷⁹⁷ whoe is in greater Securitie then the rest, dous° live soe Scandelouslie and soe unprofitablie unto himeselfe, as is a great afflictione unto his Frinds, I am tould that hee is much givene to drinkinge and to the kiepinge° of the worst Companye, that hee has very ill Sarvants and is Extremlie Cheated by them, is very much indepted° at Dublin as well as heare, soe as it is a~ great trouble to My Lord and I ^Strange^ to See that soe good an allowanse as he has from his Anewetie° and Entertainment is Soe ill Manadged by his Extravaganse and Expense as not to afford hime a desent Mantenanse, and to observe hime Soe Litell° regarded in the world as noe body dous or Cane commend hime for anye one good qualitie, I pray deale freelie with Mee and Let mee know whether you think ther bee anye thinge that Canbee done by his Frinds heare [illegible] the [illegible] of hime and⁷⁹⁸ whoe it is, if anye Sober person therbee that has anye Credit with hime, your Selfe or anye other of our relations or Frinds that might bee made uss° of to Laye befor hime the disadvantages of his course of Life and how it has Lessened hime in the worlds Estime as well as in that of his Parents whoe are very Sensible and asshamed of his Faults (though hee is Not) My Lord bid mee to desier° you to gett from hime an accompt° of all his depts° Ther and heare, for hee beleves that My Sonn Johns* Leavinge mr Osborne* to doe what hee pleased with his Mony° without Ever takinge anye accompt from hime or requiringe anye in that of the Manadgment of the Pay of the Troupe has bine° a Loss unto Many Persons and to ^himselfe and to Persons besides as well as to^ Severall of My Lords Gentellmen;

Letter 234. February 20, 1671/2, [London], the Duchess of Ormonde to Captain George Mathew (NLI, Ormond Papers, 2503, no. 86). Autograph.
For My Brother Captane Gorge Mathews [/] thes. [Endorsed]: My Ladys 26 ffebruary 1671 Lord John.

The 20 of Feb

I Showede My Lord this inclosede, whoe advises, that you should as from your Selfe in kindnes unto My Sonn John* Show hime this Leter but not Send it hime, and from it to grownd° your discourse and advise unto hime, and accordinge as hee reseves° it, to Let

---

⁷⁹⁷ Lord John.
⁷⁹⁸ Two words cannot be discerned under strikethroughs so heavy that they almost tear the paper.

uss know what your oppinion is of hime, and what hee dous° for the future propose unto himselfe, I supose you heare the generall discourse that is of the Earle of Essexe* beinge to goe over Lord Liftenant which though it has not bine° as yet publicklie declared by the kinge yet it is generalie beleved that hee willbee the Person Chossen,⁷⁹⁹ whoe beinge Soe temperate and prudent as hee is Sayede° to bee; will give Soe good Example as My Sonn John will have very Litell° resone° to beleve that hee cane have Creditt or Intrest in his Lordshipps Favour if hee Continows° to Live as hee dous; Theris a Person mr Redinge⁸⁰⁰ that pretends hee has a great intemasie with ~~hime~~ Jacke⁸⁰¹ but I hope has not, for theris not a More worthles nor unfitt Companione ~~livinge~~ for a Man of honner° liveinge then himselfe, and soe is reputed by all the world that knows hime and a Spie, for thes New undertakers; but this Caracture° I thought beter° to tell you, then write it to my Sonn, ~~of~~ ^to^ whom you may in discourse give ~~hime~~ some cautione ~~of~~ conseringe° hime

intimacy

Letter 235. February 24, [1671/2], [London], the Duchess of Ormonde to Captain George Mathew (NLI, Ormond Papers, 2503, no. 87). Autograph.
For My Brother Captane Gorge Mathews [/] thes. [Endorsed]: My Ladys.

The Post which came on wedensday Last broght mee a Leter from you of the 3 of this Month dated from kilkeny* together with Baxters* accompts° signede by hime the 2 of the Same; to ballanse which, and to reimburse the 300 that was returned mee ther appiers therby dew° only 127:7.1 though your Leter charges hime with 140 towards it, besides 67 reseved° for Accates and twentye Pound more from mr Briane;* soe as the differanse betwixt Baxters accompt and what you doe mentione I thought fitt to Let you know, that at your Lesure you may the beter° ajust it betwixt you, I doe aprove of what you propose as to the giveinge over the plowing at Dunmore* but befor it bee Layede a Side; it is My Lords desier° and Mine To;° that the Grownds° Neare unto the House shouldbee Leveled and the way that Leads straght upe unto the Hous if it bee posible to bee done

balance

---

⁷⁹⁹ Arthur Capel, Earl of Essex (1631–1683), would be appointed Lord Lieutenant on May 21, 1672, succeeding Berkeley.
⁸⁰⁰ Unidentified.
⁸⁰¹ An informal name for John, this is the only time EO uses it in reference to her youngest son.

and I shall consent hensforwarde that the Profitts of the Plase shall
Pay the Expense of it without charginge my Lords accompts therwith
[/] I perseve° the woole is upon Sayle which I hope will more then
Cleare what is behind of the 300 Pound dept° besides mr le grands*
Proportione which I am now intyteled° unto as allsoe unto his Stocke
which it willbee requisit shouldbee accompted° for and added unto
Mine [/] I desier allsoe, that when the Season of the yeare is proper
for it, that you will give order unto Baxter to Sell as many of the
wethers as are Fitt to be parted with and will yeald Mony,° for I have
some Juells° which I did ingadge° to pay the Intrest of My Lords
depts which Nether Hee nor I have bine° sense° abbell to redime,° I
have Louked° over the accompt you Sent mee of the Sarvants wayges
and doe aprove of the abaytment unless That of william Sestions*
[*two words illegible*] whoe havinge soe considerable a charge to Louke
after; as all the Goods; and than non° of his abbilitie will Sarve for
[*illegible*]⁸⁰² for Soe litell° consideringe that hee Finds himselfe, I am
of oppinion if hee bee not remiss or faultie in his imployment that
hee Shouldbee still retaynede upon the Termes as formerlie, I doe
hope My Last Leter consarninge° My Sonn John* will find you at
Dublin of whom I doe very much desier to heare; though I feare it
willnot bee such an accompt of his Livinge beter, as will give mee
anye Content, I cane send Noe derections° consarninge the Gardener
at kilkenye* to Curbe his Expense hearinge Nothinge Ether from
you or Baxter of the perticulers, but have writene to hime to send
mee word what hee dous° Now that the plantinge worke is over, and
how the Gardines are kepe, I have Sent for 2 Sutes° of Hangings of
Forest worke⁸⁰³ and one Peartia Carpett that would Cost to much   Persia(n)
to buye; and wee have ocatione° for heare; and May bee sparede
from Thense in our absense without disfurnishinge the best Romes,°
which I desier may bee Enterede ^when sent^ in the Margent of the
Inventorye Bouke° that is Left ther, and I shall doe the Like in That
which I have heare Soe Soune° as I reseve° Them to prevent anye
Mistake;

The 24 of Feb

---

⁸⁰² The illegible words are obscured by binding tape.
⁸⁰³ "a decorative representation of sylvan scenery" ("forest-work," in "forest, *n.*," *OED*).

Letter 236. April 9, [1672], [London], the Duchess of Ormonde to Captain George Mathew (NLI, Ormond Papers, 2503, no. 88). Autograph.
For My Brother Captane Gorge Mathews.

The 9 of Aprell

I doe very much wish that mr wallter Archer* may bee agreede with upon the termes that I Last Mentioned to you which was for the one halfe of his morgadge° sense° I promist hime that he Shouldbee as favorablie dealt with as anye other in his Condistione whoe I find by the copie of the Morgadgies° you Latlie° Sent over were allowede the one halfe; I have upon your Expectatione to reseve° Mony° from mr Briane* Charged a bill for 3 hundreth :pound upon you and 30 for the Exchange which you are not to ~~charge~~ ^Plase^ upon My Lords accompt° but Mine; hee haveinge allowed mee That, towards the rediminge° of My Juells° which were ingadged° to paye the Intrest Mony of Moore Parke* befor it was Solde; I find the Steward has sould° 600 of the Sheepe at Dunmore* for which hee is to reseve 200 the first of June, and intends to sell ofe° 500 more ^which I doe aprove of^ ther beinge noe wast° Land; and the increase beinge Likelie otherwiss to overstocke the Grownd° ~~which I doe aprove of~~ I have made inquirye after mr Butler of Banshaws Sone[804] and I doe not heare of anye but his Eldest that diede heare; haveinge Loukede° over the Seduell° of the Morgedges I find the inclosede returnede in that Paper as Payede; and if Soe, mr wallter Archer has but Litell° to Challenge unles therbee some mistake in it; I am Sorrye the Marchand° is fallene ofe from his bargine for the woole; it beinge some disapoyntment to Mee, and I feare the Duch warr will hinder the rest from beinge Sould ~~offe to for all~~, James Clarke* beinge Sent upon some ocatione° out of Towne, I thought fitt to acquant you that the above mentioned Bill is to bee payede at 10 days Sight unto mr Peirse Reeves[805] mr Lindsays* Corespondant

---

[804] Unidentified.
[805] Unidentified.

Letter 237. April 20, 1672, [London], the Duchess of Ormonde to Captain George Mathew (NLI, Ormond Papers, 2503, no. 90).
Autograph.
For My Brother Captane Gorge Mathews [/] thes. [Endorsed]: My Ladyes 20 / 29 April 1672.

The 20 of Aprell

Mr James Briane[806] sent mee this inclosed, which I doe heare returne, and acquant you with what further favour My Lord and I are willinge to doe hime upon his Fathers accompt° whoe was Ever a fathfull Person unto My Lord and all our Familie and one that I had a perticuler regard For haveinge found hime Frindlie to mee, in Times when Few appiered° Soe, and therfor wee Both are willinge to ade° 10 years more unto his Lease; which you may Let hime know (if you please) that you have resevede° derections° For hee knowinge nothinge of this intended Curtisie° to hime nor shallnot by anye other way then by you; Theris one Mistris Cavenagh;[807] daghter unto the widow Archer,[808] whoe has sent My Lord a Petistione that in regard of hir relatione and great Charge shee might bee continowed° in the Farme that hir Mother had upon the same Termes, which is Not thought resonable, but to Let hir bee Ther untell° shee ~~Canbee~~ Cane provide otherwise for hir Selfe, at a more Easie Rent then a Nother° would give soe that shee may bee sensible that theris a Curtisie done hir in That, and soe bee quit of hir afterwards I think willbee the best Course in that perticuler, My Lord beinge of the same opinione

Letter 238. May 7, 1672, [London], the Duchess of Ormonde to Captain George Mathew (NLI, Ormond Papers, 2503, no. 91).
Autograph.
For My Brother Captane Gorge Mathews [/] thes. [Endorsed]: My Lady Dutches about Ill bargaines 7 May 1672.

The 7 of May

you will very soune° reseve° a List of the Table of Fees Establisht in the Countye Palatine[809] Courts heare, which will I hope bee of some

---

[806] John Brian's son.
[807] Unidentified.
[808] Unidentified.
[809] "designating a county or other territory in England (and later in Ireland and other countries) of which the earl or lord originally had royal privileges, with the right

uss° unto you to forme and regulate That of Tiperarye, which as it is
now; ocations° a great Charge unto My Lord, farr above the Profitts
of it; I was as Ignorant of the bargine My Lord made with mr
Dwyer[810] for the Lands of Balacomishe as I was of that of Nenagh
but I shall hensforward bee more wachfull which I thought I nieded°
the Less bee when I had my Lords promiss after the Last mentioned
Cheate that was put upon hime that Hee would not ingadge°
himselfe anye more in things of that kind without acquantinge Mee;
which it simes° hee did forgett, haveinge ~~greater~~ ^other^ things to
think on, it has allways bine° my oppinione and I find it to bee his
To, that where ever theris anye pretentione; that you should rather
Commpound and agree with the Persons Ther, then that thay°
shouldbee Left to solisset My Lord, ^heare^ and that in Cayse° you
should Light upon anye perticuler Person ^~~heare~~^ that wouldnot
Consent to Resone° when it is offered hime, that My Lord may then
bee made acquanted with the state ^ther^ of the Cayse, wherby ther
applicatione may bee regected if thay should come over themselfs, I
had a Leter from mr walter Archer,* whoe I find is ~~rather~~ unsatisfiede
with the Length of Time takene for the payment of the halfe of his
Morgadge° though how to deale otherwiss with hime I feare willbee
very difficult ~~to doe~~ by resone of the Severall payments that you are
otherwiss to make, and the Bad comminge in of The Rents, though
as farr as hee couldbee complyede with in regard of his presant
Nesesities (I wish) sense° I know noe Pretender Now but himselfe of
anye consideratione but is Satisfiede; therfor I pray when hee comes
to you agayne,° See what you Cane doe to Ende that bussenes,° I was
allways apprehendsive that Milo Powers* want of understandinge his
owne affares would doe himselfe and others wronge; yet if you Cane
bringe hime out of hazard I pray doe; for how ever hee has ordered
his bussenes I am Confident Hee Menes° honestlie; I find my Lord
very unwillinge to Medell with what is advisede consarninge° the
Tythes,° but Soe Litell° a Time hee had to Consider of ~~that~~ what
you Mentioned Consarninge it, by resone of the Sudane° Command
hee resevede° to goe to Porchmoth ther to attend the kinge (and   *Portsmouth*
kiepe° his Table) where hee Now is, as you shall know at this returne
^but Cannot Souner°^ what his ~~resolutione~~ ^oppinione^ is, in that
perticuler; Ther Shallbee Nothinge concluded with mr Lindsye* but
what you Shall aprove of, nor with anye other without makinge you
first acquanted with it; I think it beter° to defer the settinge of the

---

of exclusive civil and criminal jurisdiction within that territory" ("palatine, *adj.¹* and *n.¹*,"
A, I, 1, *OED*).
    [810] Unidentified.

walled grownd° at Dublin⁸¹¹ untell° you doe take a veue° of it your
Selfe then to proside° further therin, sense a plase Soe well Fenst   *fenced*
and Planted with Frute Trees as that is, may questionles yealde
Somthinge were it Let but from yeare to yeare, and I doe beleve is
imployede to gardininge or Such Like uss, or at the Least might bee
if it were Louked° after, The Steward tould mee ther might bee more
of the Sheepe Parted with; then the 5 hundreth that hee had Sould°
[/] if Soe I intreate you to give hime some derections° about that and
the Sellinge of the woole; and to ~~take an~~ ^requier°^ an accompt° of
the Accats that willbee Now dew°

**Letter 239. May 18, 1672, [London], the Duchess of Ormonde to
Captain George Mathew (NLI, Ormond Papers, 2503, no. 92).**
Autograph.
For My Brother Captane Mathews [/] thes. [Endorsed]: My Lady
dated 18 received 27 May 1672 about Lord John and osborne and
whites debts.

The 18 of M[a]y
you will reseve° by this Post My Lords answar unto your Leter of
the 1 of May in all the perticulers therin Mentioned; I had a Leter
yesterday from My Sonn John* whoe denies himselfe Gilltie of
havinge dealt ill with mr Osborne,* but Charges the gentellman
of havinge wronged hime, whous Fault had bine° fitter for hime to
have proved when hee was upon the Plase (as sartanlie° hee might) if
his Cheats were soe apparent as My Sone alledges them to bee, and
convinst others allsoe of ther beinge Soe, then for want of Loukinge°
beter° into his accompts° or intrustinge some knowinge Frind to
doe it, ~~has~~ ^have^ given a disadvantage aganst himselfe which I doe
asshure° you is, and willbee much agravated to his prejudis; Hee has
promist to Send mee over a List of his depts° both in Ireland and
heare soe soune° as you come to Dublin which I desier° you will mind
hime of, My Lord has resevede° some Mony° heare from My Sonn
Arran* to bee deducted out of what mr Charles white⁸¹² is to Pay
for his halfe years Rent the perticuler of which Some allowede unto
mr white upon My Sonns accompt I desier may bee Sent mee, the
formar beinge Lost by hime; I pray remem^ber^ [/] mee unto My

---

⁸¹¹ An area of Dublin that is now St. Stephen's Green. It had been enclosed in 1664 by the Dublin Corporation, becoming the earliest and largest of Dublin's residential squares. See Casey, *Dublin*, 24.

⁸¹² Unidentified.

Sister, whoe Shall heare from mee by hir Sarvant whoe willbee with hir Shortlie

Letter 240. June 4, 1672, [London], the Duchess of Ormonde to Captain George Mathew (NLI, Ormond Papers, 2503, no. 93). Autograph.
For My Brother Captane Gorge Mathews [/] thes. [Endorsed]: My Lady dated 4 June 1672 received 9 at Kilkeny about Baxter et cetera.

I understand by a Leter that I resevede° from Baxter* that hee has sould° the Last years wooll at 9 shillings the Stone to bee payede the fifteenth of July but dous° not tell mee what the Some is, that it Comes unto; I wishe at your Leasure with the healpe of Luke Archer,* whoe knows the Last accompt° that mr Briane* gave when hee had the overseeinge of the Stocke that Baxter might bee accompted° with, as allsoe for such accates (as has bine° resevede sense° the Last ~~was~~ reckninge was Made, that what mony° dous remayne in his hands may bee sent mee by the same way that My Lord dous designe to have his; Both My Sons have I bless God Escapede with ther Lives in this Last Fight with the Duch [/] My Sonn Ossorye* beinge only a Litell° Brusede in both his Legs with a splinter, but it is soe Light a hurt as hee walks with it, and dous not make anye thinge of it [/] I am tould ther willbee some oltoratione in the Armye in Ireland which perhapes may make it Nesesarye for My Lord to recall My Sonn John* from thense, and to remove hime from that ill companye that hee to frequentlie Converses with and I heare besides that hee Loukes° ill; and is not well in his health, what it is that ocations° it I cannot tell but am afrade of the worst, and therfor I desier° that some inquirye may bee made after hime, and some Course takene to prevent anye daynger to his Life, or Blemish unto his Person sense his ~~Course~~ way of Liveinge cane promise Litell Sayftye,° but befor ther canbee anye thinge resolved upon as to the bringinge hime over, it must bee knowne what his depts° are, both ther and heare, that some Course may bee takene to Sattisfie his Creditors, I have Sent you a Copie of the Table of Fees of the Countye Palatine of Durham

The 4 of June

Letter 241. June 6, 1672, [London], the Duchess of Ormonde to Captain George Mathew (NLI, Ormond Papers, 2503, no. 94).
Autograph.
For My Brother Captane Gorge Mathews [/] thes. [Endorsed]: My Ladys dated 6 received 18 June 1672 advises transport mony aquant Lord John et cetera.

The 6 of June

The writinge you sent for My Lord to Signe and came inclosede in your Leter to mee of the 22 of May willbee dispacht to you by this Post; I think it wouldbee Nesesarye to have The Mony° that you designe to send over ~~to bee~~ in a redenes° to bee transported when the Convoye returnes that is to attend My Lord of Essexe* whoe purposes to bee goeinge for Ireland 3 weekes hense, and if you could the Mene° Time contrive to send this Suplye without Noyse° the more privatlie it were done the beter,° and the Securer it wouldbee; which posiblie might bee by putinge it into good Stronge Accavita Caskes, and Soe orderede; as ther might bee noe greater wayght in Each, then soe much of that sort of Drink might Ecquall, or send it Over in woole, which I beleve if sould° at Chester would quit[813] the Charge of Carringe° a Few Packs thether, and if this were aprovede of, I dout° not but mr Anderton[814] beinge the Chife° Costomer[815] wouldbee assistinge ~~unto~~ to uss, and would informe you, how the Rayts° dous° goe Ther and healpe Baxter* to Secure the Mony when it Lands, ~~but this is~~ ^This beinge^ only proposed by mee, but Left unto you to Manadge as you think best, I desier° that what Mony you cane reseve° for mee, May bee Sent with My lords;

aqua-vitae (whiskey)

---

[813] "To be equal to; to match, balance, redress" ("quit, *v.*," I, 3c, *OED*).
[814] Unidentified.
[815] Presumably, in the sense of "(The title of) a person who is responsible for the levying and collection of customs duties in a particular port, region, etc.; a person whose job is to collect such duties and prevent illegal or contraband goods from entering or leaving a country; a customs officer" ("customer, *n.*," 1, *OED*).

Letter 242. June 22, 1672, [London], the Duchess of Ormonde to Captain George Mathew (NLI, Ormond Papers, 2503, no. 96). Autograph.
For My Brother Captane Gorge Mathews [/] thes. [Endorsed]: My Lady Dutches 22 June 1672 about Erors Commission for one and to O'Keefe Lord Arlingon Knight Garter.

The 22 of June

Though the mistakes that were in the Tytells° of the Persons mentionede in the commistione simes° but Nisities yet the best Counsell heare dous° think it very Essentiall that a New commistione should bee forthwith Sent, and the Errors in the former rectifiede; otherwiss the adversarye may take great advantage, and put My Lord to More Charge and trouble; soe as the Souner° it bee returnede the beter,° the Exseptions are thes; which you will find in the inclosed, The Leter you desier° from My Lord unto mr keatinge* shallbee Sent you by the Next Post but cannot by this; ꝑ My Lord beinge gone ^to windsor^ this Morninge very Earlie, unto the Enstolment[816] of My Lord Arlington* whoe is made knight of the Garter, the Like honnor the kinge declarede My Sone Ossorye* should have when the Next vacansie should hapene; which Promiss Hee made in Publick upon Teusday Last when the quine° and Hee did Both supe with My Sonn in his Shipe, hir Magestye haveinge a desier to See The Fleete which Shee did; and Laye in the Dukes Shipe 2 Nights, My Sonn Arran* Continows° his Command in Irland and soe dous Sir william Flower* Though the Lord of Ranelagh* did doe all that hee could by his tricks to hinder Both; I pray write freelie to Mee consarninge° My Sonn John,* and Let mee bee informede what his depts° are, that wee may consider what Course to take with hime, for I doe beleve the Troupe of Gards willbee redust° unto an ordenarye Troupe; and the Pay to bee accordinglie

niceties

queen
(Catherine of Braganza)

---

[816] "To invest with an office or dignity by seating in a stall or official seat, as the choir-stall of a canon in a cathedral, or that of a Knight of the Garter or Bath in the chapel of his order, the throne of a bishop, etc. Hence, To instate in an office, rank, etc. with the customary ceremonies or formalities" ("unstall, v.1," 1a, *OED*).

Letter 243. July 8, [1672], [London], the Duchess of Ormonde to Captain George Mathew (NLI, Ormond Papers, 2503, no. 97). Autograph.
For My Brother Captane Gorge Mathews [/] thes. [Endorsed]: My Lady Dutches Trotter against Miller. 1672.

The 8 of July

I am very glad that you have compounded with Mr Archer,* as I thought you had done with Mr kelye* allsoe but it should Sime° hee refusses to stand to anye agreement Soe as you will reseve° from My Lord some derections° in That perticuler, I send you hearinclosed some perticulers of Trotters* complaynt aganst Millan,* which Last I find the Steward dous° beleve is wronged by the other, whoe hee beleves to bee distracted, soe as I dout° his indiscretione and Pastion° may gayne° Millan, a beter° oppinione then perhapes hee desarves sense° if noe accompt° canbee givene of the Scaffalldinge Leade and Bourds that were Left when the worke was finnisht I cannot but Suspect that Millan has bine° Ether dishonest or Negligent, soe as I have sent unto Baxter* to Examine the bussenes,° and to send mee a true accompt, I have delivrede the Copie of the Fient[817] consarninge° the Tythes° unto My Lord to bee made usse of when it may bee Seasonable, My Lord is resolved to gett a Liesense from the kinge to bringe over his Mony,° sense hee offerede 10 in the hundreth for Exchange by resone° hee was unwillinge to bringe it out of the kingdom in kind, but it could not bee had upon thous° Termes, My Sonn ossorye* is still at Sea, but well I thank God and wee all doe hope and beleve that ther willbee noe ^More^ Fightinge; My Sonn Arran* goes for Ireland the Next weeke, and Sir william Flower* begines his Journye tomorogh by whom your writings are Sent; Mr Foxen* of Limbricke° whoe has allways declared himselfe a great Frind unto my Lord and to all our Familie and an opposier of such as were My Lords Enimies; do was a Sutor to become Tenant to some thirtie or fortie Ackers° of Land whether for himselfe or his Father in Law mr Bodkine* I doe not know, which hee challenges some Promis hee ^should^ have from my Lord, but says that it is sense Let unto a Nother° [/] I asshure° my selfe if it bee Soe; therwas good resone for it which I shouldbee glad to bee informed of, to Silense his importunitie in a thinge that were not convenient to bee granted hime, or if otherwiss, how wee might Complye with the desieres° of

---

[817] "A warrant addressed to the Irish Chancery for a grant under the Great Seal" ("fiant, *n.*," *OED*).

a Person that has bine Frindlie to My Lord on all ocations° as farr as hee had Power

Letter 244. July 16, 1672, [London], the Duchess of Ormonde to Captain George Mathew (NLI, Ormond Papers, 2503, no. 98). Autograph.
For My Bother [*sic*] Captane Gorge Mathews [/] thes. [Endorsed]: My Ladyes dated 16 July 1672 received 28.

The 16 of July

My Lord haveinge procurede Liesense from the kinge to have his Mony° transported not Exsidinge° 10 Thowsand Pound ^in a^ a yeare and will have the Securitie of haveinge it Broght over to Chester in the Man of warr[818] that Carryes over the Earle of Essexe,* it would bee of a great advantage unto his affares heare, if More Mony Couldbee Sent, (and the same Charge,) For then wee Could Free our Selfs of all the Materiall depts,° and bee at Ease untell° the Next Rents dous° come in, and by that Time it may bee hopede that the Exchange of mony will Fall, which in that kingdom I doe know is very difficult to bee raysede, yet if upon anye Securitie or resonable advantage a Thowsand pound more canbee procurede it wouldbee very materiall ^important^ unto My Lord at this Time to Suport the Creditt with which hee has hetherto° Livede, without the Clamore of Creditors, which few or Non° of the Nobilitie heare but are vext with and Cryede out upon for beinge ill paymasters, I have reseved° the Copie of Baxters* accompts;° and Showede My Lord what you Mentioned consarninge° the Charge of his Courts, and the accompt of his Pay and Creatione Mony,[819] which I supose hee will say somthinge of to you himselfe, for hee toulde mee hee would write this day, I pray make Seearch for My Sister Clancarthys* writings in hope thay° may bee Found amongst My Lords; for I perseve° that thay are of great importanse to hir

---

[818] "A vessel equipped for warfare; a commissioned warship belonging to the recognized navy of a country" ("man-of-war, *n.*," 2a, *OED*).
[819] "[A] regular payment made by the Crown to a peer from the time of investiture" ("creation money," in "creation, *n.*," *OED*).

Letter 245. July 20, 1672, [London], the Duchess of Ormonde to Captain George Mathew (NLI, Ormond Papers, 2503, no. 99). Autograph.
For My Brother Captane Gorge Mathews [/] thes. [Endorsed]: My Lady 20/ 31 July 1672 compound debts Lord John et cetera.[820]

The 20 of July

you will find by the inclosed which is a Coppie of My Leter unto My Sonn John,* that My Lord has intentions to have hime over, if hee doe answar by his beter° deportment, and Care to Settell his affares ~~Ther~~ what is requirede of hime by taking a ~~Course~~ ^Course^ to pay his depts° ^Ther^ wherby to stope° the Clamor of his Creditors, and have from Thense, what may Support hime heare Soe as I must intreate you to take the trouble upon you to bee assistinge to hime, in contrivinge how hee may be healpt in what I have proposed, to whom I have Commanded hime to applye himselfe, and I hope unto a beter way of Liveinge in the world then hetherto,° which if hee canbee broght unto, ther shallbee noe incoridgment° wantinge that Canbee givene ^hime^ by his Parants

Letter 246. July 22, 1672, [London], the Duchess of Ormonde to Lord John Butler (NLI, Ormond Papers, 2355, no. 3227, p. 305). Scribal copy.
[Endorsed]: Copy of my Ladys to my Lord John 22 July 1672.

The 22 of July

I have not written often to you nor should I now, fearing you as Carelesse of your friends concernement for you as you are of most other things that might deserve your Care: But however to passe by what has been your faults, Let me prevayle with you for the time to come to live in a Way of more Decency and Temperance: to be respective in paying your Attendance upon my Lord of Essex,* who is a Derserveing person, and will I am sure be such to you, and Weane *deserving* your selfe from the Conversation of the little Sort of People, or else you must never expect that persons more valuable and of greater parts will ever have an Esteeme for you, but will Judge of you according unto the Company you most converse with and the Inclinations that appeare in you either to Actions of Honor and Prudence or the Contrary. So as it will bee much in your owne power to create

---

[820] In what may be the same hand as the endorsement are doodles featuring the words "mayd," "Love," and "James."

in your selfe a Reputation becomeing your Quality, and incourage
your friends to help you out of those Debts you have contracted
here that otherwise will still confine you where you are. And if I
could receive any Assurance from you that if some Course would be
taken to sett you free here you would for the future be advised by
your friends and conforme your Selfe unto such a Course of life as
they shall thinck most honorable and Advantagious for you, I would
upon those Termes be a Sutor unto your Father to take your Debts
here upon him, and for what you owe in Ireland you must pay by
degrees, and may do it if you will ingage my Brother Mathewes* to
advise and help you in it, by compounding with your Creditors and
so lessen your Debts in a great proportion, when Accounts shall be
examined by such as Understand businesse of that Kind; And your
Creditors be glad to make considerable Abatements to be secured the
rest: Therefore I advise you to get that affaire adjusted as soone as
you can, for untill that be, there can be no thoughts of your comeing
over. And contrive how you may be supplyed from thence for your
Maintenance for you cannot reasonably expect your Debts here
should be payd and you maintaind besides, though your Diet shall
cost you nothing if you please.

**Letter 247. August 13, 1672, [London], the Duchess of Ormonde
to Captain George Mathew** (NLI, Ormond Papers, 2503, no. 103).
Autograph.
For My Brother Captane Gorge Mathews [/] thes. [Endorsed]: My
Ladyes 13 / 31 August 1672 bills 1200 from Dublin.

The 13 of Agust
your Leter in answar unto My Lady of Clonrickerds[821] Consarninge°
mr kelye* came very oppertunlie to bee Showede unto My Lord,
whoe was at that same instant, drawinge upe the State of that Cayse°
betwixt Them, by which hee willbee much healped in a Just defense
of himselfe by the informatione that you have givene hime, and the
More if you could informe hime, upon what Termes the Ansestors of
mr kelye did hould° the Maner of Ahrime, from My Grandfather,[822]
and afterwards from wallter Earle of Ormond[823] and upon what

---

[821] Probably the second wife of William Burke, seventh Earl of Clanricarde (d. 1687): Helen, daughter of Donough MacCarthy, first Earl of Clancarty, who was JO's niece by his sister Eleanor.
[822] EO's maternal grandfather, Thomas, tenth Earl of Ormonde (1531–1614).
[823] JO's paternal grandfather, Walter, eleventh Earl of Ormonde (1569–1633).

condistions, and by whom; it was givene him in fee farme[824] and in
what yeare the severall Leasses were made; by the above mentioned
Persons and the Sayle of it afterwards by My Lord; and for what
Some° hee parted with the inheritanse of it, sense That if mr kelye
bee incoridged° to make anye Complant heare, hee may appiere° as
Litell° wisse and honnest as others has bine° whoe has bine sett on
to goe the same way [/] My Lord has resevede° Bills from Dublin
for 12 hundreth pound at 10 in the hundreth which are acsepted,
and hee, more willinge to allow that; then bringe anye Mony° out of
the kingdom, howsoever it is Convenient that My Lord has that
Liesense, in Cayse that the Exchange should rise higher agayne;° I
heare My Lord Liftenant[825] is Landed, soe as I conclude you willbee
at Dublin befor it bee Longe; and then I hope to reseve° some
accompt° from you Consarninge my Sone John,*

**Letter 248. August 17, 1672, [London], the Duchess of Ormonde
to Captain George Mathew** (NLI, Ormond Papers, 2503, no. 102).
Autograph.
For My Brother Captane Gorge Mathews [/] [thes]. To bee left with
mr Luke Archer* at Kilkenny. [Endorsed]: My Lady Dutches with
Lord Johns debts 7 September 1672.

fearinge that My Sonn Johns* Negligense has bine° Such; as not
to have kept a true accompt° of his depts° heare, I have sent you
a Copie of Them,[826] which besides Neare 5 hundreth Pound
^More^ that Hee; and I have payede sense° my cominge over, ther
remayns a greater Some then perhapes hee Expects (or I did beleve)
howsoever My Lord will undertake what Them; and free hime,
upon Condistione that hee will for the future reforme himselfe in his
Maner of Livinge; and bee more Carfull of his Expense, and for his
depts Ther; I have writene unto hime to advise with you, and the rest
of his Frinds how to pay Them by degrees, out of his Entertainment
or Anewetie,° Sense wee Cannot undertake Both

The 17 of Agust

---

[824] "That kind of tenure by which land is held in fee-simple subject to a perpetual fixed rent, without any other services; the estate of the tenant in land so held; rarely, the land itself" ("fee-farm, *n.*," 1, *OED*).
[825] Essex.
[826] A list of John's debts remains with the letter amounting to 977 pounds and 11 shillings. The largest sum, 400 pounds, is due to one Mr. Temple, hosier.

Letter 249. [August 1672], [London], the Duchess of Ormonde to Captain George Mathew (NLI, Ormond Papers, 2503, no. 104[b]).
Autograph.
[Endorsed]: about Lord John.

Brother

I send you hearinclosed My Sonn Johns* Leter to mee and My answar to hime which if you doe think it fitt I shall intreate you to Seale and get it Sent, or deliver it to hime your Selfe, I am Extremlie troubled to heare how idelie hee lives, and how Litell° hee regards anye advise that is Givene hime for his Good

idly

Letter 250. August 31, 1672, [London], the Duchess of Ormonde to Captain George Mathew (NLI, Ormond Papers, 2503, no. 105).
Autograph.
For My Brother Captane Gorge Mathews [/] thes. [Endorsed]: My Ladyes 31 August 12 September 1672.

The Last of Agust

The Commistione is returned and givene into the hand of Captane Charles Fieldinge;[827] soe as I hope it will come over time Enough; but the Gentell woman mistris kiefe[828] I doe as yet, heare Nothinge of, I doe wish you were at Dublin befor My Sonn Johns* cominge over to assist hime in the Settlinge of his affares Ther, for the payment of his depts° by degrees out of his Anewetie° or Entertainment, Sense° My Lord is indevoringe° to Compound with his Creditors heare, and free hime by takinge the dept upon himselfe; I should bee glad to know what you heare mr kelye* dous° intend sense hee has ^havinge^ refusede the offiers° that you made hime; sense his thretinge to Complane hee will find not to bee the way to doe hime anye good, My Lord intends to remove his whole Familie unto the House that hee has takene redie Furnisht in Oxfordshire about the Ende of the Next Month, Mr Arthur[829] a Marchant° of good Creditt will advanse a thowsand Pound heare to bee payede in Ireland at on 31 days sight which wouldbee very convenient for my Lords ocations° Now upon his remove, but not knowinge when out of the Next Mickelmas° Rents you canbee provided to answar anye such Bill if Charged upon you I have suspended to proside° Further

threatening

---

[827] Unidentified.
[828] Unidentified.
[829] Unidentified.

untell° I doe heare from you agayne° as I desier° I may doe as unto this Perticuler as soune° as you Cane Convenintlie

Letter 251. September 7, 1672, [London], the Duchess of Ormonde to Captain George Mathew (NLI, Ormond Papers, 2503, no. 106). Autograph.
For My Brother Captane Gorge Mathews [/] thes. [Endorsed]: My Ladyes 7 / 23 September 1672.

At My Sonn Arans* desier,° My Lord has givene order unto his Counsell Mr Philips,* to draw upe a Convayanse to Settell thous° Lands upon hime accordinge unto the agreement you made; and the valuations mentioned in the Sedwell° of thous Lands that were Sent over by you some wherof beinge Sett out to hime, with the incombranses° that are upon them; takes ofe° soe much of the dept° as rested upon My Lord and therfor wouldbee Nesesarye for uss Both to know, what dous° remayne of Morgadges° and all other sorts of depts whatsowever in that kingdom, with what has bine° payede Sense° wee Left it; that wee may See what hopes theris to bee free of thous ingadgments° that has bine Soe Longe upon uss [/] I must agayne° intreate you to bee assistinge unto My Sonn John* by advisinge hime in the Settlinge of his affares ther Soe as to take some Course for the payment of his depts Ther

The 7 of Sep

Letter 252. October 15, 1672, [London], the Duchess of Ormonde to Captain George Mathew (NLI, Ormond Papers, 2503, no. 107). Autograph.
For My Brother Captane Mathews [/] thes. [Endorsed]: My Ladyes about Lord Arran Settlement et cetera a housekeeping 15 October 21 1672.

The 15 of October

My Sonn Arran* befor hee went Last over, desiringe that thous° [Lands] that were returnede and vallewede° by you, to make upe the three Thowsand pound a yeare designede for hime, might bee settled unto hime, My Lord did in persuanse therof, Intrust mr Philips* his Counsell to draw upe a Deede of convayanse unto that Effect, which upon veuinge° of the Settellment of our whole Estate with the Artickells that were at My Sonns Mariage hee couldnot perfect untell° some queries as ^that^ hee had drawne upe; and were sent over unto My Sonn Arran were answrede; consarninge° which you were at the same time made acquanted, but haveinge not heard Nor reseved° your Sense therupon as was desirede; but only an Answar as My Sonn tells mee in his Leter drawne upe by his Sarvant mr Bagett;[830] My Lord whoe was at Newmarkett* when the Leters came and willbee untell the 19 of this Month; has made some Scrupell and soe doe I allsoe; to proside° in an affare of this importanse untell wee have transmitted a Copie of My Sonns Leter ~~unto mee~~; and sent you duplicats of mr Mr [sic] Philipes his queries and mr Bagetts answer, that out of thes, and the Sedwell and valluations you Sent uss; wee may become Sattisfiede by you what may bee fitt for uss to allow or retrench befor the writings bee drawne upe; which My Lord desiers° and I Both wee beinge Ecqualie consernede;° may be hastenede to uss, as soune° as convenientlie you Cane;

    In the State of My Lords affares in Ireland relatinge unto his Fortune which was Latlie° sent over by you I find amongst the Contingent Charges That of Entertaninge Strangers, but you doe not Mentione the Plasses° where, nor how much is disburst upon that accompt,° though if you Cane without to much of trouble to you informe mee of thes tow° perticulers it is posible when My Lord shall have considered of Them hee may think it Fitt to make some redusment[831] of that Charge; It wouldbee allsoe Nesesarye, that I might know what Suplye of Mony° you have in a redenes° for My Lords presant ocations,° and at what time more may bee Expected, that wee may accomodate our ~~selfes~~ ^affares^ Ether by stayinge to reseve° Bills from Thense or Charginge ~~you with~~ ^some upon you^ if wee cane doe it upon resonable Termes [/] I obsarve the Lands morgadged° unto Sir John Tempell* in Trust for Sir John Dinglie[832] to bee mentioned in the Seduell° of thous as are to bee Settled upon my Sonn Arran, ^(but Not Rayted°[833])^ I desier to know whether hee bee to take them with the incombranse° that is upon Them or whether the dept° must still remayne upon My Lord, and when redemed; whether My Sonn Arran bee to have the inheritanse of it free, sense° that wouldbee Three ~~thowsand pound~~ ^hundreth Pound a yeare more^ parted with, besides what the vallew of thous Lands may bee ~~when~~ improvede To when thay° are Free, which wouldbee fitt to

---

[830] Unidentified.
[831] "Diminution, lessening; abatement" ("reducement, *n.*," 3, *OED*).
[832] Kinsman of Sir John Temple.
[833] "To be assessed or valued for purposes of taxation; to be liable or subjected to payment of a certain rate" ("rate, *v.*2," 1a, *OED*).

bee considered of you Nide° not owne my haveinge Sent you a Copie of My Sonn Arrans Leter, sense it is only for your own perustiall°

Letter 253. November 3, 1672, [London], the Duchess of Ormonde to Captain George Mathew (NLI, Ormond Papers, 2503, no. 108). Autograph.
For My Brother Captane Mathews. To bee left with mr Luke Archer* at his house in Kilkenny. [Endorsed]: My Lady Dutches about Instalment Lord Ossory mr Page debt 900. 13 November 1672.

I willnot give My Sister the trouble of a Leter, beinge Latlie° tould that shee has bine° dayngeroslie sicke gives mee great feares for hir, wherfor I desier° to bee informed in what condistione shee is at the presant, the printed papers will give you an accompt° of My Sonn Ossorys* Installment at windzor[834] which has bine of some Charge unto My Lord whoe was willinge to healpe hime upon that ocatione° (and did) unto the vallew° of above 5 hundreth pound [/] heare is at this time a dept° challenged by mr Page* that I thought not of, which is 9 yeares arreares of an Annewetie of a hundreth Pound a year givene hime by My Lord in recompense of his Sarvis° when hee was Governor unto My Sone when hee was abrode° which My Lord has a great desier to pay unto hime but Finds a dificultie how to rayse such a Some though I doutnot but the Gentellman would give Time for it or take his payment by soe much a yeare as might bee thought resonable or most Convenient for My Lord wherfor I pray informe and advise what you doe Judge best in this perticuler

The 3 of November

---

[834] Ossory had been made a Knight of the Garter on September 30, 1672, and was installed at Windsor on October 25. See J. D. Davies, "Butler, Thomas, sixth earl of Ossory (1634–1680)," *ODNB*.

Letter 254. November 3, 1672, [London], the Duchess of Ormonde to Captain George Mathew (NLI, Ormond Papers, 2503, no. 109). Autograph.
For My Brother Captane Mathews [/] thes. [Endorsed]: My Ladys 16 / 27 November 1672.

[Brother]   The 16 of November
your Leter of the 23 from kilkenye* with the Severall papers relatinge unto My Sonn Arrans* conserns° came Sayfe° unto my hands one° wedensday Last, and shallbee Sent unto mr Philips* to perusse for his further Satisfactione; the Last Bills for 300 Pound though my Name was ussede, were disposed of for My Lords ocations° accordinge as you did designe Them [/] My Sonn ossory* has contracted a great dept° by his goeinge to Sea; and yet Runes° further into inconveniensies of the Like Nature Nether hee Nor his Lady regardinge the Ruene° that is Like to Fall very sudanlie° upon them which is a great trouble to Mee that am under gre Strats° of the Like kind by healpinge hime, soe as I am afrade wee Shall goe Neare to S[ink] ^Suffier°^ together, though My Lords Creditt I thank God bee beter then his, if our Suplyes from Ireland should Fayle° by resone° of the Fall of Trade in that kingdom as wee have but to much resone to feare thay° will, I had some hopes to have resevede° 4 hundreth Pound befor Cristmas for my perticuler uss, but Now hee ^Baxter*^ writs mee word that noe mony° Canbee had Nether for Sheepe Nor wooll which is a great disapoyntment to Mee; wee Shall goe within a Few days to a Plase called Burford* in Oxfordshire, where I will trye whether wee Cane Live Cheaper ther then at London, that wee may spend the most Time where wee Cane best Subsist

Letter 255. November 9, 1672, [London], the Duchess of Ormonde to Captain George Mathew (NLI, Ormond Papers, 2503, no. 110). Autograph.
To Captain George Mathew. [Endorsed]: My Lady Dutches about Lord John 19 / 27 November 1672.

what you have proposed consarninge° My Sonn Johns* depts° is sartanlie° the best Course, That hee should come away privatlie from Thense, and Leave his Creditors to bee compounded with in his absense and gayne° Time for payinge what is owinge unto Them; I will Send you what agrement has bine° made with thous° heare; but all that is indevored° to free hime willbee unto Litell° purpose, unles hee will resolve to Change the way of his Liveinge and conforme unto that Course as is by My Lord proposed unto hime, which I send you hearinclosed in writinge for you to See and afterwards to Show unto hime, and to returne his answar ~~befor~~ which willbee Expected befor hee shall have Leave to Stir from thense, and when hee Comes to bee Shure° to bringe over Non° but such Sarvants as are usfull and honnest, or Else Let his Frinds find out for hime heare, such as are Soe, which wouldbee the beter° way and Les charge unto hime, without which; hee Cane Never hope to bee well Sarvede; nor his Frinds Secure, but that hee will Exside° his allowanse and Rune° in dept as much as befor, and then you may Imagine how uneasie that willbee unto his Father that is willinge to ingadge° himselfe soe farr to free hime at a Time when his owne depts are soe presinge upon hime, which besides other Considerations my thinks ought to move hime to amendment and gratitude, By the computatione made of the yearlie charge of My Sonn Johns Sarvants wayges and Ecupage *equipage* you will Find it will Come unto 200 and 20 pound a yeare soe as out of his yearlie allowanse hee may have besides for Clothes and Pocket Mony° 300 hundreth and forcor which well manadged will *fourscore* Mentayne° hime as desentlie° as anye Man of his qualitie Nieds° to bee, and his Entertainment to goe towards the pay^ment^ [/] of his depts Ther, The greatest difficultie I apprehend to hime willbee the Layinge out of a hundreth pound for a Chariot and a payre of Horses and fiftie more for Liveres besides what Clothes hee may Nide° at *liveries* his first coming but if hee cane come provided for thes Nesesarye ocations° and some ^spendinge^ Mony ~~in his Pocket~~, I doe beleve hee will Live more unto his Credit and I hope unto his Content allsoe; then Ever hee did in his Life;

The 9 of November

Letter 256. November 23, 1672, [London], the Duchess of Ormonde to Captain George Mathew (NLI, Ormond Papers, 2503, no. 111). Autograph.
For My Brother Captane Gorge Mathews [/] thes. [Endorsed]: My Lady Dutches about my Lord John 23 November 6 december 1672.

The 23 of November

beinge to goe to Burford* on Teusday Next, ocations° soe many interuptions, as I have hardlie time to write, but heald it Nesesarye you Should know, that the State of all the accompts° My Sone Arran* broght Sayfe,° whoe arrivede heare on Monday Last [/] I touck some Care to propound a way how My Sonn Johns* depts° might bee payede, and hee to have the Satisfactione of beinge heare for a Time in hope his Frinds advise might by degrees worke some good upon hime, but sense° That, I have some grownd° to beleve that hee is as ill in health as hee is in Fortune and Consequentlie that a Nother° Climate may bee Fitter for hime then This, as you did propose in your Leter unto My Lord [Soe] as you may Suppres if you think fitt the Last Rules that were Sent unto hime, untell° my Lord shall have resolved on some other Course for hime, which must bee manadged with some privasie, and therfor untell my Lords further derections° Comes which willbee addrest unto you I desier° that Nothinge of this that I have now writene consarninge° hime May bee spokene of, nether unto himselfe nor anye other, I pray Send mee word how My Sister dous°

Letter 257. December 21, 1672, Burford, the Duchess of Ormonde to Captain George Mathew (NLI, Ormond Papers, 2356, no. 3264, p. 175). Autograph.
For My Brother Captane Mathews thes. [Endorsed]: my Lady 21 december 1672 mr winckworth Bucknally allow out of prizewines 70 pounds of mr Clarke. 21 December 1672. my Lady Dutchis Desember 21 16.

The 21 of Des

My beinge upon my remove to Burford* when I reseved° your tow° Leters of the 28 of Oct and 13 of November which Came together though of very differinge dats° did ocatione° my Not ansaringe° of them untell° Now, that I am settled heare for a while untell my Lords goeinge upe unto the Parliment which willbee the begininge of Feb Next at which time I purpose to goe To; wherby to avoyde° the Expense of kiepinge° tow Houses I was I confees desirious to trye whether the Liveinge in the Contrye for a Considerable part of the yeare would abayte° the Charge wee are at in London and I find it will very considerablie as if the wars abrode;° and the misfortune that pour Irland is in ^liklie^ to bee ^soe^ Ruened° upon all accompts° soe that wee cannot hope to resev[e] anye considerable part of our Rents bee Like to continow° in Soe ill a posture; My Lord must resolve ether to betake himselfe to Live in the Contrye heare or goe into Irland for imposible it willbee for hime to Subsist at London; I will doe what I cane to Satisfi[e] mr Page,* and will perfect what you desier° consarninge° the Commistione that was Last Sent which shallbee returnede by the time oppoyntede;° James Clarke* willbee accompable unto Mee for the Seventie pound you assigne hime to

paye ~~unto Mee~~ for which you shall reseve° an acknowlegment under
my hand within a very few days; I am in some trouble for haveinge
Excusede the giveinge of wood out of Durrow for repayringe of
the Deanes House at kilkenye* which hee did desier of Mee, The
Bushope of Osorye haveinge sense° made the same request unto
Mee for the repayre of his allsoe; My Lord thought it Not Fitt this
Last Shouldbee refusede considringe wee hould° That Land from
the Curch° and therfor has granted his desier but referede it unto
Sir william Flower* to give in qualitie and quantitie but what may
bee ^the^ ~~most~~ convenientlie sparede whoe I am Confident will
Manadge it as sparinglie as may bee when he understands how
unwillinglie it is parted with and what ocatione ~~therby~~ may bee
to made uss° of that wood for what Buildings may bee designed
hearafter at Dunmore* or kilkenye by My Sonn or whoe may Come
after, I am very impatiant to have an answar to Some Late Leters I
sent you Consarninge My Sonn John* and other Perticulers untell
when I have Litell° more to Say, I send you heare inclosede a Leter
from Captane winckworth* Consarning whous request I formerlie
writ unto you and gave hime an answar accordinge as you did
then advise mee, Soe as I desier the Gentellman may bee spokene
with and dealt favorablie with accordinge as you Judge his desiers
resonable

The oppinione of My Lords Counsell whethar My Lord bee
to allow what Sir william Bucknell* dous° Stope° out of the Rent of
the Priswins,° for dewties° payabell out of Eche June wouldbee very
Fitt to bee returned befor the Next Payment is to bee made which
willbee at our Lady day[835]

**Letter 258. January 4, 1672/3, Burford, the Duchess of Ormonde
to Captain George Mathew** (NLI, Ormond Papers, 2503, no. 112).
Autograph.
For My Brother Captane Mathews [/] thes. [Endorsed]: My Ladyes
4 January 1672 Lord John. for mony. et cetera.

            Burford the 4 of Jan

I have some cause to dout° that a former Leter of Mine has
miscaryede which was sent tow° Posts after the draft of that
methode that was proposede for my Sonn John* as to his Expense
for the future and the Manner of his Liveinge; a Stope° wherof

---

[835] March 25, the first day of the year in the Old Style calendar.

from tenderinge it to hime; (had you not done it befor) was then heald Nesesarye and is soe still, Both by My Lord and Mee upon an intematione° that was givene uss of his beinge as ill in his health as hee was in his Fortune, and therfor that Franse wouldbee a Fitter Plase for hime to goe privatlie and spiedilie° To, then come into England; wherby hee might not only have the benefitt of a Sayfe° Cure, but his Creditors in his absense bee compounded with upon more resonable Termes; a cleare accompt° of what you Could observe in hime or understand from others of the condistione of his health, beinge what I did Earnestlie Press to know, that accordinglie some Course might bee takene to presarve hime; but resevinge° noe answar from you consarninge° This perticuler, I must agayne° intreate it from you; I send you a Leter from mr Jackson* which I shall make noe answar unto, but as you shall advise Mee Nor to mr Houke,[836] whoe it should sime° My Sonn John to staufe ofe° importunitie from himselfe tells hime and the rest of his Creditors that My Lord will take a Course to paye his depts° and the mene° time reseves° his Pay and spends it as ~~idle~~ ill as hee has don° the rest, and this is all the returne wee are Like to reseve for anye intendments of favour towards ~~hiem~~ hime which is soe resented by uss Both, as has put a Stope from ^undertaking^ anye thinge for hime unto our owne prejudise, sense° hee has soe Litell° witt or gratitude to make noe beter° uss° of his Frinds kinnes to hime, James Clarke* tells mee hee has not above sixtie pound of yours in his hand, which I have not as yet resevede° but when I doe you shall know it, if you could procure mee 200 Pound to bee repayede out of the wooll or Stocke you would doe mee a spetiall° Curtisie° for soe much I owe upon My perticuler accompt; for a diamand Gorge[837] that I gave unto My Sonn Ossorye* when hee was Made knight of the Garter

stave

kindness

---

[836] Unidentified.
[837] "A representation of St George, typically jewelled or enamelled, and forming part of the insignia of the Order of the Garter" ("George, *n.*," 1b, *OED*).

Letter 259. March 21, 1672/3, [London], the Duchess of Ormonde to Captain George Mathew (NLI, Ormond Papers, 2503, no. 113). Autograph.
For My Brother Captane Mathews. [Endorsed]: [My Ladyes] 21 March [1672].

The 21 of March

I have not heard from you of Late consarninge° the disposinge of the woole, though I hope to doe ^shortlie^ it beinge of a great conserne° to our remove, which wee are providinge for as fast as wee Cane ~~the mene Time~~ though theris great perswations aganst it by som that pretends to bee our Frinds; I have writen to Baxter* consarninge the Ine° at kilkenye and what Course is thought best for a presant accomodatione and what other may bee afterwards Contrivede when wee are ther our Selfs, tell° when ther will hardlie bee anye Inkieper° gottene; The wether has bine° for this 5 or sixe weekes soe Extremlie Colde, as made mee kiepe° the House and My Chamber Ever sense° it begane which has prevented the daynger I fearede of the returne of My Coughe which I have had to Noe degree that has bine troubellsome to Mee hetherto° I thank God, I pray remember mee to My Sister of whous beinge well I shouldbee glad to heare

Letter 260. April 15, 1673, [London], the Duchess of Ormonde to Captain George Mathew (NLI, Ormond Papers, 2503, no. 129). Autograph.
For My Brother Captane Gorge Mathews. [Endorsed]: My Ladyes about Lord John and Estimat for his Retinue 15 April 1673. Duchess of ormonde to George Mathew.

My unhapie Sonn John* has bine° much the Subgect of my Leters to you of Late, as This must bee To upon the accompt° of somthinge consarninge° hime and his afares that I resevede° from himeselfe and Baxter* some weekes sense,° which I could not at that Time give anye answar unto beinge ~~but~~ then much weaknede by a Plurisie[838] I had of which I thank God I am Now recovrede and gotene abrode agayne° [/] I am Satisfiede that My Sonn is well in his health for Soe Doctor Mara dous° sertifie° under his hand, but cannot aprove of his kiepinge° thous° at killkenye upon his Fathers Charge and putinge uss unto the unnesesarye Charge of kiepinge his owne

---

[838] "pain in the chest or the side, esp. when stabbing in nature and exacerbated by inspiration or coughing" ("pleurisy, *n.*," 1, *OED*).

and Strangers Horses in Towne which was not done when wee our
Selfs Livede Ther and therfor my thinks it shouldbee as much as
hee could resonablie desier° to have the allowanse of Hay where it
is ^at Dunmore*^ and where he may kiepe° his Horses if hee please
and Let others send Thers to the Ine° for soe thay° ought in good
manners to doe; I do as for his diete I know noe Course beter;° then
that all his Foutmen and Gromes should bee put to Bourd wages *footmen;*
and hee to give Soe much a weeke for his owne and his Mans diete *grooms; board*
and Lodginge at Baxters House which would kiepe hime whilst hee
Stays in thous Parts from beinge ever pesterede with companye and
by that Menes° reduse his Expenses unto a Sartantie° and this Course
I desier you will give your best [at di]stanse to Settell hime in; for
otherwiss the Charge that will falle upon uss by his Extravaganse
willbee unlimeted, but for what is Past my Lord willbee Content to
allow for it, My Sonn John writes mee word that with some Monys°
hee has payede at Dublin to his Creditors ther, and compounded
with the rest; his depts° is now redust° unto 18 hundreth Pound soe
as if hee bee a Litell° healpt by my Lord as hee desiers hee proposes
to overcome the unease of his depts in a while and to Live within
the Compas of his allowanse for the time to come, but My Lord has
made hime Noe promise in that perticuler nor willnot but accordinge
as you shall advise; I pray consider well the Last perticuler of My
Lords Leter for it is of a great importanse to hime, I have Sent you a
Copie of the computatione of My Sonn Johns presant Expense and
the Nomber of the Sarvants and Horses that hee proposes to kiepe;[839]

The 15 of Aprell

Letter 261. May 13, 1673, [London], the Duchess of Ormonde to
Captain George Mathew (NLI, Ormond Papers, 2503, no. 115).[840]
Autograph.
For My Brother Captane Gorge Mathews. [Endorsed]: My Lady 13
May 1673.

The 13 of May

If you have not heard soe frequentlie from mee of Late as you might
expect you will the Less wonder, when you heare of tow° Mariages in

---

[839] This is enclosed, dated March 1672. No day is provided, but it must be prior to Lady Day, March 25.

[840] There is wear and tear to the left-hand side of the leaf meaning the text is lost on the left-hand margin of the first page and the right-hand margin of the second.

My Familie that are Neare concluded; the one for My Sonn Ossoryes
daghter unto the Earle of Darby,[841] the other My Sonn Arran* to the
daghter of one Mr Feries one of the best and Antiantist Families of   *most ancient*
England formerlie Earles of Essex,[842] the Portion is 12 Thow^sand^
[/] Pound and but one Sicklie yonge Man hir Brother betwixt hir
and 3 Thowsand a yeare after hir Fathers desease, how thes workes
are Compast[843] [*two words missing*] incoridgment° givene uss of
Suplies from Ireland is some [*two words missing*] to venter° upon; yet
where theris presant and Future ^advantages^ in [them] My Lord
and I were for Strengthninge of our Familie by the best allianse
to [forti]fie it aganst the Mallis° of Mene° and Litell° Pepell° that
has Labored [all tha]y could to Ruene° uss, My Lord has sould° his
unsartane° Pentione of [a] Thowsand pound a yeare as Gentellman
of the Bedchamber for 6 Thowsand Pound 3 wherof is to bee payede
in hand for My Lord of Darbys [and] the other sevene beinge 10
Thowsand in all that wee are to give to bee payede in a yeare and
a halfe from November Next or when My Lord of Darby comes of
Age whoe is at presant in his 18 yeare This perticuler beinge not
as yet fullie agreede upon, one Thowsand of this Mony° My Lord
has givene unto My Sone Osory* and designed 15 hundreth of the
remayninge to satisfie some Nesesarye depts° of his owne; and the
other 5 to pay the Fees of the Exchecker and the Charge that attends
[proc]edinge for That, hee has takene upon himselfe; Soe as unto our
[owne] Suport you are desirede to uss° your best indevours° as I am
Shure° you will to send uss over Suplies as soune° as you Cane gett
them In; I pray show this Leter unto My Sister beinge I cannot at
this time write unto hir My Selfe for I beleve this Neuse° willnot bee
unacseptable to hir, This is a greate yeare of wedings Generalie soe as
I doe not dispare but that My Sonn John* may gett a wife To for Soe
hee makes mee beleve; if his Frinds will assist and Countenanse hime
as upon some condistions that I have intemated° to hime and to My
Lord Angers* whoe is Now goeinge over and will make knowne unto
you when hee comes Ther My Lord and I shallbee very inclinable To;

---

[841] Ossory's eldest daughter, Lady Elizabeth Butler (1660–1717), would be married to William Stanley, ninth Earl of Derby on July 10, 1673. See John H. Rains, III, "Stanley, William George Richard, ninth earl of Derby (1655–1702), nobleman," *ODNB*.

[842] Arran would be married to Dorothy Ferrars (d. 1716), daughter of John Ferrars of Tamworth Castle and his wife Anne, daughter of Sir Dudley Carleton, before June 7, 1673. See Harman Murtagh, "Butler, Richard, first earl of Arran (1639–1686), army officer," *ODNB*.

[843] "To contrive, devise, machinate (a purpose)" ("compass, v.1," 2a, *OED*).

Letter 262. April 22, 1673, [London], the Duchess of Ormonde to Captain George Mathew (NLI, Ormond Papers, 2503, no. 116).[844] Autograph.
For My Brother Captane Mathews. [Endorsed]: [My Ladyes] 21 March [1673].

[*Two lines missing*] came unto your hands that I knew Nothinge of My Sonn Johns* kiepinge° House at killkenye* untell° the first time of his beinge Ther that Baxter* Sent mee an accompt° in generall that it came unto 20 ode° Pound whether in redie Mony° besides accates I doe not know; sense° which time I understand hee has bine° Ther Sense ^agayne°^ without anye derectione° of Mine, or makinge you acquanted therwith, as I thought thay ^Baxter^ had done; otherwiss it was Strange in Baxter ^hime^ beinge but a Sarvant, to draw on such an Expense upon his Master without Order for it; This, and the Sellinge ofe of the Stocke at Donmore* without advisinge with you is what I doe soe Litell° aprove; as gives mee Cause to Second my desiers° to you that Hee may bee broght unto an accompt for what hee has resevede,° sense the perclose[845] of the Last, and that you will Louke° upon the inclosed petistione sent mee from the poure° Tenants of Dunmore and accordinge as you Find what thay° doe alleadge° to bee True or False that you will take such a Course therin as may bee Just and resonable towards all ^all^ the Persons conserned,° the answar unto mistris kieffs[846] Bill was Longe sense sent away by one mr Prisse[847] a Marchand° of Dublin, whoe did ^whoe was goeinge Thither, and did^ asshure° uss that hee would ride Post to Holyhead* and make noe Stope° by the way but it should sime° hee olltorede° his Mind; and in That, desevede° uss; otherwiss you should have had noe Cause to Complane of the delaye that has hapenede though I doe hope hee is arrivede in Ireland befor this time; My Lord will answar That Part of your Leter consarninge° the dept° pretended to bee dew° unto the Lord of Taragh[848] to which I am soe much a Stranger as I never heard of it befor as hee will, what Consernes° Mr Martine* whoe has not bine a Litell [*three lines missing*][849] hee is redie to Starve by his owne visses;° if wooll dous°

---

[844] There is significant wear and tear to the top of the leaf resulting in the loss of most of two or three lines of text at the top of each page.
[845] "To bring to a close; to close, conclude" ("parclose, *v.*," 2, *OED*).
[846] Unidentified.
[847] Unidentified.
[848] Thomas, third Viscount Tara (d. 1674).
[849] Words that are discernible in each line through the damage are "but daylie importunes," "has bine givene," "Man bringing [...] selfe."

yeald anye Prisse° I think Mine had beter° to bee Solde then kept for
I dout° others has not that Care that mr Brian* had of thous° small
Consernes, I doe hope My Sonn Johns Ague willnot Continow°
Longe upon hime, if hee doe Take Care of himselfe which I am
afrade hee willbee fayllinge in;

The 22 of Aprell

**Letter 263. May 27, 1673, [London], the Duchess of Ormonde to
Captain George Mathew** (NLI, Ormond Papers, 2503, no. 117).
Autograph.
For My Brother Captane Mathews [/] thes. [Endorsed]: My Lady 27
May 1673 about Lord John.

The 27 of May

The Neuse° of My Mothers death[850] was resevede° by My Lord, My
selfe and all hir relations heare with that Sense of hir Loos,° as was
dew° unto a Person soe much beloved and vallewed° as shee was;
and deservede to bee; by all hir Familie [/] I give you many thanks
for beinge assistinge unto My Sonn John* in the way proposede for
his Liveinge, which if hee willbee soe prudent as to Submitt unto;
willbee the only way to put hime out of the unease of his depts° and
incoridge° My Lord to healpe hime hearafter as hee is abble, which at
the presant cannot bee Expected; I dout° therwas but small grownd°
for some Late hopes that hee tould mee hee had of obtaninge the
Lady that it was belevede that hee might onse° have had if his owne
Neglect had not Lost hime that good Fortune, which I find hee
would Now take more paynes For, if it were to bee Compast by anye
indevores° of his; therfor I pray informe your Selfe and afterwars Mee
what incoridgment° has of Late bine° givene hime, and by whom
in that Perticuler. The tow° wedings of My Sonn and Grandchild
willbe Soune° (but private). My Sonn Osorys* goeinge to Sea was a
great Surprise to Mee and all his Frinds whoe had not soe much as a
thought of it, Nor hee himselfe as I doe beleve, untell° hee Came to
Rye where the Fleete then was; that wanted a Reare Aderall unto one   *Rear*
of the Squadrans; and findinge it wouldbee gratfull unto the kinge   *Admiral*
and the Duke[851] did offier° himselfe whoe is at the Presant upon the

---

[850] EO's mother-in-law, Elizabeth, née Poyntz, Lady Thurles.
[851] James, Duke of York. Ossory's biographer points out that his appointment "was a stopgap due to the unexpected absence of the designated flag officer, John Narbrough; Ossory's appointment prevented the post from becoming a focus for ambitious claimants

Duch Cost, God Send uss good Neuse of hime and the rest untell *Dutch Coast*
when, his relations are but in an uneasie Condistione; My Lord bid
mee tell you that hee couldnot write unto you by this Post but would
by My Lord Angers* whoe goes from hense with^in^ a day or Tow

**Letter 264. June 7, 1673, [London], the Duchess of Ormonde to
Captain George Mathew** (NLI, Ormond Papers, 2503, no. 118).
Autograph.
For My Brother Captane Mathews [/] thes. [Endorsed]: My Lady
Dutches 7 June 1673 mr Hamltons death et cetera. Duchess of
ormonde to George Mathew.

The 7 of June

I doutnot but you have heard of My Nephue James Hambeltons*
havinge Lost a Lege in a ^the^ Late Fight at Sea whoe diede of
that wound yesterday at 4 of the Clocke in the Morninge and is to
bee burede at 10 this Night [/] hee was a great Loos° unto his owne
Familie (and ours) by whom hee is very much regreted; and by Many
more whoe will find the Loss of soe generous a Frind (for soe hee
was) to all that hee could Sarve that Nieded° his kindnes, I couldnot
prevall with my Selfe to write unto My Brother Hambellton* or My *prevail*
Sister upon a Subgect that I well know willbee ~~hard to~~ ^greatlie^
afflictinge to Them; I cannot Say hee diede in his Senses for ~~hee~~ his
Fever and the Gangerine of his wond made hime Rave Soune° after *wound*
hee was broght on Shore, untell° ~~in~~ a Few howers° befor hee diede,
that hee Lay quiet, and as thous° that weere about hime thought was
in a Sleepe and breathinge Swete, and soe Ended without speach or
aperanse of payne, Hee showede the greatest patianse° in the payne
that hee indurede that was posible for Man to doe, and Sayede°
nothinge that was ill in his Ravings but of the bussines of the Sea
and would bee Sillent when hee was desired; and knew Pepell,° but
was not Capable of anye thinge that was Serious, the desease havinge
soe farr Seasede° his Spirets, Ther has bine° a Second Fight at Sea,
but I bless God My Sonn Ossorye* has Scapede anye Harme and is
well, and Come ~~with~~ ^in^ the Fleete unto the Boy of the Nore[852] ~~as~~
a Plase where thay° are to ~~ust~~ take in Provistions, I pray remember
mee to My Sister ~~and~~ whoe shall heare from mee by the Next Post,

---

and faction-fighting." See J. D. Davies, "Butler, Thomas, sixth earl of Ossory (1634–
1680)," *ODNB*.

[852] The Buoy of the Nore is a sandbank at the mouth of the Thames Estuary.

My Sonn Arran* is Latlie° Maryede and I hope very hapilie unto the yonge Gentellwoman that I formerlie acquanted you[853]

Letter 265. June 10, [1673], [London], the Duchess of Ormonde to Captain George Mathew (NLI, Ormond Papers, 2503, no. 95). Autograph.
For My Brother Captane Gorge Mathews [/] thes. [Endorsed]: My Lady 10 June [1673].

The 10 of June

I find by a Leter I resevede° yesterday from My Sonn John* dated the 1 of this Month that hee continows° still his hopes of obtayninge the yonge Lady,[854] grownded° upon the incoridgment° that divers persons gives hime of good Suckses° in his addresses if hee and his Frinds, doe apiere° consernede° as hee pretends to mee to bee very much for the Person of the Lady, and desiers,° that hee may bee assisted with such a Suplye as may bee requisit for hime to apiere as hee ought upon such an ocatione;° wherin if ther bee a provabilitie° ansarable° unto what hee Fansies, hee shallnot want all the resonable healpe that his Frinds cane give hime; of which I shouldbee glad to know your oppinione befor My Lord or I doe apiere to ingadge° in this affare; consarninge° which Hee proposes that his Father Should write unto hirs; and to a Nother° that I shall forbeare to Name that is much trusted in all that Lords consernes;°[855] but which my Lord wouldbee willinge to doe; if from you or hee can bee Satisfiede that anye such adrese wouldbee acsepted; therfor I pray Let mee know your oppinione as soune° as may bee conserninge° this perticuler and whether hee Lives more orderlie and within Compas then hee did; and Now that My Sonn Arran* is Maryed and Bety Butler[856] Like to bee very soune; I have nothinge Left to wish of good unto My Familie and Joy unto My Selfe as to See My Sonn John as hapilie disposede of as the rest of his Brothers are; as I dout° not but hee wouldbee if hee could ^Cane^ obtane that yonge Lady that hee pretends to Like very well of, My Sonn Ossorye* havinge bine° in both the Fights at Sea has I thank God Escaped anye harme in his

---

[853] Dorothy Ferrars.
[854] Anne Chichester (d. 1697), daughter and co-heir of Arthur Chichester, first Earl of Donegal (d. 1675), and Letitia Hickes (d. 1691).
[855] Carol Bolton? For a comprehensive discussion of the marriage negotiations, which outlines Bolton's instrumental role in brokering the marriage, see O'Keeffe, 65–67.
[856] Ossory's daughter Elizabeth.

person, and is Expected heare Evrye hower,° I resevede Baxters*
accompt° of My Sonn Johns Expenses at kilkenye but dous° not
Mentione how Longe hee Stayede ther which amounts in all unto
65:09.01 which my Lord will take upon himselfe, and not abayte° it
out of his allowanse, but desiers that ther may bee noe more of the
Like ill Manadged expenses in which the Steward ought to have bine
more warye then I perseve° hee was; to admitt or incoridge° anye
such thinge without Order; Sense° you have takene woole from the
Tenants for ther Rent, I think it wouldbee ~~be~~ a beter° way for you to
deale with Some Marchand° to Buye all the quantitie you have then
Leave it to Baxter from whom I have not as yet had anye accompt of
what hee resevede for the wethers hee Sould° Nor of the Acates, Mr
Martins* Povertie and Continowell° importunitie has prevayled with
My Lord to Charge a Bill upon you to pay hime a Nother hundreth
Pound much agaynst my will if I could have healped it; for hee is the
ocatione of his owne Misirie by spendinge all hee Cane upon persons
as vitious as himselfe, and tormentinge uss to healpe hime, when   *vicious*
wee cannot procure Mony° for our owne ocations;° It is of soe great
importanse My Lords Stay heare untell° the Next springe as hee
and his Frinds are Convinst of the Nesesitie of it, for some ~~wayghtie~~
Resons, that you Shall know by some other way before it bee Longe
Not fitt to bee Mentioned in a Leter, Soe as ~~you must~~ ^I hope you
will^ uss° all your indevours,° to healpe towarde our Subsistanse for
soe Longe a time, and then wee hope you will find that wee shall
give a good accompt of our Stay, I wish you would discourse with My
Lord Angers* Consarninge this affare of My Sonn Johns whoe I doe
beleve may bee assistinge in it by his advisses to hime with whom I
find hee has some Creditt

**Letter 266. June 24, 1673, [London], the Duchess of Ormonde to
Captain George Mathew** (NLI, Ormond Papers, 2503, no. 119).
Autograph.
For My Brother Captane Mathews [/] thes. [Endorsed]: My Lady
Dutches 24 June 1673. Duchess of ormonde to George Mathew.

The 24 of June

Some howers° after I had writene to you this day, and Sent away My
Leter, I fortuned to reseve° one from ^you^ of the 17 of this Month
which I doe supose was intended mee by the Last ^Post^ Soe as all
The time that is allowede mee to answar it, is only to tell you that I
think theris soe much provabilitie° of My Sonn Johns* good Suckses°

in his pretentione sense° you Find the knight[857] soe well disposede
~~to befrind~~ ^towardes^ hime ~~in it~~ whoe I know has power both with
the Lord and Lady,[858] as hee must bee incoridged° by the hopes
of reward to befrind hime in it; which you are to Manadge in that
perticuler as you See Cause; to whom My Lord ~~has [resolved to write
soe] soune this night,~~ ^intends to write by the Next Post^ and to the
Father of the yonge Lady allsoe, and Soe I doe intend to hir Mother
and doe hope from the accompt° My Lord Angeres* and your
Selfe has givene mee of this affare, that it will take Effect, which
wouldbee beyond anye thinge the most unto my Sattisfaction, if it
may be Compast; as the Menes° to Make My Sonns Fortune, and
take hime ofe° from a Course of Life that was soe much disaproved
of by his Frinds [/] It is my Lords desier° and Mine, that My Sonn
John shouldbee reimburst what Mony° hee Layede out of his owne
when hee went unto Clonmell* upon his Fathers ocations,° and that
hee may bee suplyede beyond That; when hee goes into the North,[859]
where it willbee Nesesarye that hee should take some Sober Frind a
Longe with hime, and tow° or three of his owne Sarvants only; the
Chife° Person to bee Chosene must bee Left unto My Lord Angers
and your Selfe to picke upon ~~Sense~~ whoe will doe it beter,° then I
cane derect° at this distanse, for the other parts of your leter I cannot
answar it Now, it beinge Soe Late, but Shall by the Next Post

**Letter 267. July 15, 1673, [London], the Duchess of Ormonde to
Captain George Mathew (NLI, Ormond Papers, 2503, no. 120).**[860]
Autograph.
For My Brother Captane Gorge Mathews. [Endorsed]: Dutches
[missing] Dunmore [missing] July 1673. Duchess of ormonde to
George Mathew.

The 15 of July

I have omited writinge a Post or tow° upon the ocatione° of the Late
wedinge of My Lord of Darby* to My Sonn Osorys* Eldest daghter,

---

[857] Sir Audley Mervin, broker for the marriage.

[858] The Earl and Countess of Donegal, Arthur and Letitia Chichester.

[859] Joymount, Carrickfergus, was the principal seat of the Earl of Donegal, but from the 1660s he was more often resident in Belfast Castle. See J. M. Rigg, "Chichester, Arthur, first earl of Donegal (1606–1675)," rev. R. M. Armstrong, *ODNB*.

[860] There is severe wear and tear to the left-hand side of the leaf, which has resulted in the loss of text in the left-hand margin of the one-page letter, as much as one or two words in each of thirteen lines of text.

which was upon Thursday Last, whoe is to [go] for Franse tow days
hense; and is a very Considerable [and] well Naturede yonge Man;
Soe as this Mach° promisses [much] hapenes° to hir and to hir
Familie, for whom hee [prot]est[s] soe great kindnes and respect as
hee has Chosen [My] Lord to bee his Gaurdiane and put himselfe
Intyrelie [in] his hands;[861] I have resevede° a Nother° Complaynt *entirely*
from [the Te]nants of Dunmore* whoe dous° alleadge° that
Notwithstanding [the or]der you gave in June Last consarninge° ther
Settellment [they] are Sense° warnede to bee gone, and ther Housses
to [be pulled]e downe by Baxters* derections,° I cannot tell whye [this
beje done, but doe supose theris some Nesesitie possiblie that may
ocatione it by Scarsitie of Grase for the Stocke that is upon it, but *grass*
I think it had bine° beter° to have made uss° of Some [wast°] Land
wherof I beleve theris but to great Store then put [such] distrese upon
the poure° Pepell° to Forse ther remove on [*missing*], in Soe hard a
time as this is, therfor I pray give your Selfe [Leave] to inquier° after
this perticuler, and to the Ende that Noe wronge may bee done unto
the Tenants

**Letter 268. July 22, [1673], [London], the Duchess of Ormonde to
Captain George Mathew** (NLI, Ormond Papers, 2503, no. 100).
Autograph.
For My Brother Captane Gorge Mathews [/] thes. [Endorsed]: My
Ladys letter about Lodowick Jackson. 22 July.

Brother

I have Sent the Controwler a Note of mr Jacksons* disbursments
for the Lead, which I desier° you will repaye unto hime; as soune°
as you Cane Convenientlie whoe is not very presinge for his Mony°
soe ^Soe^ hee may bee but Secure of it, Hee has an offiss° in the
Coustom House of yoghall and has a very Suffisent Corespondant *Youghall* (Co.
heare on° mr Lindsie* whoe has made a Proposall for the Exchange Cork)
of Mony at 4 in the hundreth but I am very confident will take 3

---

[861] William George Richard Stanley, ninth Earl of Derby, was eighteen when he married; his wife, Lady Elizabeth Butler (1660–1717), was just thirteen. JO served as Derby's guardian for the rest of his minority, and sent him on the customary grand tour of France and Italy until the summer of 1675. See John H. Rains, III, "Stanley, William George Richard, ninth earl of Derby (1655–1702)," *ODNB*. On the difficult education of the young Earl of Derby see Burghclere, II, 235–45, and O'Keeffe, 78–79. According to his second governor, Colonel Thomas Fairfax, to JO: "I am sorry to say I am the unhappiest man alive to have had anything to do with him" (quoted in O'Keeffe, 78–79).

throughout the yeare if you doe think that allowanse resonable, mr Jackson is desirious to Farme the Priswins° and if you and hee dous° come to anye agreement will give you good Securitie and ~~I doe beleve will~~ ^will I doe beleve^ if you insist upon it, bee oblidged Ether to pay you ther or heare, and advanse you the halfe years rent in hand as the First Farmers did, though I have not discourst of perticulars with hime, but Left that unto you, as what was Judged Fittest by

                 your affectionat Sister

The 22 of July   E:ormonde

Letter 269. August 4, [1673], [London], the Duchess of Ormonde to Captain George Mathew (NLI, Ormond Papers, 2503, no. 101). Autograph.
[Endorsed]: My Lady 4 / 11 August 1673 about woull.

The Gentellman with whom My Lord did make agrement for the Exchange of his Mony° sent mee word yesterday that if hee might bee informede what quantitie of wooll My Lord had to Sell ~~that~~ and the Rayte° you would put upon it, that hee would Buy it Ther or pay the Mony heare allowinge the Exchange; which I thought Fitt to Let you know, that you may consider whether this way that hee proposes or the Sendinge of it over hether wouldbee best, theris some discourse of a Pease, but noe sartantie° of it as yet that I cane Find, but it beinge now soe Late in the yeare; it is to bee hopede that the Fleete cannot bee Longe abrode ^and^ that ther willbee noe Fightinge; I Niede° not desier° your care to hastene over some suplye of Mony to uss, sense° I know theris noe indevour° of yours wantinge in that perticuler; but the imposibilitie of gettinge ~~Mony~~ it in that Contrye, it beinge allsoe heare more Secarse then Ever,   *scarce*
The Boouks⁸⁶² you Sent by Mr Turner Came Sayfe° and are put in Exzact° Methode,

The 4 of Agust

---

⁸⁶² Account books (see "book, *n.*," II, b, *OED*).

Letter 270. August 9, 1673, the Duchess of Ormonde to Captain George Mathew (NLI, Ormond Papers, 2503, no. 104[a]).
Autograph.
For My Brother Captane Gorge Mathews [/] thes. [Endorsed]: My Ladyes 9 / 18 August 1673.

I am advised for my health to goe to the Bayth° which I am resolvede upon the Next weeke and to Staye accordinge as the drinkinge of thous° hote° waters shall agree with Mee which has done Cures Ecquall unto the Burbone waters in Franse to thous whoe have had Coughs Like Mine and are Now [More] Cryede upe[863] then anye Sort of Phisicke;[864] Baxter* writs Mee word that ther willbee a Nesesitie of sellinge 8 hundreth Sheepe out of my Stocke at Dunmore* at Mickellmas° Next, but I doe hope at beter° Raytes° then the Last were parted with or Else it willnot quitt the Cost of kiepinge° a Stocke and Loousinge the Rent of soe much good Land; I have not as yet Seene thous accompts° of his that you toulde mee shouldbee Sent over, Nether doe I desier° them untell° you have first takene them and made your Exseptions if anye you find grownd° For, and when perfected and approvede of by you I ~~may~~ ^will^ give hime a discharge which otherwiss I shall not doe mr John welch* has recomended on° Ogane[865] for a Farme consarninge° which my Lord has writene unto you; and Left it to you to favour hime in ~~the bargine such as hee will not but~~ ^his Arrears and in the Bargine^ as you find hee desarves, I wish that ^all such^ ~~as desarves~~ ^as pretends to Merit^ anye Consideratione would transmitt ther desiers over to uss rather then come themselfes for besides what is done to satisfie them Ther, thay° importune uss for mony° to Carrye them Backe; which has Cost uss more then wee had to spare Captane Power* still complaynes that hee Cane Nether reseve° anye part of the Mony dew unto hime; Nor Securitie, I know not how that intangeled affar is, but I wish ther were an Ende of it, for the trouble is the greater to have anye dispute with a Person that soe Litell° understands bussenes° as hee dous,° that ~~perplexes~~ ^perplexes^ it to himselfe and others by his ill manadginge of it, soe as it wouldbee great Charitie to advise and healpe hime in it, as farr as you may without prejudis

Bourbon

losing

---

[863] "Extolled" ("cried-up, *adj.*," *OED*).
[864] Thomas Guidott popularized the spa waters at Bath, publishing in 1669 the third edition of Edward Jorden's 1632 *A Discourse of Natural Bathes* with his own *Appendix Concerning Bathe* (London: Thomas Salmon, 1669). Several other publications about the Bath waters followed. See Mark S. R. Jenner, "Guidott, Thomas (1638?–1706)," *ODNB*.
[865] Unidentified.

unto My lords Intrest, I wish you would Send mee at your Leasure a List of all the depts° remayninge upon My Lords Estate and all other whatsowever that is dew° in that kingdom that upon the whole both ther and heare wee may know what our ingadgments° are

The 9 of Agust

Letter 271. September 13, 1673, [London], the Duchess of Ormonde to Captain George Mathew (NLI, Ormond Papers, 2503, no. 122). Autograph.
For My Brother Captane Mathews. [Endorsed]: My Lady Dutches 13 September 24 October 1673 about mr Baxters and Sessions Kate ffox. Duchess of ormonde to George Mathew.

The 13 of September

I returned from the Bayth° on wedensday Last, haveinge resevede° much benifit in my health by drinkinge of thous° waters, I made some Stay at Burford* to put ofe° that Plase which I found Nesesarye to Stope° the Charge of kiepinge° it, Sense° My Lord cannot bee at Libertie to bee ther this yeare; and was drawene to Leave James Clarke* ther for a Few days after Mee Soe as I cannot (wantinge hime) bee abble ^Fullie^ to answar your Leter of the 22 of this Month which I found heare at my Cominge Home, whoe could give (and shall by the Next) a beter° accompt° then I cane of mr Lentrops* payments, some of them havinge bine° for my Lords perticuler uss° unto which I am a Stranger I doe beleve you willnot find hime deale for wooll but upon very hard Termes, and that the best way will bee to transport it over, though you doe very well to Trye what bargine you cane make Ther to prevent the hazard of the Sea, which may bee somthinge at this ill time of the yeare, but for other daynger ther willbee Litell° Sense My Lord is Shure° of haveinge a Convoy, I wonder that Baxter* shouldbee soe backward in makinge upe his accompts that has soe Litell to doe and that ther should bee soe great a proportione of Cast wooll as you Mention which is More by 3 parts of Fower then ever was in mr Brians* Time; Soe as I have *four* Just Cause to Suspect a Fault in hime or thous that are imployed under hime, soe as ^therfor^ I pray bringe hime to a Strict accompt for I am not Satisfiede with his way of prosidinge,° I desier° to know from you whether the Letinge of the Land and Stocke of Dunmore* might not bee beter then to kiepe° it as it is; provided I could Light upon a good English responsable Tenant; the greatest Scrupell I should have in what I now propose, is the Feare of ther spoylinge the House and prejudisinge the Plantings ~~which~~ Nether of which I wouldbee willinge to hazard for anye profitt, Sense ~~Both~~ ^Thay°^ are Now of great delight, but if I couldbee Secure in both thes, perhapes it wouldbee beter to have some Sartantie° then kiepe it, as it is to benifitt others, and not my Selfe, I heare that william Sestions* is not Like to Live, which willbee a great Loos,° and not Easie to Find a Sarvant of his kind that may in my absense bee trusted with the Charge of all the Goods though I am indevoringe° by my inquiries how I may Light of one, theris a poure° Madwoman kate Foxe[866] that torments mee with ^beginge^ Leters in verse and the Strangest superscriptions in the same Style that Ever was Siene, I pray give hir 4 Stone of the Cast wooll and 2 or 3 Barells of Corne if ther bee anye, upon condistione that Shee writs verses to mee noe More

Letter 272. September 20, 1673, [London], the Duchess of Ormonde to Captain George Mathew (NLI, Ormond Papers, 2503, no. 121). Autograph.
For My Brother Captane Gorge Mathews. [Endorsed]: My Ladyes 20 September 14 October 1673 about Milen and Woolls. Duchess of ormonde to George Mathew.

The Ballife° of Dunmore* william Millan* was heare whoe went from hense this day, Hee broght mee a Leter from Baxter* and in it a generall accompt° of the 2 Last years wooll, which I Cane make Litell° Judgment of, Nor will; untell° the perticulers of his accompt have bine° Examined by you as I desier° it may, as allsoe; what hee Stands Charged with for Accates and the Rent of Dunmore; Sense° you know all that I have resevede° from hime Sense hee had the Manadgment of That affare

The 20 of September

Letter 273. October 28, 1673, [London], the Duchess of Ormonde to Captain George Mathew (NLI, Ormond Papers, 2503, no. 123). Autograph.
For My Brother Captane Gorge Mathews. [Endorsed]: Her Graces Letter Dated 28 October 1673 for 4 or 500 pounds against Christmas. Duchess of ormonde to George Mathew.

The 28 of Oct

---

[866] Unidentified, but probably a tenant at Dunmore.

It beinge soe Longe befor I cane Expect anye Suplye By the woole, and noe profitt by the Acates untell° Cristmas at the Sounest° and ~~That beinge~~ this Last beinge to reimburse the 200 formerlie advanst in Febuary Last upon that Found; Leaves mee under some dificultie how to gett mony° aganst That Time for my perticuler ocations,° which of anye other throughout the yeare willbee the most chargeble to Mee, and therfor if you could find anye way how I might bee accomodated with 4 or 5 hundreth pound I would Secure the repayment of it by the Sayle of Sheepe or anye thinge ~~Else~~ that cane become dew° to Mee, and to that Ende wouldbee contented that you should Stope° My Proportione of woole for the Securitie of Soe much of that Some as it will answar, or Else I will oblidge my selfe to make returne by Bill of Exchange thether of soe much as I shall reseve° from you heare when the woole shallbee broght over and Sould,° therfor I pray uss° your indevour° for mee in this Perticuler and Let mee heare from you conserninge° it as Soune° as Convenientlie you Cane

Letter 274. November 8, 1673, [London], the Duchess of Ormonde to Captain George Mathew (NLI, Ormond Papers, 2503, no. 124). Autograph.
For My Brother Captane Gorge Mathews. [Endorsed]: my Ladyes about mr Pages debt 8 November 1673. Duchess of ormonde to George Mathew.

The 8 of November

I have at this presant only time to tell you that the List of the payments unto mrs Hoare[867] and that of My Lords depts° Exsept the Morgadges° came yesternight Late unto my hands in that of the depts I find 0900 dew° unto mr Page* I desier° to know whether it bee the arreares of his Annewetie or anye other private dept of My Lords or of my Sonn Osorys* to hime [that] if it bee not upon the first mentionede of thes I am a Stranger unto it, The ingadgments° of the Estate that is upon Morgadge wouldbee very requisit ~~wee Both~~ My Lord and I both should know and therfor I desier you willbee pleasede to Let Mr wellch* know that it is Expected from hime to produse to you what Booukes of Entrye or other accompt° that hee Cane give of Them,

---

[867] Unidentified creditor.

Letter 275. December 5, 1673, Hampstead, the Duchess of Ormonde to Captain George Mathew (NLI, Ormond Papers, 2503, no. 125). Autograph.
For My Brother Captane Gorge Mathews. [Endorsed]: My Lady Dutches 5 and 13 december 1673. Duchess of ormonde to George Mathew.

Hamsted the 5 of Desember

as I remember I acquanted you formerlie with Captane wineworths* request that hee might surrender his Farme or bee abayted° somthinge of his Rent, I have agayne° bine° Solisited by hime, That as hee was by his Lease for the first 10 years to pay 18 pense the Acher° (and after tow° Shillings) that hee might hould° it accordinge to the first rayte° that hee was to pay, in regard of his improvments, at the Least, untell° the Times doe Mend and the warrs sease;° otherwiss it may bee apprehended our Looses may prove greater if Hee quit the plase; for The Tenants provablie° beinge English and some of them Duch will doe ~~Soe To~~ ^the Same^, but without your advise and oppinione what were best to bee done in this perticuler I shall suspend the returninge hime an answar, and therfor I desier° I may know your Sense hearof as soune° as you Cane convenientlie [/] I thank you for consarninge° your Selfe by your indevours° to procure what suplye canbee had for my ocations;° of whous Care and Frindship I Never douted,° (nor will you I hope) of my beinge as Sensible therof as your kindnes has obligdged mee to bee, I begane about a Fortnight sense,° to Find a returne of My Cough which to prevent my growinge worse I came for beter° Ayre° to Hamsted some 5 Milles from London to a pretie House Furnisht which I touck Soe from Mickellmes° last unto our Lady day for fortie Pound which Plase and ^the^ quietnes of it has givene mee greater advantages in My health then all the remidies° the Doctors could have precribede° Mee; soe as I intend God willinge to Continow° heare untell the worst of the winter bee Past, and to goe some times when the wether is Faire to vissit My Familie at Clarington House, and to inquier° after the affares of it, I pray remember mee to My Sister, whoe I writ to befor I Left London, which Leter; I should bee glad to know were Come unto hir hands

Letter 276. February 3, 1673/4, [Hampstead], the Duchess of Ormonde to Captain George Mathew (NLI, Ormond Papers, 2503, no. 126). Autograph.
For My Brother Captane Gorge Mathews. [Endorsed]: My Ladyes 3 february 1673 about the peace et cetera. Duchess of ormonde to George Mathew.

The 3 of Feb

All that I have time to tell you this day, is that the Pease with Holland is resolvede upon By the kinge ^with^ and the Concuranse of Both Housses;[868] and that an Express goes away this Night unto the Prinse of Oringe [/] The Next Neuse° wee Expect is, that Lissense° willbee givene for the bringinge over of Irishe Cattell, and that wee are Like to have very good Marketts for our woole Soe Soune Soune° as the declaratione of Pease shall make it more Sayfe° then hetherto° it has bine° to bringe it over; wee Still Continow° our resolutions of goeinge for Ireland

Letter 277. February 6, 1673/4, [Hampstead], the Duchess of Ormonde to Captain George Mathew (NLI, Ormond Papers, 2503, no. 127). Autograph.
For My Brother Captane Gorge Mathews [/] thes. [Endorsed]: My Ladyes 6 / 17 february 1673 To Send over bed hanging feathers et cetera. For a good Inn. Duchess of ormonde to George Mathew.

The 6 of Feb

I have this day writene unto Baxter* about the Furniture of a damaske Bed that had resevede° some Staynes by Salt water which I would have to bee olltored° and mended heare; and to that Ende I have sent for it, and the Plumes of Fethers to bee made upe heare accordinge as thay° are now ussed, which I bid hime to acquant you of, I would not have anye other of the Furniture belonginge to it, but the out and inside of the Bed only; in regard I purpose to returne it Backe with my other Goods which I intend within thes 2 ^Few^ Months to Send by Longe Sea[869] to waterford,
My Lord thinks it very requisit to have a good Indkieper° at kilkeny and is indevoringe° to Find one for that purpose but befor

---

[868] The Treaty of Westminster, signed by the King on February 9, stipulated that New York (formerly New Netherland) would be an English possession, and that Suriname, which had been captured by the Dutch in 1667, would remain their colony.

[869] "[S]hort for long sea passage" ("long sea" in "long, *adj.* 1 and *n.* 1," *OED*).

wee proside° further it willbee Nesesarye to bee informed whether the House, that wright[870] is Now In, may be Free to bee disposed of, or anye other as Convenient, and in what repayre, as allsoe what Staybelinge Sellers° Gardines and other accomodations dous° belonge to it and what Rent it now yealds, Sense° it wouldbee of soe great an advantage to the Towne to have a good Ine Ther, as it would draw a great resort, which for want of Entertainment Ther are forst to goe other Rodes

stabling (stables)

Letter 278. February 14, 1673/4, [Hampstead], the Duchess of Ormonde to Captain George Mathew (NLI, Ormond Papers, 2503, no. 128). Autograph.
For My Brother Captane Gorge Mathews. [Endorsed]: My Ladyes 14 / 27 february 1673 Millins place. The Wooll. Duchess of ormonde to George Mathew.

The 14 of Feb

you will within a Few days have a full asshuranse of Pease upon the returne of the ratificatione from Holland which is sudanlie° Expected, soe soune° as I understoud of Millans* beinge soe dayngeroslie Sicke I sent unto an acquantanse of Mine in Oxfordshire by whous Menes° I dout° not of beinge provided of a good Sarvant in his Plase, James Clarke* will by this Post informe you what offiers° are made heare for the wooll by mr Lentrope* and others, the Time beinge now Expirede for allowinge a 11 in the hundreth for Exchange ^which^ will now I hope bee had upon much Easier Termes

---

[870] Unidentified.

Final Decade, 1674–1684

Letter 279. August [1674?], [Kilkenny], the Duchess of Ormonde to the Duke of Ormonde (NLI, Ormond Papers, 2484, no. 248, p. 315).[871] Autograph.
For the Duke of Ormonde. [Endorsed]: Lady Dutchesse of Orm[onde].

The [*missing*] of Agust

The wind has crost° mee from hearinge this 2 Last Posts out of England, soe as I am at this presant Ignorant whether you have Left London and are at the Bayth° or Not, by which you May imagine my unease when I am prevented by anye acsident from hearinge from you, and espetialie° sense° you have proposed a Journye for your health am soe much the More Consarned° to know how the watters dous° agree with you, which I doe not dout° but you willbee Soe kind as to Find some way to Let mee know from thense, and when I may Expect you heare, My Sonn and daughter Arran* are still at Dublin; and ther I doe beleve will Staye, the Landinge of mrs Feris* and ther Litell° Boy that comes over together, My former Leter will give you all the accompt° I had or have Sense resevede° of my Sonn Johns* affare, and for other relatinge to the olltorations° of this plase and the works you oppoynted° to bee don° in your absense I willnot heare insert the perticulers; hopinge you willbee a wittnes of it your Selfe Shortlie and aprove therof for soe I please; This yeare is like to prove very plentifull and is very healthfull to all the inhabitants God bee thanked for it [/] The Mesenger I sent to See My Brother Hambellon[872] is not as yet returned soe as I cannot at the presant give you anye furthar accompt of hime, My Brother Mathew* desirede mee to tell you that the Game has bine° Soe well presarvede in your absense as theris great Store of Partridge Everye where Neere the Towne

---

[871] There is minor wear and tear to the top of the leaf.
[872] JO's brother-in-law, Sir George Hamilton.

Letter 280. November 3, 1675, Kilkenny, the Duchess of Ormonde to Sir George Preston (Birr Castle, Rosse Papers, A/1/48). Scribal: signed.
For Sir George Preston Knight at his house [/] Lymricke.
[Endorsed]: The Dutches of Ormonds Letter to Sir George Preston about the Lordship of Dingwell belonging to her Grace—and Sir George his own affaire: 1675.

Cousen[873]   Kilkenny 3rd November 1675

Itt beeing the Opinion of the Kinges Advocatt and other Lawyers in Scotland that I have a right to the Lordshipp of Dingwell[874] as well as to the Titles and would be recovered if looked after occations the trouble of the inclosed doubts and queryes to bee resolved afore I can proceed farther therein which I desire you will give mee an account of as soon as you can,

There is all [Serch] possible made at Dublin for the resolve of the Lord Lieutenant and Councill in your concern uppon whitch mutch of your advantage depends besides all indeavors used in England to secure your Intrest Soe as wee hope to bring this affayre to a good Conclution wherein there shalbee noe indeavor omitted or Charge spared by

      your affectionat Cousen

      E:ormonde

I desire to bee remembered to my Cousen your Lady

Letter 281. November 11, 1675, [Kilkenny?], the Duchess of Ormonde to Valentine Smith (Birr Castle, Rosse Papers, A/1/46). Autograph.
For Mr vallantine Smith [/] thes. [Endorsed]: my Lady Dutchess about Sir George Preston 11/17 November 1675.

vallantine Smith*   The 11 of November

yesternight I reseved° the inclosed from the Aturnye° Generall,[875] but not the co draft of the kings Leter that hee Mentions, and this

---

[873] Sir George Preston was EO's paternal cousin.

[874] EO was *suo jure* Lady Dingwall through her father, Richard Preston, Lord Dingwall, first Earl of Desmond.

[875] William Domvile (1609–1689) served as Attorney General for Ireland througout the reign of Charles II.

day I had an advertisment from Sir Gorge Preston* whous Lady is
Now heare, that hee has bine° Sarved with a writ by the Corporation
of Limbericke;[876] which soe Soune° as you have perussede; I desier°
you will put into Such a way as my Cousen may not bee disposest of
the Plase, untell° the kings Leter bee obtayned which I dout° not to
procure, his Lady has broght mee divers papers, which I send you
to the Ende that such of them as are materiall for his Counsell May
bee Transmited to them, as I desier may a Note from you ^to Mee^
of such as you Now reseve,° and that I may know when you think
you Cane bee heare, the Last Post brought noe Leters from England
which I pray Let My Brother Mathews* know from

EO

**Letter 282. May 27, [1677], [London], the Duchess of Ormonde
to the Countess of Cork and Burlington** (BL, Additional MSS,
Althorpe Papers, 75356). Autograph.
For the Countis of Burlington. att Launsbrough [*illegible*] to bee left
with Mr ffotthewgill dyer in Walmegate of Yorke.[877] [Endorsed]:
Duchess Ormond.

Madam[878]   The 27 of May

---

[876] Sir George Preston had an interest in a number of fisheries along the west and south-west coast of Ireland. In 1662, he was granted the Lax (salmon) weir and fishery by Charles II, which lead to a long legal battle between Preston and the Corporation of Limerick. The courts eventually ruled against Preston, but to prevent further litigation, the Corporation agreed to make a payment to him in acknowledgment of his claim. See J. A. Place, "History of the Lax Weir," *Journal of the Limerick Field Club* 3.9 (1905–1908): 25–31, especially 28. Some verse, which seems to date from the seventeenth century, was written on the subject, and quoted in John Ferrar, *The History of Limerick, Ecclesiastical, Civil and Military* (Limerick: A. Watson & Co., 1787), 117.

[877] Londesborough was the Earl of Cork and Burlington's Yorkshire seat. Walmgate Bar was one of the four main medieval gateways to the city of York.

[878] The Countess of Cork and Burlington, Elizabeth Boyle, née Clifford (1613–1691), was the wife of Richard Boyle, first Earl of Burlington and second Earl of Cork, and the daughter and heiress of Henry, Lord Clifford (later Earl of Cumberland). There was evidently a warm friendship between the two women, which probably dates back to the 1640s and 1650s when first, they found refuge in Caen, and second, successfully recovered their respective estates from confiscation; both spent the rest of the Interregnum living quietly on these estates in Ireland. For the Countess of Cork's petition to Cromwell, see *Original Letters and Papers of State, Addressed to Oliver Cromwell*, ed. by John Nickolls (London: William Bowyer, 1743), I, 84–85; also SAL, MS 138.

I reseved° with great Satisfactione the honner° of a Leter from you
of the 20 of this Month it bringinge mee the wellcome Neuse° of
your beinge come sayfe° unto your owne House and beinge in health;
which I pray and wish you may Long injoye; to your owne comfort
and the Contentment of all your relations and Frinds; that Cannot
but have a great conserne° for you; as I am Shure° I have in my
perticuler, as much as for anye person, Non° desarvinge it more from
mee then your Ladyshipp dous;° whous good companye I am soe
Sensible of the want of, as I Fansie That Ende of the Towne[879] dous
not apiere° what it did at the Least to mee, sense° you Left it, makes
mee the Less troubled more willinge to goe for Ireland; as my Lord
thinks hee shall the Next Month but I dout° hee Cane hardlie bee
redie to begine his Journye untell° July [/]
    I was indisposed in My health sense your Ladyshipp went
away, made mee spend some days at Rohampton[880] with the ustiall°
advantage that I have reseved from the Goodnes of that Ayre;° Soe
as That, and the Hote° wether which has agreede beter° with Mee
hetherto° though it bee troubelsome then it has done with Manye
others; inables° mee to bee heare at presant, where I shall and in all
plasses° bee; with a perfect respect, and Fathfullnes

            Madam

                your Ladyshipps oblidged and most humble Sarvant

                      E:ormonde

Madam I bege the Favour to have by you my Sarvis° presented unto
My Lord of Burlington*

**Letter 283. August 11, [1677], Chatsworth, the Duchess of
Ormonde to the Countess of Cork and Burlington** (BL, Additional
MSS, Althorpe Papers, 75356). Autograph.
For the Countis of Burlington. [Endorsed]: from the Duchesse of
Ormond August 11th ([16]77).

Madam   Chathswood[881] the 11 of Agust

---

    [879] Presumably Piccadilly, London, where Burlington House, the couple's London residence since 1668, stood.
    [880] Possibly the Devonshire house in Roehampton, Surrey.
    [881] Chatsworth House was the seat of the third Earl of Devonshire, the father of Lord Cavendish, and father-in-law of EO's daughter, Mary. It is where the younger couple also resided.

I Came hether to Chadsworth on Thursday Last where I had the
good Fortune to Meete My Lord Burlington* and to reseve° the
honner° of a Leter from your Ladyshipp, and in it; the Expretione°
of your continowed° favour and good wisshes for Mee, which I
Estime my selfe soe hapie in, as I shall goe with much the greater
Chierfullnes° the remayninge part of my Journye,[882] though it bee
the most difficult to Mee; I have bine° a Litell° indisposede sense°
my Cominge hether, but hope to find some benefitt by the beinge
Sicke at Sea, though I thinke the Rockinge by Land in the worst
Coche way° that Ever I past in cominge hether, did much ocatione°
my distemper, together with the acsident of Breakinge one of my
Shines, which My Lord Burlington was Soe charitable as to precribe°
mee a remidie° for, which provede more Sucksesfull° in givinge
mee Ease; then Mine did his Lordshipps for his hearinge though
I Meant it as well, This Plase is much improvede by My Lady of
Devonshires[883] Care and Ingeneuite; which is much disernede in the
great amendments shee has made both without doure,[884] and in the
House, ~~which is~~ the great worke of all still remaynes unperfected,
which I hope Shee will make hir Selfe a hapie instrument in, of
makinge Pease betwixt My Lord of Devonshire and his Sonn,[885]
without which I cannot beleve anye thinge will prove prosperous to
ther Familie; My Lord of Darby* and his Lady[886] are gone to ^ther^
owne House, whoe I shall Meete at Chester within a Few days,
which is all the accompt° that I Cane give your Ladyshipp from
hense untell° I come one° the other side of the water and then I shall

---

[882] To Ireland, where the Countess of Cork and Burlington had recently returned.

[883] Devonshire's wife, Elizabeth, née Cecil, Countess of Devonshire (1620–1689), was the mother of Lord Cavendish, EO's son-in-law.

[884] "Out of doors, outside the house, in the open air" ("wi☒thout ☒doors, *adv.* (and *adj.*).," 1, *OED*).

[885] Father and son had a very strained relationship, which in her detailed analysis of JO's mediating role with his in-laws, O'Keeffe, 112–14, attributes to the fact that William was not financially independent from his father. As she outlines, the dispute in 1677 was over Cavendish's attempt to purchase a house in London, which he intended to do by disposing of an annuity left him by his grandmother, but he needed his father to consent to the purchase. In a letter to JO, Cavendish wondered why his father "should be so offended at my design of living by myself, nor can I imagine what can make him so averse from it, unless he thinks that because I have been content to pass the best part of my life uneasily I am obliged to spend the rest so too" (NLI, Ormond Papers, 2367, no. 3909, p. 257).

[886] EO's seventeen-year-old granddaughter, Elizabeth, daughter of her eldest son, the Earl of Ossory, who had married William Stanley, ninth Earl of Derby.

take the Libertie ~~you have~~ ^of^ given^ge^ ~~mee of~~ your Ladyshipp a further address from

 Madam

  your Ladyshipps fathfull and Most humble Sarvant

   E:ormonde

I bege my Sarvis° may bee presented unto My Lady Jeane Cliford[887]

Letter 284. September 29, 1677, [Dublin], the Duchess of Ormonde to the Earl of Ossory (NLI, Ormond Papers, 2368, no. 3993, p. 49). Autograph.
For the Earle of Ossory [/] thes. [Endorsed]: Lady Duchesse to My Lord Ossory 29 September 1677. Lord Ossory.

         The 29 of September

At my goeinge to killkenye I writ to you; and doe hope from what I heare out of England that this may find you Ther, I stayede in the Contrye but a Few days, where I found all things beter° then I Expected, I hope My Lords affares are Now soe regulated, as hee willbee abble Evrye yeare, to pay ofe° a Considerable part of his dept,° and yet suport the dignitie of his Plase ~~besides~~ in a way of honner° and Creditt to hime [/] I find Noe appieringe dissatisfactions as yet; but ~~what~~ what Time and inconstantsie of Humor may produse at Longe Runinge I cannot tell, for this world is Subgect to Change [/] My Lord and Lady Straford[888] are Expected heare within a Few days, the yaght beinge Sent to bringe them over, whoe Shallbee reseved° and Treated by all of your relations with the respect that is dew° to Them and ~~the~~ ^our^ Frindshipe and relation unto ther Familie upon your daghters accompt,°

---

[887] Lady Jane Clifford, youngest daughter of William Seymour, second Duke of Somerset (1637–1679), was the Countess of Burlington's daughter-in-law, wife of her eldest son, Charles, third Viscount Dungarvin.

[888] William Wentworth, second Earl of Strafford, and Lady Henrietta Mary Stanley, the daughter of James Stanley, seventh Earl of Derby. Ossory's daughter had married into Lady Strafford's paternal family.

Letter 285. July 13, 1678, [Dublin], the Duchess of Ormonde to the Earl of Ossory (NLI, Ormond Papers, 2375, no. 4469, p. 491). Autograph. For the Earle of Ossory. [Endorsed]: 13 July 1678 Dutchess of ormonde.

The 13 of July

I was doutfull of your beinge at London, untell° I reseved° your Leter of the 2 of this Month, as I hope you have done ~~mine~~ a Late Leter of Mine, which I sent you soe soune° as I heard of your arrivall in England, I take very kindlie [your] intendment to have made My Lord and mee a visset° if ther had bine° Pease, which it beinge now takene for granted willbee otherwise I cannot resonablie Expect nor will desier;° untell you may bee at more Libertye to afford mee the Satisfactione of Seeinge you in this Contrye the mene° Time; I shall pray for your Sayftie and hapie Suckses° in all your undertakings; Monsieur de Lange your Sonns Governor[889] gives mee great hopes of his perfect recovrye, which I am the apter to beeleve, by resone° I heare Hee is much Growne and Loukes° well; soe that as soune° as Barington[890] returns it willbee then Convenient to Consider of removinge hime where hee may bee put to Learne his Exsiersies,° and reseve° such other advantages, as willbee Fitt for one of his Qualitie which I supose cannot bee in anye Plase soe well ^Taught^ as at Paris, and therfor I wish I knew your oppinion whether you aprove of putinge hime into an Academie ^Ther^ or otherwise; sense° ther shallbee nothinge wantinge towards his Educatione and Mantenanse that shallbee requisit nor anye Course takene therin (with My Consent) but with your approbatione therfor I pray Consider well of it, and Let My Lord know what your desiers are in this perticuler

---

[889] Monsieur de Lange was the governor of Ossory's eldest son and heir, Lord James Butler, who was thirteen. The governor was later dismissed from his post after being accused of financial corruption, isolating James from his peers, and keeping him "shamefully low and wanting of clothes and all necessities." For a detailed discussion of James's education, see O'Keeffe, 76–82.

[890] Robert Barrington, companion to Lord James.

Letter 286. October 26, [1678], Dublin, the Duchess of Ormonde to the Earl of Ossory (NLI, Ormond Papers, 2484, no. 247, p. 307).[891]
Autograph.
For the Earle of Ossory [/] Thes. Endorsed: Dutchess of Ormond.

Dublin the 26 of [Oct]

I have bine° heare sense° Monday Last where I had the Next day the good Fortune to reseve° a Leter from you that gave mee intemation° of your arrivall, and of your good Fortune of havinge acquited your selfe with Sattisfaction, unto all that you were ~~instructede with the care of~~ ^to Conduct^ and that the Duches[892] was soe oblidginge as to owne your Sarvisses° performed to hir, which I am Shure° has bine a full recompense to you, as well as a great Satisfaction unto your Frinds; I conclude that your Sonn is by this time come to Parris, where it willbee of absolute nesesitie that hee shouldbee soune° ~~pl~~ supplyede with a Governor that may take Care of his Person and Educatione to redime° The Time that hee has Lost in Learninge of his ocationed° by his ill health, and the Solitarines of the Plase that hee was In; My Lord Chamberlane[893] and Sir Robert Southwell[894] were indevoringe° to gett one mr Hindshaw[895] that is [*missing*] without Exseption if hee would undertake such an imployment as I much feare hee willnot, and in that Cayse;° I offier° to you to Consider, whether mr Forbus[896] might not bee as proper as anye other that you could have ^and^ if soe; you would doe well to inquier° at a distanse whether hee bee not otherwise ingadged;° and how Duke Hambellton[897] is Satisfiede with hime whoe Traveled with his Eldest Soon,° for the other Perticuler of the Mach° I shall deferr Sayinge anye thinge therin; untell° the Next Post by resone° theris much to bee considerd in an affare of that great importanse only this I am positive in ~~My advise is,~~ that the Name shouldnot bee

---

[891] Minor wear and mending tape have obscured some text in the MS.

[892] Presumably, Mary of Modena, who had become the second wife of James, Duke of York, in 1673.

[893] Ossory's friend and brother-in-law, the Earl of Arlington.

[894] Sir Robert Southwell was a confidante of JO, who entrusted the education of his grandsons to him. See Toby Barnard, "Southwell, Sir Robert (1635–1702)," *ODNB*.

[895] Unidentified.

[896] Unidentified.

[897] William Hamilton, third Duke of Hamilton (1634–1694).

Changed[898] upon anye Termes whatsomever, I pray speake with My daughter Ossory* and know hir opinion consarninge° mr Forbus

Letter 287. September 4, 1679, [Dublin?], the Duchess of Ormonde to Captain George Mathew (NLI, Ormond Papers, 2391, no. 5448, p. 195). Scribal: signed.
[Endorsed]: my Lady Dutches order to Sett Balliline to mrs Austacie Comerford.

Having promised mrs Comerford* of Callan the preference of a ffarme and Shee desiring to bee Tenant to Ballilyne as most contiguous to her I desire you will preferr her to the Sayd ffarme uppon the Rates you have Sett down for Setting the farme

dated the 4th of September 1679   E:ormonde

To my Brother Captain George Mathew / These[899]

Letter 288. July 13, 1680, [Dublin], the Duchess of Ormonde to the Duke of Ormonde (NLI, Ormond Papers, 2400, no. 5991, p. 123). Autograph.
For My Lord the Duke of Ormonde. [Endorsed]: Dutchess of Ormond 13 July 1680.

the 13 of July

My Brother Mathews* came to Towne yesternight with whom I had some discourse consarninge° your Intent to take upe Mony,° to bee in a redenes° in Cayse° of anye Nesesitie you may bee driwene° unto, Ether for your owne or the kings Sarvis,° and I find hime to bee of opinione that whatsowever Some° you designe to rayse were beter° to bee takene upe from one Person, if it may bee soe had, then from severall, by resone° the Layter,° will make much Noyse,° which

---

[898] This perhaps relates to EO's daughter-in-law, Anne, widow of EO's youngest son, John, Earl of Gowran, who had died in 1676. She would marry Francis Aungier, first Earl of Longford, shortly after this letter was written.

[899] Enclosed with the above letter is the following signed bond dated from March 1649:
> I Confesse to have receaved att the hands of mr Jespar Bennett marchant of Rouen the Some of a thousand Liveres tournois ["2000 pounds" inserted in the left margin] is by order of mr patricke Archer marchant of waterford in Ireland as wittnesse my hand the 24 march 1649
>   Elis:o

may prove inconvenient, in many respects, Sir Robert Collvin[900] I doe beleve both Cane and will Furnish you with a Considerable Some, which My Brother would have to bee proposed to pay ofe° the Second great dept;° ^you owe^ that to Sir Robert viner* beinge discharged which hee thinks a beter pretense, then to have it thought you wanted it, or would have it, upon anye other accompt,° and if you please to write your Selfe unto Sir Robert[901] or make Sir Mawris[902] To do it for you, I maye Not question of your suckses° in that affare, I pray send mee word when you think to bee heare,

Letter 289. January 26, [early 1680s?], [Dublin], the Duchess of Ormonde to the Lord Chief Justice John Keating (Birr Castle, Rosse Papers, A/1/40). Autograph.
For the Lord Chife Justis Keatinge. Endorsed: Hir Grace the Dutches of Ormonds Letter to the Lord Chief Justice Keating.

My Lord   The 26 of Jan

I take soe kindlie Sir Lawranse Parsons[903] great Sivelitie to mee, in not presinge the sudane° payinge of my kinswomans Portion,[904] as nothinge could soe much ingadge° mee to a Conserne° of doeinge it spidilie° to accomodate his ocations,° then his beinge soe oblidginge to Mee; and therfor Hee may depend upon resevinge° tow° Thowsand ^pound^ at ~~Ester~~ the Time of Ther Mariage, which I desier° may bee at Ester,° and the rest hee shallbee Shure° of at Midsomer, at the Farthest; but I hope Souner,° I doe beter° aprove of my Cousens goeinge to Thomastowne[905] then mr Parsons[906] cominge to Dublin,

---

[900] Sir Robert Colvin, perhaps of Lough Eske, Co. Donegal.
[901] Sir Robert Viner, presumably.
[902] Possibly Sir Maurice Eustace (d. 1708), nephew and heir of JO's friend of the same name.
[903] Sir Lawrence Parsons, ancestor to the earls of Rosse, had been created baronet in 1677. See Piers Wauchope, "Parsons, Sir Lawrence, first baronet (c. 1637–1698)," *ODNB*.
[904] Her kinswoman is Elizabeth, one of Sir George Preston's daughters, who would marry Sir Lawrence Parsons's son and heir, William. Preston's other daughter, Margery, had married John Eyre of Eyrecourt, Galway, in 1677.
[905] Thomastown, Co. Tipperary, was George Mathew's residence, which he had built in 1670.
[906] Presumably, William Parsons, the groom.

and therfor shall order it accordinglie, to have hir invited thether, and will allways remayne

    My Lord

        your Lordshipps reall Frind and Sarvant

           E:ormonde

Letter 290. January, [early 1680s?], Roehampton, the Duchess of Ormonde to Sir William Domvile (Birr Castle, Rosse Papers, A/1/41). Autograph.
For Sir william Dumbuile his Magestis Atturnye Generall of Ireland.

Sir[907]   Roehampton the [*blank*] of January

I am shure° you are noe stranger unto My Conserne° for My kinsman Sir George Preston;* that has resevede° formerlie the trouble of some addresses from mee upon his accompt,° whous Cause, is now Like as I understand, to come Shortlie unto a Tryall° betwixt hime and the Corporatione of Limbricke,° I therfor doe at this time renew my request unto you to afford hime your Favour, and the advantage of your advise, which I sett soe great a vallew° upon; and thous° many testimonys of your Frindshipe and Regard Exprest unto Mee and all my Relations; as noe Person canbee more sensible therof then I am, and therfor shall hope for the good Fortune of some ocatione;° that may inable° mee to make the same apiere;° more to my owne Sattisfactione, and your Merit, in the mene° Time I desier° the Justiss from you to beleve I am, and allways bee

    Sir

        your very asshured° Frind and Sarvant

           E:ormonde

Sir I desier that my Sarvis° may by you bee presented unto My Lady Dumbuile[908]

---

[907] Sir William Domvile (1609–1689), Attorney General for Ireland. See Hazel Maynard, Patrick H. Kelly, "Domvile (Domville), Sir William," *DIB*.

[908] Brigid, Lady Domvile, a daughter of Sir Thomas Lake (1567–1630). See Hazel Maynard, Patrick H. Kelly, "Domvile (Domville), Sir William," *DIB*.

Letter 291. July 16, [early 1680s?], [London?], the Duchess of Ormonde to Lady Jean Preston (Birr Castle, Rosse Papers, A/1/43). Autograph.
For My Lady Preston. Endorsed: The Dutches of Ormonds Letter to the Lady Preston.

Madam[909]   The 16 of July

Sir Gorge Prestons* conselinge the ingadgment° of the Lexe weere;   *lax weir*
and makinge ^afterwards^ a Diede of Sayle ^of it^ to My Brother   *deed*
Mathews* and Jeames Clarke* of That and other his Intrest [for]
afterwards, has soe Intangeled the bussenes° as it is Like to undoe
all the Settellment that was made for his Securitie, which had I but
understoud the worst of, which I did allways desier° both from you
and hime, might have bine° otherwiss Contrived but as it is; I desier
that what papers or the Copies of such as vallantine Smith* dous°
Now send unto you For, may bee transmited to hime, which is all at
presant from

   your Ladyshipps affectionat Cousen

      E:ormonde

Letter 292. July 17, [early 1680s?], [London?], the Duchess of Ormonde to Sir George Preston (Birr Castle, Rosse Papers, A/1/42). Autograph.
For Sir Gorge Preston [/] thes at Limbrick. Endorsed: Lady Duchess Letter to Sir George Preston about his Sutte with the Corporation.

Cousen   The 17 of July

I reseved° your Leter of the 13 of this Month, and shall uss° all the
Intrest I have with thous° that you desirede mee to write unto, to
befrind you in your Conserns;° wherin the want of an abble Lawyer
may bee of a great disadvantage to you, and therfor I have prevayled
^with^ mr Shee[910] that is a Counselor and a ve has the reputatione
of a very abble and an honnest ^Man^ one much imployed in My
Lords affares, to goe downe on purpose to pleade and Manadge
this bussenes° of yours, whoe is knowne unto the Judges and well
Estimede by them; whoe willbee at Corke the 29 of this [/] This

---

[909] Jean Preston, née Gibson, daughter of Sir Alexander Gibson of Durie. She married Sir George Preston in around 1640. See *Burke's Irish Family Records* (London: Burke's Peerage, 1976).
[910] Unidentified.

^Month^ to Meete your Counsell, and informe himselfe of your Cayse° and how the prosidings° has bine,° whoe is to Sarve you without Fees for I have takene upon my Selfe to gratifie hime and a Nother° I send ~~one m~~ Mr vallantine Smith* that Follows My Lord[s] bussenes, and willbee a very ussfull person to you, ther beinge some industrye and Experiense requirede in Carryinge on a bussenes of this kind, agaynst a whole Corporation that you have now to Contend with, by whom I intend to write unto the Lord Busshope of Corke[911] and some other of My Frinds in your behalfe and will doe what Ever Else I cane ~~doe~~ to Expres my selfe

        your affectionat Cousen

          E:ormonde

Letter 293. September 9, [early 1680s?], Roehampton, the Duchess of Ormonde to Valentine Smith (Birr Castle, Rosse Papers, A/1/44). Autograph.

vallantine Smith   Roehampton the 9 of September

If you bee remembred befor my Cominge out of Ireland, beinge in dispayre of gettinge what was desirede in the Consarne° of Sir Gorge Preston* by obtayninge a [*illegible*] Couranto[912] to Compell the Sitie of Limbricke° to take out ther Charter ther was a draft of a Nother° Leter drawne for the kinge to Signe; to the Chife° Governer in Favour of Sir Gorges Patent that Nothinge in the New Charter should Pass unto his Prejudis; which Copie I thought I had broght over with mee but cannot Find, wherfor I desier,° if you have anye on° of them by you that you will Send it to mee with all Spide for I will make uss° of all the Intrest I have Both heare and in Ireland to Suport My kinsmans Intrest; and doe hope to Send you the oppinione of the best Lawyers heare, which I doe beleve will have Some Creditt Thar° in this Cayse° of his; if I find it willbee for Sir Gorges ^advantage^ and however, will obtanyne the kings Leter, in his Favour; and what other to anye perticuler Persons Ther from My Lord; that you think May bee Nesesarye; upon whous Care in this affare I doe prinsepalie relye; and therfor doe desier you to disburse what you think may bee requisit to Fee Lawyers or otherwise and I

despair

city

---

[911] Edward Wetenhall, Church of Ireland Bishop of Cork and Ross, from 1679. See John Cronin and Patrick A. Walsh, "Wetenhall, Edward," *DIB*.

[912] "A letter or paper containing public news; a gazette, news-letter, or newspaper" ("co⊠ranto, *n*.2," *OED*).

will write unto My Brother Mathews* to repaye it you, ~~that~~ it beinge
not My intent that you should Rune° the Least hazard by anye thinge
that is imposede upon you by Mee, but on the Contrarye ~~bee~~ have
your Paynes requited by

your asshured° Frind

E:ormonde

I pray Let Sir Gorge Preston bee made acquanted with such Part
of this Leter as you Judge Nesesarye to Satisfie hime that I am not
Negligent of his Conserns°

**Letter 294. September 16, [early 1680s?], [London?], the Duchess
of Ormonde to Valentine Smith** (Birr Castle, Rosse Papers, A/1/45).
Autograph.
For Mr vallantine Smith.

vallantine Smith*   The 16 of September

I send you hearinclosed a ~~Pet~~ Copie of a Petistione presented some
time Sense° unto the kinge in Sir Gorge Prestons* Name, his
Magesties referanse upon it unto the Lord Liftenant with his Report;
which I knew Nothinge of untell° the Last weeke that Gascogne[913]
acquainted mee with it, Nether cane I Judge whether it willbee of
anye advantage unto hime or Not, however I thought it Fitt to Send
~~it~~ ^them^ to you, that upon your perusstiall° of Both it may bee
considered whether the kings Leter grownded° upon ~~all~~ thes; may
bee of uss° unto My Cousens presant Conserns° which, I dout° not
to obtayne; if anye such shallbee thought Nesesarye, a draft wherof I
desier° may bee transmitted from thense with as much spiede° as you
Cane, and that Sir Gorge Preston may bee maded acquanted with
what is allredie procured, and what Shallbee further indevored° for
hime

---

[913] Unidentified.

Letter 295. November 1, [early 1680s?], [London], the Duchess of Ormonde to Sir George Preston (Birr Castle, Rosse Papers, A/1/57).
Autograph.
For Sir Gorge Preston at Limbricke. Endorsed: The Dutches of Ormonds Letter to Sir George Preston about his Daughters dangerous voyage.

Cousen   The first of November

To prevent anye report that might make you beleve your daghter to bee Cast a way, I have takene the first oppertunitie to asshure° you that Shee is Sayfe,° though presarvede by noe Less then a Merickell; the Shipe wherin shee wass beinge wracked on the westterne Coust; and Shee broght on Shore upon a Mans Backe and afterwards carryede unto the Earle of Bayths House; where shee was very kindlie resevede,° and went from thense to Minhead;[914] I heard of this but yesterday; and this Morninge; I am takinge ~~Care~~ ^order^ to have hir broght to towne; where I shall take Care of hir persone and breedinge; and doe hope that God whoe has soe Emenentlie presarved hir out of this Late daynger, will make hir a Comfort unto you and hir Mother, to whom I pray remember ^Mee^ and asshure your selfe of my beinge

miracle

eminently

        Sir

               your asshured° Frind and Cousen

                   E:ormonde

Letter 296. May [16], [1682], [London], the Duchess of Ormonde to the Earl of Arran (NLI, Ormond Papers, 2420, no. 7277, p. 29).
Autograph.
For the Earle of Arran.

                                       [16] May

---

[914] Minehead, Somerset, on the west coast of England. Given its relative proximity to Minehead, presumably the "Earl of Bath's house" is the Earl of Bath's Devon seat, Tawstock Court, although after the fifth Earl had died in 1654 without issue, the Tawstock estate had come into the hands of the Wrey family through Anne Bourchier, one of the three daughters and co-heirs of the fourth earl, who had married Sir Chichester Wrey, third Baronet (1628–1668). See Victor Stater, "Bourchier, Henry, fifth earl of Bath (c. 1587–1654)," *ODNB*.

My Last Leter to you was from London beinge then redie to goe to windsor, and this day, are upon our returne backe; in order unto our Continowanse° heare; for soe Longe as my Lord intends to Stay; findinge it more Convenient in all respects to bee where the kinge is, and to kiepe° one House then to devide our Familie, I had Just Now a Leter from you dated the 10 of this Month that gives mee an accompt° of Sir Lawranse Esmonds[915] ill Suckses° in his affares in having[e] a Judgment givene against hime, and some Feare of the Like in the Conserne° of My Lord of Clonrickerd[916] both which I am very Sorrye For, though Satisfiede, that all was, don° in the first Cayse;° that warantablie couldbee, in favour of hime, and shallbee beleve the Like willbee in the Second allsoe, whatever the Suckses bee; Soe as to such misfortuns as are ^are^ not in the Partys owne Power nor that of ther Frinds indevours° to prevent, must bee by them, and others submitted unto,

Letter 297. [May/June 1682], London, the Duchess of Ormonde to the Earl of Arran (NLI, Ormond Papers, 2420, no. 7316, p. 283).[917] Autograph.
For the Earle of Arran.

[Lon]don the [*date missing*]

I went on thursday Last to [See your] Litell° S[one] whoe I found very well, and as I think a Childe very Like to live for hee thrives very well God bee thanked hetherto,° and [*missing*] that hee is at some distanse from the Doctors and mrs Fereres* whouse over much conserne,° without the [least] Resone° ^resone^ in what she Manages; dous° often times more hurt then Good though I doe beleve shee Menes° well, your Lady is as well in hir health as Ever I saw hir, The Duke and Duches[918] is Everye day Expected but not as yet come, that I doe heare My Lord goes the Next weeke to windsor and soe doe I where I purpose to bee for soe Longe as I shall Stay in this kingdom,

---

[915] Sir Laurence Esmond, second Baronet (d. 1688).
[916] William Burke, seventh Earl of Clanricarde (d. 1687).
[917] The top of the leaf is worn away and partially repaired with mending tape.
[918] James, Duke of York and his second wife, Mary of Modena.

Letter 298. December 16, [1682], [London], the Duchess of Ormonde to the Earl of Arran (NLI, Ormond Papers, 2427, no. 7703, p. 1). Autograph.
For the Earle of Arran.

The 16 of Desember

I am very glad to heare as I did by your Leter of the Second of this Month that My daghter Arran* Landed Sayfe° at Dublin, whoe has befor this Time I hope recovered the wearenes and Toyle of that Longe Journye; and willbe deverted with Litell° Sharlots[919] companye, whoe I conclude is much improved in hir discourse, sense° I Left hir; as your Litell Soon° is in his health and Grouth sense his Last Sicknes and is a very Livelie child; and If upon Deane Jones[920] his preferment, therbee anye Senacure[921] heald by hime that is in your Gift, I desier° you will bistow it upon Mr Rydier* the Scoulmaster at kilkenye for his greater incoridgment° to continow° still ther, otherwiss I feare without some such healpe hee will quitt that Plase, and then That Scooule° will Breake; which has hetherto° had great Creditt, and bine° ag an advantage unto the Towne; My Lady Dunegall* was yesterday to See mee; and did discourse of hir daghter to mee with more Consernednes° then I Expected, soe as I hope Shee willbee kind to hir at Last, I heare my daghter Longford* was resolved to Trye My Lady Rochesters* Doctor whoe has don° great Cures to Severall that had Paynes in ther Stomacks, but I feare My Lady Rochesters recovrye is Not Perfect, for Shee has had returnes of hir ill; Sense hir Landinge and is Extreme Leane; I pray remember My Sarvis° to My daghter[922] to whom I intended to have writene this day but that my Coughe is soe troubelsom this Mistie° wether, that I must deferr it untell° I bee beter,°

weariness

growth

misty

---

[919] Arran's daughter, Charlotte (1678–1725).
[920] Unidentified.
[921] "Any office or position which has no work or duties attached to it, esp. one which yields some stipend or emolument" ("sinecure, *n.* and *adj.*," 2, *OED*).
[922] Lady Arran.

Letter 299. January 6, 1682/3, [London], the Duchess of Ormonde to the Earl of Arran (NLI, Ormond Papers, 2427, no. 7735, p. 225). Autograph.
For the Earle of Arran. [Endorsed]: 6 of Jan 82/3.

6 of Jan

Tow° of your Leters came together to my hands upon wedensday Last the one of the 21 of [Decem]ber the other of the 23 of the Same; with an accompt° of My daghter Arrans* health and Sattisfaction, and the prudent resolutions shee has takene, which I am infinitlie satisfiede with, as what will make you Both hapie, which I pray God may Continow° to the Ende of both your days, and that Evrye yeare of your Liufs,° may increase your vallew° one of a Nother,°   *lives* your Litell° Soon° is very well, and grows a Fine stronge Childe, but Betie* is Lady Blouse⁹²³ still, you willbee I supose surprised to heare that your Father is become a Purcheser of my Lord St Allbans House⁹²⁴ which hee gives 9 thowsand pound For but is thay° Say a good bargine; for it cost above fiftine thowsand Pound the Buildinge, and will Sett for as much or more then the Intrest of his Mony,° I thank you for your good intendment to Mr Ryder* which if it may bee by giveinge hime a Senecure it cane noe ways hinder his presant undertakinge but incoridge° hime to Continow it, as I find hee is resolvede, and never to Louke° for further preferment, if hee may obtane some adistionall° healpe to what hee has, ~~for hee is an~~ ^whoe is a^ hospitable Man; and much valewed in the Plase where hee Lives, The Mach° for Betye Stanope⁹²⁵ is broke ofe° on hir Side, whoe could by noe Menes° bee perswaded to Like of the Person, that was proposede to hir, whoe I never saw but is I heare; farr more Considerabell in his understandinge then in his outward Figure and for his Fortune, theris non° Now, to bee had that Ecqualls hime,⁹²⁶ but upon the whole Matter that affare is at an Ende It beinge the Part of hir Frinds to propound; but Not to Compell aganst hir owne inclination, The Lord Belemont Diede 2 days a goe, and Left My

---

⁹²³ "A beggar's trull, a beggar wench; a wench" ("blowze, *n.*," 1, *OED*).
⁹²⁴ Lord St. Albans' town house was the largest in the recently built St. James's Square. The purchase came after JO's elevation to English duke.
⁹²⁵ Elizabeth Stanhope (1663–1723), EO's granddaughter by her eldest daughter, Elizabeth, Countess of Chesterfield (d. 1665).
⁹²⁶ The proposed match for Betty Stanhope was Lord Camden, the Earl of Gainsborough's son; it was the third proposal for Betty. For a discussion of the efforts to find her a husband, see O'Keeffe, 118–19.

Lord of Chesterfilds Second Soon⁹²⁷ His Ayre° of all his Reall and personall Estate

Letter 300. January 20, 1682/3, [London], the Duchess of Ormonde to the Earl of Arran (NLI, Ormond Papers, 2427, no. 7766, p. 423).
Autograph.
For the Earl of Arran. [Endorsed]: My Lady Duchesse 20 Jan 82/83.

The 20 of Jan

I have not [heard from you] sense° I [writ] Last thar° beinge some Packets from Ireland dew,° but doe am asshured° by Sir Robert Hambelton⁹²⁸ whoe arrivede heare within thes Few days, that hee Left you and my daghter very well; which is the prinsepall Conserne° that I doe inquier° after, I had a Leter upon Monday Last from My daghter Longford,* whoe complayns of ill health notwithstandinge the tryall° shee has made of My Lady Rochesters* Doctor, whoe has done hir ^this Last^ but Litell° Good; for shee is still under a great impayre, and it is fearede cannot recover; the Duke of Buckingham* it is sayede° for Sartane;° has parted with all the Estate that hee has Left, for 6 thowsand a yeare duringe his owne Life and 3 thowsand ^a yeare^ to his Lady, if shee doe Survive hime, The Duches of Richmond* has had hir House Seasede° upon for dept° which the kinge did redime° for hir very Latlie,° but hir other ingadgments° are soe great, that hir best Frinds dous° feare that shee willbee in a condistion to want bread, befor it bee many Months soe very imprudent shee has bine° in hir Expenses Sense hir Husband diede; your Litell Boy is very well thanks bee to God and soe is Betie;* My Lord has hetherto° Scapede the Goout,° and I begine to bee beter° then I was, sense the Fare wether, though I have not ventured downe stayrs as yet for feare of a relapts, I was tould Just Now, that My Lord Connowway⁹²⁹ is to quitt his Plase and My Lord S[unde]rland⁹³⁰ to bee Secretarye

stairs; relapse

---

⁹²⁷ Philip Stanhope, later third Earl of Chesterfield (1673–1726).
⁹²⁸ Unidentified.
⁹²⁹ Edward Conway, third Viscount Conway (c. 1623–1683). See T. C. Barnard, "Conway, Edward 3rd Viscount Conway 1st earl of Conway," *DIB*.
⁹³⁰ Robert Spencer, second Earl of Sunderland (1641–1702), was appointed Secretary of State on January 31, 1683. See W. A. Speck, "Spencer, Robert, second earl of Sunderland (1641–1702)," *ODNB*.

Letter 301. [1683?], [London], the Duchess of Ormonde to the Earl of Arran (NLI, Ormond Papers, 2484, no. 245, p. 293).[931]
Autograph.
For the Earle of Arran. [Endorsed]: Dutchesse of Ormond.

on the 10 of Feb

I am much conserned° for My daghter[932] [*four words missing*] more surprised at it, that it shouldbee without anye acsident that might ocatione° it, of Fright or other; but doe hope the Next leters will bringe a beter° accompt° of hir health, which hir Frinds heare dous° with some impatianse° Expect; I ventured to take the Ayre° upon wednesday Last, beinge the first time that I have bine° abrode this many weeks past, and find my Selfe rather beter, then worse for it, though I went only in a Cheare, my Next attempt, soe soune° as I cane gett a Fare day; shallbee to go to Chelsie to See your ~~Litell~~ Soon,° whoe is very much improvede as I am tould by all that Sees hime; and such as I send to vissit the Litell° Man; whoe I doe hope willbee ~~to her~~ a Comfort to you, for hee apiers Liklie; to Live Longe, I pray asshure° My Cousen Farfaxe[933] that I both doe and will put my Lord in mind of hime; whoe I find to bee as much his Frind, as Hee cane wish hime, soe as I am Shure° hee willnot fayle° in his pretention, when it falls, as I doe beleve it will
[*one line missing*] the person that is in the imployment at the presant, dous decaye very fast unto an aparant degree

chair (chariot or car)
Chelsea

Letter 302. May 27, [1684], [London], the Duchess of Ormonde to the Earl of Arran (NLI, Ormond Papers, 2484, no. 243, p. 279).
Autograph.
For the Earle of Arran. [Endorsed]: Dutchesse of Ormonde 27 May.

I conclude that My Lady Fingall[934] and My Brother Fitspatricke* are arrived in Irland beefor This Time, and will have givene you an

---

[931] Text is missing from the first line of each of two pages of the letter due to wear and tear in the MS.
[932] Presumably, Lady Arran.
[933] Henry Fairfax, fourth Lord Fairfax of Cameron (1631–1688).
[934] Margaret Plunket, née MacCarthy, was the wife of Luke Plunket, third Earl of Fingall (1639–1684). EO's niece, Lady Fingall was the daughter of EO's sister-in-law Eleanor, Lady Clancarty. She was among a group of Catholics found at Somerset House and Whitehall during a search of the royal palaces in 1678 after the revelations of the Popish Plot, but there are no records of her imprisonment or expulsion from court. See Anne Creighton, "Plunket, Luke, 3rd earl of Fingall," *DIB*.

accompt° of all things heare; sense° whous goeinge from hense theris Litell° of Change, soe as I have noe Neuse° to Send you, but that My Lady Dunegall* and My daghter Longford* begins ther Journye together on wedensday or thursday Next to Chester, and from thense the Elder Lady goes to Bellfast and hir daghter to Dublin, your Lady takes the waters heare whether as a preparitive to hir goeinge to Tunbridge or Not I cannot tell you because Shee says nothinge of it to Mee hir selfe, when shee dous,° I shall then tell hir ^speake^ my opinione tell° then I shall say Nothinge, the tow° Boys are very well and Bety* is beter° then shee was the Last yeare, soe as I hope Time, will make hir out grow hir former ills, My Lady [Ororye] the yonger[935] goes very soune° over to Ireland; Shee speakes very well of you as I heare in all Companyes, the Frindshipe that was onse° betwixt hir and a Lady of your acquantanse is offe Now, or at the Least growne very Could° [/] what has made the distanse I cannot tell not haveinge willinge to make anye inquires into that Matter, I suppose you know both ther humors beter then I doe, and therfor I shall say noe More but Leave you to your owne conjecturs, Just Now I reseved° Neuse that Luxen^Burk^ was takene by the French[936] and that your Nephue Osory[937] had Scaped without anye hurt, though hee was in the Trenches and in all the Attacks, sense the first day that hee came to the Campe, but mr Howard the Earle of Carliles Soon° whoe went over with hime it is beleved is Dead, for hee was ^dayngeroslie^ wounded;[938] Mr Penrose the Mersier[939] came to mee yesterday to desier° Mee to put you in mind of 6 hundreth pound dept° that is owinge him 2 hundreth wherof, hee has your Bond For, consarninge° which hee tells mee that hee has writene oftene but never could obtayne anye answar from you, I hope you have a Note by you of all your depts both heare and in Ireland that Soe you May as you are abble paye offe such of them as are the most Nesesarye

---

[935] Mary Boyle, née Sackville (1648–1710), wife of the second Earl of Orrery and daughter of Richard Sackville, fifth Earl of Dorset. Her husband predeceased his mother when he died in March 1682, which means that there were two dowager countesses.

[936] In 1684, Luxembourg was besieged by the armies of Louis XIV, and until 1697 remained under French rule.

[937] EO's grandson, and her husband's namesake and heir, James Butler (1665–1745), who had succeeded to the title of Earl of Ossory after his father's death in 1680.

[938] Frederick Christian Howard, son of Charles Howard, first Earl of Carlisle, was killed at the Siege of Luxembourg (April/June 1684).

[939] "A person who deals in textile fabrics, esp. silks, velvets, and other fine materials; *spec.* a member of the Worshipful Company of Mercers, a livery company of the City of London. Also (occasionally): a dealer in haberdashery" ("mercer, *n.*," *OED*).

Letter 303. July 5, 1684, Hampton Court, the Duchess of Ormonde to the Earl of Arran (NLI, Ormond Papers, 2439, no. 8491, p. 119). Autograph.
For the Earle of Arran. [Endorsed]: Lady Dutchess 5 July 84.

Hampton Court the 5 of July

By your Leter of the 22 of the Last Month I understand that by some accompt° you had reseved° from my Lady Longford,* of your Ladys Intent to goe into Irland and what shee had writene unto your ^Selfe^ unto the same Efect, that you find cause to beleve that shee intends it, but that you are in dout,° what to doe in the disposinge of the Chilldren; which in your Fathers oppinion and Mine is; that Thay° shouldbee all Broght over, with hir Selfe unless shee dous° deferr hir goeinge Longer then whilst the ways and wether° continows° Good; of which I see noe Resone° for in a winter Season I would by noe Menes° advise the hasardinge of Them; I doe not dout,° but you have befor this Time bine° made acquanted with My Lords goeinge into Irland, whoe intends to begine his Journye befor the Ende of this Month, but where to bee I know not ^when wee Land^ untell° wee do heare from you; whoe I feare will find as great a trouble in your perticuler affars as wee shall doe to accomodate our Selfs, but Nesesitie must bee obayede your Nephue Osory is not as yet Come; but is daylie Expected

List of Correspondents

Archer, Patrick	Letter 5 (1 letter)
Bennet, Henry, Earl of Arlington	Letters 128–130 (3 letters)
Boyle, Elizabeth, Countess of Cork and Burlington	Letters 282–283 (2 letters)
Bramhall, John, Bishop of Derry	Letters 20, 25–26 (3 letters)
Brian, John	Letter 188, 206 (2 letters)
Browne, Sir Richard	Letter 15–16, 19, 21–24 (7 letters)
Burdon, John	Letters 33–38, 40–41, 43–69, 71–81, 84, 89–90, 104–107, 111, 117, 125 (56 letters)
Butler, Edward	Letters 140–141 (2 letters)
Butler, James, first Duke of Ormonde	Letters 82, 85–87, 91, 93–95, 97–98, 100–103, 131, 166–170, 279, 288 (22 letters)
Butler, Lord John	Letter 246 (1 letter)
Butler, Margaret, Viscountess Mountgarret	Letter 32 (1 letter)
Butler, Richard, Earl of Arran	Letters 296–303 (8 letters)
Butler, Thomas, Earl of Ossory	Letters 83, 284–286 (4 letters)
Butler, Walter, eleventh Earl of Ormonde	Letter 1 (1 letter)
Catherine of Braganza	Letter 126 (1 letter)
Comerford, Edward	Letter 2 (1 letter)
Cromwell, Henry	Letters 39, 42, 70 (3 letters)
Cromwell, Oliver	Letter 29 (1 letter)
Domvile, Sir William	Letter 290 (1 letter)
Fairfax, Sir Thomas	Letter 9 (1 letter)
Fleetwood, Charles	Letter 31 (1 letter)

Flower, Sir William, and others	Letters 108, 110, 112, 113, 115–116, 118–119 (8 letters)
Graham, Sir James	Letter 123 (1 letter)
Hamilton, George	Letter 88 (1 letter)
Hume, Anne	Letter 99 (1 letter)
Hyde, Edward, Earl of Clarendon	Letters 122 (1 letter)
Keating, John	Letter 289 (1 letter)
Kennedy, Edmund	Letter 4 (1 letter)
Legge, Colonel William	Letters 132–139 (8 letters)
Mathew, Captain George	Letters 142–145, 147–165, 171–187, 189–205, 207–245, 247–278, 287 (129 letters)
Meredith, Sir Thomas	Letter 109 (1 letter)
Nicholas, Sir Edward	Letters 7–8, 11–14, 17–18, 27–28, 30, 120–121, 124, 127 (15 letters)
Perceval, Sir John	Letter 92 (1 letter)
Perceval, Sir Philip	Letter 6 (1 letter)
Preston, Lady Jean	Letter 291 (1 letter)
Preston, Sir George	Letters 146, 280, 292, 295 (4 letters)
Sheffield, Edmund, second Earl of Mulgrave	Letter 10 (1 letter)
Smith, Stephen	Letter 96 (1 letter)
Smith, Valentine	Letters 281, 293–294 (3 letters)
Wale, William	Letter 3 (1 letter)
Walsh, John	Letter 114 (1 letter)

Persons and Places

Abbott (Aboot), Colonel Daniel (fl. 1656–1660), EO's tenant and one of the trustees responsible for assigning confiscated land to the army for arrears of pay.

Acton (Iron Acton), Gloucester, home of JO's maternal grandfather, Sir John Poyntz, where EO and JO lived when they first married, and where EO found refuge during the 1650s.

Anglesey, Earl of. See Annesley, Arthur.

Annesley, Arthur, first Earl of Anglesey (1614–1686), Irish landowner, vice-treasurer and receiver-general of Ireland from August 1660 until June 1667, and JO's ally at court.

Archer, Captain James (fl. 1632–1680), a military engineer and architect, employed for the couple's building program; he was also a Roman Catholic and native of Kilkenny.

Archer, Luke (fl. 1668–1672), servant at Kilkenny.

Archer, Patrick (fl. 1646–1649), Waterford merchant.

Archer, Walter (fl. 1671–1672), dispossessed Kilkenny landowner and petitioner.

Ards, Viscount of. See Montgomery, Hugh.

Arlington, Earl of. See Bennet, Henry.

Arran, Countess of. See Ferrars, Dorothy.

Arran, Countess of. See Stuart, Mary.

Arran, Earl of. See Butler, Richard.

Aungier (Angers), Francis, first Earl of Longford (c. 1632–1700), vice-treasurer of Ireland (1670–1675), acted as agent for the Ormonde Butler family in Lord John's marriage negotiations with Lady Anne Chichester, whom he married after John's death.

Bath (Bayth), spa town visited by EO.

Bathurst, Samuel (fl. 1658–1663), postmaster of Dublin, recommended to the position by EO.

Baxter (fl. 1670–1674), steward at Kilkenny Castle.

Bellingham, Daniel (1620–1672), one of EO's creditors during the 1650s, he became alderman of Dublin in 1656 and served as lord mayor of Dublin in 1665–1666. See Robert Armstrong, "Bellingham, Sir Daniel," *DIB*.

Bennet, Henry, Earl of Arlington (*bap.* 1618, *d.* 1685), Secretary of State to Charles II, and friend and brother-in-law of EO's eldest son, Thomas, Earl of Ossory. He married, on April 16, 1666, Isabella van Nassau (bap. 1633, d. 1718), sister to Aemilia, Countess of Ossory.

Berkeley, John, Lord Berkeley of Stratton (1607–1678), Lord Lieutenant of Ireland from January 1670 to May 1672.

Blood, Colonel Thomas (1617/18–1680), adventurer and spy, involved in a plot to seize Dublin Castle in May 1663 as well as an attempt on JO's life in December 1670, and stole the crown jewels in May 1671.

Bodkine, Mr. (fl. 1670–1672), EO's prospective tenant, and father-in-law of Foxen.

Boyle, Elizabeth, née Clifford, Countess of Cork and Burlington (1613–1691), friend of EO, daughter and heiress of Henry, Lord Clifford (later earl of Cumberland), and wife of Richard Boyle, first Earl of Burlington and second Earl of Cork.

Boyle, Michael (1615?–1702), Church of Ireland archbishop of Armagh. See James Maguire, "Boyle, Michael," *DIB*.

Boyle, Richard (1612–1698), first Earl of Burlington and second Earl of Cork, he spent some time in exile in Caen with EO and remained a lifelong friend.

Boyle, Roger (1621–1679), Earl of Orrery, formerly Lord Broghill, supporter of EO in the 1650s but JO's political rival in the 1660s.

Brabazon, Edward, second Earl of Meath (1610–1675), ally of JO, his estates were confiscated but subsequently restored, and during the 1650s he built a new house at Kilruddery.

Bramhall, John (1594–1663), Bishop of Derry, and later Archbishop of Armagh, friend of JO, in exile with EO in Caen.

Brian (Bryan), John (d. 1671), valued agent at Kilkenny.

Bridgeman, Sir Orlando (1609–1674), a renowned lawyer who helped EO and other royalists to protect their estates from alienation or forfeiture.

Bristol, city in the south west of England from which EO often made her journeys to and from Ireland. It was also a starting place for voyages to the New World.

Broghill, Lord. See Boyle, Roger.

Brown, Mr. (fl. 1658–1660), an attorney for EO.

Browne, Sir Richard (1605–1683), Charles II's ambassador in Paris during his exile, and correspondent of EO.

Bucke, James (fl. 1657–1666), EO's servant.

Buckingham, Duke of. See Villiers, George.

Bucknell, Sir William (1633–1676), alderman of London.

Burdon, John (fl. 1655–1671), trusted agent of EO, particularly during the 1650s.

Burford, Oxfordshire, JO and EO's home during part of the 1670s.

Burke, Helen, née MacCarthy (1641–1722), Countess of Clanricarde, JO's niece by his sister Eleanor and her husband Donough MacCarthy, first Earl of Clancarty.

Burke, William, seventh Earl of Clanricarde (d. 1687), took as his second wife Helen MacCarthy, JO's niece by his sister Eleanor and her husband Donough MacCarthy, first Earl of Clancarty.
Burlington, Countess of. See Boyle, Elizabeth.
Burlington, Earl of. See Boyle, Richard.
Butler, Betie (fl. 1683), granddaughter of EO and JO, daughter of their son Richard, Earl of Arran, and his wife, Dorothy Ferrars, who died in childhood.
Butler, Charlotte (1678–1725), granddaughter of EO and JO, daughter of their son Richard, Earl of Arran, and his wife, Dorothy Ferrars; she was their only child who survived into adulthood.
Butler, Edward (Ned) (1656–1671), receiver for EO.
Butler, Elizabeth (1640–1665), eldest daughter of EO and JO, she married Philip Stanhope, second Earl of Chesterfield.
Butler, Elizabeth (1660–1717), daughter of Thomas, Earl of Ossory, she married William George Richard Stanley, ninth Earl of Derby.
Butler, Elizabeth, née Preston (1615–1684), Duchess of Ormonde, wife of James Butler, twelfth Earl and first Duke of Ormonde, and only daughter of Richard Preston, Baron Dingwall, Earl of Desmond, and Elizabeth Butler, daughter of Thomas Butler, tenth Earl of Ormonde.
Butler, Frances, née Touchet, wife of JO's younger brother, Richard Butler of Kilcash, she was the sister of James Touchet, third Earl of Castlehaven, and a daughter of Mervin Touchet, second Earl of Castlehaven (1593–1631), who was convicted and beheaded for rape and sodomy.
Butler, James (1610–1688), twelfth Earl and first Duke of Ormonde, son of Thomas Butler, Viscount Thurles (1596–1619), and grandson of Walter Butler, eleventh Earl of Ormonde, he married Elizabeth Preston.
Butler, James (1665–1745), grandson of EO and JO, and eldest surviving son of Thomas, Earl of Ossory, and his wife, Aemilia van Nassau; he would succeed his father as seventh Earl of Ossory, and then his grandfather as second Duke of Ormonde.
Butler, John (1643–1676), first Earl of Gowran, youngest son of EO and JO.
Butler, Margaret, née Spencer (d. 1655), Viscountess Mountgarret, widow of JO's uncle, third Viscount Mountgarret (1578–1652/3), EO testified on her behalf in support of her petition to the Commonwealth.
Butler, Mary (1646–1710), youngest daughter of EO and JO, she married Lord William Cavendish.
Butler, Richard (1639–1686), first Earl of Arran, second surviving son of EO and JO.
Butler, Richard, of Kilcash (c. 1616–1701), younger brother of JO, he fought with the Confederate Catholics.
Butler, Richard, third Viscount Mountgarret (1578–1651), JO's uncle, President of the Supreme Council of the Confederate Catholics, he gave EO and her family protection and ensured her safe convoy to Dublin in 1642.

Butler, Thomas (1634–1680), sixth Earl of Ossory, the eldest surviving son of EO and JO.
Butler, Walter (1559–1633), eleventh Earl of Ormonde, JO's grandfather, who lost much of his estate to EO's parents.
Caen, France, where EO and other Irish royalists found refuge during their exile.
Capel, Arthur, Earl of Essex (1631–1683), succeeded Berkeley as Lord Lieutenant on May 21, 1672.
Carr, George (fl. 1655–1657), EO's agent.
Carrick. See Ormond Castle.
Carteret (Cartwright), Sir George (1610?–1680), vice-admiral of the navy and lieutenant-governor of Jersey during the 1650s and vice-treasurer of Ireland during the 1660s.
Catherine of Braganza (1638–1705), consort to Charles II.
Cavendish, Christian (Christiana), *née* Bruce, dowager Countess of Devonshire (1595–1675), friend and supporter of EO during the Interregnum, she was the widow of William Cavendish, second Earl of Devonshire, who died in 1628. Her grandson would marry EO's youngest daughter, Mary.
Cavendish, Elizabeth, née Cecil, Countess of Devonshire (1620–1689), mother of William, Lord Cavendish, EO's son-in-law; she was the wife of the William Cavendish, third Earl of Cavendish, and daughter of William Cecil, second Earl of Salisbury.
Cavendish, Lady Mary. See Butler, Mary.
Cavendish, William (1641–1707), son-in-law of EO and JO, husband of their youngest daughter, Mary, he inherited the earldom after the death of his father, William Cavendish, third Earl of Devonshire (1617–1684), and was later elevated to a dukedom.
Cavendish, William, third earl of Devonshire (1617–1684), the father-in-law of EO's daughter Mary.
Cawfield (Cawfild), Mr. (fl. 1657), EO's prospective tenant at Arklow.
Chapelizod, Dublin, one of the official lodgings of the Irish Lord Lieutenant.
Charles II (1630–1685), restored as King of England, Scotland, and Ireland in May 1660.
Chesterfield, Countess of. See Butler, Elizabeth.
Chesterfield, Earl of. See Stanhope, Philip.
Chichester, Lady Anne (d. 1697), daughter-in-law of EO and JO, wife of their youngest son, John, first Earl of Gowran, and later married the Earl of Longford. She was the daughter and co-heir of Arthur Chichester, first Earl of Donegal.
Chichester, Letitia, née Hickes (d. 1691), widow of Arthur Chichester, first Earl of Donegal (d. 1675), was the mother of EO's daughter-in-law, Anne. She was a patron of protestant dissent, in Ulster, Dublin, and London.
Clancarty, Countess of. See MacCarthy, Eleanor.
Clanricarde, Countess of. See Burke, Helen.

Clanricarde, Earl of. See Burke, William.
Clarendon House, Piccadilly, the grandest private London residence of its era, owned by Edward Hyde, first Earl of Clarendon; part of the residence was lent to JO and EO in 1670.
Clarke, James (fl. 1666–1674), EO's household steward.
Cloghrennan Castle, Co. Carlow, one of the Ormonde residences. Arran had been created Baron Butler of Cloghrennan in 1662.
Clonmel, Co. Tipperary, one of the Ormonde residences; EO's son, Richard, Earl of Arran resided there during the 1670s.
Cole (Coole), Captain (fl. 1671), JO's tenant at Nenagh.
Comerford, Austacie (1657–1679), widow of Edward Comerford (d. 1649) of Callan, Co. Kilkenny.
Comerford, Edward (d. 1649) of Callan, Co. Kilkenny, agent of the Ormonde Butler family.
Commin, Mr. (fl. 1670), petitioner to JO.
Connoway, Mr. (fl. 1668), Clerk of the Kitchen.
Corbett, Mr. (fl. 1658–1660), EO's tenant.
Cromwell, Henry (1628–1674), son of Oliver Cromwell, he served as Lord Lieutenant of Ireland, remaining in Ireland from summer 1655 until spring 1659.
Cromwell, Oliver (1599–1658), Lord Protector of England, Scotland, and Ireland.
Crooke (Crouke), Ompton (fl. 1668–1669), EO's tenant.
Davies, Sir Paul, Secretary of State for Ireland and Keeper of the Signet, or Privy Seal, 1661–1672.
Derby, Earl of. See Stanley, William George Richard.
Devonshire, Countess of. See Cavendish, Elizabeth.
Devonshire, Dowager Countess of. See Cavendish, Christian.
Domvile (Domville), Sir William (1609–1689), Attorney General for Ireland throughout the reign of Charles II.
Donegal, Countess of. See Chichester, Letitia.
Dublin Castle, the official lodging of the Lord Lieutenant.
Dunmore House, EO's favorite residence, inherited from her mother, her planned dowager home, and the location for the marriage of her daughter, Mary; EO lived there during the Interregnum and engaged in extensive renovations of the building and gardens during the 1650s and 1660s.
Ely (Ellye), second Viscount Loftus of. See Edward Loftus.
Esmond, Ellice (Alice) (fl. 1629), aunt and advisor of EO, she was the granddaughter of James, ninth Earl of Ormonde and EO's mother's cousin. She took as her third husband, Laurence Esmonde, before December 1628, and survived him.
Esmond, Sir Laurence, first Baron Esmond (c. 1565–1645), agent, in Ireland, to EO's father Richard, Earl of Desmond and advisor to EO, overseeing the negotiations that led to her marriage.

Essex, Earl of. See Capel, Arthur.
Eustace, Sir Maurice (1595–1665), Lord Chancellor of Ireland.
Fairfax, Thomas, third Lord Fairfax of Cameron (1612–1671), Parliamentarian army officer. Edmund Sheffield, second Earl of Mulgrave, was his cousin.
Fennell, Gerald (d. c. 1666), physician to JO and member of the Supreme Council of the Confederate Catholics.
Ferrars (Farers, Fereres, Feris), Anne, née Carleton (fl. 1668–1682), mother-in-law of Richard, Earl of Arran.
Ferrars, Dorothy (d. 1716), Countess of Arran, daughter-in-law of EO and JO, second wife of their second son, Richard, Earl of Arran, and daughter of John Ferrars of Tamworth Castle and his wife, Anne, daughter of Sir Dudley Carleton.
Fitzpatrick, Colonel John (d. 1693), JO's brother-in-law, he married to JO's sister Elizabeth (d. 1675), widow of Nicholas Purcell.
Fleetwood, General Charles (c. 1618–1692), appointed Commander-in-Chief of Ireland in July 1652.
Flower, Colonel William (fl. 1656–1672), Cromwellian officer and tenant and agent of EO, he was a beneficiary of the restoration land settlement.
Floyd, Mr. (1669–1670), JO's receiver.
Folia, Captain (fl. 1658), Cromwellian officer and EO's tenant.
Foxen (Foxton), Captain (fl. 1670–1672), Cromwellian soldier, JO's tenant, impacted by the restoration land settlement, son-in-law of Bodkine.
Freeman, Sir Ralph (fl. 1667–1671), client of JO and tenant of Ormond Castle, Carrick-on-Suir, he was probably the son and heir of Sir Ralph Freeman (d. 1667) who had served in Ireland under JO during the civil wars.
Gookin, Vincent (c. 1616–1659), Surveyor-General of Ireland, he worked alongside Sir William Petty in setting out forfeited land for plantation.
Grace (Grase), Mr. (fl. 1671), brother-in-law and supporter of Walter Archer.
Graham, Sir James (fl. 1663–1683), son of the seventh Earl of Menteith, he married Isabel, daughter of John Bramhall.
Hackett, Mrs. (fl. 1671), widow and prospective settler and tenant of EO.
Halsey, Captain William (fl. 1657), a newcomer who had been awarded lands in Kilkenny and Tipperary and would later become Mayor of Waterford.
Haly, William, of Limerick (fl. 1661–1669), petitioner at the Court of Claims.
Hamilton, James (c. 1642–1679), nephew of JO, eldest son of his sister Mary and Sir George Hamilton. Unlike the rest of his family, James was a Protestant.
Hamilton, Mary (d. 1680), JO's sister and wife of Sir George Hamilton.
Hamilton, Sir George (c. 1608–1679), JO's brother-in-law and husband of his eldest sister Mary.
Hampstead, village near London where EO spent time during the early 1670s.
Hampton Court, Surrey, royal palace.
Harman, Sergeant Major Thomas (fl. 1661), EO's agent.
Harrison, Matthew (fl. 1657–1670), EO's agent and comptroller.

Hassells, Captain (fl. 1659–1670), Cromwellian officer.
Hawley, Sir Francis, Baron Hawley of Duncannon, maternal grandfather of the Elizabeth Malet, whose inheritance he held in trust.
Holyhead, town in Wales and important Irish Sea port through which people and post traveled to and from England and Ireland.
Hume, Anne, née French (d. 1701), an heiress who had been EO's ward. She married first Thomas Hume and second Captain George Mathew, JO's half-brother.
Hume, Thomas (d. 1668), the husband of EO's friend Anne, née French, and her agent, he had been a favorite of EO's father and was knighted by JO in 1665.
Hyde, Edward, first Earl of Clarendon (1609–1674), Lord Chancellor, and friend of JO.
Hyde, Henrietta, née Boyle (1645/6–1687), wife of Laurence Hyde, first Earl of Rochester, and daughter of the Earl of Cork and Burlington.
Inchiquin, Countess of. See O'Brien, Elizabeth.
Inchiquin, Earl of. See O'Brien, Murrough.
Jackson, Lodovick (1660–1673), merchant and one of EO's creditors.
Jacques (Jackas, Jackuis), Captain Joseph (fl. 1669–1670), petitioner.
Jones, Katherine, *née* Boyle, Viscountess Ranelagh (1615–1691), friend and supporter of EO; she was the fifth daughter of Richard Boyle, first Earl of Cork, and sister of the Earl of Orrery, and associated with the Hartlib circle, the correspondence network set up by Samuel Hartlib, an intelligencer based in London.
Jones, Richard, first Earl of Ranelagh (1641–1712), politician and son of Katherine, Viscountess Ranelagh.
Keating, John (d. 1691), Lord Chief Justice of Ireland, friend of JO and his son Arran.
Kelye, Mr., of Aughrim (fl. 1669–1672), complainant.
Kennedy, Edmund (fl. 1643), servant of EO.
Kilkenny Castle, main residence of the Ormonde Butlers; during the 1640s it was the headquarters of the Confederate Catholics, and in the 1660s it was transformed into a seat of the viceregal court.
Kilkenny College, John Street, Kilkenny, established c. 1666 by JO, the "school" mentioned by EO.
Lane (Layne), George, first Viscount Lanesborough (1620–1683), JO's secretary. He kept all the poetry that came to Ormonde, which is now found in the Beinecke Library at Yale University.
Lane, Susannah (1627–1671), second wife of Sir George Lane, whom she married in 1655, and daughter of Sir Edward Nicholas.
Le Grande, Monsieur, a painter and musician in EO's employ, he set the fourth song of Katherine Philips's play *Pompey* to music.
Legge, Colonel William (1607/8–1670), old friend of JO and his family, and correspondent of EO, he represented the family in the potential marriage

of their youngest son, John, to Elizabeth Malet. A royalist army officer, he possessed a sizeable estate in Ireland, which was augmented by the restoration land settlement.

Legge, Elizabeth, née Washington (c. 1616–1688), wife of EO's correspondent William Legge, she was the eldest daughter of Sir William Washington of Sulgrave Manor, Northamptonshire.

Legge, George (c. 1647–1691), eldest son of EO's correspondent William Legge and his wife Elizabeth, he would later become first Baron Dartmouth.

Lentrope, Mr. (fl. 1673–1674), creditor.

Leslie, Henry (1580–1661), Church of Ireland Bishop of Down and Connor, and potential household chaplain for EO.

Lindsie, John (fl. 1670–1673), creditor.

Loftus, Sir Edward, second Viscount Loftus of Ely (fl. 1643), second son and heir of Adam Loftus (1568–1643), first Viscount Loftus of Ely.

Longford, Countess of. See Chichester, Lady Anne.

Ludlow, Mr. (fl. 1671), creditor.

MacCarthy, Eleanor, Countess of Clancarty (1612–1682), sister of JO, and wife of Donough MacCarthy (1594–1665), second Viscount Muskerry, first Earl of Clancarty.

Malet, Elizabeth (d. 1681), heiress and prospective wife for EO's youngest son, Lord John, she was the only child of John Malet of Enmore, Somerset, and Untia, née Hawley.

Mandevile, John (fl. 1657–1669), served as EO's rent collector but dismissed in 1669.

Martin, Captain Nicholas (fl. 1650), commander of JO's ship, the St. Peter.

Martin, Mr. (fl. 1661–1673), creditor.

Mathew, George (d. 1689), EO's brother-in-law and JO's half-brother and the couple's estate manager; he was the second son of JO's mother, Elizabeth Poyntz's second marriage to Captain George Mathew. In 1670 he built Thomastown on sequestered abbey land received from JO. He took as his first wife Eleanor, daughter of the third Baron Dunboyne, by whom he had two sons, one of whom survived to adulthood; his second wife was EO's friend Anne Hume.

Mathew, Theobald (d. 1699), EO's brother-in-law and JO's half-brother, George Mathew's elder brother.

Meath, Earl of. See Brabazon, Edward.

Meredith, Sir Thomas (d. c. 1677), had been knighted in Ireland by the Lords Justices in 1630. He was the son of Richard Meredith, Bishop of Leighlin.

Mervin, Sir Audley (1603–1675), broker for the marriage of Lord John and Anne Chichester.

Millan, William (fl. 1670–1674), bailiff of Dunmore.

Monmouth, Duke of. See Scott, James.

Montgomery, Hugh, third Viscount of Ards (1625–1663), eldest son of Hugh Montgomery, second Viscount Montgomery (1598/9–1642), he was created first Earl of Mount Alexander in 1661. He had been recommended by EO in 1660.

Moor Park, Hertfordshire, countryside residence purchased by JO and EO in the wake of their elevation to ducal status in the early 1660s. It would be sold in 1670 to help to alleviate debts, bought by Charles II for his illegitimate son, the Duke of Monmouth.

Moore, Captain (fl. 1657), Cromwellian soldier with a competing claim to land on EO's estate.

Mordaunt, Elizabeth, née Howard, dowager Countess of Peterborough (1603–1671), friend and supporter of EO during the Interregnum; her husband, John Mordaunt, first Earl of Peterborough, had died in 1643.

Morgan, Sir Anthony (1621–1668), a trusted supporter of Charles Fleetwood and Henry Cromwell, he had been involved in the early stages of the land settlement in Ireland.

Morton, Captain John (d. 1669), contractor and possibly an architect, commissioned for work on the Ormonde properties.

Mountgarret, Viscount. See Richard Butler.

Mountgarret, Viscountess. See Butler, Margaret.

Mulgrave, Earl of. See Sheffield, Edmund.

Nassau, Aemilia van (d. 1688), Countess of Ossory, daughter-in-law of EO and JO, wife of their eldest son, Thomas, Earl of Ossory, and daughter of Lodewyk van Nassau, heer van Beverweerd, governor of Sluis, an illegitimate son of the stadholder Maurits van Nassau.

Newmarket, location of Charles II's sporting palace and racing stables.

Nicholas, Lady Jane, née Jaye (d. 1688), wife of Sir Edward Nicholas, and daughter of Henry Jaye, draper and alderman, of London.

Nicholas, Sir Edward (1593–1669), Secretary of State to Charles I and II, correspondent and friend of EO.

O'Brien, Elizabeth, Countess of Inchiquin (d. 1685), wife of Murrough O'Brien, first Earl of Inchiquin, and daughter of Sir William St. Leger, Lord President of Munster, to whom her husband had been ward.

O'Brien, Murrough, first Earl of Inchiquin (c. 1614–1674), royalist army officer, he had defected to Parliament in July 1644 but returned his allegiance to the king in May 1648. Inchiquin had been born into a prominent Catholic family but taken as a ward and brought up in the Protestant faith.

O'Neill, Daniel (c. 1612–1664), friend of JO, he was the stepfather of JO's son-in-law, Philip Stanhope, second Earl of Chesterfield.

Ormond Castle, Carrick-on-Suir, was built by Thomas, tenth Earl of Ormonde, in the 1560s. JO and EO lived there during their early married life, and there is a carving of their arms and the date 1641 over a fireplace on the ground floor.

Ormonde House, St. James's Square, London, a great townhouse purchased by JO in 1682, where EO died in 1684.
Orrery, Earl of. See Boyle, Roger.
Osborne, Charles (1668–1672), advisor to Lord John, and of his troop.
Ossory, Countess of. See Nassau, Aemilia van.
Ossory, Earl of. See Butler, James.
Ossory, Earl of. See Butler, Thomas.
Page, Thomas (fl. 1649–1659), secretary and confidante to Thomas, Earl of Ossory.
Perceval, Sir John (1629–1665), eldest son and heir of Sir Philip Perceval.
Perceval, Sir Philip (1605–1647), Master of the Irish Court of Wards.
Petty, Sir William (1623–1687), natural philosopher and administrator in Ireland; also responsible for the Down Survey of Ireland in the 1650s.
Philips, Mr. (fl. 1672), JO's legal counsel.
Phoenix, country house, official viceregal residence, built on present day Magazine Hill in Phoenix Park, Dublin.
Pierrepont, née Stanley, Katherine, Marchioness of Dorchester (b. 1631), friend and supporter of EO during the Interregnum; she was the daughter of the dowager Countess of Derby and the second wife of the Marquess of Dorchester, whom she had married in 1652.
Plunkett, Walter (fl. 1664–1671), EO's agent.
Power, Captain Milo (fl. 1660–1673), a merchant and creditor to EO.
Poyntz, Elizabeth (c. 1588–1673), Viscountess Thurles, EO's mother-in-law, JO was her son by Thomas Butler (1596–1619). After her first husband's death she married George Mathew (d. 1636) from Radyr/Llandaff in Wales, by whom she had two sons and a daughter. She was Catholic, as were most of her children.
Poyntz, Sir John, JO's maternal grandfather.
Preston, Lady Jean, née Gibson (fl. 1640–1680), daughter of Sir Alexander Gibson of Durie and wife of EO's paternal cousin, Sir George Preston.
Preston, Richard, first Lord Dingwall and Earl of Desmond (1570–1628), EO's father, a Scottish favorite of James I.
Preston, Sir George (fl. 1640–1672), EO's paternal cousin, he had EO's support during a legal battle with the Corporation of Limerick over Lax weir and fishery.
Purcell, Philip, of Balyfoyle (fl. 1671), dispossessed landowner, threatened to murder JO.
Ranelagh, Earl of. See Jones, Richard.
Ranelagh, Viscountess of. See Jones, Katherine.
Redmond, Major (fl. 1657–1659), Cromwellian officer.
Reynolds, Sir John (1625–1657), one of the trustees of EO's estate. He was a valued supporter of successive commanders in Ireland, including Henry Cromwell, to whom his wife's sister was married.

Rich, Sir Henry, first Earl of Holland (1590–1649), had been awarded the wardship of EO. He was a regular tournament companion of her father and may have been his friend.

Richmond, Duchess of. See Villiers, Mary.

Robartes (Roberts), John, second Baron Robartes of Truro, later first Earl of Radnor (1606–1685), served briefly as Lord Deputy of Ireland in 1660, and was appointed Lord Lieutenant on May 3, 1669, succeeding JO. He was recalled in May 1670.

Robartes (Roberts), Lady Letitia Isabella (d. 1714), second wife of Lord Robartes, was daughter of Sir John Smith of Bidborough, Kent, and his wife, Isabella, daughter of Robert Rich, first Earl of Warwick.

Roche, Lawrence (fl. 1668), hired to work on EO's estate, perhaps a craftsman.

Rochester, Countess of. See Hyde, Henrietta.

Ryder (Rydier), Mr. (fl. 1682–1683), schoolmaster in Kilkenny.

Savile, Lady Anne, née Coventry (d. 1662), widow of Sir William Savile (1612–1644), third baronet of Thornhill, who died in arms for the king. She became celebrated as a heroine of the civil war and was a friend and supporter of JO.

Scott, James, Duke of Monmouth (1649–1685), illegitimate son of Charles II and Lucy Walter, and purchaser of Moor Park.

Sestions, William (d. 1673), servant at Kilkenny Castle.

Sheffield, Edmund, first Earl of Mulgrave (1565–1646), brother of EO's maternal grandmother, Elizabeth, the second wife of Thomas, tenth Earl of Ormonde.

Sheffield, Edmund, second Earl of Mulgrave (1611–1658), parliamentarian nobleman, he was the grandson of the first Earl of Mulgrave, and therefore a distant kinsman of EO. The parliamentarian General Lord Fairfax was his cousin.

Sixe, Adam (fl. 1668–1670), gardener for EO.

Slingsby, Mr. (fl. 1670–1671), merchant.

Smith, Stephen (fl. 1656–1660), agent of EO.

Smith, Valentine (1672–1675), of Damagh, Co. Kilkenny, steward to JO.

Standish, James (fl. 1649–1661), Cromwellian Vice-Treasurer of Ireland.

Stanhope, Elizabeth ("Betty") (1663–1723), granddaughter of EO and JO, only daughter of their daughter, the Countess of Chesterfield.

Stanhope, Katherine, née Wotton (d. 1667), mother of the second Earl of Chesterfield, her third husband was JO's friend, Daniel O'Neill.

Stanhope, Philip (1633–1714), second Earl of Chesterfield, son-in-law of EO and JO, whose daughter, Elizabeth, was his second wife. After her death he married Lady Elizabeth Dormer (1653–1677), daughter and co-heir of Charles Dormer, second Earl of Carnarvon.

Stanley, Charlotte, *née* de La Trémoille, dowager Countess of Derby (1599–1664), friend and supporter of EO during the Interregnum. Her husband James Stanley, seventh Earl of Derby, had been executed in 1651 for his loyalty to Charles I.

Stanley, William George Richard (1655–1702), ninth Earl of Derby, ward of JO, and husband to Elizabeth Butler (1660–1717), daughter of Thomas, Earl of Ossory.

Stowell, George (fl. 1670–1671), creditor.

Stuart, Mary (1651–1668), Countess of Arran, daughter-in-law of EO and JO, first wife of their second son, Richard, Earl of Arran. Baroness Clifton of Leighton Bromswold in her own right, she was the daughter of James Stuart, third Duke of Richmond, and his wife, Mary, daughter of George Villiers, first Duke of Buckingham. She married Arran at court in September 1664.

Temple, Sir John (1600–1677), one of the trustees of EO's estate in the 1650s, and author of *The Irish Rebellion* (1646).

Thurles Castle, the residence of JO's mother, Viscountess Thurles, and his half-brother, Theobald Mathew.

Thurles, Viscountess of. See Poyntz, Elizabeth.

Thynne, Lady Isabella, née Rich (b. 1623), friend of EO and mother of JO's illegitimate child, she is said to have facilitated the courtship and marriage of EO and JO. She was the daughter of Henry Rich, first Earl of Holland, to whom EO was appointed ward, and Isabel Cope. She married and was later divorced by Sir James Thynne, son of Sir Thomas Thynne and Maria Audley.

Tichburne, Sir Henry (1581?–1667), soldier and Lord Justice. EO had some interactions with him in the 1650s and 1660s.

Tollemache, Elizabeth, née Murray, Countess of Dysart (1626–1698), friend and supporter of EO during the Interregnum, she was the eldest of the five daughters of William Murray, first Earl of Dysart (d. 1655).

Treswell, Sir Daniel (d. 1670), army commander and creditor to JO and EO.

Trotter, Robert (fl. 1672–1686), a Dutch painter who acted as EO's building overseer.

Villiers, George, second Duke of Buckingham (1628–1687), son and heir of George Villiers, first duke of Buckingham (1592–1628).

Villiers, Mary, Duchess of Lennox and Richmond (1622–1685), mother of Mary Stuart, Countess of Arran. The eldest child and only daughter of George Villiers, first duke of Buckingham (1592–1628), and his wife, Lady Katherine Manners (1603?–1649).

Vyner (Viner), Sir Robert (1631–1688), one of England's largest-scale bankers, he lent money to JO.

Wale, William (d. 1677), wine merchant, became an alderman , he was conferred a knighthood in May 1660.

Waller, Sir Hardress (c. 1604–1666), parliamentarian army officer and regicide, with long-standing connections to Munster.

Walsh [Wellch], John (fl. 1661–1673), JO's lawyer and accountant.
Warre, Sir John (1636–1669), stepfather to Elizabeth Malet, he had married her mother, Untia (or Unton), née Hawley, after her father's death.
Warren, Captain Edward (fl. 1659), EO's tenant.
Wemyss (Wemes), Sir Patrick (1604?–1661), EO's cousin, the nephew of her father, Richard, first Earl of Desmond, by his sister, Elizabeth.
Wentworth, Henrietta Maria, née Stanley, Countess of Strafford (d. 1685), friend and supporter of EO during the Interregnum, she was the daughter of the dowager Countess of Derby and the sister of the Marchioness of Dorchester. She married the second Earl of Strafford in 1654.
Wheeler, Jonas (fl. 1656–1661), EO's tenant at Kells.
Wheeler, Oliver (1669–1671), EO's tenant, agent, and native of Kilkenny.
Willoughby (Willoby), Lady Cassandra, née Ridgway (fl. 1610–1658), wife of Sir Francis Willoughby, daughter of Thomas, Earl of Londonderry, and creditor to EO.
Winckworth (Wineworth), Captain (fl. 1672–1673), EO's tenant.
Worsley, Benjamin (1617/18–1677), Surveyor General of Ireland.
Yarner, Abraham (1598–1677), physician who became president of the College of Physicians in Dublin.

Glossary

a Nothar, a Nother	another
a peese	apiece
abatted, abayte, abayted	abate, abated
abell	able
abrode	abroad
Abye	abbey
accompt/s	account/s
accomptabill, accompted	accountable, accounted
Acher, Ackars, Ackers	acres
acquitanse	acquittance
ade	add
adistionall, adistione	additional, addition
Adventerors	Adventurers
adward, adwarded	award, awarded
agayne	again
alevene	eleven
alleadge	allege
Allhol(l)antyde	All Saints Day (Nov. 1)
amont/s	amount/s
ane	an
Anewetie	annuity
ansar, ansarable, ansared(e), ansaringe	answer, answerable, answered, answering
antiant	ancient
ap(p)iere, apieringe, appiered(e)	appear, appearing appeared
Arckloe, Arcklow, Arclo(e),	Arklow
assartanede	ascertained

asshure, asshured(e)(d), asshuredlie	assure, assured, assuredly
Aturnye	Attorney
avoyde, avoyded, avoydinge	avoid, avoided, avoiding
ayme/s	aim/s
Ayre	air, heir
ballife	bailiff
Bayth	Bath
Beare, biere	beer
berar(e)	bearer (of letters)
betar, beter, Beters	better, betters
bin(e)	been
Bouke	book
bouth	both
brife, brifelie, briffer, briuefer	brief, briefly, briefer
bus(s)enes(s)	business
Car(r)acture, Carracterede	character, charactered
Carringe	carrying
cayse/(s)s	case/s
Chierfull, Chierfullie, Chierfullnes	cheerful, cheerfully, cheerfulness
chife	chief
chuse, chusses, chuseres	choose, chooses, choosers
Clame/s	Claim/s
Coche, Coche way	coach, coachway
Confyne, Confynede	confine, confined
consarned(e), conserned	concerned
consarning(e), conserninge	concerning
consarnment/s, consernment/s, concernement/s	concernment/s
consern(e)/s, consarn(e)/s	concern/s
consernedlie, consernednes	concernedly, concernedness
conseve/s, conseved(e)	conceive/s, conceived
Contenowede, continowed(e)	continued
continow/s	continue/s

continowanse	continuance
continowell	continual
continowinge	continuing
could	cold
couldnes	coldness
Cous(s)ened(e)	cozened
crost	crossed
Curch(e)	church
Curtesie, Curtisie, Curtisies(s)	courtesy, courtesies
dept(e), depts	debt, debts
derect, derectede, derection(e)s	direct, directed, directions
derectlie	directly
desentlie	decently
desevede	deceived
desier/(e)s	desire/s
deue, dew(e)	due
devistione	division
dewtie/s, dewtye	duty, duties
dier(e)	dear, deer
disingadge/d	disengage/d
dismist	dismissed
distroctive, distroction(e)	destructive, destruction
don	done
doue, dous	do, does
doupt, dout(e), douted, doutles, douptfull	doubt, doubted, doubtless, doubtful
driwene	driven
dueringe	during
dune	done
Eie	eye
Espetialie, Espetialye	especially
Ester	Easter
ethar	either

expretione, expretions	expression, expressions
Exs(i)ersie/s	exercise/s
Exsequitor, Exsequtors	executor, executors
Exside, Exsidinge	exceed, exceeding
Exzact, Exzactlie	exact, exactly
Fase	face
fayl(l)e, faylede, fayler	fail, failed, failure
forfited, forfitt, forfiture	forfeited, forfeit, forfeiture
forse/s	force/s
Frutles	fruitless
Gallowaye	Galway
gayne, gaynede, gayner	gain, gained, gainer
gees, gess(t)	guess, guessed
gide	guide
Goout	gout
Gould	gold
grife	grief
grownd/s	ground/s
grownded	grounded
growndless	groundless
hapenes	happiness
hast, hastie	haste, hasty
heare	here
heather, hethar	hither
hetharto, hetherto	hitherto
hir, hirs	her, hers
honner	honor
hote	hot
hould(e), houlds, houldinge	hold, holds, holding
hower, hower(e)s	hour, hours
impatianse	impatience
impossede	imposed
improvabell	improbable

inabell/s, inable/s, inablede	enable/s, enabled
incombranse/s	encumbrance/s
incoridge, incoridged(e), incoridgment/s	encourage, encouraged, encouragement/s
indepted	indebted
inderect	indirect
indevo(u)r(e)/s, indevoringe	endeavor/s, endeavoring
indevored(e)	endeavored
industerious, industerouslie	industrious, industriously
Ine, In(d)kieper	inn, innkeeper
inga(y)dge/d(e), ingadginge, inga(y)dgment/s	engage/d, engaging, engagement/s
Injoyne	enjoin
inquier	enquire
intemate, intemated, intemation(e)	intimate, intimated, intimation
intyteled, Intytell, intytled	entitled, entitle
juells	jewels
kiep(e)/s, kipe/s, kiepers, kieping(e), kipinge	keep/s, keepers, keeping
latar, layter, laytest	later or latter, latest
Latlie	lately
Least	lest
Lew	lieu
Limbricke	Limerick
Lissense	license
litell	little
loos	loss
louk(e)/s, louked(e), loukinge	look/s, looked, looking
mach(e), maches	match, matches
Machinge	matching
Mallis, mal(l)itious	malice, malicious
mantane/s, mentane, mentayne, mentaynede	maintain/s, maintained
Marchand/s, marchant	merchant/s

Mater/s	matter/s
mayne	main
mene, menes	mean, means
Mickel(l)mas, Mickellmes	Michaelmas [Sept. 29]
Monster	Munster
mony(e), monys	money, monies
Morgadge, Morgadg(i)(e)s, Morgadginge	mortgage, mortgages, mortgaging
my thinks	methinks
Neuse, Nuse	news
Nide/s, Niede/d	need/s, need/ed
Niedfull	needful
Niedles	needless
Nombar	number
Non	none
Notis(e), Nottis(e)	notice
Nots	notes
Noyse	noise
obstakell/s	obstacles
ocatione, ocationed(e), ocations	occasion, occasioned, occasions
ode	odd
of(e)	off
offier/s, offiered	offer/s, offered
offiss(e), offisier/s, offisies	office, officer/s, offices
olltor, olltored(e)	alter, altered
olltoratione, olltorations	alteration/s
on/s	one/'s
one	on, own
onse	once
oppoynt, oppoynted(e), opoyntment	appoint, appoint(ed), appointment
othoritie, othorit(i)ye	authority
o(u)ght	owed
outhar/s, outharwise, outharwiss	other/s, otherwise

Glossary

overtoucke	overtook
parsell/s	parcel/s
Pastion(e)	passion
patianse	patience
Pepell/s	people/s
perseve	perceive
perus(s)tiall	perusal
Phisistions	physicians
plas(s)e, plas(s)es(s)	place, places
plassede, plast	placed
poure, pourer	poor, poorer
precribe, precribede	prescribe, prescribed
presanse	presence
president	precedent
prest	pressed
pris(s)e/s	price/s
Priswins	prise wines (wines taken as prisage)
proside/s	proceed/s
prosidinge, prosidings	proceeding, proceedings
provabilitie(s), provabilitye	probability, probabilities
provable, provablie	probable, probably
raysede, rayser, raysinge	raised, raiser, raising
rayt(e)/s, rayted	rate/s, rated
redenes, redynes	readiness
redime, redimede, rediminge	redeem, redeemed, redeeming
redust	reduced
Reekninge, Reeknings	reckoning, reckonings
releufe	relief
remidie/s, remidye, remided	remedy/ies, remedied
requier/s	require/s
res(s)ept/s	receipt/s
res(s)eptione	reception

reseve/s, receved(e), recever/s, resevinge	receive/s, received, receiver/s, receiving
resone/s, resonede	reason/s, reasoned
Rome/s	room/s
Ruene, Ruened(e), Rueninge	ruin, ruined, ruining
Ruenous	ruinous
rune(s)	run(s)
Sallerye	salary
sartane, sartanlie, sartantie, sartantye	certain, certainly, certainty
Sarvis(e), Sarvis(s), Sarvises, Sarvissis	service, services
Sarvisabell, sarvisable	serviceable
sayede	said
Sayfe, sayfest, sayf(f)ier, sayflie, Sayflye, Sayftye	safe, safest, safer, safely, safety
Sco(o)ule, Skooule	school
Seariouslie, Seariouslye	seriously
sease	cease
Seasede	seized
Seduell, Sedwell	schedule
sellers	cellars
sence, sense	since
Senight	sennight (one week)
Sertifie	certify
Sevilitie, Sevilit(i)es(s), Sevilitye	civility, civilities
Sevilitye, Sevilit(i)e(s)(s)	civility/ies
Seville, Sivell	civil
Shiphier	cipher
shure	sure
sielense, Sielensinge	silence, silencing
Siene, Sine	seen
sime/s, simede	seem/s, seemed
Sinsearlie	sincerely
Sivelie	civilly

some, somede, somonede	sum, summed, summoned
Soon	son
sould	sold
Soulderye, Souldirye	soldiery
Souldiers, Souldiors, Souldyors	soldiers
soune, Souner, Sounest	soon, sooner, soonest
spe(a)sifiede	specified
speatialle, spetiall	special
spiede, spidie, spidier, spidiest, spi(e)dilie	speed, speedy, speedier, speediest, speedily
Spight	spite
Stats	State's
stope	stop
stoud	stood
Strate, strats	strait, straits
Suckses(s), Sucksesfull	success, successful
Suckside, Sucksided, Sucksidinge	succeed, succeeded, succeeding
sudane, sudayne	sudden
sudanlie, Sudanlye, Sudaynlie	suddenly
suffier	suffer
surcomstanses	circumstances
Sute/s, Sutabell	suit/s, suitable
tell	till
thar	their, there
Thatht	thatched
thay	they
thayr	their
then	than
thethar	thither
thous	those
to	too
toucke	took
tow	two

Trusties	trustees
tryall	trial
tuche, tuching(e)	touch, touching
tyme	time
tyrede	tired
Tytell/s	title/s
Tyth(e)s	tithes
unabell	unable
unconsarnede	unconcerned
undertoucke	undertook
unkell	uncle
unsartane, unsartantie/s, unsartantye	uncertain, uncertainty, uncertainties
untell	until
unusstiall	unusual
us(s)tiall, usstialie	usual, usually
uss	use
vallew/s, vallewabill, vallewed(e), vallewing	value/s, valuable, valued, valuing
venter, ventered(e)	venture, ventured
vertew/s	virtue/s
veue, veuede, veuinge	view, viewed, viewing
visse/s	vice/s
visset/s	visit/s
wa(y)te	wait
warine	warren
wast	waste
wethar, wether	weather
wich	which
yaught	yacht

SELECTED BIBLIOGRAPHY

Primary Sources

Manuscripts

Birr, Co. Offaly, Birr Castle, Rosse Papers, A/1.
Dublin, National Library of Ireland, Ormond Papers, 2321–26, 2332, 2342, 2352–53, 2355–56, 2368, 2375, 2391, 2400, 2420, 2427, 2439, 2482, 2484–86, 2499–2500, 2503.
Kew, National Archives, State Papers, Ireland, 320.85, 321.31, 321.37.
London, British Library, Additional MSS., Egmont Papers, 46931, B46938; Althorpe Papers, 75356; Evelyn Papers, 78199 (827A).
———, Egerton MSS., 2533–34, 2538.
———, Lansdowne MSS., 823.
London, Society of Antiquaries of London, MS 138.
Longleat, Wiltshire, Longleat House, Thynne Papers, IX.
Oxford, Bodleian Library, Carte Papers, 4–5, 18, 24, 30–31, 213–14, 243.
———, Clarendon Papers, 79, 92.
San Marino, California, Huntington Library, Hastings-Irish Papers (Rawdon Papers), HA 14109, HA 14110, HA 14112.
Stafford, Staffordshire Record Office, Dartmouth Collection, D(W)1778/I/i.

Printed Works

An Account of the Solemn Funeral and Interrment of the Right Honourable the Countess of Arran. [London]: Thomas Newcombe, 1668.
A Pastoral upon the Death of Her Grace the Dutchess of Ormond. London: N. Thompson, 1684.
A[rmaker], E[dward]. *An Elegy on her Grace Elizabeth, Duchess of Ormond, who died July the 21ˢᵗ, 1684*. London: Thomas Newcomb, 1684.
Carte, Thomas. *An History of the Life of James Duke of Ormonde*. 3 vols. London: J. Bettenham, for J.J. and P. Knapton, in Ludgate-Street; G. Strahan, in Cornhill; W. Innys and R. Manby, at the West End of St. Paul's; F. Giles, in Holbourn; and T. Wotton, in Fleetstreet, 1735–36.

Cavendish, Margaret. *A True Relation of My Birth, Breeding, and Life*, in *Natures Pictures Drawn by Fancies Pencil to the Life*. London: J. Martin and J. Allestrye, 1656.

Ferrar, John. *The History of Limerick, Ecclesiastical, Civil and Military*. Limerick: A. Watson & Co., 1787.

Gookin, Vincent. *The Great Case of Transplantation in Ireland Discussed*. London: I. C., 1655.

Guidott, Thomas. *Appendix Concerning Bathe*. In Edward Jorden's *A Discourse of Natural Bathes*. London: Thomas Salmon, 1669.

Hamilton, Anthony. *Memoirs of Count Grammont*. London: S. and E. Harding, 1794.

Leslie, Henry. *A Discourse of Praying with the Spirit and with the Understanding*. London: John Crooke, 1660.

Morrice, Thomas. *The Life of the Earl of Orrery*. In *A Collection of the State Letters of the Right Honourable Roger Boyle, the First Earl of Orrery, Lord President of Munster in Ireland*. London: James Bettenham for Charles Hitch, 1742. 1–50.

Nickolls, John, ed. *Original Letters and Papers of State, Addressed to Oliver Cromwell*. London: William Bowyer, 1743.

Pomfret, Thomas. *The Life of the Right Honourable and Religious Lady Christian, Late Countess Dowager of Devonshire*. London: William Rawlins, 1685.

Shirley, James. *Poems &c.* London: Humphrey Moseley, 1646.

The Occasion and Manner of Mr. Francis Wolleys Death, Slaine by the Earle of Chesterfield at Kensington, January 17 1659. London: IC, 1660.

Tichborne, Henry. *A Letter of Sir Henry Tichborne to his Lady, at the Siege of Drogheda*. Drogheda: John Fleming, 1772.

Williamson, Joseph. *A Modest Essay upon the Character of her late Grace, the Dutchess-Dowager of Devonshire*. London: A. Roper, 1710.

Editions

"An Epistolary Account of the Irish Rising of 1641 by the Wife of the Mayor of Waterford." Edited by Naomi McAreavey. *English Literary Renaissance* 42.1 (2012): 90–118.

"Anonymous Account of the Early Life and Marriage of James, First Duke of Ormonde." Edited by James Graves. *The Journal of the Kilkenny and South-East of Ireland Archaeological Society*, N.S. 4.2 (1863): 276–92.

Boyle, Richard. *The Diary of Richard Boyle, 2nd Earl of Cork and 1st Earl of Burlington, 1650–73*. Edited by Coleman Dennehy and Patrick Little. Dublin: Irish Manuscripts Commission, forthcoming.

Calendar of the Manuscripts of the Marquess of Ormonde. 3 vols. London: Her Majesty's Stationery Office, 1895–99.

Calendar of the Manuscripts of the Marquess of Ormonde, N.S. 8 vols. London: His Majesty's Stationery Office, 1902–20.
Evelyn, John. *The Diary of John Evelyn*. Edited by E. S. de Beer. London: Everyman, 2006.
Fanshawe, Anne. *Memoirs of Lady Anne Fanshawe*. Edited by Charles Robert Fanshawe. London: Colburne and Bentley, 1830.
Field Day Anthology of Irish Writing, IV and V: Irish Women's Writing and Traditions, The. Edited by Angela Bourke and others. Cork: Cork University Press, 2002.
Giffard, Martha. *Martha, Lady Giffard, Her Life and Correspondence (1664–1722)*. Edited by Julia G. Longe. London: George Allen, 1911.
HMC, *The Manuscripts of the Earl of Dartmouth*. 3 vols. London: His Majesty's Stationery Office, 1887.
Osborne, Dorothy. *The Letters of Dorothy Osborne to William Temple*. Edited by G. C. Moore Smith. Oxford: Clarendon, 1947.
Philips, Katherine. *The Collected Works of Katherine Philips*. 3 vols. London: Stump Cross, 1990–93.
Verse in English from Tudor and Stuart Ireland. Edited by Andrew Carpenter. Cork: Cork University Press, 2003.

Secondary Sources

Barnard, Toby. "The Viceregal Court in Later Seventeenth-Century Ireland." In *The Stuart Courts*, edited by Eveline Cruickshanks. Stroud: Sutton, 2000. 256–65.
Barnard, Toby, and Jane Fenlon, eds. *The Dukes of Ormonde, 1610–1745*. Woodbridge: Boydell & Brewer, 2000.
Beckett, J. C. *The Cavalier Duke: A Life of James Butler, 1st Duke of Ormond, 1610–1688*. Belfast: Pretani, 1990.
Berwick, Edward. *The Rawdon Papers: Consisting of Letters on Various Subjects Literary Political and Ecclesiastical to and From Dr John Bramhall, Primate of Ireland*. London: John Nichols and Son, 1819.
Burghclere, Winifred. *The Life of James First Duke of Ormonde*. 2 vols. London: John Murray, 1912.
Burke, John. *A Genealogical and Heraldic History of the Commoners of Great Britain and Ireland*. 4 vols. London: Henry Colburn, 1836.
Burke's Irish Family Records. 5th edn. London: Burke's Peerage, 1976.
Carpenter, Andrew. "A Collection of Verse Presented to James Butler, First Duke of Ormonde." *The Yale University Library Gazette* 75 (2000): 64–70.
Carrigan, William. *The History and Antiquities of the Diocese of Ossory*. 4 vols. Dublin: Sealy, Bryers and Walker, 1905.

Casey, Christine. *Dublin: The City within the Grand and Royal Canals and the Circular Road with the Phoenix Park.* New Haven: Yale University Press, 2005.

Clarke, Aidan. *Prelude to Restoration in Ireland: The End of the Commonwealth, 1659–60.* Cambridge: Cambridge University Press, 2004.

Condon, James. "Elizabeth, Lady Thurles – Her Ancestry and Her Role in the Rebellion of 1641." In *Thurles: The Cathedral Town; Essays in Honour of Archbishop Thomas Morris,* edited by William Corbett and William Nolan. Dublin: Geography Publications, 1989. 40–45.

Coolahan, Marie-Louise. *Women, Writing, and Language in Early Modern Ireland.* Cambridge: Cambridge University Press, 2010.

Costello, Vandra. *Irish Demesne Landscapes, 1660–1740.* Dublin: Four Courts, 2015.

Cunningham, John. *Conquest and Land in Ireland: The Transplantation to Connacht, 1649–1680.* Woodbridge: Boydell and Brewer, 2011.

Daybell, James, ed. *Early Modern Women's Letter Writing, 1450–1700.* Basingstoke: Palgrave, 2001.

Daybell, James. *The Material Letter in Early Modern England: Manuscript Letters and the Culture and Practices of Letter-Writing, 1512–1635.* London: Palgrave Macmillan, 2012.

Duffy, Damien. "The Ormond Women: Family, Power, and Politics, c. 1450s–1660." Ph.D. diss., Maynooth University, 2018.

Eckerle, Julie A., and Naomi McAreavey, eds. *Women's Life Writing and Early Modern Ireland.* Lincoln: University of Nebraska Press, 2019.

Edwards, David. *The Ormond Lordship in County Kilkenny, 1515–1642: The Rise and Fall of the Butler Family.* Dublin: Four Courts, 2003.

Fenlon, Jane. "The Duchess of Ormonde's House at Dunmore, County Kilkenny." In *Kilkenny: Studies in Honour of Margaret M. Phelan,* edited by John Kirwan. Kilkenny: Kilkenny Archaeological Society, 1997.

———. "'Her Grace's Closet': Paintings in the Duchess of Ormond's Closet at Kilkenny Castle." *Bulletin of the Irish Georgian Society* 36 (1994): 30–47.

———. *Kilkenny Castle.* Dublin: The Office of Public Works, 2007.

———. *Ormond Castle.* Dublin: Stationery Office, c. 1996.

———. "The Ormonde Picture Collection." *Irish Arts Review Yearbook* 16 (2000): 142–49.

———. *The Ormonde Picture Collection.* Dublin: Dúchas / Heritage Service, 2001.

Fraser, Antonia. *The Weaker Vessel: Woman's Lot in Seventeenth-Century England.* London: Weidenfeld and Nicolson, 1984.

Gibson, Jonathan. "Significant Space in Manuscript Letters." *The Seventeenth Century* 12 (1997): 1–10.

Globe, Alexander. *Peter Stent, London Printseller, circa 1642–1665: Being a Catalogue Raisonné of his Engraved Prints and Books with an Historical and*

Bibliographical Introduction. Vancouver: University of British Columbia Press, 1985.

Graves, James. "Some Additional Facts as to the Marriage of James, Viscount Thurles, afterwards Duke of Ormonde, and the Lady Elizabeth Preston." *The Journal of the Kilkenny and South-East of Ireland Archaeological Society*, N.S. 6.1 (1867): 232–38.

Jameson, Anna. *Court Beauties of the Reign of Charles II*. London: J. C. Hotton, 1872.

Kirwan, John. *The Chief Butlers of Ireland and the House of Ormonde: A Guide to the Genealogical History*. Dublin: Irish Academic Press, 2018.

Leonard, John. "Dublin and the Duke of Ormonde." *Journal of the Butler Society* 3 (1994): 555–60.

Loeber, Rolf. *A Biographical Dictionary of Architects in Ireland, 1600–1720*. London: Murray, 1981.

———. "The Rebuilding of Dublin Castle: Thirty Critical Years, 1661–1690." *Studies: An Irish Quarterly Review* 69 (1980): 45–69.

MacCurtain, Margaret, and Mary O'Dowd, eds. *Women in Early Modern Ireland*. Dublin: Wolfhound, 1991.

Maguire, J. B. "Seventeenth-Century Plans of Dublin Castle." In *Medieval Dublin: The Making of a Metropolis*, edited by Howard Clarke. Dublin: Irish Academic Press, 1990. 193–201.

Manning, Conleth. "The 1653 Survey of the Lands Granted to the Countess of Ormond in Co. Kilkenny." *Journal of the Royal Society of Antiquaries of Ireland* 129 (1999): 40–66.

Marshall, Alan. "Colonel Thomas Blood and the Restoration Political Scene." *Historical Journal* 32 (1989): 561–82.

McGuire, J. I. "Why Was Ormond Dismissed in 1669?" *Irish Historical Studies* 18 (1973): 295–312.

Moore, Lucy. *Lady Fanshawe's Receipt Book: An Englishwoman's Life during the Civil War*. London: Atlantic Books, 2018.

Nolan, Frances. "'Jacobite' Women and the Williamite Confiscation: The Role of Women and Female Minors in Reclaiming Compromised or Forfeited Property in Ireland, 1690–1703." Ph.D. diss., University College Dublin, 2015.

Nolan, William, and Kevin Whelan, eds. *Kilkenny: History and Society: Interdisciplinary Essays on the History of an Irish County*. Dublin: Geography Publications, 1990.

O'Brien, Conor. "In Search of the Duke of Ormond's Wine Cistern and Fountain." *The Silver Society Journal* 15 (2003): 63–67.

O'Dowd, Mary. *A History of Women in Ireland, 1500–1800*. Harlow: Pearson, 2005.

Ohlmeyer, Jane. *Making Ireland English: The Irish Aristocracy in the Seventeenth Century*. New Haven: Yale University Press, 2012.

Ohlmeyer, Jane, and Steven Zwicker. "John Dryden, the House of Ormond, and the Politics of Anglo-Irish Patronage." *The Historical Journal* 49.3 (2006): 677–706.
O'Keeffe, Eleanor. "The Family and Marriage Strategies of James Butler, 1st Duke of Ormonde, 1658–1688." Ph.D. diss. University of Cambridge, 2000.
Ó Siochrú, Micheál. *God's Executioner: Oliver Cromwell and the Conquest of Ireland.* London: Faber & Faber, 2008.
Place, J. A. "History of the Lax Weir." *Journal of the Limerick Field Club* 3.9 (1905–8): 25–31.
Rankin, Deana. *Between Spenser and Swift: English Writing in Seventeenth-Century Ireland.* Cambridge: Cambridge University Press, 2005.
Sinsteden, Thomas. "Household Plate of the Dukes of Ormonde." *The Silver Society Journal* 23 (2008): 123–29.
Steen, Sara Jayne. "Behind the Arras: Editing Renaissance Women's Letters." In *New Ways of Looking at Old Texts*, edited by W. Speed Hill. New York: Binghamton, 1993. 229–38.
Treadwell, Victor. "The Irish Court of Wards under James I," *Irish Historical Studies* 12 (1960): 1–27.
Wilks, Timothy. *Of Neighing Coursers and Trumpets Shrill: A Life of Richard, 1st Lord Dingwall and Earl of Desmond (c. 1570–1628).* London: Lucas, 2012.
Williams, Mark R. F. *The King's Irishmen: The Irish in the Exiled Court of Charles II, 1649–1660.* Woodbridge: Boydell, 2014.

Databases

British History Online http://www.british-history.ac.uk/.
Dictionary of Irish Biography Online http://dib.cambridge.org.
Early Modern Practitioners http://practitioners.exeter.ac.uk/.
Oxford Dictionary of National Biography http://www.oxforddnb.com.
Oxford English Dictionary http://www.oed.com.
Oxford Reference http://www.oxfordreference.com.
The 1641 Depositions http://1641.tcd.ie/.
The Diary of Samuel Pepys: Daily Entries from the 17th-Century London Diary. http://www.pepysdiary.com.
The Down Survey of Ireland http://downsurvey.tcd.ie/.
The Hartlib Papers http://www.dhi.ac.uk/hartlib/.
The History of Parliament: British Political, Social & Local History http://www.historyofparliamentonline.org/.

Renaissance English Text Society

Officers and Council

President, Joseph L. Black, University of Massachusetts Amherst
Vice-President, Mary Ellen Lamb, Southern Illinois University
Second Vice-President, Beth Quitslund, University of Ohio
Secretary, Jaime Goodrich, Wayne State University
Membership Secretary and Treasurer, William Gentrup, emeritus ACMRS
Publisher, William R. Bowen, Iter Press

Reid Barbour, University of North Carolina
Victoria Burke, University of Ottawa
Clare Costley King'oo, University of Connecticut
Joshua Eckhardt, Virginia Commonwealth University
Gregory Kneidel, University of Connecticut
Arthur F. Marotti, Wayne State University
Steven May, Emory University
Susannah B. Monta, University of Notre Dame
Jason Powell, Saint Joseph's University
Anne Lake Prescott, Barnard College
Mark Rankin, James Madison University
Cathy Shrank, University of Sheffield
Raymond G. Siemens, University of Victoria

The Renaissance English Text Society publishes nondramatic literary texts from the period 1475–1660. For inquiries about proposals please contact Joseph L. Black at jlblack@umass.edu. For information about membership in the Society please see the RETS website at retsonline.org. For information on the availability of earlier volumes, please see the Iter Press website at IterPress.org.

I. *Merie Tales of the Mad Men of Gotam* by A. B., ed. Stanley J. Kahrl, and *The History of Tom Thumbe* by R. I., ed. Curt F. Bühler, 1965.

II. *Thomas Watson's Latin 'Amyntas' (1585)*, ed. Walter F. Staton, Jr., and *Abraham Fraunce's translation: 'The Lamentations of Amyntas' (1587)*, ed. Franklin M. Dickey, 1967.

III. *The Dyaloge Called Funus, A Translation of Erasmus's Colloquy (1534)*, and *A Very Pleasaunt & Fruitful Diologe Called The Epicure, Gerrard's Translation of Erasmus's Colloquy (1545)*, ed. Robert R. Allen, 1969.

IV. Thomas Rogers, *Leicester's Ghost*, ed. Franklin B. Williams, Jr., 1972.

V–VI. George Wither, *A Collection of Emblemes, Ancient and Moderne (1635)*, introd. Rosemary Freeman; bibliographical notes by Charles S. Hensley, 1975.

VII–VIII. *The Most Pleasant History of Tom a Lincolne* by R. I., ed. Richard S. M. Hirsch, 1978.

IX. George Cavendish, *Metrical Visions*, ed. A. S. G. Edwards, 1980.

X. *Two Early Renaissance Bird Poems: The Harmony of Birds, The Parliament of Birds*, ed. Malcolm Andrew, 1984.

XI. Francis Quarles, *Argalus and Parthenia*, ed. David Freeman, 1986.

XII. *Marcus Tullius Ciceroes Thre Bokes of Duties, to Marcus His Sonne, Turned Oute of Latine into English, by Nicolas Grimalde*, ed. Gerald O'Gorman, 1990.

XIII. Thomas Moffet, *The Silkewormes and Their Flies*, ed. Victor Houliston, 1989.

XIV. John Bale, *The Vocacyon of Johan Bale*, ed. Peter Happé and John N. King, 1990.

XV. *The Nondramatic Works of John Ford*, ed. L. E. Stock, Gilles D. Monsarrat, Judith M. Kennedy, and Dennis Danielson, 1991.

XVI. George Herbert, *The Temple: A Diplomatic Edition of the Bodleian Manuscript (Tanner 307)*, ed. Mario A. Di Cesare, 1995.

XVII. Lady Mary Wroth, *The First Part of The Countess of Montgomery's Urania*, ed. Josephine A. Roberts, 1995.

XVIII. Richard Beacon, *Solon His Follie, or, A Politique Discourse Touching the Reformation of Common-Weales Conquered, Declined or Corrupted*, ed. Clare Carroll and Vincent Carey, 1996.

XIX. An Collins, *Divine Songs and Meditacions*, ed. Sidney Gottlieb, 1996.

XX. Lady Anne Southwell, *The Southwell-Sibthorpe Commonplace Book: Folger Ms. V.b. 198*, ed. Sr. Jean Klene, 1997.

XXI. *The Collected Works of Anne Vaughan Lock*, ed. Susan M. Felch, 1999.

XXII. Thomas May, *The Reigne of King Henry the Second: Written in Seauen Bookes*, ed. Götz Schmitz, 1999.

XXIII. *The Poems of Sir Walter Ralegh: A Historical Edition*, ed. Michael Rudick, 1999.

XXIV. Lady Mary Wroth, *The Second Part of The Countess of Montgomery's Urania*, ed. Josephine A. Roberts, completed by Suzanne Gossett and Janel Mueller, 1999.

XXV. *The Verse Miscellany of Constance Aston Fowler: A Diplomatic Edition*, ed. Deborah Aldrich-Watson, 2000.

XXVI. *An Edition of Luke Shepherd's Satires*, ed. Janice Devereux, 2001.

XXVII. Philip Stubbes, *The Anatomie of Abuses*, ed. Margaret Jane Kidnie, 2002.

XXVIII. *Cousins in Love: The Letters of Lydia DuGard, 1665–1672: With a New Edition of 'The Marriages of Cousin Germans' by Samuel DuGard*, ed. Nancy Taylor, 2003.

XXIX. *The Commonplace Book of Sir John Strangways (1645–1666)*, ed. Thomas G. Olsen, 2004.

XXX. *The Poems of Robert Parry*, ed. G. Blakemore Evans, 2005.

XXXI. William Baspoole, *The Pilgrime*, ed. Kathryn Walls, with Marguerite Stobo, 2008.

XXXII. *Richard Tottel's 'Songes and Sonettes': The Elizabethan Version*, ed. Paul A. Marquis, 2007.

XXXIII. *Cælivs Secvndus Curio: His Historie of the Warr of Malta: Folger Ms. V.a. 508 (Formerly Ms. Add. 5 88), Translated by Thomas Mainwaringe (1579)*, ed. Helen Vella Bonavita, 2007.

XXXIV. *Nicholas Oldisworth's Manuscript (Bodleian MS. Don.c.24)*, ed. John Gouws, 2009.

XXXV. *The Holgate Miscellany: An Edition of Pierpont Morgan Library Manuscript, MA 1057*, ed. Michael Denbo, 2012.

XXXVI. *The Whole Book of Psalms Collected into English Metre by Thomas Sternhold, John Hopkins, and Others: A Critical Edition of the Texts and Tunes Vol. I*, ed. Beth Quitslund and Nicholas Temperley, 2018.

XXXVII. *The Whole Book of Psalms Collected into English Metre by Thomas Sternhold, John Hopkins, and Others: A Critical Edition of the Texts and Tunes Vol. II*, ed. Beth Quitslund and Nicholas Temperley, 2018.

XXXVIII. *Averrunci, or, The Skowrers: Ponderous and New Considerations upon the First Six Books of the 'Annals' of Cornelius Tacitus Concerning Tiberius Caesar (Genoa, Biblioteca Durazzo, MS. A IV 5) by Edmund Bolton*, ed. Patricia J. Osmond and Robert W. Ulery, Jr., 2017.

XXXIX. *The Lyrics of the Henry VIII Manuscript*, ed. Raymond G. Siemens, 2018.